Black Dog Publishing Limited

Special thanks
Phyllida Barlow expresses her special gratitude to the help, encouragement and support of her husband, Fabian Peake.

Dedication
For my family.

Page 4
Studio work
Brown paper bag with supporting timber length and plaster lump
240 x 150 x 240 cm
1999-2000

Page 6
Studio work
Two 8 x 4 sheets hard board, rubber tubing, plaster/ cement wedges
120 x 110 x 150 cm
1999-2000

Page 8
Studio work
Plywood, hard board, filler, canvas, paint
110 x 80 x 150 cm
1999-2000

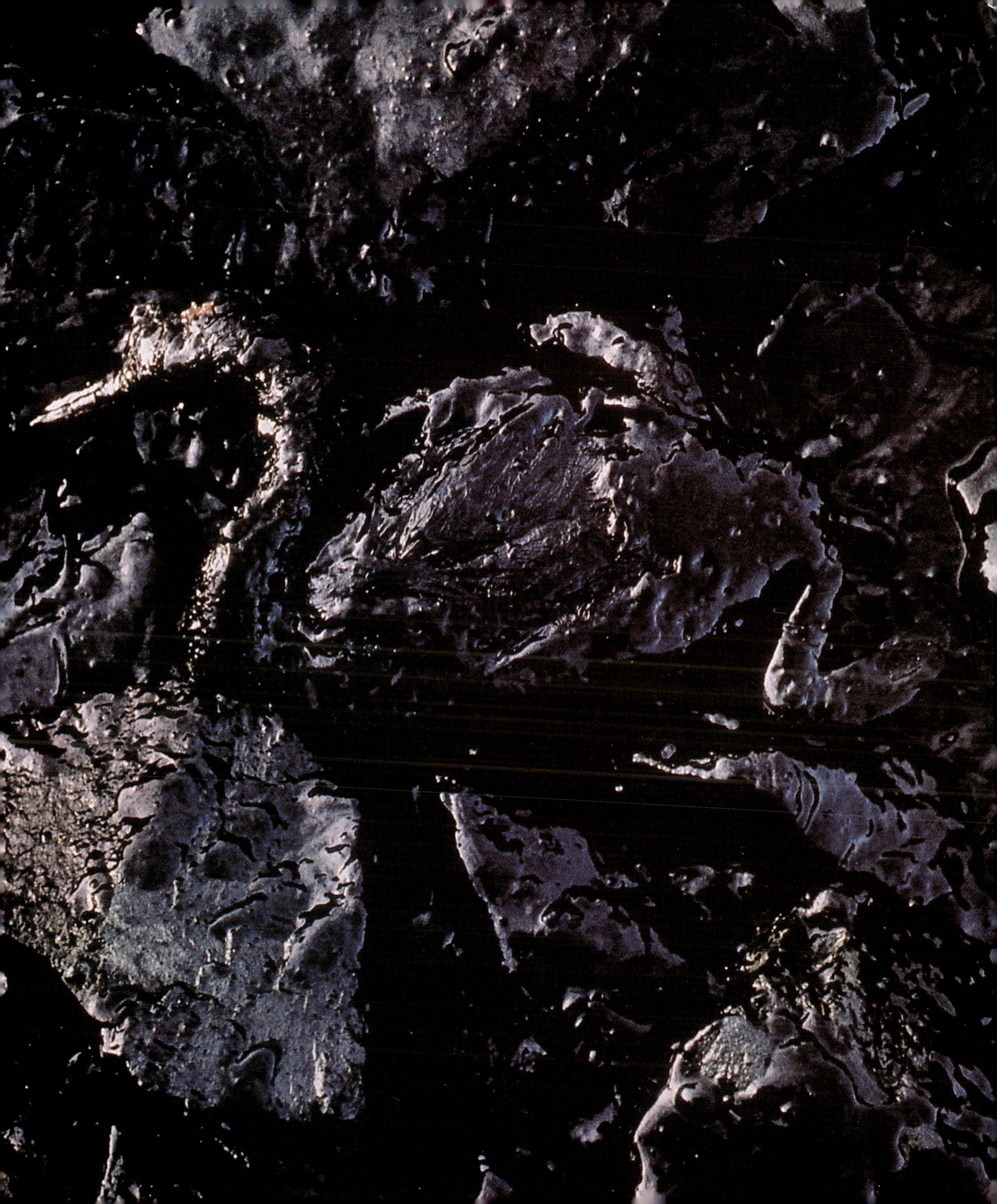

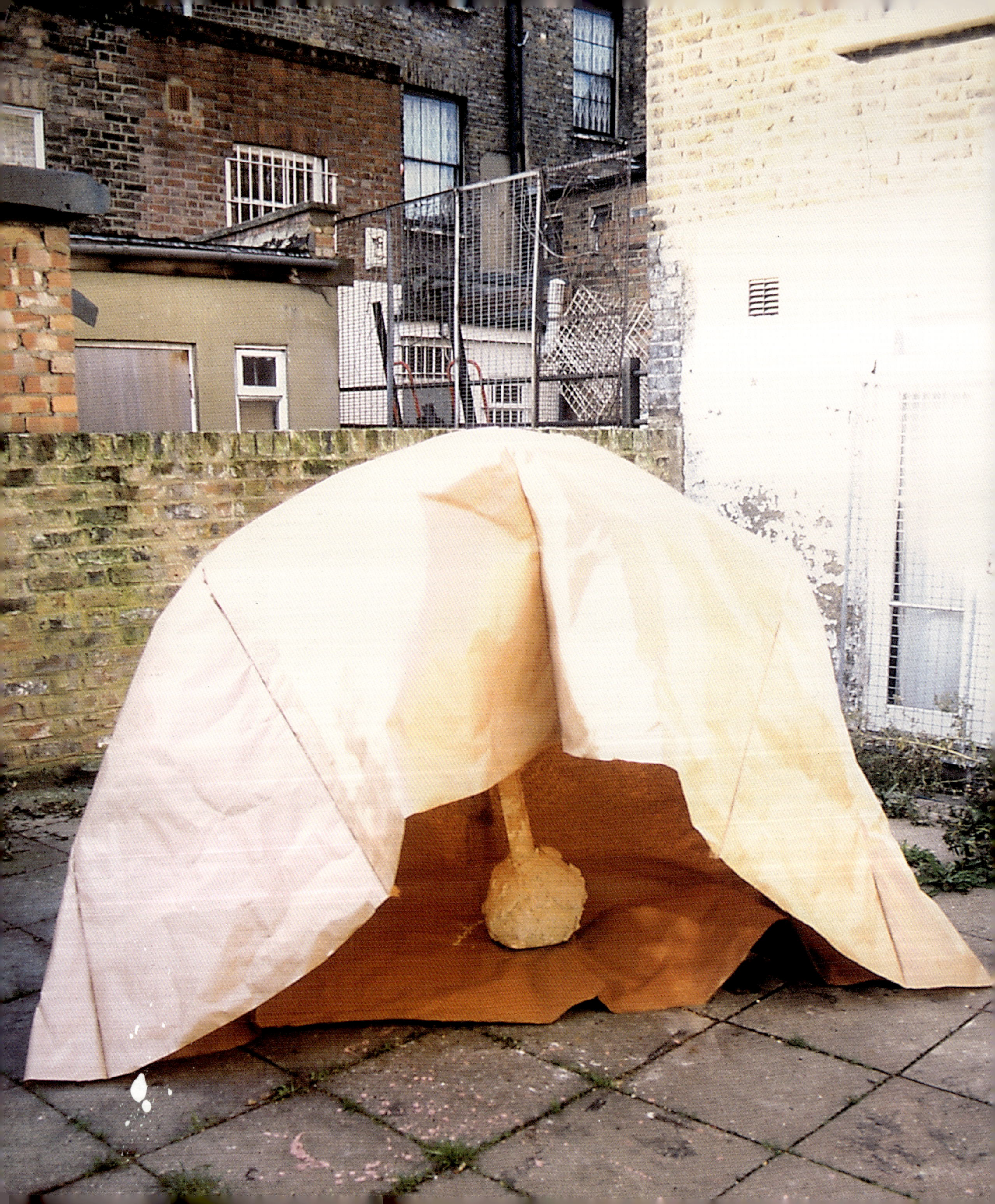

OBJECTS FOR... AND OTHER THINGS

PHYLLIDA BARLOW

Objects for... and other things
Phyllida Barlow

Designed by Gavin Ambrose

Architecture Art Design
Fashion History Photography
Theory and Things

Black Dog Publishing Limited
Unit 4.4 Tea Building
56 Shoreditch High Street
London E1 6JJ UK
T 44 020 7613 1922
F 44 020 7613 1944
E info@bdp.demon.co.uk
www.bdpworld.com

ISBN 1 901033 59 7

British Library Cataloguing-in-Publication Data.

A catalogue record for this book is available from the British Library.

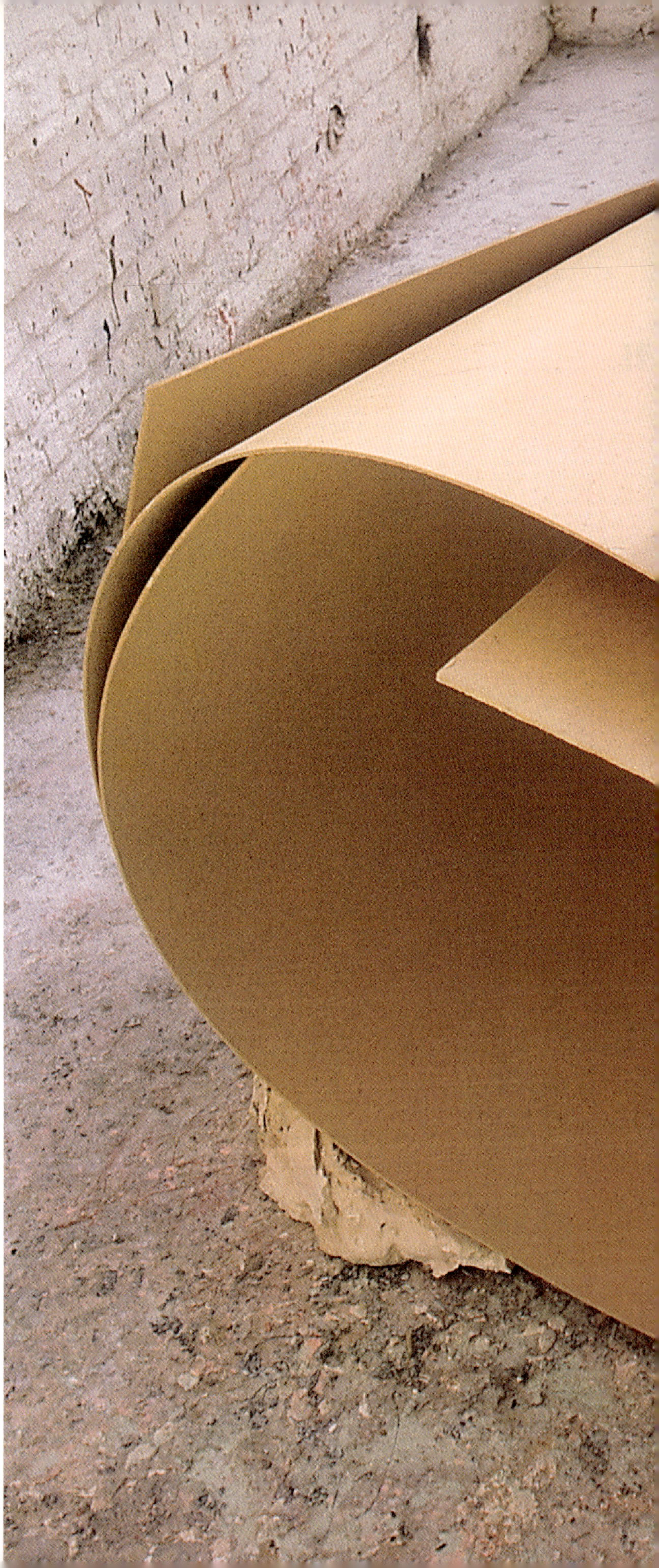

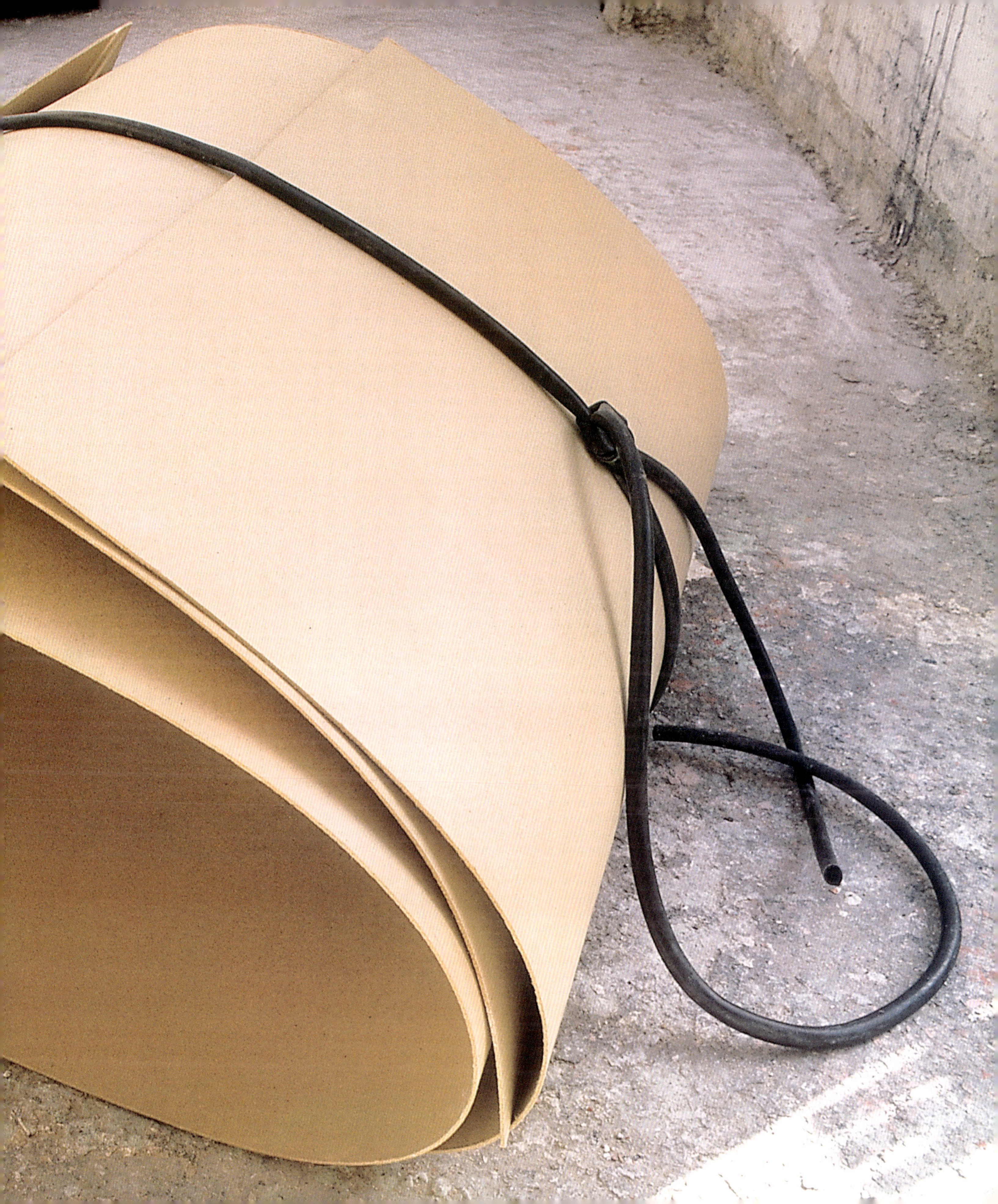

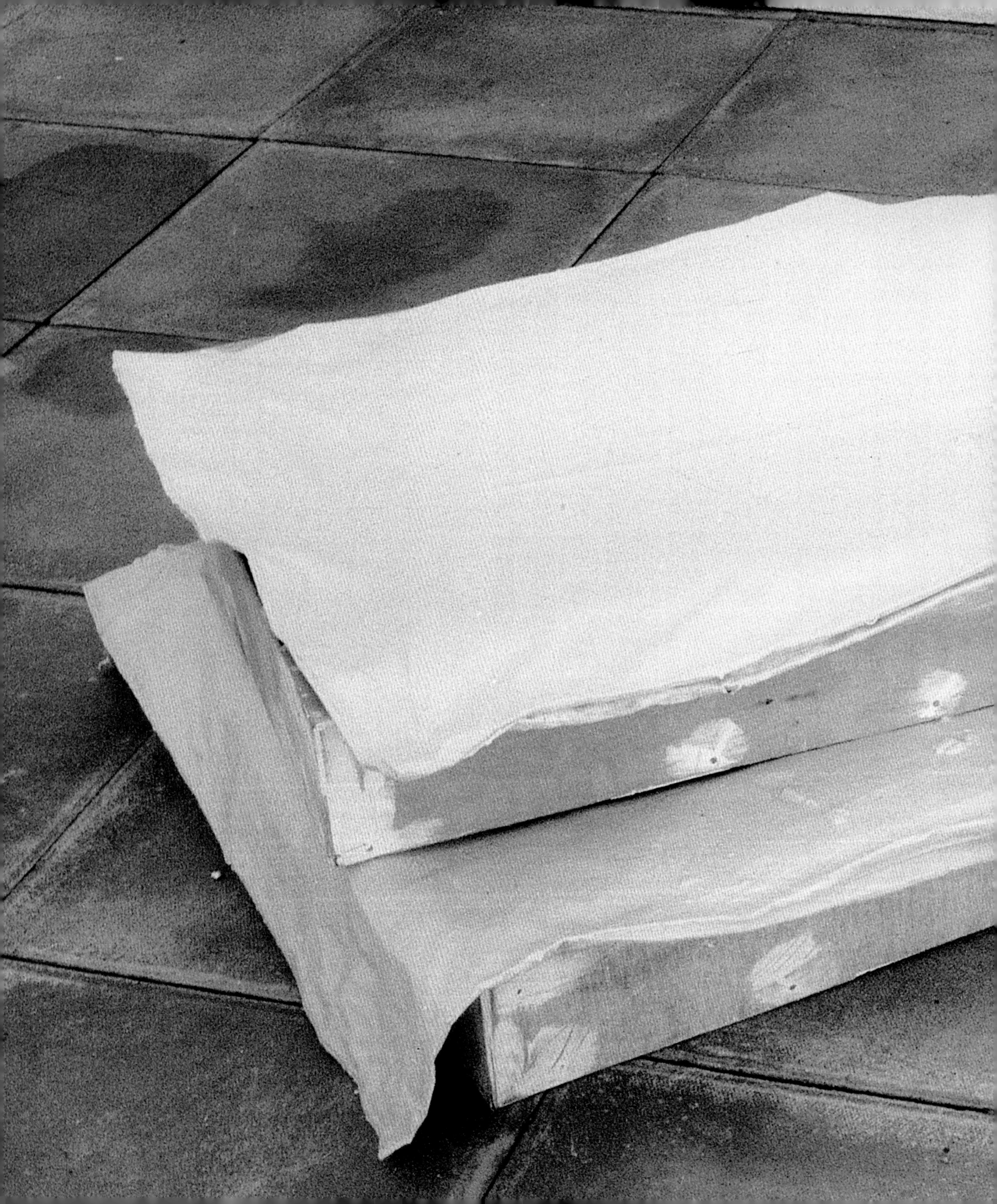

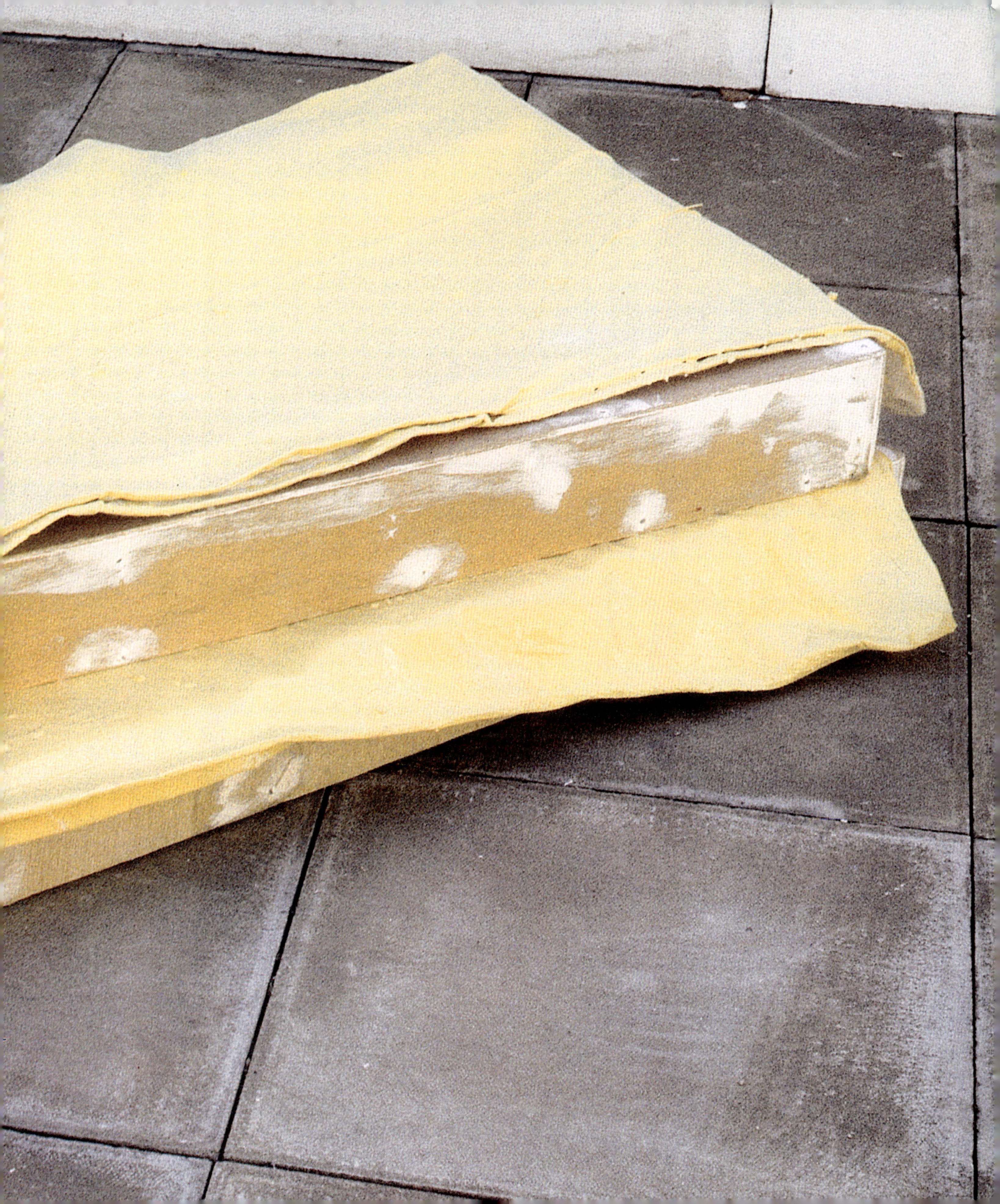

Contents

Far Away
Painted wood, fabric, felt, polystyrene, hardboard, brown paper, red tape, industrial PVC tubing, black plastic tube, casters
540 x 300 x 660 cm
1999
Lieu D'Art Contemporain, Narbonne, France for 'O Pas La' curated by Aude Herail Jaeger

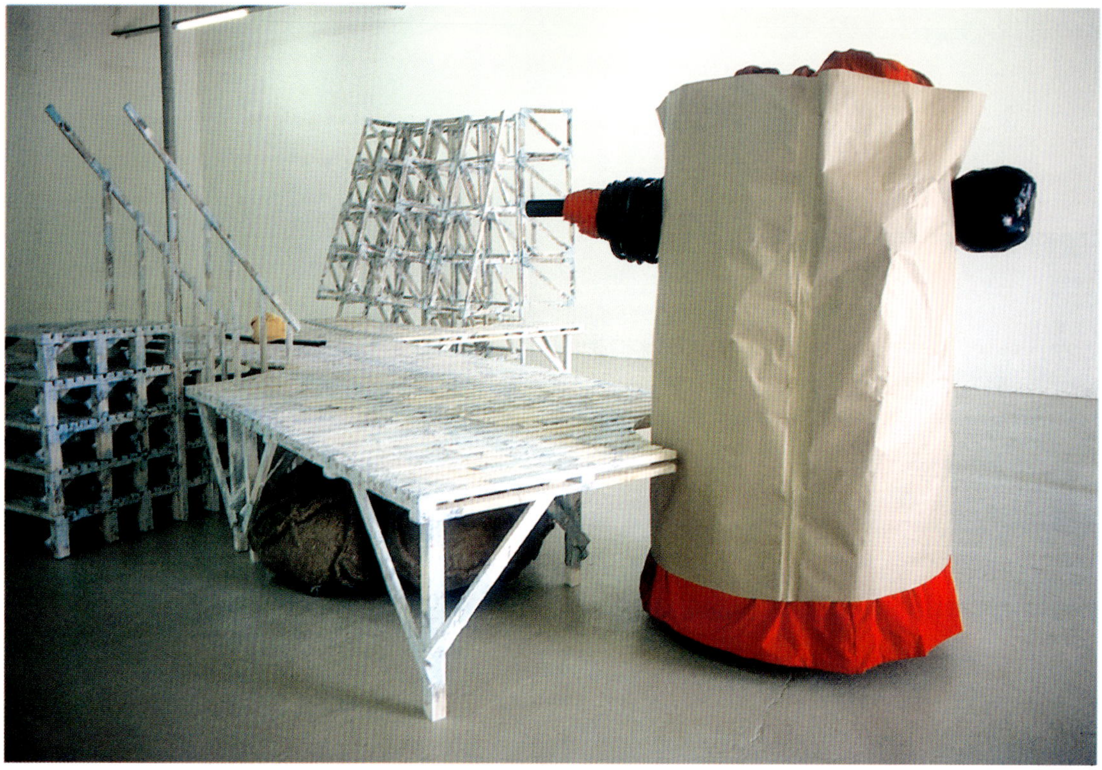

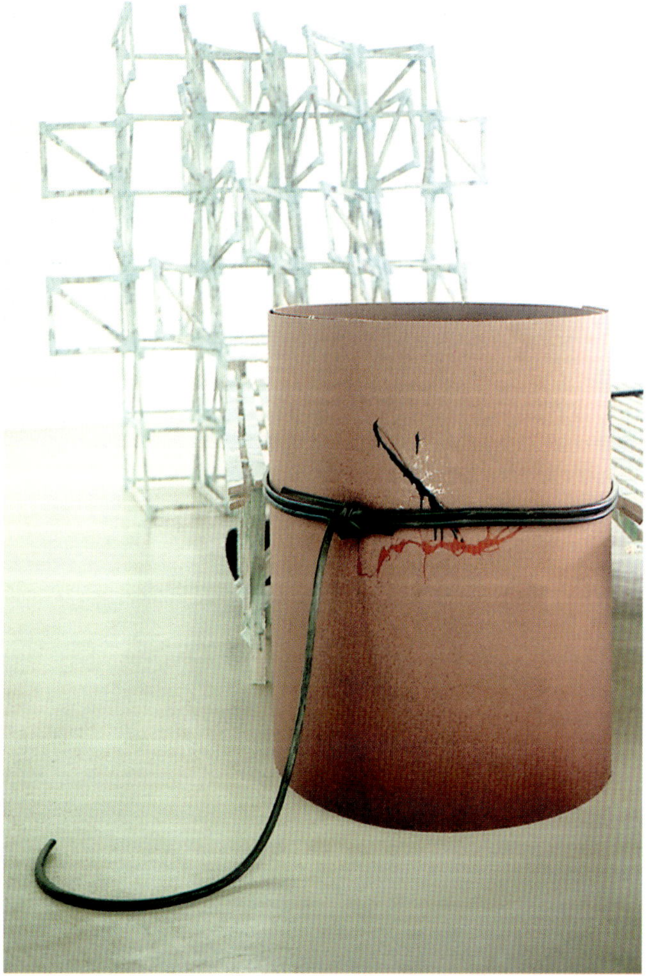

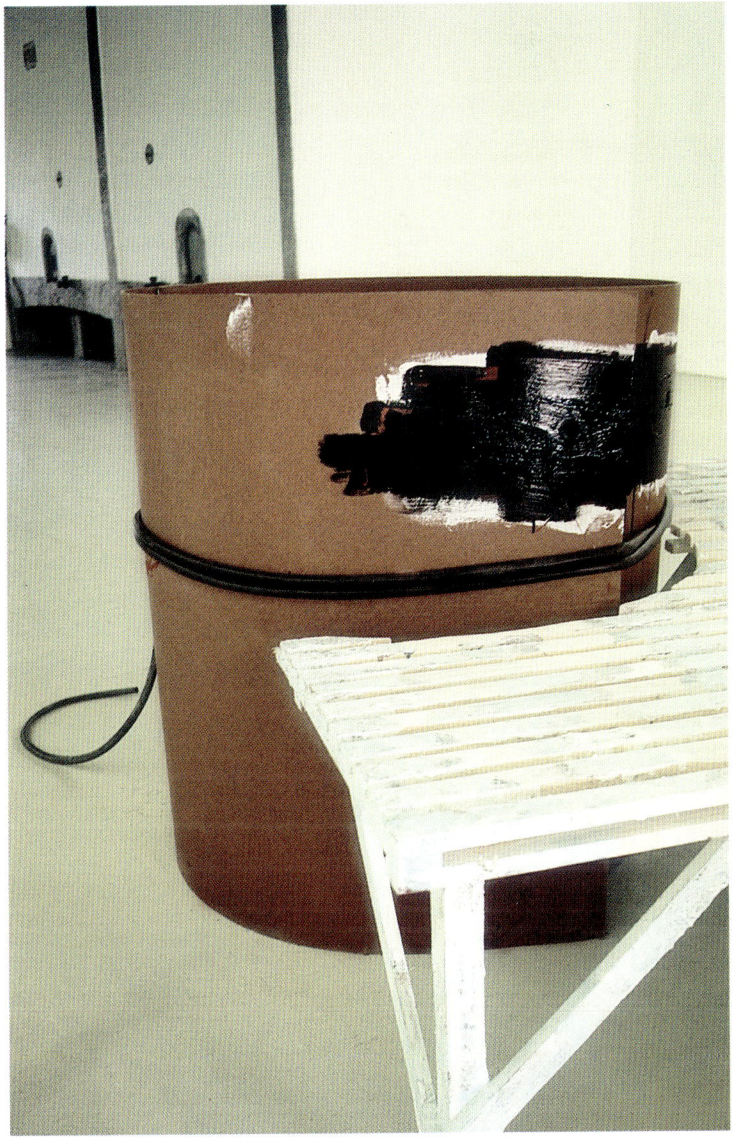

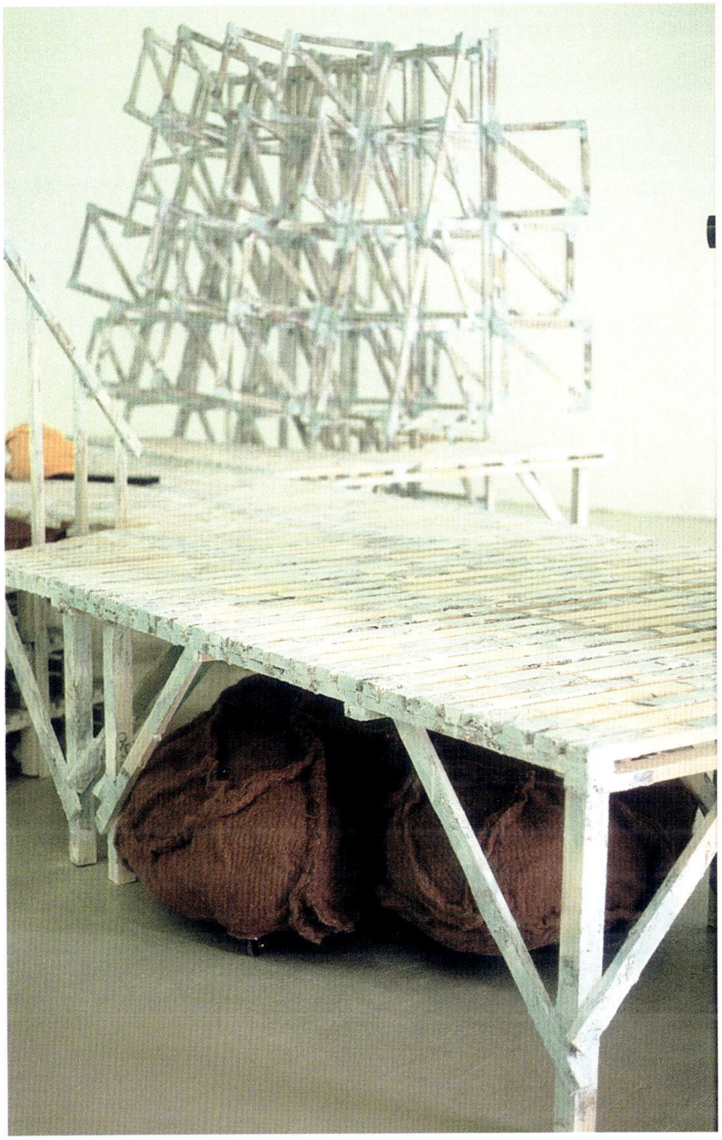

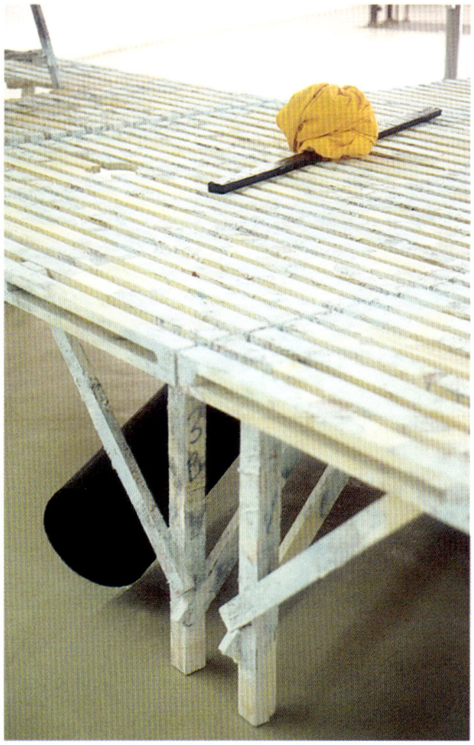

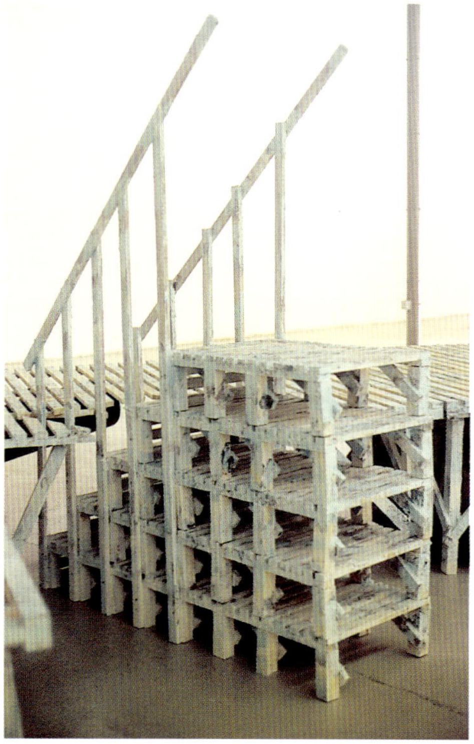

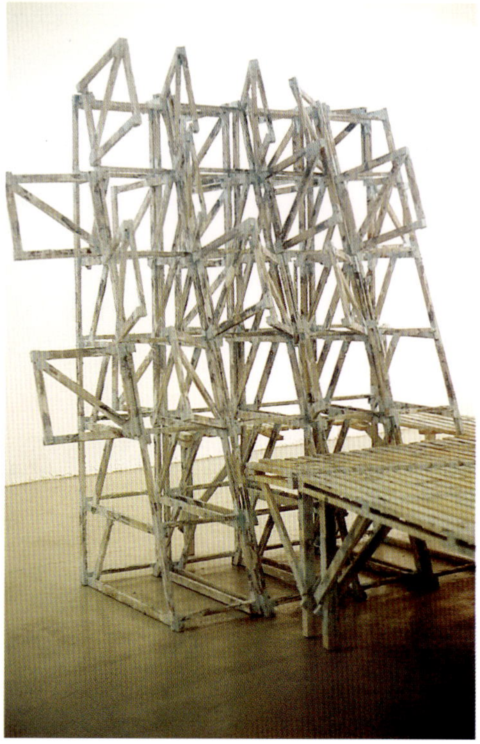

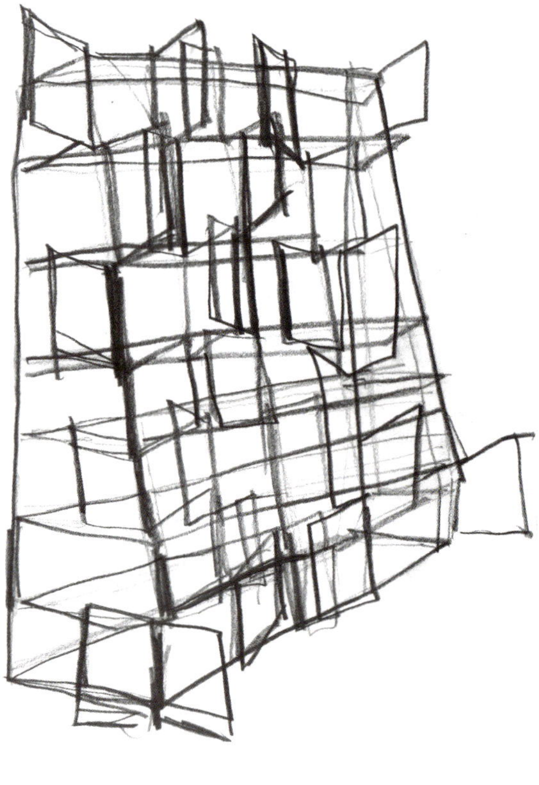

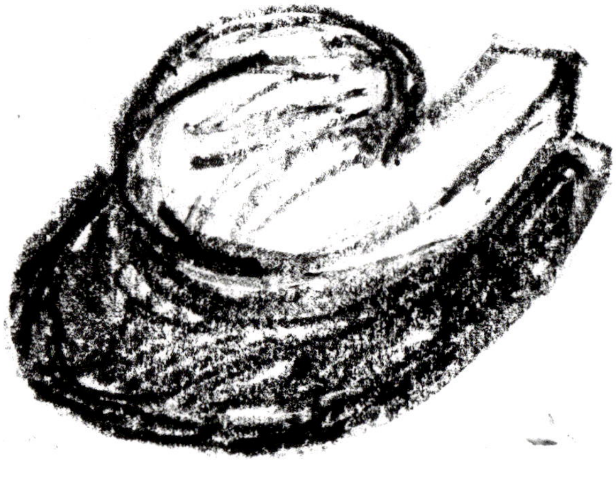

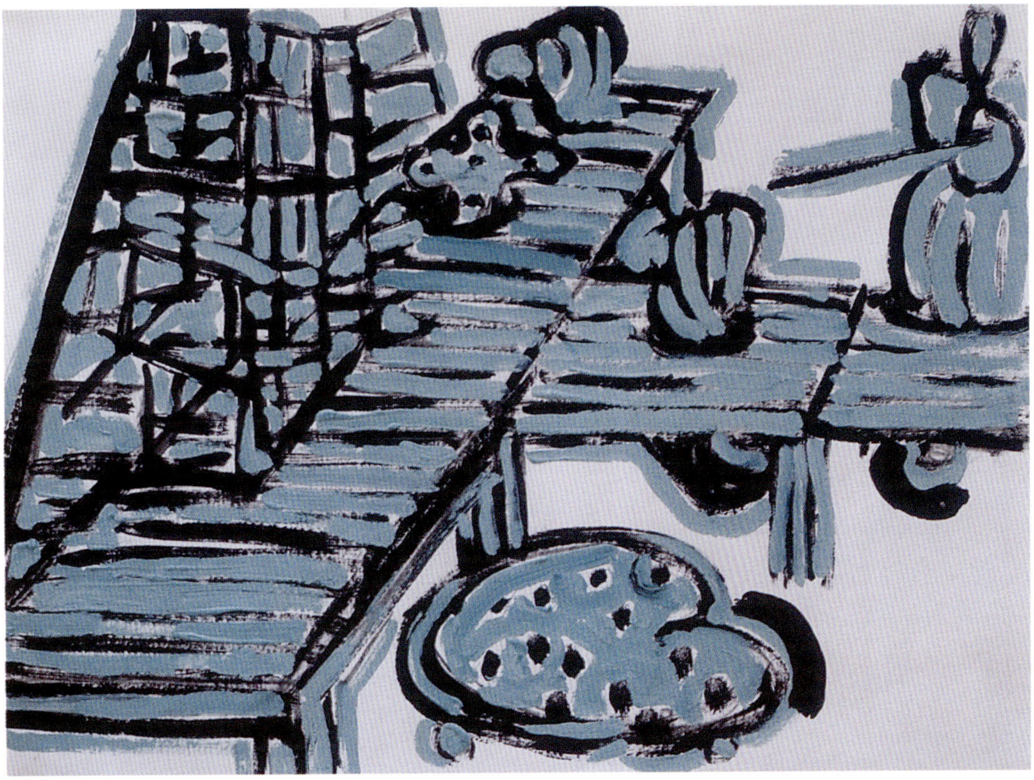

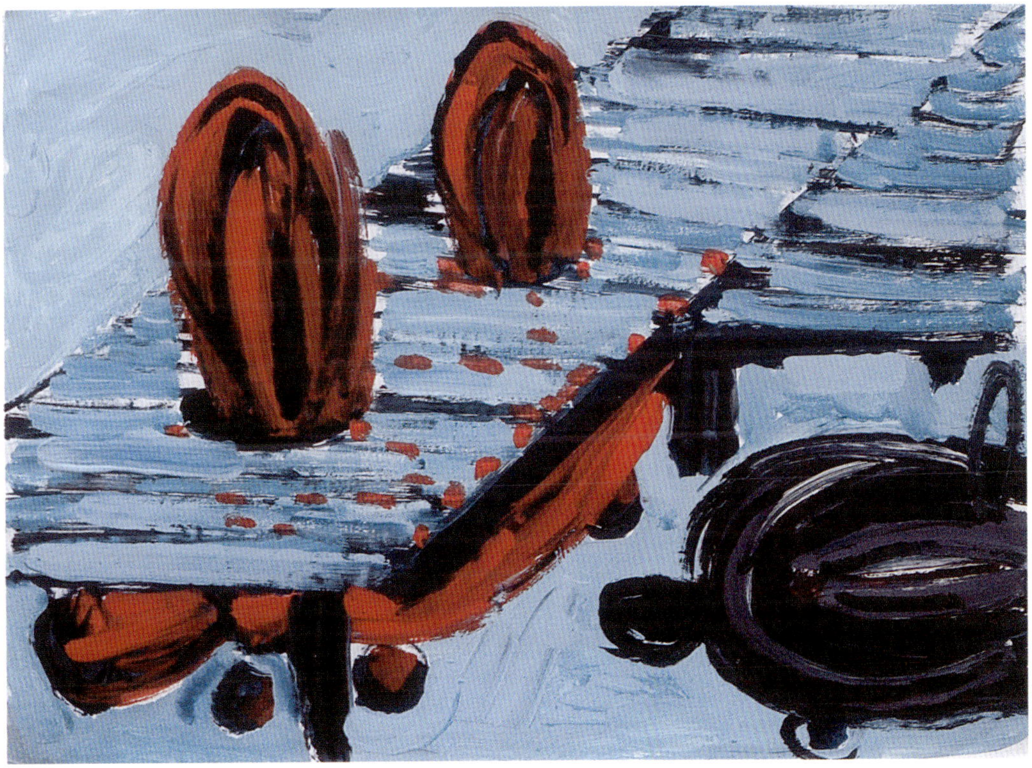

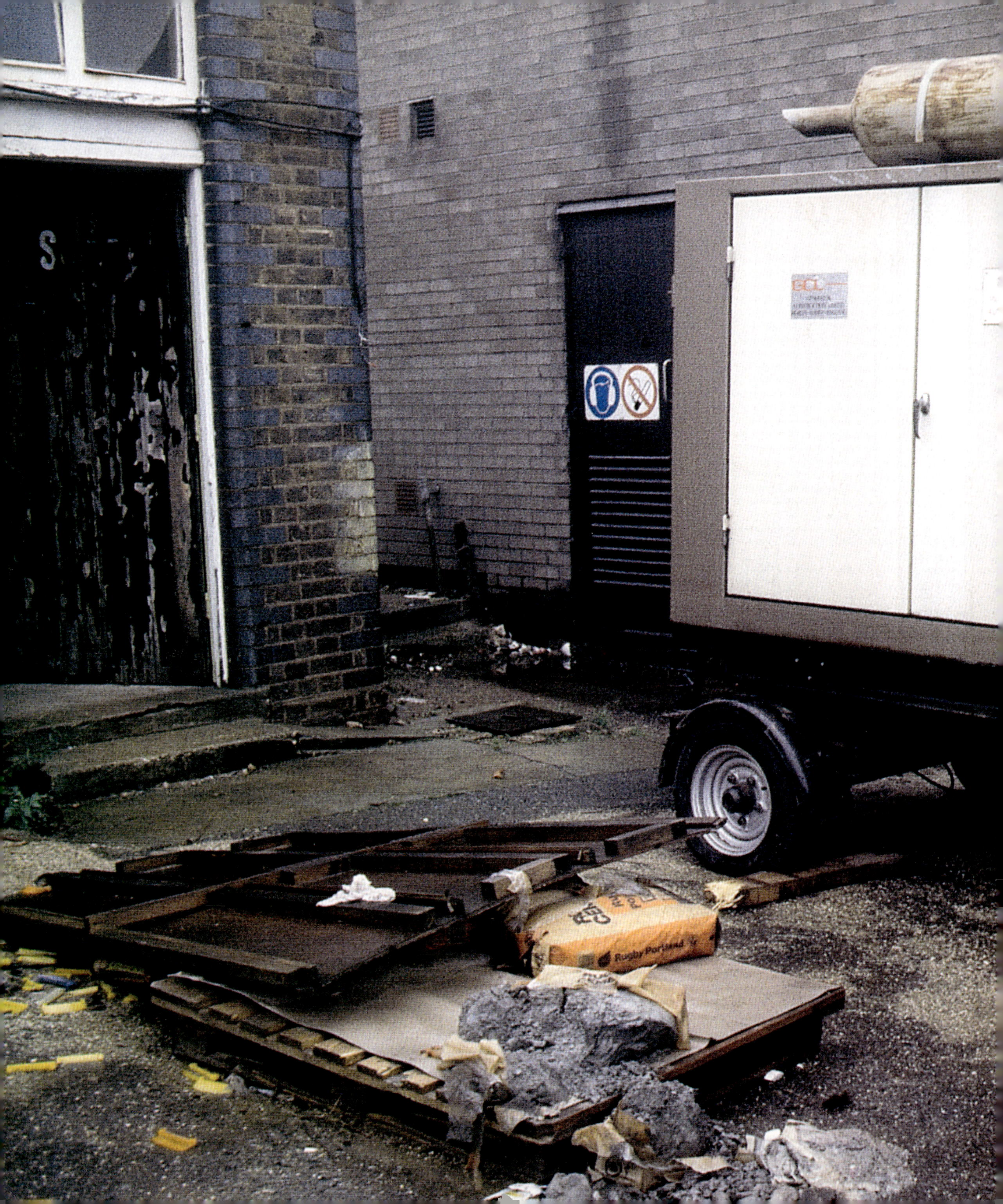
Rugby Portland

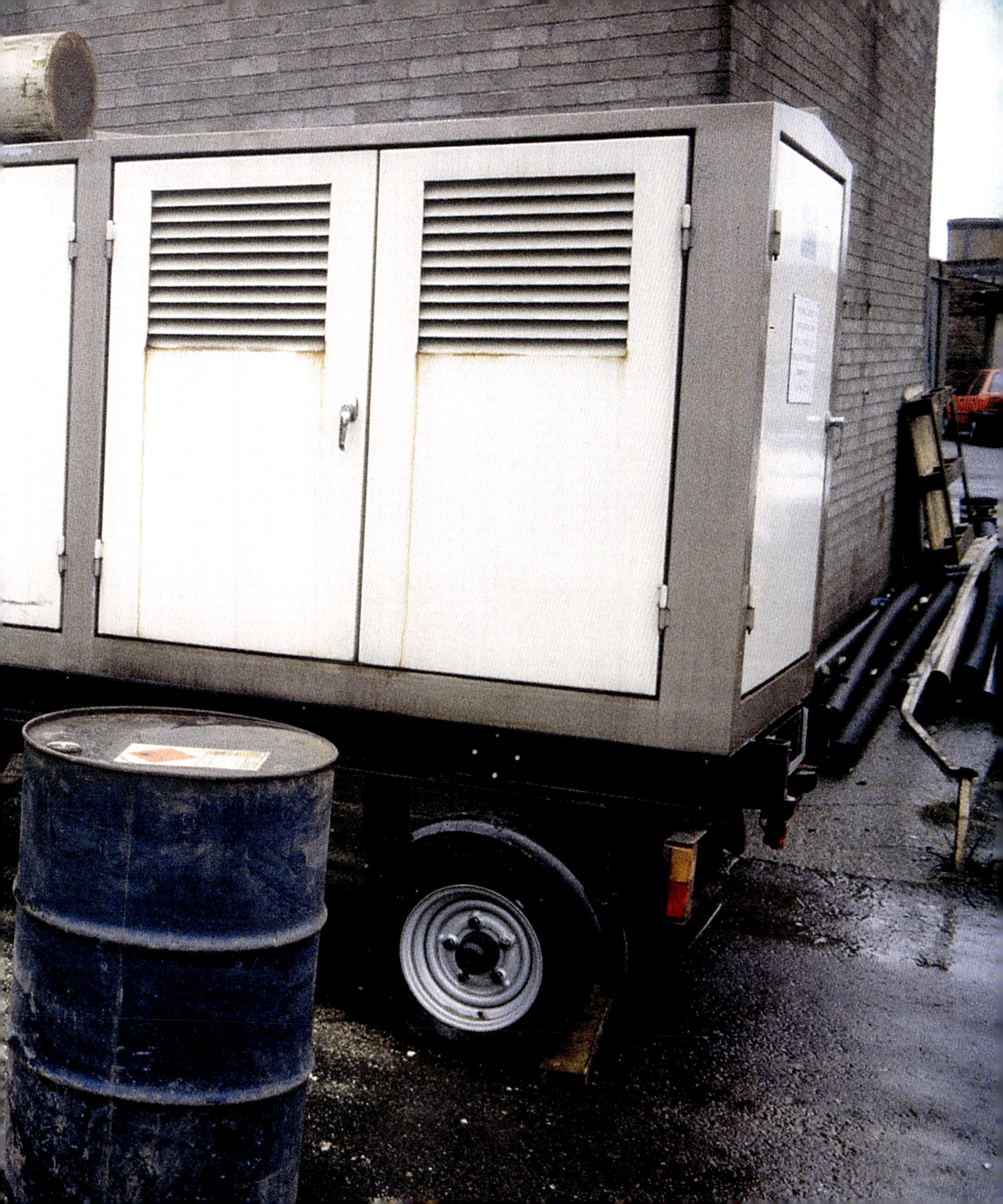

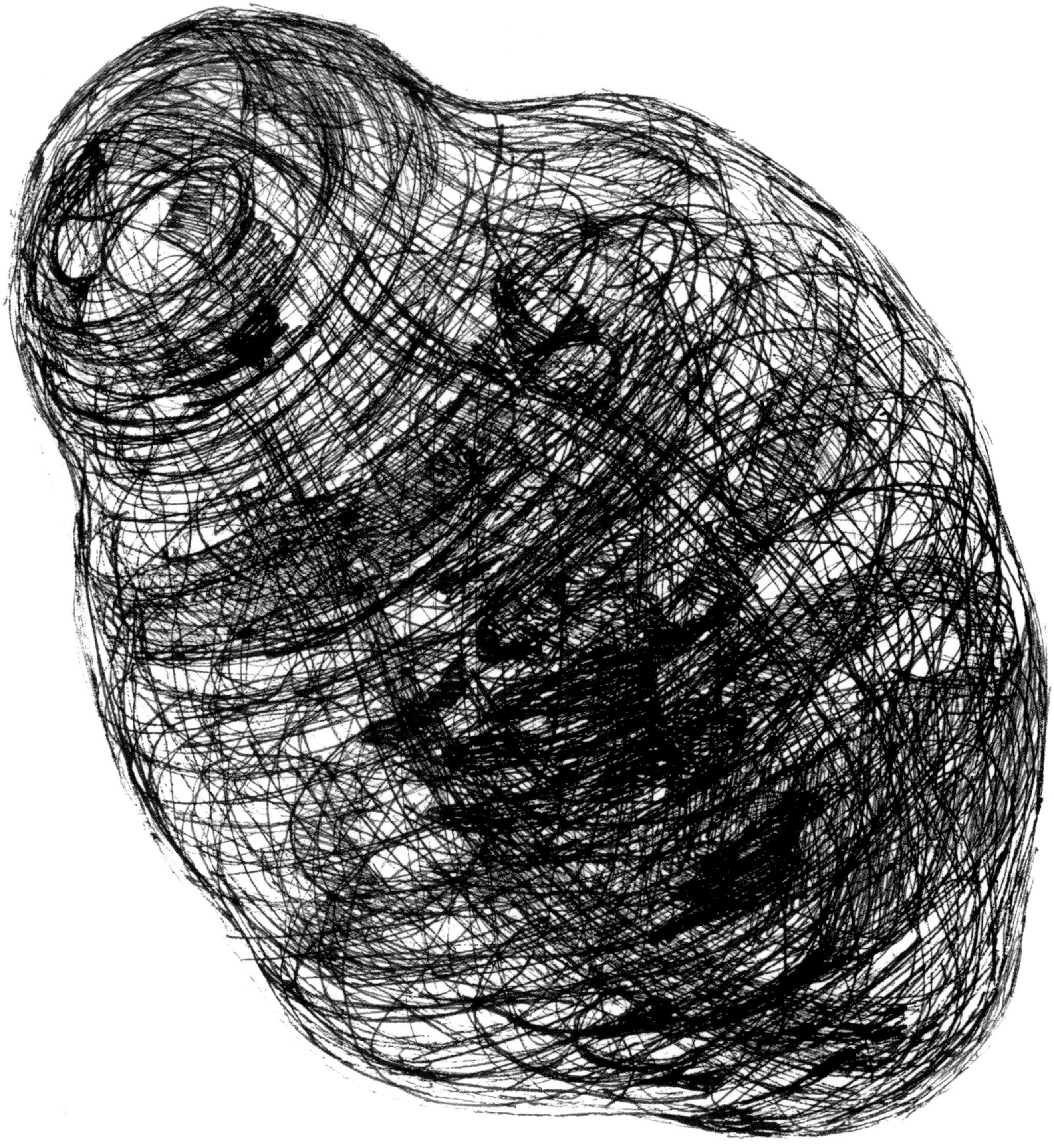

Phyllida Barlow's Sculptural Imagination

Mark Godfrey

Anti-Form and Process

1 Barlow, Phyllida, "Hearsay, Rumours, Bed-sit Dreamers and Art Begins Today", unpublished lecture given at the Whitechapel Gallery, *Early One Morning* seminar, 20 July 2002.

Shedmesh, 1976, like almost all Phyllida Barlow's work, no longer exists except as an image in a photograph. In the shot the sculpture appears centrally, almost filling the frame, seemingly installed in a group show in a low-budget space whose naked bulbs fail to light paintings that in the photo register only as black monochromes. To make the work, Barlow started with the abandoned materials of painting – old timber stretchers and bits of canvas. Six lengths of wood were tied together with canvas rags to form an initial small cube that sits in the interior of the final sculpture. Around it Barlow built a second cubic structure, this time with extra horizontal and vertical slats, and then another and another, so many latticed boxes on top of each other. Hanging off the outermost slats are irregularly shaped and different sized lengths and widths of foam, covered in grey canvas. They splurge out from the inner recesses of the work. It is as if the cube had been flayed.

Recalling British sculpture of the 1960s and 70s, it becomes clear how out of place this work was in the national context. When Barlow began teaching sculpture at Chelsea School of Art in the 1967, having been a student there from 1960-1963, and then at the Slade from 1963-1966, the British scene was dominated by Anthony Caro's 'New Generation' students busily welding across town at St Martins. Barlow was hardly sympathetic to their work. "Despite the brightness and so-called newness of the New Generation", she remembers,

> there was an instant familiarity about it. A dullness took over: the stillness of the sculpture was bland, not atmospheric; its weight was leaden rather than illusionary; its colour, although its greatest asset, too reminiscent of what had been shown in the previous year's New Generation painting exhibition.... As an all male preserve, the New Generation exhibition offered a collection of workshop practices, born out of essentially male-based activities; welding, fibreglass and resin casting and construction, and semi-industrial assemblage.[1]

Shedmesh
stretchers, canvas, foam
180 x 180 x 180 cm
1976
Camden Arts Centre, London

cf Jan Voss

*

organic, like 3D ptg.
'truth to materials.
temporary, impermanent

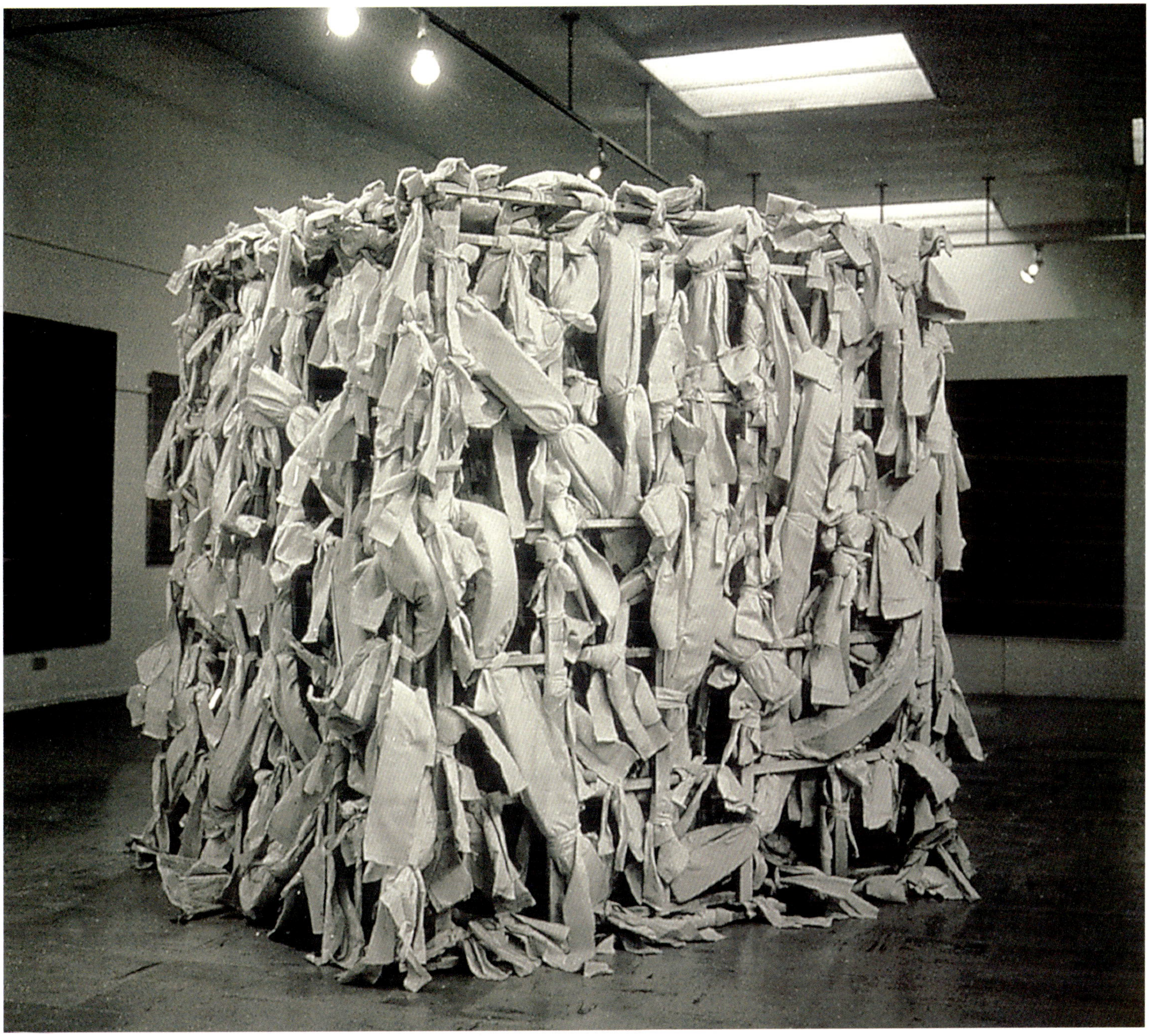

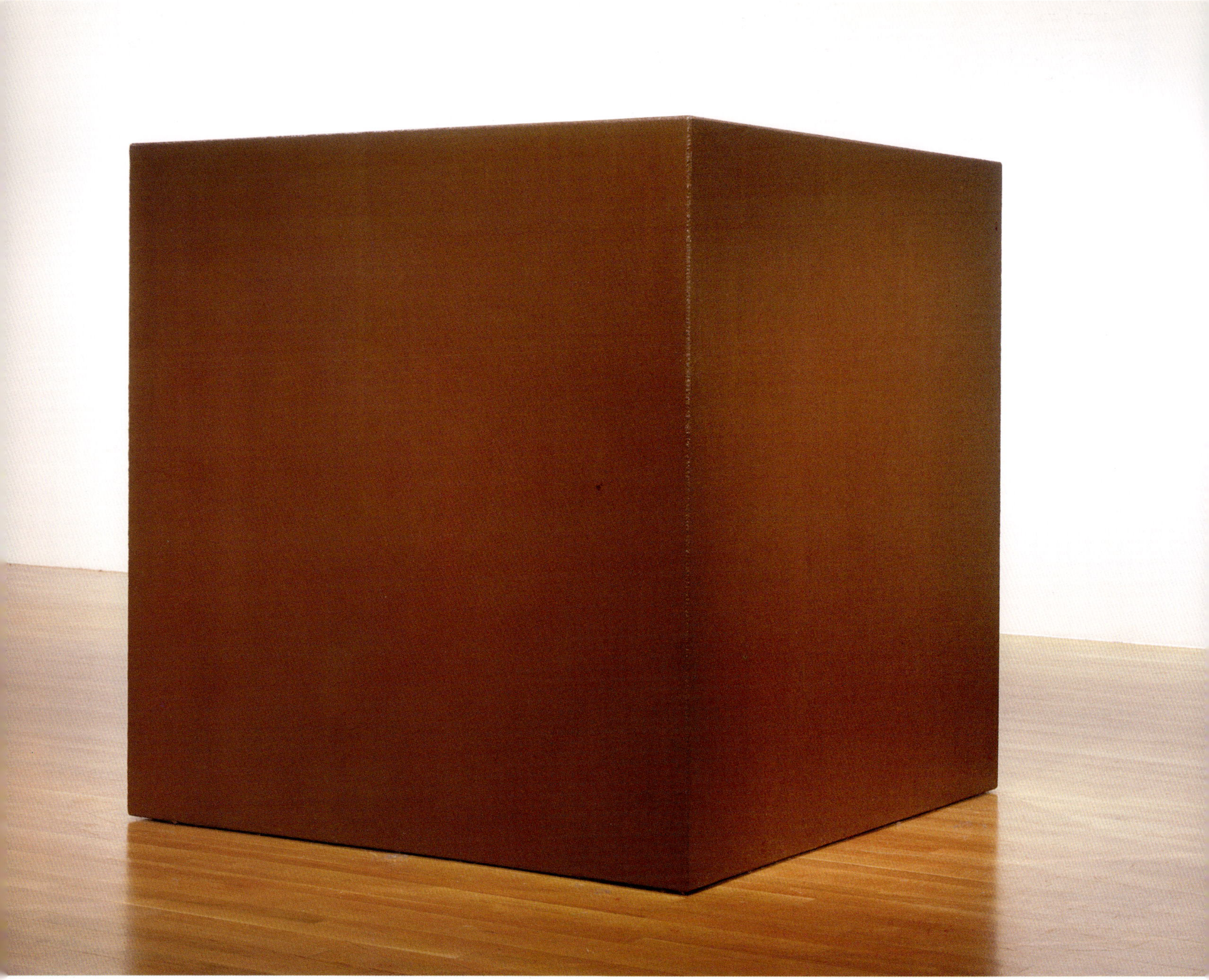

Tony Smith
Die
Steel
183 x 183 x 183 cm
1962 (fabricated 1998)

2 Wadley, Nicholas, "Against Inertia", in *The Sculpture Show*, London: Hayward and Serpentine Galleries, 1983, p. 11.

3 Barlow, Phyllida, "Travelling Light: a brief analysis of the end of the work and the triumph of the photographic colour transparency", in Naomi Salaman and Ronnie Simpson, eds., *Postcards on Photography – Photorealism and the Reproduction*, Cambridge: Cambridge Darkroom Gallery, 1998, p. 57.

As she predicted, the New Generation's dominance was short lived, but *Shedmesh* was equally at odds with British work of the 1970s. In *The Sculpture Show*, 1983, the 70s generation was represented by Paul De Monchaux, Ken Draper, Nigel Hall, Roger Partridge, and others. Nicholas Wadley, writing in the catalogue, noted their reaction against "truth to materials", coupled with a "growth of the sense of the pictorial in sculpture". Wadley selected quotations that could not have been more distant from Barlow's sensibilities: De Monchaux: "Whatever the stone is, I want it so that the material isn't the first thing the spectator responds to." Partridge: "I want to get away from people looking at my work from the point of view of how it was made."[2]

The text in which Barlow remembers the New Generation is called "Hearsay, Rumours, Bed-sit Dreamers and Art Begins Today". It is a wonderfully vivid series of recollections describing how a young British artist learnt about avant-garde American art at a time before cheap transatlantic flights and websites. In it, Barlow recalls the tales which ignited her sculptural imagination:

> stories of works in deserts and excavations in derelict warehouses employing a different kind of labour: straight manual labour as seen on the street and building site… whilst at the opposite end of the scale, resin and a new material, latex, were being used like paint, not as a substitute for bronze, but as stuff in its own right, to be dunked into, painted on cloth to make it rigid, moulded off rigid forms to make them soft, poured, spilt and thrown.

The wonder of these rumours did not mean that Barlow went on to emulate Robert Smithson, Gordon Matta-Clark, or Eva Hesse, yet if *Shedmesh* is to be situated, surely the important comparisons should be with American work. Whilst the structure calls to mind Sol LeWitt's lattices, the overall final shape and scale (the work is just over six foot high) summons the single sculpture that by the early 1970s might have stood, at least in the UK, for the beginnings of minimalism: Tony Smith's *Die*, 1962. Barlow has described a photograph of the work published in the catalogue for *The Art of the Real*, the show that toured to the Tate in 1969:

> The image of Smith's *Die* shows the infamous black steel cube situated in a woodland setting. The cube itself is streaked and stained, anything but pristine, and placed awkwardly within the boundaries of the photograph; a black and white photograph printed on thin, now slightly yellowing, glossy paper.[3]

Though this text dates from the late 90s, one imagines that Barlow even in 1969 would have been struck by the image in which this most pared down of sculptures appeared spoiled and awkward. Already a ruin in representation, *Die* is recast in *Shedmesh*. The cube now has an interior that can be seen into but not seen through, an interior that seems to spill out beyond its boundaries. Floppy foam appendages droop over neat edges: gravity, not geometry, rules.

Shedmesh shares little with British work of its time, but it does have affinities with the American work that followed in the wake of Smith's and Donald Judd's minimalism. In her "Accession" series, 1967-1968, Eva Hesse had opened up the cube, drilling a grid of holes in its aluminium faces and threading through lengths of tubing to create a bristling almost living inside of innumerable protuberances and interiors. As Richard Serra succinctly remembered, "Eva added subjectivity, obsession, metaphor, psychology, and sexuality to Judd's exquisitely tooled rarefied container."[4] In 1971, Jackie Winsor had made *Bound Grid*, using hemp to tie together lengths of wood whose quirky bends and differing thicknesses clearly upset the order the grid arrangement would seem to promise. Faith Wilding made her *Womb Room (Crocheted Environment)* in 1972, knitting a main grid structure but differentiating each square with individual circular or spider's web patterns. Brenda Miller had hung different lengths of fibre from a grid of nails on a wall to make *Diandrous* in 1973. Commenting on Winsor's work in 1974, and possibly thinking about these other pieces, and even Jo Baer's radiator paintings, Lucy Lippard wrote that:

'Grid' makers & manipulators

4 Serra, Richard, "Donald Judd", *Artforum*, Summer 1994, p. 113.

5 Lippard, Lucy, "Jackie Winsor", *Artforum*, February 1974, p. 56.

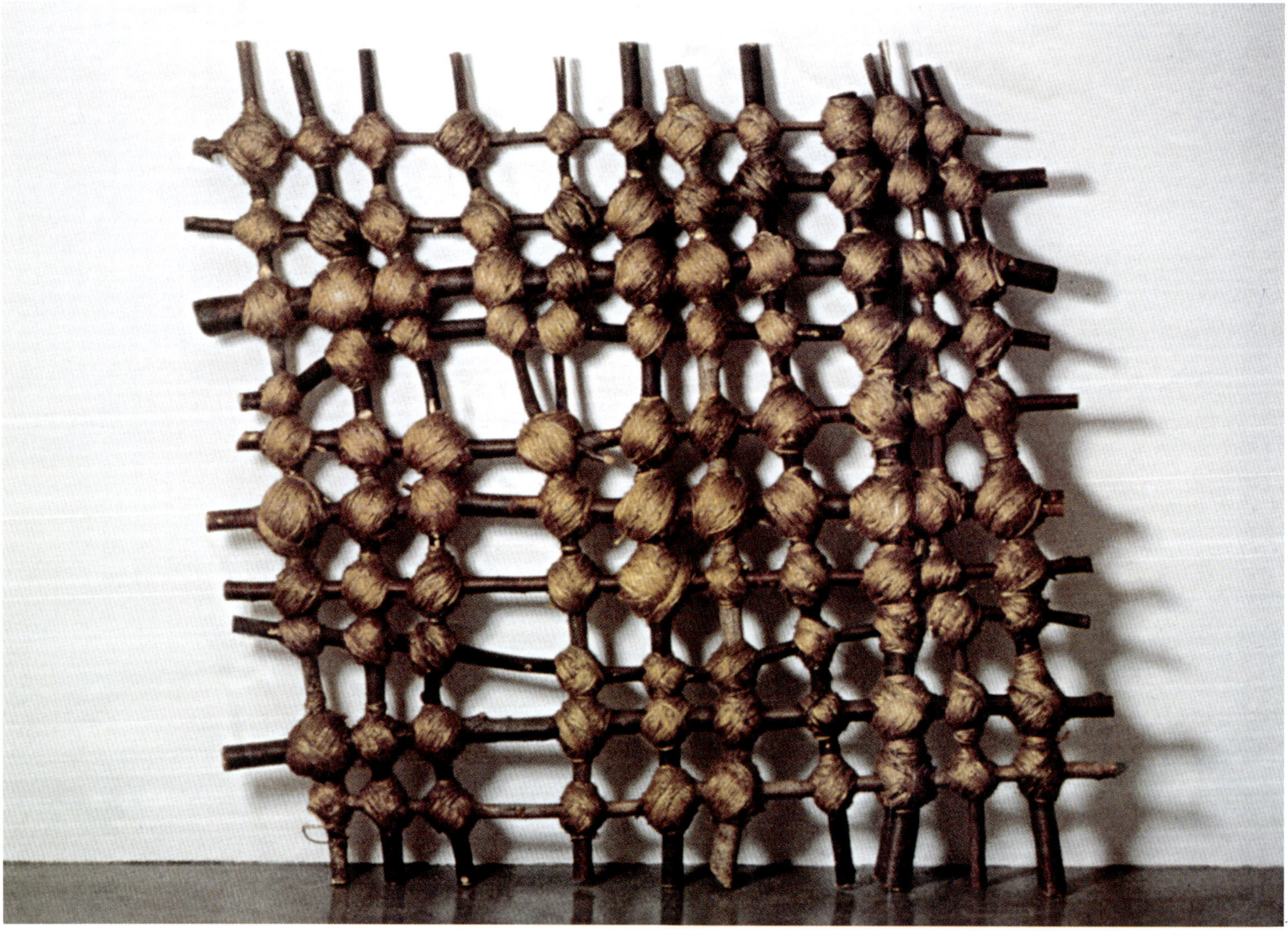

Jackie Windsor
Bound Grid
Wood and hemp
1971-1972
Courtesy Paula Cooper Gallery, New York

Barry Flanagan
Heap 4
Hessian and sand
1967

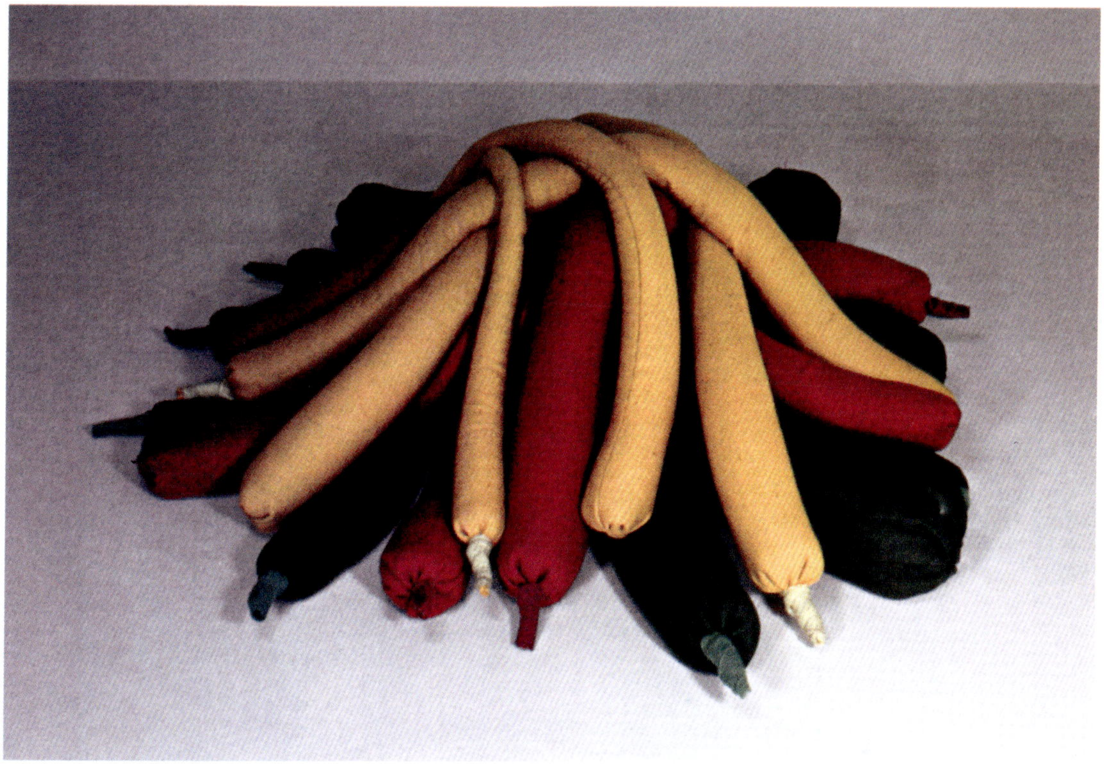

women make more 'emotional' work?

> Many women artists working with geometry and obsessive repetition (at its extreme, fragmentation), have come into their own by using a rectilinear framework primarily to contradict it, or within which to perpetrate mysterious rituals of process or emotive content. There is a certain pleasure in proving oneself against perfection, or the order that runs the world, despoiling neat edges and angles with "homemade" or natural procedures that relate back to the body and personal experience.[5]

Lippard's analysis, which is very much of its time, does speak to the work Barlow would show two years later. *Shedmesh* certainly uses a "rectilinear framework to contradict it", but one should beware of feminising the strategies that are so clearly in play in the work, for the use of loose foam could just as easily mark the importance for Barlow of the one prominent British sculptor whose work must have seemed experimental, forward-looking, and yet still resolutely material. At a moment when Richard Long, Hamish Fulton, Bruce McLean, and Gilbert and George were pointing forward out of the New Generation mode to performance and a textual sculpture which could only be represented through photography and language, Barry Flanagan had been hanging coloured cloths off a rope line, stacking and folding coloured blankets, trailing rope across a gallery floor, stuffing hessian bags with sand and drooping them over each other. Though Flanagan soon moved into stone carving and bronze casting, his weighty, colourful early sculpture with its use of everyday materials would provide an important British precedent for Barlow's.

6 Morris, Robert, "Anti-Form", *Artforum*, April 1968, p. 35.

Flanagan's work was not illustrated in Robert Morris's 1968 essay "Anti-Form" but it could have been. Morris's essay is highly appropriate for a consideration of *Shedmesh* but it also points well beyond it to later works Barlow made like *Fill*, 1981 and *Expanse*, 1987. Morris's essay began by describing the "well-built thing" – a sculpture such as Smith's *Die*: "To achieve a cubic or rectangular form is to build in the simplest, most reasonable way, but it is also to build well." For Morris, the move to the cubic solved the problem of sculptural composition, eliminating the problems of subjectivity, but the move away from the cubic was not back towards the personal (as in Lippard's feminist reading) – it was as a further means of divesting authorship. Materials would not be chosen in advance to construct a pre-planned shape: materials would determine form. "Recently, materials other than rigid industrial ones have begun to show up", wrote Morris, thinking of Oldenburg's vinyl, Serra's vulcanised rubber, his own felt. "Considerations of gravity", he continued,

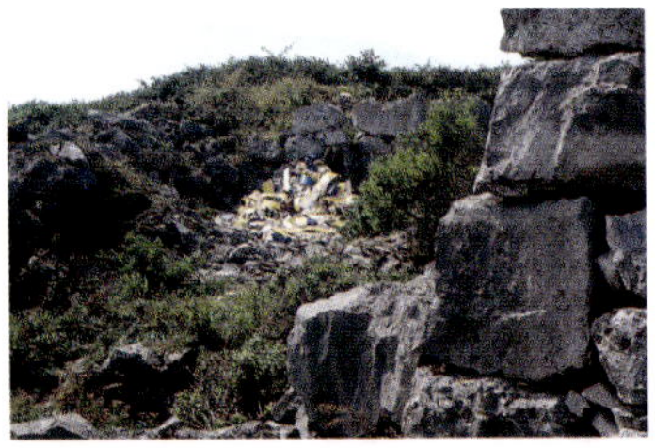

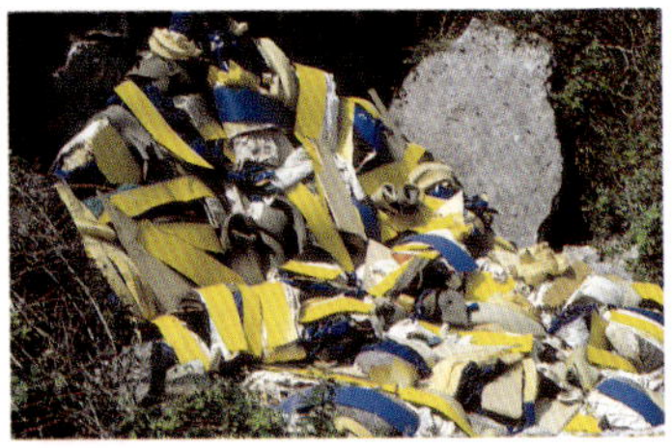

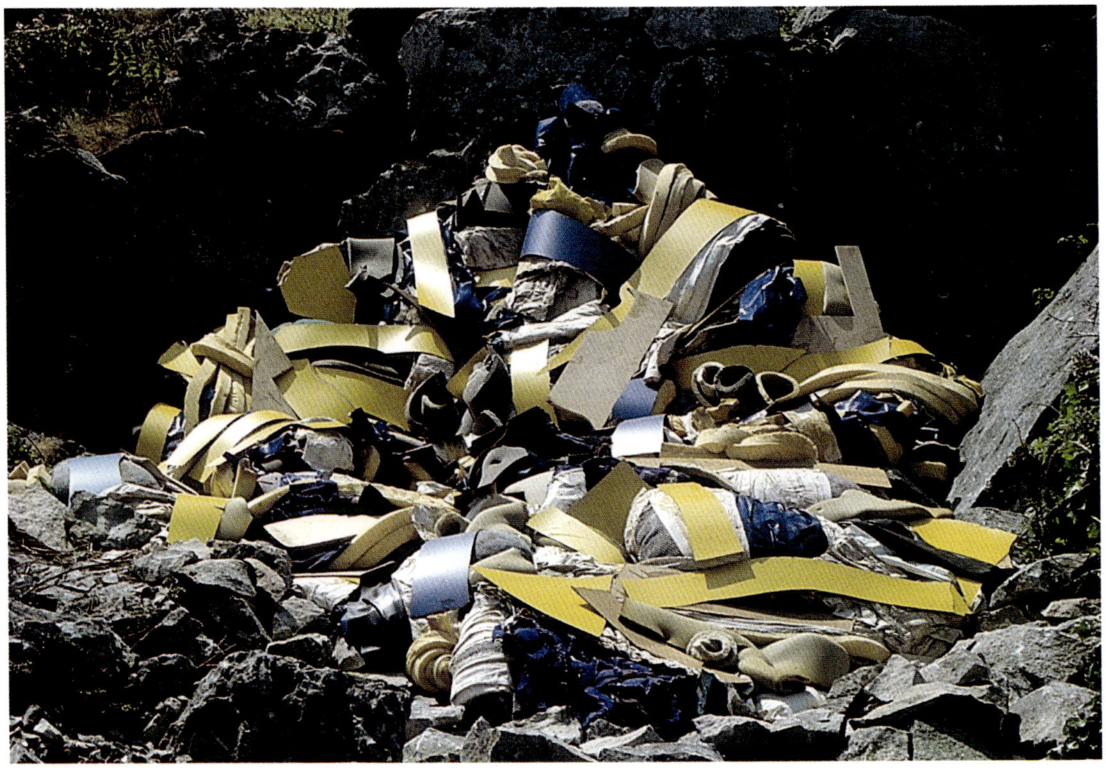

This page
Fill
Tout Quarry, Portland, Dorset.
Formica, canvas, timber lengths, string, studio debris, hardboard, chip board, upholstery foam
900 x 450 (depth of hole) x 1200 cm
1983

Opposite
Four
Upholstery foam, hardboard, sugar, stitched twine, steel frame
Overall of site:
900 x 300 (of tallest work) x 1000 cm
1977
Gloucester Cathedral Close, Gloucester Festival

> become as important as those of space. The focus on matter and gravity as means results in forms that were not projected in advance. Considerations of ordering are necessarily causal and imprecise and unemphasised. Random piling, loose stacking, hanging, give passing form to the material. Chance is accepted and indeterminacy is implied, as replacing will result in another configuration.[6]

Whilst *Shedmesh* combines the 'well-built cube' with the anti-form attitude, Morris's words might read as a kind of mission statement for Barlow's later postminimalist works of the late 1970s, in which building all but disappears.

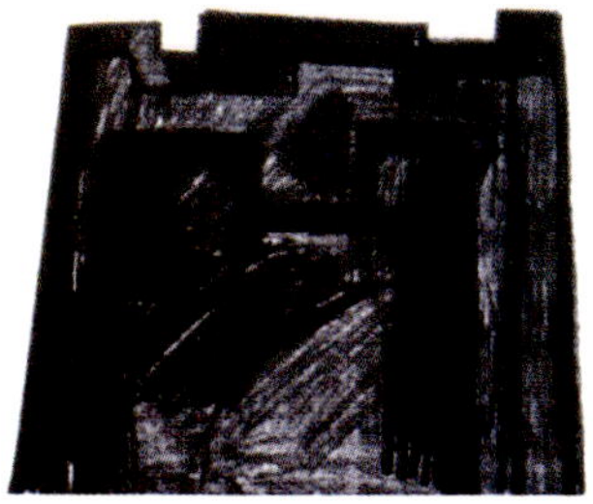
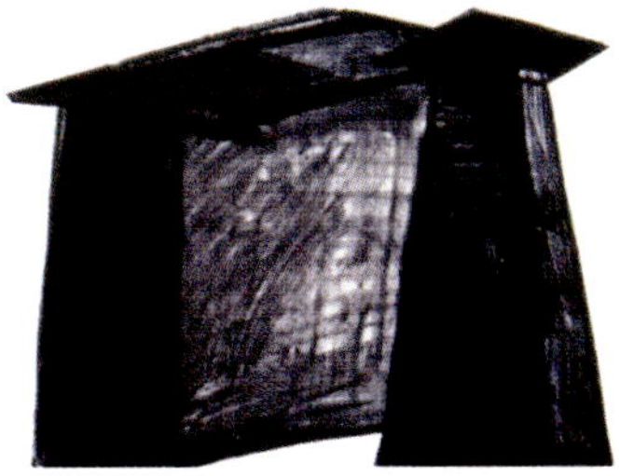
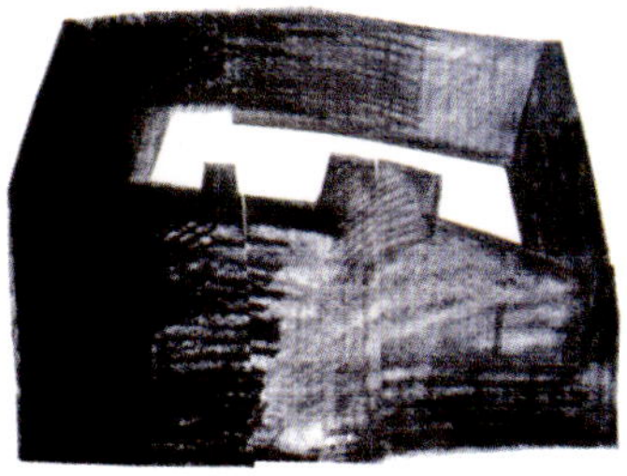
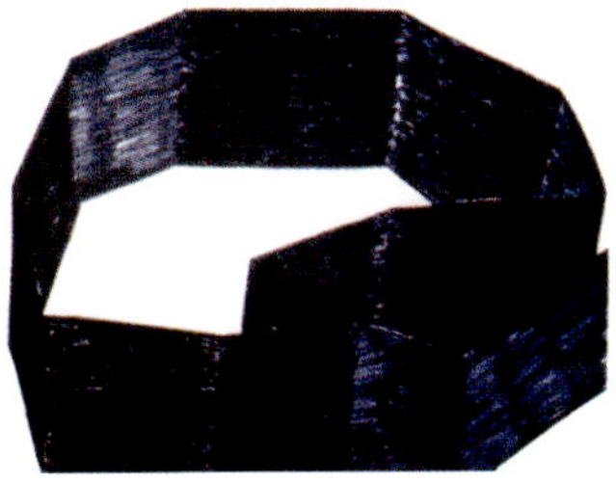
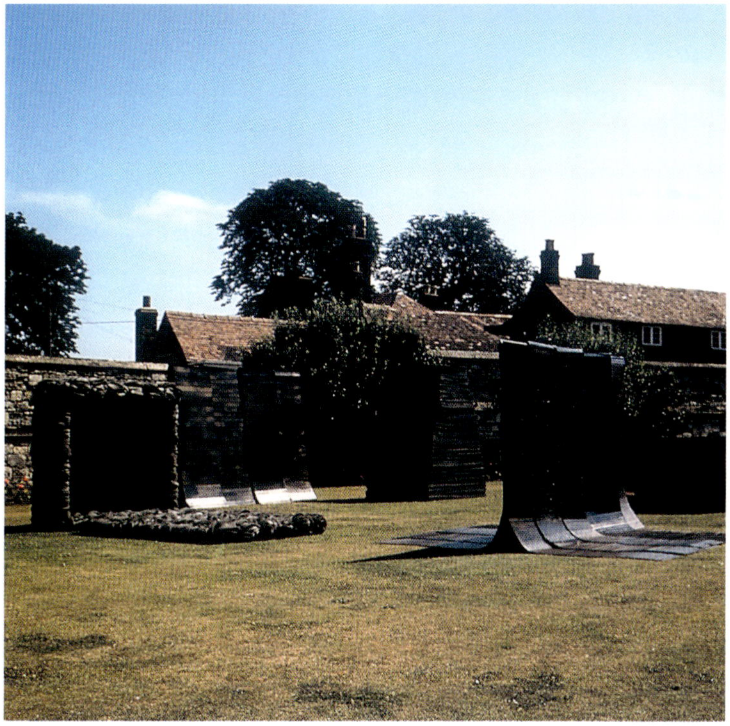
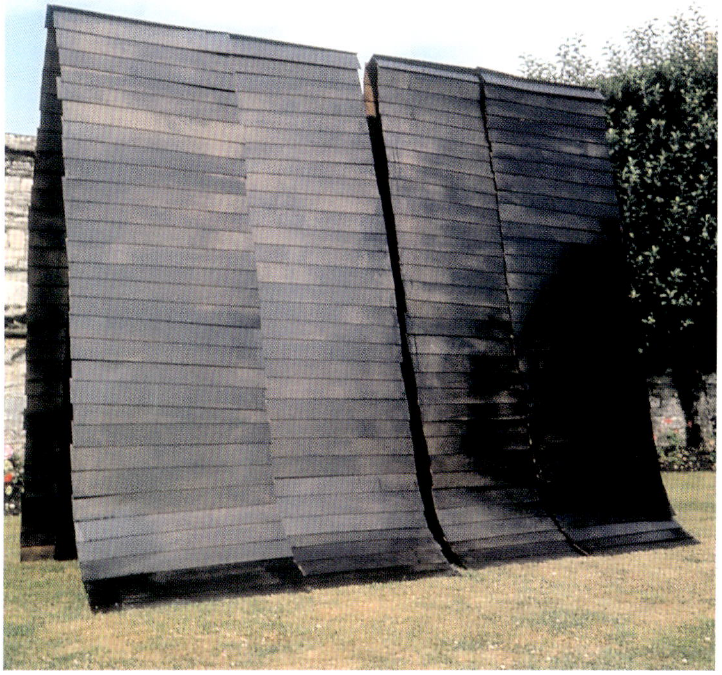
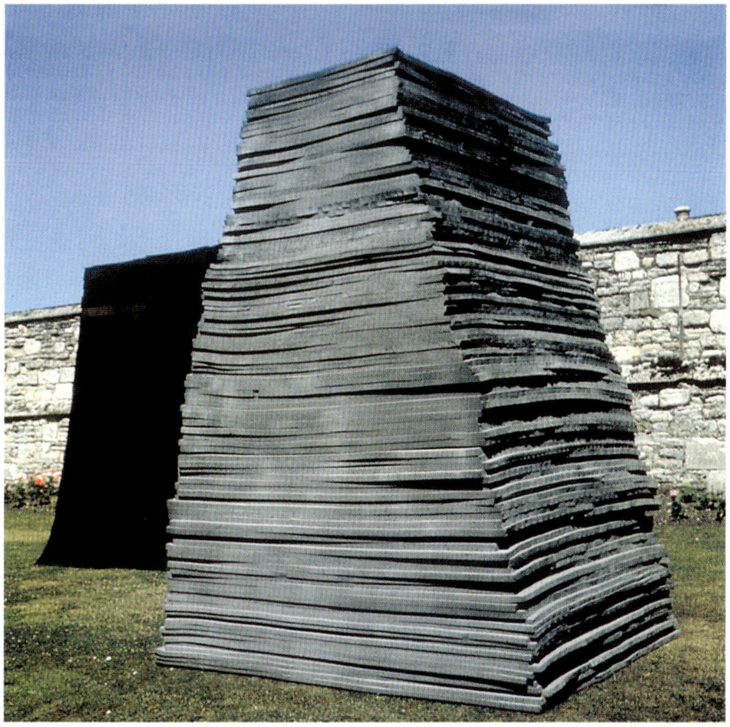
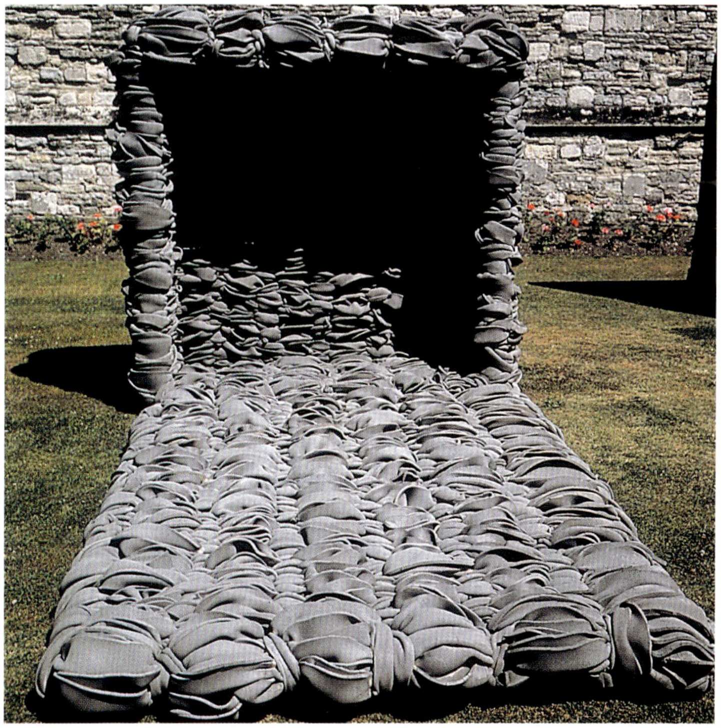

7 Serra, Richard, interview with Art 21, www.pbs.org/art21/artists/serra/clip1.html.

Morris's verbs ("Random piling, loose stacking, hanging...") give a sense of a messy, unwieldy sculpture such as his own *Threadwaste*, 1968. *Shedmesh* is also messy but for all its difference from a sleek, Donald Judd-like box, the work is also very restrained. Compared with *All and Everything*, 1973, whose very title describes a sense of excess, the number of processes in *Shedmesh* is very limited (tying, hanging) in a manner that makes its own title quite apt (two nouns economically crammed together). What is noticeable in Barlow's work between 1976 and 1990 is not just the way hands-on sculptural activities are in play, but that only a small number of activities are in play at any time. To make one of the four structures of *Four*, 1977, hardboard was soaked, stitched, and hung. To make another, foam slabs were cut and stacked. Rags were bleached, sewn and wound around themselves (*x 2*, 1978), felt was slumped over a railing (*Threat*, 1986), upholstery foam was gathered and bunched (*Engulf*, 1987), tarpaulin was propped over thin planks (*Slope*, 1988). The activities might have been painstakingly repetitive or strikingly casual but they were always immediate and immediately recognisable: there was no transformation of matter, no welding, casting, carving, forging, setting, just so many different ways of arranging, all perfectly evident to the viewer. And for every activity that could be read allusively (sewing) there was another that is more simply physical (cramming).

Many of Barlow's processes had been included in Richard Serra's 1972 *Verb List*: to crease, to fold, to twist, to crumple, to knot, to support. Serra has said that of his early work "I really just worked out pieces in relation to the verb list physically in a space", and this work was, it should be stated, a useful bridge to his eventual concerns, a way out of minimalism.[7] His 1968 *Tearing Lead from 1:00-1:47* was made using a sheet of lead just over a metre square. There was just enough lead, then, for Serra to be able to show clearly in the finished sculpture that the only action involved had been tearing. For all their correspondence with Serra's verbs, Barlow's works would never merely be demonstrations of sculptural processes: Barlow would always use far more stuff than a demonstration would require.

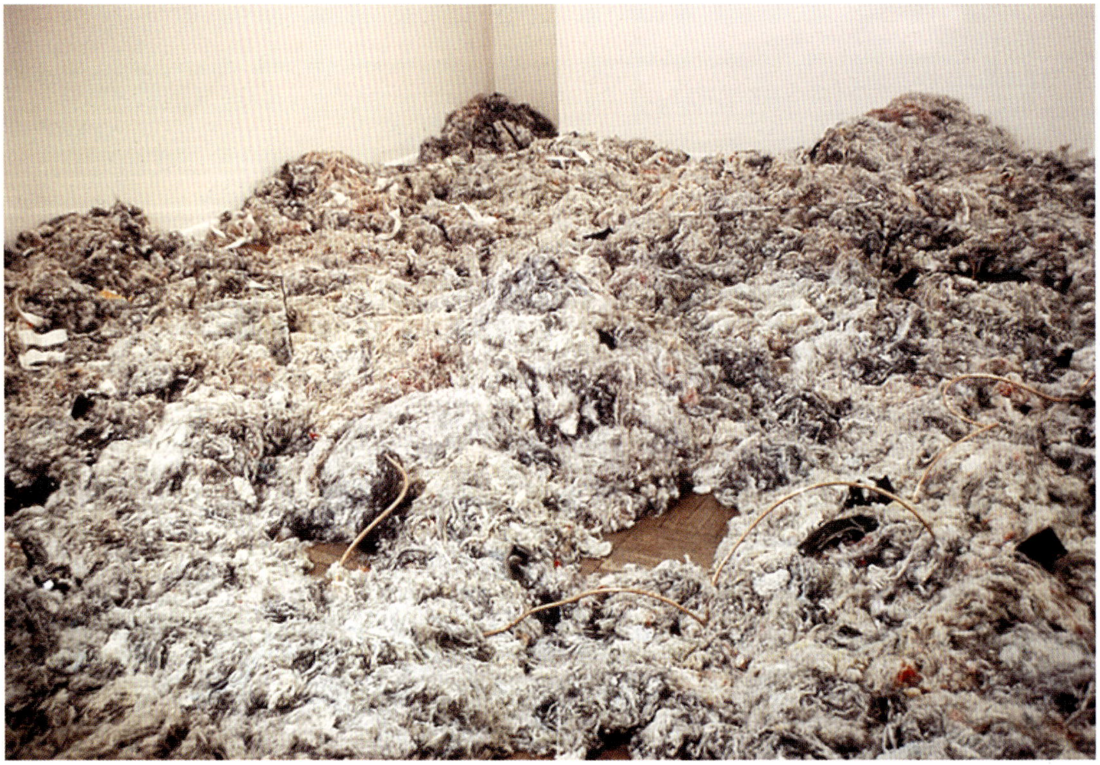

Robert Morris
Untitled (Threadwaste)
Threadwaste, asphalt, mirrors, copper tubing and felt
1968-1969

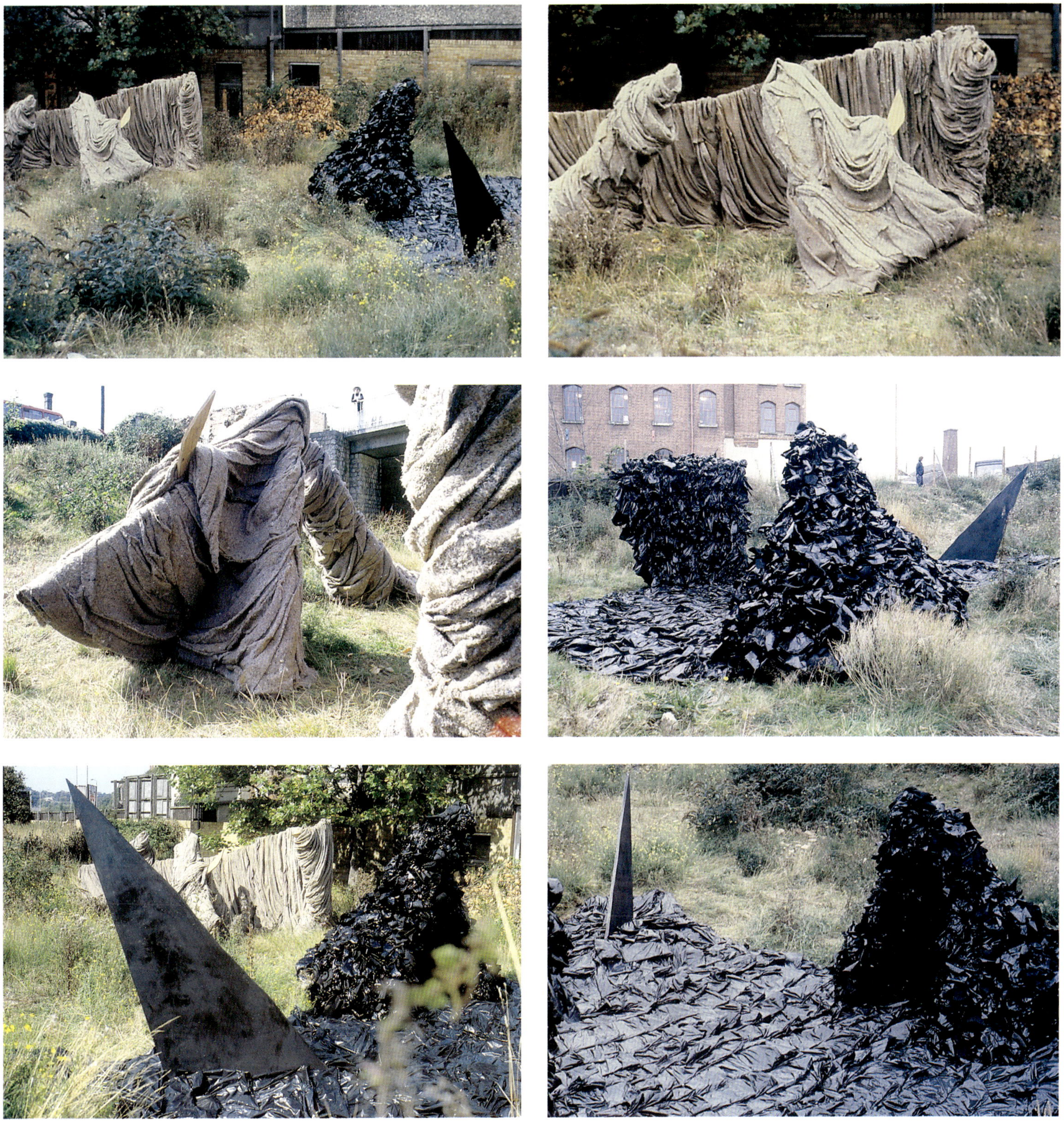

Threat
Timber stakes, carpet felt, refuse sacks, bitumen, paper, polythene
1200 x 270 (tallest work) x 1500 cm
1986
Canterbury

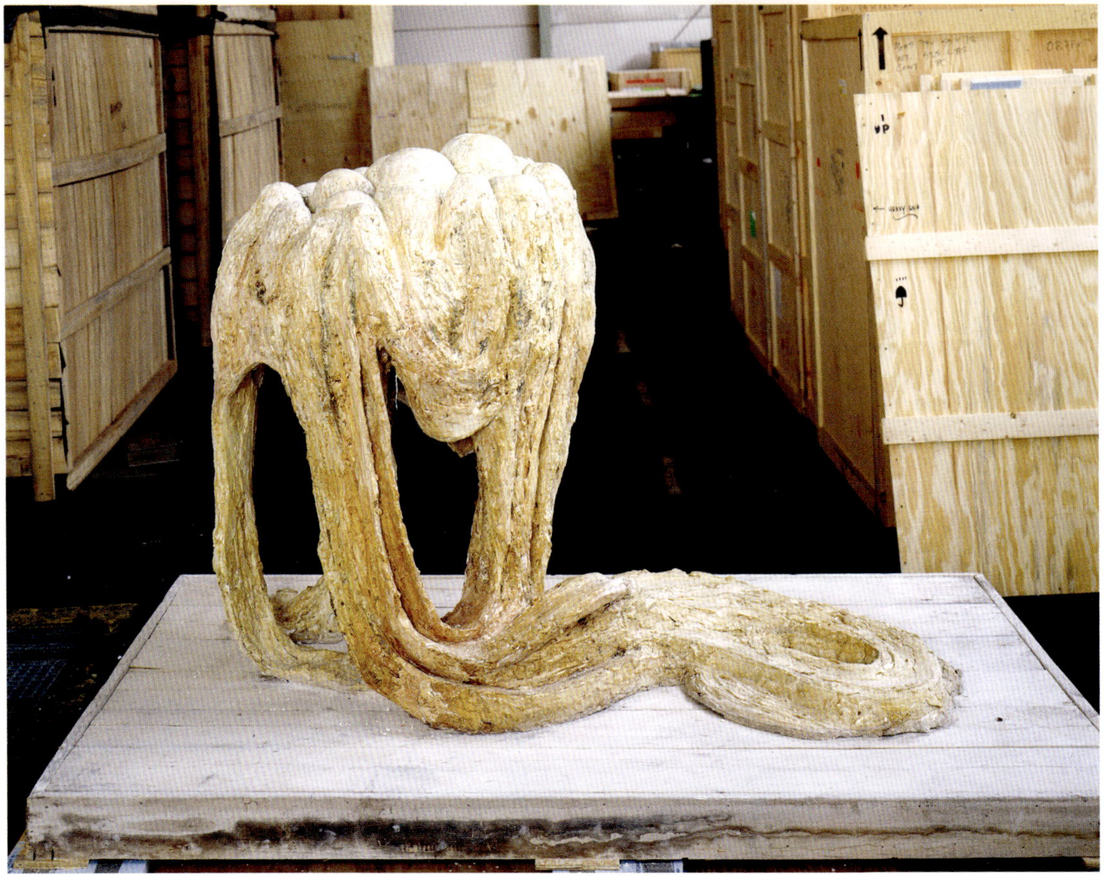

Louise Bourgeois
Avenza Revisited II
Plaster, plastic and wire on wooden base
1968-1969

Processual restraint was continually coupled with material excess and it was perhaps also the sheer expansive amount of stuff that distanced Barlow's work from the American for whom she felt the most admiration – Louise Bourgeois. *Untitled*, 1968 – later called *Avenza Revisited II* – has been of recurrent interest to Barlow. The work, she writes, is "redeemed by its fluidity, its spillage and its sensual tactility, qualities which have the potential to give beauty to the monstrous".[8] "The back of it cascades down in very carefully modelled folds. Her whole relationship with the folded shape is extremely erotic and sensual, where she incorporates both the absolute female side of the folded shape, the cavernous empty womb-like space, with the rippling eroticism of the phallic forms on top."[9] Many of Barlow's own works of the mid-1980s were also often folded – think of *Engulf*, 1987 or *Folds*, 1988 – but because these work so far exceeded the size of discreet objects, the sense of the body was always at a further remove. When Barlow described her own work, she related the folded form not so much to the body but to stage curtains, which is not to say the forms were inert: "*Threat* had the idea of the curtain as a sensual form because of the folds in it. A folded shape has an inside that you can't quite get to, you are offered it but it is often hidden, and the curtain seems to replicate this folded form over and over again."[10] A work could suggest the theatrical as well as the geological, or the architectural as well as the bodily. Perhaps the ease of such associations means they should be held at bay. Barlow was not dealing with metaphor so much as matter.

8 Barlow, Phyllida, "The Sneeze of Louise", in *Museum of Modern Art Papers, Volume One, Louise Bourgeois,* Oxford: Museum of Modern Art, 1996, p. 8.

9 Barlow, Phyllida, "Big Bad Ugly", in *Cloth*, Norwich School of Art and Design, Documents 01, 1998.

10 Barlow, "Big Bad Ugly".

Fold
Carpet felt, stitching,
scaffolding pole
450 x 210 x 450 cm
1988
for 'Housework',
Clarynge Road, Bristol

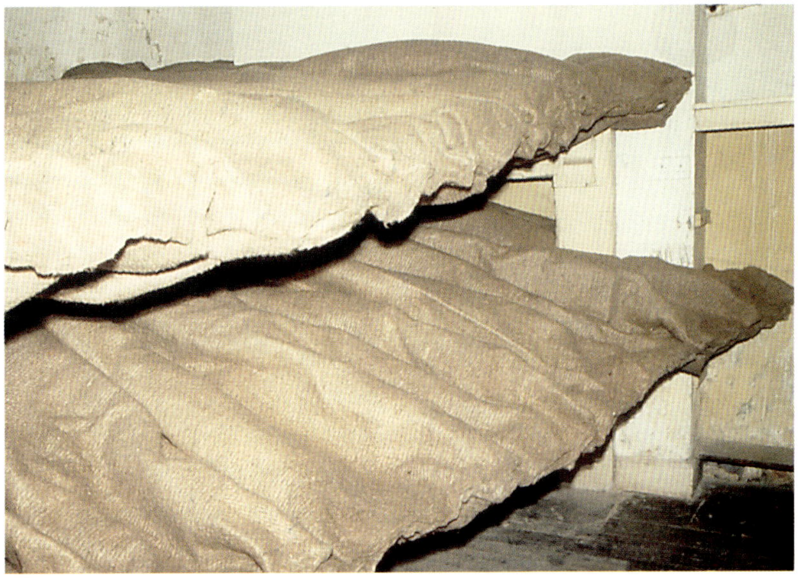

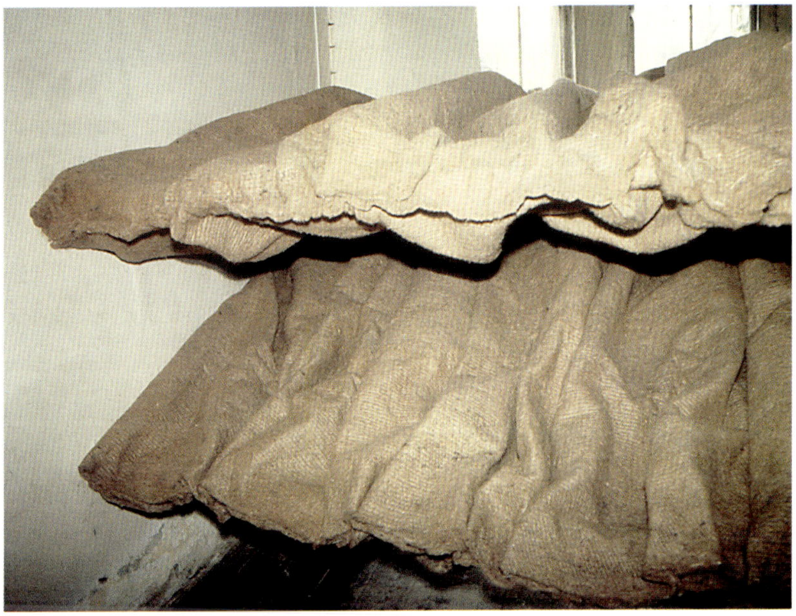

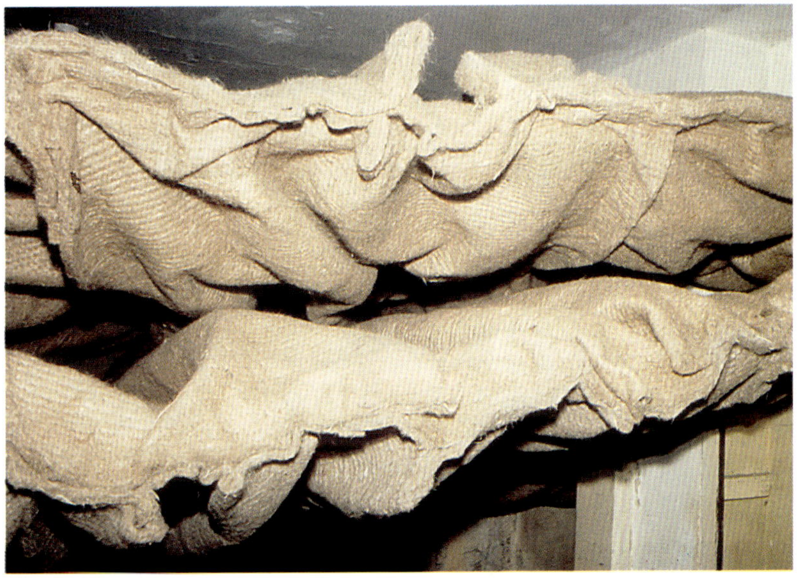

Right
Tarpaulin
Canvas, rubber tubing.
Paint, tarpaulin, concrete,
timber lengths
100 x 330 x 200 cm
2001

Opposite
Slope
Black paper, black gaffer tape,
roofing timbers, polythene,
tarpaulin, staples, wire
1200 x 450 x 1200 cm
1988
Dean Clough, Halifax

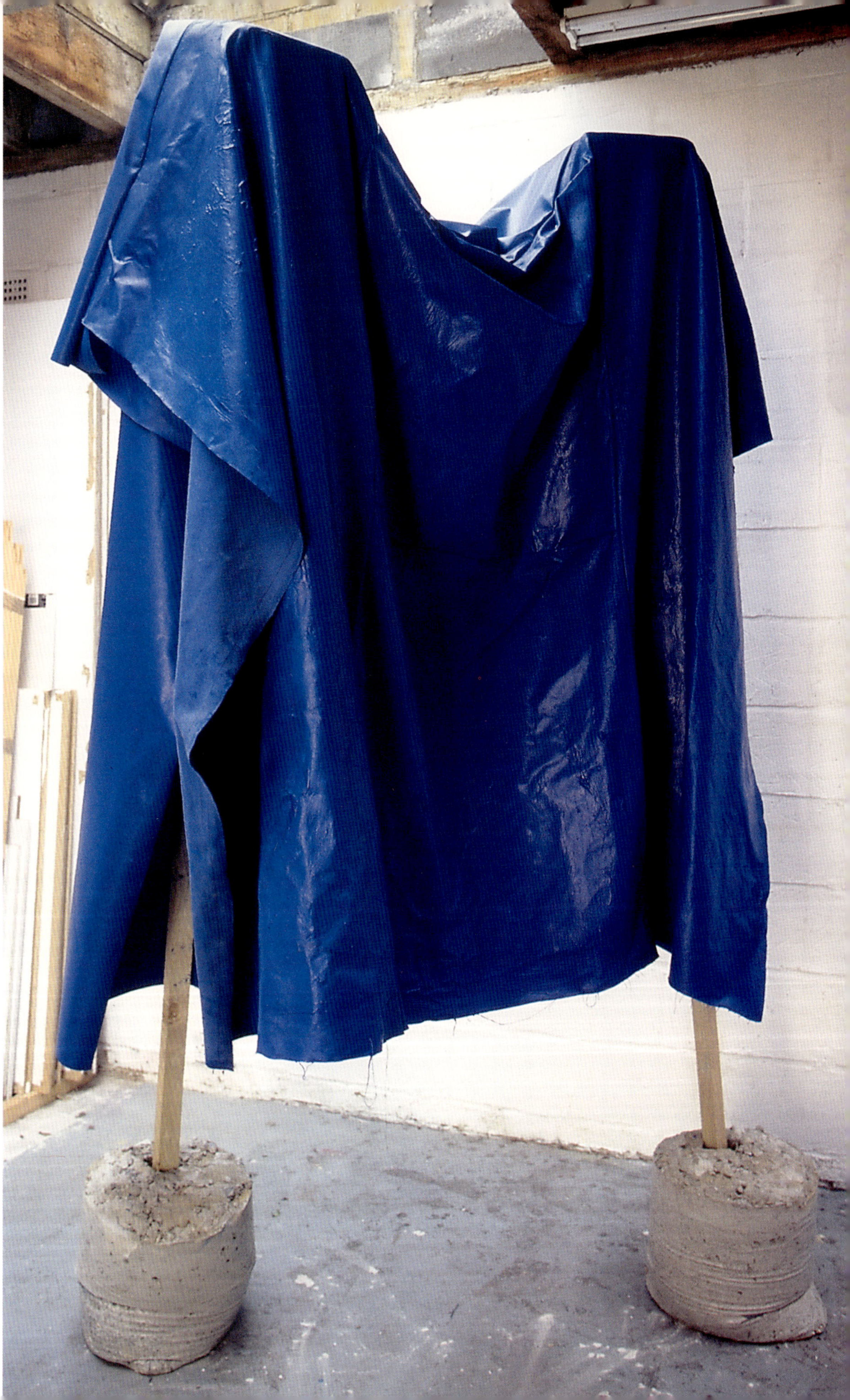

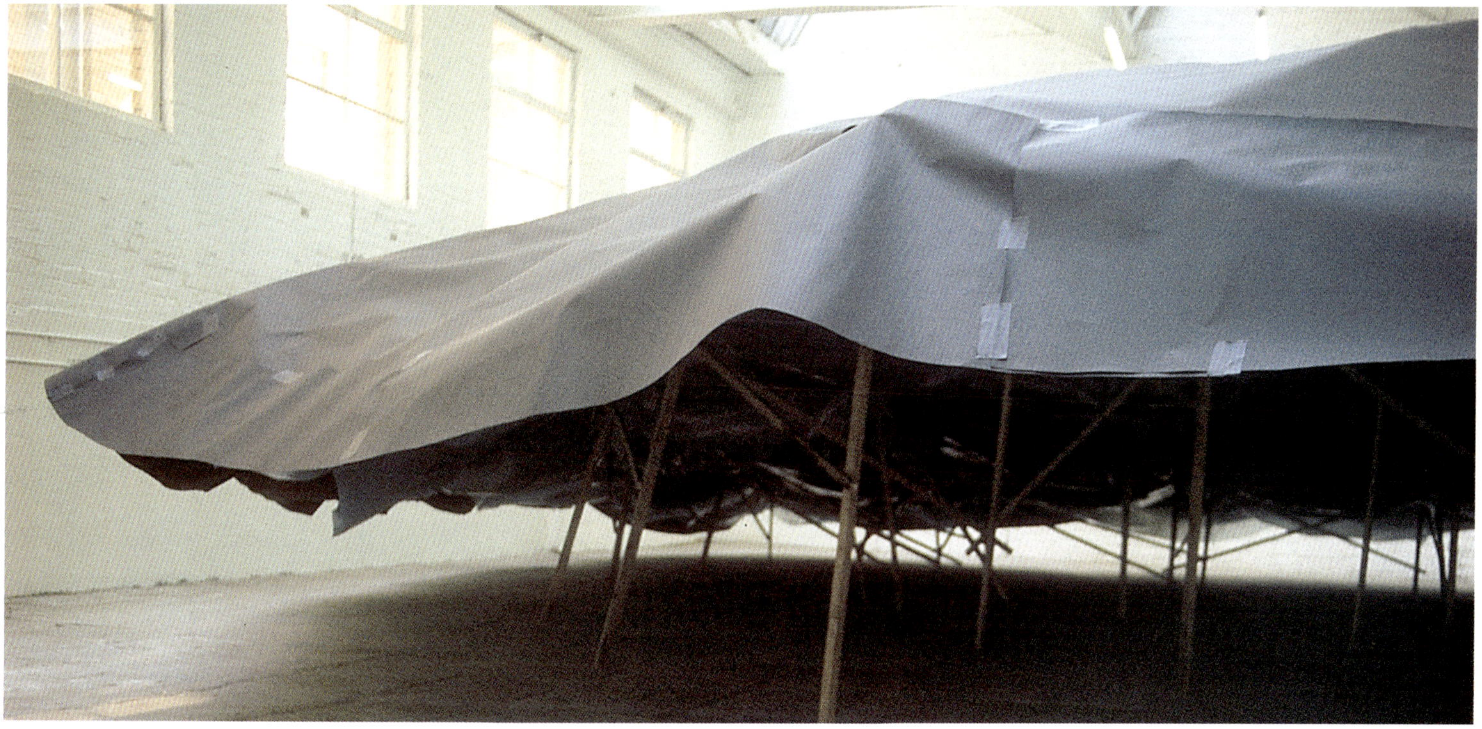
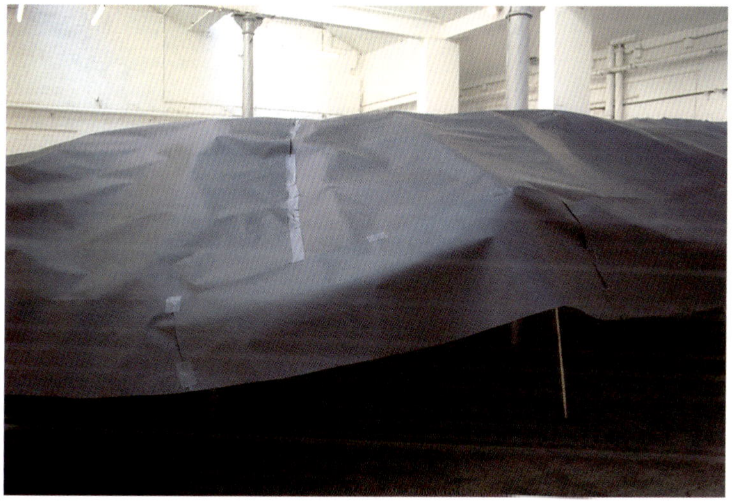
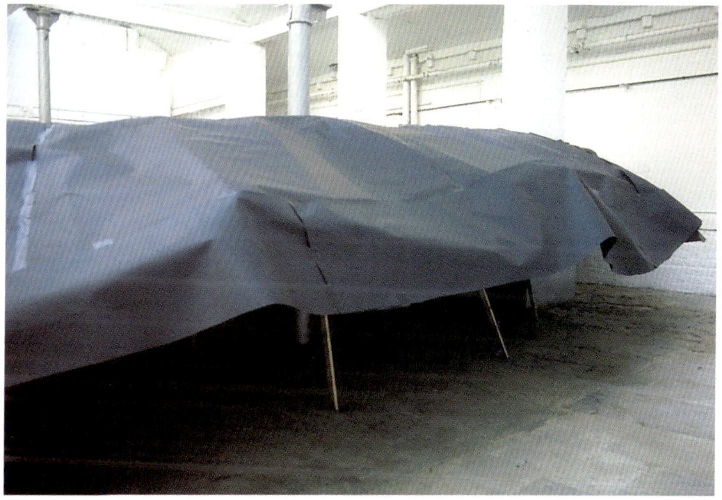
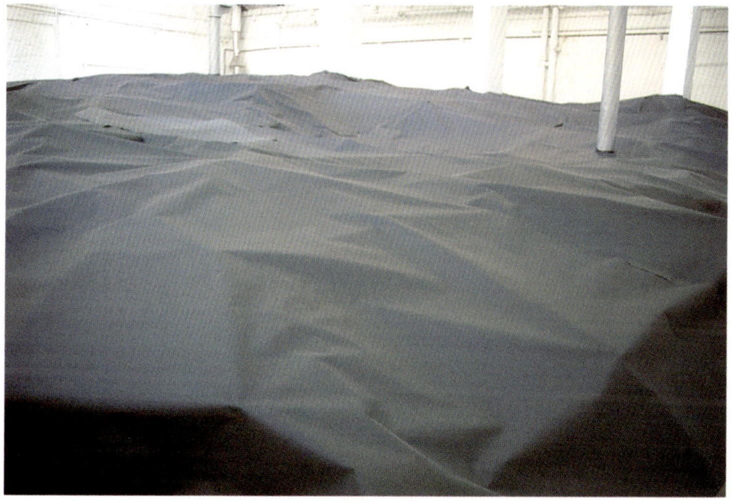
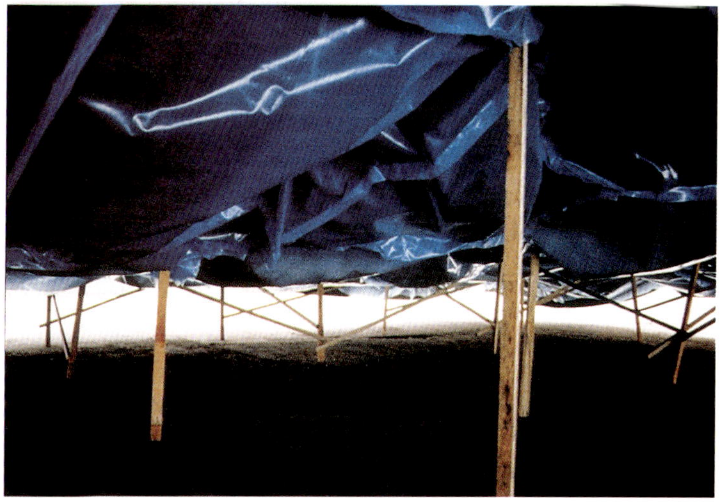

Untitled – Bollard
Hardboard, wood, paint,
cement and wire netting
100 x 110 x 100 cm
2000
Studio work

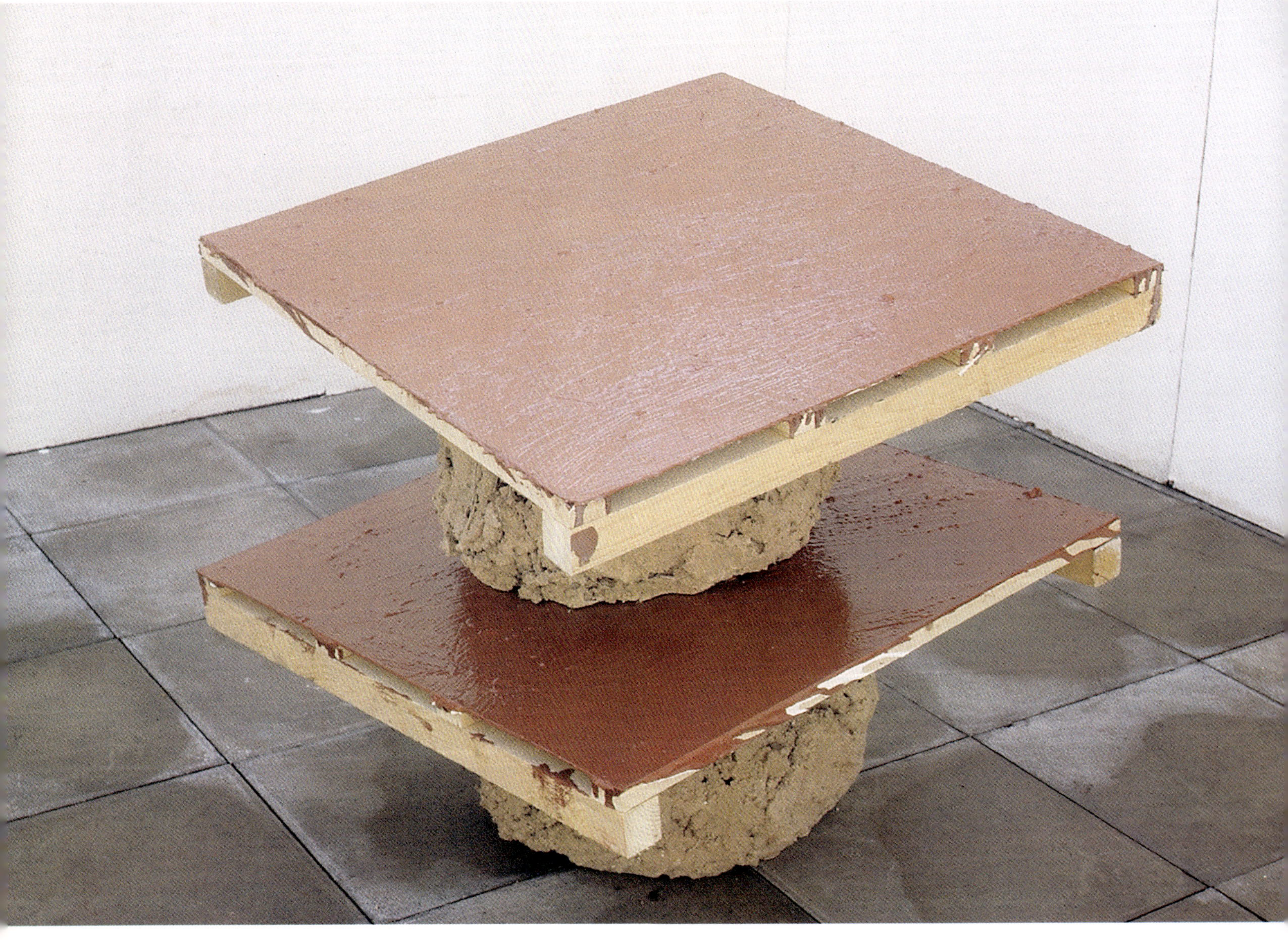

Matter/Material

There are not many published portrait photographs of Phyllida Barlow in front of her work but those that do exist are instructive as they are hardly of Barlow, and certainly not of discrete works. You could be forgiven for not noticing Barlow's face on the invite card for a Camden Arts Centre show from 1971: she is all but pushed out of a shot crammed with rope ends, sheets, folded blankets, cushion covers. One hand stretches out towards the camera perhaps to stop the pile of stuff to the left from toppling; the overexposed fingers of her other hand in the bottom right rhyme with the white folds in the top left corner. In a later shot taken for the *Twelve Sculptors at West Surrey* show from 1978 Barlow stands much more centrally, but still it's not so much her figure that grabs attention as the mass of rubber mats around her, some slightly cracked, some rolled, but most sagging this way and that. What we don't see in these photographs is the artist in front of finished work (think of Eva Hesse by *Expanded Expansion* at the opening of the Whitney *Anti-Illusion Procedures/Materials* show) or an artist in the process of making (think of Richard Serra throwing lead in the catalogue for that same show). What we do see is materials, and lots of them.

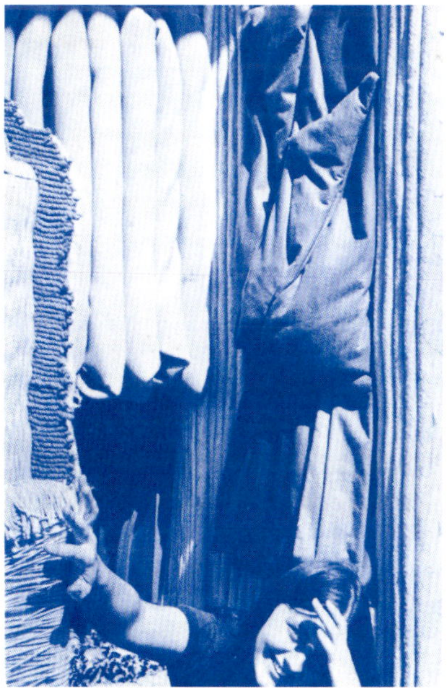

Invitation card,
Phyllida Barlow – exhibition
1971
Camden Arts Centre

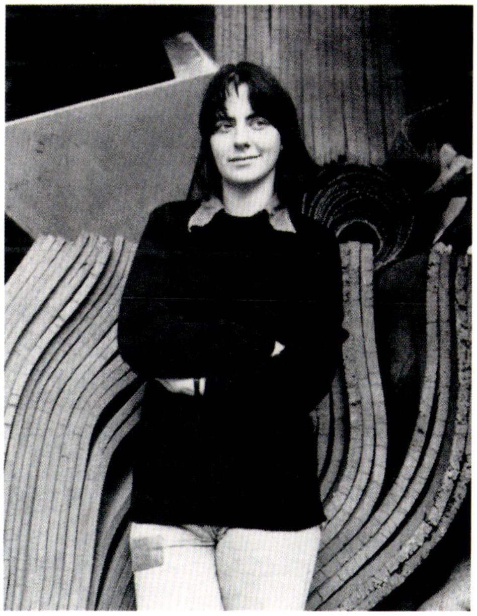

Invitation card
Twelve Sculptors at West Surrey
exhibition
1978

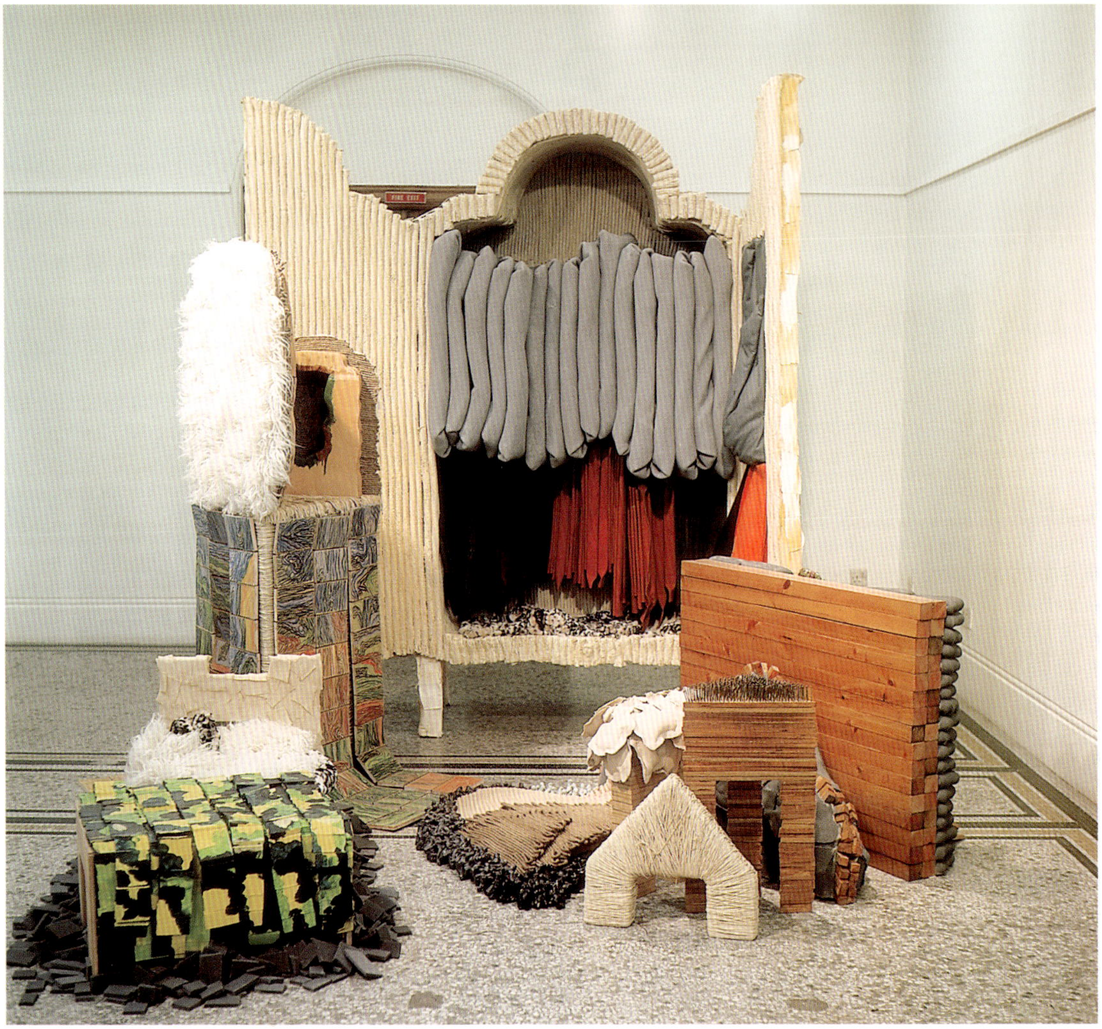

Above
Wardrobe
Timber frame, paper, felt, upholstery foam, plywood, wool, clay, matting, hardboard
300 x 260 x 320 cm
1971
Camden Arts Centre, London

Opposite
View
Canvas, pant, charcoal, upholstery foam, clay, stainer, plywood blocks
210 x 240 x 300 cm
1971
Camden Arts Centre, London

Looking at images of *Engulf*, 1987, *Expanse*, 1987, or *Vigil*, 1989, it is pretty obvious that Barlow's work – at least until the mid 90s – could be characterised by its material expansiveness, and also quite clear that the materials in play are not the traditional ones of wood, metal and stone. Even though at least eight of the 12 West Surrey sculptors with whom she had showed in 1978 *were* represented with work in these materials, noting Barlow's rejection of them (but for the armatures of some works) will not get us very far when trying to locate her work in the context of adventurous, serious sculpture. A partial inventory of the materials of Barlow's works of the 1980s includes carpet felt, polythene, rags, rubber tarpaulin, bitumen, upholstery foam, handkerchiefs, sellotape, canvas, paper, timber, silk, foil, canvas, plaster. Hard and fast rules fall apart before this list: traditional fine art materials are not wilfully expelled; industrial materials dominate but not to the exclusion of organic ones; most do not change from liquid to solid, but plaster sets and bitumen hardens; some materials are bought, but some are found, and some become available by chance: the carpet material in *Threat* came from a fire-damaged factory.

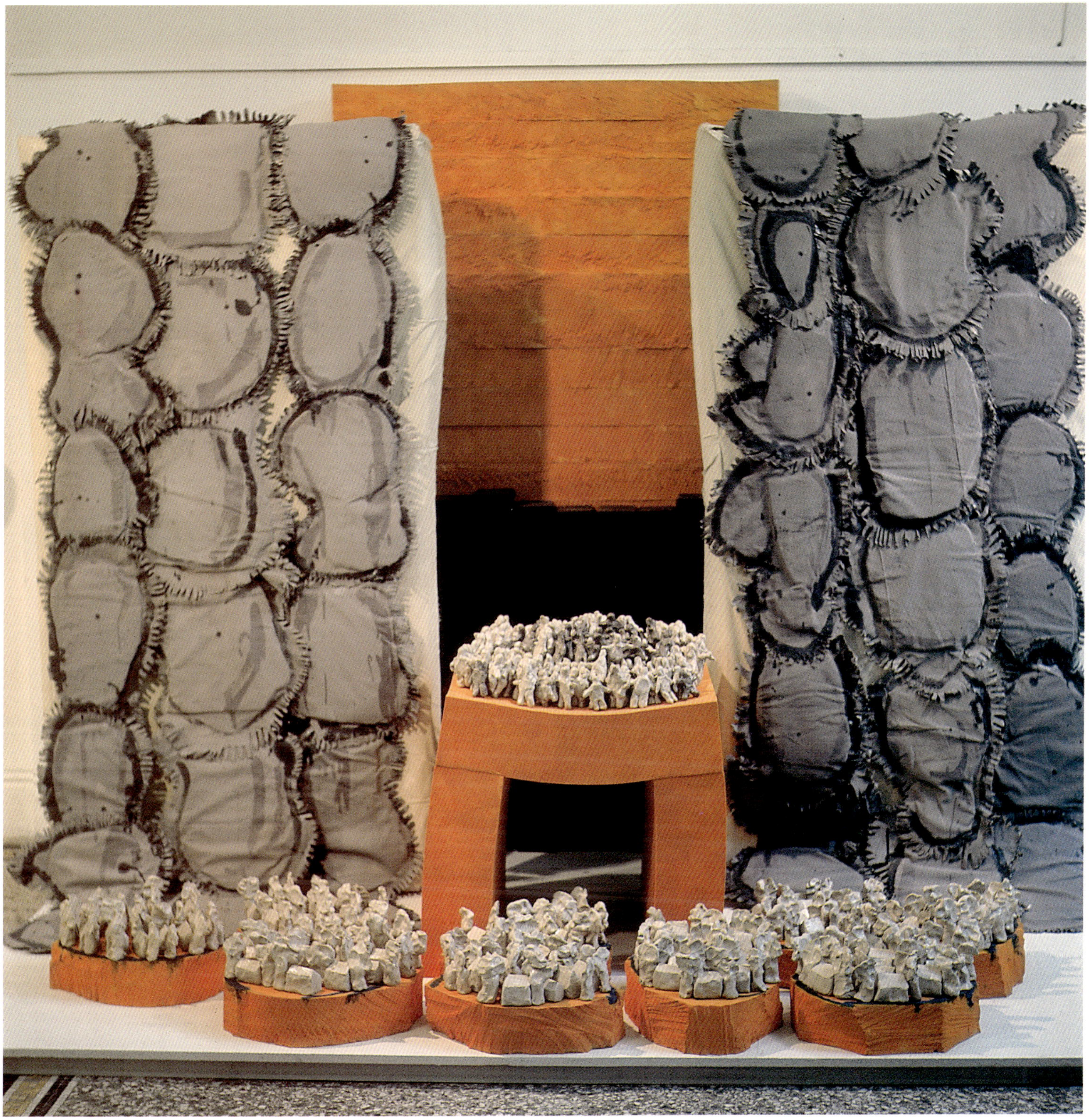

11 Cooke, Lynne, "Between Image and Object: The 'New British Sculpture'", in *A Quiet Revolution: British Sculpture Since 1965*, London: Thames & Hudson, 1987, p. 40.

However, it is still possible to distance Barlow's approach to materials from other practitioners. As Lynne Cooke has noted, many British sculptors of the 70s "were variously involved with landscape, natural cycles, and organic form. Roger Ackling, Hamish Fulton, and David Tremlett, along with David Nash and Nicholas Pope, were its major exponents."[11] Nash in particular represented a somewhat romantic attitude to the 'natural', building primitive stoves from tree trunks or with slates, carving a fake rocky boulder out of wood. Though Barlow used wood at times, it was usually already processed either as hardboard or as factory cut planks, and on the rare occasion when work was situated in a rural area, it was actually in a stone quarry. At a site where a mineral had been prised from the earth as raw matter for future transformation into the aesthetic object, Barlow rather appropriately built a pile out of formerly useful detritus – Formica, canvas, and timber. *Fill*, 1981, might be said to reverse the operation of Richard Long's work – taking urban waste matter to an outdoor site instead of bringing stones into galleries.

Chair
Upholstery foam, clay, varnish, paint, fabrics, paper, wool, paint, wood
300 x 180 x 350 cm
1971
Camden Arts Centre, London

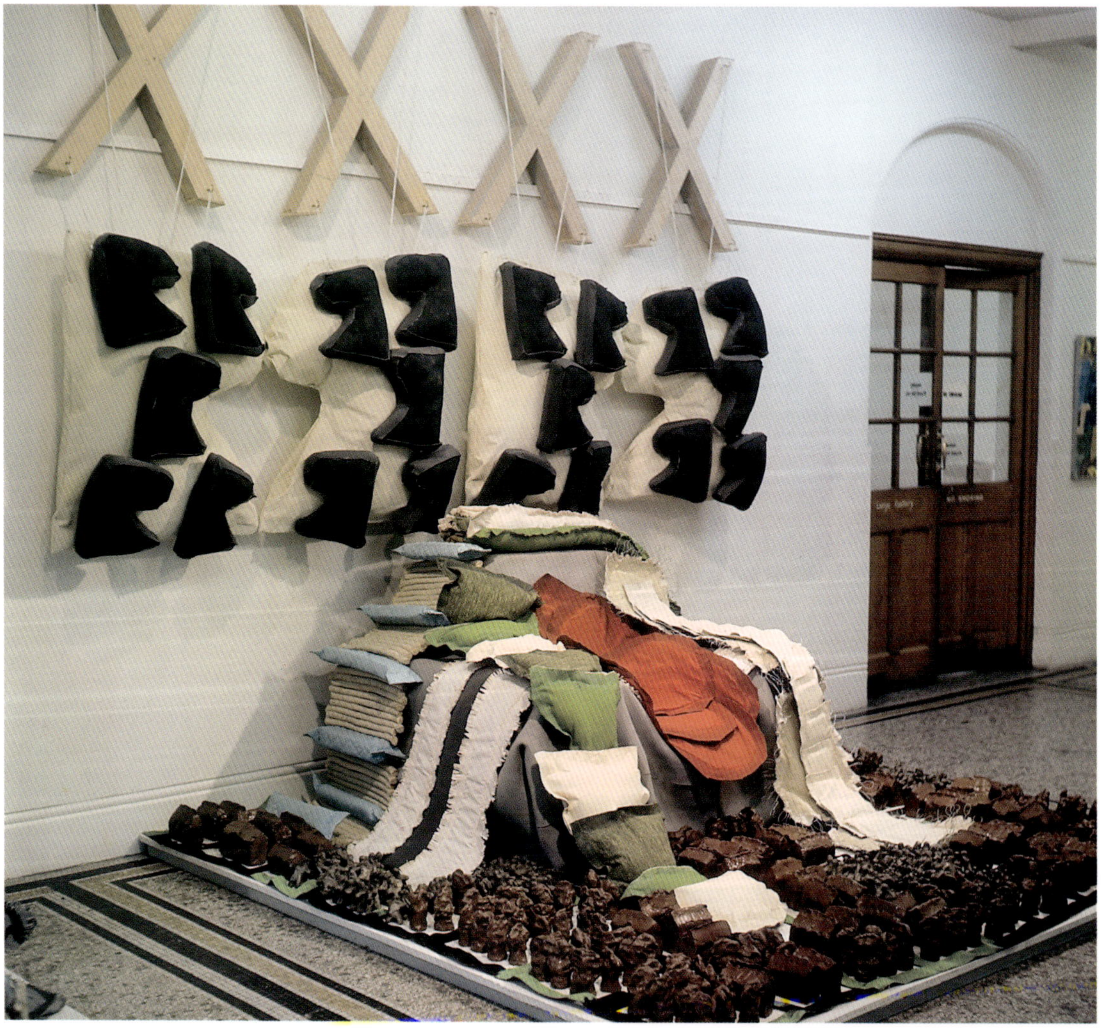

Vigil 1
Paper, bitumen, polythene,
sellotape, vinyl, vinyl tape
Overall of space:
900 x 210 (tallest work) x 1500 cms
1989
Disused churchyard, Windsor

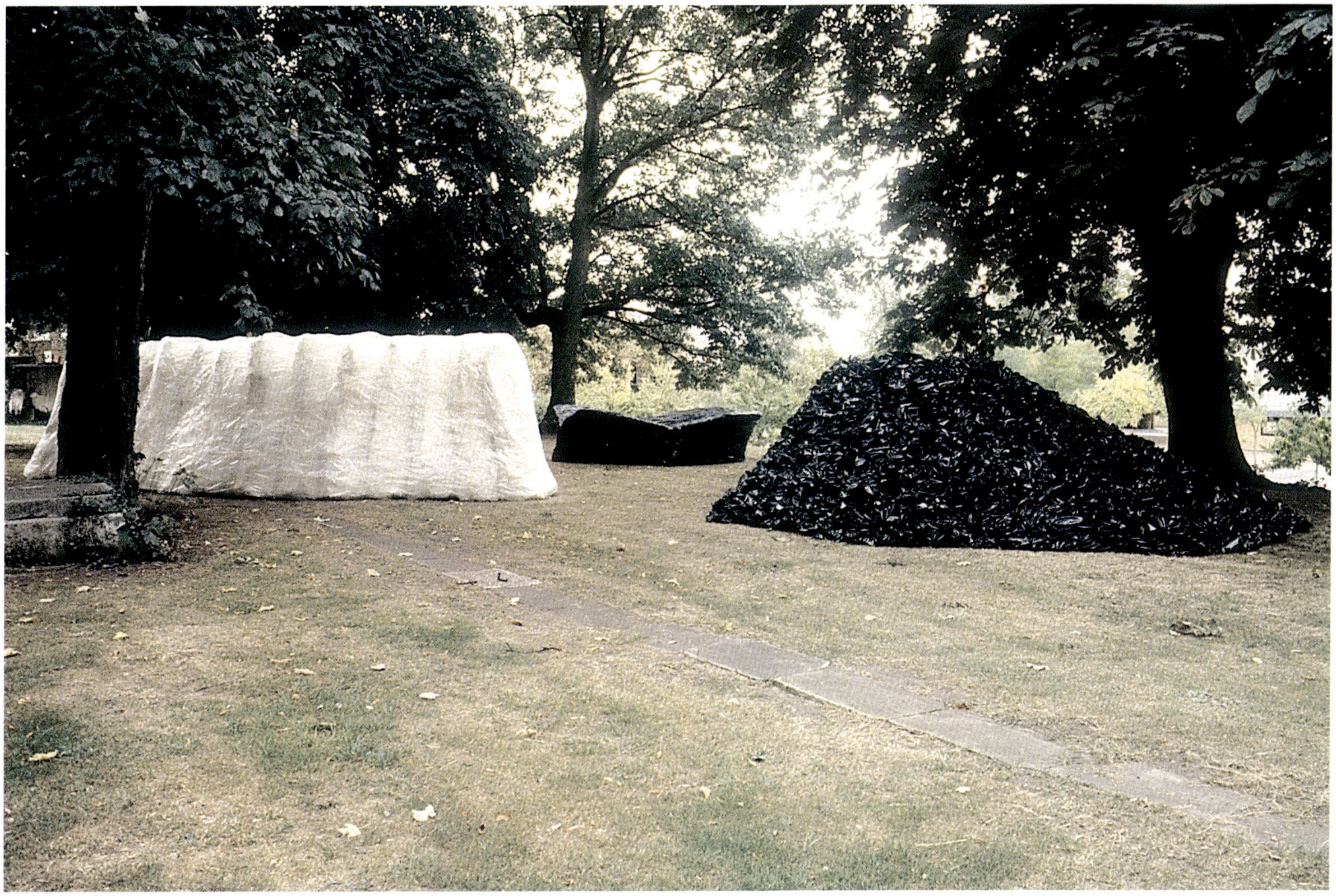

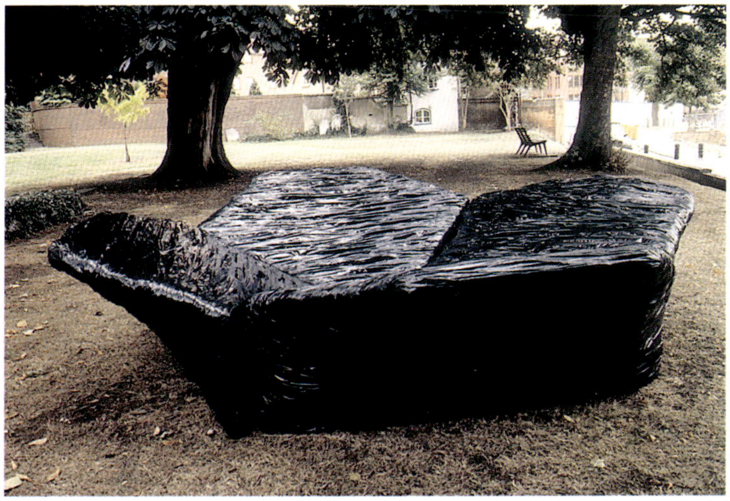

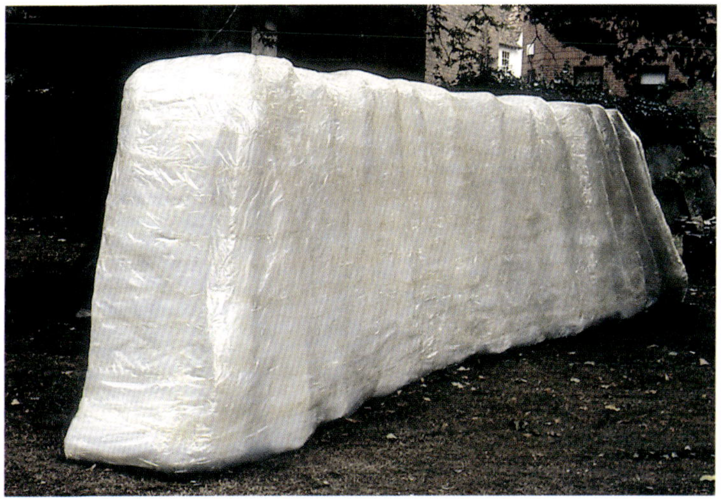

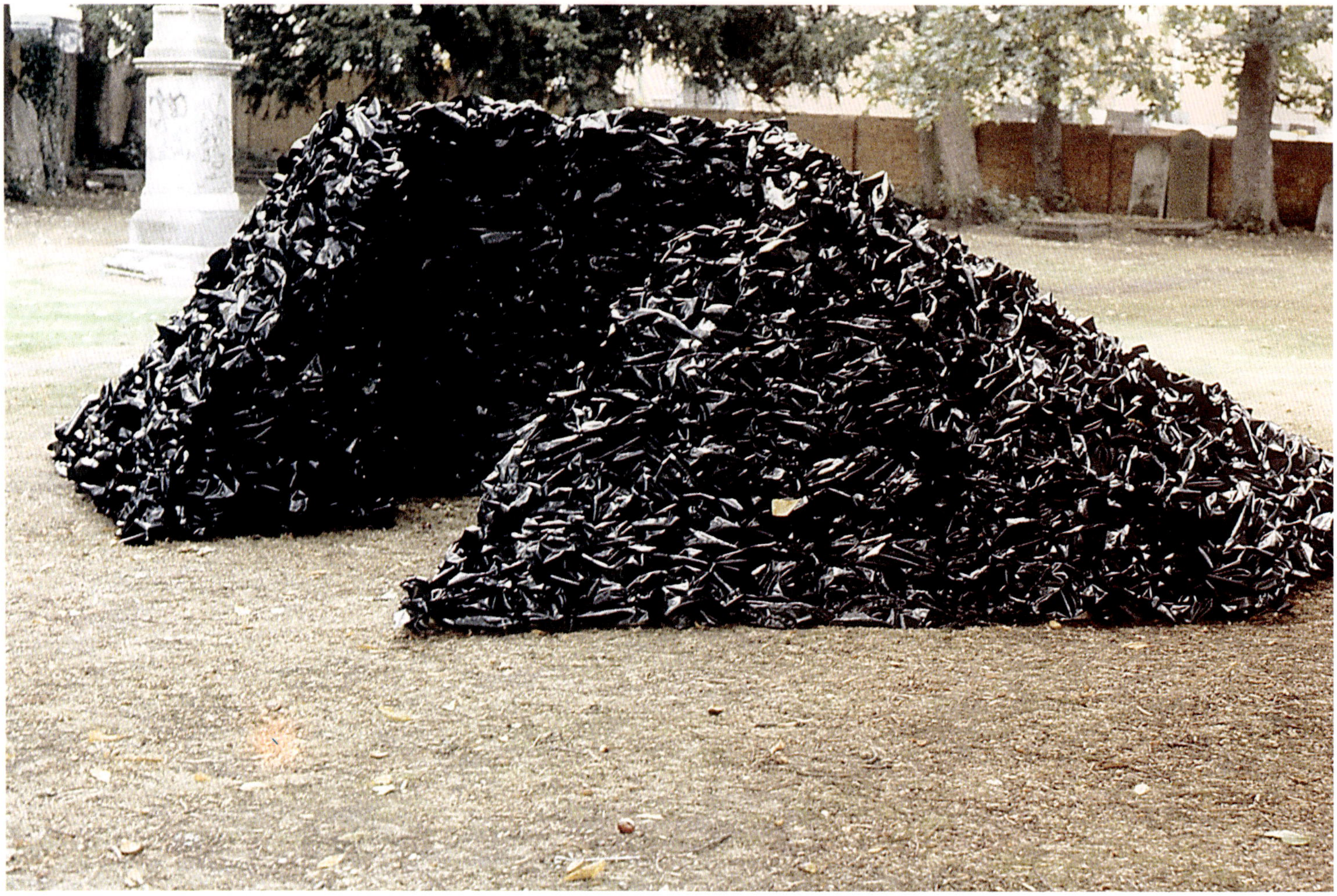

In the same years as many British sculptors turned to 'natural' materials, industrial materials such as Cor-ten steel and Plexiglass continued to guarantee a kind of workmanlike seriousness to the sculpture of Americans such as Richard Serra and Donald Judd. Barlow's materials were mainly industrially manufactured but their regular, non-art place and purpose was not in heavy industry and construction. Rather, her materials would be found within the household. Barlow tended to use everyday stuff that hardly registers, materials just beyond the edge of what we notice. She employed materials that line the perimeters of everyday interior spaces: carpets and foams which cover and insulate the floors and roofs, tarpaulin sheets that cover temporary living spaces, Formica, stuff that contains rubbish (polythene bin bags), stuff that stuffs furniture (upholstery foam). These materials might hold the memories of their everyday uses but they never function metaphorically, in the manner, for instance, of Joseph Beuys's felt. Indeed a soft material which would usually offer comfort and protection can appear in Barlow's work in such vast quantities to be ugly and threatening.

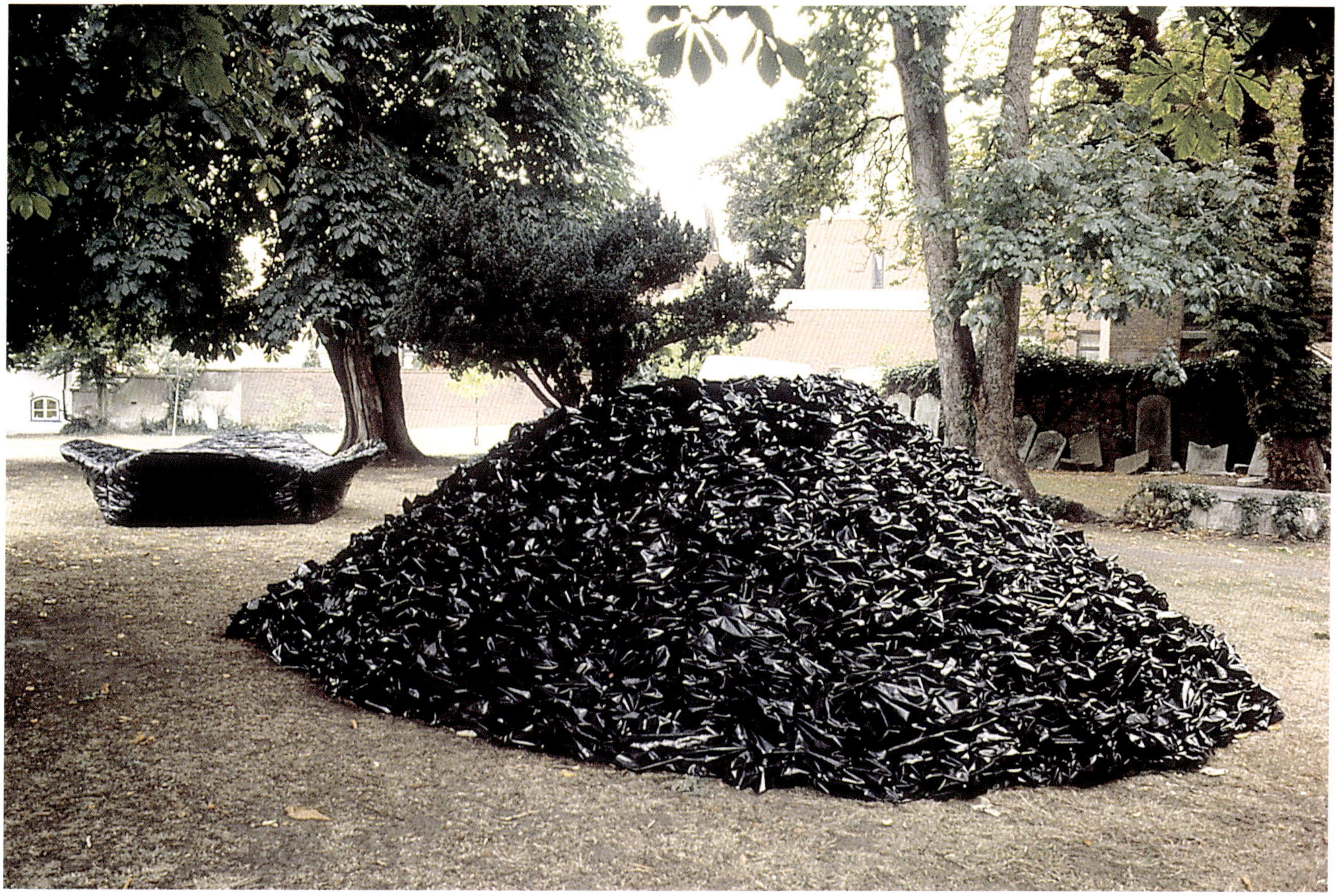

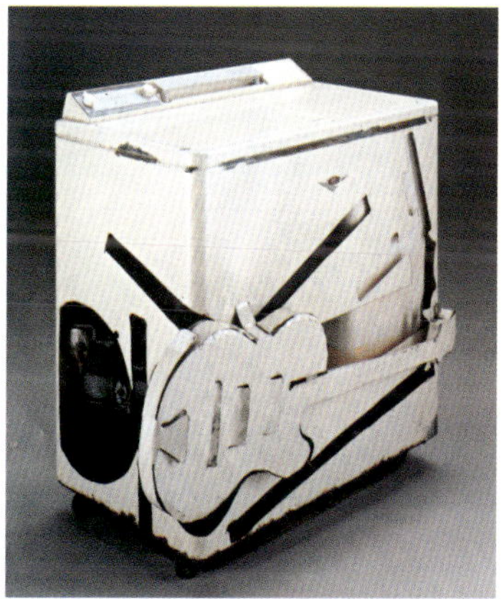

Bill Woodrow
Twin Tub with Guitar
1981

Expediency seems to have determined Barlow's choices: these were the materials most cheaply available in abundance. Sometimes she would just use what was to hand. To make the most Bourgeois-like of her work, the white bulbous part of *x2*, Barlow took household rags and old clothes and bleached them. *Ghosts*, 1984 was made from another collection of household waste, tightly wrapped and covered in bin bags and tape. In these two works, rubbish is covered up, but when Barlow came to make *Strangers* in 1985, the identity of the waste material was no longer in doubt. A mound of clothes was built up, covered by a black, rubber tarpaulin, the rags poking through a slit and spilling out the bottom. A recent room display at Tate Modern is called "Trash Into Art". It includes Kurt Schwitters's *Relief in Relief*, c.1942-1945 and Jacques Villeglé's *Jazzmen*, 1961, and one can imagine as well John Chamberlain's car metal sculptures or Tony Cragg's collages of found plastic objects. The room's title implies a kind of alchemical transformation that Barlow would surely resist. Her non-redemptive use of trash should also be specified in relation to other practices. In the same years she made these works, a former student of hers, Bill Woodrow, was scavenging London's streets and skips for obsolescent metallic household appliances out of which he would cut objects of desire such as electric guitars and walkie-talkies. Later, Rachel Whiteread, another of Barlow's students, would gather discarded mattresses and furniture to imprint their surfaces in her rubber and resin casts. For Barlow, trash was mere matter, not a raw material to be cleverly transformed, nor a material repository of memory. Rubbish was readily available, and cheap. If the expansiveness of her work of the 80s looked forward to Jason Rhodes, her material sensibility actually points forward to an artist like Thomas Hirschhorn who builds his pavilions and altars in the most expedient manner possible with cardboard, foil and packing tape.

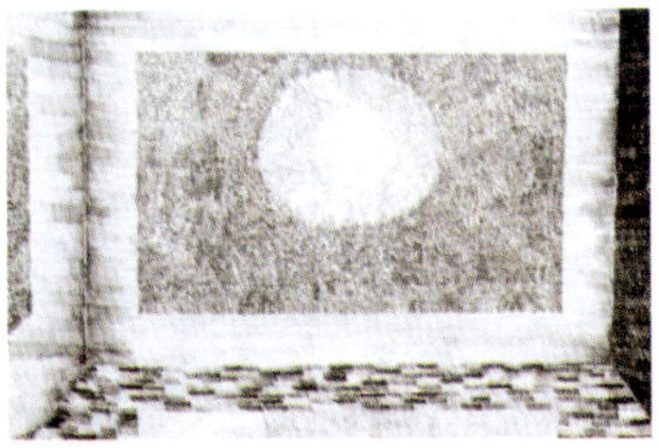

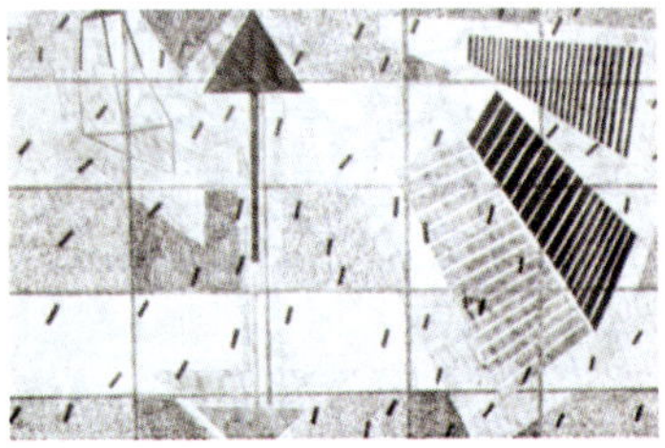

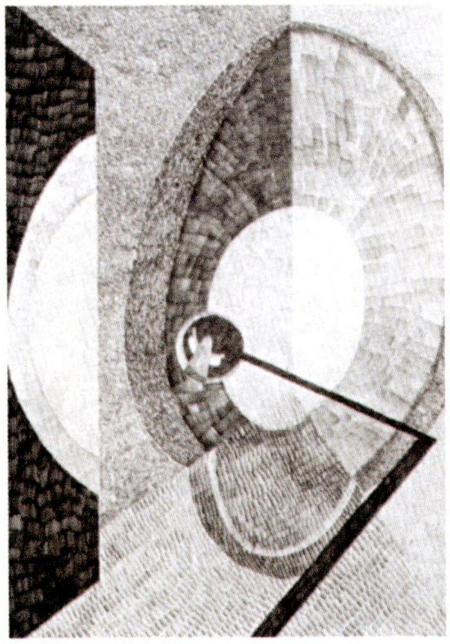

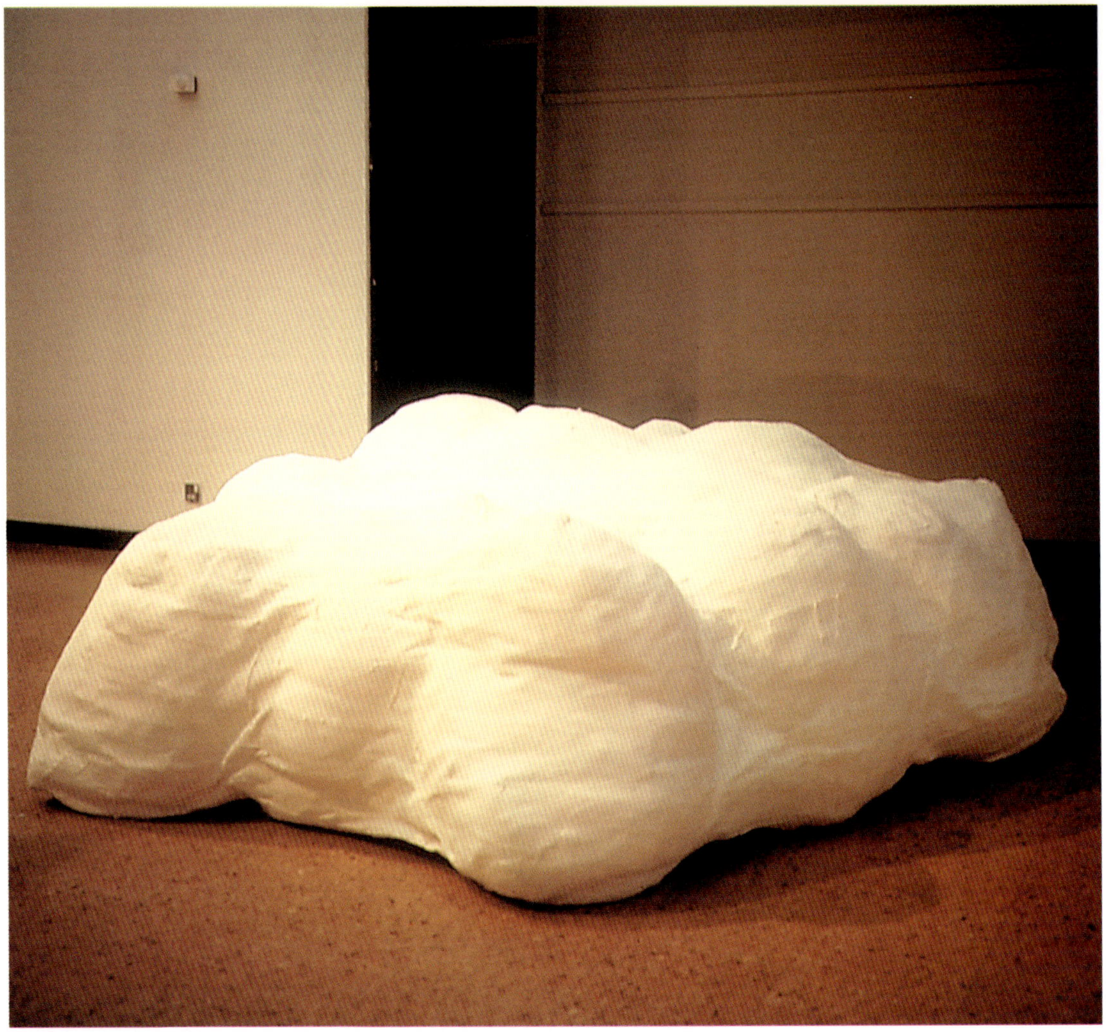

x 2
Hardboard, sugar, stitched twine, steel frame, bleached fabrics/ clothes, latex, stitching
540 cms x 350 x 600 cm (above)
360 cms x 120 x 420 cm (right)
1979
Farnham School of Art

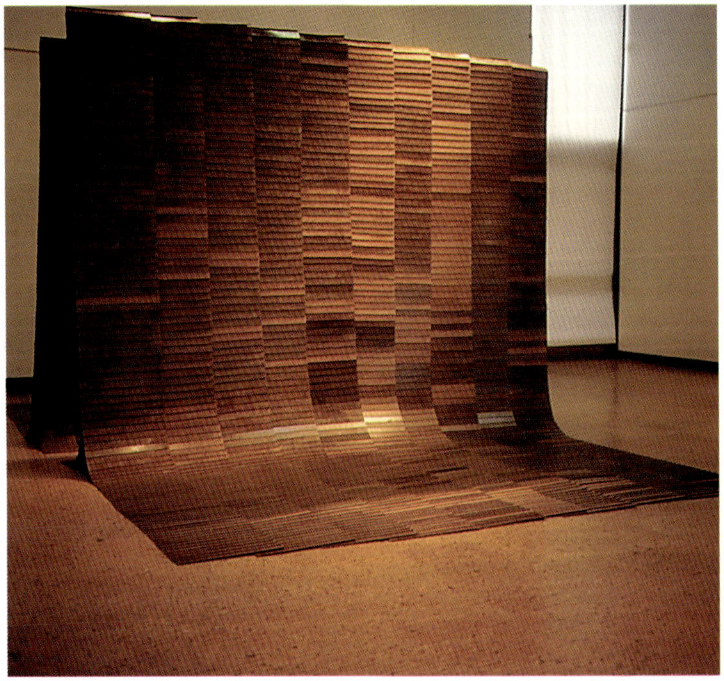

12 "At Sea: a conversation by fax between Phyllida Barlow and Alison Wilding" 22.08.98-02.09.98, for the catalogue *Grounded* which accompanied the solo exhibition of Alison Wilding's sculpture at the Northern Gallery for Contemporary Art, Sunderland, 1998.

13 Barlow, "Big Bad Ugly".

One of Barlow's most illuminating comments about her materials comes from a faxed interview with Alison Wilding. In it she explains her attraction to "the malleability of certain materials, like clay, where there can be a quick response from the material to a change of thought. Though I no longer work with clay, that particular attitude towards materials remains: A relationship which assumes that materials can be easily changed, even at the eleventh hour, into something else, better, right."[12] The comment inflects what one might say about her materials. It is not just their cheapness and abundance that appeals. Because they are not precious, more or less can be used right up until the show opens, the work is complete, just as more clay can always be added or removed without financial care. The main point of Barlow's comment, however, was to address the question of modelling. Even *Threat*, a work made of polythene, bitumen and paper could be modelled:

> The actual way these objects are made is as if the material was clay. They are built up with the bitumen and the polythene, stuffing and filling, pushing and pressing in a very direct moulding process which I think goes back to my early experience with clay.[13]

As Barlow relates her use of industrial materials to working with clay, another question arises. Do Barlow's materials, like clay, bear the marks of process, and what of the issue of expressionism and touch here?

Ghosts
Domestic rubbish, polythene, tape, sellotape
Overall space:
300 x 240 x 1500 cm
1985
Factory, Mare Street, London

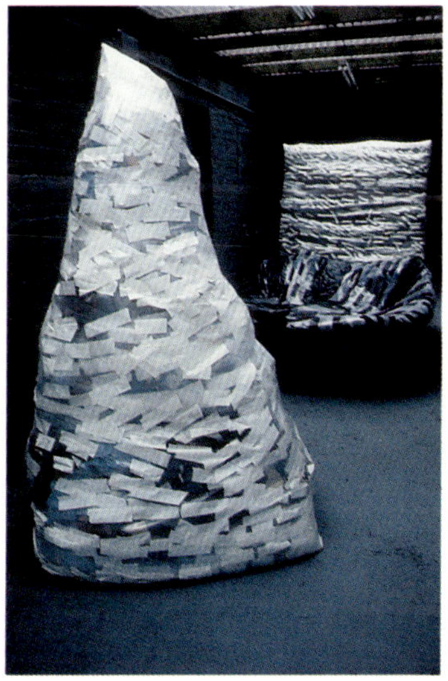

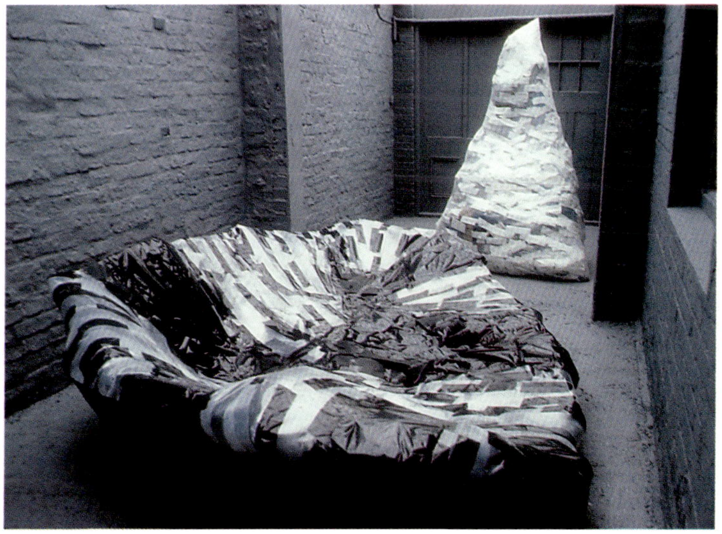

Scar
Upholstery foam, tape, paint, painted clay, painted polythene, chairs
300 x 270 x 750 cm
1984
Abandoned attic, North London

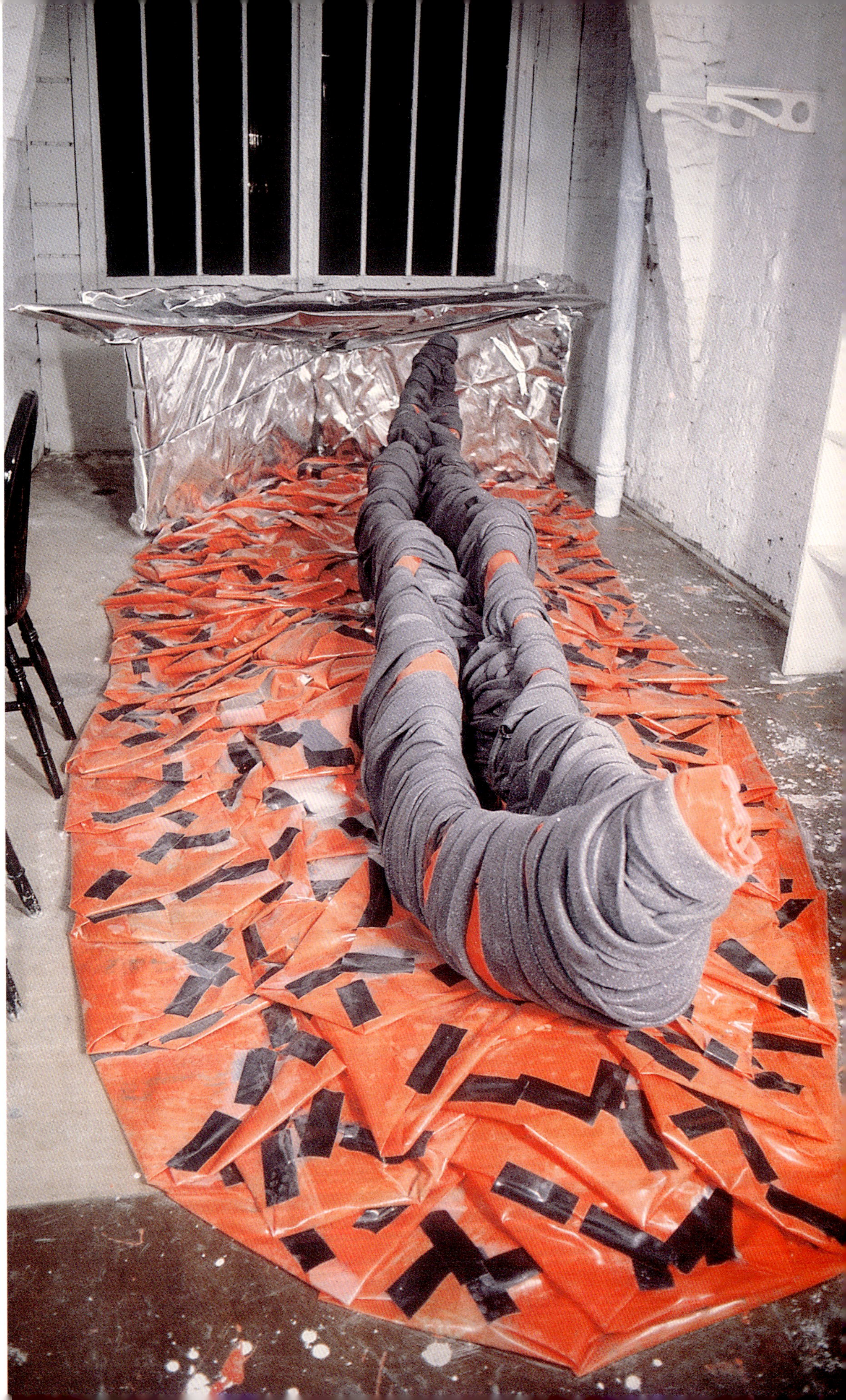

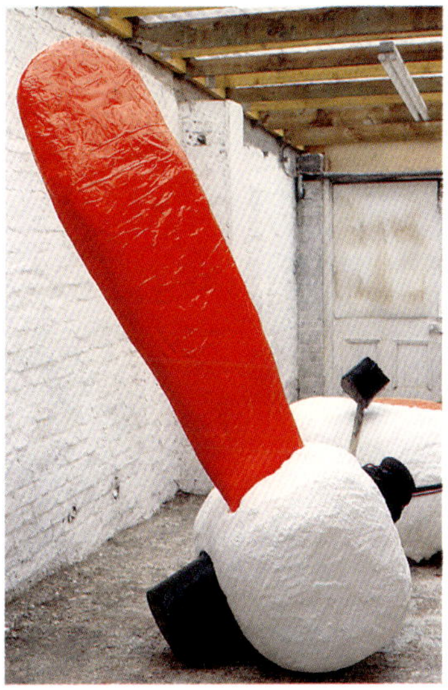

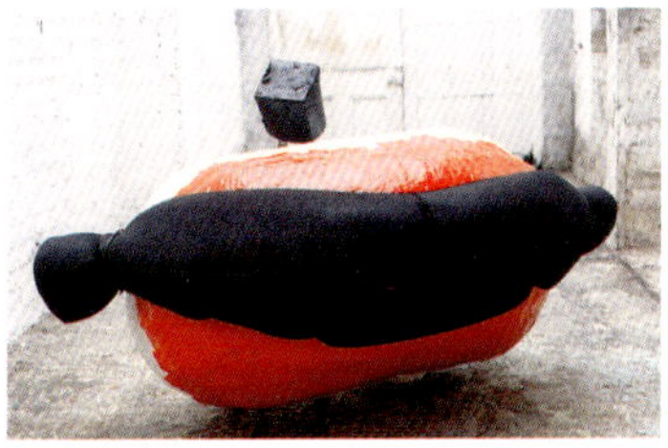

Ugly mugs
Polystyrene, upholstery foam, lead weight, casters, tape, plywood, plaster, black drainpipe
200 x150 x 200 cm (top)
150 x 210 x 150 cm (bottom)
1998
For the Ugly Edge Conference, curated by Elizabeth Rosser for the Henry Moore Institute Galleries, Leeds

Back to Bourgeois. In another text, "Big Bad Ugly", Barlow notes how the plaster of *Avenza Revisited II* "is covered in her finger marks, striated all over with the places where she has actually modelled and clawed at the surface".[14] "Like all such marks", she writes elsewhere, "they make evident her presence in the work, as if her emotions are drawn into the body of the sculpture."[15] The risks such work takes are well described in yet another text: "the hot object – that is, the object loaded with the all-too-visible signs of the act of making, can repulse through its desperate need to attract. It becomes an object of emotional blackmail, persuading us to feel for it because it shows so clearly the marks, wounds perhaps, caused through its struggle to come into existence."[16]
It is probably in her *Nightworks* from 1982-1983, a sub-group of her *Touchpiece* series (on-going from 1982 to the present), where Barlow most clearly runs the risks described here. These works were made while she was a mother of young children, in her brief spare time, at night in the dark. Finger marks did show on the surfaces but these were actually the result of holding the object with one hand whilst working on it with another, rather than scratching or clawing a freestanding object with both hands, *pace* Bourgeois. Barlow recalls clearly that "the marks were not intended to be 'expressive' but were merely the accidental deposits from dirty hands".[17] Yet though not expressionist, the *Nightworks* still do speak to the frustrations of maintaining artistic production during active motherhood – to use Barlow's terms, the works do exhibit their "struggle to come into existence". Given her personal circumstances, only night work was possible, only small works could be fashioned. And more than ever, new work had to be made expediently, with whatever was to hand. The *Nightworks* were actually dense collages of bits of material recycled from dismantled former works – *x 2*, *Foursome*, *Stack*. Briony Fer has described how the principle of recycling structured the connections between many of Eva Hesse's works, how, for instance, the moulds for *Repetition Nineteen III*, 1968 were used to produce *Area*. Fer is interested in contrast of the "extraordinarily beautiful" containers of the former and the ugliness of the latter, and there is a similar contrast between the grace of *x 2* and the haste of a *Nightwork*.[18] In terms of recycling, however, a more devastating, less delicate principle was at work in Barlow's practice: the only materials it was possible to use to make new sculpture were actual parts of already-shown works.

To return to the question of touch, in the work that followed the *Nightworks*, this issue became more complex, for though they can be modelled, polythene, tarpaulin, rags, foam, or felt will not bare the imprint of the maker's hands, or if they do, only as one dip or fold that could as easily have been caused by another source of pressure, or by the weight of the rest of the material. Barlow's materials tend neither to be resistant to touch like stone nor easily marked by touch like wet plaster. But in relation to sculpture, what is touch exactly? The question is complicated by Barlow's own comments on other artists. Recently, Barlow contrasted Eva Hesse and Lynda Benglis with Donald Judd and John McCracken. Her remarks were very surprising. Most historical accounts would compare the hands-on approach of the first two with the hands-off approach of the second pair. But approaching the subject as only a maker could, Barlow pressed a different point. "Tactility is duplicitous and misleading. Liquid to solid materials only have so much time in which they can be handled whilst they are setting: it is a one-hit relationship. And with a material like resin, if it has not set, due to a faulty mix, or too cold conditions, the process of restoring the surface to how you want it is excruciating…." So a work like Hesse's *Untitled* 1970 rope piece "would have been as deftly, and as quickly manipulated as possible, in fact, as hands-off as possible", whilst "those supposedly coolest of cool objects of Judd or McCracken, of Koons or Hirst, have every inch of them handled, touched, manipulated, not necessarily by the artist but certainly by the fabricator."[19]

14 Barlow, "Big Bad Ugly".

15 Barlow, "The Sneeze of Louise", p. 8.

16 Barlow, Phyllida, "The Hatred of the Object", in *Sculpture Method Research* Matrix 3d conference, 1997, London: Lethaby Press, pp. 25-26.

17 Correspondence with the author, July 2003.

18 Fer, Briony, "Treading Blindly, or the Excessive Presence of the Object", *Art History*, vol. 20, no. 2, June 1997, p. 270.

19 Barlow, Phyllida, "Lost for Words", unpublished talk given at the Eva Hesse symposium, Tate Modern, 15 November 2002.

John McCracken
Plank
Polyester resin, fibreglass
and wood
96 x 29 x 4 cm
1966 (remade 1988)

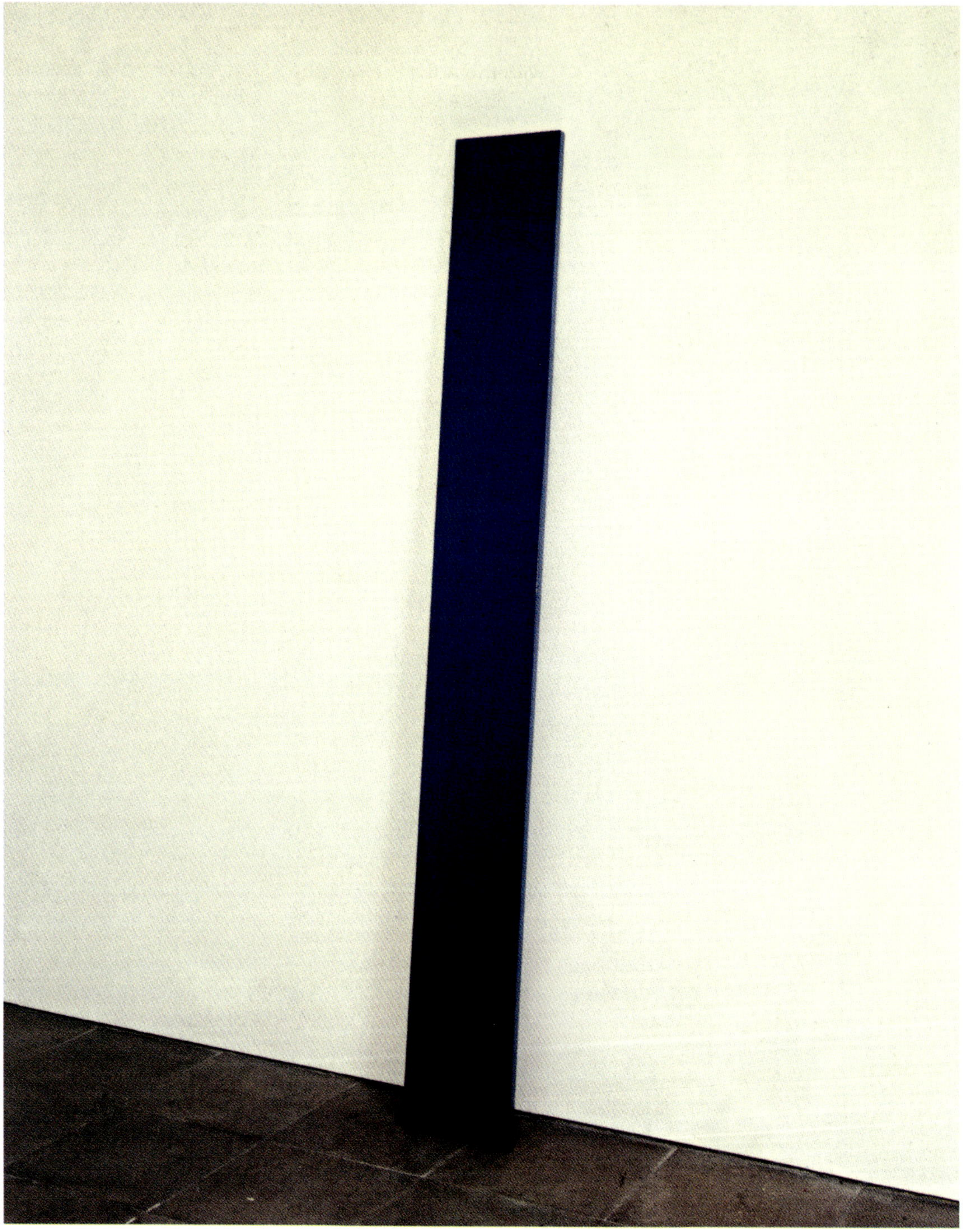

Eva Hesse
Untitled (Rope Piece)
Latex and filler over rope and string with metal hooks, dimensions variable
1969-1970
Whitney Museum of American Art, New York, purchased with funds from Eli and Edythe L Broad, the Mrs Percy Uris Purchase Fund, and the Painting and Sculpture Committee 88.17a-b
Photo: Geoffrey Clements
© The Estate of Eva Hesse
Courtesy Galerie Hauser & Wirth, Zurich

It is strange to think that an object which would look spoiled with a finger print is in fact rubbed and polished to gleaming perfection, whilst another, which has been in direct contact with the artist during fabrication, could not be touched as it set. But what of Barlow's own work in this context? Actually, the debate would not seem of relevance. Materials were certainly not polished, touched until they will bear not one touch more, nor did they set so quickly that a wrong touch in the process of making would have ruined them. Looking at the work before 1992 it is hard to imagine an accident in the process of making spoiling a Barlow sculpture, a slip that would have cost all, just as it is hard to think that the look of the work would be risked if brushed into: the opposite is the case in fact. This was work that would easily survive movement, the impress of a body. The question of a viewer touching the work will be important later. For now, thinking about the touch of the artist, and thinking forward, one might surmise that by the early 90s, Barlow must have found her materials were not registering her physical touch in the way she then wanted. For at that moment she started to work with paint, using the material to index her touch on surfaces that would formerly have been left alone. She began, that is, to touch her surfaces with colour.

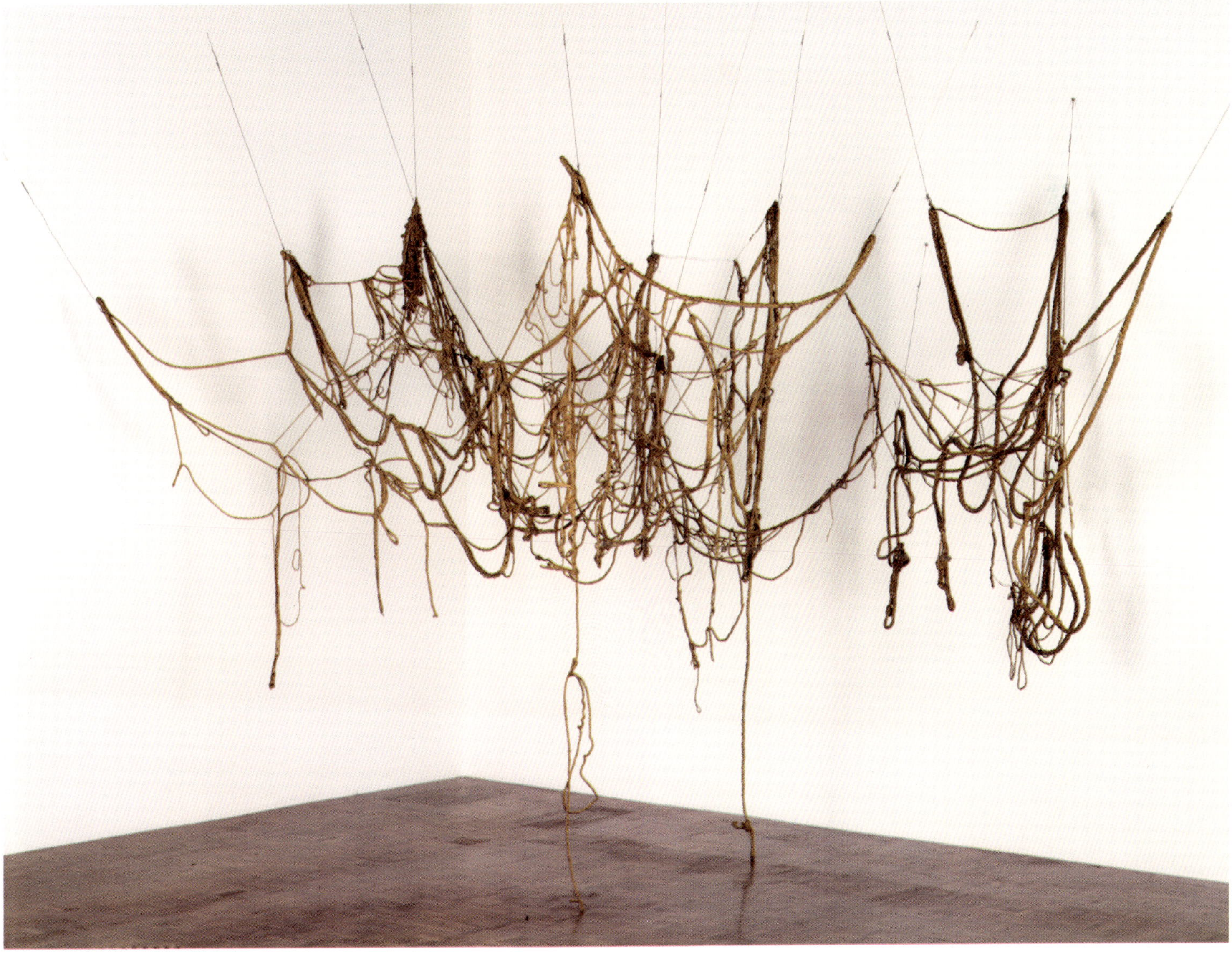

The Problem of Colour

20 Barlow, "Hearsay, Rumours, Bed-sit Dreamers and Art Begins Today".

Paint was deployed as an important physical material, but it was also a very versatile one – its colour, after all, was unrestricted and changeable. In order to get a better sense of both of the functions of paint and what paint has enabled in Barlow's recent work, we should not only attend to the way it resolved a problem of touch, but to the way it solved a problem of colour.

What 'problem of colour'? We need only recall the early work to see that colour has been a problematic issue for Barlow, as is frequently the case in sculptural practice. The works around *All and Everything* were not just materially but chromatically exuberant. *Stuff*, for instance, is a free-falling fete of primary coloured fabrics. By 1976, however, Barlow had abandoned chromophilia for the greyed restraint of *Shedmesh*. The rejection of colour was a step in the direction of 'serious sculpture', and a further means of distancing her work from the look of the New Generation. Barlow has written that the colours of this work were already second-hand, borrowed from American art of the early 1960s. Though she does not make the point, American artists from Andy Warhol and Roy Lichtenstein to Frank Stella and Kenneth Noland were employing the colours of brash new post-war products. Even Pollock had used car enamel paint. So the colours of the New Generation sculpture were taken (albeit through the intermediary of the American artists) from the world of consumerism; in turn, the New Generation sculptures would inspire a new wave of British products:

> The New Generation sculpture had become fodder for designers who had plundered its bright, toy-like style for their own ends, making the [New Generation] work indistinguishable from the burgeoning Habitat domestic commodities, Galt's faddish, pseudo crafted toys, as well as packaging, textiles and new innovations with easy to assemble furniture and DIY. [20]

Untitled 1 and 2
Spray painted fibreglass and
resin, painted plywood
Left: 220 x 200 x 250 cm
Right: 200 x 170 x 220 cm
1966
Slade School of Fine Art, London

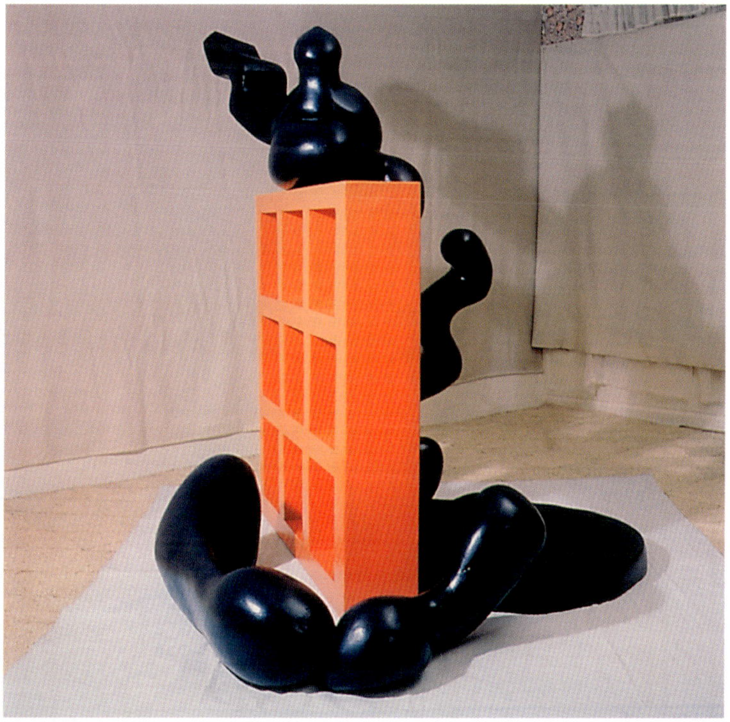

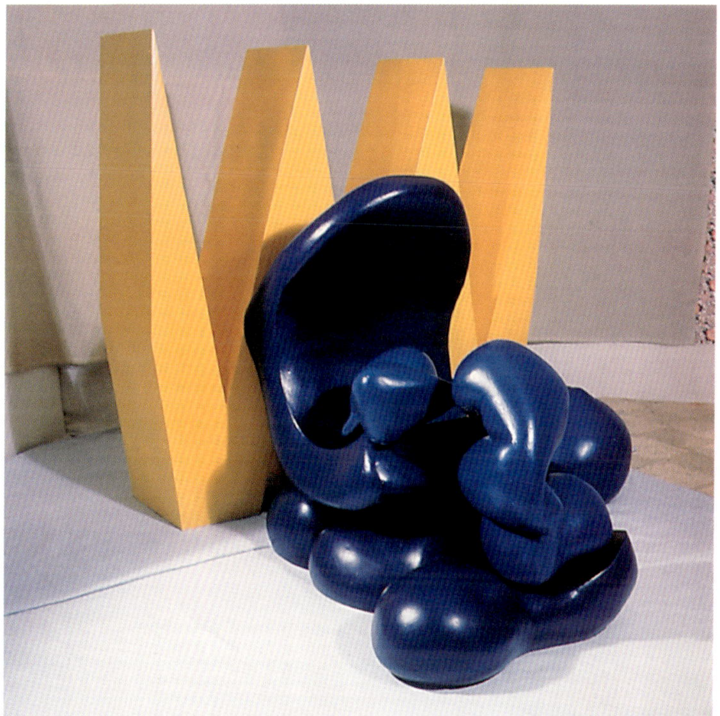

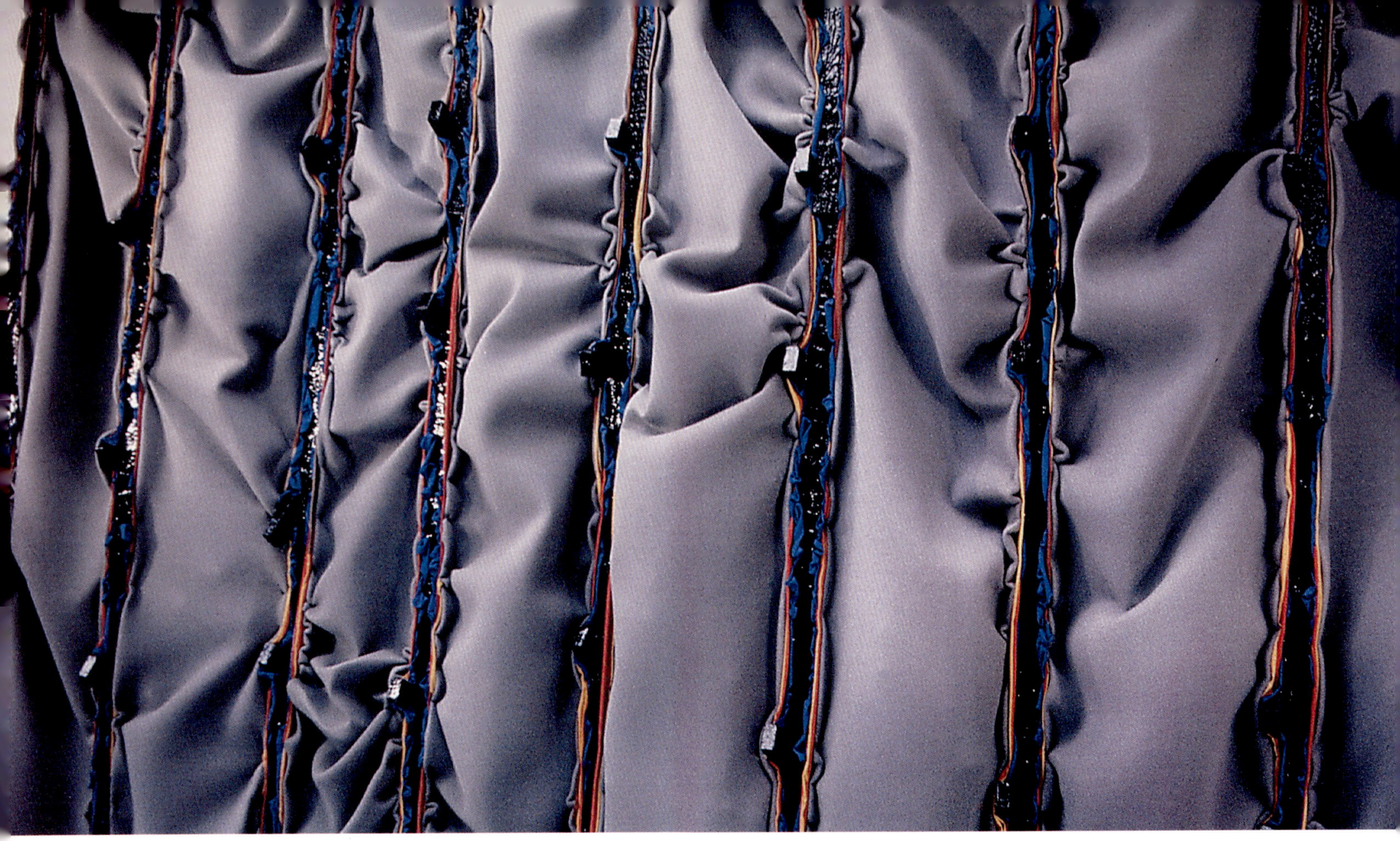

Barlow's eschewal of bright pop colours would have been a means of distancing her work not just from the previous generation but from the objects of desire increasingly dominating 1970s life. Yet her choice should also be seen positively: by abandoning the wild colours of her early 70s work, Barlow could direct a viewer's attention to the materials and forms of her new work. Colours would only change when the material changed, colours would be *of* the material and not added to it.

Sellotape ball

Shedmesh and the works that follow were grey, white, brown, black. Chromatically, they related to the bulk of post-minimalist work, with the exception perhaps of Lynda Benglis's pigmented latex and Keith Sonnier's coloured neon. Of course the limits of the colours of Barlow's sculptures did not correspond to the limits of the colours of the materials of which they were made. Barlow's dedication to the crumpled and folded form meant that a monochrome material would lighten and darken across its surface. Many of the works would also juxtapose reflective and mat materials: a harsh white light glinted off the black polythene parts of *Engulf* whilst the grey felt muffled the light that fell on it, so it appeared in places almost pink. Barlow rarely mobilised translucent materials but in *Torso*, 1989, a later work of the *Touchpiece* series, she wrapped huge lengths of sellotape around and around themselves to form a gob of plastic and glue. It shines and darkens, where thickest, to deep amber. Simply by doubling and redoubling an almost colourless everyday material, Barlow conjured an intense and rich colour, one reminiscent of the fibreglass and resin of Hesse's *Sans II*, 1968.

Fall
Painted wooden struts; red, yellow, blue, orange silk, upholstery foam
150 x 300 x 450 cm
1991
Commissioned work for architect's office, Caledonian Road, London

The visible colours of a well-installed and well-lit work were certainly more varied than the grey or black of its material, yet the chromatic conservatism of Barlow's work of the 80s still gives no clues as to how Barlow's present sculpture came to be so colourful. Yes, *Expanse*, 1987, included one strata of red polythene, *Slope*, 1989, an under-layer of blue tarpaulin, but in the first case, grey and black were predominant, and in the second work, the blue was darkened by virtue of its placement within the work's structure: it faced the floor, hardly a light underside of the black paper on top. To account for the shift to the work of the mid 90s, we could start with *Fall*, 1989. Ten black gloss-painted wooden props lean up against a wall, the spaces in between them mainly occupied by regular narrow rectangles of crumpled grey upholstery foam. Such a work would not seem surprising given what had come before but between the black props and the grey upholstery run ripples of red, yellow and blue silk. It is as if the grey foam was concealing the silk that was just escaping from underneath it at its edges; as if, were one only to flip the work around, these politely peeking primary colours would not 'fall' so much as cascade.

More than almost any other work by Barlow, *Fall* occupies the space of painting, propped at such a steep angle against the wall. It invites associations with the history of modernist painting, most importantly, Morris Louis's work. Whilst its composition relates rather crudely to the late stripe paintings, it is the relationship to the *Veils* that is more compelling. In those paintings, successive washes of thinned acrylic were poured onto untreated raw canvas, merging in the massive central areas. Each colour was translucent, so where many overlapped new colours would be created. However, at the peripheries, where each wave had reached different limits, the individual colours were distinct. At a distance, *Fall*'s viewer might have seen orange and purple where yellow and red, or red and blue silk appeared to merge, but close up, the three colours would have all been quite separate.

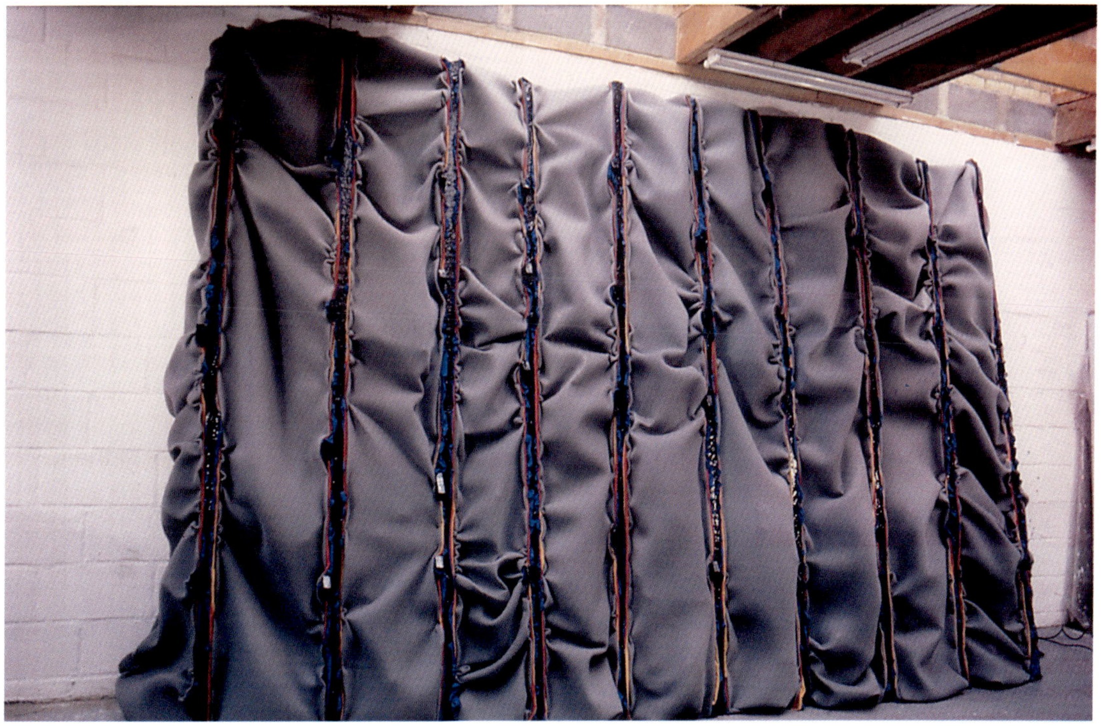

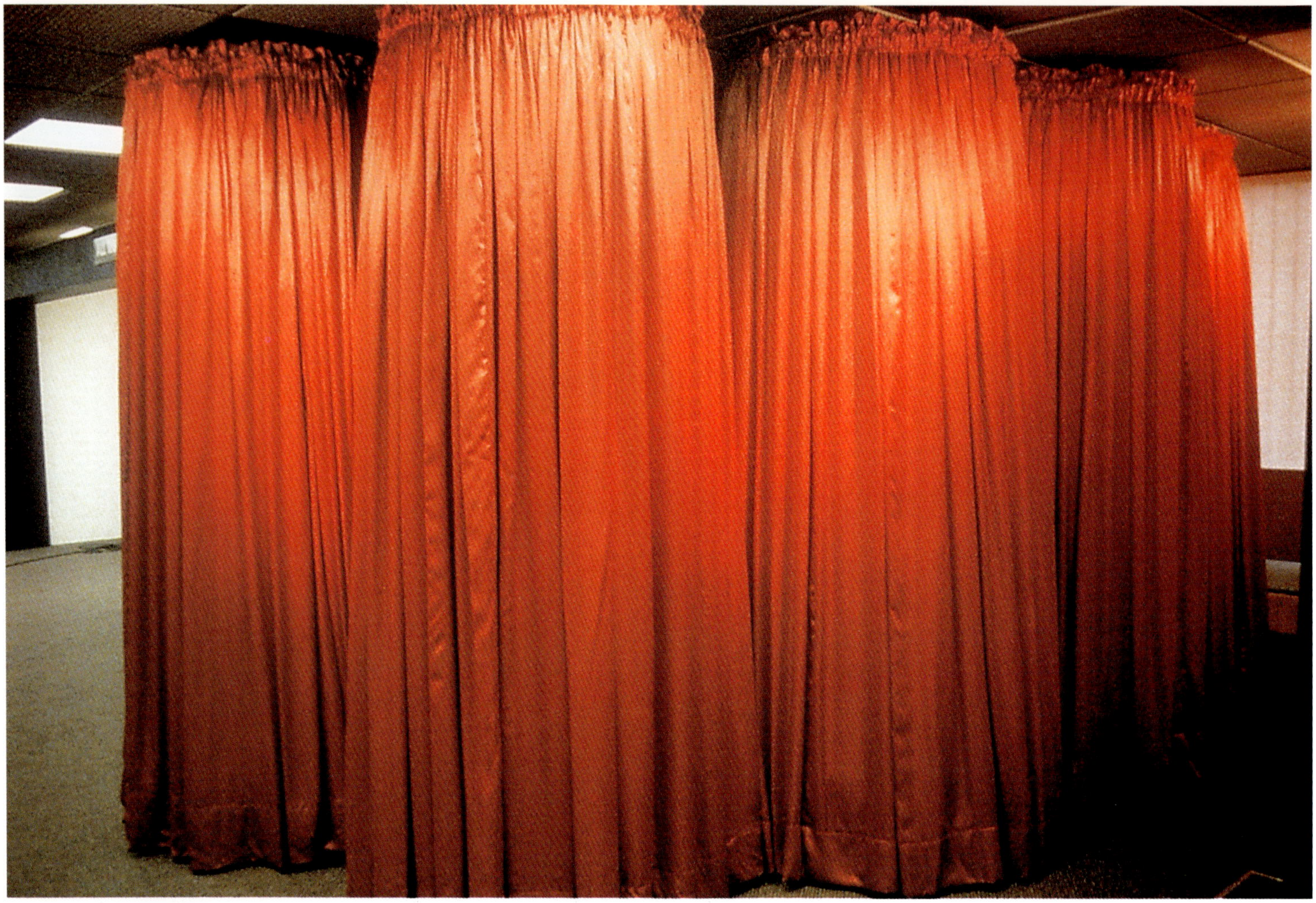

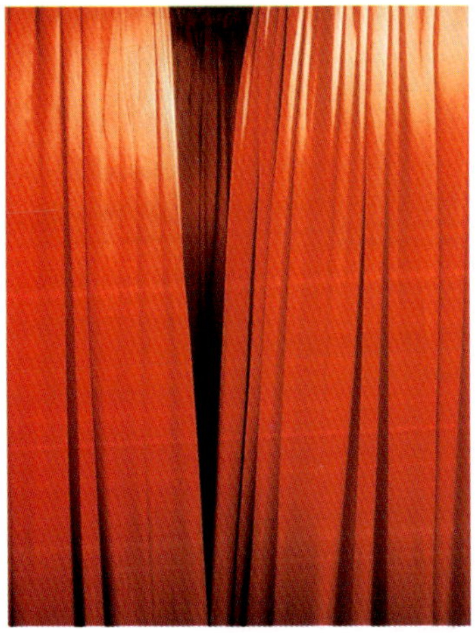

Colour is at its most sensuous in *Home*, 1992, a work made for a travelling exhibition called *Shopping Sensations* that toured to shopping centres in the UK and Europe. The curator wanted work to accommodate all the senses, for the consideration of the unsighted, the deaf, and for those in wheelchairs. Barlow installed fourteen red lining-satin curtains, or skirts, tightly gathered, sewn and pinned to the top of 2.5 metre high circular, timber-built armatures. The densely folded, shiny red columns were grouped close together and the satin dropped in such as way as to totally conceal the supporting structure beneath. The fabric was sprayed with lavender oil, and buried in the middle column was a cassette recording playing the distant sound of children's voices recorded at the local school. For the able-bodied viewer, smell and sound were secondary to the intensity of colour that darkened in the folds of the curtains and in the shades between the columns.

Home
Red lining satin, timber frames,
recorded sound, lavender oil
360 x 240 x 400 cm
Fourteen columns, each
120 diameter x 240 cm high
1991-1992
Gulbenkian Gallery, Whitgift Centre,
Croydon, London
Toured to: Bradford, Brussels,
Belgium, Nantes, France

Right
Anish Kapoor
At the Edge of the World II
Fibreglass and pigment
800 x 800 cm
1998

Below
David Annesley
Swing Low
Painted steel
1964

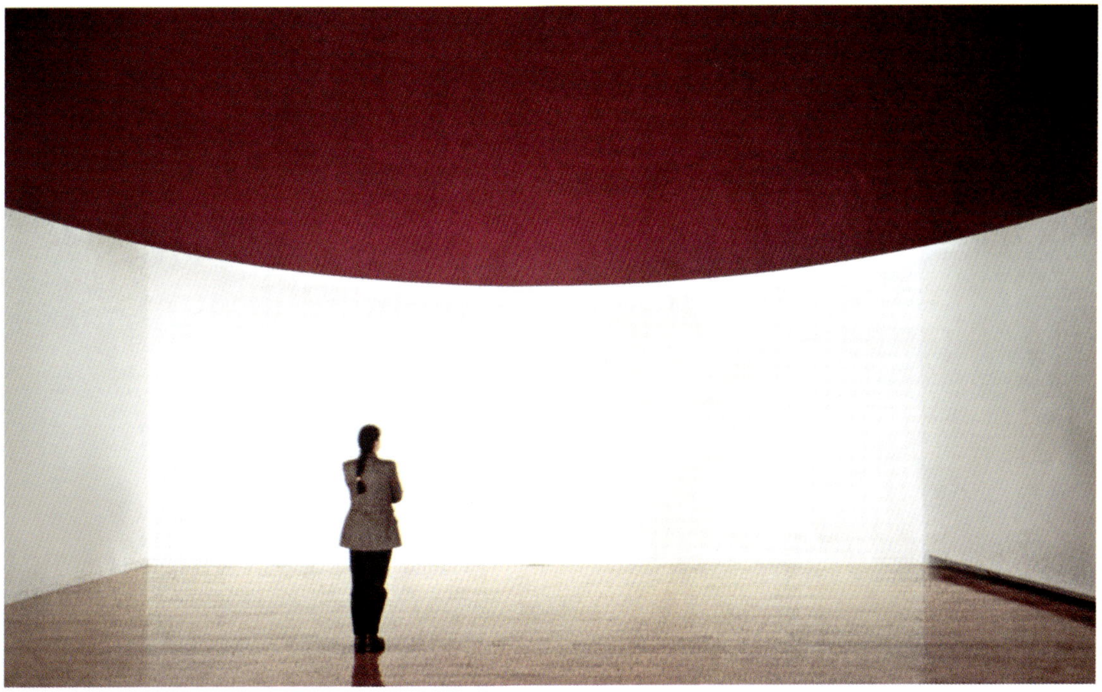

Fall and *Home* help explain the introduction of paint a few years later, but not because the colour question was resolved in these works. Rather, in the two works, the problems of particular ways of mobilising colour became apparent. *Fall* might have used a range of colours, but in far too discrete and pretty a manner. The spectre of the designed product haunted this kind of use of colour. These were the products to which Barlow had related the work of Michael Bolus, Philip King, David Annesley, et. al., and they were being newly staged in galleries at the time in the work of neo-pop Americans such as Jeff Koons, whose *Vacuum pieces* were included in London in the *New York Art Now* exhibitions at the Saatchi Gallery in 1987 and 1988.

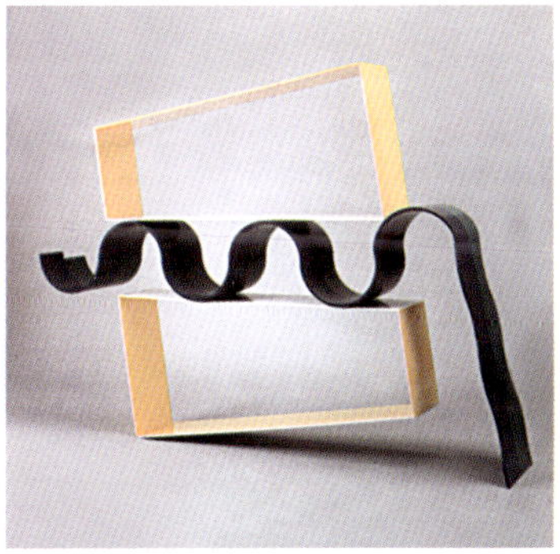

Home, meanwhile, might have risked making colour purely atmospheric, intangible and immaterial. Of course, many artists treat colour in precisely this manner. Standing in front of an Yves Klein monochrome painting, it is hard to know exactly where the surface lies. Anish Kapoor is closer to Barlow's generation. In the early 80s, Kapoor would sprinkle pure pigment over shaped objects in a manner that tended to dematerialise their physical bulk. Mark Francis compared Kapoor's use of colour to the "powdered facial masks of the *pierrot*, Indian dancers or Japanese Kabuki players, where the human personality is covered over, disguised and universalised.... The texture of the powdered skin has a very powerful effect, accustomed as we are, when looking at sculpture, to the rougher or glossier surfaces of stone or plastic, metal or wood."[21] Later, Kapoor's colours would no longer be used to disguise materials, but, impregnated into the materials of his strange biomorphic constructions, or into the cavities of roughly hewn rocks, they would defy a viewer's knowledge of the sculpture's physical limits. A bell-shaped structure would seem far deeper than its actual bulk would permit; whilst "A cavity [would be] set so deeply in a stone that its pigmented pitch defies the depth of the rock, and floats weightless to the surface."[22] Illusionism was courted and infinity replaced materiality. Returning to *Home*, for sure, the material limits of the fabric were evident to a viewer. After all, he or she would brush up against the red satin whilst walking through the columns and even touch the satin to enter the hollows. Yet still it is fair to surmise that colour came dangerously close to simple effect here. For an artist who wanted sculpture "Big Bad [and] Ugly", chromatic atmospherics would not do.

21 Francis, Mark, "Illuminations", in *Transformations: New Sculpture from Britain*, XVII Bienal de SãoPaulo, 1983, p. 49.

22 Bhabha, Homi K, "Anish Kapoor: Making Emptiness", in *Anish Kapoor*, London: The South Bank Centre, 1998, p. 12.

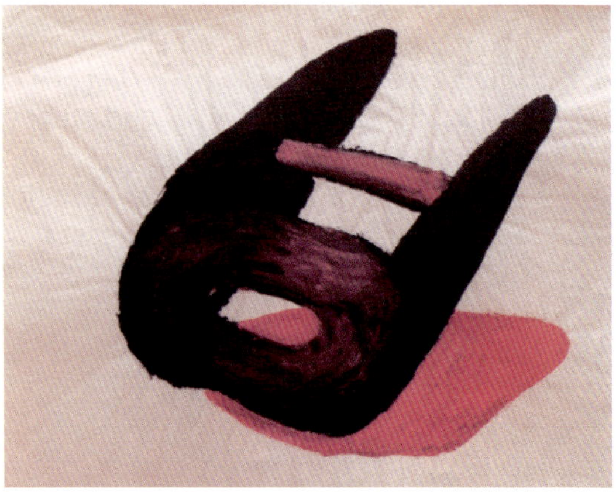
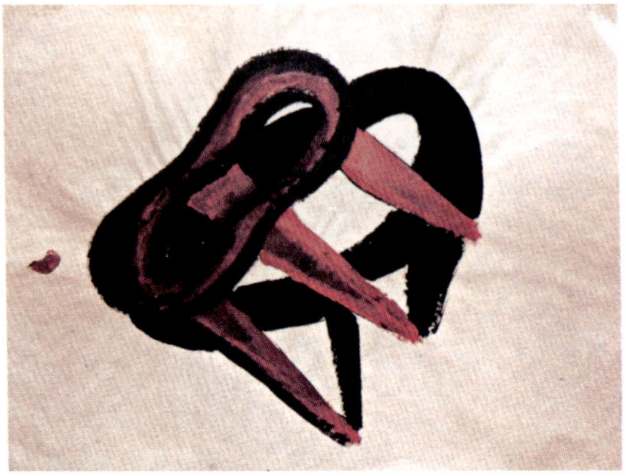
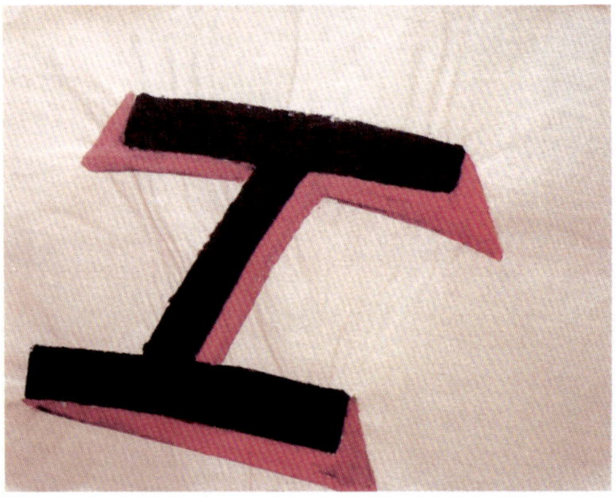
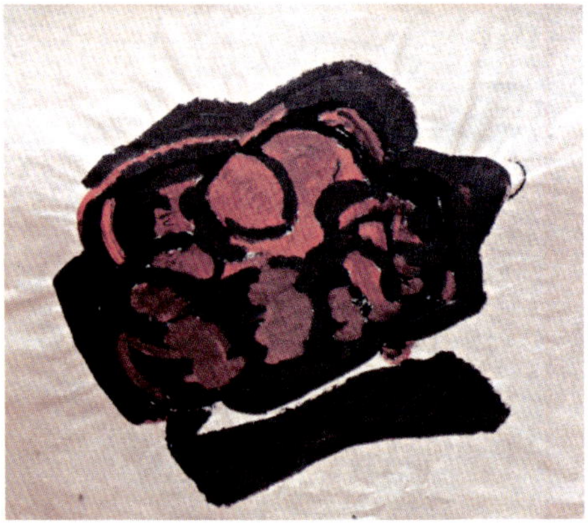
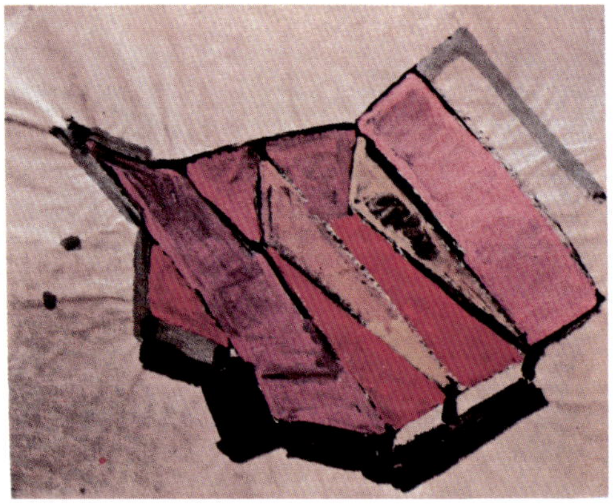
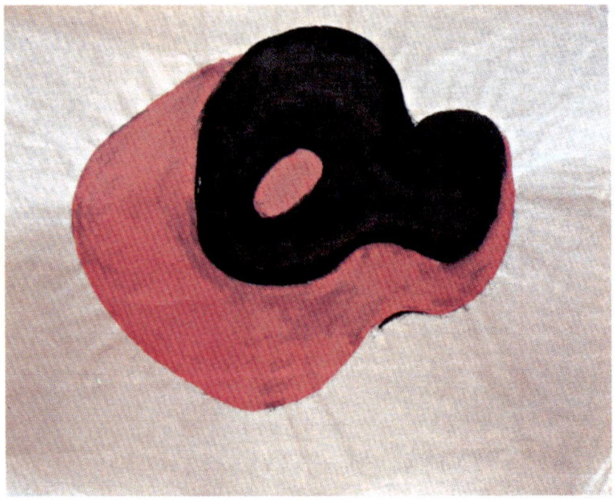
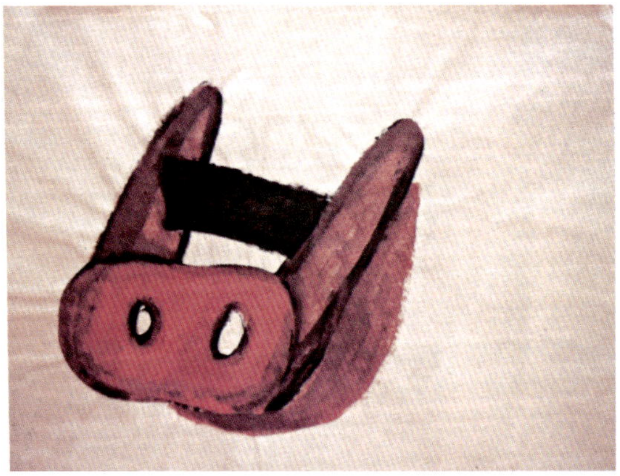
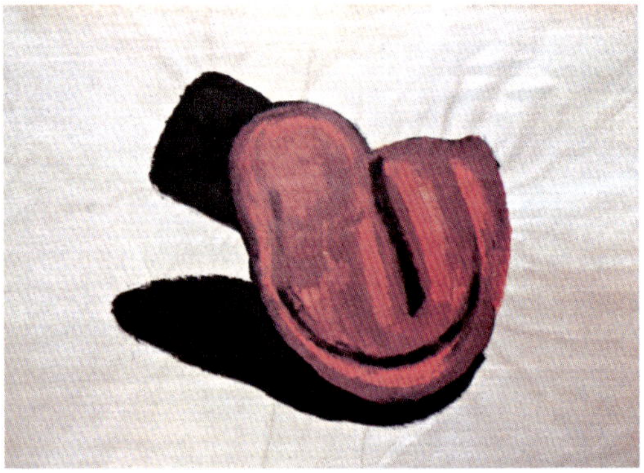

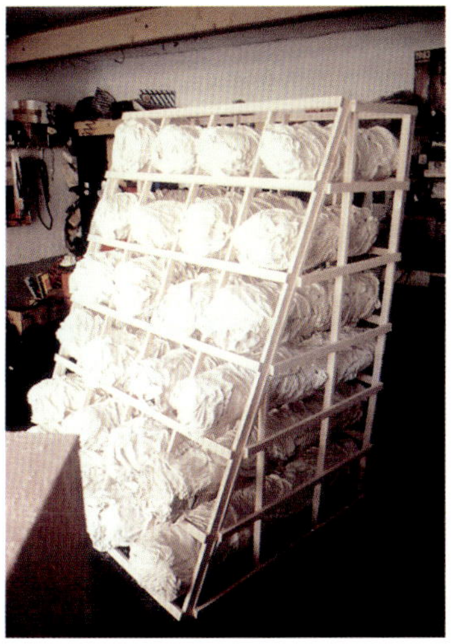

Installation for a Car Mechanic's Garage
Paint, hardboard, timber, plaster, muslin, mixed fabrics
Overall of space:
300 x 450 x 600 cm
1994
Kings Cross, London

With paint, colour could become physical. Paint was not only a coloured cover of the sculpture's surface but a fundamental material part of the construction, its adhesive qualities mobilised in every bit as important a way as its colour. The lattices of *Across*, 1992, *Installation for a Country House Hallway*, 1994, *Depot*, 1995 and other works were glued together by paint. Paint did not join the slats of plywood that form *Undercover*, 1996 but traversed these joins, not disguising them but declaring them like a highlighter. The same gesture occurred in *Stand-off*, 1996. So paint had a structural job; it is also important to see how it was applied. Barlow tended to slap it onto a surface, hastily sponging or, in her words, "smearing" it on. It was never sanded (chunks of encrusted paint stick out) and nor did it coat the entire surface: a central area might be covered but towards the edges the surface material tends to remain uncovered or streaked with drips.

Paint brings Barlow's sculpture away from the smooth cleanliness of Kapoor's work and much closer to the anarchic polychromy of Jessica Stockholder's. Barlow's colours even resonate with the ketchup and mustards of Paul McCarthy's performances. Paint has also opened up the range and possibilities of colour. As it is used in such a physical way, the threat of the association to design is diminished. Colour can be used with as much confidence as it is by an artist like Koons but without the ensuing association with the consumer product. And because of the way paint is used, Barlow can happily bring in readymade colours – notable, in particular, in her frequent use of bright red masking tape.

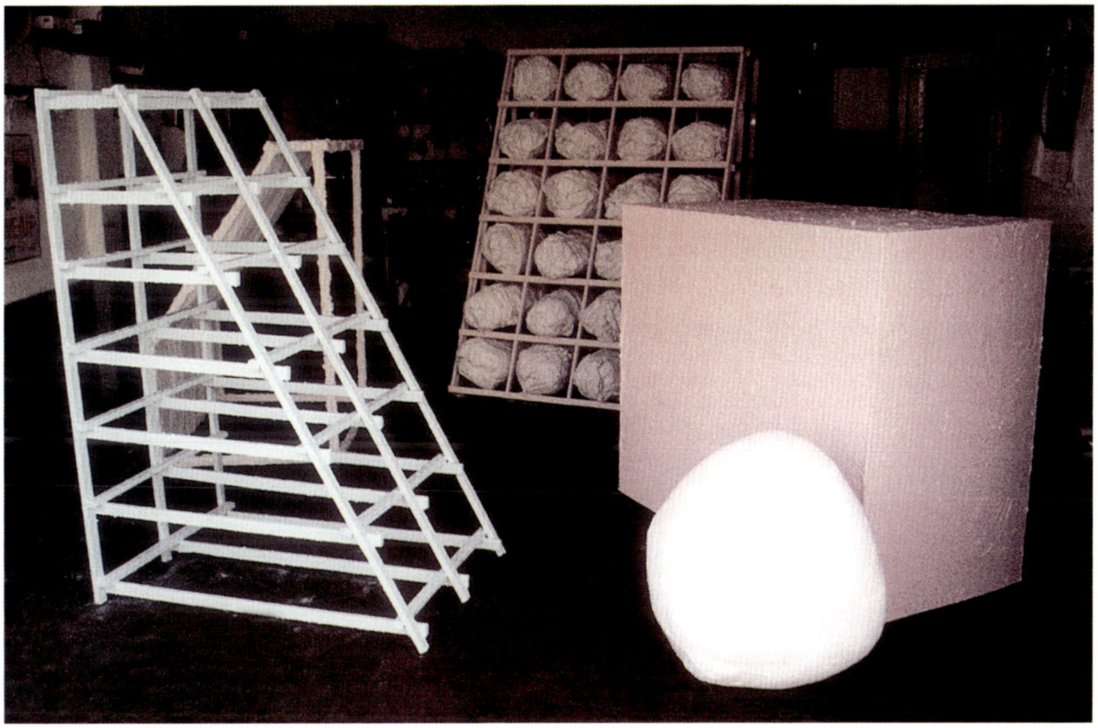

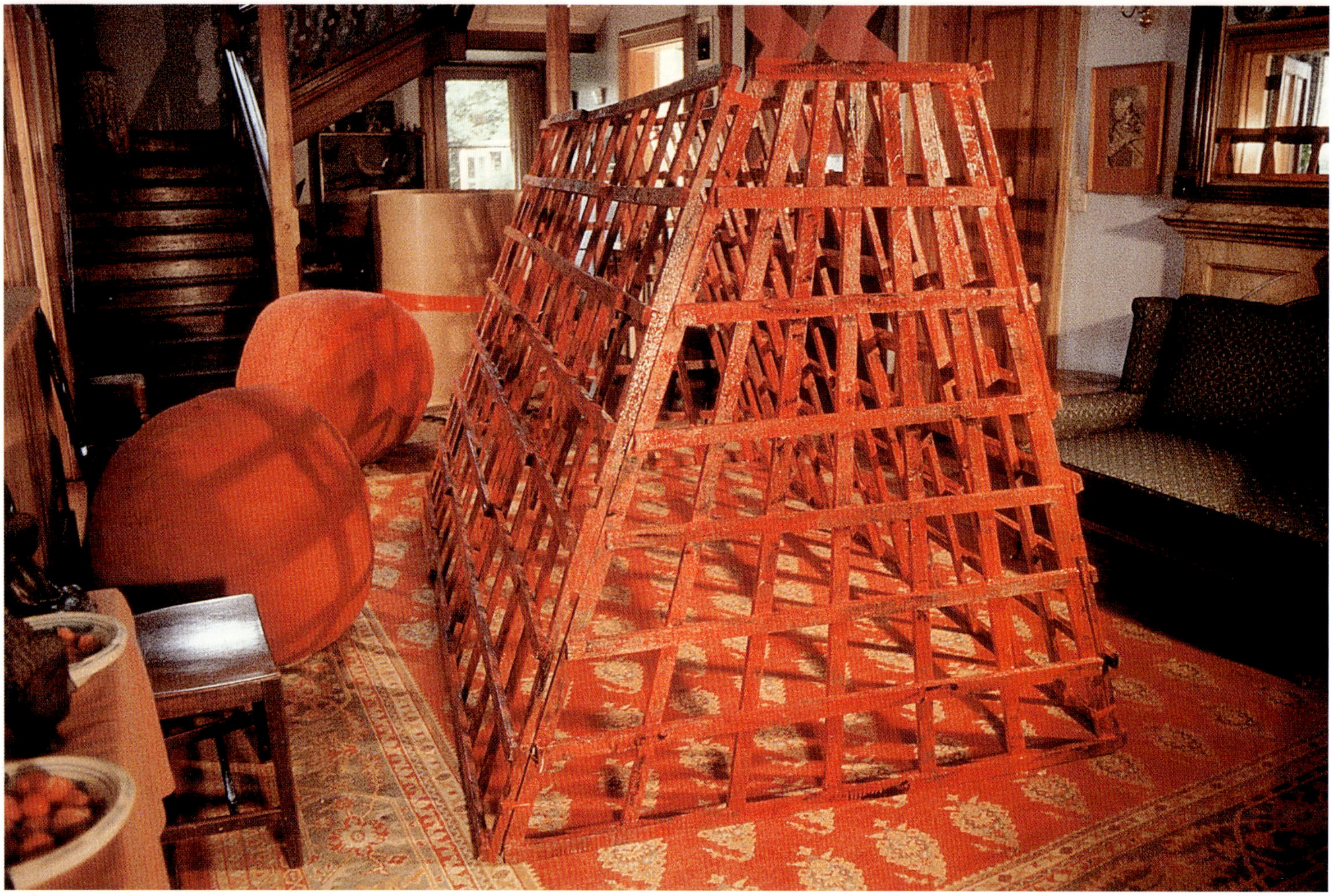
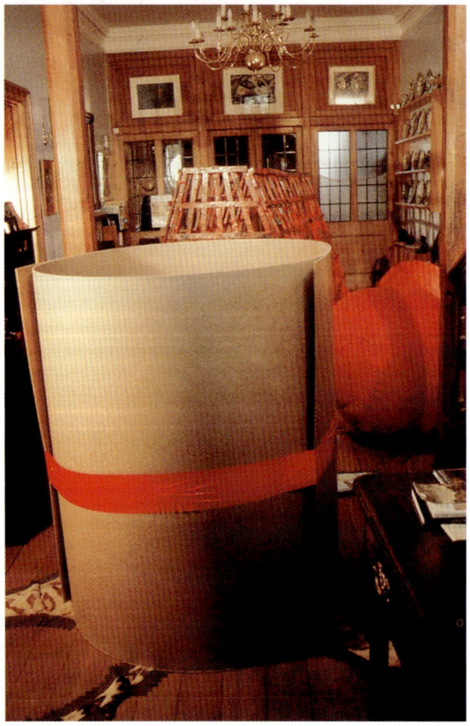
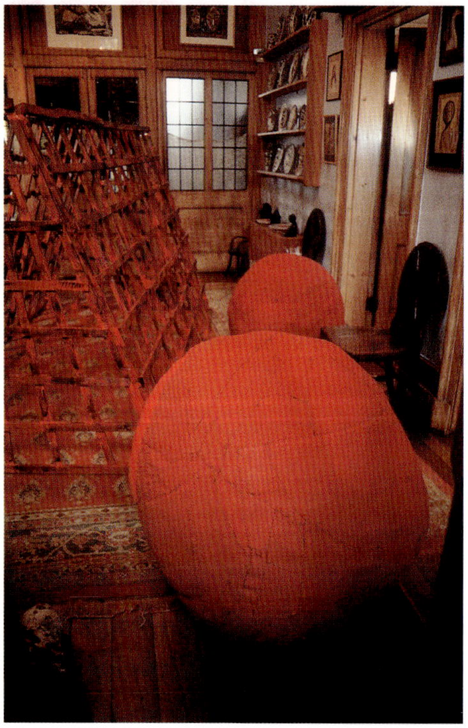
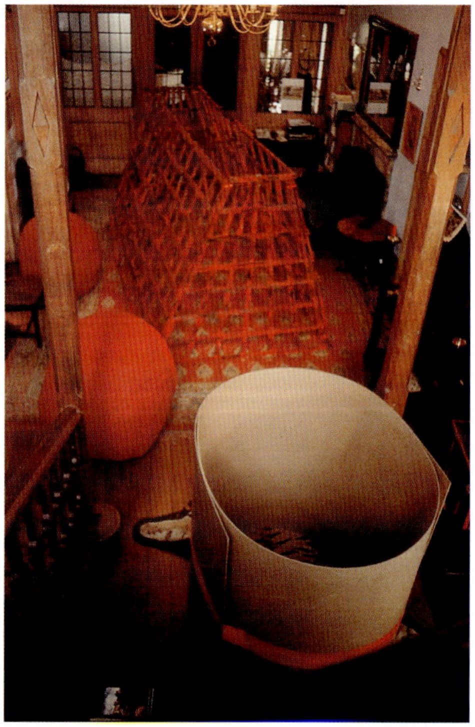

Opposite
Installation for a Country House Hallway
Paint, roofing struts, assorted fabrics, felt, hardboard, red tape
Overall of space:
600 x 420 x 700 cm
1994
Private house, Hertfordshire, UK

Top right
Stuff
Dyed canvas, felt, fabrics, laths, string, elastic, latex
Overall of space:
600 x 300 x 1800 cm
1973
Gulbenkian Calouste Gallery, Newcastle-upon-Tyne, UK

Bottom right
All and Everything
Dyed canvas, paper, fabrics, felt, vinyl, sliced plywood, hardboard
Overall of site:
900 x 400 x 1200 cm
1972
Guildford University, UK

Overleaf
Ramp
Wood boards, filler, paint, canvas, plastic tube
300 x 120 x 360 cm
2001

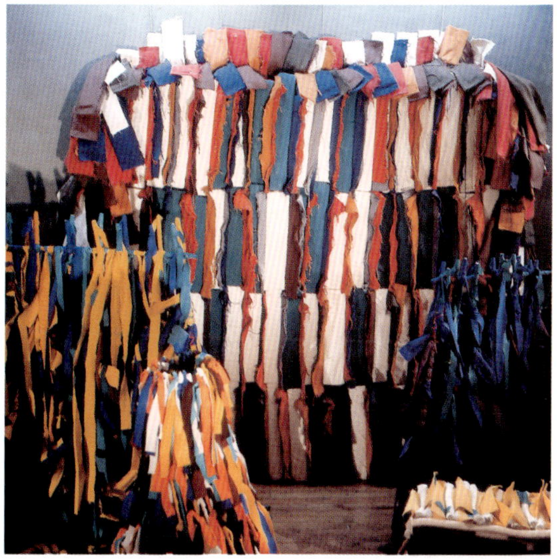

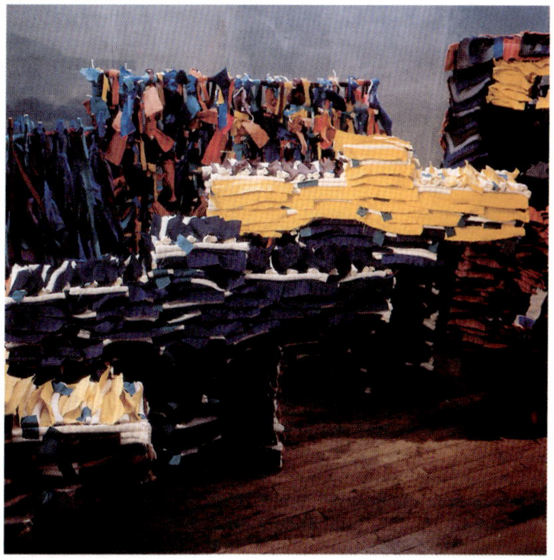

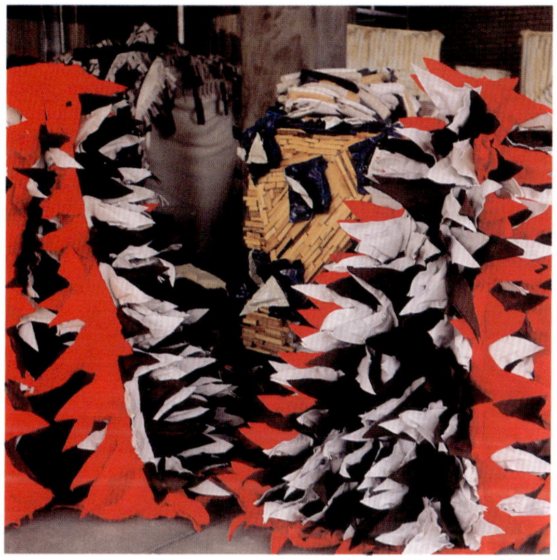

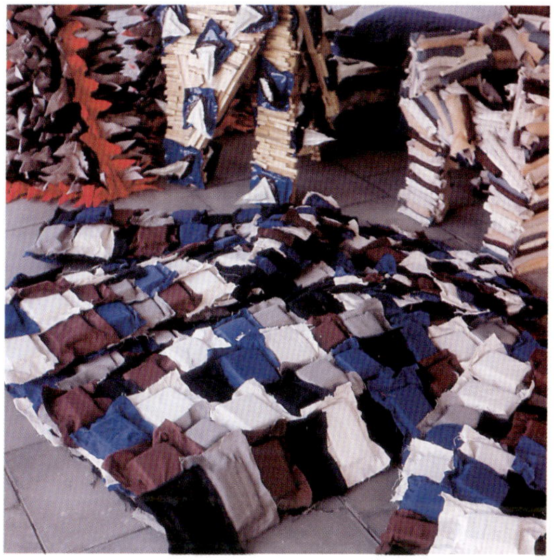

Four of Barlow's most recent works have been shown in a disused mill in Chilworth for Albury Arts. In *holed-up: pink*, 2003, a readymade colour – the scarlet of store-bought fabric – pokes out of a hardboard structure that has been painted with a totally invented and roughly mixed pinky purple which actually fluctuates from mauve to white to dark red. In *holed-up: green*, 2003, the same readymade red (but this time, the red of a piece of masking tape) stretches over an area of paint which is also readymade as it is unmixed, applied straight from the can. This paint is a pale and sickly green, so there is an awkward and rude juxtaposition: this is not the complimentary bold green the bright red tape would deserve. In *holed-up: red*, 2003, however, the combination of maroon, red and orange is incredibly subtle. In *holed-up: yellow*, 2003, the hue is kept constant through the sculpture, and the difference of the areas does not have to do with colour shifts but with reflectivity (gloss paint's shine next to matt fabric). Barlow sometimes uses evocative colours to summon memories, describing the pale green as institutional – the colours of hospital wards. Elsewhere, colour can be used to destroy memory: for instance, we totally forget the brown of wood when it appears next to the yellow cloth and gloss in *holed-up: yellow*. These works have emerged at a moment where coloured abstract sculpture is newly celebrated in Britain with another "New Generation" that includes Jim Lambie and Gary Webb. In contrast to the polite cacophony of appropriated colours in their works, Barlow's found and created colours seem more subtle yet ruder, more versatile and more challenging.

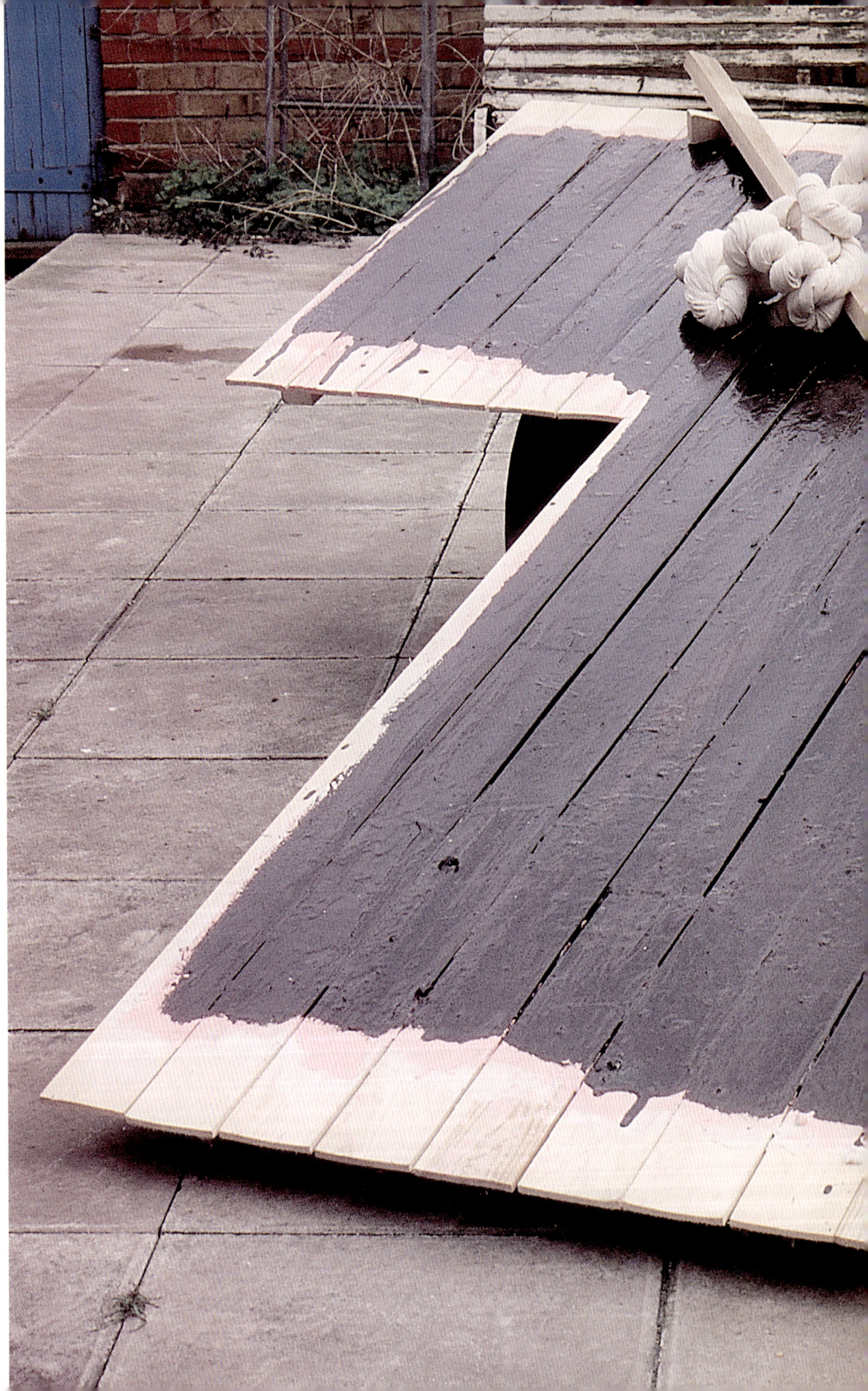

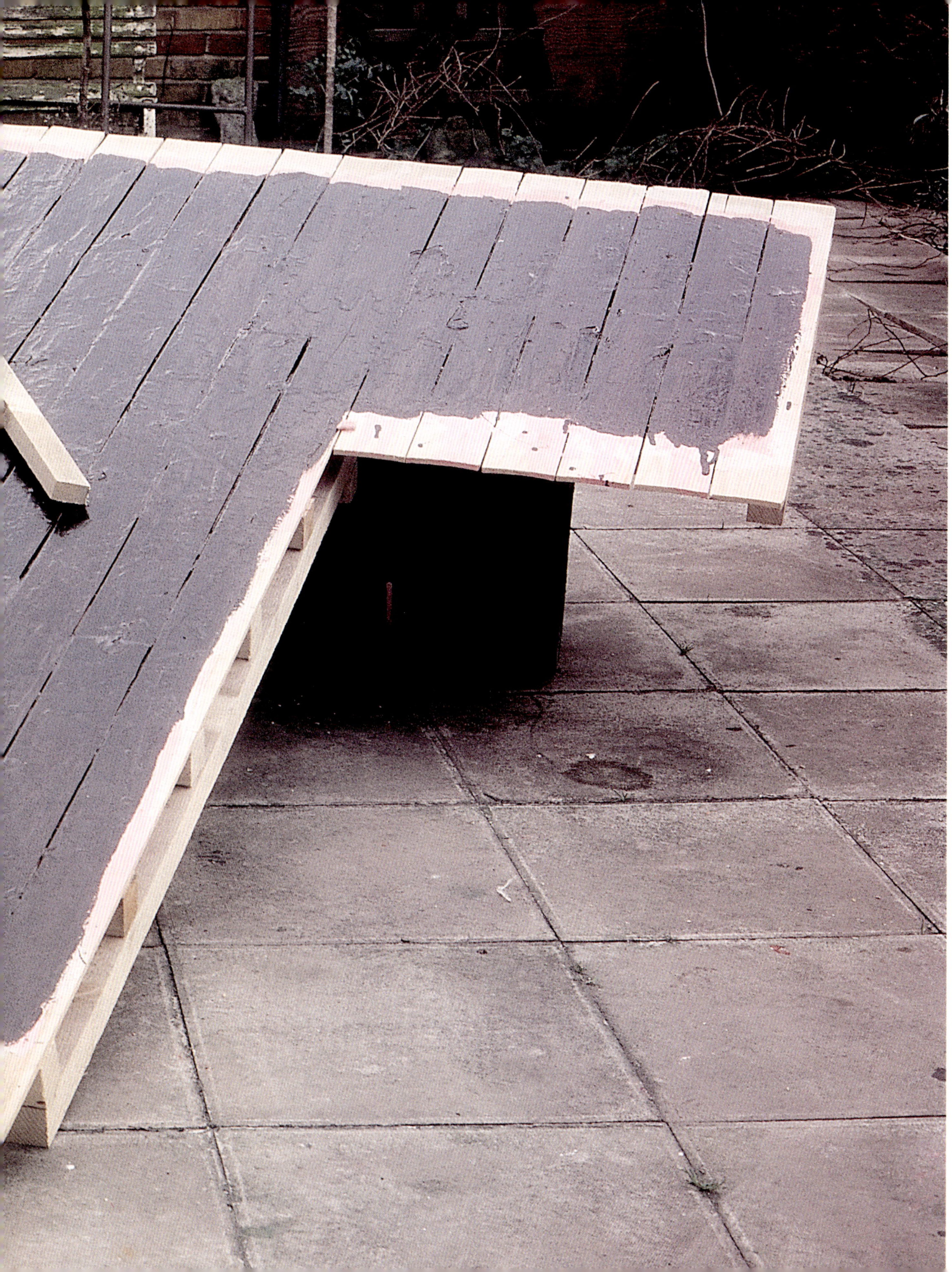

The Encounter

If we can draw two points from the discussion of colour, they would be that its function is to magnify the physical and imaginative dimensions of the viewer's encounter with Barlow's work, and it is the encounter that I now wish to discuss. It is hardly difficult to locate the artists who were important to Barlow in developing her interest in the physical, as opposed to the pictorial, encounter. Even though she had to move her work away from the minimalists', their exploration of the physical dimension of spectatorship was crucial for her. As Michael Fried, minimalism's most famous critic noted, the work was theatrical and durational. The viewing situation now included "the beholder's *body*" and was an experience that "*persists in time*".[23] In his book *Minimalism*, James Meyer has clarified how each minimalist artist considered spectatorship in different ways. Where Morris "relocat[ed] perception in a corporeal self, a body that could see", Carl Andre "sought a more haptic spectatorship [and] declared that tactility was the medium's distinctive feature". Sculpture was "something you "trip over" after "you shut off the lights"."[24] Andre also extended Morris's concern with space: in his Styrofoam show of 1965, by deliberately filling the Tibor de Nagy gallery with his expanded Styrofoam pieces, Andre forced the viewer to realise their movement around the work, but also drew attention to the specific dimensions of the room in which the sculpture was housed. Donald Judd's stacks, meanwhile, would not be walked around, but they did measure out the space between floor and ceiling, declaring the limits of the gallery space in which the viewer was standing.

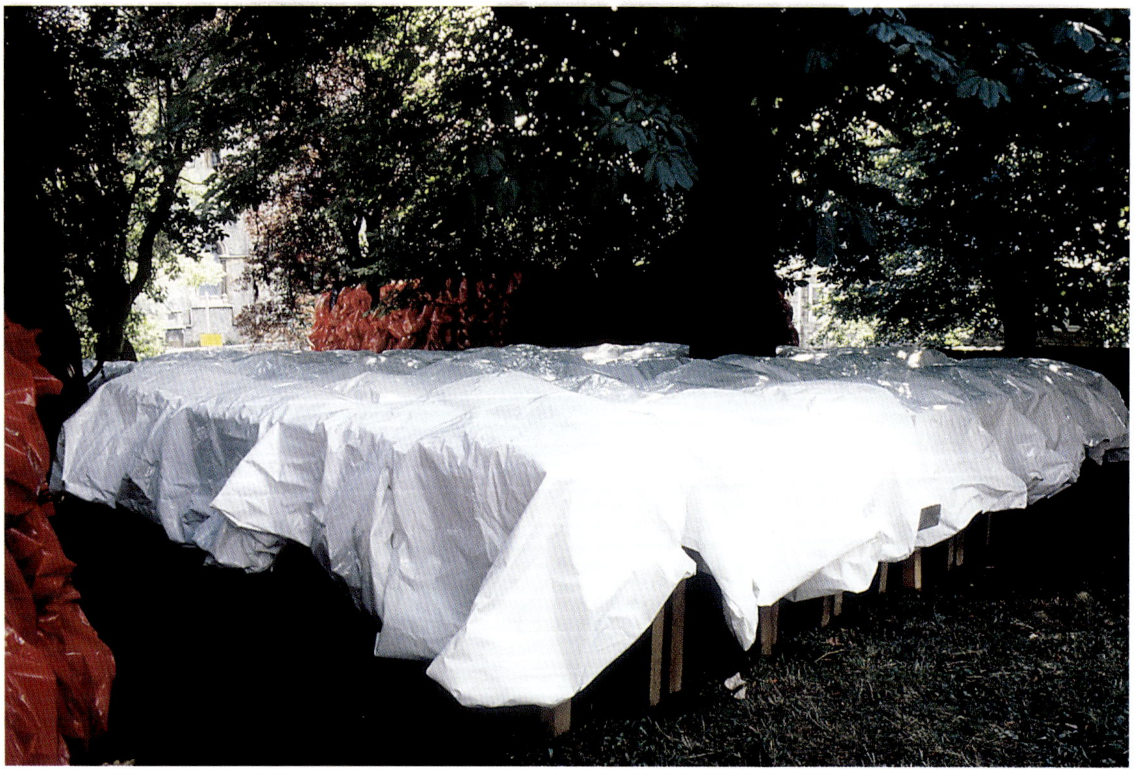

Right
Oracle
Polythene, timber, canvas
300 x 1800 x 1800 cm
1987
St Peter's Church Yard,
Kettle's Yard, Cambridge

Below
Richard Serra
Snake
Cor-ten steel
1998-1999

23 Fried, Michael, "Art and Objecthood", *Artforum*, June 1967, p. 16 and 22.

24 Meyer, James, *Minimalism– Art and Polemics in the Sixties*, London and New Haven: Yale University Press, 2001, pp.197-198.

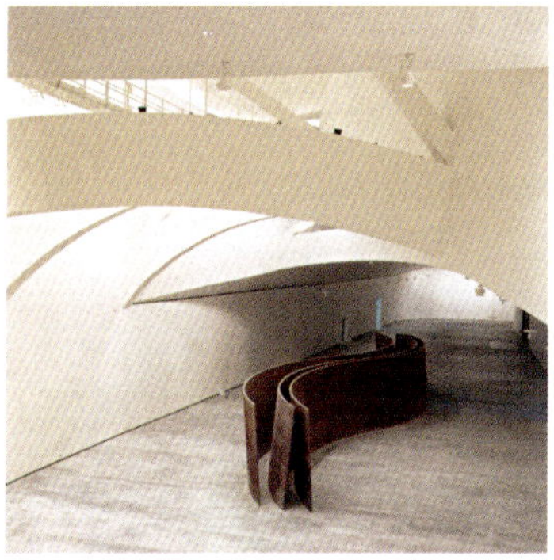

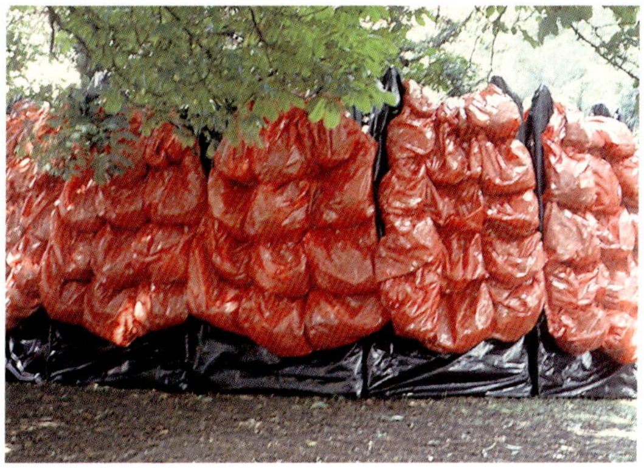

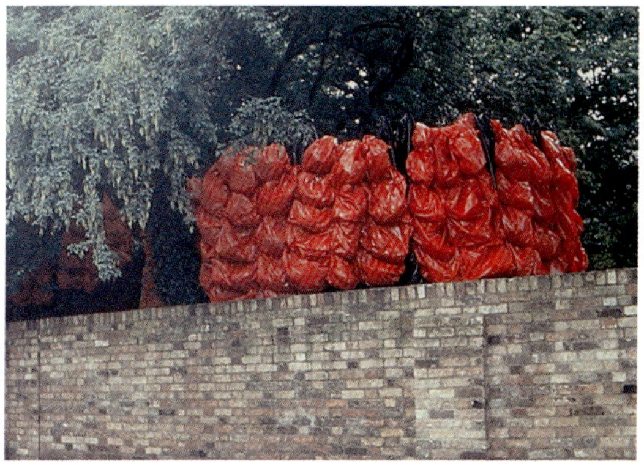

Barlow's work expands all these investigations. Works like *Ghosts*, 1984, almost filled the spaces they were in, whist in *Storm*, 1987 and *Folds*, 1988, material stretched from one vertical wall to another. Stuff was squashed and pushed against the walls blocking the viewer's way and making them feel constrained in the space. The space between the polythene and felt sections of *Engulf*, 1987, was a narrow corridor whose walls fell away on one side and bent over a viewer on the other, whilst for *Slope*, 1988, Barlow made a low space into which a viewer would walk, bending their necks as they cautiously stepped in. Earlier I discussed the importance of process in Richard Serra's early work, but in terms of the phenomenological encounter, his late work is the most significant of the late twentieth century. I imagine that walking through the passages of *Engulf* might have felt a little like walking through his *Snake*, 1998-99, whose walls similarly curve around, compressing and opening up space. Barlow's soft materials might have created even more of a sense of imbalance: empathising with the wavy crumpled foam all around them, the viewer might have felt their own stability was on the verge of collapse.

The encounter with Barlow's work is never simply a negotiation of stuff in space: the imaginative dimension of the encounter is crucial. The material that is visibly present before the viewer matters, but so do the fantasies that are provoked by its shapes, its colours, its associations. Barlow wants the sculptural encounter to be one of enchantment, and just what this means will become clearer soon, but the importance of the imagination for Barlow is marked quite clearly by quasi-architectural works such as *Slope* and *Vigil*, 1989. These are less like Dan Graham's pavilions, which are actual architectural spaces, and closer to Mario Merz's igloos, which demand their viewer imagine inhabiting them without literally doing so. *Slope* and *Vigil* promised a temporary shelter and provoked the memory of secure spaces. *Deep*, 1991, consisted of two stepped mounds of white boxes arranged at either end of a gallery space carpeted with black polythene. The mounds appeared like overcrowded cities, rising and falling again towards the ground. They recall the futuristic architectural projects of the 60s like Moshe Safdie's *Habitat 67*. Hoping the interiors of the boxes would shine like the polythene, Barlow had poured paint in and then tipped it out of some boxes, and the viewer could look into the lowest boxes to see their pale blue gloss surfaces. But despite the importance of colour and light in the work, the viewer would still have had a rather literal sense that the mounds looked like buildings. Though this might have initiated a fantasy that they were giants peering over an abandoned Lilliputian city, this literalness was problematic.

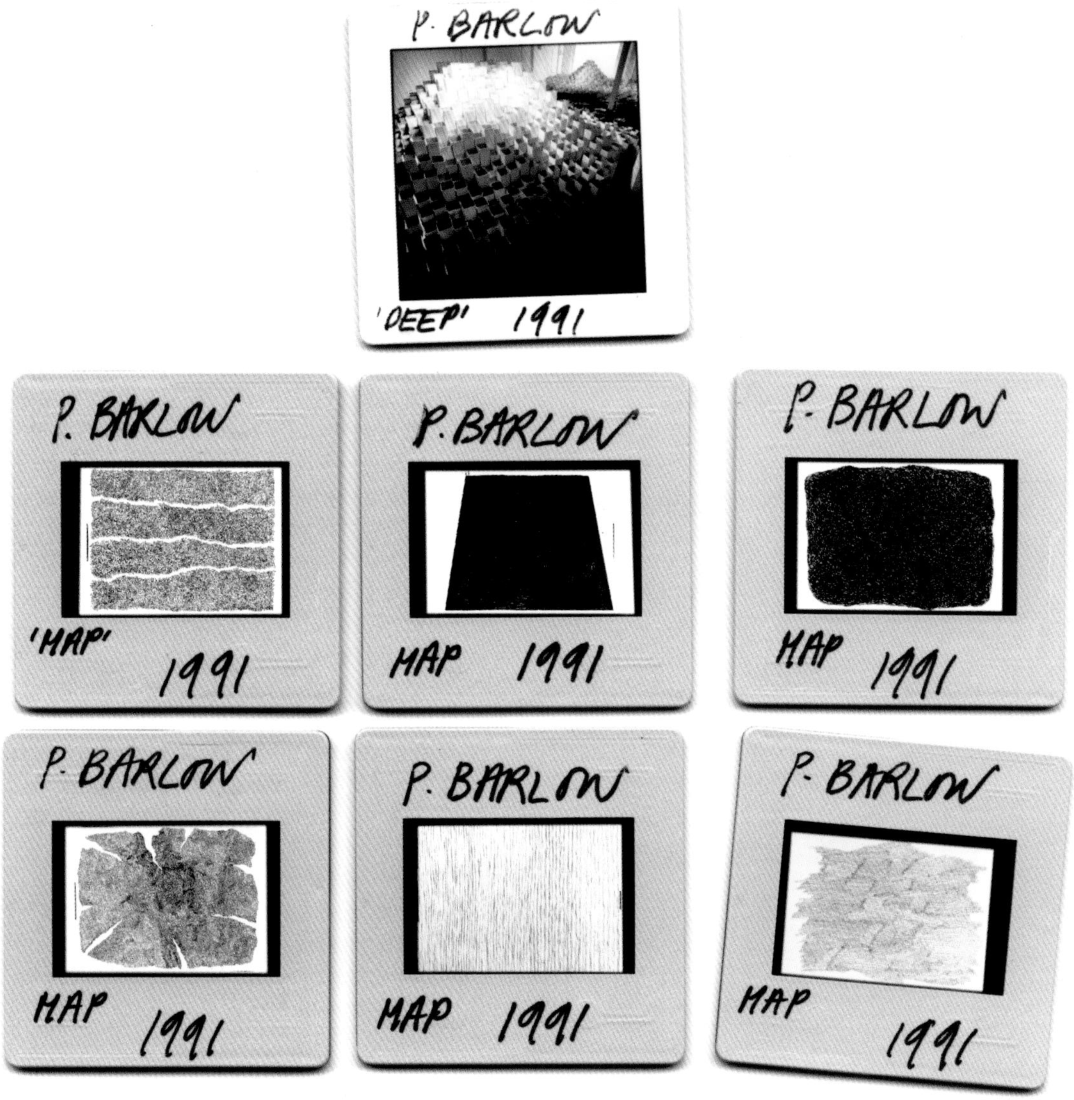

Like *Fall* and *Home*, *Deep* is a bit of an anomaly in Barlow's work. This is because if it triggers the imagination, it does so through resemblance and simile. In her more recent works, the imaginative dimension of the encounter has little to do with resemblance, relying on more abstract principles. These have to do with potential and memory, absurdity and sense, artifice and honesty, concealment and revelation, awkwardness and ease. But before looking at the works to see how these ideas come into play, it is instructive to think about Barlow's comments on other artists, for these reveal the nature of her sculptural imagination.

Counter-intuitively, we can begin by thinking about work that Barlow feels deadens the sculptural imagination. In perhaps her most powerful text, "The Hatred of the Object", Barlow invented a wonderful phrase, the 'made-easy', whilst discussing work that is easy to make and easy to consume. Barlow does not name names when discussing the 'made-easy' object, but given that the text appeared in the years following *Sensation*, it is not hard to spot whose work she had in mind. The 'made-easy' object is appropriated from the world of consumerism, fabricated by assistants rather than built by the artist, easily nameable and cleverly titled, installed in a vitrine so

25 Barlow, "At Sea".

26 Barlow, "The Hatred of the Object".

Alighiero Boetti
Lampada Annuale (Yearly Lamp)
Steel
78 x 40 x 40 cm
1966

Marcel Duchamp
Why not sneeze… Rrose Selavy?
1964 (replica of the 1921 original)

separated from the viewer, best seen from one spot and quickly recalled as image, pictorial and simple to photograph. Made-easy objects are press-friendly and easily marketed, yet for Barlow, they are the disappointingly pathetic progeny of Duchamp's more imaginative readymades.

It is whilst describing her anxieties about and differences from the 'made-easy' artists and their strategies that Barlow reveals her most passionate and firmly held opinions on sculpture: "Sculpture is essentially wordless – that is part of its vulnerability. Is this why readymades score so effortlessly in comparison to sculpture? [It is] as if displacing an object with verbal/written language is a plus – much easier than the complicated act of looking."[25] Discussing the problem of the vitrine she writes "as a device, it deadens opinion, rendering the status of the object as a wild, messy, unpredictable, ugly, difficult thing to being cleansed, tamed, glamorised, polite. A shift from raw experience to managed spectacle."[26] So sculpture is to be wild, wordless, unpredictable and ugly – but this is not to say that the only work to fascinate her would be *Threadwaste* or *Avenza Revisited*. For Barlow, the sculptural imagination is provoked as much by Morris or Bourgeois as it is by the work of Marcel Duchamp and Hans Haacke, artists conventionally associated with the readymade and institutional critique.

Temporality is an important sculptural element for Barlow. Not just the slow time it takes to look at a work or move around it (the duration Fried disliked in minimalism), but the past time the work seems to hold in store or the future event it seems to promise. The subtitle of Alighiero E Boetti's *Lampada Annuale (Yearly Lamp)*, 1966, reveals that it illuminates for eleven seconds a year but does not say when this will happen. The work dramatically instantiates the sense of anticipation one might have before a sculpture, the sense of an imminent but perhaps impossible and constantly withheld event. Another Italian work that Barlow has referred to is Giovanni Anselmo's *Torsione (Torsion)*, 1968. This stages the irretrievability of past time: the leather that was being prised from wet concrete is now stuck mid-twist. In a text that focussed on Louise Bourgeois' *Cell (Eyes and Mirrors)*, 1989-1993, Barlow described her interest in the way she "experience[d] a suspension of time through objects which act as instruments of measurement". In the Bourgeois, these objects were the mirrors which "seem to record, hold, and trap every movement beyond their immediate environment". Barlow compared the work with Marcel Duchamp's *Why not sneeze, Rrose Selavy*, 1921, "an object held in time, poised to explode":

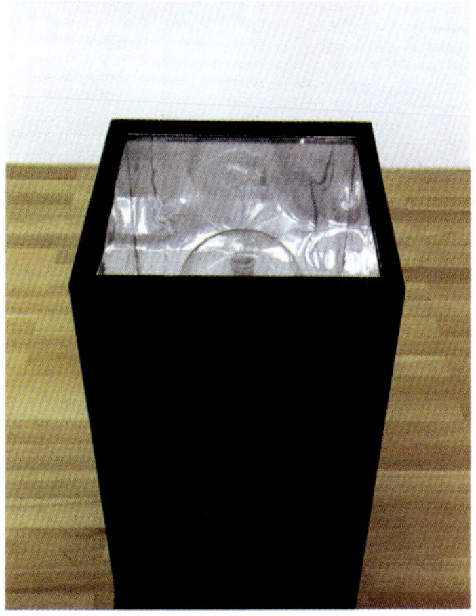

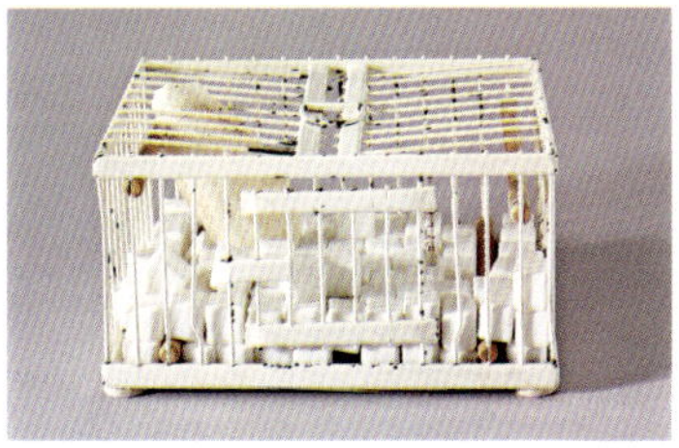

Deep/Map series
1991

> The thermometer waits in anticipation for any change which indicates the impending explosion. What is the role of the cuttle bone? A cuttle bone… is the central bone of the cuttle fish, a squid-like animal which ejects black ink when alarmed. Like the thermometer, this residual object also indicates anticipation, but in its case it is the anticipation of fear, and the volatile consequences of that fear, an eruption of black ink. Gradually this small, portable cage object becomes more and more like an ambiguous instrument with a sexuality which its title begins to reveal. More particularly, it reveals its absence of sex, its hoping for sex…. Duchamp's object is an object of measurement. It is in suspense, held in time, unfolding itself continuously at the same moment, a constant reminder of the longed for and the about to be.[27]

For Barlow, the question of time is the question of what is not evident now, but what might have happened or might happen. But this is not to say that what is present before the viewer is always revealed in the here and now of the encounter. For the sculpture can also conceal, or refuse to disclose its contents. Given the way institutional critique and land art are kept quite distinct in recent art histories, it was surprising to see her bring together Hans Haacke and Walter De Maria in a talk given at the Royal Academy. For Barlow, both De Maria's *Vertical Earth Kilometre*, 1977 and Hans Haacke's *Standort Merry Go Round*, 1997 "reveal a sculptural language rooted in the undisclosed, the hidden, the contained, the unfinished, the impossible to grasp, and the defiance and repudiation of an image and its inevitable optimum view."[28] Whilst De Maria buried a huge brass pole into the earth's crust, so only its top end remained on Kassel's street level, Haacke enclosed the carousel within a huge slatted wooded stockade. Both works conceal objects but as a result of the act of concealment, the viewer has not only to imagine the hidden objects themselves but the space around them and the consequences of their potential revelation. Of course the nature of the imaginative content is different in each work, given the two artists' different concerns. So the *Vertical Earth Kilometre* draws us to imagine "the bowels of the city and beyond… the dark viscera…. There is the thought of what happens when the kilometre length is extracted, what will ooze from the hole?" The imaginative questions Haacke's work provokes are more political, having to do with the nature of the culture industry and the usurpation of formerly public spaces by the screens of advertising. Barlow suggests precisely by raising a façade around a somewhat antiquated object of popular entertainment, Haacke draws attention to the façades that are omnipresent in the contemporary city, and the loss of authentic space. The sculpture "seems to refer to the stark realities of what becomes of a cosmetically constructed world, reciprocated by the city and its system of facades, and what happens when such facades collapse".

Hans Haacke
Standort Merry-Go-Round
(German Merry-Go-Round)
1997

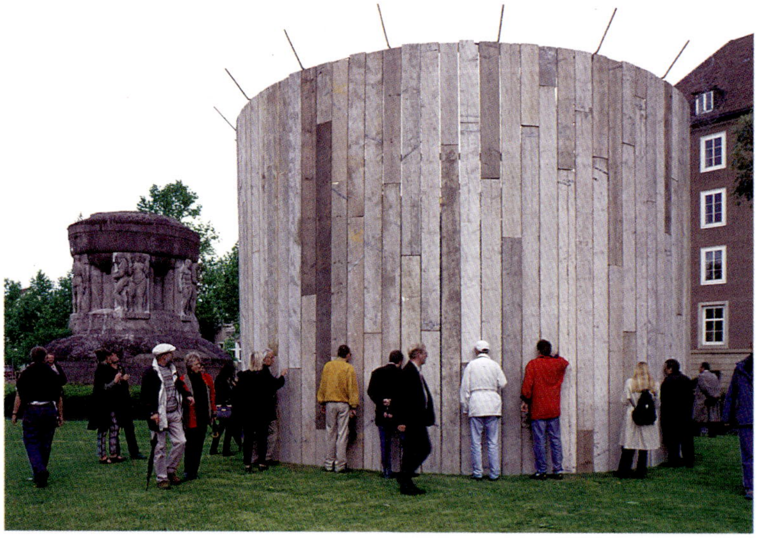

27 **Barlow**, "The Sneeze of Louise", pp. 4-5.

28 Barlow, Phyllida, talk published in *The City as Sculpture*, London: Royal Academy of Arts, 2002, p. 6.

29 Importantly, Barlow will not make 'references' to other famous works in the eclectic, knowing, post-modern manner of someone like Gary Webb (who might refer in one work to Malevich, Judd, or Andre). Barlow instead uses historical sculptural discoveries as tools. Barlow commented that the legs of *holed-up: yellow* were "A direct lift from [Louise Bourgeois's] *The Blind Leading the Blind*" and explained "It's such a brilliant device that she used for getting something to stand up and I've had that difficulty myself with knowing how to make a horizontal platform.
It is a very sculptural thing in all sorts of ways – it's a kind of plinth, it's a base, it's a platform, it's a stage – how do you raise it up, how do you get it off the floor and give it a dynamic which is balanced, poised, on tip-toes? Having really loved that work [*The Blind Leading the Blind*] I decided to plagiarise it." (Conversation with author, June 2003).

Let us now return to Barlow's most recent work to see what kind of a sculptural encounter it sets up. The works in the mill at Albury are placed in such a way that the viewer feels compelled to walk around them rather than to view them from a fixed central point as so many static images. Entering the space the viewer first sees *holed-up: yellow*. Its top board slopes upwards from the horizontal platform like the lid of a grand piano but the viewer cannot tell what is inside so to satisfy their curiosity they must start walking: movement starts with a question mark. The horizontal platform is raised on precarious legs which narrow as they reach the ground, a device inherited from Bourgeois's *The Blind Leading the Blind*, 1947-49.[29] Seeing these whilst moving on their feet, the viewer becomes alert to their own balance. *holed-up: yellow* is placed at some distance from the walls of the mill but *holed-up: green* and *holed-up: red* squeeze the spectator as they walk around them. *holed-up: pink*, meanwhile, sends the viewer's glance upwards, following its length to the heights of the wood-beamed roof.

Taken as a group, then, the works in the installation alert the spectator to his or her own movement and balance and to the horizontal and vertical extension of the architectural setting around them. Yet as we know, the physical experience is only one element of the encounter. Of the four works in *holed up: red, yellow, green, pink*, 2003, three seemed to suggest a future event. You could imagine the red tape blob falling off *holed-up: red*, placed as it was so awkwardly upon the rectangular object which itself rests somewhat provisionally on three unpainted wooded slats. *holed-up: green* is a circular object made from six huge sheets of hardboard bent around into a cylinder. These boards seem to be held in place by red masking tape but should this snap, they would spring out violently. On top of the upper gloss-painted board of *holed-up: yellow*, two wooden sticks have already acted as a crank to wind out the yellow cloth that lies between the boards. This quotes Anselmo's *Torsion* but there, leather is encased in set concrete: here the cloth remains loose. Turn the handle more and the boards will snap shut.

holed-up: red's wooden box is covered by an orange sheet, stitched in five sections to fit over the top but hanging loosely. We do not know whether the maroon paint visible at the bottom coats its whole surface or just stops underneath the orange blanket, but nor can we tell what is in the box. That we should ask the question at all has to do with the way this work is charged by the sculptures that surround it: two have insides which visibly spill out. Barlow is fascinated by the way close objects affect each other, thinking for instance of Roni Horn's *Pair Objects*, but the point I want to pick up here concerns concealment. Physical elements of the sculptures are concealed but so are the mechanical ones. When Barlow began making work, like other artists of the late 60s she tended to make evident the armatures of her works, confronting illusionism and trickery. If a sculpture stood up, it was obvious how. But such values might no longer be important, and whilst Barlow is committed to a sculpture of space and materials, she has become interested in the ideas of deceit and artifice. Is the yellow fabric *really* propping the lid of *holed-up: yellow*? Or is there a hidden armature? The red tape of *holed-up: green seems* to rein in the hardboard, keeping it cylindrical, but is it? (In fact, hidden luggage straps perform the task the red tape pretends to do.) The idea of deceit relates to the notion of the fake. *holed-up: pink* seems to be a solid plank like the beams it touches but look closely and it turns out to be hollow, made of four lengths of hardboard.

During a conversation in the mill at Albury, Barlow described one of the problems facing the contemporary sculptor. "We are in a world that's stuffed with fascinating things. We are competing with materialism that's on such a gigantic scale. There's a gigantic global industry of objects, and how do we compete with that? What is left for the maker of things to do that can be different from this wealth of stuff in the world? I think [this situation] forces the maker of things to become excessively contrived, almost to the point of it being absurd."[30] From photographs of recent works, it might indeed seem that the sculptural encounter Barlow stages is in essence an encounter with the absurd, with 'things' utterly distinct from the objects of materialism, utterly out of place in the world of useful products. It is not that simple. *holed-up: pink*, for instance, is both in- and out-of-place: it bonds the four sculptures with architecture of the mill, drawing the viewer's attention to the wooden roof. At the same time, the work presses home the unbridgeable distance that separates the functional world of a mill and the enchanted world of Barlow's sculpture, and importantly, it does so with greatest power at precisely the place where physical distance diminishes, where there is contact between the wood of the mill and the wood of the sculpture. Here, at the top, red fabric spills out of the plank's hollow. The juxtaposition of the functional and useless – perhaps loosely inherited from Surrealist works like Dali's *Lobster Telephone*, 1936 – has been important to Barlow since works like *Object for an Ironing Board*, 1993 and *Object for a Television*, 1994. Though neatly placed on their provisional plinths, the objects were visually ridiculous. In the manner of Caro's 1966 *Table Pieces*, they parodied the politeness of domestic sculpture, the quiet kitsch of the decorative souvenir. But the force of these works was as much directed to the objects they replaced as to their supports.

Where *Object for an Ironing Board* prevented ironing, *Object for a Television* must have distracted the TV viewer. Barlow was not simply declaring the uselessness of the sculptural object but stressing the very idea of uselessness by rendering the functional object obsolete, a mere plinth. Which is to say that the encounter Barlow imagines is not simply wild and absurd. Barlow keeps in play the notion of use in order to suggest by contrast what enchantment might be, what another kind of world might be.

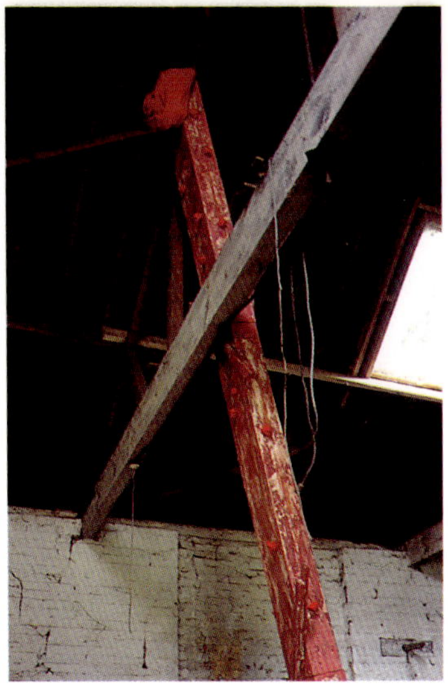

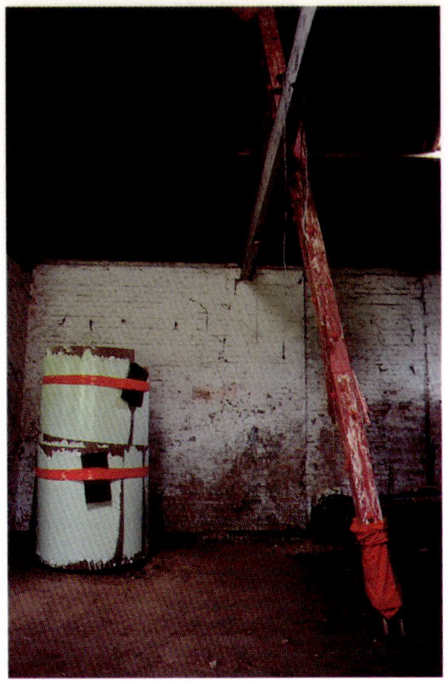

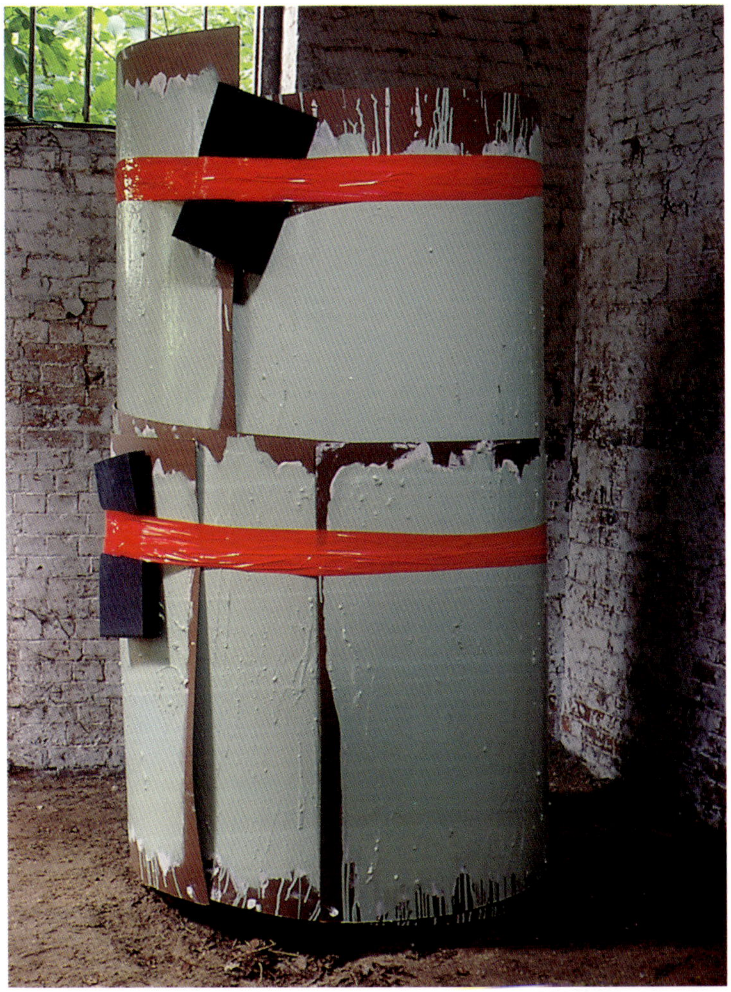

holed-up: yellow, red, green, pink
Hardboard, plywood, paint, fabric, tape, foam, tubing
750 x 1200 x 1200 cm
2003
Albury, Surrey

The red blob on the orange sheet over the maroon box has two plastic tubes penetrating through its middle and sticking out on both sides. Barlow is fascinated by the idea of a sculpture seeing you, notably thinking of Bourgeois's *Nature Study (Velvet Eyes)*, 1984. Despite the fact that *holed-up: red* also brings to mind Philip Guston's late paintings of hooded Klansmen, what I want to address here is less the possibility that these tubes are the eyes of the wobbly shape than the way the tubes manoeuvre the viewer to look through them like telescopes. But only *like* telescopes. The viewer cannot actually hold the tubes to his or her eyes – there are no rings to twist or knobs to turn. To conclude the discussion of the encounter, I want just to note that though totally theatrical, the encounter with Barlow's work is not literally participative. (*Home*, in passing, must have seemed simply *too* theatrical: just as Barlow's experiments with sound and smell did not continue, nor did her viewers ever again literally enter a sculptural space.) The viewer does *not* knock *holed-up: red*'s blob off its support, just as they do not actually twist the wooden crank in *holed-up: yellow*, pull the red stuffing from the plank of *holed-up: pink*, or snap the red masking tape of *holed-up: green*. From Lygia Clark and Helio Oiticica to Angela Bulloch and Carsten Holler, sculptors have encouraged a participative encounter with their objects, but Barlow prefers to keep any action in the realm of the imagination. Importantly, Barlow's viewer leaves her work with a sense of longing, with unfulfilled desires to carry to the world beyond.

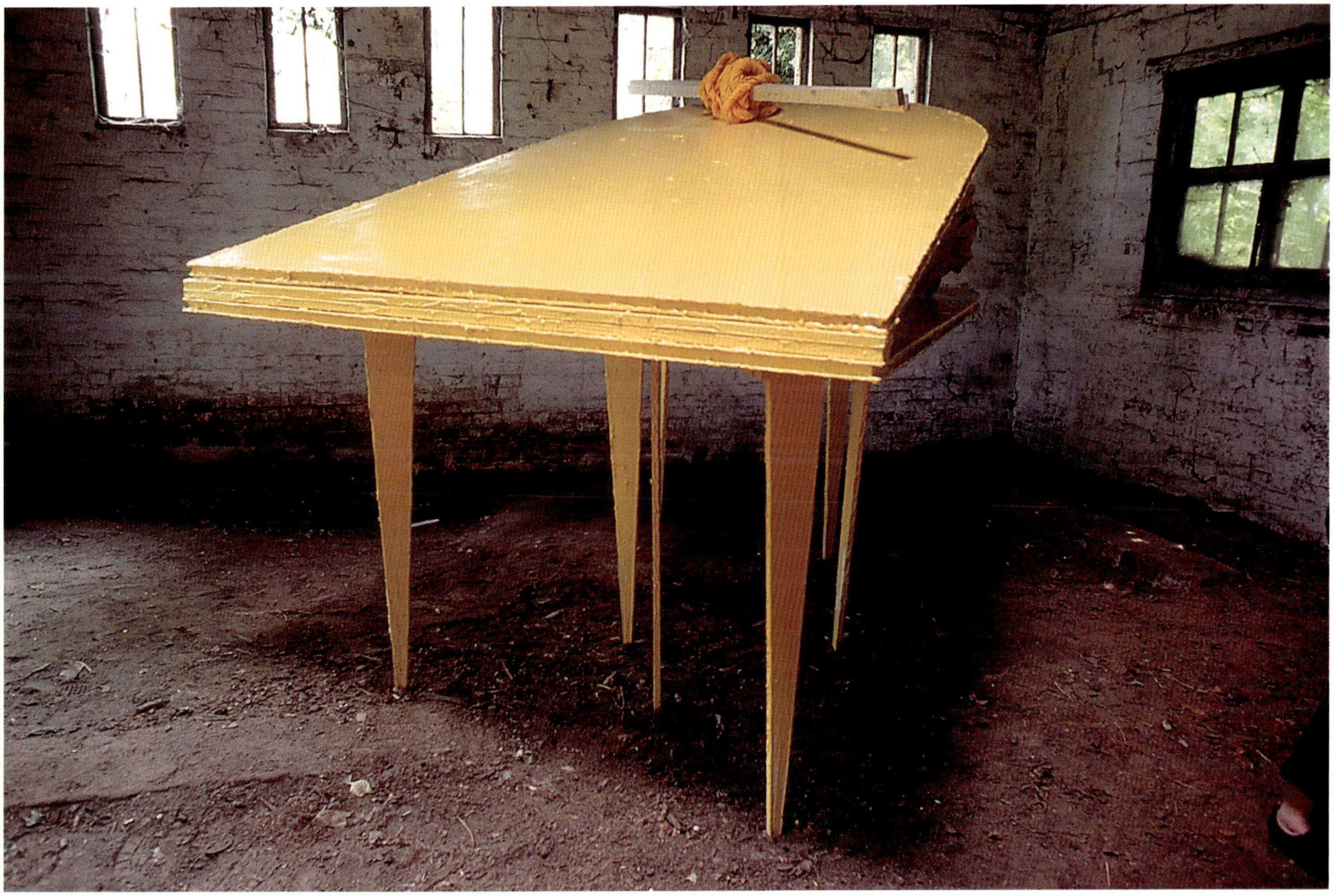

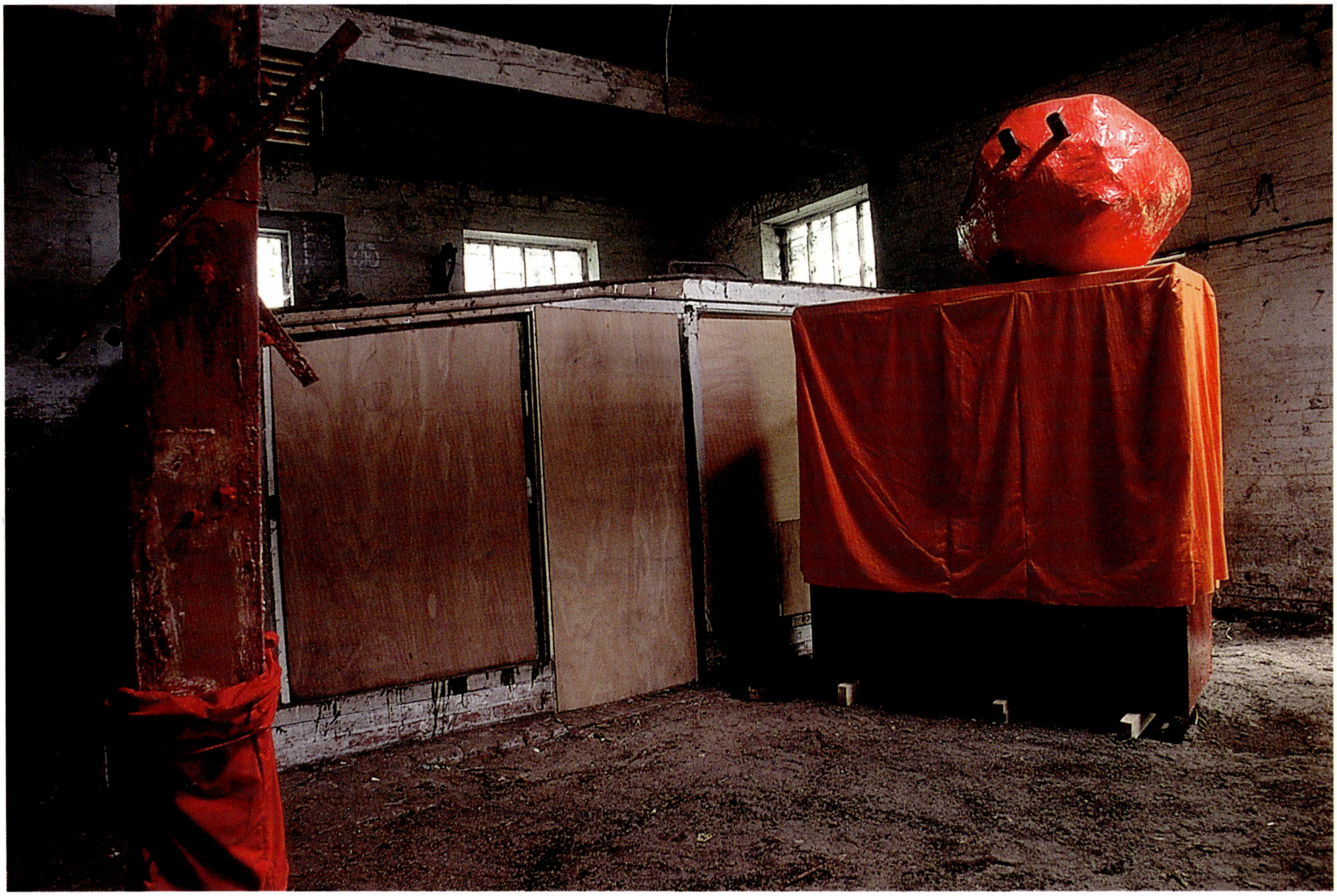

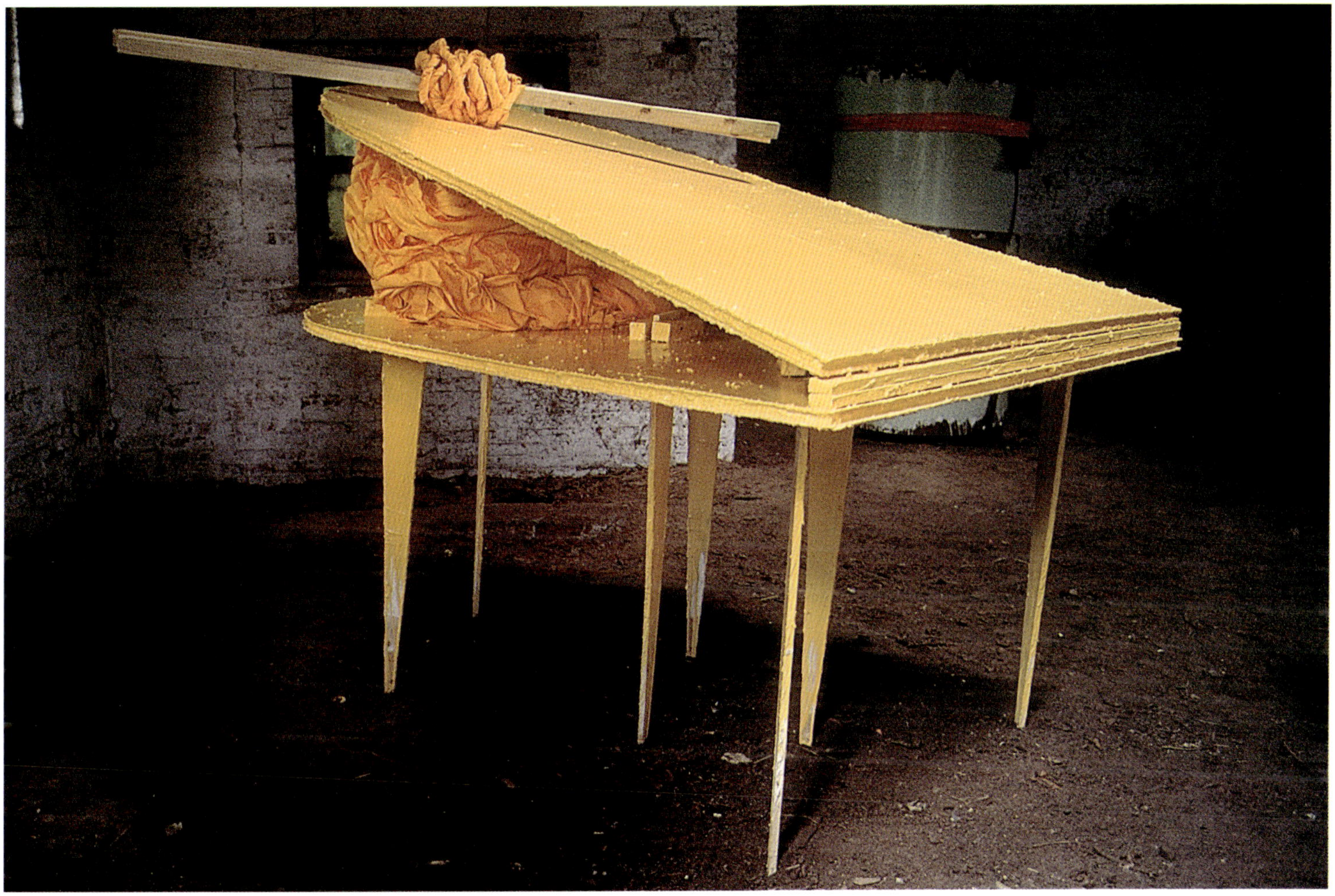

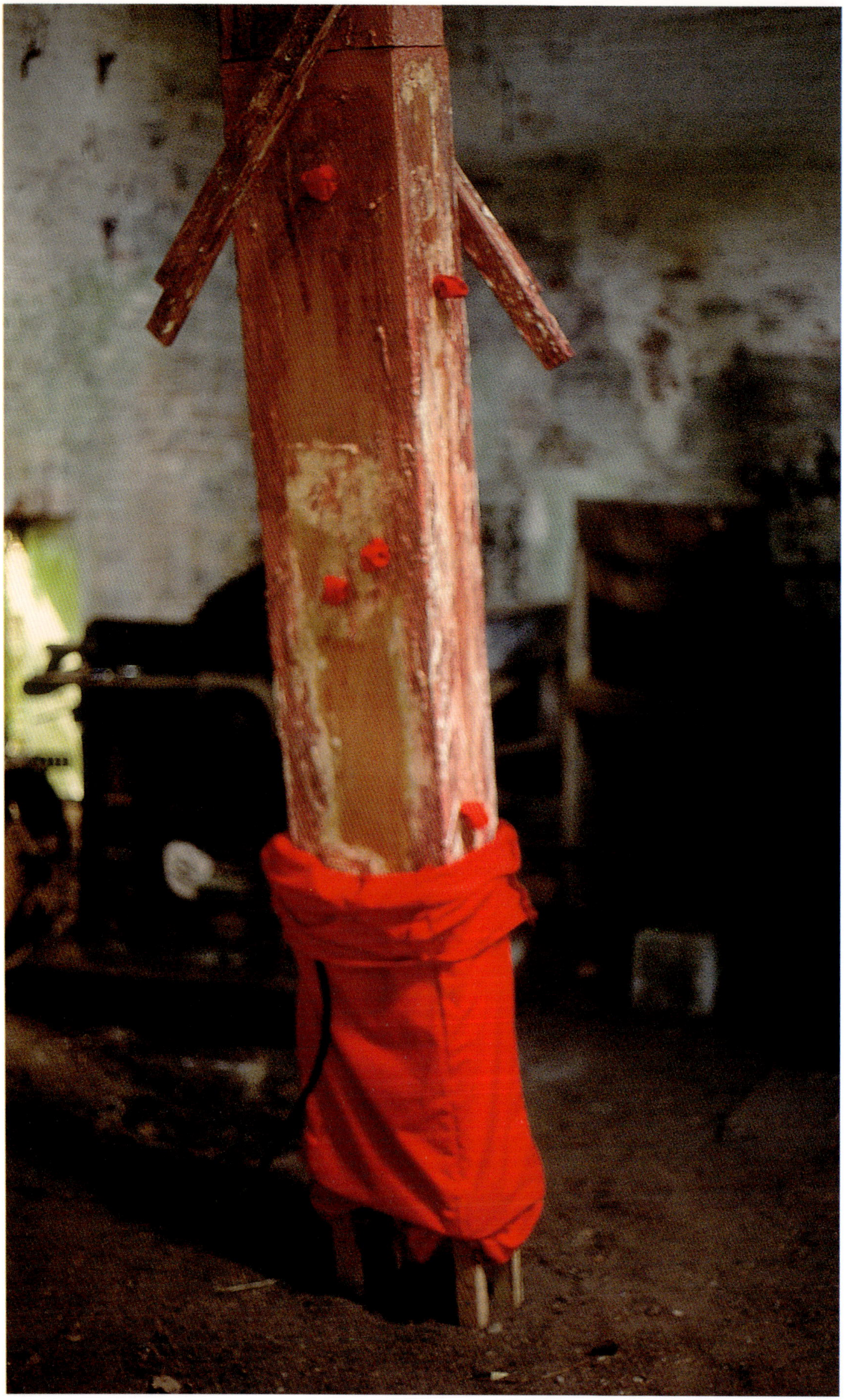

Photography/ Pedagogy

And much as a viewer might long to revisit a work after the time of its exhibition, they cannot. Once shown, Barlow's sculptures are dismantled, destroyed, their materials sometimes recycled to make new works, sometimes more simply discarded. Importantly, disintegration does not actually take place in the space of exhibition. Throughout the period of Barlow's work, artists have staged ephemeral objects which melt, evaporate, rot, disintegrate, darken, or dissipate over time. Consider Rafael Ferrer's *Ice* installed in the 1969 *Anti-Illusion* Whitney show or Anya Gallaccio's *Intensities and Surfaces*, another melting ice piece made 25 years later, Bruce McLeans' *King for a Day*, 1972 or Felix Gonzales-Torres 1991 piled corner of wrapped and removable sweets, *Untitled (Portrait of Ross in LA)*. The hardboard of Barlow's early works began to crumble in the rain, but this was untypical: ephemerality has not been the subject of Barlow's work, and her objects have never been literally transient.

Three factors explain why Barlow dismantles her works. Practically, of course, it would be impossible to store works like *Threat* and even the more contained, recent works would demand huge and hugely expensive storage spaces. The second factor is political: Barlow reached artistic maturity during the Thatcher years, and her refusal to create stable, storable, saleable sculpture was a strategy of resistance shared by a number of British artists. But just as American conceptual artists of the 70s had to realise how easily their photography and text work could be collected, so British installation artists were soon made to realise the naivety of their anti-market positions. Emasculating oppositional installation practices, collectors just learned to buy the room: Barlow describes Charles Saatchi's acquisition of Richard Wilson's *20:50*, 1987, as a wake-up call.

More positively, the disappearance of Barlow's work should be seen as the flipside to her insistence on the here-and-now event of the encounter. In *Open Ends*, the millennial group show at The Museum of Modern Art, New York, three of the stars in the Barlow sculptural canon came face-to-face. But Morris's *Threadwaste*, Serra's *House of Cards*, and Anselmo's *Torsion* were now just packaged and pigeon-holed – neat historical examples of postminimalism, anti-form, and Arte Povera. Pushed together in one room, they were juxtaposed with contemporary works indebted to this history: Janine Antoni's *Gnaw*, 1992 and Gonzales-Torres's *Untitled (Placebo)*, 1991, with Rachel Whiteread's *Water Tower*, 1998, visible through the window. No doubt at the cost of greater repute, Barlow has staked a position against the potentially deadening effect of the museum on sculpture, directing energies towards the creation of new work and never to the preservation of old.

30 Conversation with author, June 2003.

Whilst the museum threatens sculpture on one flank, photography attacks it on the other, rendering the three-dimensional object a picture. Recently, artists such as Gabriel Orozco and Guiseppe Gabellone have complicated the relation of sculpture and photography: Orozco photographs sculptural events to emphasise the transience of their physical manifestation.[31] Gabellone builds elaborate constructions just to dismantle them after they are photographed, mourning the contemporary impossibility of the purely phenomenological encounter in a world where images displace physical experience. Despite acknowledging in her texts and teaching the embattled position of sculpture, despite her anxieties about its obsolescence, Barlow still has faith in the possibilities of the physical sculptural encounter so for all her fascination with these artists, the photograph remains for her a problem. This is all the more the case because of the way sculptures are now photographed. In "Travelling Light", Barlow notes that whilst photographs of sculptures in the 1960s were casual and expedient (such as the shot of Smith's *Die*, now pristine colour slides show works alone, cleaned up, well lit in gleaming white spaces. The result of this orthodoxy is that "there is no need to be there with the work because its idealised photographic image can be believed to communicate the work". The photograph is only half of the problem:

> The contemporary catalogue with its outstanding photographic representation is, in the context of a take-away culture, the take-away exhibition. So superbly does it not only represent the work, but re-present the work in compact, portable book form that the art objects within, whatever their original form, become idealised portraits.[32]

And so, with this book, we are faced with the greatest of ironies. Barlow's anti-pictorial, aggressively physical work can now only be known through the photographs gathered here. Barlow would be the first to remind us of the inadequacies of these representations. But rather than ending by stuffing humble pie down Phyllida's throat, in conclusion I want to think about the happy consequences of the physical disappearance of her works.

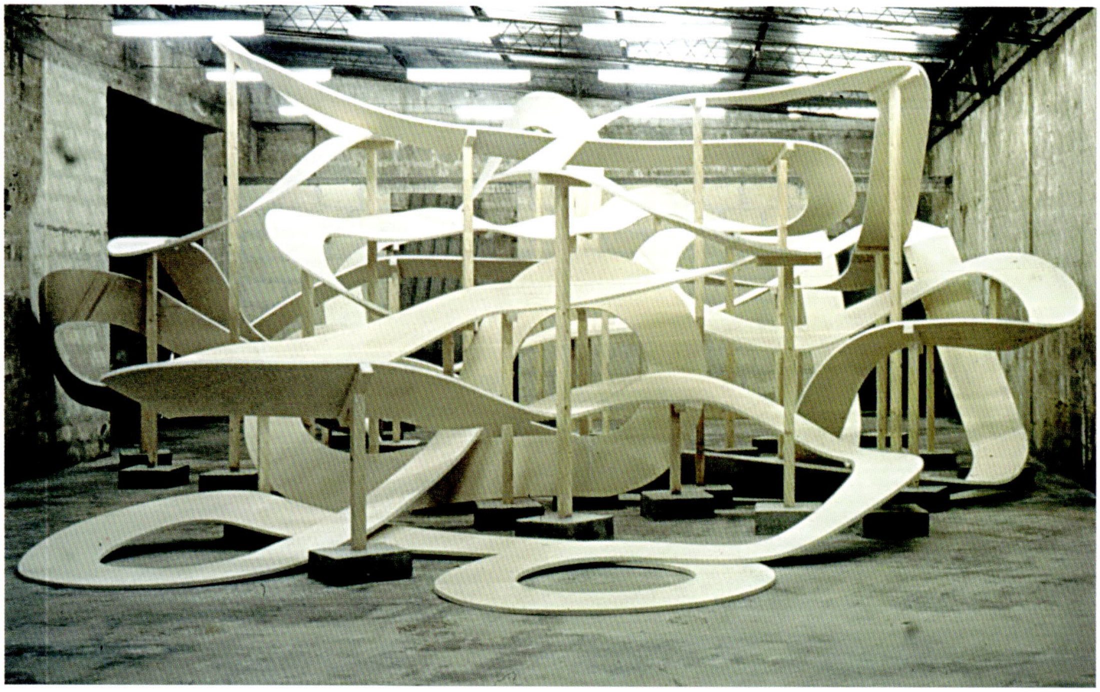

Guiseppe Gabellone
Untitled
1999.

31 Anthony Hudek in the roundtable describes Barlow's work as "snapshot sculpture". This is an extremely interesting phrase, and a fascinating way of characterising Barlow's approach to the transient, as it also gives the sense of the casual and awkward. It should be clear of course that Barlow's sculptures are never as transient as works like Orozco's *Breath on Piano*, 1993. The elegance of Orozco's more immediately ephemeral sculpture would mean the phrase "snapshot sculpture" ill-suits his work, and interestingly, Orozco's own elaborately composed photographs of such works are anything but snapshots.

32 Barlow, "Travelling Light", p. 58.

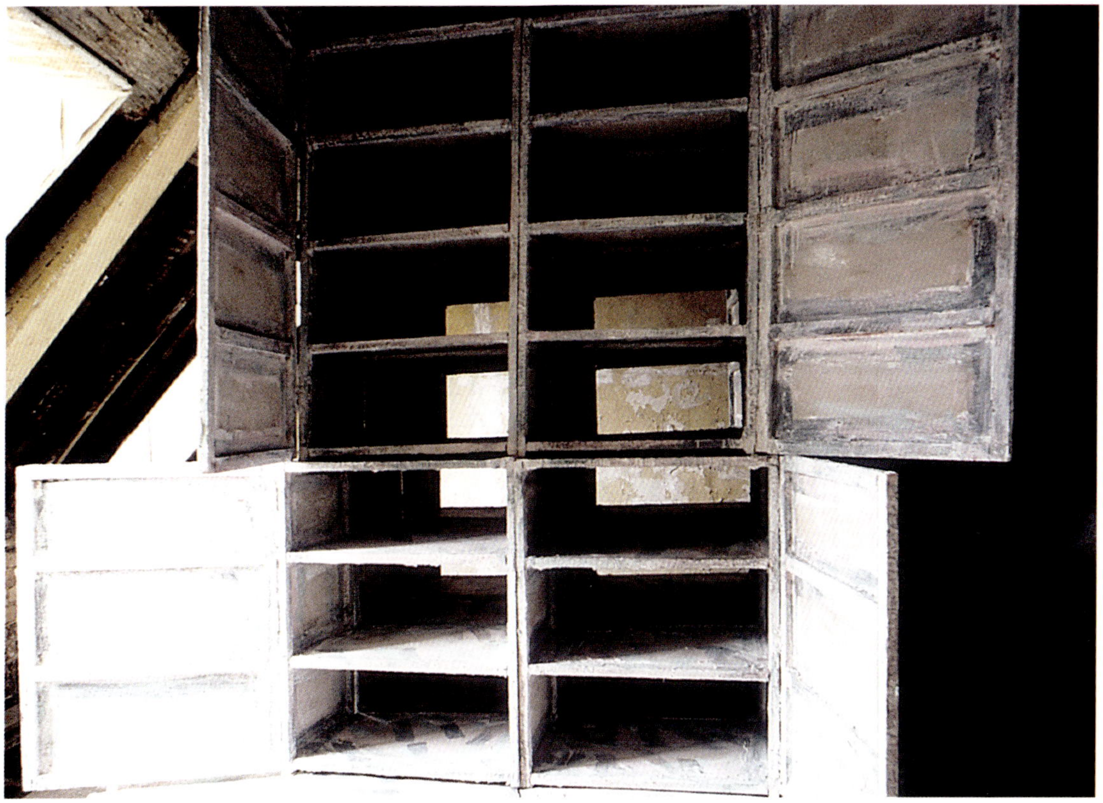

after dark
Painted hardboard platforms, painted plywood, paper, fabric, felt, tulle, foil, cord, canvas, plaster, drainpipe, painted fabric, ventilation tube, rubber tubing, casters.
Seven rooms, one work per room
Approximate dimensions of each room:
four rooms at 300 x 300 x 300 cm,
two rooms at 300 x 360 x 300 cm,
one room at 360 x 300 x 540 cm
1998
The Master Shipwright's House, Deptford, London.

Being neither willing nor able to preserve past works has meant two things: first, without the burden of past works in the studio, or masterpieces in museums, Barlow has been remarkably free to reinvent her practice. Free to experiment, to challenge her interests, to acknowledge rather than repress her anxieties about sculpture, even to fail and to use failure constructively. The first work of Barlow's that I saw seemed to me a failure, and I later learnt that she agreed.[33] *after dark into black*, made in 2000-2001 for the British Art Show simply seemed too big, bad, and ugly. Everything was here, and in such quantity: lattices, crumpled canvas, steps cutting through a slanted painted platform, strange furnishings wrapped round with tied mattresses, giant blobby objects which held oversized matches – and it was all just one work! Excess smothered enchantment. It was as if, pressured by the opportunity to show alongside a younger generation, Barlow had to cram in all her material and structural ideas, overstressing her commitment to the sculptural to confront what she might have feared would be the tyranny of the 'made-easy'. As it happened, though, there were other sculptors (as opposed to 'made-easy readymakers') in the British Art Show, and they made works with which Barlow would have had much sympathy: Lucy Gunning's highly charged installation of found and disabled furniture, Jim Lambie's paint-dripping plastic bags. The restraint of such works might have tempered Barlow's since that time. The self-containment and smaller scale of the works in Albury has certainly not come at the cost of their success.

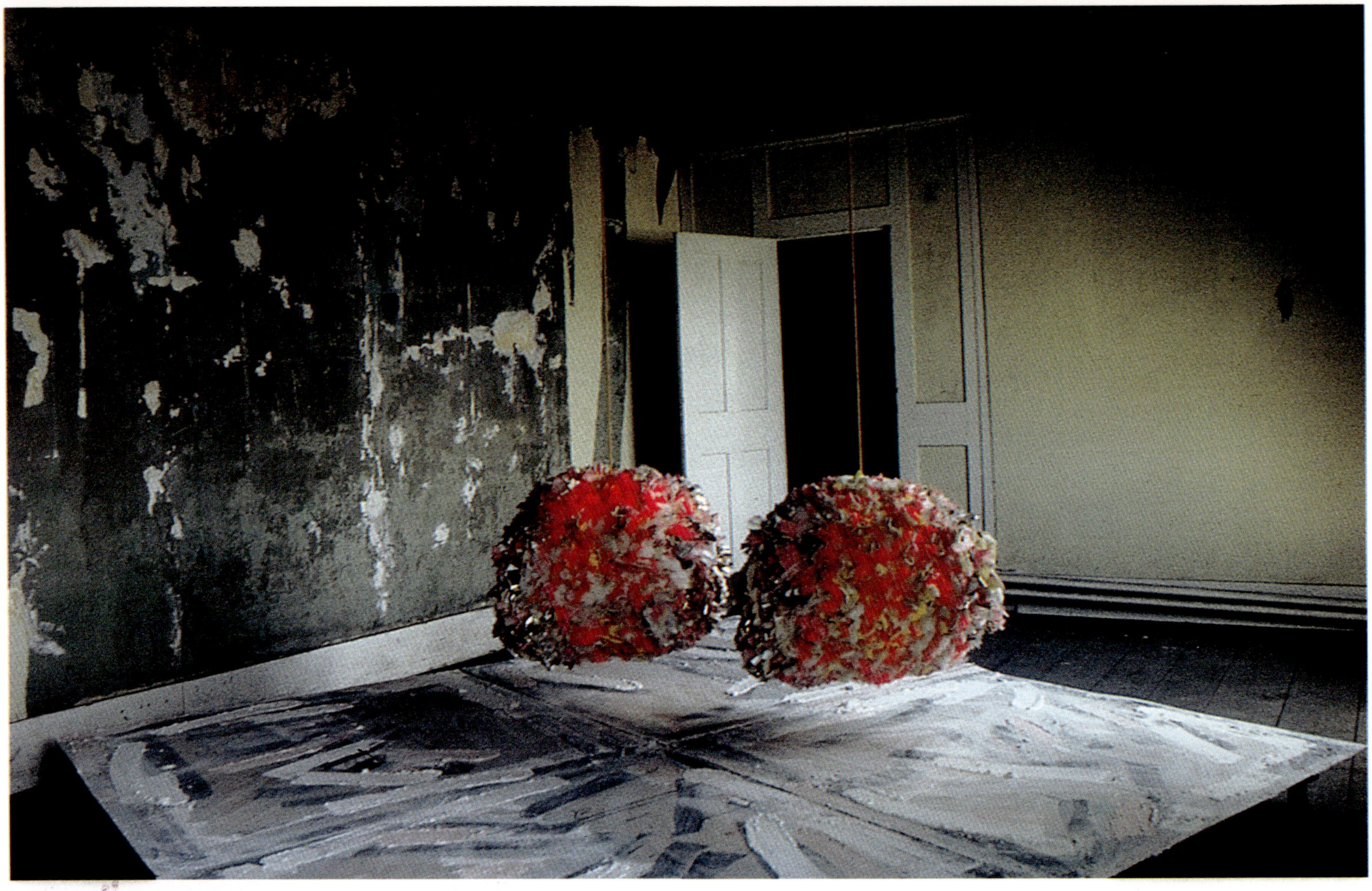

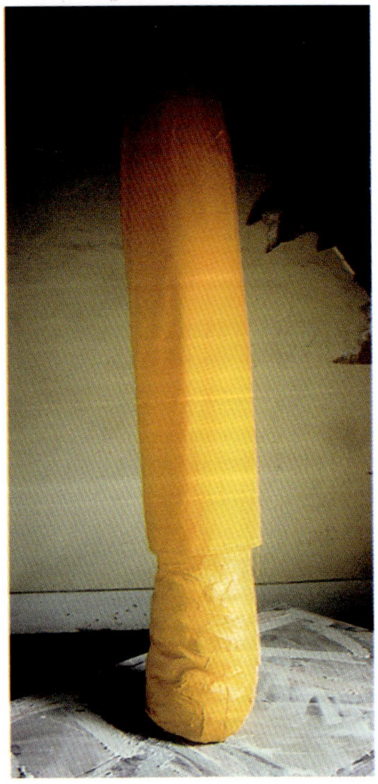

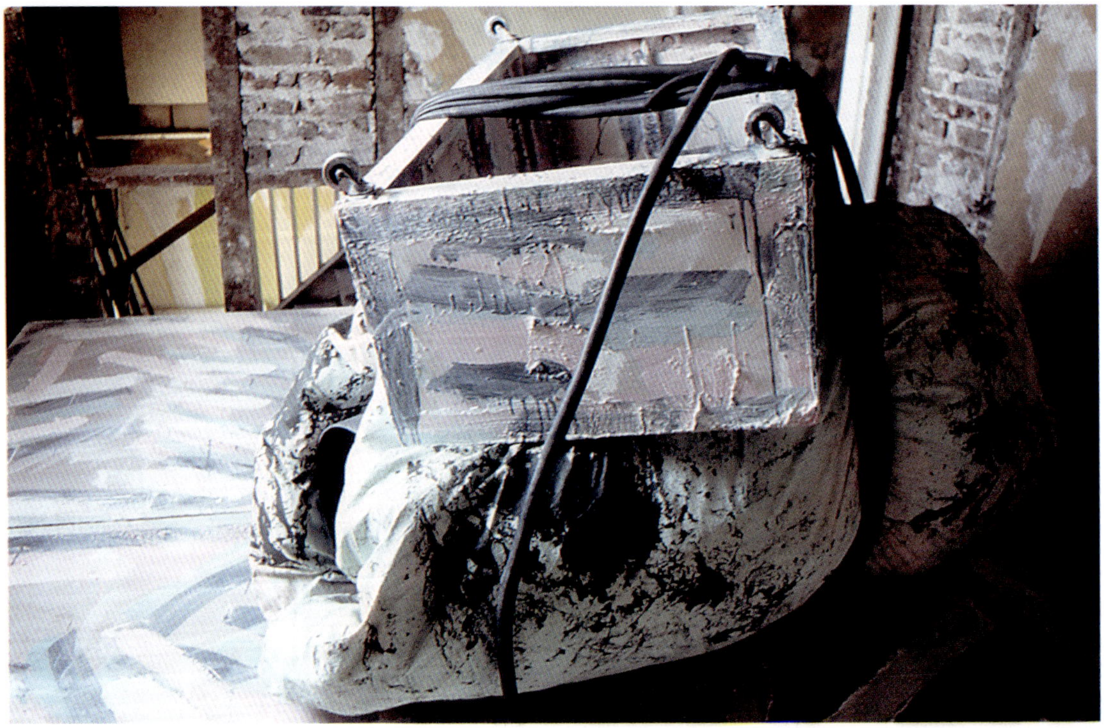

The second consequence of the commercial difficulty of Barlow's work is that she has had to teach. That teaching has been necessary to sustain and fund her work should not be taken to suggest that pedagogy is a grind.[34] As has hopefully been apparent throughout this essay, Barlow's work has never simply responded to the work of her generational predecessors. Perhaps the most appropriate way to end is to note how much Barlow has learnt from students even whilst they have learnt from her. Barlow teaches by asking questions rather than giving answers, and she asks because she is curious. Questions come from unexpected directions and reveal the nuanced breadth of her thinking: "Is the work honest?" she asks of a circular wooden construction. "Are they tonal?" she asks of metallic shapes painted around the Slade's steps and banisters. The next works to perplex and challenge her sculptural imagination, the next works to push her own work forwards might well be made by the nonagenarian Louise Bourgeois, but equally they might come from any number of artists in their twenties – Carinan Bjldenstein, Elliot Milbourne, Madi Boyd, Alison Joyce, Helen Dewhurst, Ian Dudley, Helen Watson, Steve Cornford, Megan Broadmeadow, Mar Fazenda, Will Potter, Laura Cull, Ben Youngman, Sana Halverssen-Green…. or perhaps even one of next year's intake…. Who knows?[35]

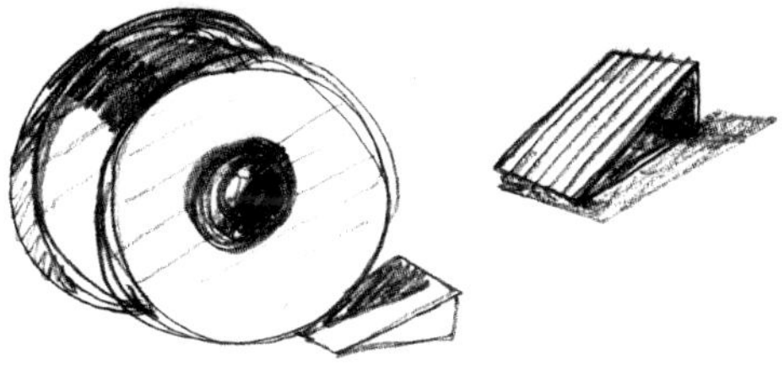

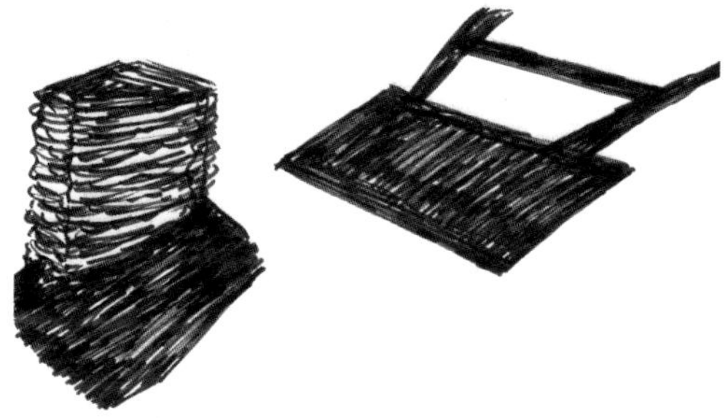

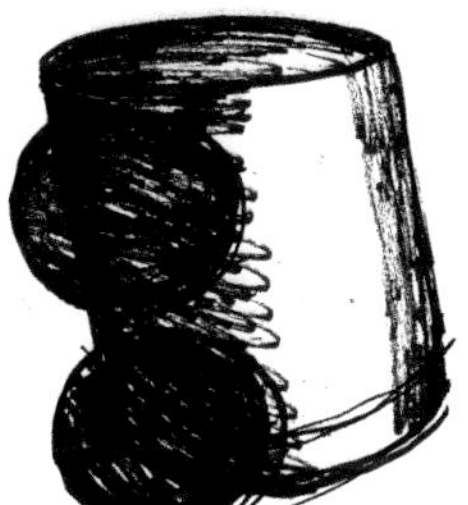

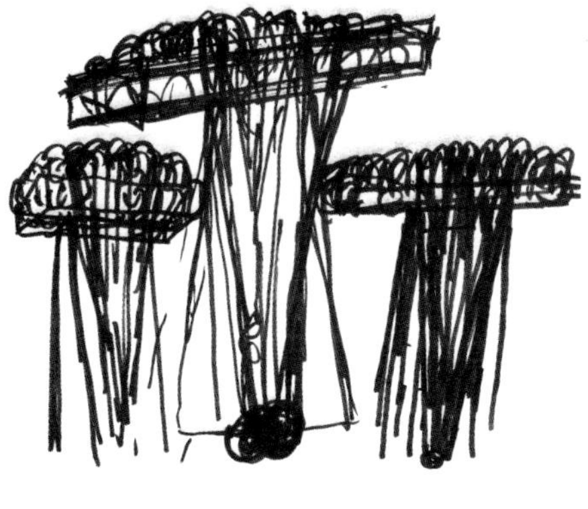

33 I should also note that Phyllida encouraged me to explain why I thought the way I did. Can you imagine another artist pleading a critic to say what they *didn't* like?

after dark
Painted hardboard platforms, painted plywood, paper, fabric, felt, tulle, foil, cord, canvas, plaster, drainpipe, painted fabric, ventilation tube, rubber tubing, casters.
Seven rooms, one work per room
Approximate dimensions of each room:
four rooms at 300 x 300 x 300 cm,
two rooms at 300 x 360 x 300 cm,
one room at 360 x 300 x 540 cm
1998
The Master Shipwright's House, Deptford, London.

34 In the roundtable discussion Charles Harrison makes the reverse point about teaching which of course is also true: teaching has given Barlow financial security, and since she now does not have to sell work to make more, she can afford to make temporary work and pay little attention to questions of the long-term robustness of her sculpture.

35 Barlow notes that the list is endless – named above are only students from the last two years.

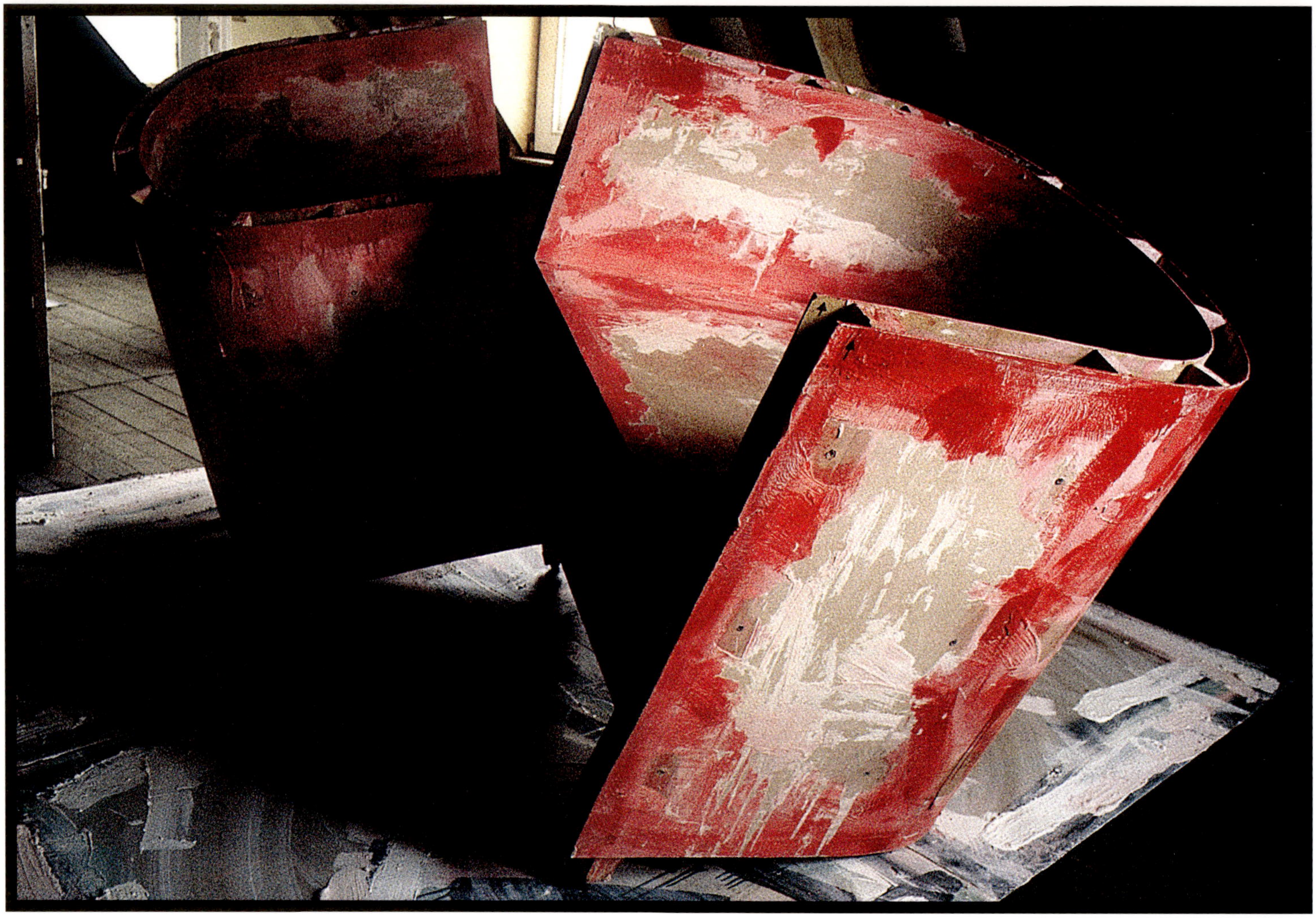

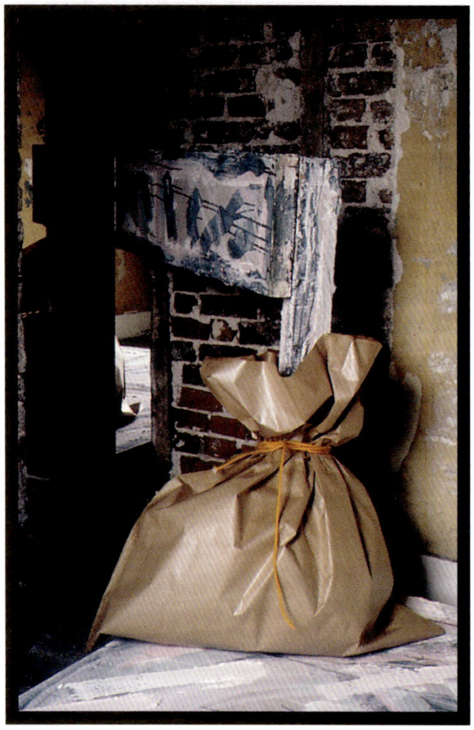

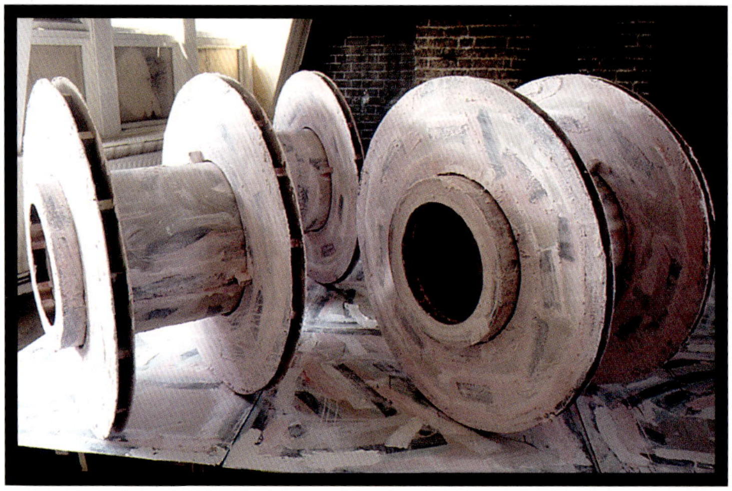

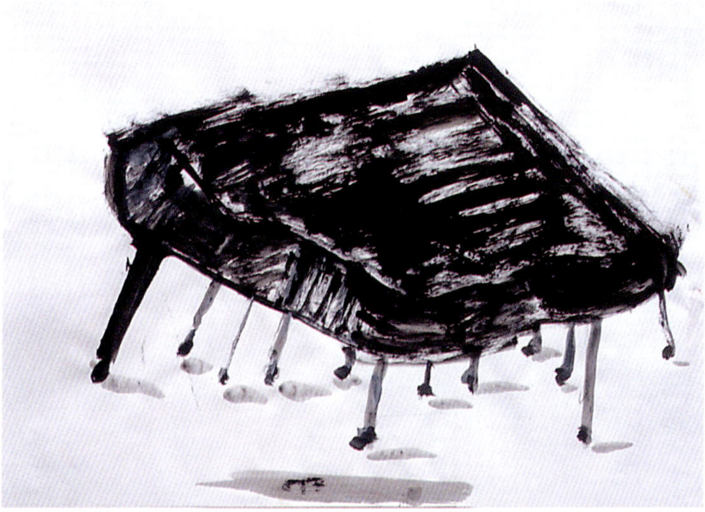

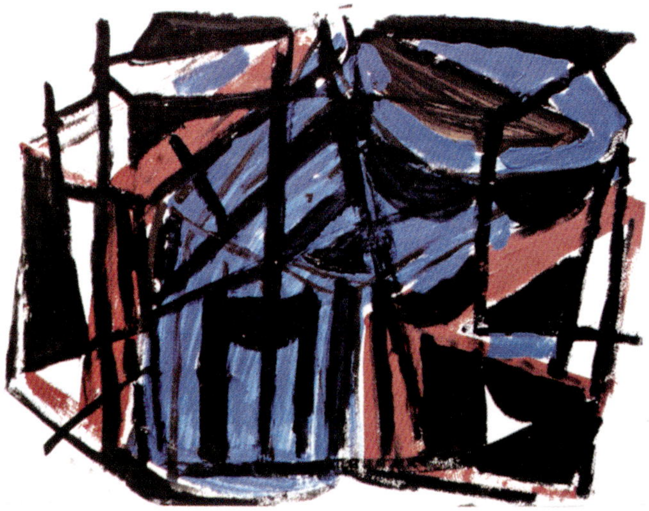

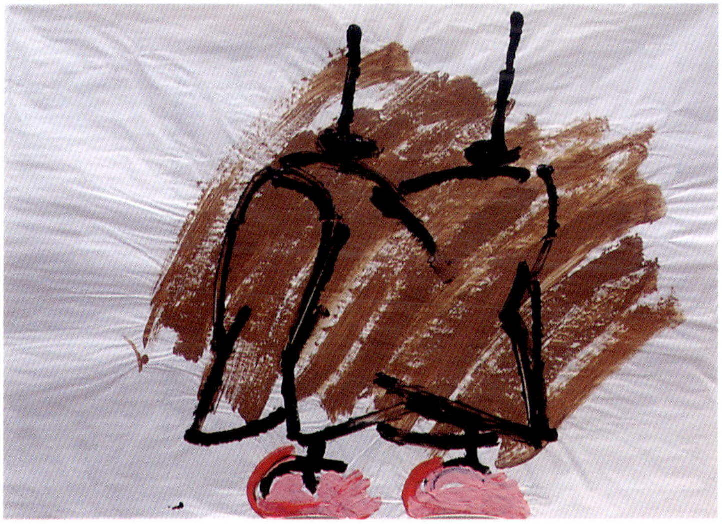

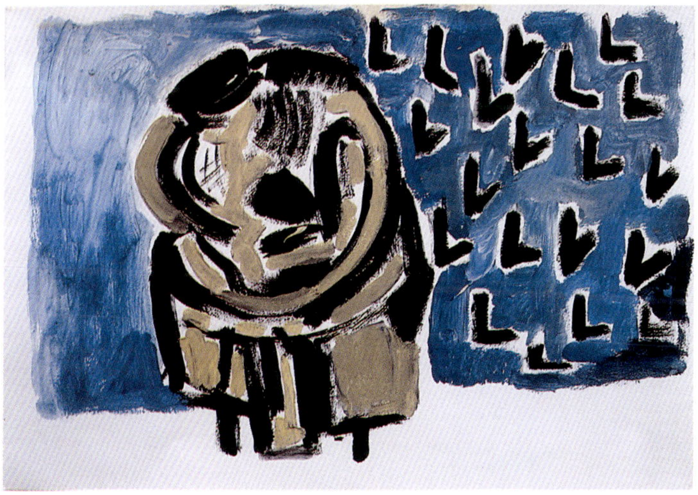

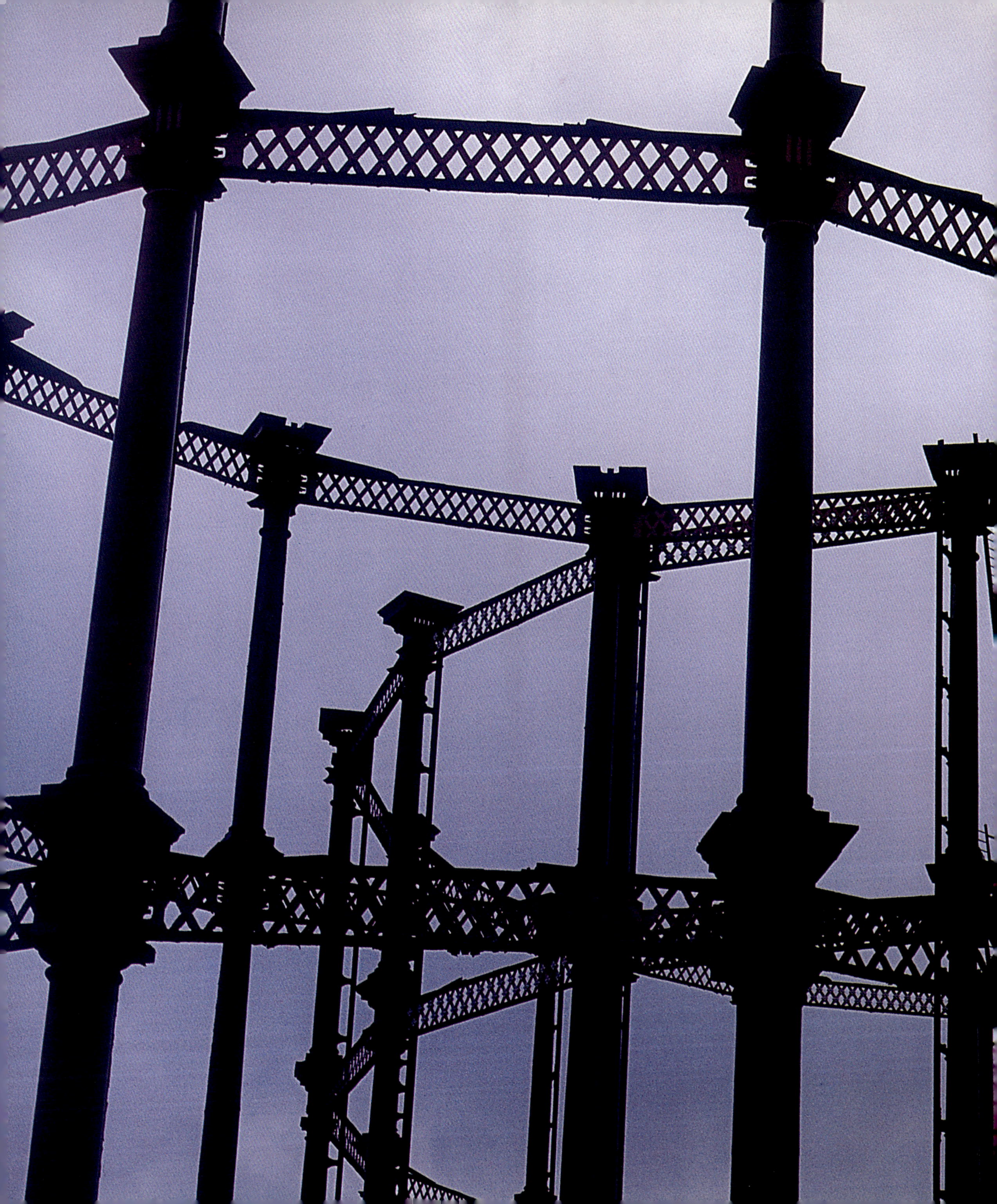

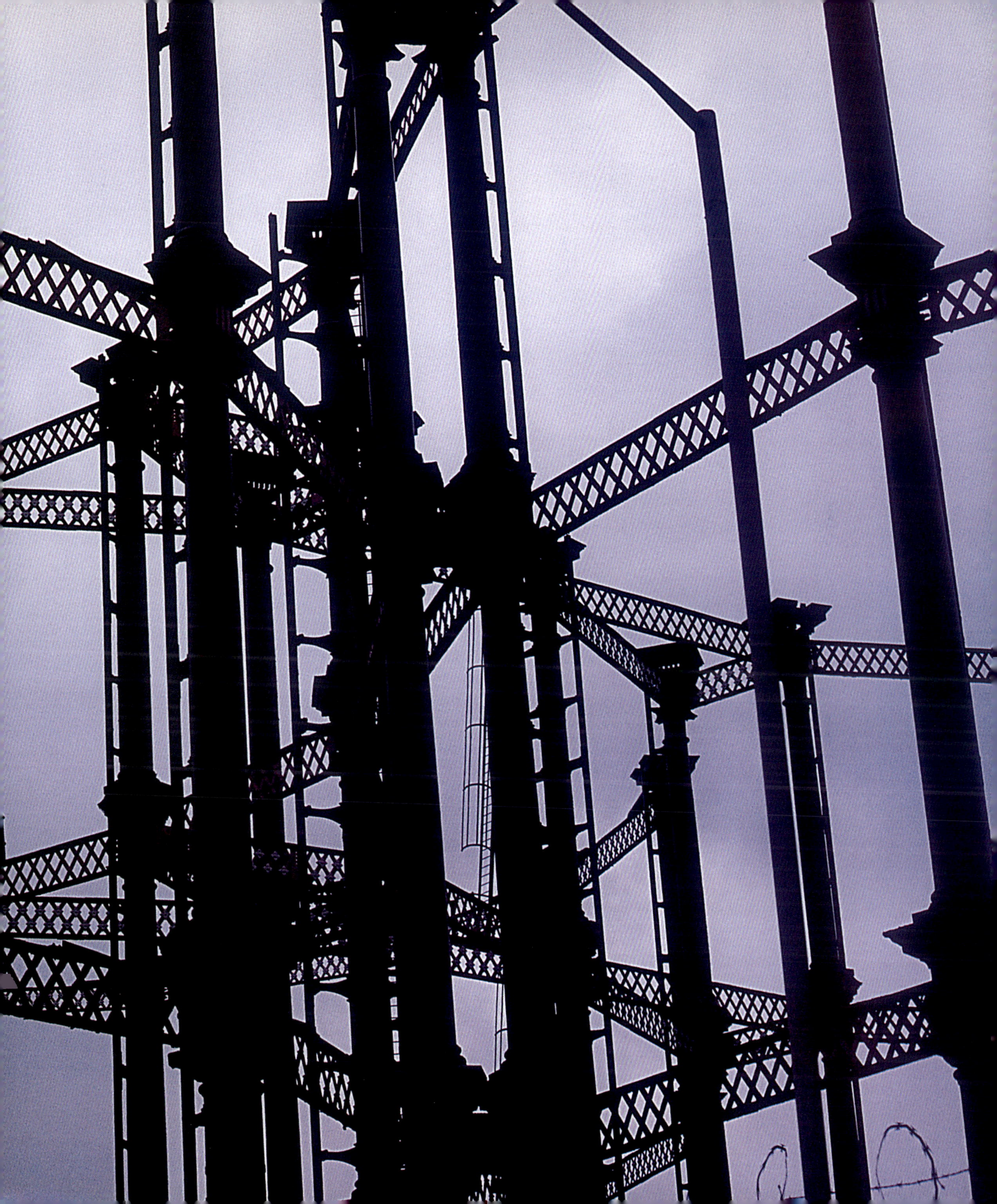

Plantation
Shuttering ply, varnish, dowling,
polythene, tape, timber lengths
600 x 100 x 600 cm
1991
Islington Design Centre, London

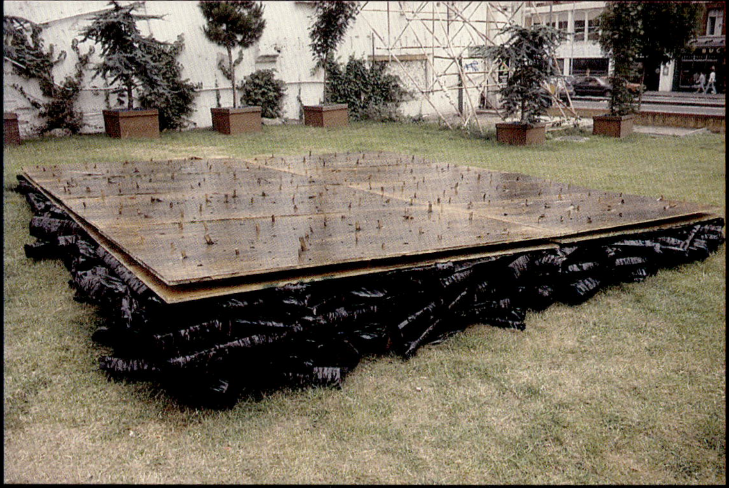

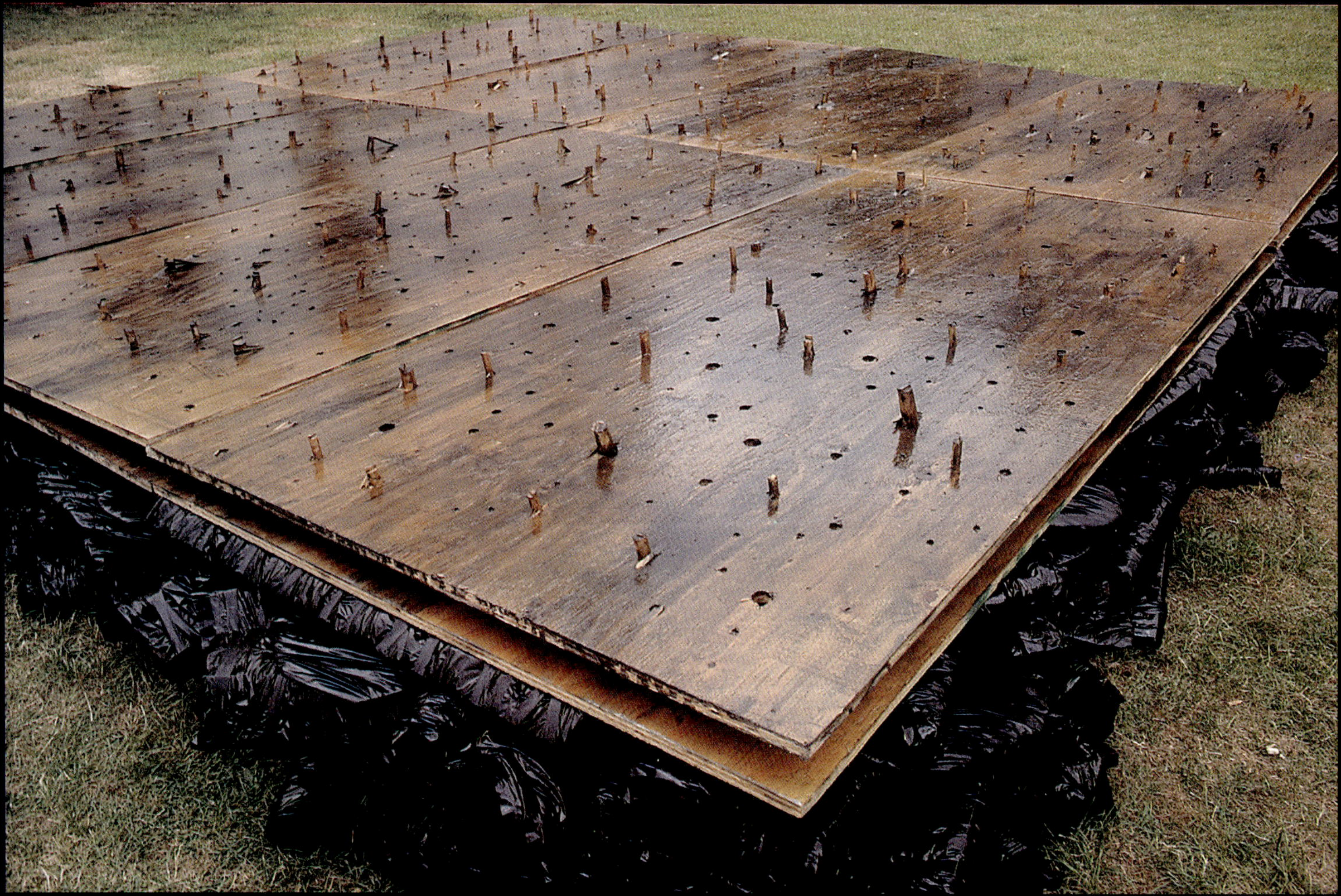

At Sea: a conversation by fax between Phyllida Barlow and Alison Wilding 22.08.98 – 02.09.98

1 Henry Moore Fellow in Sculpture. The British School at Rome, 1998.

2 Public Commission, River Wear, Sunderland.

3 artranspennine 98.

4 "In Pieno Sole", 1998.

PB You talked about 'this time'. Is there something different or changed about the way you are working and thinking about your work now, 'this time'?

AW Your fax really spooked me – until I realised it was from you… ! I think it is only now, three months after returning from Rome, that I am back in the studio and working.[1] O.K., there is 'Ambit',[2] and the new work in Skipton Castle[3] and the two sculptures I made in Rome.[4] So this time is about starting again, now – doing it, getting it right but finding it slipping through my fingers. ('it', what is it?). 'This time' has a sense of urgency. There is also a sense of repetition, if 'this time' then what was 'last time'? Last time was here – working in the studio – it went well, slowly, but well. This time it didn't do that – but I think I worked through a lot of stuff that I do not want in order to get where I am now (i.e. today and doing it, and it's fine). A bit like you and I talking rubbish into the tape when we tried to record an interview. You have to do a lot of what you know is no good in order to get rid of it, to get it out of the system.
Love, Alison.

'Getting it right' and 'talking rubbish': Control is important – is it? (school m'am) How do you know when you are getting it right? How experimental are your processes – or are they more reactive than experimental? Even if you 'get rid' of a lot of what you think is no good, do you remember it, store it in some way for future use? Is the process of 'doing a lot of what is no good' part of some kind of ritual courtship to familiarise yourself with something that takes time (more than anything else), to make itself known to you? Why do you need to be familiar with what you do? Is the feeling of urgency because there is a dread of the time this courtship process consumes?

Could you do without it – this courtship?
Phyllida.

P.S. : Essential listening: Sunday, Radio 3, St. Matthew Passion (plus weather like November in August)

'Getting it right' or 'finding it' is dependent upon a loss of control. I don't want to be in control in those evolutionary beninnings to making something – I want to catch up with it – or catch it. I do not know if the processes can be described as 'experimental' – probably something must be either experimental or pro-active, as a way of kick-starting it, and the rest follows. 'Getting rid' of stuff means that it's not for now – maybe it will be there, ready, waiting for the future; it seems to be important to make those decisions early on – before anything becomes really concrete. I do not want an elephants' graveyard in my studio! It is a necessary ritual – or courtship as you called it – it means I hold on to something I want to do and the rest can wait and if necessary it is there waiting for later – if by that time it has not been superseded by something else. I don't think about needing a familiarity with something – more a rush of excitement that is perhaps the opposite of that – the unknown factor. Urgency is a fear of it disappearing – of time passing so fast anyway these days, and maybe that the 'ritual courtship' will not go anywhere. Is there another expression for 'ritual courtship'? Ritual implies that I know it's not for real, but it is. I used to think that it was a struggle being acted out or rather a conflict. And sometimes it is.

If St Matthew Passion was last night I missed it but I watched a bit of 'Drugstore Cowboy'.
Love, Alison.

Yes, 'courtship' is probably not the right word – too prudish… I was thinking of restraint and self-control, not surrendering to the first thing that comes along – leaping into bed with anyone, so to speak – Instead the ability to eliminate and edit before, rather than after the event.

I have been sorting slides of the work I am showing at the Chapter Art Gallery in Cardiff, 'Time and Time Again' – and sorting out my doubts about it. The objects overfill the space as I wanted – but I do not know if it works or not. Should there be more objects, to really crush the space, or fewer objects doing more with the space? The work has been greeted with silence, except for those ambiguous comments such as 'Are you pleased with it?' or 'I must come back for a longer look.' Suspicious statements inferring dissatisfied viewers! Mental focus is enviable; the determination to seek out. And the urgency rather than desperation, my equivalent, which is a recipe for mistakes that later will need correcting. It takes time, 'it' being a kind of recognition of ease between myself and the proposed work, or the debris of try-outs, results of the desperate need to engage with physical stuff, without any clear idea of what to do. Boredom and disappointment – how do you respond?
Phyllida

Do you think that your frustration with what you have just done is because there can be no dress rehearsals – like life, actually? And there is rarely enough time or favourable conditions to do it in – it is a very tough thing to take on, you know, partly because it is a very public act. Well, fuck the dissatisfied viewers. They have got it all wrong – they want a map and they do not realise that they have to throw all this away. 'My way' seems inevitably more cautious, yes, more edited out, in private; but the confrontation with the public is the same. Lots of people in Skipton saying 'what is it', 'Excuse me for asking but what is the point?', and at the same time they are grabbing hold of that frail piece of alabaster as if it was a handle. Boredom and disappointment: Where does the boredom fit in? Perhaps with the same dull responses. Is it possible to excite people, or are there always only going to be a minority who are open and brave enough to confront this kind of unknown? I am bored when I need a buzz from what I am doing and not getting it. Perhaps this accounts for the popularity of the YBAs, their ability to instant gratification.
Love from Alison

Is boredom more static than disappointment? I can recover, sort of, from disappointment because it is more organic, and its anger creates a kind of hope for the next excitement.

I love the title (and what I can see of the work from the slides you showed me): 'In Shadow'. It sums up 'privacy'. The sculpture appears rooted in its place, almost hidden, recalling those sleeping tomb figures. Is privacy to do with nakedness? Being naked, not just undressed, but stripped down bare. Different from that dismal quest for 'truth'. Because, as a compulsive liar, being stripped is terrifying when things are uncovered. Therefore, showing work is fearful. It is being scrutinised when the protective lies have been removed. The maps, like symptoms of tourism and its fantasies, are protective, and the thrill of showing work is because the maps have been thrown away, leaving the work isolated for the full scrutiny of the public eye.

Is privacy central to art making? And especially non-making? Is stalking something within one, which has this thrilling possibility of revelation, only to be done in private? Is art-making a kind of birth, pain and pleasure precipitating a dread of the death of the new-born thing? Are we, am I, perversely savouring pain in order to experience pleasure?

Increasingly I long for elitist places to show work, very protected but not exclusive. Also, in the present climate, the object, more particularly sculpture, is in the doldrums. The non-visual qualities of sculpture need acknowledging as do its lineage and its history, in order for it to be considered as a serious contender to the quick-fix-approach of so much contemporary art.
Love, P.

All my life I have been an obsessive truth-teller and envied those who lived according to their version of events, but like you I think that the search for truth in art is utterly pointless (I didn't know you were a compulsive liar!) The more stripping, exposing I can do in privacy, the easier it is in public. Though of course, it is never that easy, but neither, to be fair to the observer, is the act of looking: it can be like swimming for land in the middle of an ocean with nothing in sight – for me, that is the most physically terrifying thing I can think of. Looking at art is – or perhaps should be – that scary.

The thing about elitist places – though we all hate them (well, not all of us) – is that they do the difficult work for the artist. They may not be the best places to show work but at least the viewer knows they are not on a building site, in a hardware shop or a waiting room.

I remember conversations, in the Eighties, about whether making sculpture was analogous with having children (for women, that is). Obviously I only understand half the equation, but there is undeniably something very fierce and strong about producing a new thing. I have never felt that it was a surrogate. Has having children also gone out of fashion?

5 Eric Peskett (1914-1997), sculptor, Head of the Sculpture Department at Ravensbourne College of Art and Design, where Alison Wilding studied 1968-1971.

Tell me about the non–visual qualities of sculpture – Eric Peskett[5] used to talk about the presence of objects in the dark.[5] I have always liked this idea…

PRIVACY IS NOT ALWAYS THE CORE OF MAKING, but making must be born out of that condition at least at some point. Hermaphroditic.
Love, Alison.
P.S.: I agree with you about boredom and disappointment. Boredom is like low pressure, disappointment is a keen physical thing, it hurts. It is not fatal but can linger if not watched.
xxx A

It is not knowing that makes me a compulsive liar. I do not know where my work comes from. I can only guess that it is some sort of play with something out there; visible and in there; invisible. Whether this is true or not I do not know and I do not care. The new thing (certainly not a surrogate child) is neither one or the other; it gets revealed like talking to myself, rather secretly, and as such, might be only half heard and therefore misunderstood.

But what of understanding, of being understood? Understanding what? Does it matter? Why should art be 'understood' (and what does 'understanding' mean in this context)? That over-used word 'experience' is a catch-all, and too limp and pathetic. Yet it is the significant word because it allows for imagination and speculation, which I believe the non-visual qualities of sculpture depend upon – anything, that is, other than what is literally visible: weight, density, unseen surfaces, what do they do? What are they in contact with? The interior – where is it? The time it takes to walk around it, and its space/location, the place/placing, next to, on, by, with, from, away, near, far, here, there; size: the space it owns; does the work claim more or less space than its dimensions? What if touched? Cold, damp, warm, scratchy…

Absolutely, experiencing sculpture in the dark – and as an imagined state for the work. Darkness reveals the sound and movement inherent to sculpture: Not literally so, but as locked into the substance as a memory of its making. All such qualities get obliterated by the scramble to justify and explain through verbal language

The viewer: my guilt. I never consider the viewer. When swimming without sight of land are you the maker or the viewer? Or both? Is that what is so terrifying? Yes, terror, dread, fear – they are familiar as ongoing states, but I am never sure why they are there. In fact, letting go of the work is comparatively painless; I relish it, and once gone, in its place, I no longer feel vulnerable on its behalf. It is me who becomes vulnerable. A kind of longing to forget it. Instead there is accountability, which is where all the feelings of privacy and intimacy come in, and an embarrassment of having to speak about things which should remain contained in the work. But speaking and writing is a rich resource – everything which is not 'it' can be written and spoken.

6 'Desormais': Title of the installation at Skipton Castle for artranspennine 98. "Desormais" is the motto of the Clifford family, translated as "From Here On – Henceforth".

7 Adrian Searle is the art critic of *The Guardian* newspaper.

'The New Thing': I have never equated my work with my children as such, but touching the work has reminded me at times of touching them – especially when they were little. It is another thing now – not easy to talk about. My reference to giving birth was to do with bringing into the world a new thing, nameless, a different thing; but different from what? Then placing it, finding a place for it. You said once that you did not think about the placing. I cannot believe that!
Honesty and truth – they seem different – are they? Longer and longer.
Love, Phyllida.

Yes, truth and honesty are not the same thing, are they? I should have said that I have been obsessively honest (or straightforward) in my life, whilst the 'truth' is out there somewhere.

Don't we all make work for ourselves? The best experience with the work is when it is in the right place and we are alone with it and it is not exactly alive, but sentient, open to speculation, responding to daylight then darkness and somehow breathing. A good way, I think, to measure the presence (or not) of a piece of work. Meaning, understanding, total immersion is locked into that situation. Which is why for me, nipping into the National Gallery, say, to look at Titian's Portrait of a Young Man for two minutes will always be satisfying. I want to see it when I wake up, when the lights are out, when I am having a drink. Is this why people buy art?

More on truth, lies and inconsistencies: A student has sent me a list of questions to answer. Most of them are either unanswerable, e.g. 'Do you have an overriding aim in your work?', or so complicated that it would take days to think about them. I have suggested that she goes to Skipton to see 'Desormais'[6], but apparently that is not possible. Why should it matter what I have to say, when there is a chance to see what I do? She obviously does not know (but I will tell her) that I am so inconsistent and contradictory in what I say as to be downright untruthful at times. (Did I really say that thing about not caring about the placing of work? I did not mean it!) The sculpture is not inconsistent. But at the same time I do not think that the artists should be so arrogant and removed as to let the work exclusively speak for them at all times, hiding behind its myth or theory. First of all though it must be seen at first hand. I suppose I am just annoyed at having to answer her questions.

Swimming: Out of depth without sight of land is my own personal nightmare, and there is nothing exhilarating in it. Whereas being out of my depth in my work is. Is this the flipside of boredom? Being the viewer need never be that bad, even after having thrown away the map. I think that is what Adrian Searle[7] is very good at doing – he throws himself at the mercy of the art he is looking at and describes his experience.
Love, Alison.

I want to discuss that not-being- able-to-work place you have referred to in the past. It seems linked to the 'horror of being out of depth without sight of land'... (I remember

you telling me that your father threw you into the swimming pool to teach you to swim. Is that correct?) But can one's personal horror be a touchstone? Is it somehow, incomprehensibly, reassuring to know what one's personal terror is? What is it like to be terrified and not know, to have no image which mirrors the paralysis of fear? From your description, which is exhilarating and sensual, your personal nightmare has a metaphorical energy. It is alive and vividly represents the state of absolute isolation, where survival depends on summoning unknown sources of energy, intuition and improvisation, all with the full knowledge that these might be of no help. But not-being-able-to-work is like that, isn't it?

Can retrieving deeply buried responses and resources trigger creative survival? To somehow carry on working through that time – but then when-you-cannot-work, you cannot!

How to rediscover land: very biblical – I keep thinking of the dove with the olive branch in the Old Testament. Not-being-able-to-work seems to me a place of no security: the awful, awesome weight of water beneath your barely floating body, not you but the sea in control.

Words and lying. Writing about places makes me think about the gap between myself and the work, and the descriptions I attach to my work which seem to fill this gap ambiguously. The feeling I get from these descriptions is like lying. Telling what the work is about, or what it refers to, creates a separate, rival object, which does not equate with what is there, and can become enhanced with glamour and expectation, something words are so capable of doing, and which the task of looking and remembering, is not.

I so agree with you about looking at the Titian. There is a real need to allow one's act of looking to carry on, like a kind of story-telling which has no beginning, middle or end, just a continuous state of arousal. Looking, I think is a slow burn, a gathering up of curiosity, into which fall, gradually, those qualities of expectation, glamour, excitement, etc.. Words are quicker.

Yes, being alone with the work when it is in its place is like meeting with it for the first time. A brief encounter which can go either way – love or hate. It is a relationship, however brief, but the meeting in that place is always a surprise: Something I thought I knew well becomes something I do not know at all and which I cannot recognise. Again, like stalking – from the making to the place: stalking something that is not there, or something that is there, but is unknown, and then, when it is there, still not knowing.

Is not-knowing like not-being-able-to-work?

I have a recurring dream about drowning: Dark blue sea, brilliant sky, people drowning – my children – no hope of rescue – all to do with having witnessed a drowning, aged 8. xxx, Phyllida.

Not-being-able-to-work continued: There is a dull dread which feels a bit like being a child with something unpleasant to look forward to; a foreboding; and being at sea, treading water – more apt than the personal nightmare of swimming without horizons – put perhaps a watered-down version of it. (Yes, my father did throw me into the swimming pool, and I could not swim until I was 14 – my recurring sea dream is being caught between huge, towering, frozen waves.)

I think you have put your finger on it exactly with the question 'How to re-discover land?', by digging deeper into your hidden resources, yourself. There is another option, which is to stop looking inwards, close the system down, get out, see, do and go. Do you ever do that? I don't. It is like an itch I must scratch, I cannot leave it alone (Digging deeper). Like a dog that follows a smell I return to the studio. That's the fear, I think, that the smell will go away, taking It with it.

So there is the water (the fear) and the earth, we are uncovering the elements at last. I loved your image of the dove – which makes the connection between the sea and the land – which are of course in a kind of conflict. For me, the sea is fear, dread, but also movement, potential, weightlessness, sensuality, CREATIVITY. Where land and sea meet is forever shifting territory – the ultimate edge.

The image of the bird/dove makes this connection between sea and land look like an act of faith but it is of course in the genes: Migrating across oceans (no precedent, no horizons). It is not in our genes, but we have to develop an instinct, a technique which enables us to cross land and sea at will. The land is where the territory is staked out, what we know – the sea is where it happens, where we drown or not.

I like the slow burn, it is the missing element.

Doesn't the glamour of words seem like top-dressing?
Love, Alison.

My equivalent to your straightforwardness could be hardworkingness. I do not see this as any great virtue because it can blind and mask what is really there and the essentials to be done. I have worked hard, overworked, when standing back, waiting and watching would have been infinitely productive.

My hardworkingness is not as ordered as a Protestant work ethic, it is, unfortunately, more hysterical, panic-stricken, as if driven to exorcise something. So yes, I do keep

8 Marcel Duchamp 'Why not Sneeze Rrose Selavy' 1921, The Museum of Modern Art, NY. Shown in 'Objects of Desire: The Modern Still Life'. The Hayward Gallery, London 1997-1998.

going, and, like you, I cannot close the system down. With this drive to work comes the desire to push the work, to work something through, however inadequately. It is connected to the malleability of certain materials, like clay, where there can be quick response from the material to a change of thought. Though I no longer work with clay, that particular attitude towards materials remains: A relationship which assumes that materials can be easily changed, even at the eleventh hour, into something else, better, right. Working at it, being unable to leave it alone, seems very deep-rooted within me and, at times, something I long to shake off, in order to find another, easier way, which allows for short-cuts. Hence my fascination with appropriations and ready-mades. They exemplify for me the divorce between thinking and doing and between hands on and hands off. The appropriators and the ready-makers seem to have translators who do their work for them whilst I have to slog it out word by word, getting things wrong, not knowing the pronunciation, spelling, etc, etc. Their's is a seamless process, where the thinking is the creative act and where the results appear cleaner, more sensible and more shrewd, with fewer mistakes and less abuse of material. Their struggle is done away from the work; they can stand back and wait; altogether a more reliable activity. But in the end, I am not fully convinced, envious yes, but the clinical nature and the coldness of what they are doing is more often than not repelling. I want hard evidence of who is saying what and not be fobbed off with the messenger, a kind of servant to the hidden artist. Appropriation and ready-mades have changed into something else – Duchamp's *Why not Sneeze, Rrose Selavy*[8] is so scuffed and worn, full of muffled noises, unlike the new army of shiny and glossy appropriations and ready-mades. Do ready-makers and appropriators make mistakes? How do they try things out? How do they 'push' the work? Maybe the answer to this is Duchamp's long, self-imposed silence. Still, I do envy them. I feel I have to rely on the flukes that emerge from physical making, endless, often frustrating revision and the perpetual turmoil in the studio – all this is so far removed from the intellectual neatness of the ready-made.
xxx, Phyllida.

Words and Ready-mades, re: top-dressing. Verbal language and written language are so close to the ready-made and complement it so well. By comparison, sculpture is essentially wordless – that is part of its vulnerability. Is this why ready-mades score so effortlessly in comparison to sculpture. As if displacing an object with verbal/written language is a plus – much easier than the complicated act of looking.

Let's get back to water, swimming and places beyond the horizon!
Love, Phyllida.
Next: 'acts of faith', 'edges', 'digging deeper' – lots more to talk about.

Overworking: I do it with drawings, especially when at the moment it feels as if I am chasing a chimera. I think I deliberately push them over the edge to see if there is anything at all I can salvage. Inevitably, they all go into the bin. I know when to stop, but until then I

9 The Chinati Foundation in Marfa, Texas.

cannot leave them alone. They make me very angry. It reminds me of shooting a take for a film – you can do it a 100 times in the hope that the 101st time will be it (how do I know) I think that's similar to working with clay?

Ready-mades and appropriations: I think you should relax about them. They are here to stay. On one level you can displace an object with language and as you said, it's seductive, glamourising, mythologising and very persuasive, but I think that deep down we both find it not totally nourishing. Sculpture is that oddball thing that can side-step language – this is why it frustrates writers – . The more I think about it the more anachronistic I could make it sound. When I think about how baffling sculpture is to many people I think of those time machines in SF books and films which are always seamless monoliths made of unknown materials with no obvious way in, (and when they open there is usually a gremlin-thing inside which is not so interesting).

Yes, let's return to 'acts of faith', 'edges', etc..
Love, Alison.

On Edges; Another anachronism; the longing to make edges without structure and physical materiality, knowing full well that the character of sculpture's physicality makes this an impossibility: therefore light, distance, fogging, fracturing become essential aesthetics as a means for diffusing edges and challenging the solidity of material. Heroic attempts to blur and dissolve the rigidity of sheet materials and the density of solid materials. I try to do this by using paint on surfaces while you seem to do it by choosing particular materials: polypropylene, rubber, metal or alabaster. They all seem to react with or to light, but for what?

Someone described to me their visit to Donald Judd's emporium at Marfa.[9] He went into one of the large spaces, a converted barn, and there appeared to be nothing there. In fact the shininess of the metallic surfaces of the objects had fused with the intense brilliance of the desert light, dissolving the objects into invisibility. The edges and the space had magically become one. Is this a sculptor's ultimate ambition, or desire for edges? To push them to the edge of their existence and to liberate the edge of its edginess?

Drawing and Drawbacks

I never know what to draw=dull

I end up drawing the things I am going to make=boring

I think of other artists' drawings=confusing

10 Tabitha Peake; youngest daughter of Phyllida Barlow and Fabian Peake.

11 Louise Bourgeois; sculptor, born 1911 in Paris. Lives and works in New York.

I become self-conscious, I draw my feelings=ugh!

I must begin with the materials and get rid of images=incompetent

Discover that I am back to 1=hopeless

A rush of indifference=hope

Yes, I get angry with drawing, and paranoid and defensive. A nagging voice taunts me with the whisper 'Drawing is the epitome of being an artist. If you cannot do it then you are not an artist'. So, if I am not an artist what am I? Tabby[10] recently asked a little boy what he wanted to be when he grew up. 'A person', he replied. I feel like that with drawing. If I am not an artist because I cannot draw then I will make do with being a person.

Violence and Edges: Making edges by cutting, slicing, stitching, pinning, pinching, filing, sawing, nailing, breaking, tearing, etc etc. These acts, like touch, can go either way, gentle or violent; mending or wrecking; the surgeon or the murderer; the lover or the abuser. I know Madame Bourgeois[11] has gone through all this in depth, but it does seem apposite. Who are we when we cut, slice, nail, hit? Which character are we assuming? And does that character become part of the work as much as the formal aesthetic-conscious decisions? I am sure that my acts of making are a series of sublimated double-sided acts. Dyonisian and Apollonian, split between the repairer and the destroyer, between the caress and the hit (another horror of mine besides drowning: hitting children), but brought together like a dissonance. Do you think your acts of making as purely functional, as a means to an end or as loaded with insignificance well beyond this?

Last word on appropriation and ready-mades: Here to stay and very much (for me) about here and now. It is my conflict of wanting to be here and now, but recognising that I could be a member of a tribe on the verge of extinction, which has not yet invented the wheel, always making, making, making, with no noticeable results. Meanwhile, the neighbouring tribe picks up what is lying around and produces innovative and progressive objects… with ease, simplicity and elegance. Yet there remain doubts… lots of love, P.

Edges: If you wanted to make edges without structure then I have wanted to make objects without edges – rather to achieve dissolution between solid and liquid. Like you I admit to difficulties with this one. I can see (although I have not been there) how Judd succeeds with this in Marfa – in those carefully controlled conditions and it makes me realise that I have probably never really seen a Donald Judd! Which of us would not like that ultimate control? But – inconsistent again – I like the mutability of certain materials and how they react in unheated spaces – like a concrete floor sweating or a wall dripping; alabaster sweats, changes colour. As volatile as changing light conditions. A material like polypropylene helps in distancing, dissolving, but inherently it traps a dangerous aesthetic (as I see it), and I am afraid of it – and alabaster can do a similar thing. You asked if these materials react with or to light, but for what? I think it is a question of velocity. Some materials are dense and matt and deadening and stop you – like black rubber (unless the intention is otherwise), others slow down or suspend light. And then of course they also reveal something inside, beyond, expanding, opening out. You used to talk a lot about cutting through things. This is a way of revealing without cutting (more stroking than whipping).

Edges again: Twice, as a student, and at different times, I made a work specifically without edges. Both of them were installed outside in fog, which solved the problem for a photograph. But it was The Emperor's New Clothes when the sun came out. Conceptual art has no edges. Discuss.

I have always been obsessed with how much space my sculpture can hold – and maybe this is an indication of its true edge, an invisible field around it. What you have headed 'Violence and Edges' refers to what I mean by the work coming about through conflict. We are all the things you describe when we make the work (cutting and stroking). Nowadays I have more distance on it, perhaps I am more knowing and I need to do less physically, but that makes it sound like a bag of tricks with a load of special effects – which is not true either.

The conflict is very much there in drawing where a need to find a subject or a meaning fights with a desire to explode things in a rather infantile way. I feel an awful pressure to make the same or similar, drawings, which I resist. But the breakthrough to the next series is rare. I am also embarrassed by the activity – it seems so private – why is that? (not the finished thing but the doing of it).

I went for years not drawing without being troubled by it. Now I draw more regularly, I worry much more about it. Your work seems so direct and immediate which is what drawing should be.

Sometimes I have a physical urge to draw, usually when the studio is least set up for it.
I have always equated drawing with discipline, and felt the lack of it.
All for now, Alison.

I want to return to fear and fright in order to respond to the edgelessness of conceptual art. As the camera becomes the most convenient, desirable and fashionable means through which the object and its physicality can be dissolved, fractured and then captured, it seems to have become more and more questionable (and dangerous, not to

say risky) to make physical objects – a sculpture – as an end in itself which has all those qualities of light, movement, sound, temperature, locked within it, which are revealed imaginatively rather than literally. And instead of it being a passive engagement to unlock those qualities, it demands an active engagement. You have a walk around, stand back, approach, stalk the space the sculpture occupies in order to extract, step by step, the information it contains, its non-visual qualities. Not so with camera art. Therefore the affrontery of sculpture, its inherent obstructiveness, that it exists at all generates hostility from the viewer who can expect to be rewarded only by a prescribed system of looking. And to complicate matters further, sculpture does not conform to an ordered process of looking: look, then think, then understand: 1+1=2. Sculpture is a 1+1=3 experience.

Conceptual art has been devoured by advertising; think, for example of the ongoing Silk Cut campaign in the Eighties which has generated an endemic style. The public now knows how to 'solve' the conceptual element of an art work. It has become fun, like working through a puzzle book, or doing a crossword.

Seventies conceptual art did not have edges, and would not be trapped, and the camera and text became vital props to substantiate it, and probably initiated its demise as 'radical' art at the same time. And since the 1980s and the rise and rise of the pictorial object (vitrines, framed objects and objects on plinths), conceptual art has become subsumed within the image. The edgeless nature of much conceptual art has been replaced – probably because of a lack of economic value – with actual objects – which have glamour and commercial value. It is as though that vital curiosity to find ways of fracturing form has become extinct. Your experiment of photographing sculpture in the fog when you were a student is such a vivid description of the crucial ambivalence which makes making such an uncertain, but alive activity. The very thing that gets made is the very thing that is desired to be dissolved: Life and death. What is form?

You don't have to answer. Sometimes I feel as though the forms I use have been reduced to '101 ways of using an 8 by 4 sheet' or wrapping, where the inevitable 'bundle' results. What is the use of innovation and invention? And where does invented form fit in? – i.e. a form which is not just the result of bending sheet materials, or scrunching fabric etc?

Is geometry a way of giving the amorphic form a familiar order, disciplining it? To remove it from its sculptural inheritance and from nature? Habitually I return to plaster – great bursts of energy, mixing up buckets of the stuff with absolute conviction, and, two days on, exhausted by the physical slog involved, there is nothing there other than over-worked, laborious 'forms': dead things, which tell me to go and get a life somewhere else. You have found a very precise way of using the liquidity of plaster – poured very directly, then into bronze, its essence of wet to dry held tight. I want to be up to my neck in the stuff with a miraculous result forthcoming. But it is not like that. Fabrics, etc. have

12 Jonathan Callan; sculptor, student at Goldsmiths College, then at the Slade School of Fine Art 1987-1989.

13 Michael Craig-Martin: Artist and Millard Professor of Fine Art at Goldsmiths College.

fulfilled something of that desire, but it is a kind of mimicry, and very clean. What is the longing for filth, mess and spillage?
Phyllida.

The longing for dirt: Does it go back to a time, or evoke a feeling of sheer pleasure that has nothing to do with meaning or process (is this what they call a pre-cognitive experience? but let's not get into that!): getting your hands dirty or like a good shit. It's also a beginning, a state of flux, a formlessness – pre-form, pre-anxiety. And a reaction against the clean, the hard, mechanical edge; but it doesn't preclude a transformation into that latter state. My favourite stuff, although it's not dirt, is sand; either as the tide has gone out leaving it packed hard, silvery and ridged, or sand as the tide comes in and is undergoing a transformation, a total collapse. Very, very sexy.

Fears and forebodings: Yes, I think geometry is a way of circumventing invention – disciplining amorphic form – very severe discipline.

I remember Jon Callan[12] repeating one of Michael Craig-Martin's[13] mantras that art is about observation not innovation. How annoyingly right that turned out to be! Yes, it's all one: advertising, fashion, music, conceptual art. Personally I like going against the grain. Your description of being part of a tribe on the verge of extinction (I nearly wrote distinction) was brilliant but neighbouring tribes also get wiped out by the common cold...

If, as seems likely, we are about to go into world recession or worse, it will be interesting to see how this affects the next big thing in art – or not. But I sense a hiatus, not stasis: hold on – anything might happen!
Love, Alison.

Is the tragedy of sculpture, (its doom), the fact that it can never be that pre-form, pre-anxiety state, and when it tries to be, it ends us being that surrogate that you referred to earlier; a paltry illustration and imitation, and altogether an unfulfilling second-hand experience? And is sculpture's closeness, materially and physically, to that territory of the basic reflexes and urges of animals, (including humans) and nature which makes it feared and scorned – in a lot of cases understandably so – as an art form? As though its next of kin is all those functions of animals, humans and nature which are without thought: raw, basic, uncontrollable.

But I don't trust or respond to those acts of making which have been forced to elevate themselves to the supposed integrity of craft as a bid to civilise sculpture. I'm sure the viewers who latched onto the alabaster as a 'handle' to an understanding of the work were ever hopeful that it was 'crafted', and then it – the work – would have a use, and would be civilised, removed from its primeval state. In those terms 'Harbour'[14] fails

14 'Harbour' 1994-1996. Part of Desmorais installation at Skipton Castle for artranspennine 98.

magnificently! Is the ambivalence of where and how sculpture exists because of its anarchic rejection of fulfilling the expectation of its materials? It thwarts rational resolution, always destabilising expectation.

(Digression, ref. M.C-M[13]: I don't see observation and innovation as mutually exclusive. Surely observation requires innovation to translate it, doesn't it?)

More about Making: Isn't the desperation and urgency something to do with finding the shortest route for an act of making: to be economic with craft, if not with time or labour?

Sand, Sea and Edges: Your consistent return to the sea's edge is fascinating. Is the sand, as evidence of the mutability of edges because of its state of flux, also an ultimate object, because it can't be edged? The fact that it drinks up its other edge, the sea, affirms the fallibility of edges as always rigid, which they are not; they are capricious and the sand's reaction to the tide is an ideal example of why there is a compulsion to argue with the fixity of materials and how they become sculpture, and where the edges should, could be.

Sculpture!: Sculpture's verticality and horizontality is something I have succumbed to over the last few years, and increasingly with enthusiasm. I have used structure as a strength, and support, on to which I can fling all kinds of slippery things – mess – and see if it sticks. The cool, calm upright and horizontal posture of structure is, for me, an equivalent to geometry: it permits autonomy, isolation, independence, and as a strength, it can take all kinds of assaults and remain standing, or lying, refusing to die, unless murdered in cold blood.

I love that strength, which I interpret as masculine and sexy. The assault I understand as myself, and I'm not clear what that is, but it is all the stuff that gets flung at, smeared and hung on these structures. What ends up on the floor is a rich potential, nagging for attention, and possibly threatens to be more interesting than the object it has escaped from. Removing the work from the evidence of its making, from the surrounding mess, is always a relief, and enables me to know whether these structures have been able to survive the assaults inflicted on them. Like the ridged sand being the evidence of the force of the tide. I like the idea of a structure being a restraint (what you call a discipline?) to emotive gestures: both the labour intensiveness of making the structures, (tedious, rational, organised) combined with their resulting strength – which can control and restrain what can be done to them, and the limits to which they can be pushed. For me, the structures are like the land, and the stuff that gets flung on them is anything that isn't land: weather, emotions, mess, memories…
Love, Phyllida.

Craft: Is well-made the same as crafted? I don't think so. I hate the crafty. I think there's a balance, rough edges are O.K. I hate craft processes – like the interminable 50 stages of making a beautiful mould. I love short cuts even though sometimes they don't work.

Your voice: I'm glad you have found it – you sounded very positive and optimistic about what you do and you make a great case for making sculpture and the need for it. It's not cool is it! Too much passion? Not enough irony?

Dazed and confused: This morning I've done 2 things.

Flicked through the pages of the above magazine which I take to be a microcosm of hard edged cultural high spots. Couldn't tell what I was looking at – art, advertising. A batch of photos of disabled people wearing amazing clothes superficially no different from the models in other articles. I thought it was a totally hermetic magazine 'noir', glamorous, dangerous, a text book for today.

Spent the rest of the morning losing control of bowls of plaster and pieces of thin alabaster. What I thought I saw coming towards me, an eventual resolution of seeing bulk through transparent stone which also formed part of it – has come to nothing. I feel like a spider being dropped from its web and then laboriously climbing up it again, except that's a totally inept analogy – the spider must climb its web, but I'm stalking something which has no edges or guidelines and each time I find myself in this place its as though it were for the first time instead of for the thousandth.

What a pity this is the last fax.
Love, Alison.

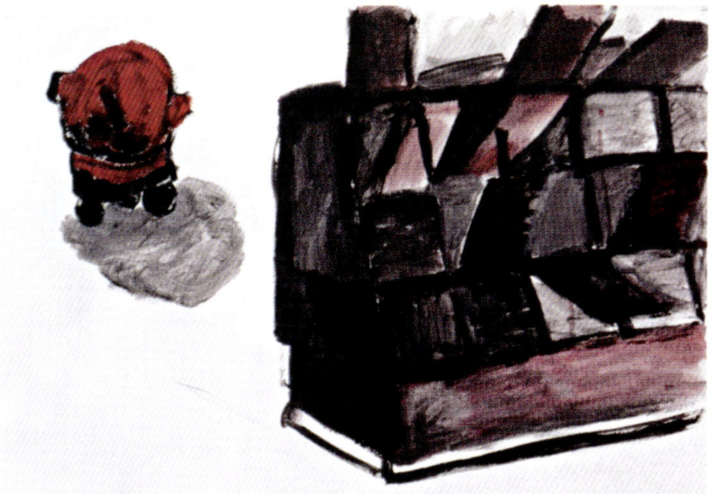

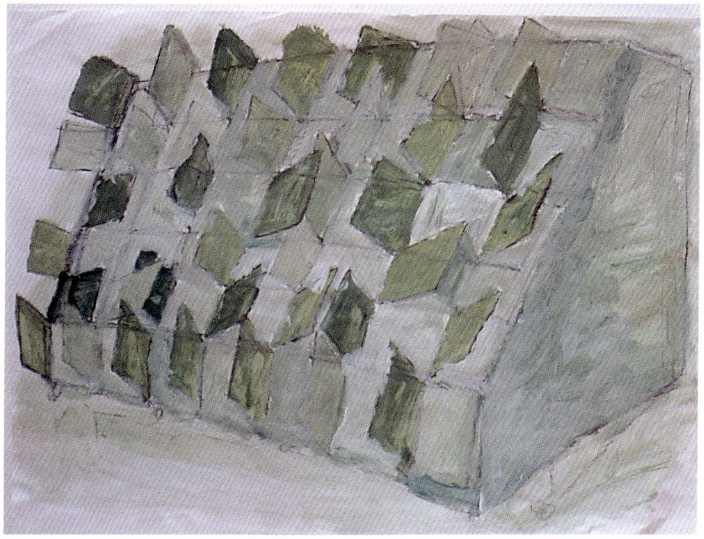

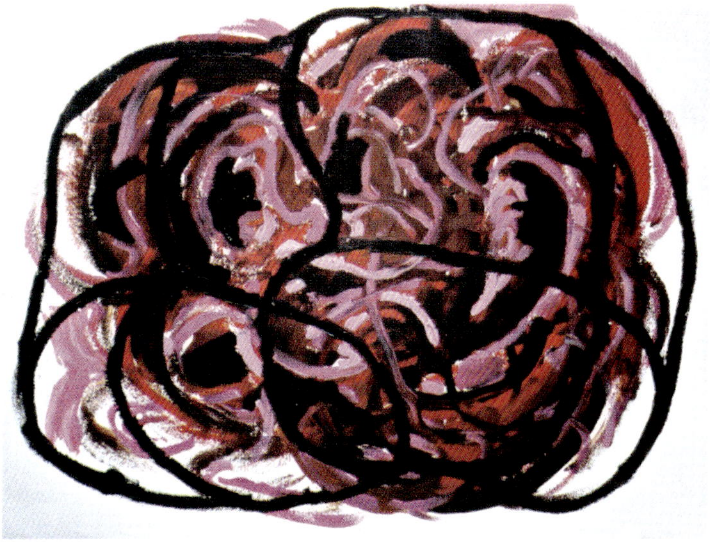

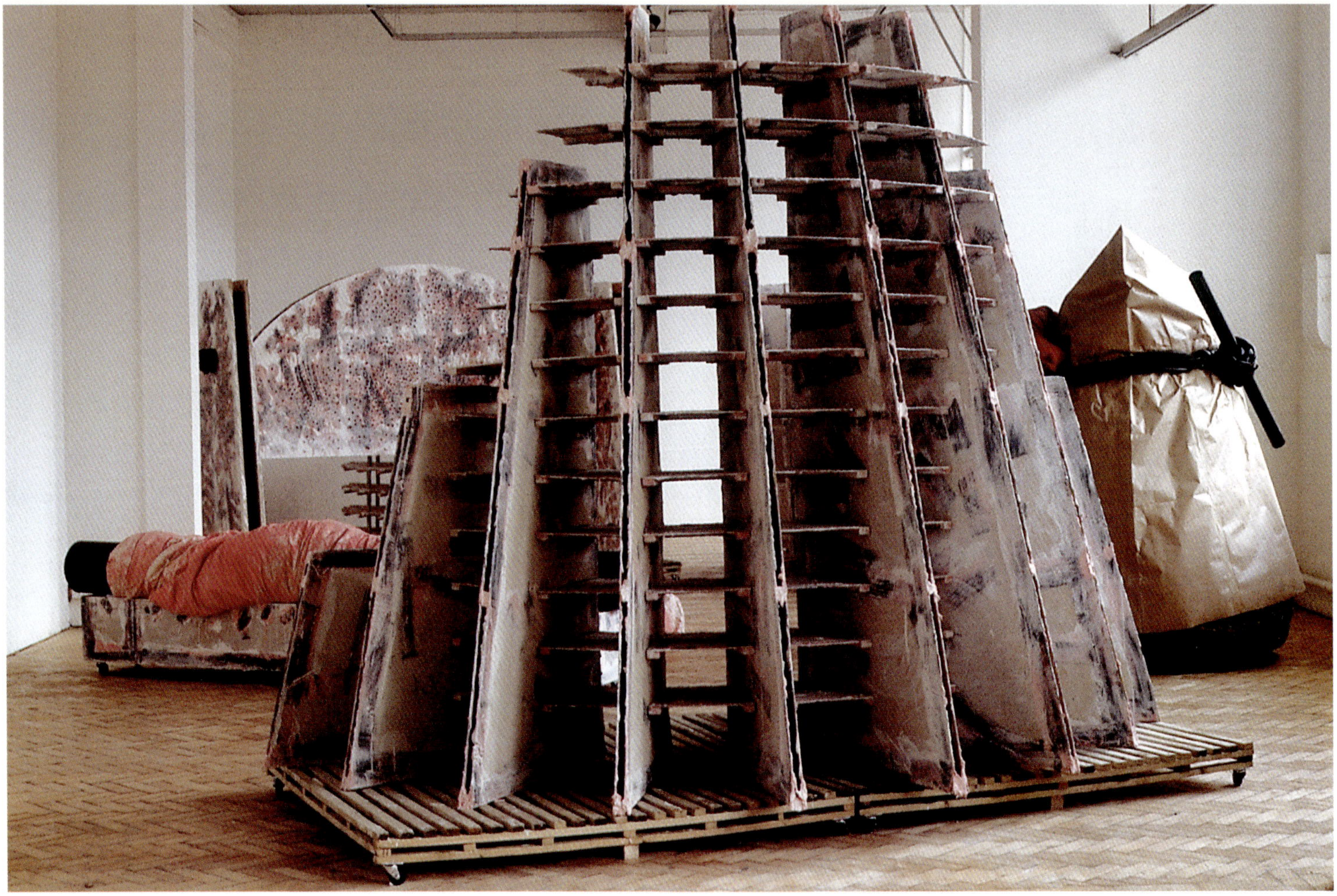

Time and time again
Painted wood, painted fabrics, felt, industrial PVC tubing, rubber tubing, brown paper, painted hardboard, palettes, casters
Overall dimensions of work/space: 600 x 420 x 600 cm
1998
Chapter Art Gallery, Cardiff, for *Out of Place*, curated by Nilofar Akmut

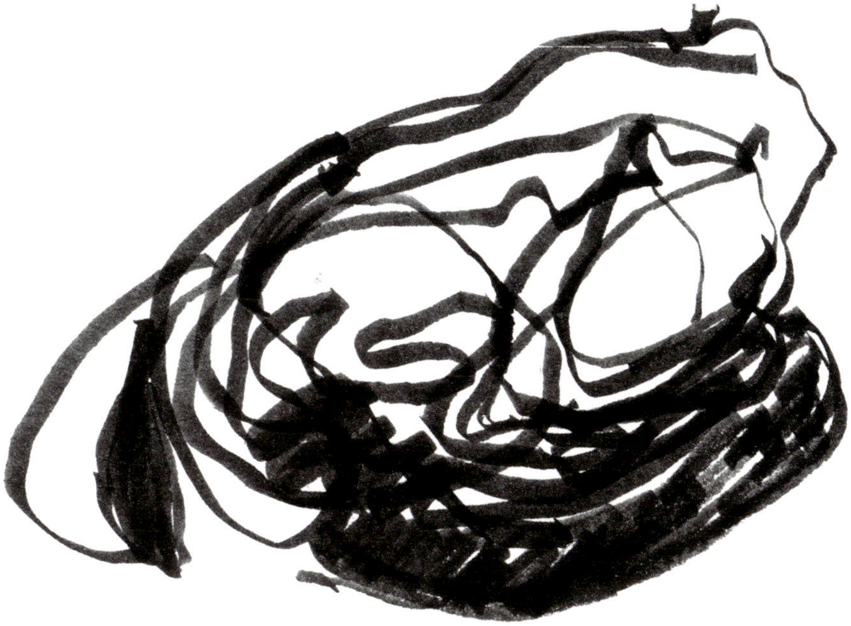

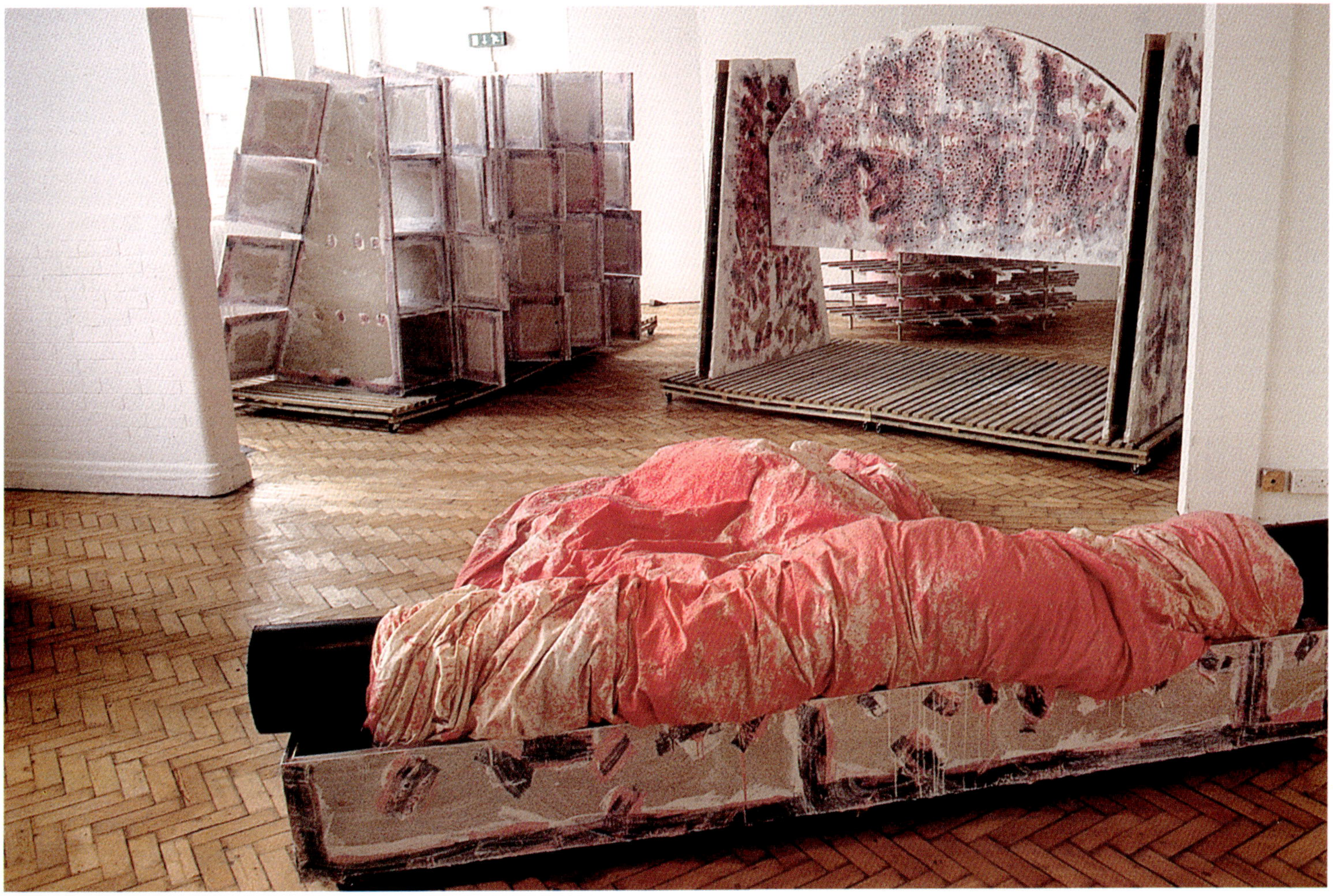

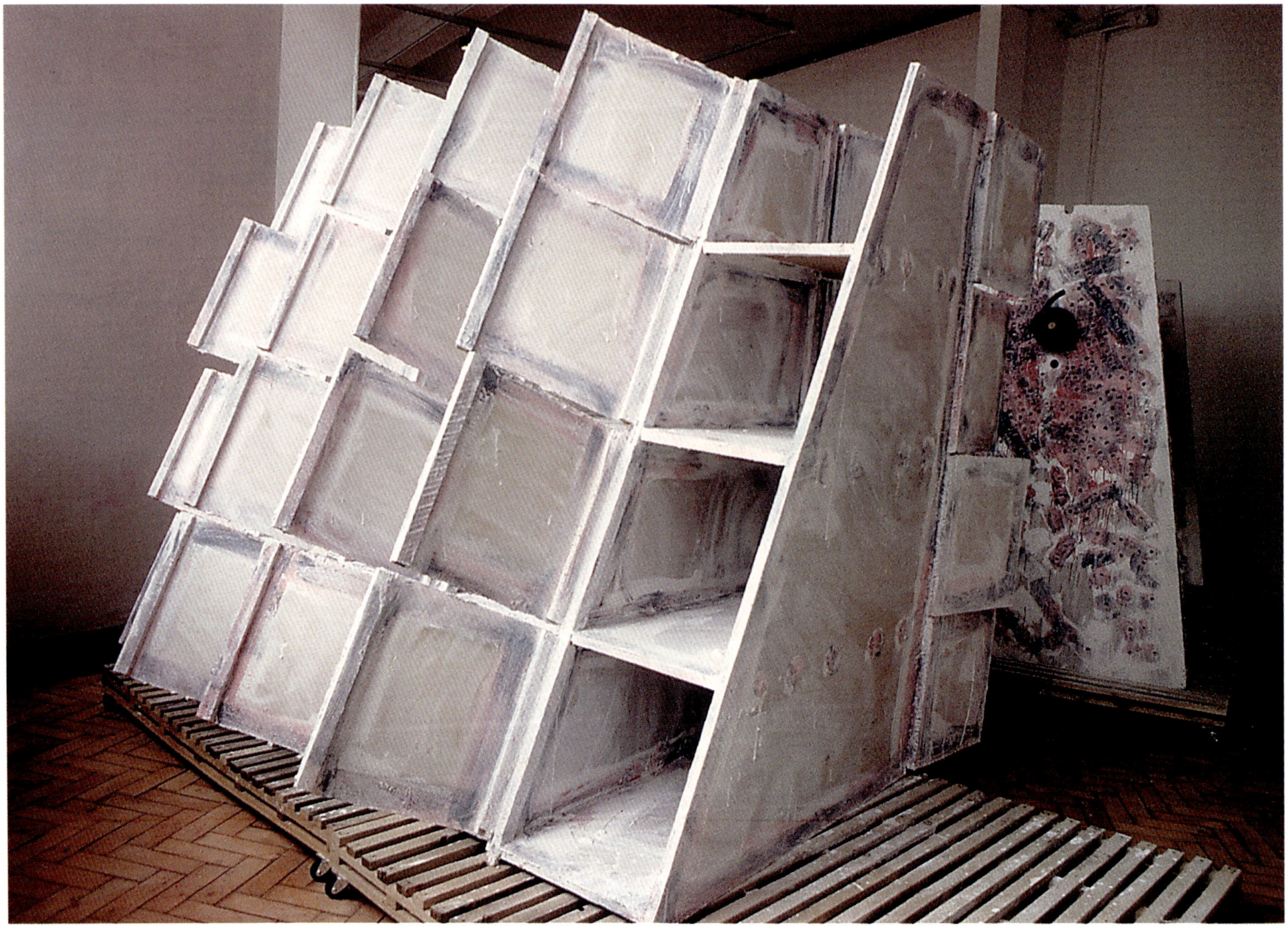

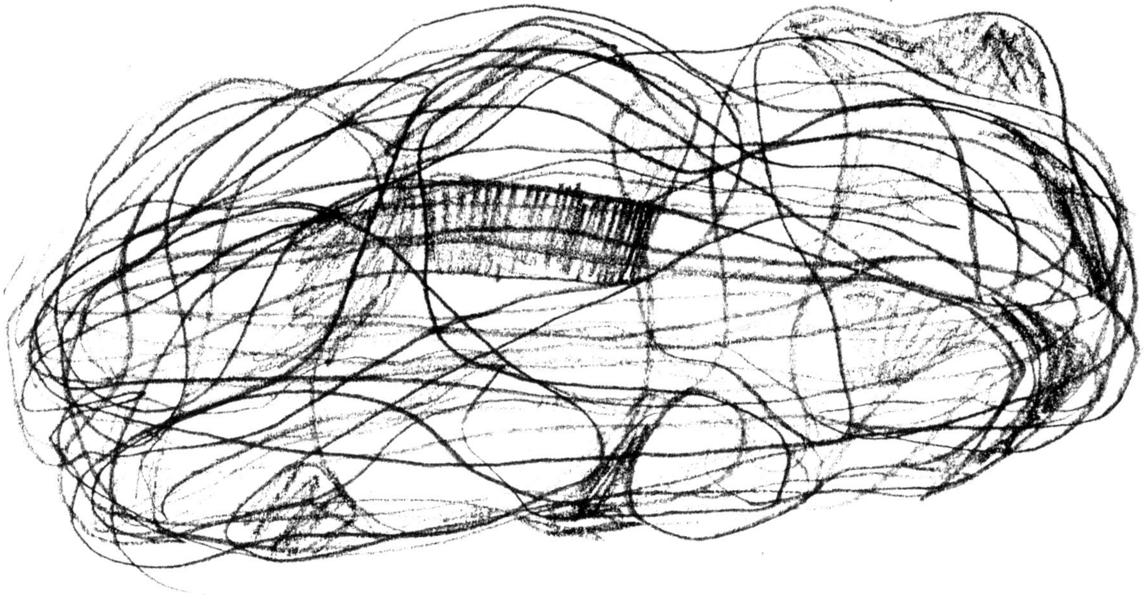

July 25.

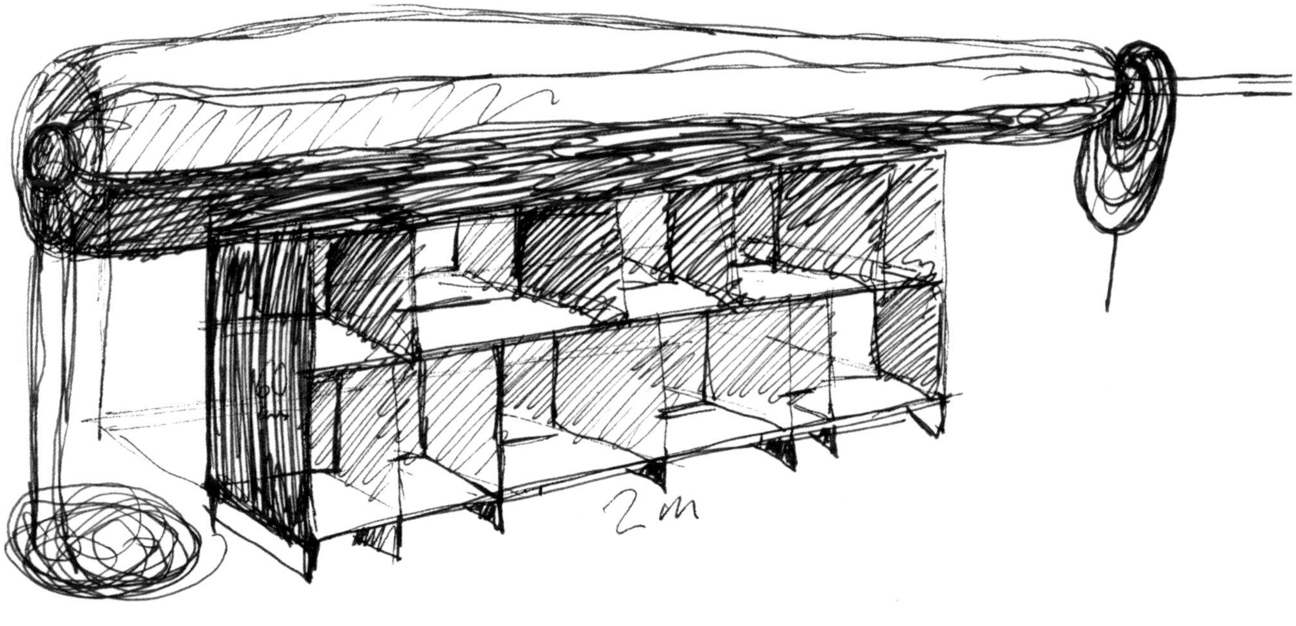

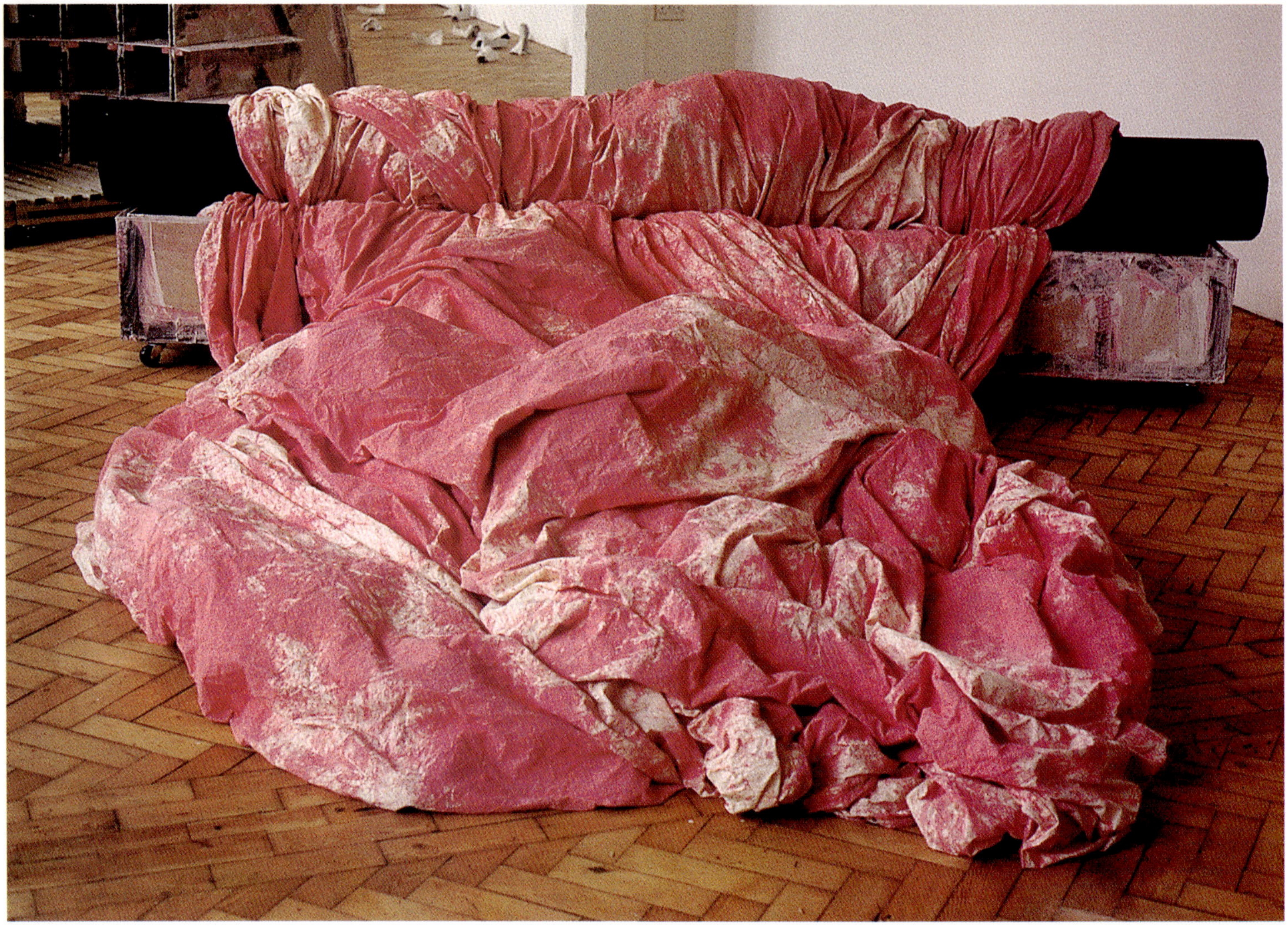

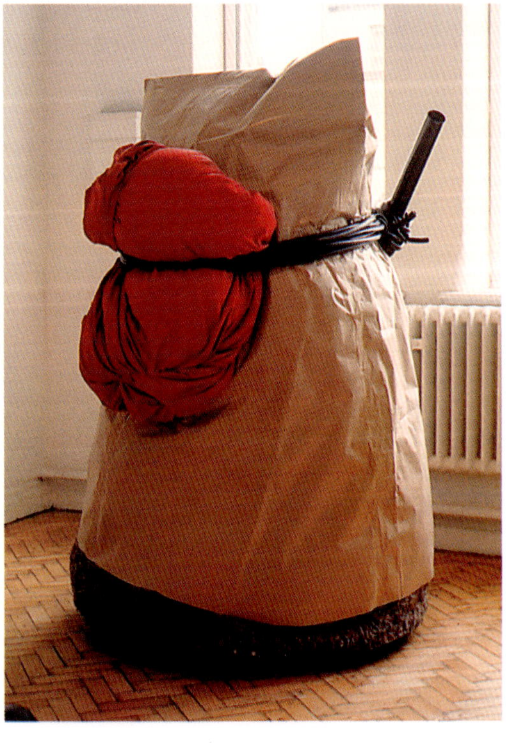

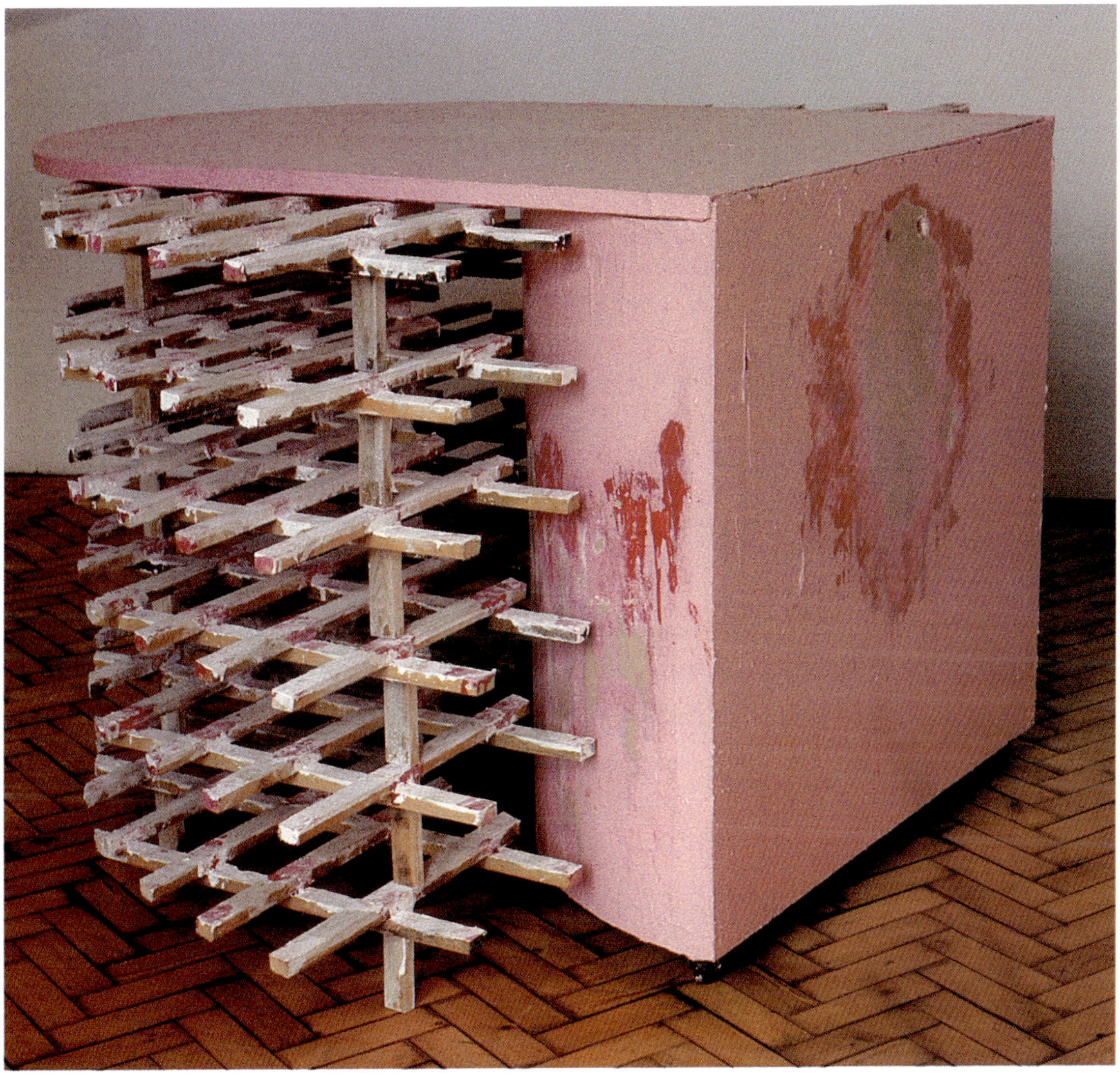

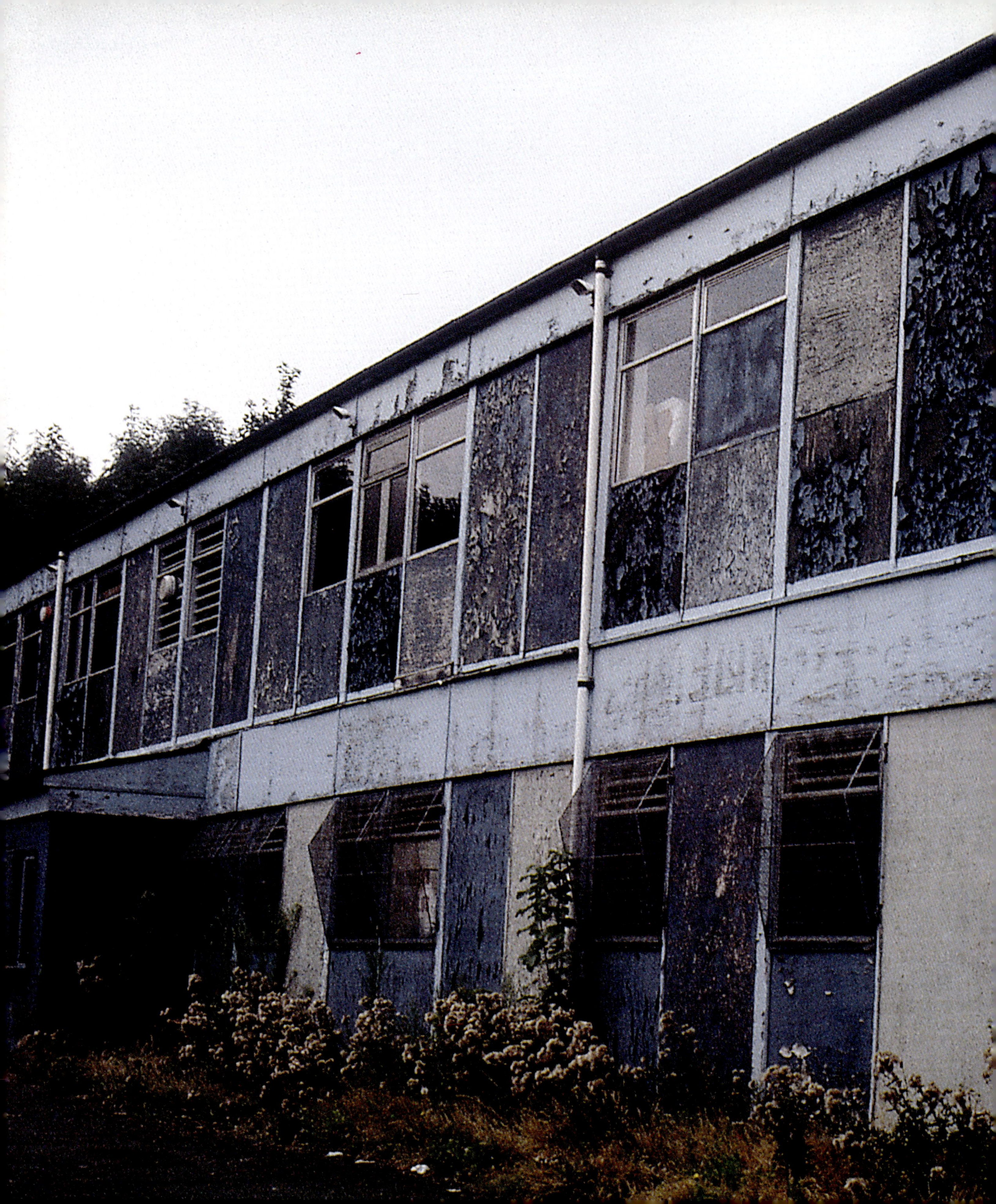

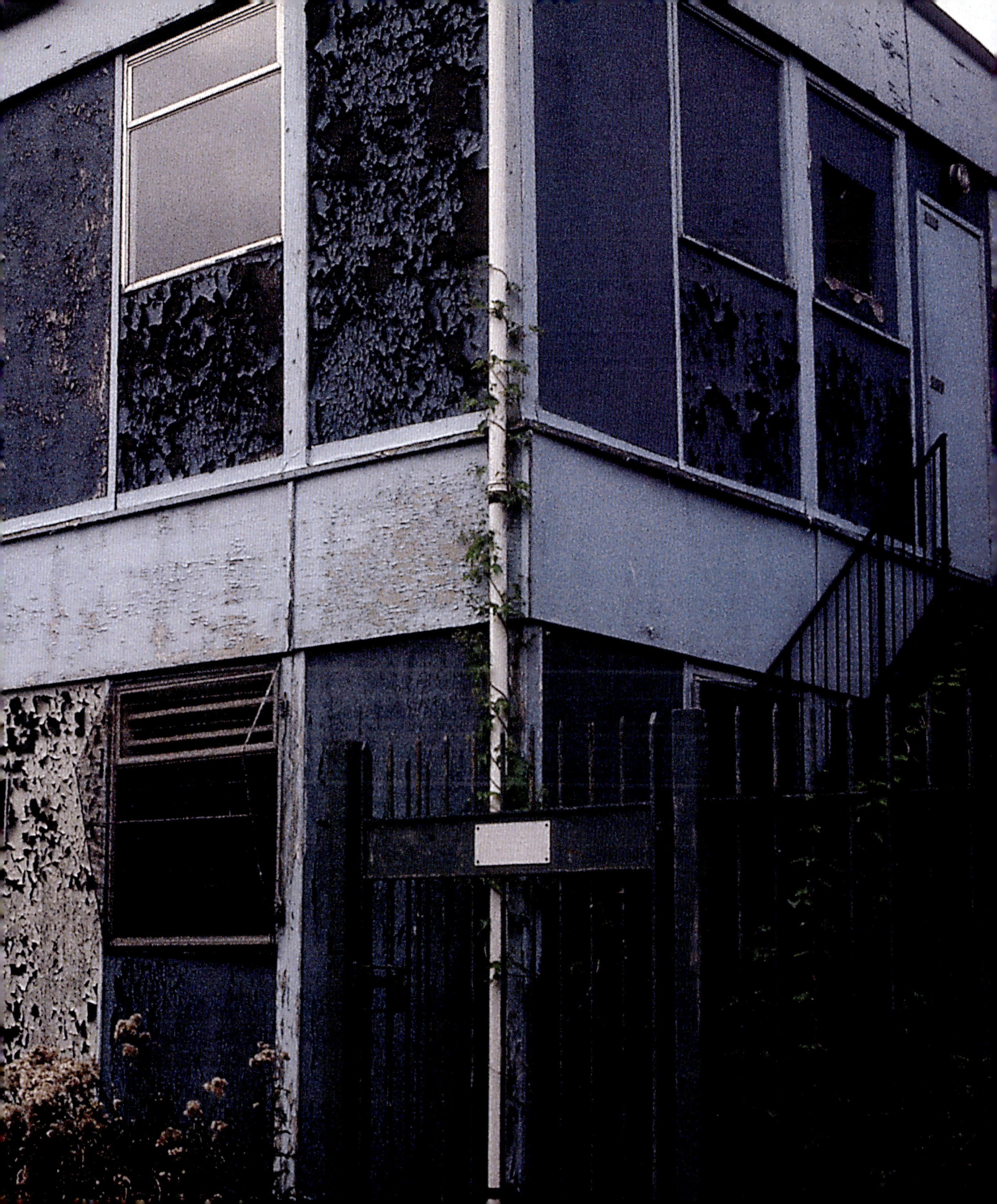

Untitled, Dallas: 2003
Plywood, timber, concrete, polystyrene, plastic, newspaper, strapping, tape, felt, rubber, foam, paint
750 x 900 x 1800 cm
2003
Visual Arts Gallery, University of Texas, Dallas, USA
Photographs: Kevin Todora, University of Texas at Dallas

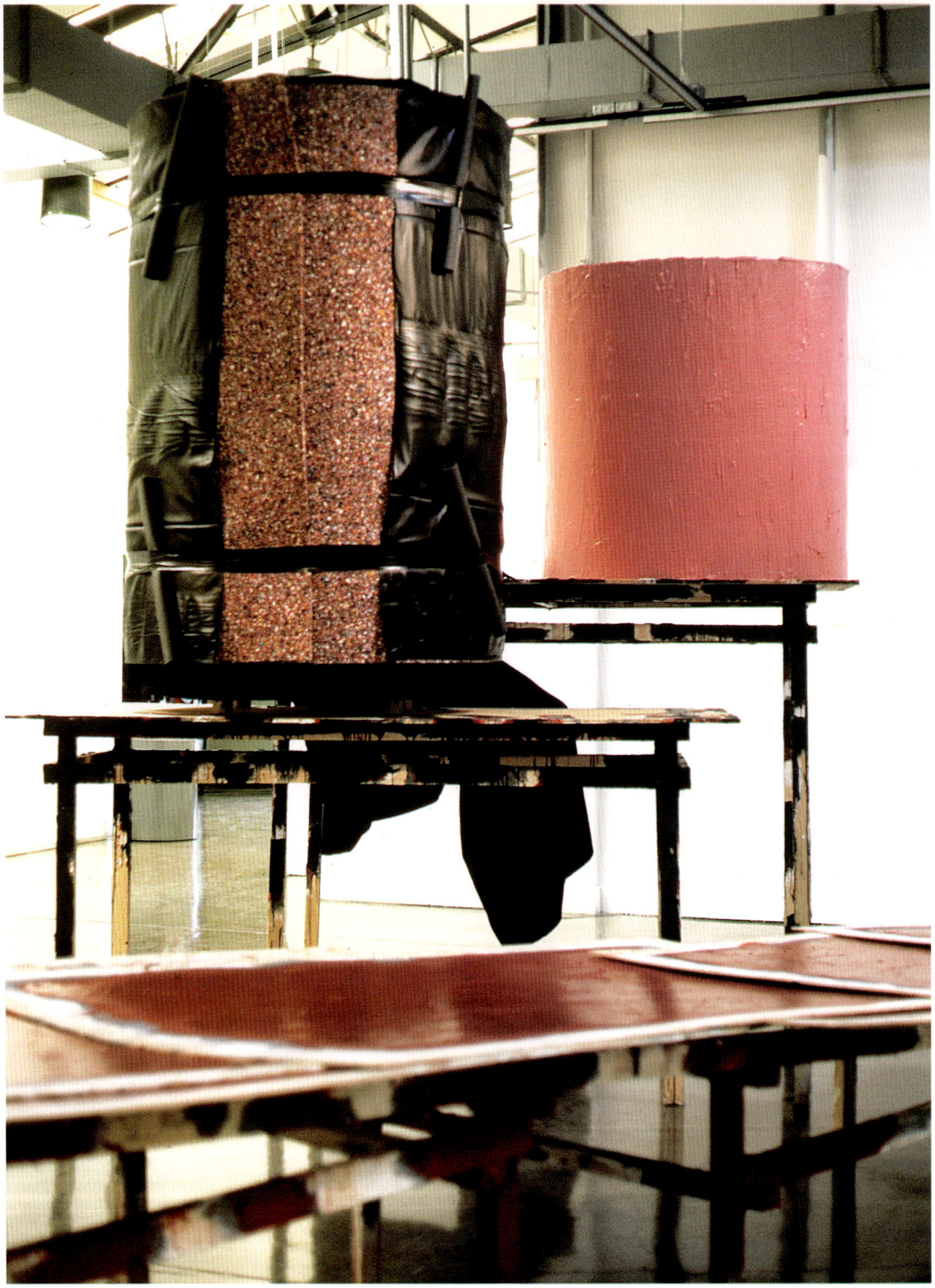

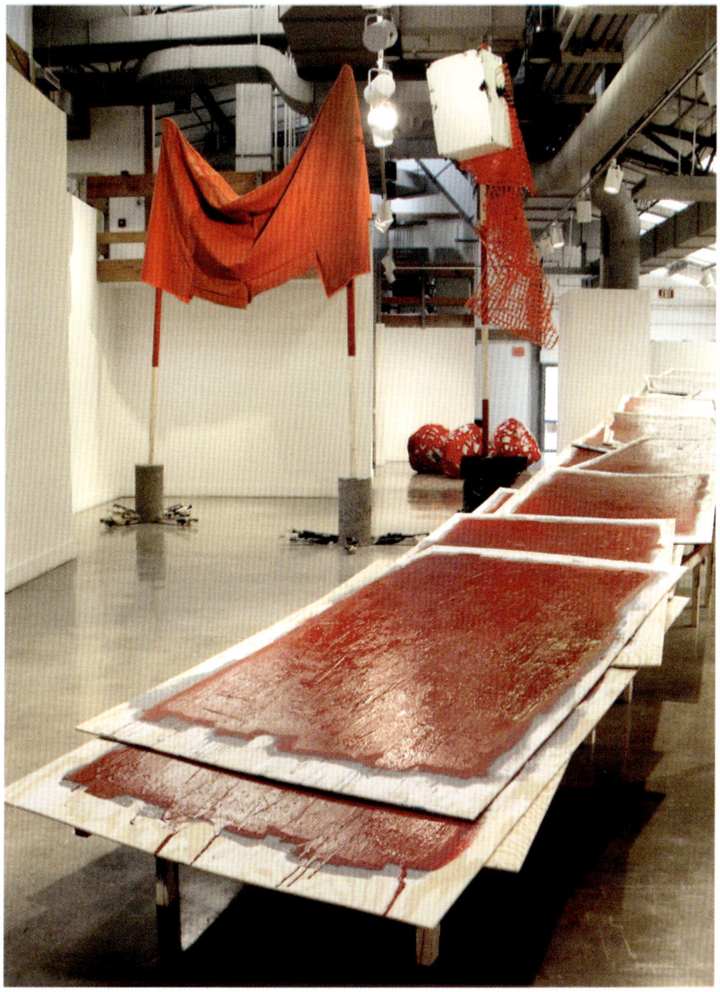

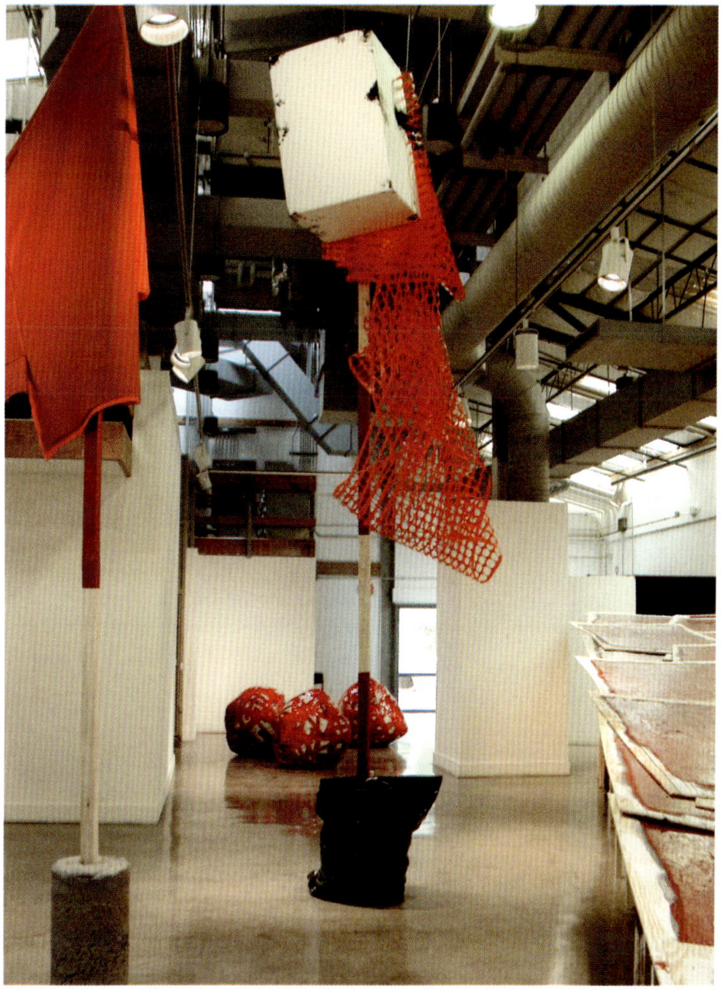

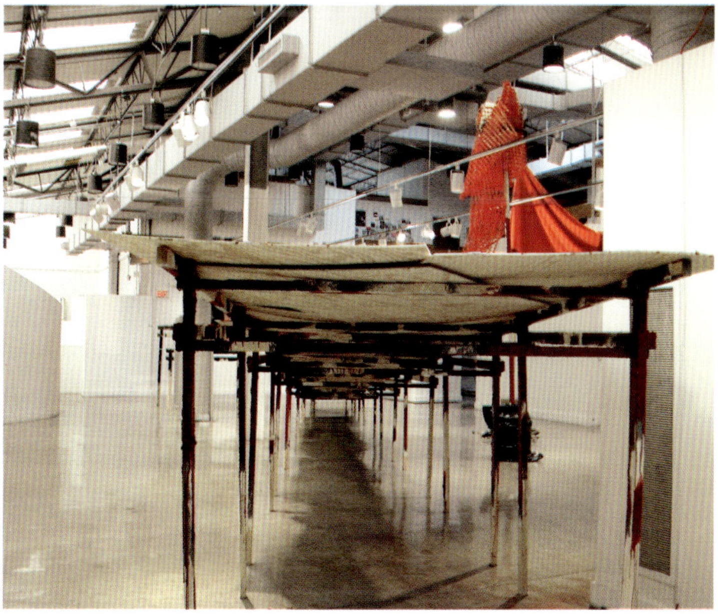

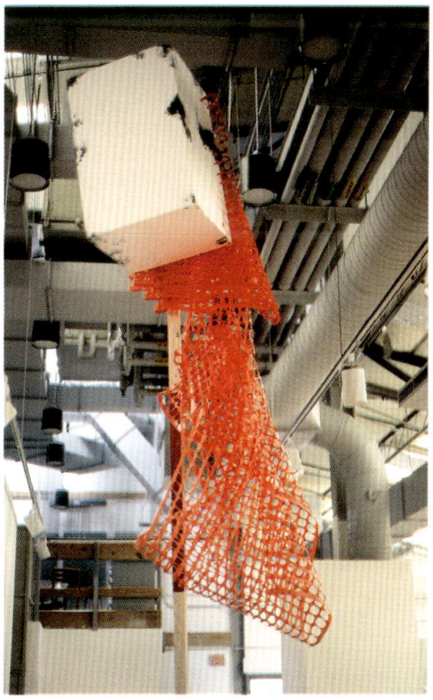

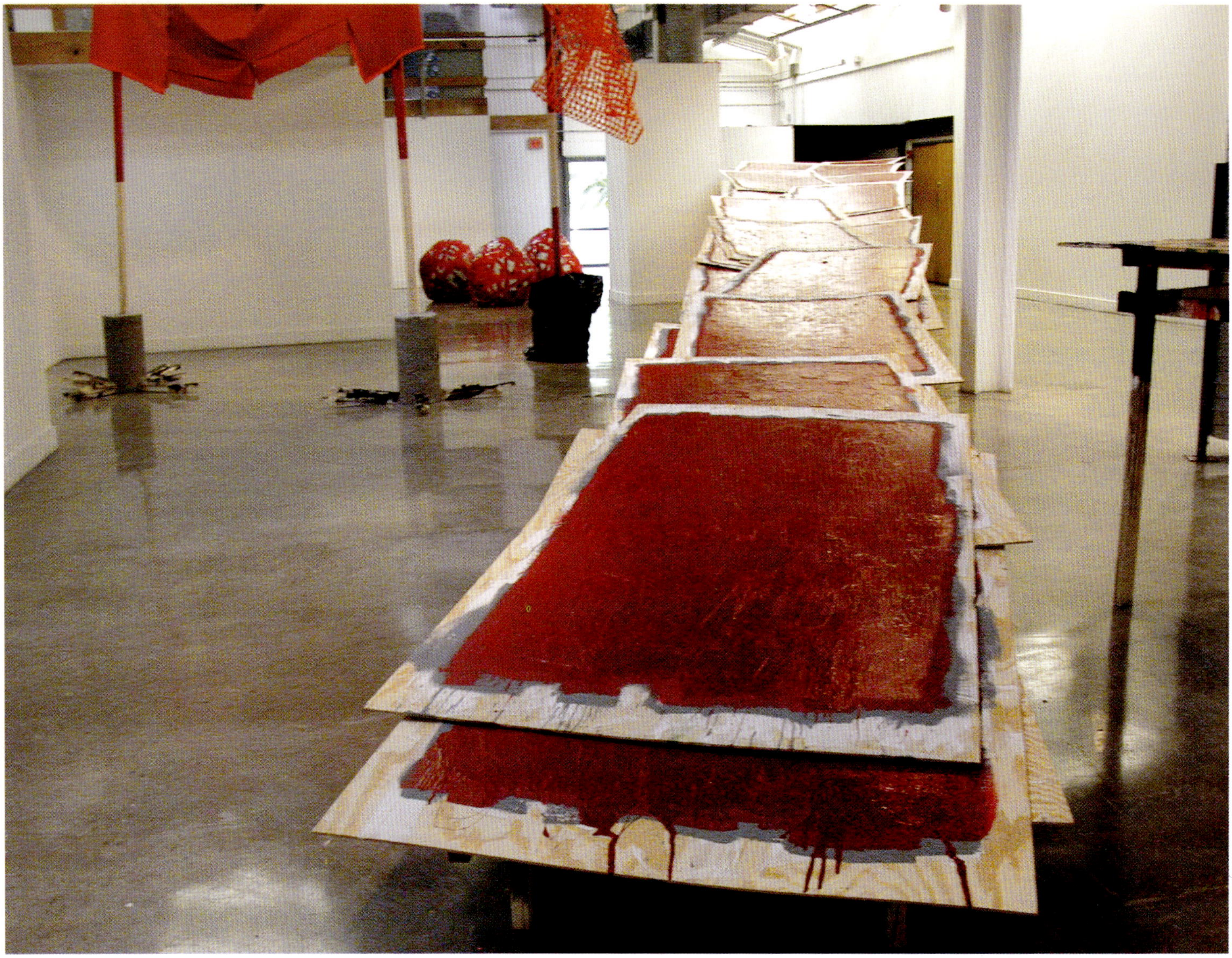

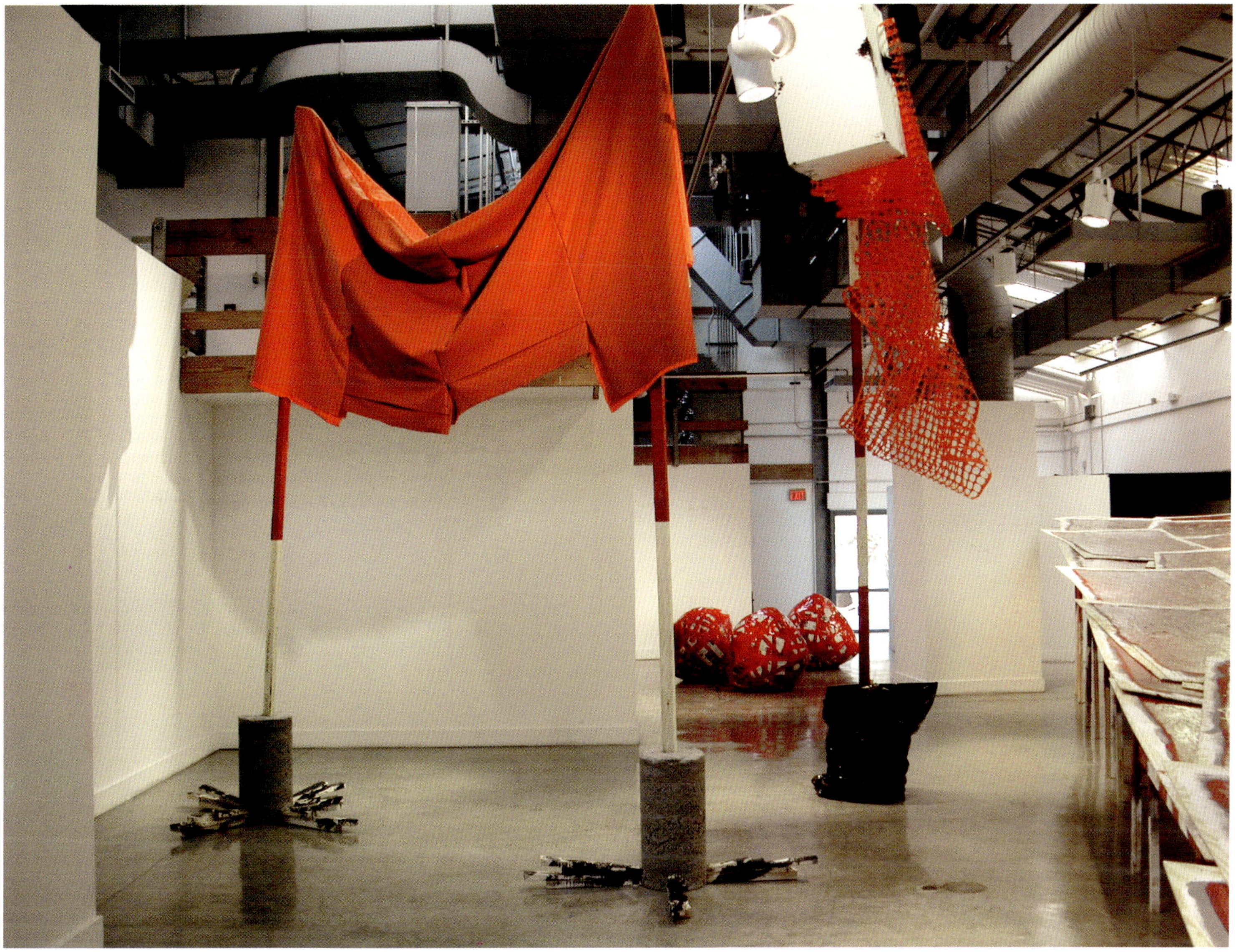

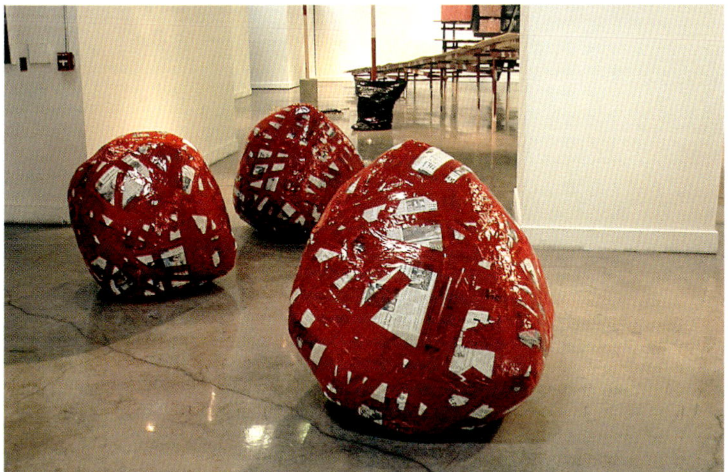

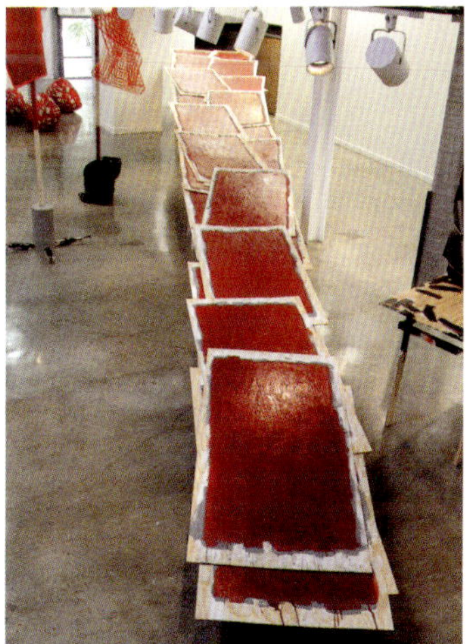

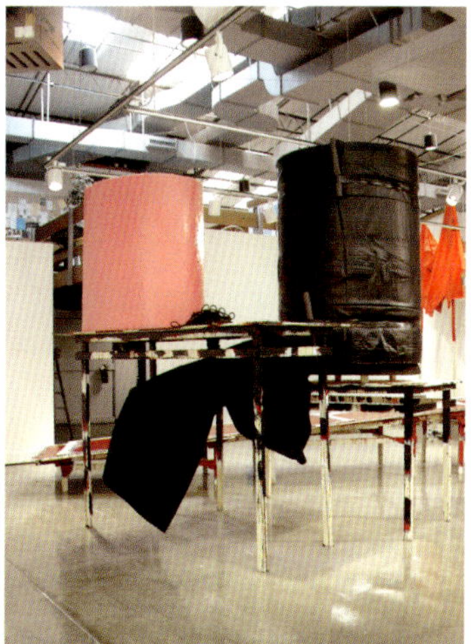

Below:
Stacks
Sliced chipboard
100 x 270 x 360 cm
240 x 270 x 240 cm
1979
Bracknell Park

Right:
Sofa, floor & drawings
Canvas, paint, wooden frame,
hardboard, plywood, drawing,
fibreglass and resin, pigment, clay
360 x 240 x 500 cm
1970-1971
Spectrum, Alexander Palace,
London

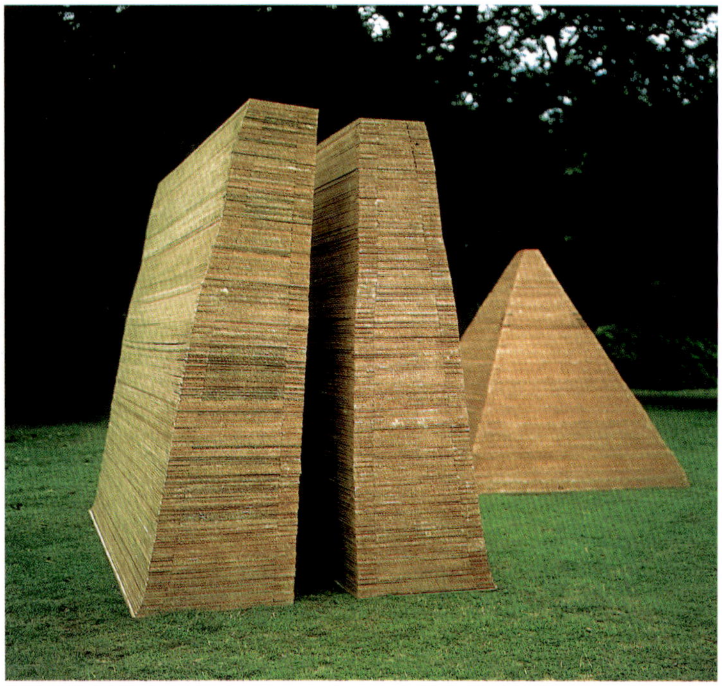

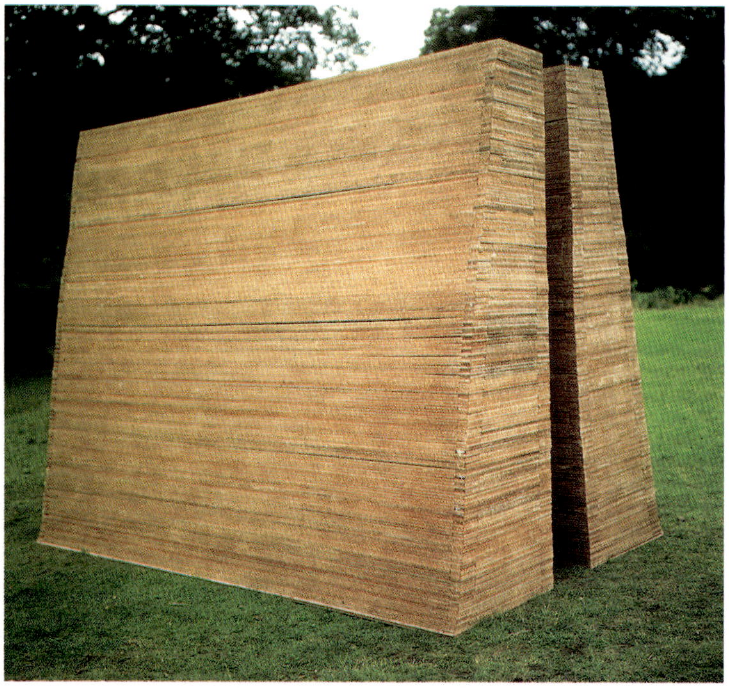

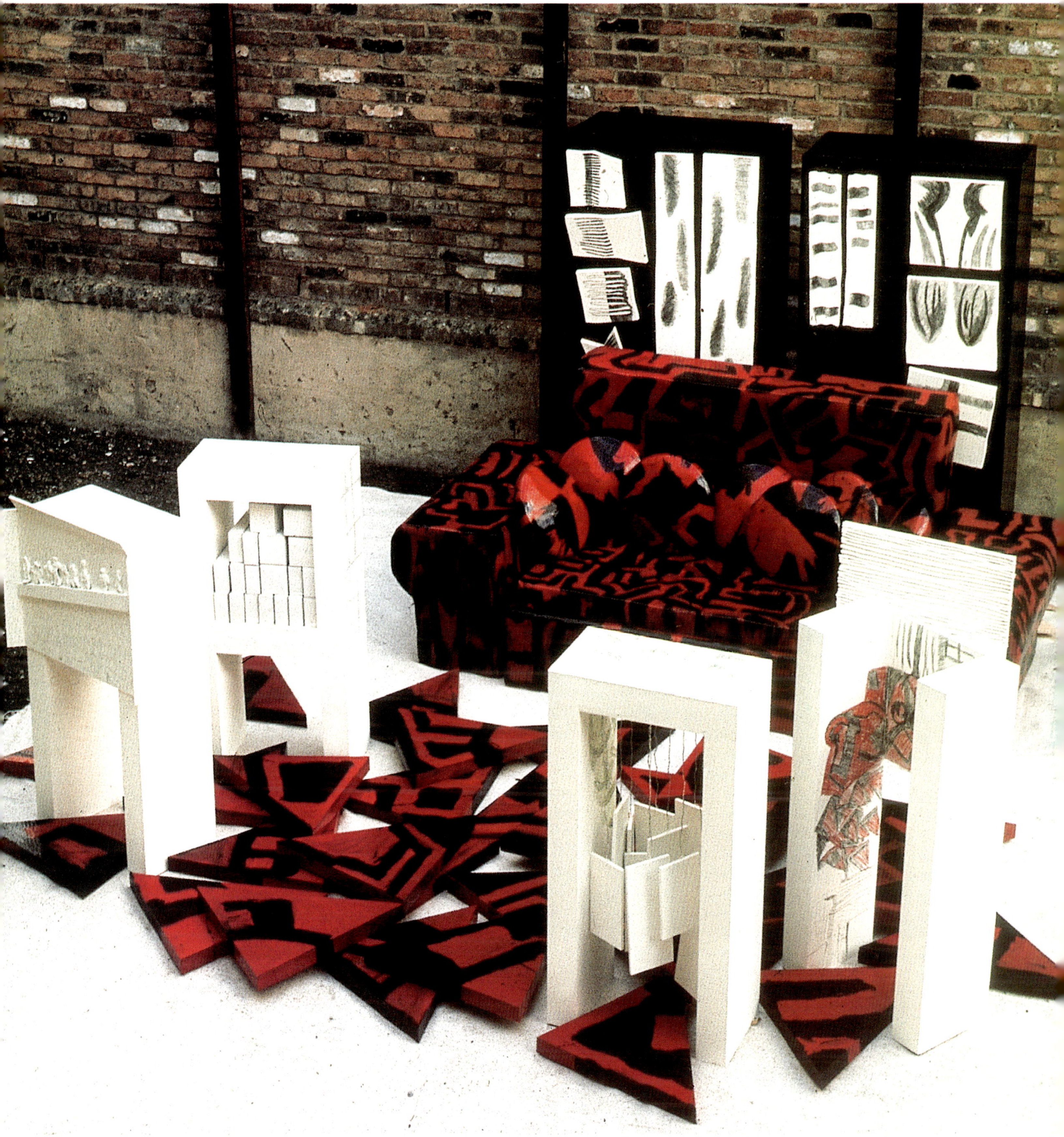

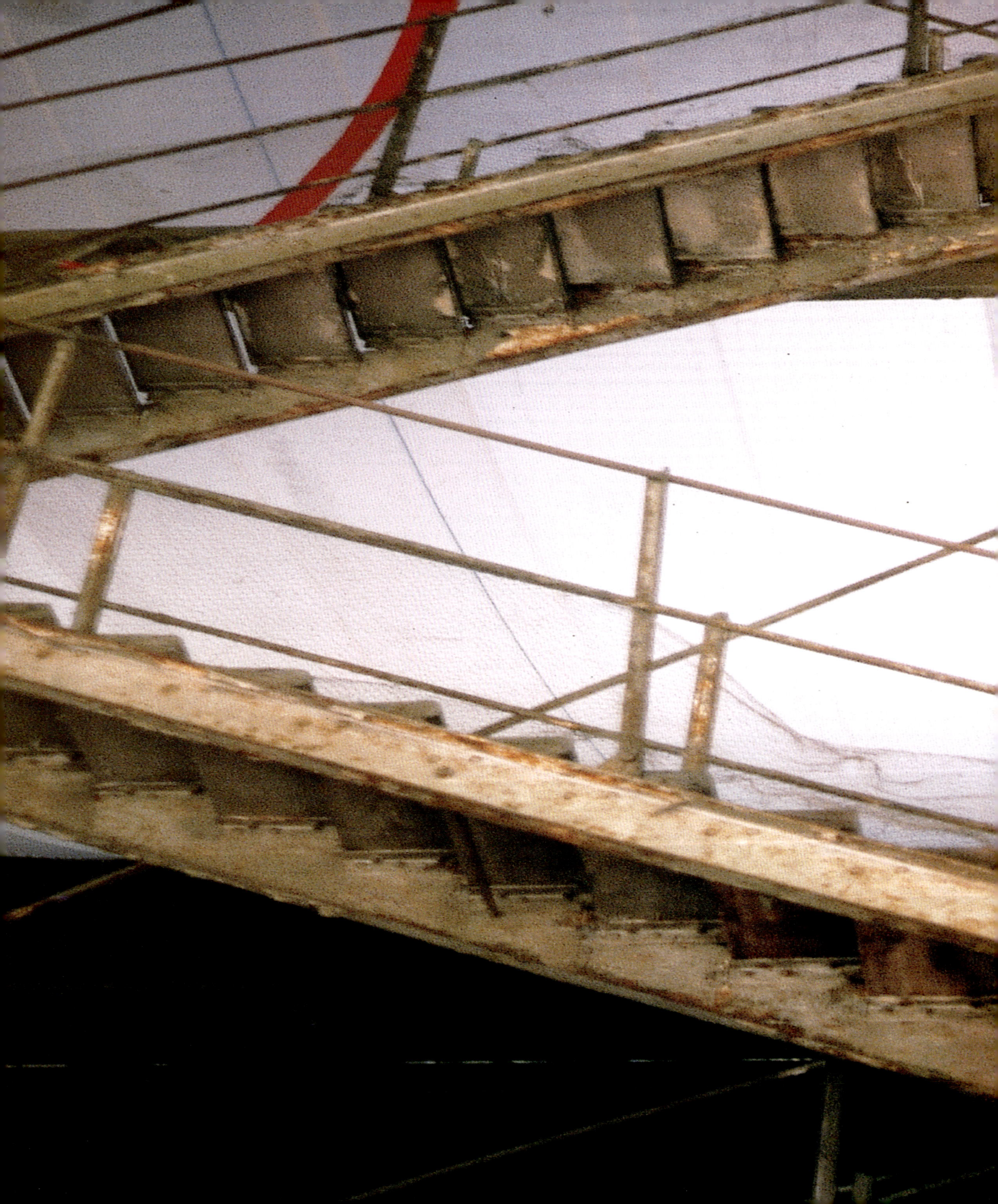

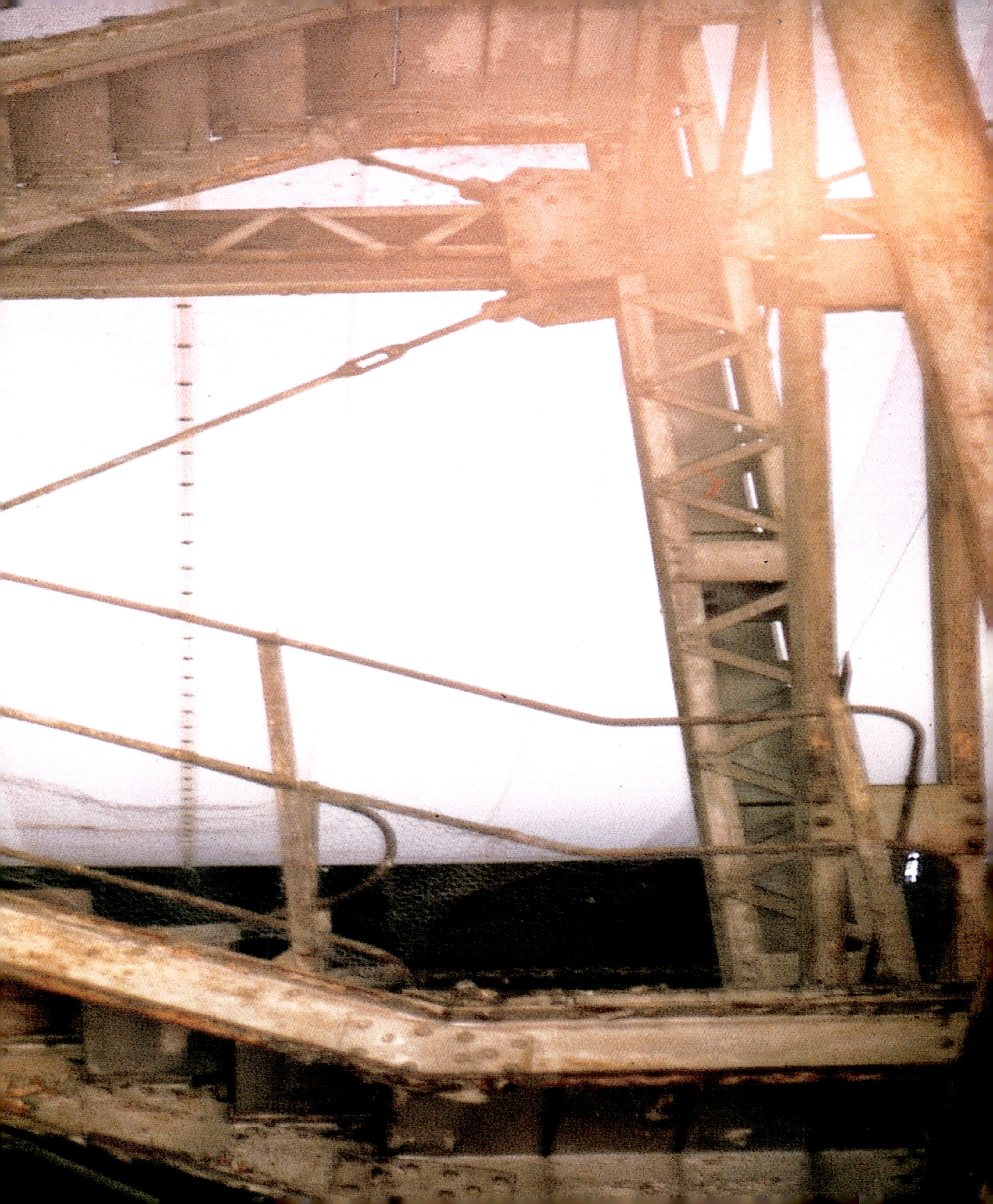

Storm
Polythene, wire, vinyl tape,
bitumen, paper, paint
Overall of space:
300 x 270 x 600 cm
1987
Studio work

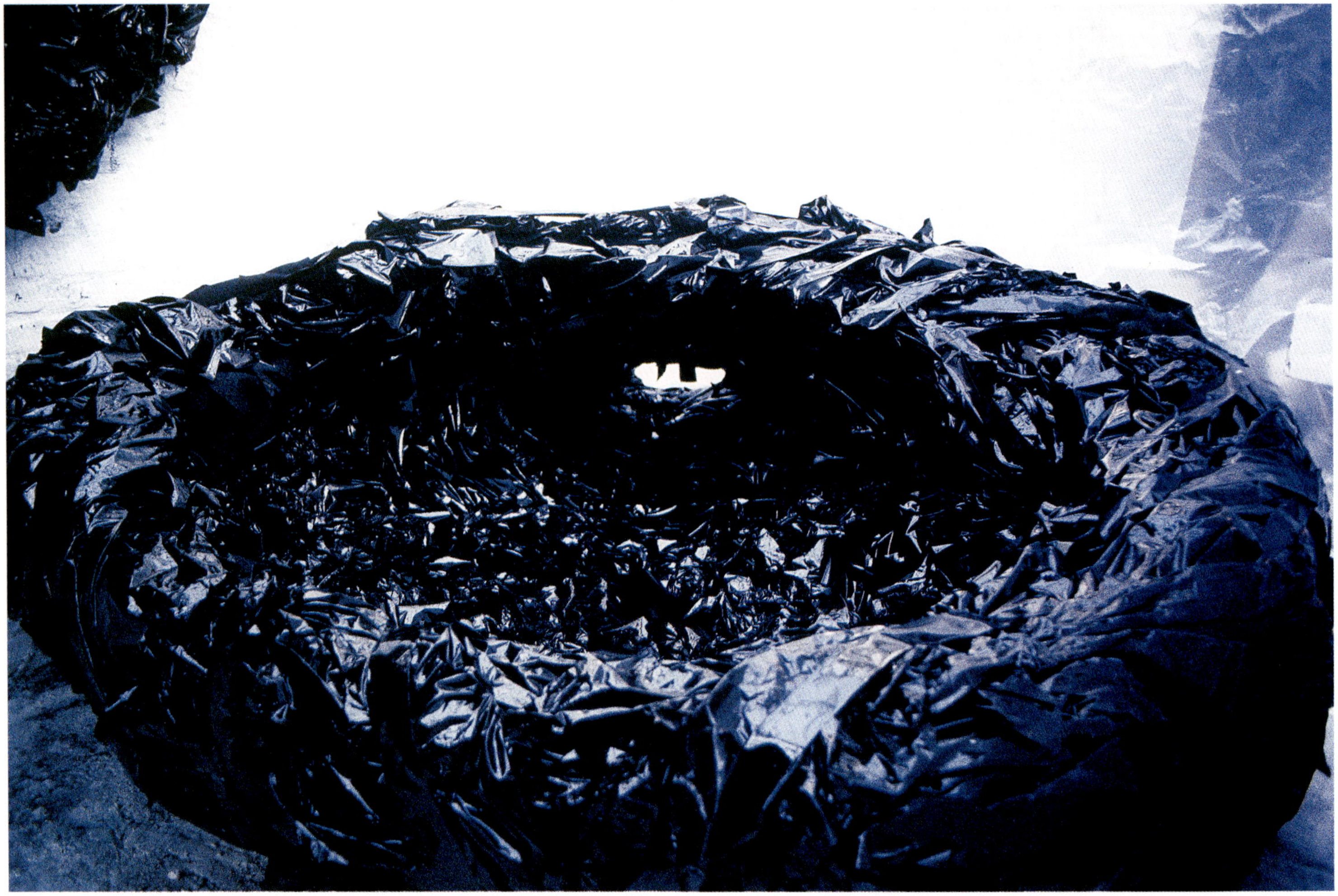

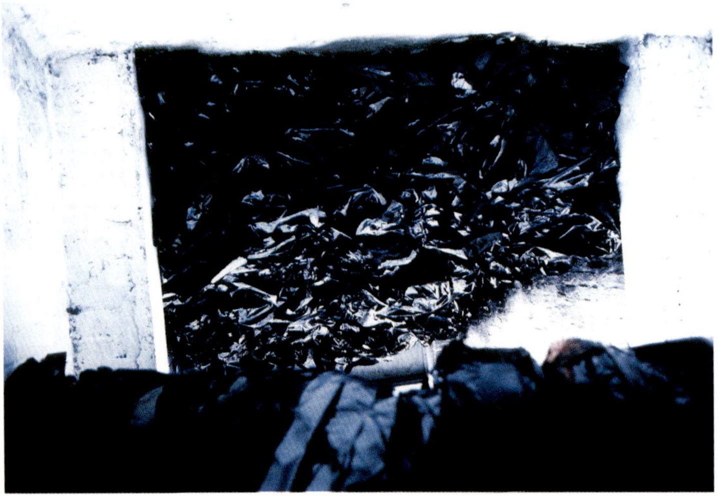

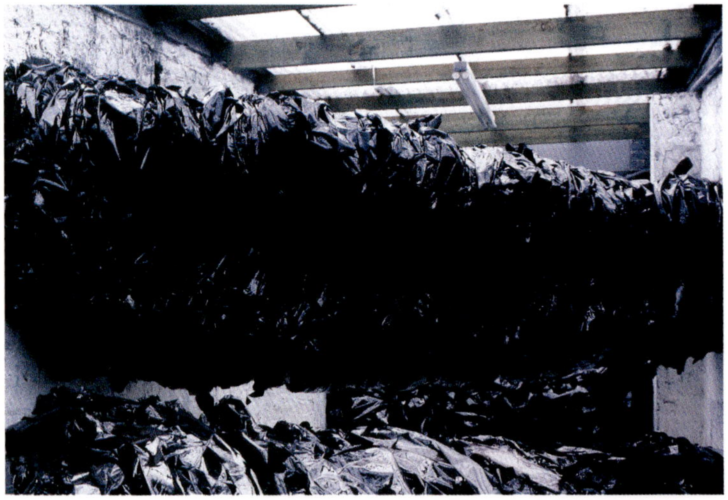

The Sculpture of Phyllida Barlow

Jon Wood

What's in a Sculpture?

1 Barlow, Phyllida, "The Hatred of the Object", in Stuart Evans, Joanna Greenhill and Ingrid Swenson, eds., *Sculpture Method Research,* Matrix 3d conference, 1997, London: Lethaby Press, p. 23.

Jacques Lipchitz
Figure
1926-30

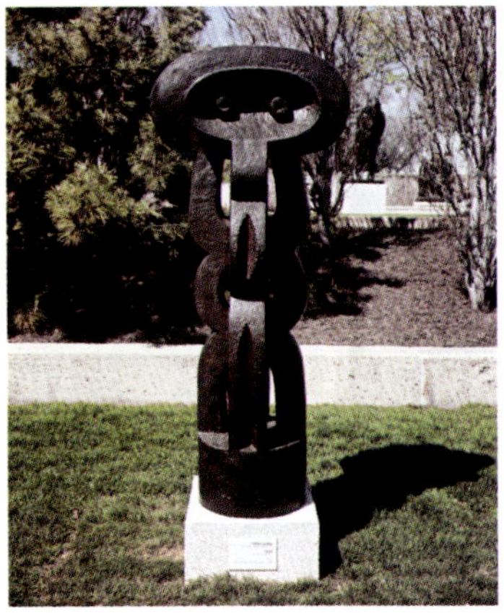

Phyllida Barlow's *Truce*, 1997, is an extraordinary work. For me, it's one of those pieces that artists make from time to time that seems to sum up or condense a lot of what their work is preoccupied with. *Truce*, and the title itself is telling (in its denotation of a pact or a cessation in the conflict), says a great deal about what Barlow's sculpture is up to. The upright cylindrical component of this five-part ensemble is particularly so. A cross between a punch bag, a huge rolled up offcut from a carpet warehouse and an industrial container, this strange object immediately reminded me of Jacques Lipchitz' *Figure,* 1926-1930) when I first saw it. It was the size of the thing, its verticality, its stubbornness and its comic and ugly absurdity that struck me and rang bells. It had incredible presence, but of a highly ambiguous and problematic kind. It was at once alien and yet familiar. So what exactly was this enigmatic thing doing? Why did this bundle appear so monumental, bold and proud? It seemed to be so 'full of itself', but full of what? What was inside? How and why was it floating off the ground? What was keeping this thing upright? If the bolster was removed, would the whole thing spring open and collapse, or would it keep its shape and remain upright?

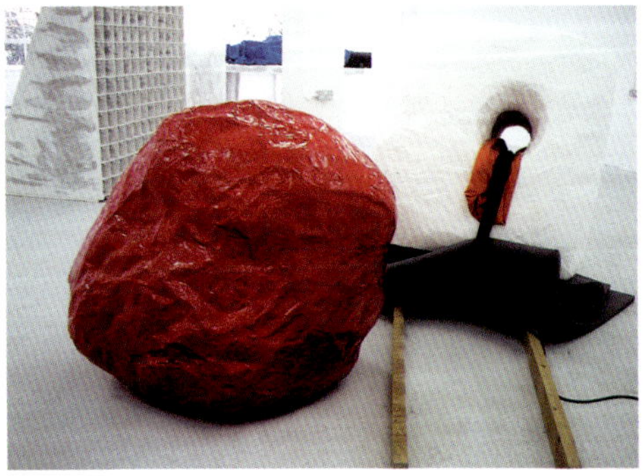

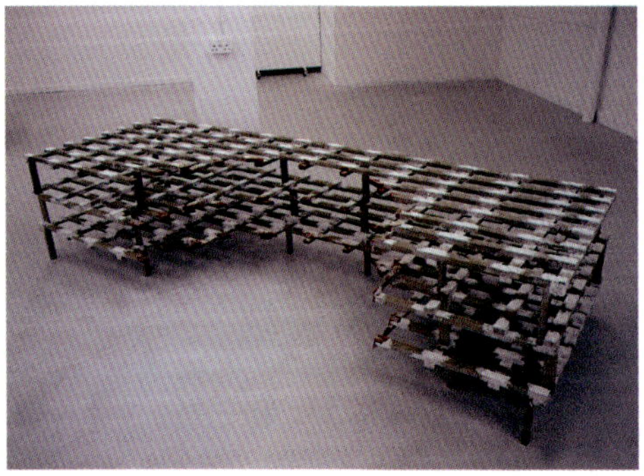

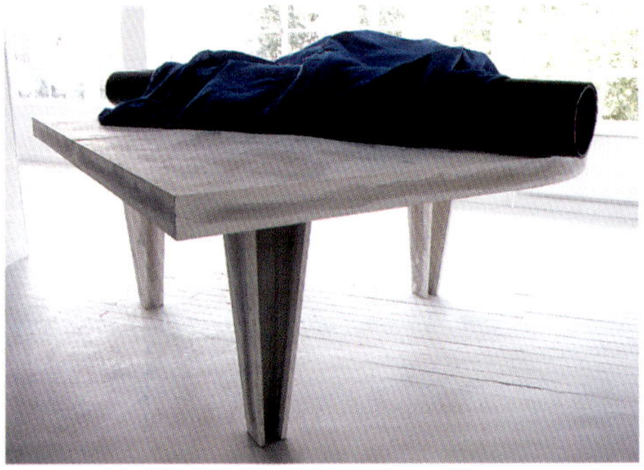

Truce
Painted hardboard, painted wood, fabric, industrial PVC tubing, felt, tubing, casters, polystyrene, rubber tubing, timber lengths, upholstery foam
Overall space / work:
1200 x 240 x 1200 cm
1997
The Sculpture Studio, Norwich School of Art, for EAST International selected by Tacita Dean and Nicholas Logsdail

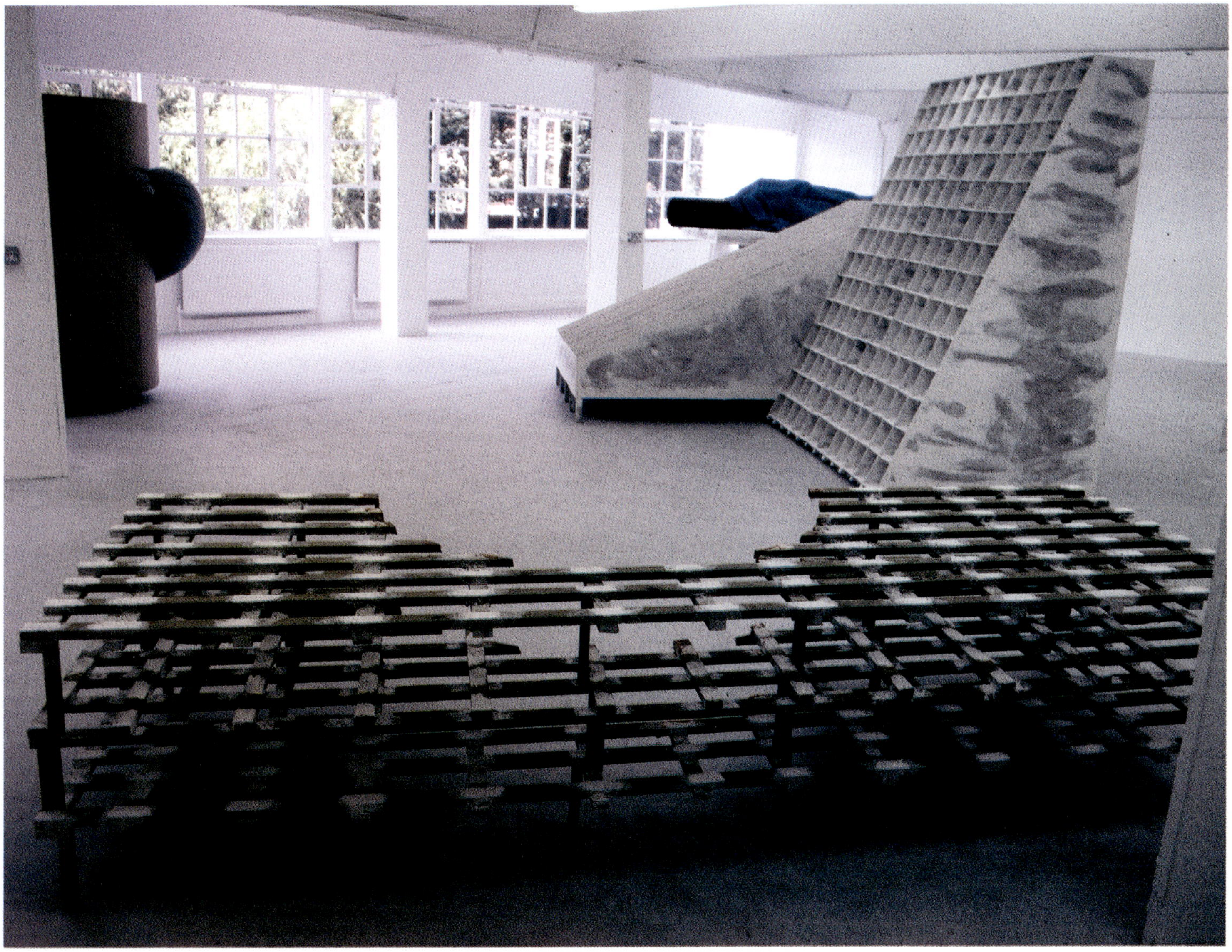

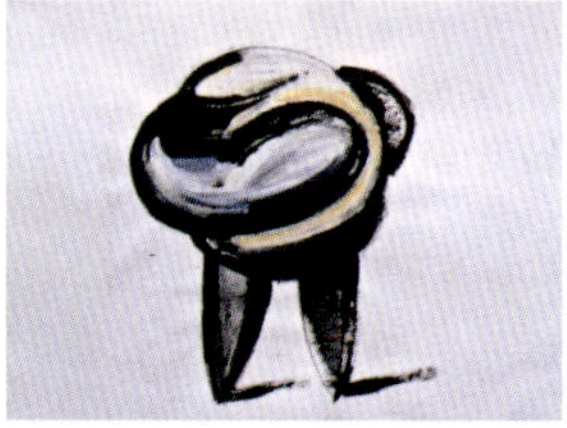

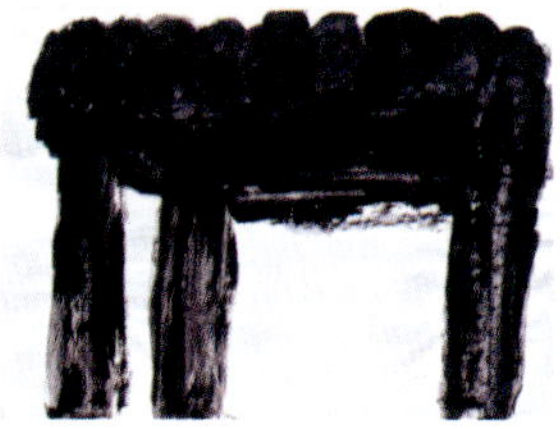

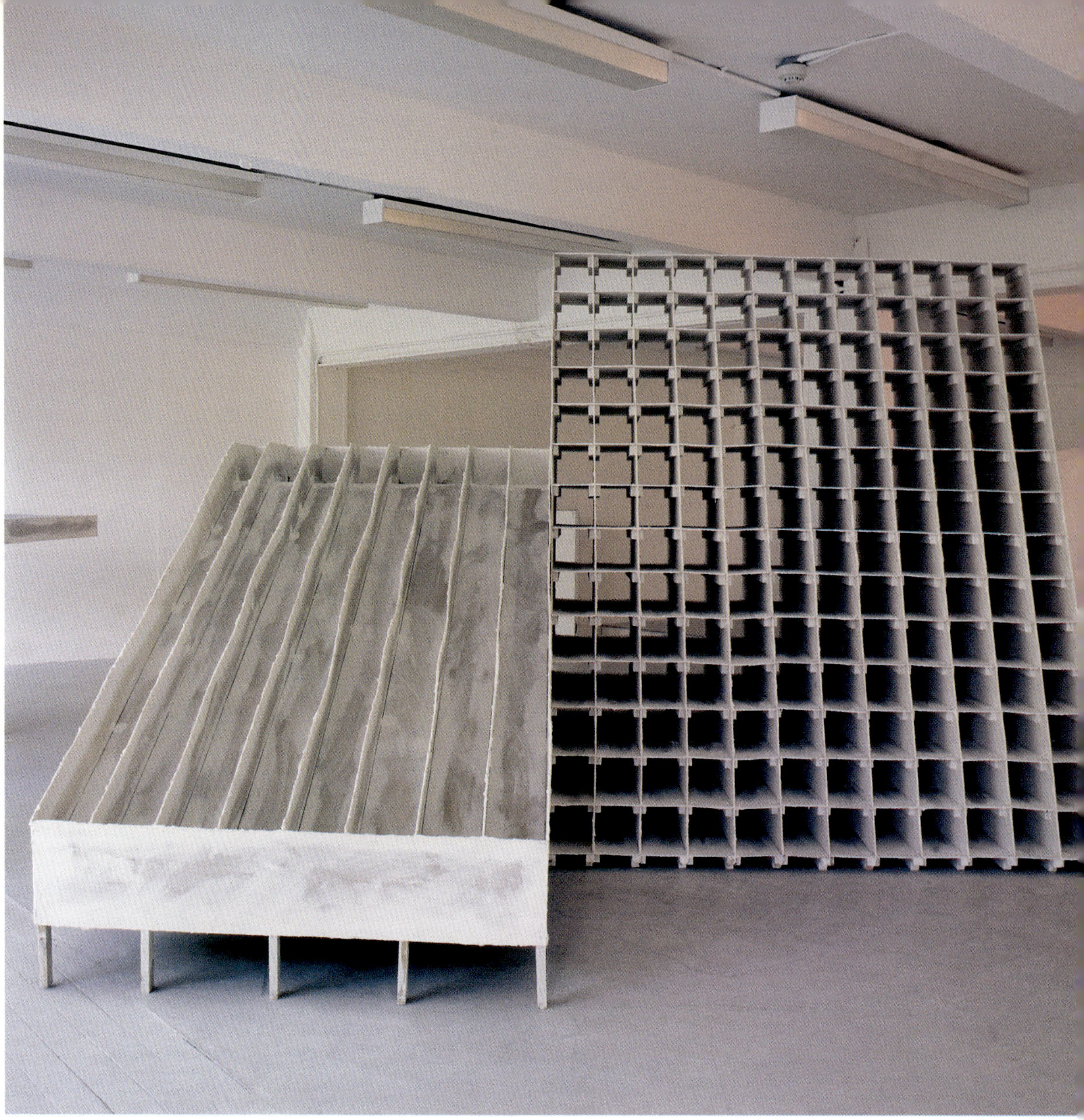

These kinds of questions are typical to encountering Barlow's work. Here, in this instance, it wasn't just a case of walking around this thing to get the gist of it, but of getting on your hands and knees to look under it, and then jumping up and down to try and peep in. Barlow has sometimes used the word 'stalking' to characterise this nosy curiosity that the viewer has to know more about the material constitution and physical construction of a sculpture.[1] Stalking, for Barlow, denotes a kind of persistent interrogation into its presented and staged 'integrity' and 'truth' as an object – sussing out its outsides and insides, its surfaces and innards. If Barlow thinks viewers can give a sculpture a hard time, casing it by stealth and attempting to unravel its artifices, devices and mechanisms, then *Truce* seems to deliberately invite this kind of interrogation – to invite us to take things personally. *Truce* at once asks us to search for that part of a sculpture that is always withheld, and at the same time celebrates and revels in the instruments of withholding and in the deceitful packaging and secretive skins of sculpture. What you see is "what you get", but of course it isn't. Barlow wouldn't want us to have her cake and eat it. In any case, a sculpture is not a cake. This is, as it happens, an important sculptural idea that runs through much of her work.

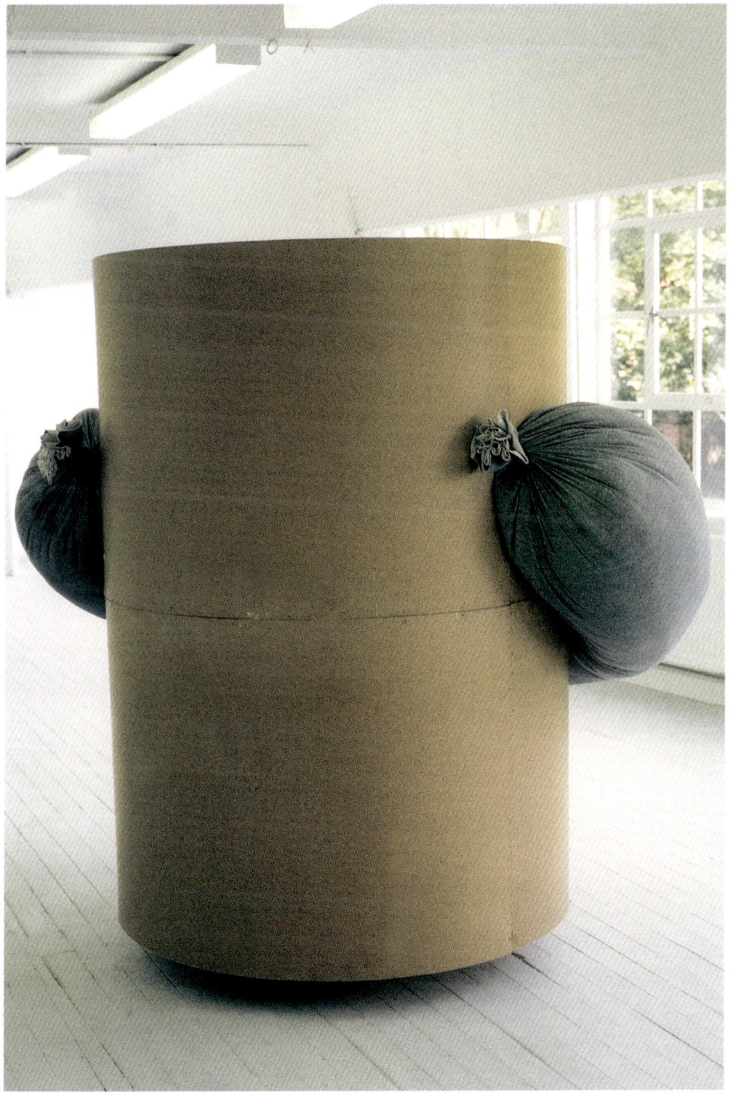

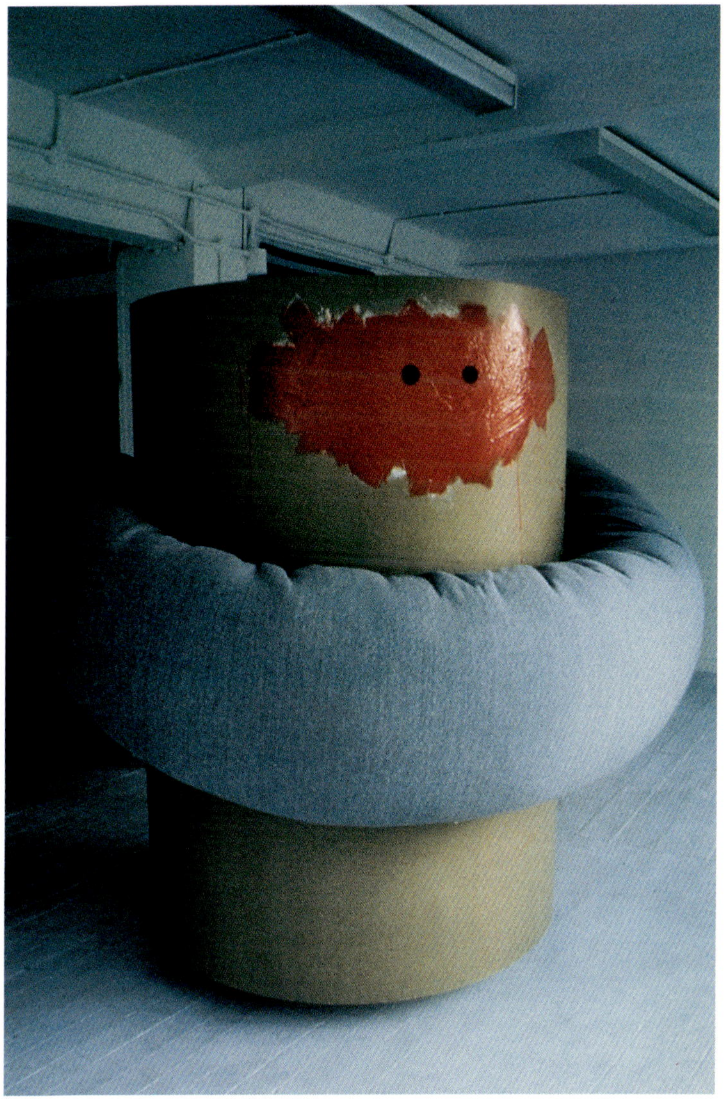

2 Potts, Alex, "Louise Bourgeois – Sculptural Confrontations", *Oxford Art Journal*, 22, 2, 1999, p. 42.

Louise Bourgeois
Nature Study, (Velvet Eyes)
marble and steel
1984

It doesn't, however, end there, for with its two dot eyes, this strange object seems to return the compliment and echo the kind of surveillance and examination that we have subjected it to. Lipchitz's *Figure* also has two dot eyes. Like those of Barlow's *Truce* they stare back at us, keeping watch, monitoring our looks. Painted onto the curve of this cylinder, they look like they could almost follow us around the room. Barlow's black dots on a red face are also warnings and advise us to keep our distance. These eye dots give hers and these other objects an anthropomorphic character and are thus also tricks. They are not holes or openings that allow us to look inside, but markings, dots, circles – signs for eyes, blind spots. It is amazing what two dots can do to and for a thing – as the work of Picasso, Bourgeois and others demonstrates. Bourgeois's *Nature Study, (Velvet Eyes)*, 1984, is one of Barlow's favourites pieces. It is a curiously attention-seeking sculpture, as Alex Potts's description nicely highlights: "The low-lying block has an immediate presence that commands attention as one approaches: it is implacably there, blocking and obstructing one's passage, as well as projecting a strong fixed gaze out into the surrounding space."[2]

All three works exact similar commands, but in different ways, partly courtesy of their material constitution. Lipchitz's is bronze, Bourgeois's is grey marble and Barlow's is board and fabric. None of them are really 'lookers', but each play different games to convince us that they are. Barlow doesn't use bronze or stone; she doesn't carve and she doesn't cast her work in metal. Nevertheless, she has always been very highly sensitive to the expectations that both convey. Her work, and *Truce* is a key example here, is in a way a response to these expectations and to the weight and the myths that such materials and techniques carry. Barlow's work is an ongoing rejection not only of these permanent, hard, inflexible and rigid materials, but also of the symbolic baggage and 'sincerities' that they claim. Bronze is not solid but hollow, and the only thing that is inside stone is stone. There is, in a sense, nothing to look into and yet, "what's in a sculpture?" is Barlow's constant question. It resonates throughout her oeuvre, from the 1960s to today. But the question is not just about "what is inside sculpture?", but ultimately "what's in it?", "what's the point?", "why make it?" and "what is it exactly that sculpture can do... what's it for....?"

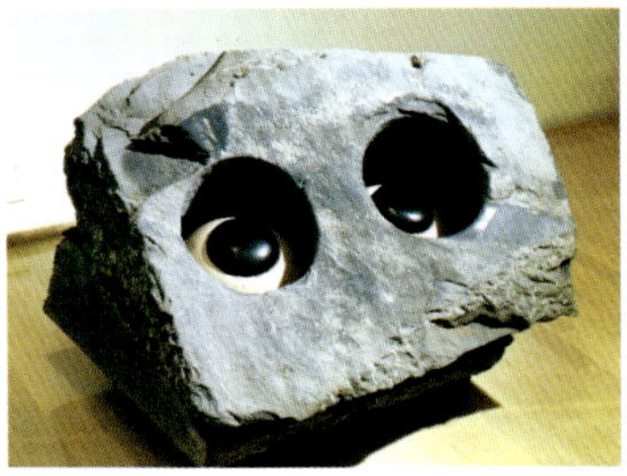

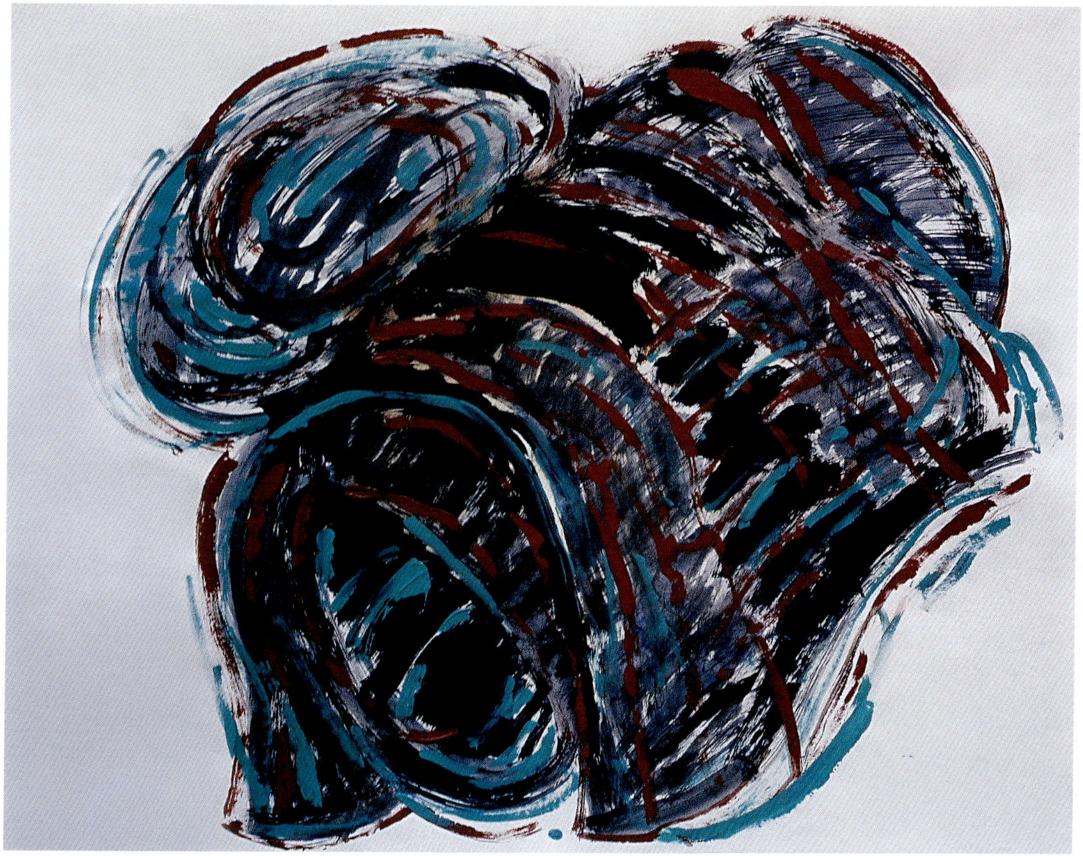

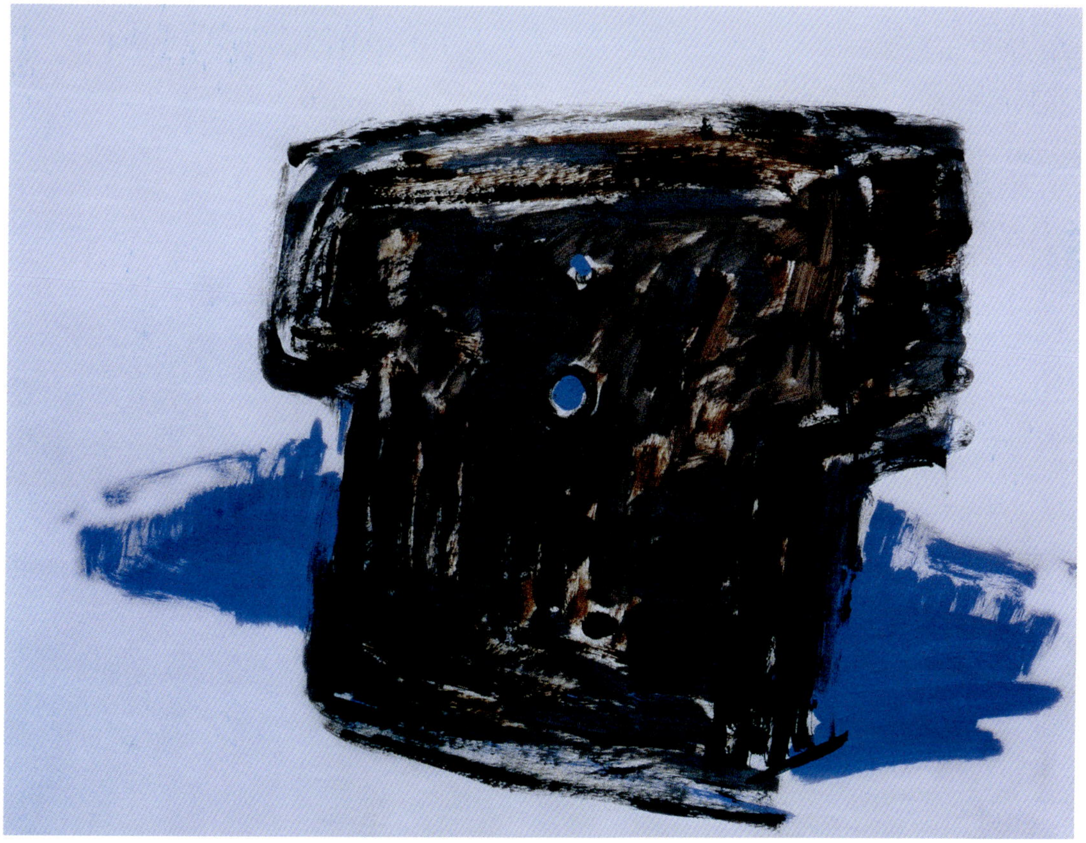

Sculpture in the Making

3 Phyllida Barlow talk at the Henry Moore Institute, Leeds, in the "Studio Lives – Contemporary Views" series, October 2001. This series included talks by Simon Starling, Graham Gussin, Keith Tyson and Keith Wilson.

Interior
Resin impregnated canvas, paint, fibreglass, resin, enamel, paints
180 x 180 x 240 cm
1967

I have an uneasy and very problematic relationship with making.[3]

Barlow is best known for using fabric, but looking at the full range of stuff she uses reveals that her sculpture has a much broader material repertoire. Alongside sheets, blankets, curtains and other fabric material, she has used plastics, linoleums, latex, rubber, wool, string, polythene, cling film, sellotape, aluminium foil, tarpaulin, concrete, glue, plaster and paint. These artificial and synthetic materials have a flexibility and a manipulability that makes them somewhat akin to clay. Though she has, to all intents and purposes, stopped working in clay now, it is a material from which Barlow has learned a great deal and from which much of her work quietly takes its coordinates. She has often described the way she uses materials as being 'like clay', even down to the description of the grey of a foam sheet.[4] Unlike stone carving and metal welding, clay modelling for Barlow is often seen as a "second-rate process" and much underestimated as a result.[5] For Barlow, it is often perceived as being too quick, too easy, too approximative, too sensual, too passé and too 'feminine'.

She was reintroduced to clay whilst a student at Chelsea School of Art by George Fullard, a sculptor whom she has great respect for and fond memories of. Fullard instilled an experimental, personal and highly inquisitive attitude to this traditional studio material in his students. Along with Picasso, Germaine Richier was the sculptor whose take on the stuff he most advocated and quoted: "Clay is hysterical, it reacts to everything: take care when you touch it that it knows what you want."[6] This statement, already past down and across the channel, has stuck with Barlow and has found itself refigured in her own writings (and teachings) about her work, as something which from time to time she has called "reciprocity". The role of the hand is central to this. Barlow takes materials, as she might clay, and works with them, doodles with them, manipulates them. This making process she reads as a two-way one, a process of give and take, in which the material responds, returns, gives and pays back, replicating the actions, gestures and manipulations that she subjects her materials to. The line between 'replication' and 'reciprocation' is a very interesting and difficult one to draw here in Barlow's work and in her reading of it. It reads as a kind of self-regulating, balancing system: you push a bit here and it comes out there, impression and expression. There is always a physical consequence to modelling that the material itself immediately demonstrates and evidences, generating further dialogue and adaptation, further balances and compromises. In clay, such processes leave behind fingerprints, traces of DNA and the personal, physical evidence of being worked upon, embedded in and embodied on the surface of the work.

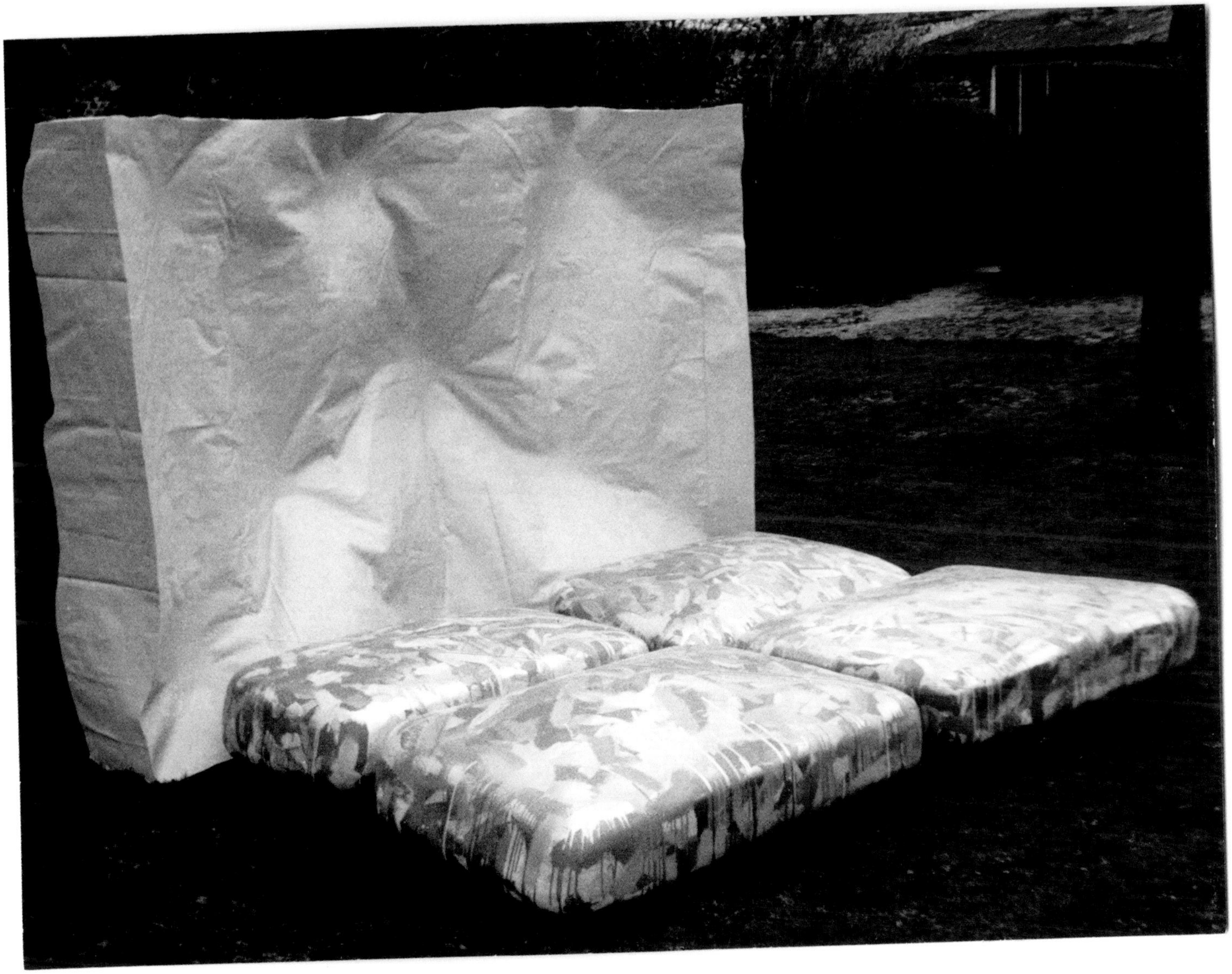

4 In for example, Phyllida Barlow, "Big Bad Ugly", *Cloth, Norwich Documents 01*, Norwich: Norwich School of Art and Design, 1997, pp. 36-41.

5 Phyllida Barlow talk, "Studio Lives – Contemporary Views" series, October 2001.

6 Barlow, Phyllida, "Touching the Past", p. 4. Opening talk given on 6 May 1998 at the Mappin Gallery, Sheffield to coincide with the exhibition *George Fullard: Playing with Paradox.*

7 Quotation from private letter, 20 December 1993.

8 Barlow, Phyllida "The Sneeze of Louise" in Ian Cole, ed., *Louise Bourgeois: Museum of Modern Art Papers*, Volume One, MOMA: Oxford, pp. 4-11.

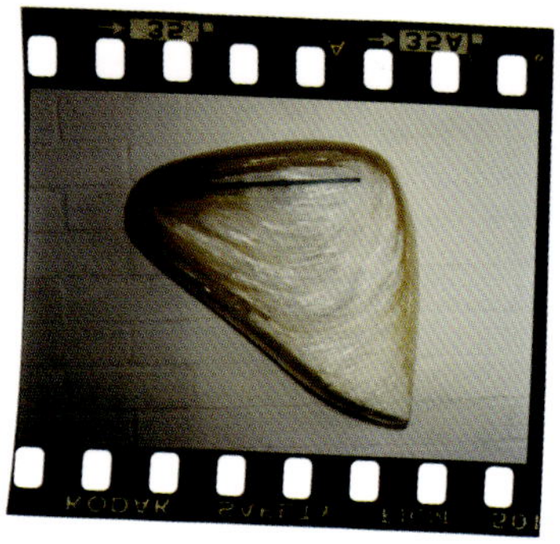

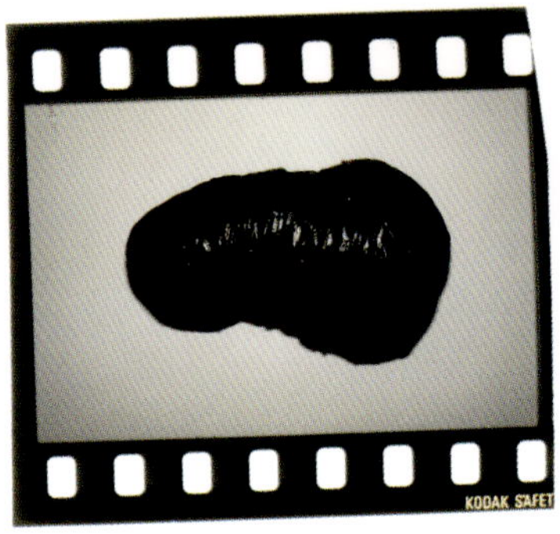

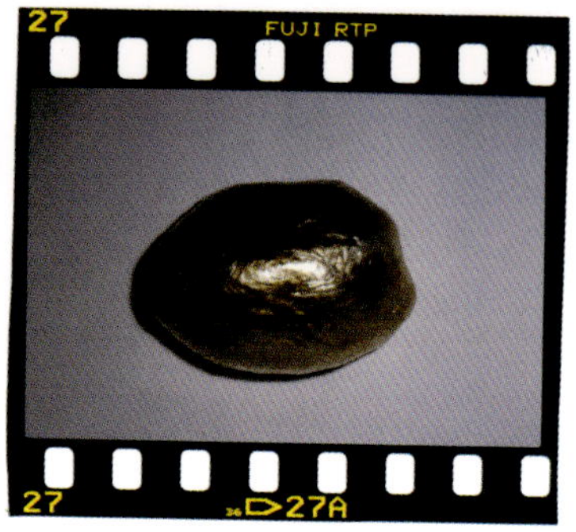

Above from left
Muscle and bone
Kettle's Yard
Sellotape, polythene, glass
20 x 55 x 45 cm
1987

Clench
Bitumen, canvas
20 x 30 x 50 cm
1989
Kapil Jarawala Gallery, London

Torso
1989
Sellotape
20 x 40 x 50 cm
Kapil Jarawala Gallery, London

Barlow's less messy synthetic materials are freed of this organic symbolism, but are nevertheless both worked on with it in mind, and imaginatively folded into the work. (And it is important to say here that I am talking about a more messy handling of clay, not the kind of accumulative 'rabbit dropping' clay modelling favoured by many academic portraitists.) This is not a regressive belief in the animistic life of the material or anything like that, rather one that feels the inside of things is also on the outside: that the surface of a work is where it is at and is not merely a varnish or a garnish to catch the eye. Take, for example, a small series of works from the late 1980s, which include *Muscle-bone*, 1986, *Clench*, 1989, and *Torso*, 1989. These sculptures are all surface: they are built up through layer upon layer of plastic, wrapped around, over, under and into the work. Through repetition these layers have gradually accumulated a thing: the surface(s) is the sculpture. They are partially translucent (teasingly partially transparent) and, as their titles suggest, have a strange corporeal identity, as if imaginary body parts or abstractions of body gestures. The gestural references are highly important because these objects have themselves been modelled and built up through the circular hand and arm actions of wrapping. These objects are, in fact, *replications* of the activity of wrapping; they are what you can get if you do this with your hands with plastic. Pass the parcel for one, on rewind. Wrapping has taken the place of modelling, but as a kind of surrogate process. It is telling that Barlow herself describes the achievement of this way of making with reference to temperature, as a kind of "freezing of process". They are 'hot' with 'just done' life, but once done, once 'finished', are then 'cold' concretisations, fossils, records and documents. This does not mean they are failures, rather that they are bursting with memory and (most importantly) that nothing, for Barlow, quite beats the heat: the raw, unformed, messy, unresolved and uncontrolled forms, energies and actions of making.

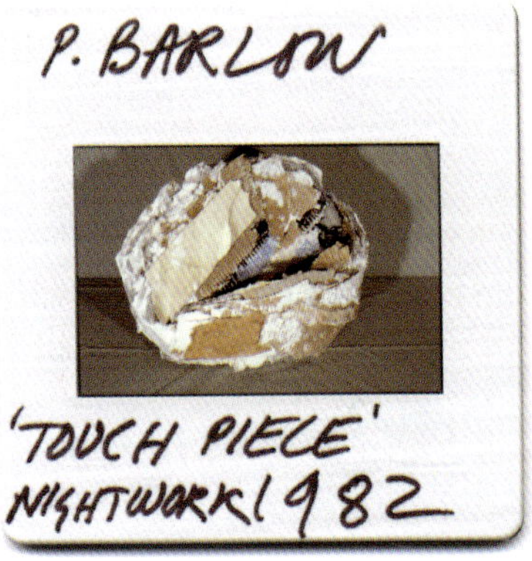

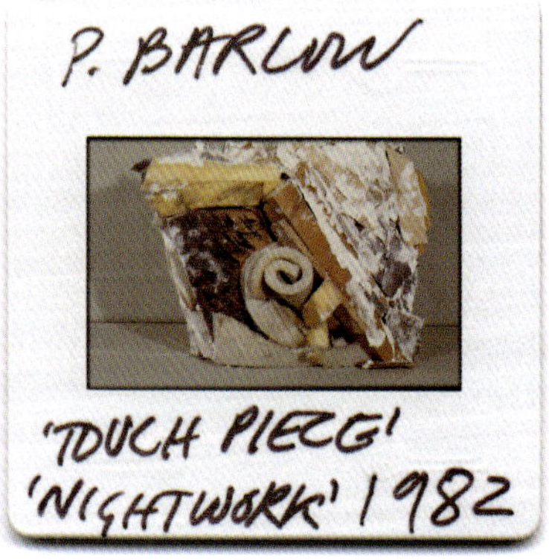

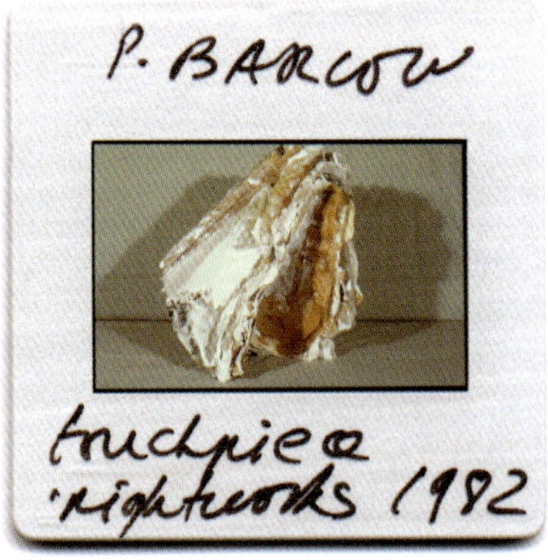

Below from left
Nightwork series
Touchpiece I
1982

Nightwork series
Touchpiece II
1982

Nightwork series
Touchpiece III
1982

Closed (Vigil ii)
Gloss paint, paper, timber frames, fabric, latex
80 x 40 x 360 cm and
450 x 240 x 450 cm
1991
RIBA, Great Portland Street, London, W1

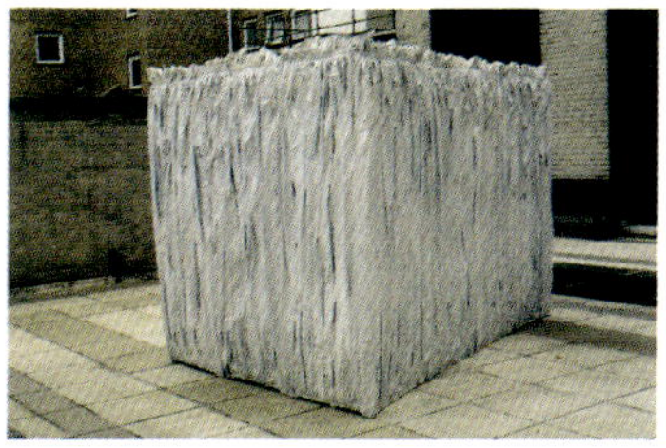

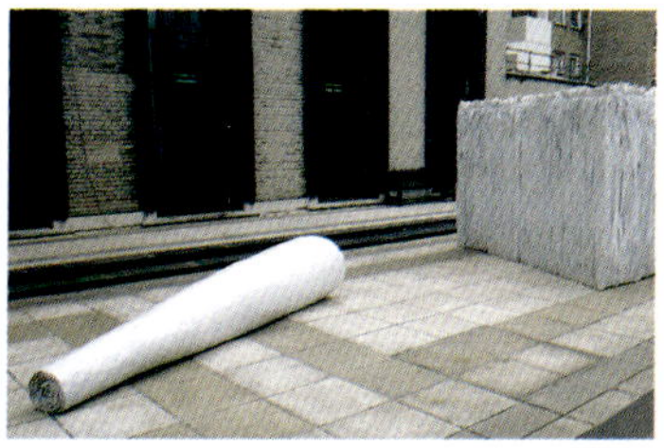

At times, Barlow's work seems to have tried to capture or 'replicate' the heat of raw and uncontrollable processes with the most minimal of touches and restraint. Her early 1980s *Touchpiece* works (from the "Nightwork" series) are a good example of this. These sculptures have not been built up layer by layer, skin by skin, but sandwiched and jammed together piece by piece in a haphazard and self-perpetuating, crazy-paving assemblage way. These are unpredictable works whose unpredictability is borne out of experimentation, from learning by trial and error, as it and she goes along. The blind leading the blind (another of her favourite Bourgeois'). This is a deliberately strategy, as Barlow herself has said: "In challenging my own 'hands on' practice I have recognised the need to root my activity in experimentation determined by my own intentions and inventions. The unpredictability of experimentations seems to be some kind of antidote to dogmatic methodologies."[7] The alliance of the *Touchpiece* works is a tentative but strong one, each dunked piece held together by their paint and paste soaked and sodden parts. This is a typical technique of Barlow's: glue and paint are often used 'like clay' (or indeed plaster), lavishly, as a sculptural material of conjunction, keeping layers of newspaper or slabs of foam together. Painting can be a kind of sculpture: impregnating material with liquid that dries, joins and becomes integral. This is something we also find in *Closed*, 1990, *Undercover*, 1996, *Stand Off*, 1996 and *Recall*, 1996. Though very different, Barlow's *Touchpieces* are also reminiscent of Fullard's assemblages. "Before you must use a nail, you must reinvent it", Fullard used to say to his students, quoting Picasso. Barlow reinvented the nail by not using it. No more nails.

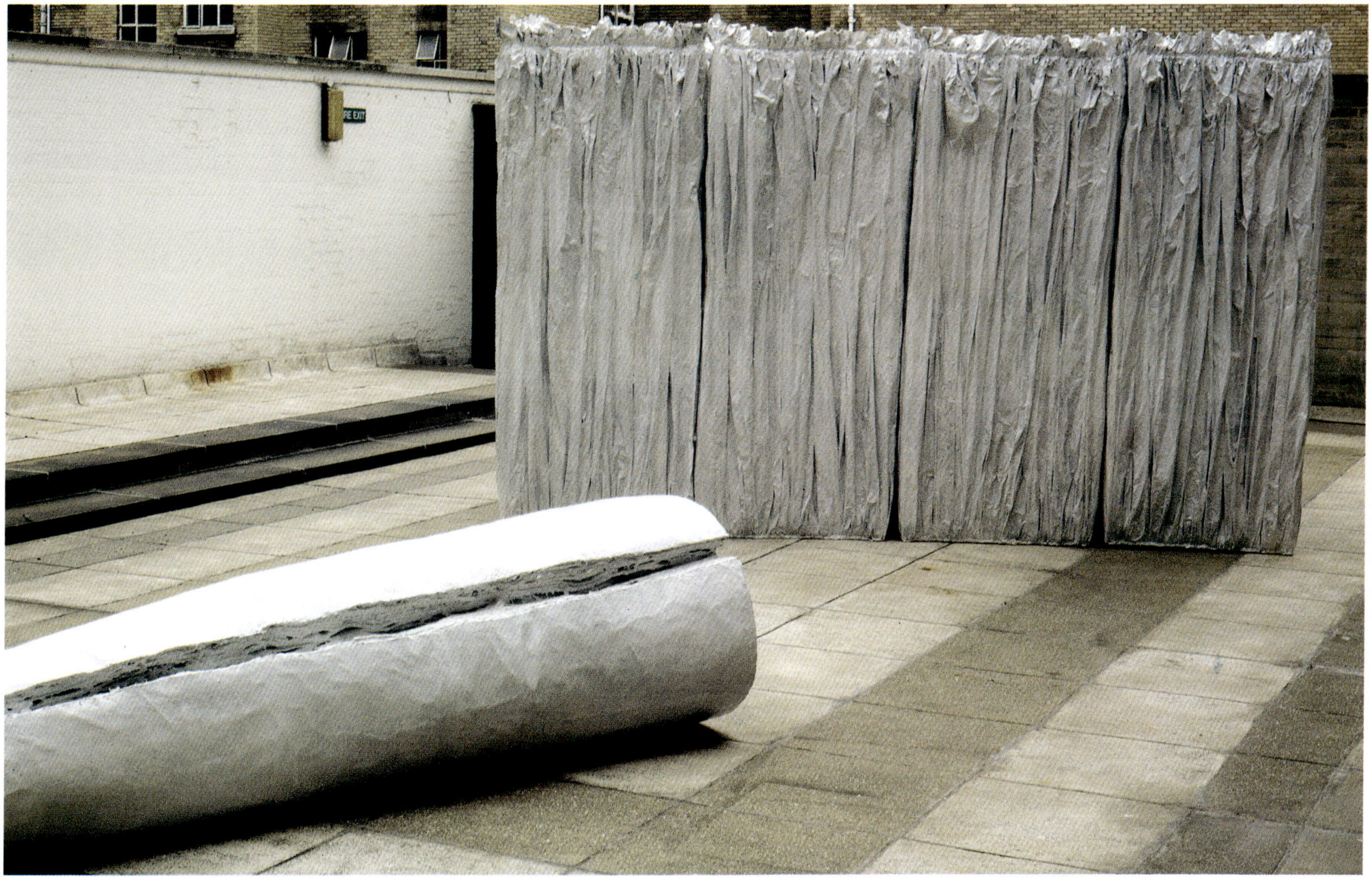

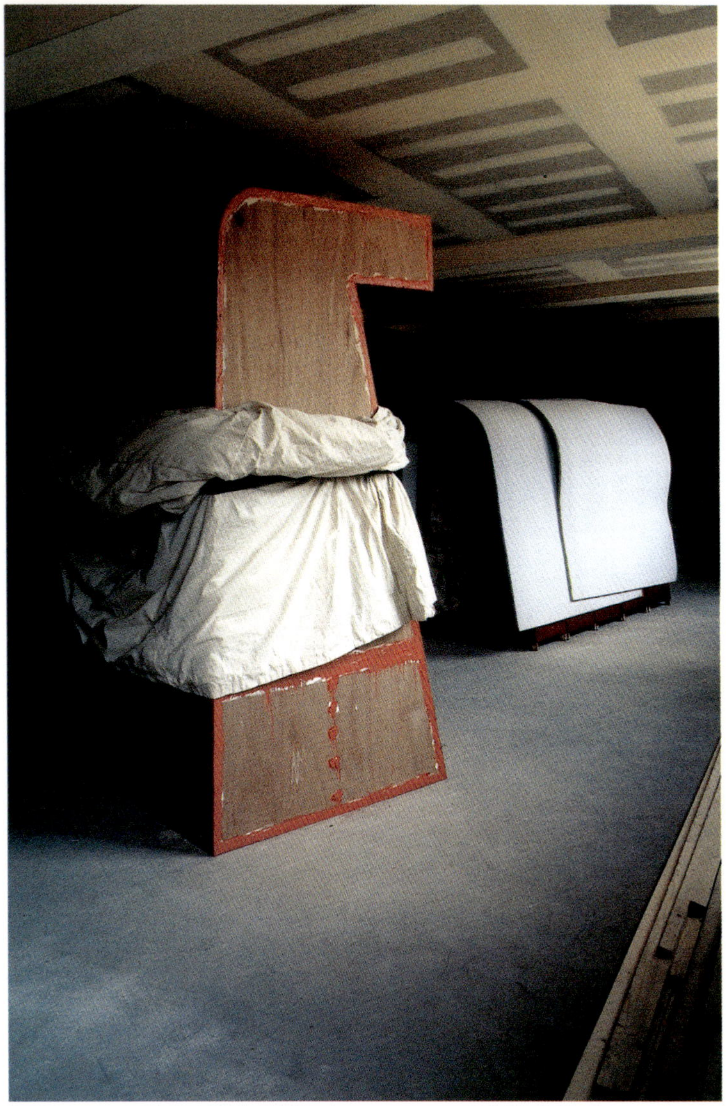

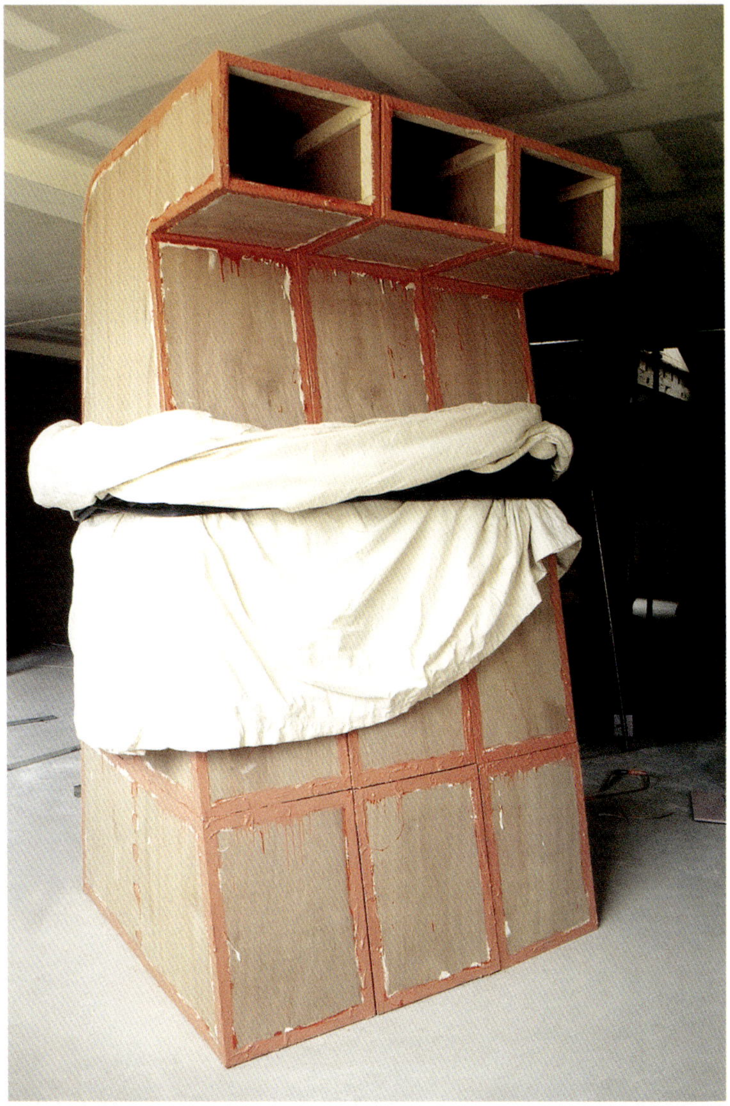

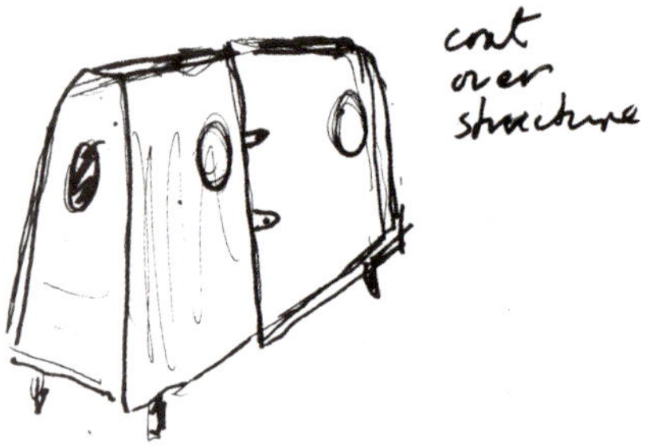
coat
over
structure

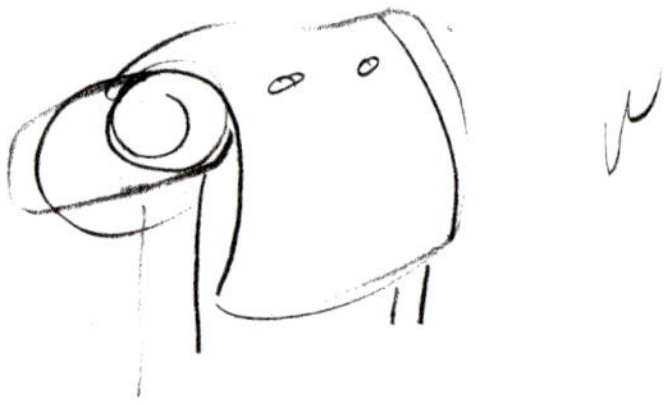

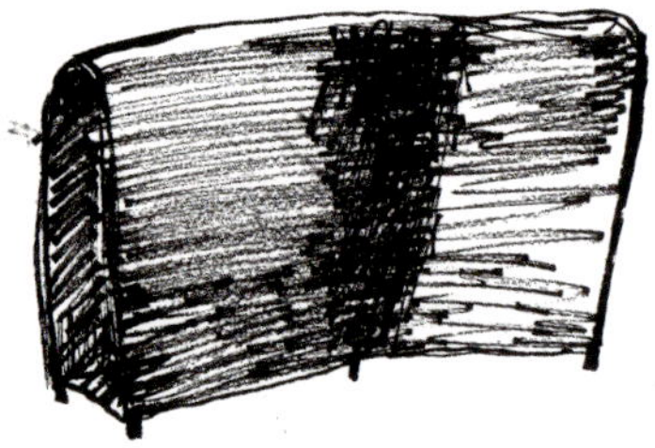

Undercover
Painted, plywood, canvas,
rubber tubing, upholstery foam,
paint stripper, hardboard
Each work: 180 x 300 x 200 cm
and 180 x 600 x 270 cm
1996
Manhattan Lofts, Bankside, London

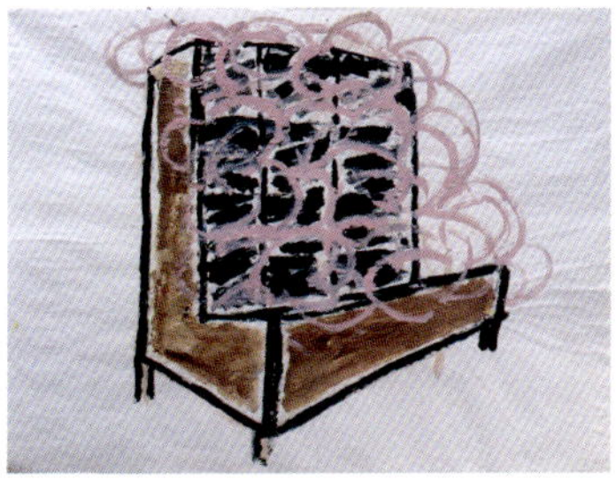

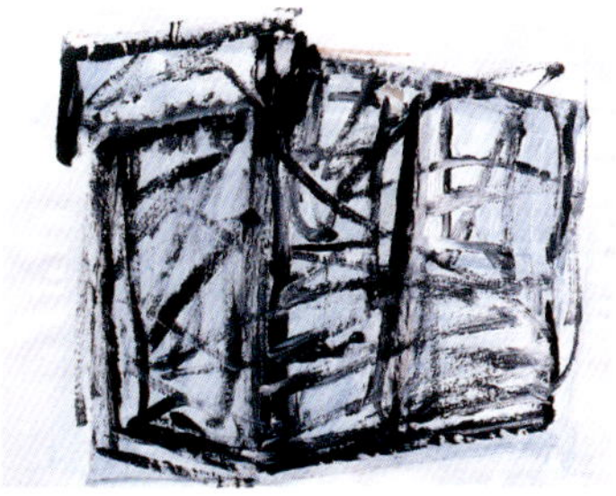

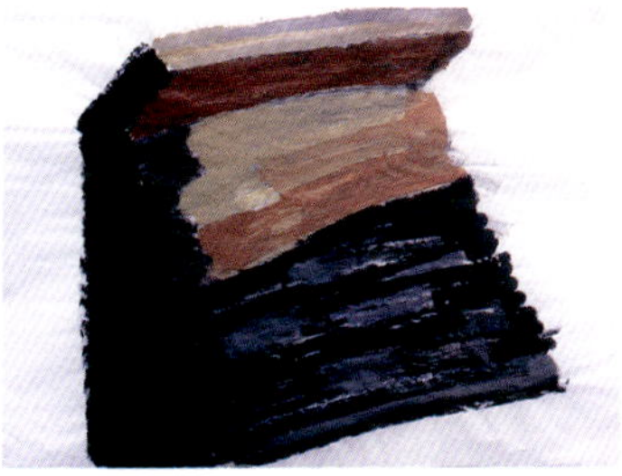

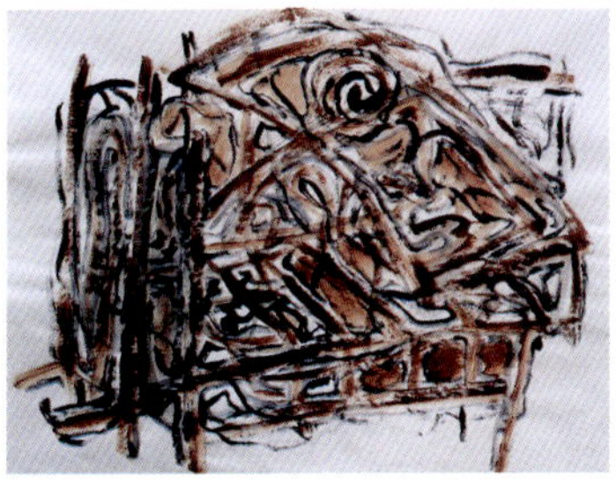

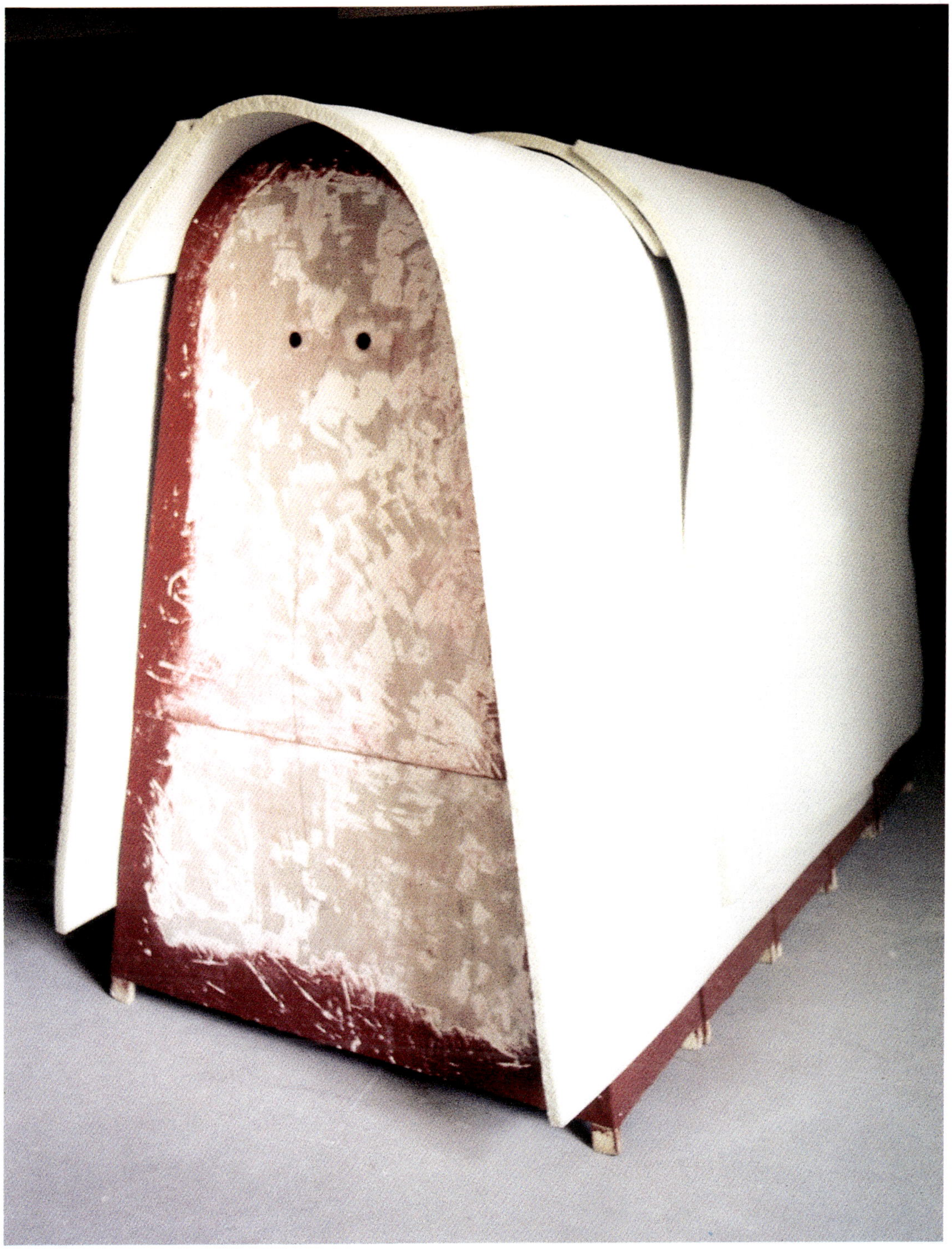

Some have linked such experimental practice to her materials being 'ephemeral'. I don't think her materials are ephemeral at all. What is ephemeral about foil, latex or foam? Are these any more ephemeral than plaster, that traditional sculptural material? I think that she just isn't interested in hanging on to things once they are done, or in spending time and money keeping them on a drip. True, Barlow does a bit of recycling, a bit of reincarnation work here and there, but she isn't interested, really, in storing these cumbersome and friable things once they've come to the end of their journeys, once they have had their moment.

Sculpture is thus, for Barlow, about doing things and about making, and many of her sculptures are, in turn, about making and doing. This is one of the reasons why Barlow has such a profound anxiety about the ready-made. The ready-made is too untransformed and unmediated – at once too premature and too posthumous. It can be arrived at too instantly and can be finished too late – just 'by adding water'. It not only short-cuts, but also expels all 'hands-on' processes of thinking and making. It is a mean art: finders-keepers. The ready-made can, for Barlow, be at once too sexless and too precious a thing, as her writing on Duchamp serves to remind us.[8]

This is not to say that Barlow does not use short cuts in her own work. On the contrary, the idea of reciprocity *entails* short cuts, experimentation and immediate, direct application. Her 1998 dialogue with Alison Wilding, "At Sea: A Conversation by Fax", provides excellent insight into her thoughts on these issues. The collected faxes of both sculptors have a wonderfully raw and diaristic quality to them. At one point Barlow asks: "More about making: Isn't the desperation and urgency something to do with finding the shortest route for an act of making: to be economic with craft, if not with time or labour?" In between these impatient lines we find not only a snub to the passionless, asceticism of ready-made 'makers', but also to the sweaty and smug, macho work ethic of the male sculptor, a real and stereotypical figure that Barlow has struggled with for years.

She positions herself between the 'mean' ready-mades & the smug, macho male sculptor.

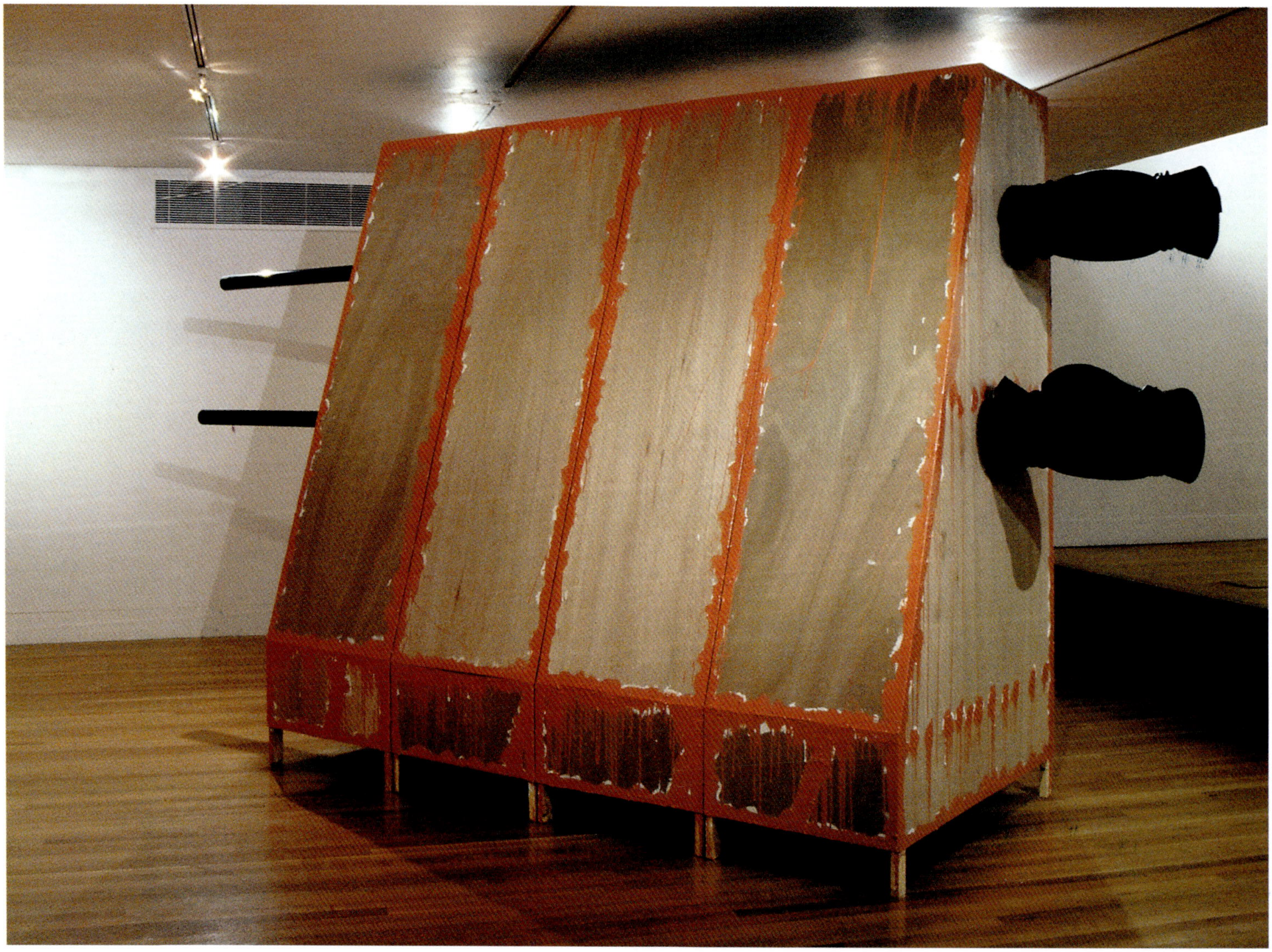

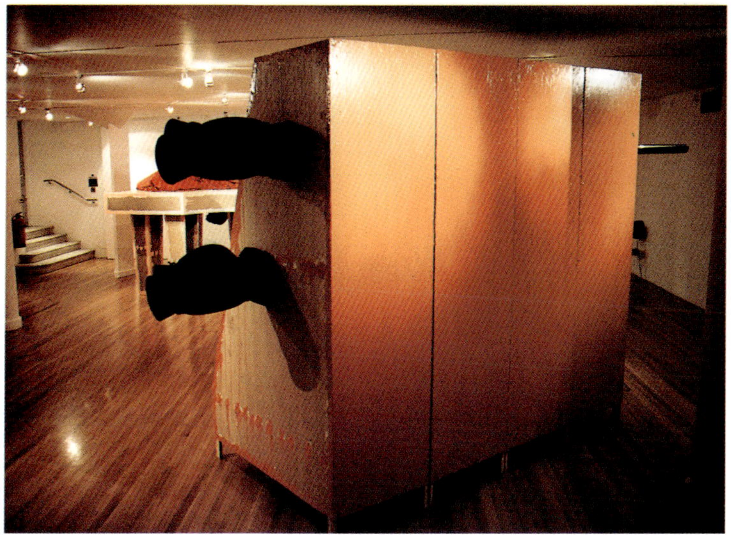

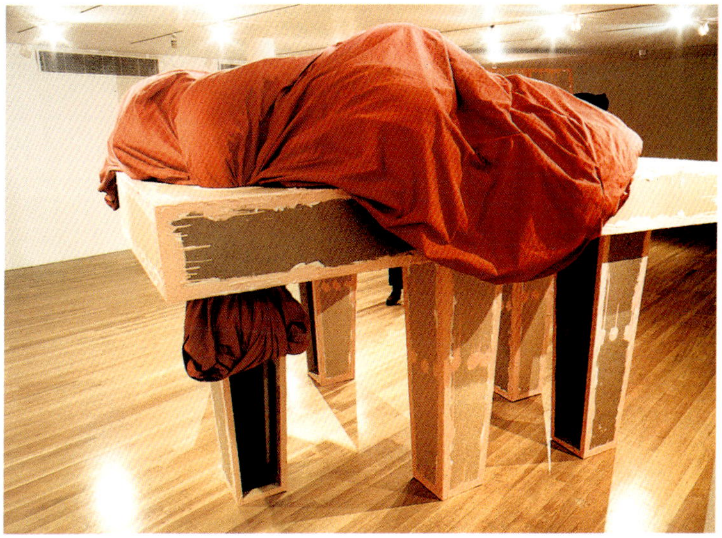

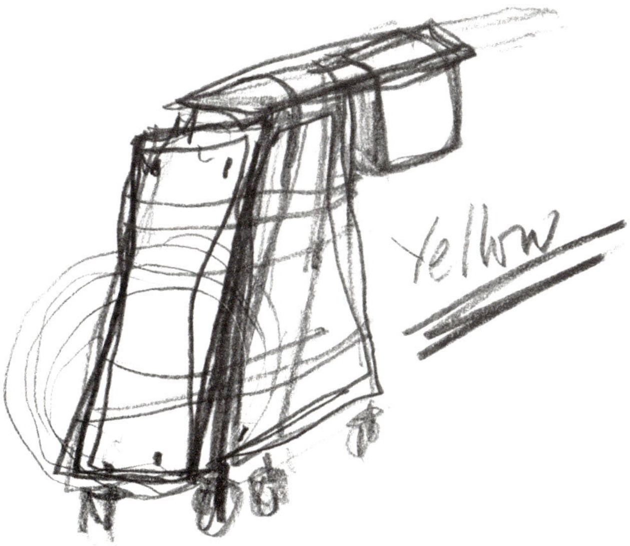

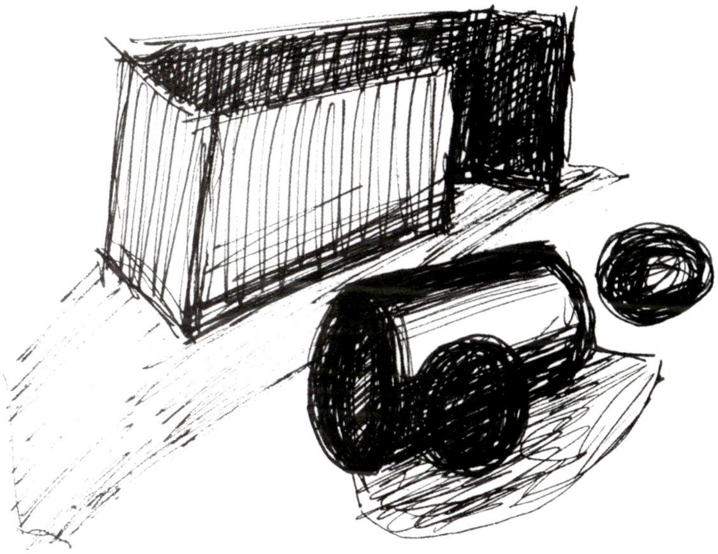

Stand Off
Paint, plywood, hardboard, red fabric, rubber tubing, plastic pipe, upholstery foam
Opposite and top left:
300 x 180 x 400 cm
Top right: 180 x 210 x 400 cm
1996
Henry Moore Galleries,
Royal College of Art, London

Recall
Painted hardboard, painted plywood, fabric, cord, plaster over wire netting
Overall of space / work:
900 x 360 x 1200 cm
1996
Marshall's Mill, Dean Clough, Halifax

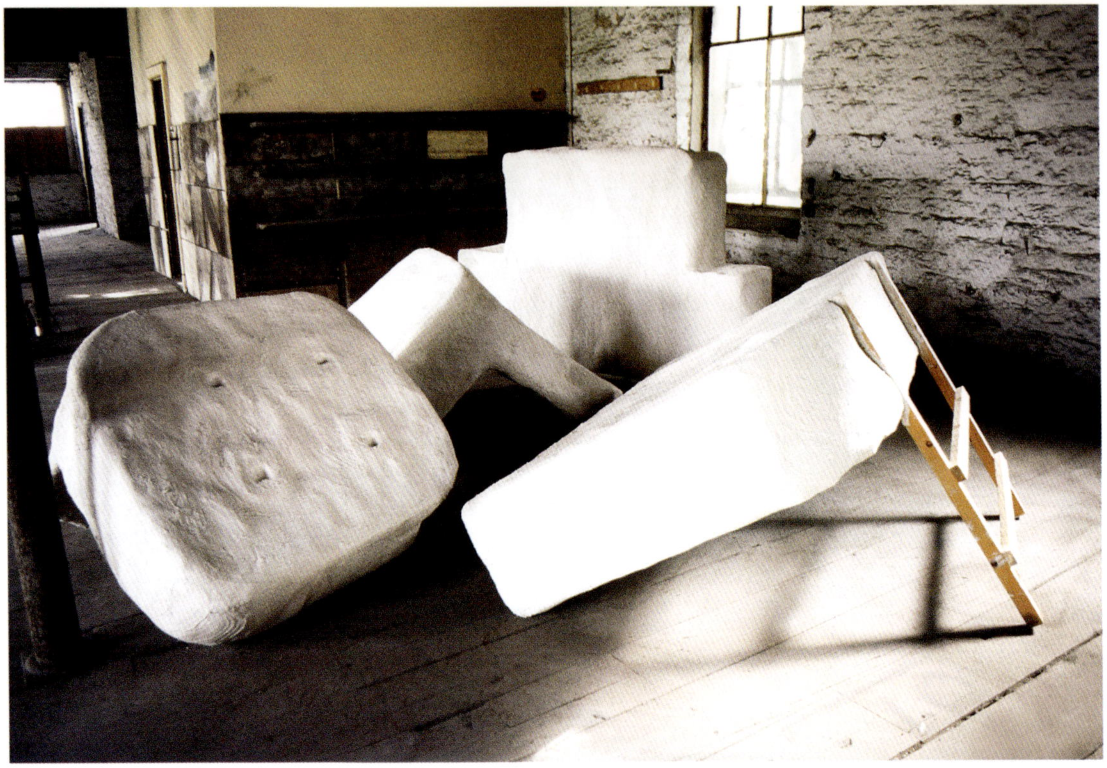

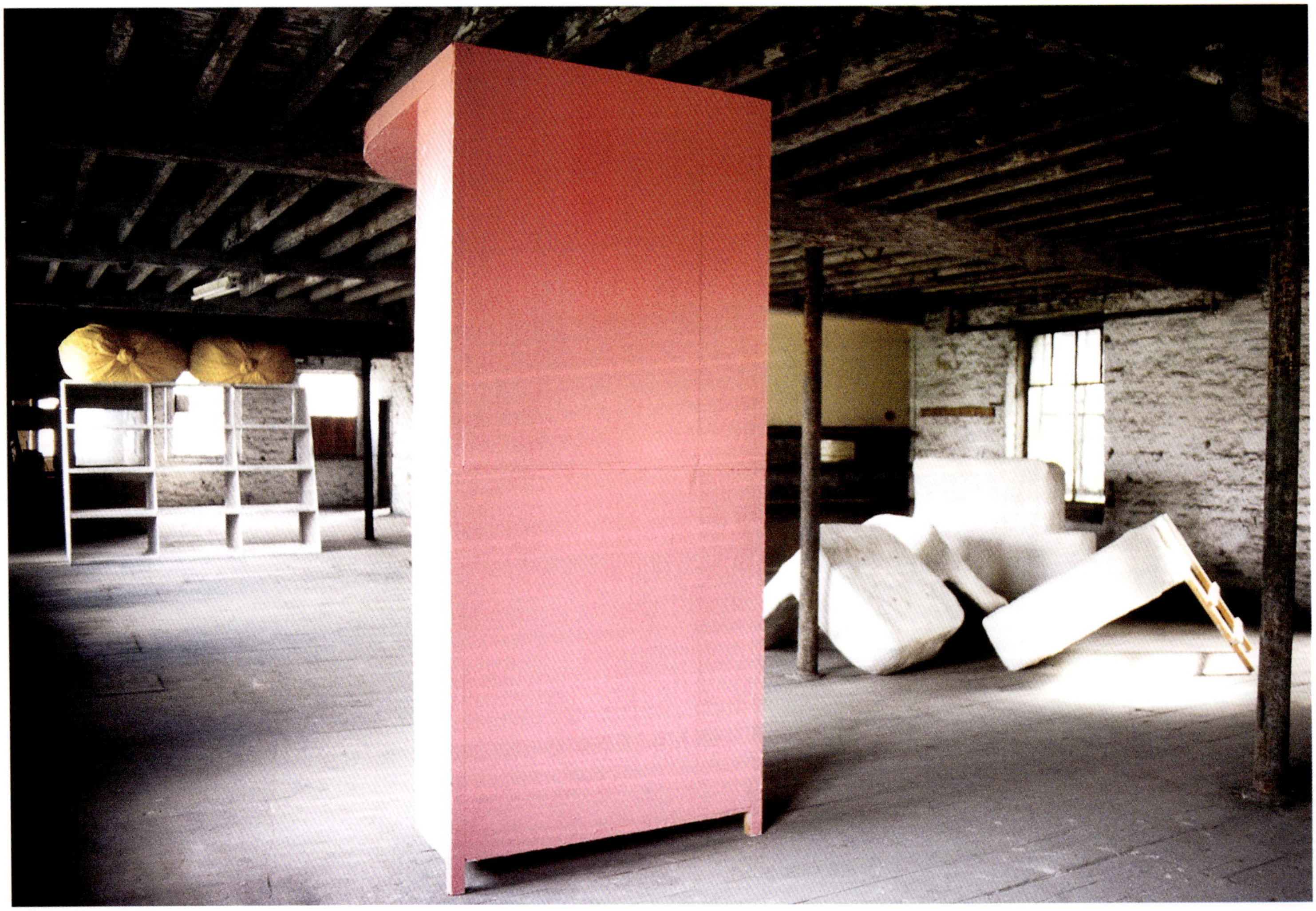

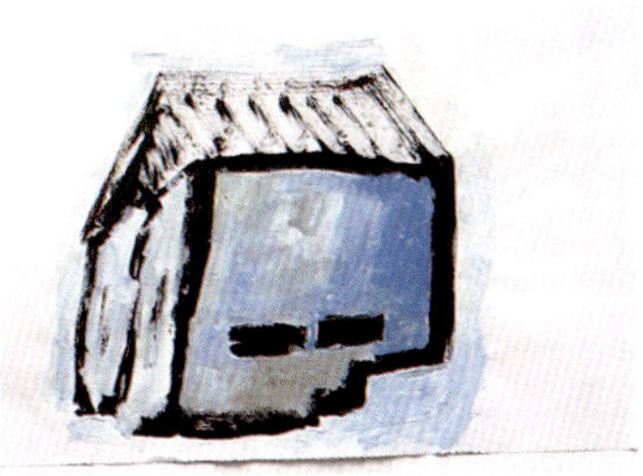

To this end, Barlow often creates sculptural body using components that either already contain volume, presence and space or that can be hung, draped, folded, bent, twisted, looped, rolled, ruffled or plumped up to suggest them. It is a knowing, deliberate and purposeful 'cheating', as we have seen with *Truce*, and its nods and winks can be spotted in works such as *Engulf*, 1987, *Oracle*, 1987, *Storm*, 1987 and *Vigil*, 1989. There is also an excited, cavalier flamboyance to such strategies. 'Exuberance' is a word that Barlow has often used to describe a mood in sculpture in Britain in the early 1980s. I think 'exuberance' is at the heart of this flamboyance in Barlow's work: in her hands, it is a kind of lavish and overflowing material abundance. Exuberance is part of reciprocity, yet here with this idea, there is necessarily a shift from the small-scale to the large-scale. Exuberance is not hand-held: that's the point. Two works in particular demonstrate this sensibility: *Expanse*, 1987 and *Seam*, 1990, one indoors and the other outdoors. *Expanse* is an indoor landscape of plastics and fabrics, gathered, flounced and pleated together in interlocking layers. The layers of grey, black, brown and white materials are packed together, but billow in and out like tiny sails, giving the whole heap of stuff a gorgeous life of its own. It has a rhythm and a movement that leads the eye from left to right, up, across and down. The entire work is generously crammed with creases, folds, hollows, bulges and protuberances that make it dance with real and imaginary volumes, and play hide and seek with our perceptions. The excessiveness of this work, curiously however, is connotative of what is piled up below ground, as much as what is piled above, since *Expanse* has a powerfully geological and archaeological appearance. It is like a trench dug up, replicated and approximated, and moored above ground to the gallery floor.

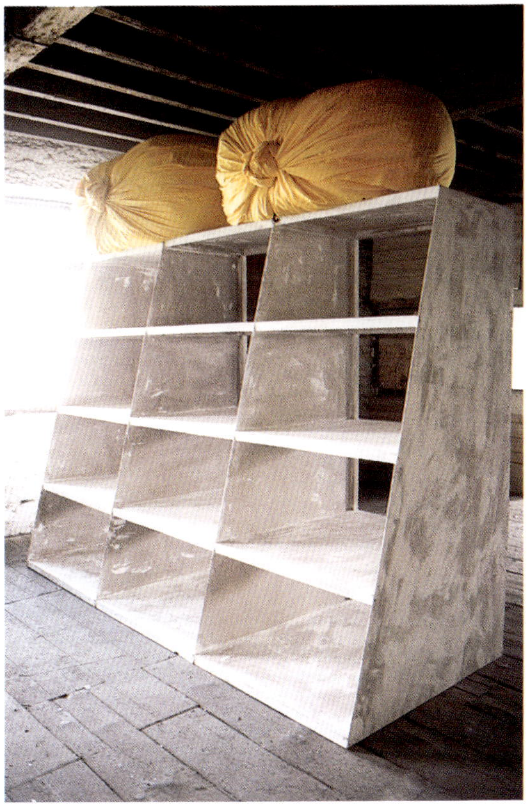

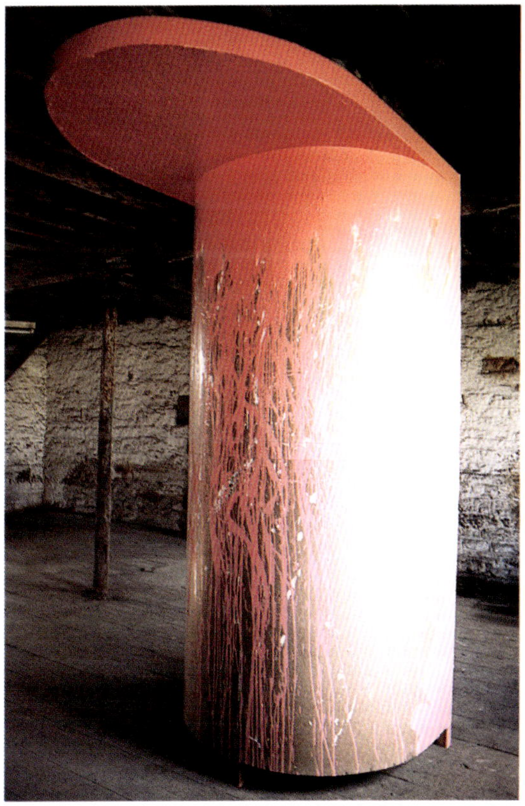

Expanse
Polythene, PVC, carpet felt, paper, upholstery foam
200 x 300 x 1500 cm
1987
Unit 7, Peckham Road, London

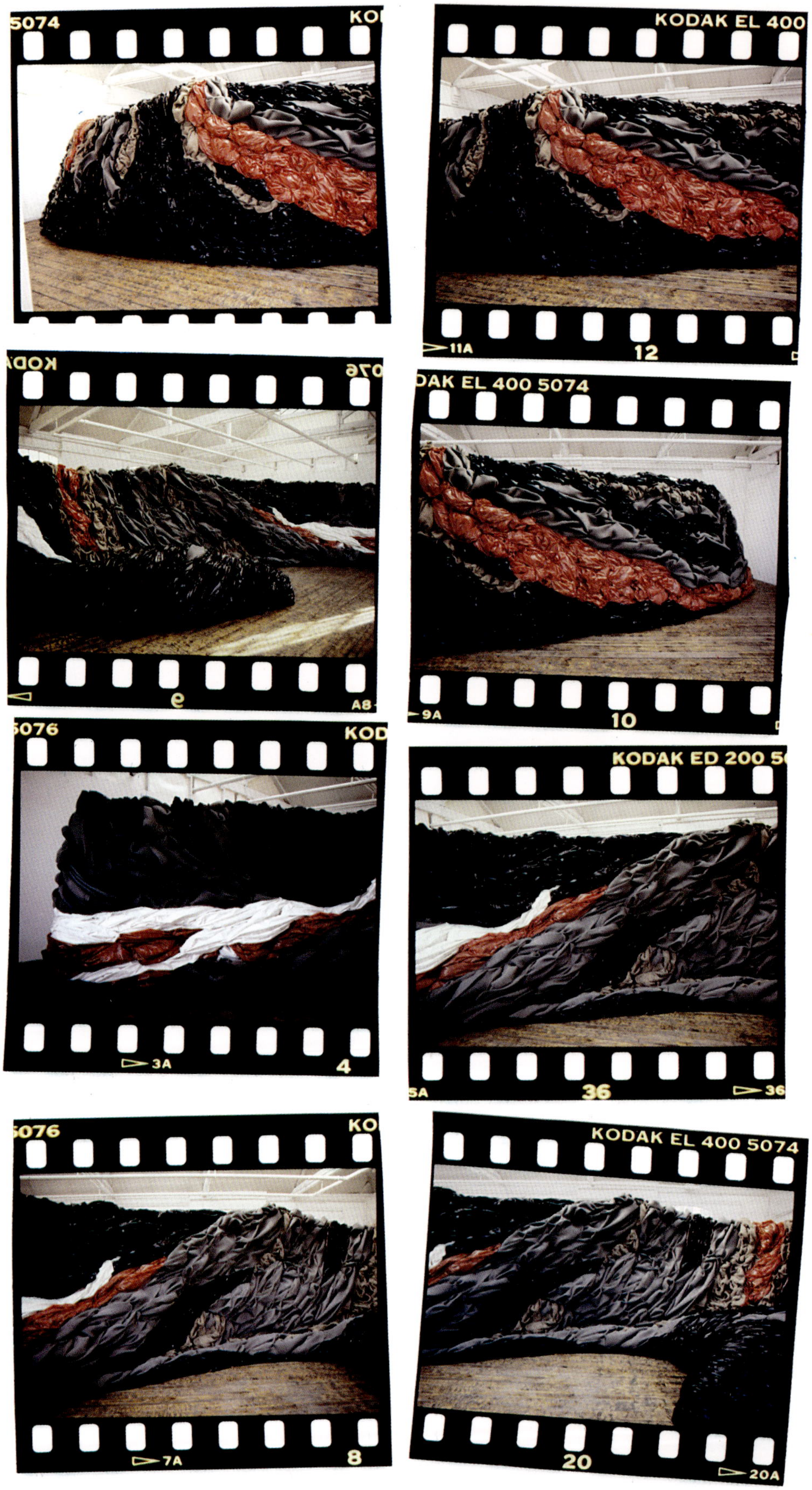

Engulf
Black polythene, tape,
upholstery foam, plywood, cord,
white knotted handkerchiefs
Overall of space:
900 x 240 x 1200 cm
1987
Cornerhouse, Manchester

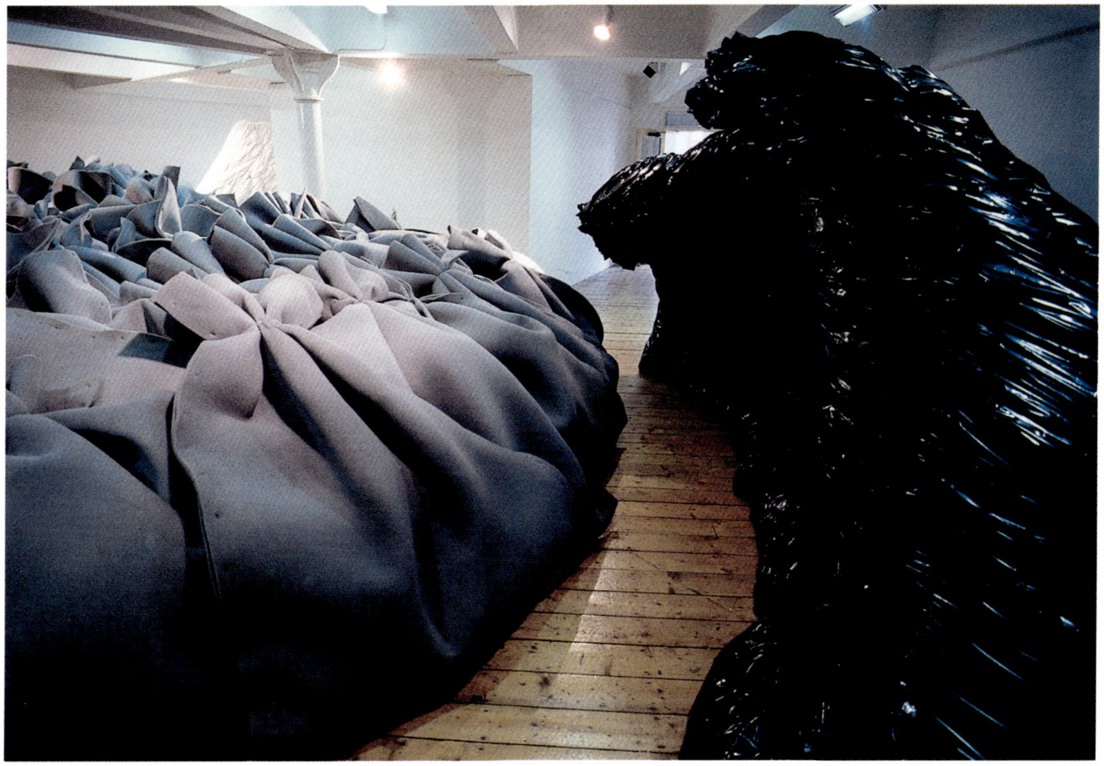

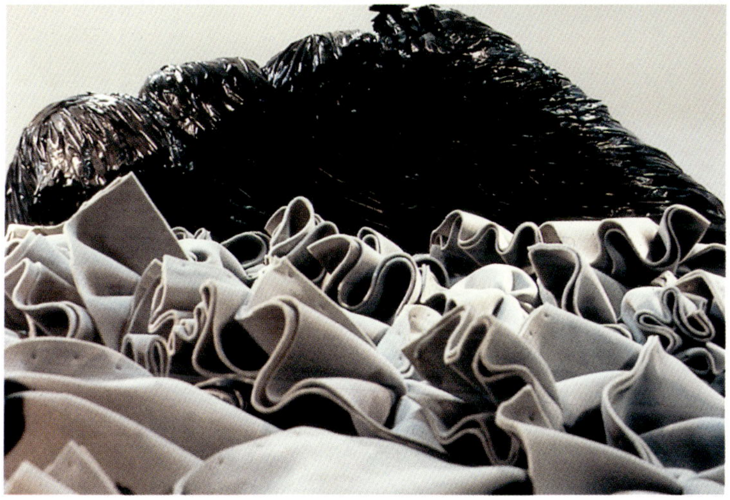

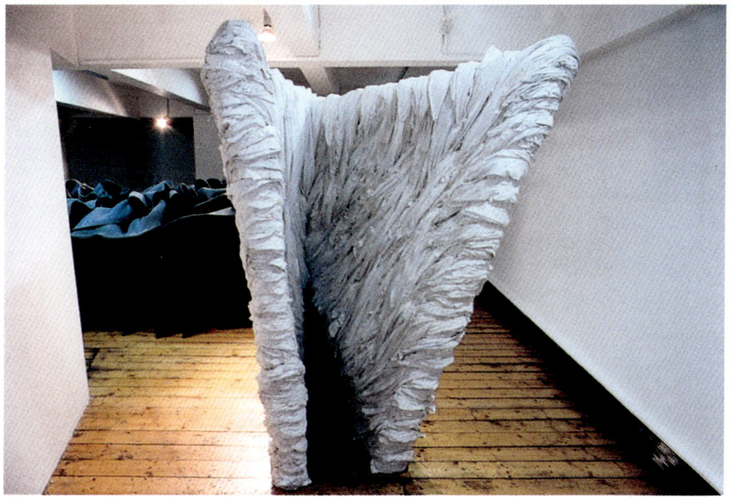

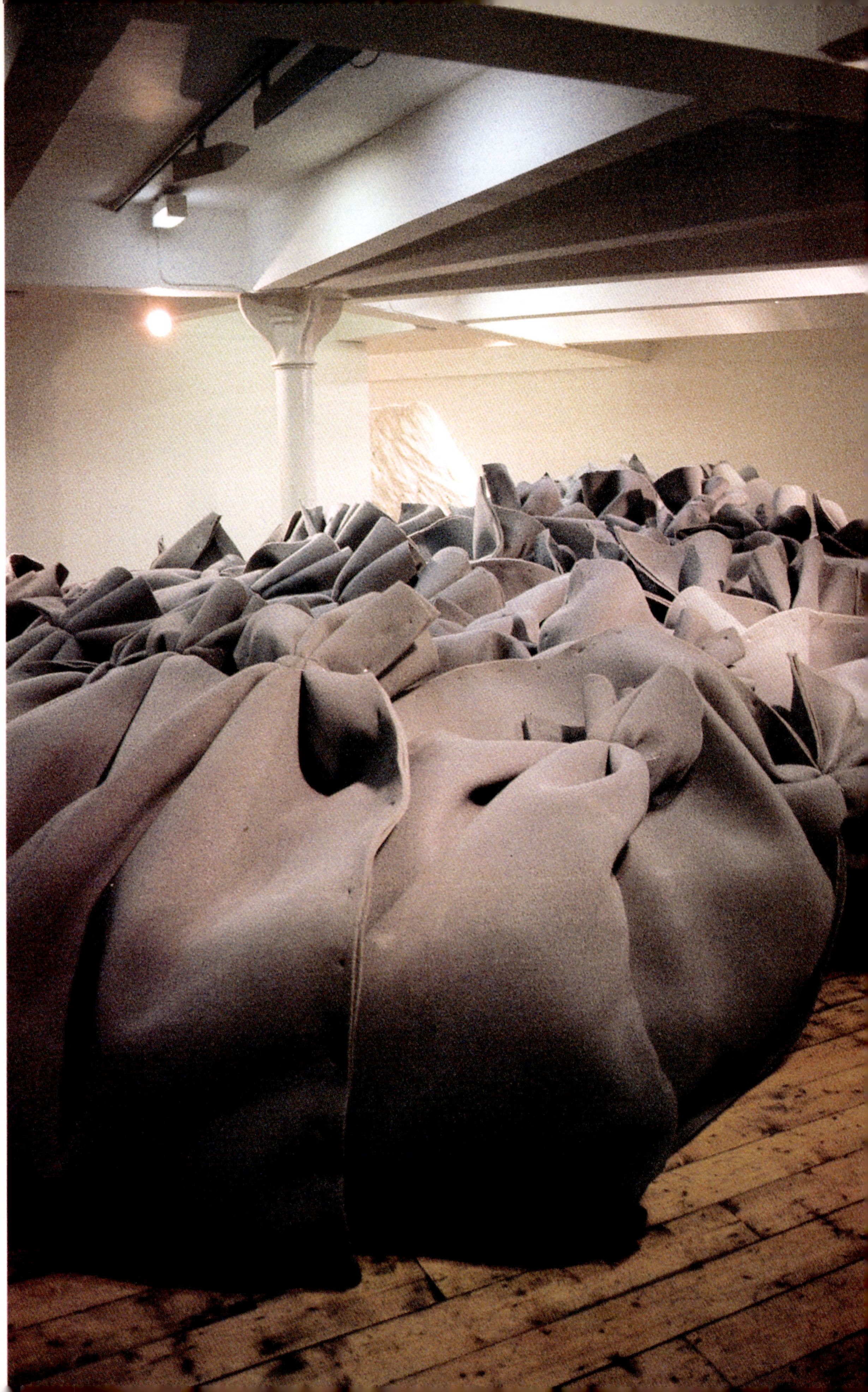

In *Seam*, 1990, made in Gateshead three years later, the archaeological metaphor was taken a step further. *Seam* was a curtain wall of plasticised gold foil, which was supported underneath (and along its entire stretch) by a wooden structure and pinned into the ground with large tent hooks. *Seam* was placed onto a long mound of clinker which had been cosmetically enhanced with a layer of turf. Barlow, as she has recalled, was struck by this 'polite' gesture and in turn by the sound and sensation of walking on top of this grassy mound, hearing and feeling the clinker underneath. *Seam*, her response to this outdoor sculpture-park invitation, was born out of this experience. Rather than dig up the grass, she decided to crown it with a gold foil curtain, highlighting and celebrating what was lying beneath. It was a poignant and ceremonial gesture, rare in public art of the time.

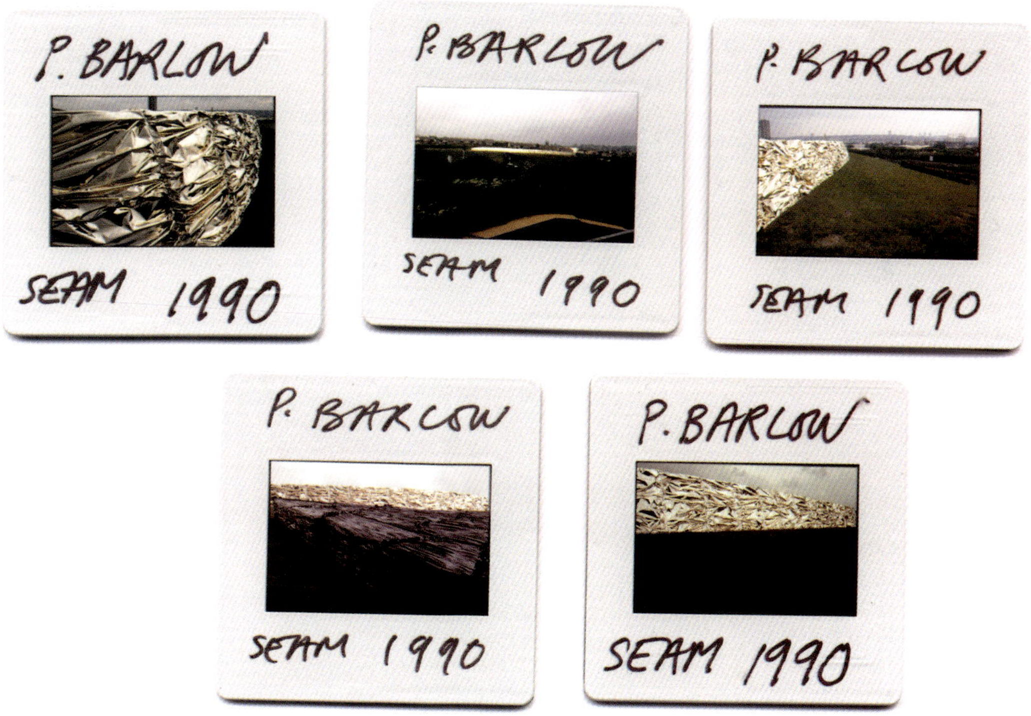

Seam
Gold PVC foil, timber frames, staples, stretched black polythene
200 x 120 x 3000 cm and
600 x 100 x 1200 cm
1990
National Garden Festival, Gateshead

The studio and its enemies

9 **Barlow**, "The Hatred of the Object", pp. 24-25.

10 Barlow, "The Hatred of the Object", p. 31.

11 Barlow, "The Hatred of the Object", p. 31.

> For me, the studio is deeply important: emotionally and practically. But it speaks trouble, and although I would not, could not, have it any other way, it can seem to be a shaming thing to be lumbered with, as if the party is going on elsewhere.[9]

For Barlow there is an inextricable link between object making and the studio. The two go together like fish and chips and newspaper. She has written a great deal about the studio and what it means to her, and is highly sensitive to its mythology, its murky history and its career enhancing operations. Perhaps her most interesting (and amusing) reading of the status and function of the studio can be found in an essay called "The Hatred of the Object" published in 1995. In it she argues that the "Hatred of the Object is manifested through the mistrust and abdication of the studio. The demise of the studio equates with a shunning, a hatred of the object."[10] Barlow sets up two kinds of traditional studios, "the enlightened studio" and "the grim studio". The latter is a place of routine, rules and regulations, education and labour, the former is what Barlow sees and hopes her own studio to be like:

> In the enlightened studio curiosity is fundamental to how ideas are explored, manifested through the physical manipulation of material, privately and intimately, where there is a slow evolution of processes, intellectual and practical, involving experimental approaches to concepts, techniques, forms and aesthetics. My experience of such a studio is that the artist is at the centre of this self-created world, independently selecting and discarding, and in control of the development and eventual showing to the outside world of their individual expression.[11]

Barlow's defence of the studio is thus a defence of the making of sculpture. But there is more to it than this. The studio is not just a private, intimate place and space to get on with things, but is an environment which feeds into the meaning and making of her work. It is not just about scale (you can only make something as big as you can get in and out of your studio): it bespeaks a mood, an atmosphere, a vibe and a value and is there embedded in the work she makes. The studio is implicated in the work: Barlow's sculpture evokes studio ruminations and is packed with indoor life. Her work is full of motifs of containment and enclosure, which is effectively what a studio is.

Tent
Canvas, timber, paint, resin, fibreglass, found objects
150 x 210 x 150 cm
1967

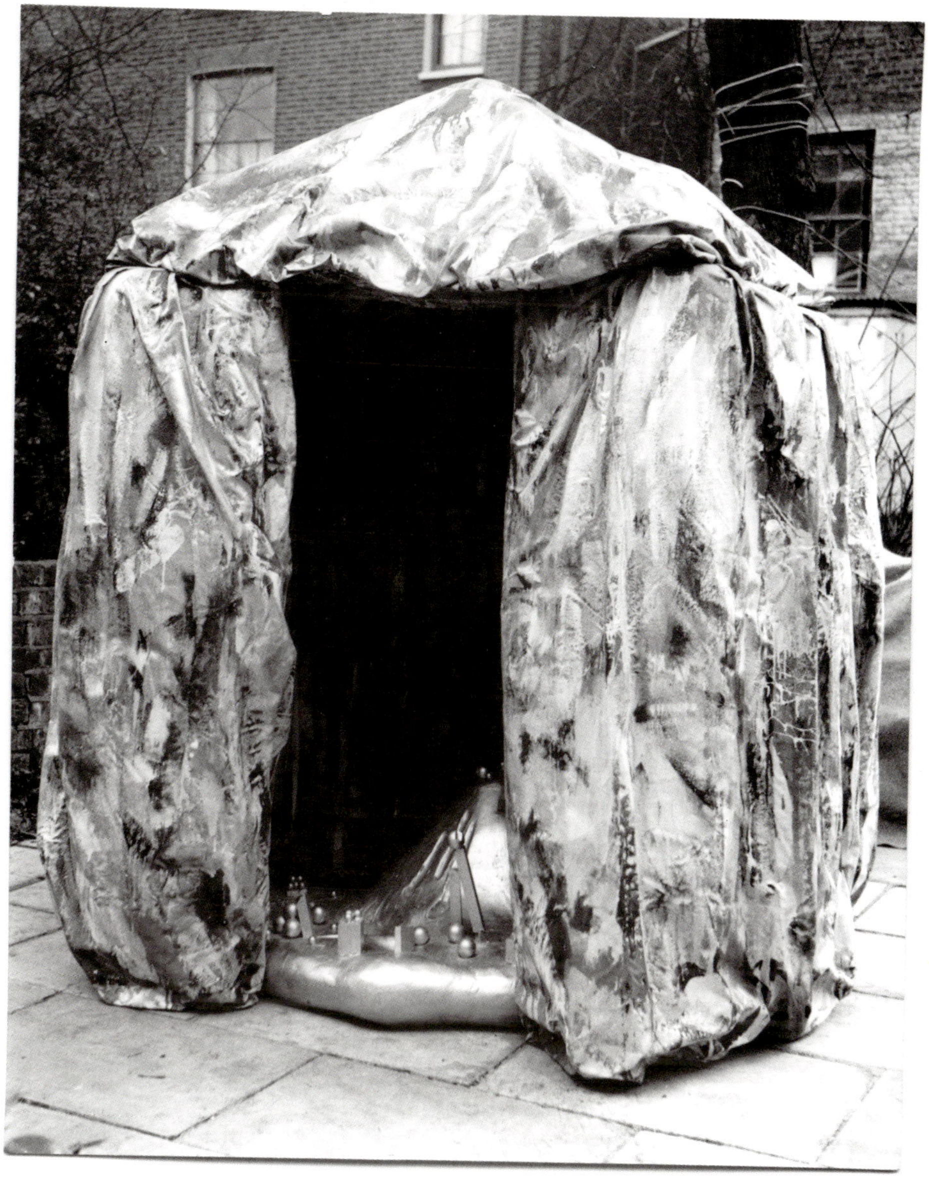

Let's start with the raw materials, the foams, cardboards, fabrics, sheeting and plastics. These ordered, spotted and salvaged materials are first outdoors and then brought indoors. Many of them are water resistance, weather proof and designed to withstand the elements. Once indoors, this function is immediately made redundant. From now on, they will be used for everything else except what they were designed for. Tape will not just bind two things together but will bind itself to itself in one large ball. Bubble wrap will not protect, but function as stuffing. Wood will not make a chair or a chest of drawers, but scaffolding and shelving for nothing in particular, or at all. Barlow customises materials when she brings them into her studio. Led by the hand, she inverts the normal rules that materials have been taught. There is a kind of blindness here at work, a blindness to materials' functions. This blindness is a condition of the studio and nowhere is this made more evident than in Barlow's "Nightwork" series of the early 1980s. Barlow made this work in the studio at night when her children we asleep. Her account of the process is important and worth quoting in full:

Strangers
Rags, rubber tarpaulin, tape,
upholstery foam, street debris,
plaster, rubbish, paper
Overall of space: 3000 cm square
Works: 210 x 210 x 240 cm (approx)
1985
School playground, Finsbury Park,
London

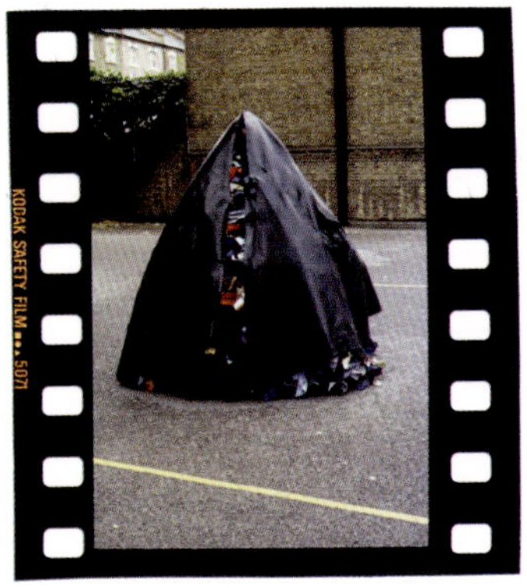

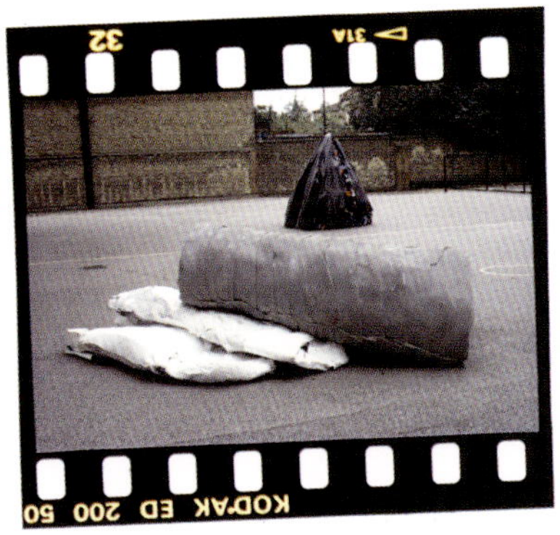

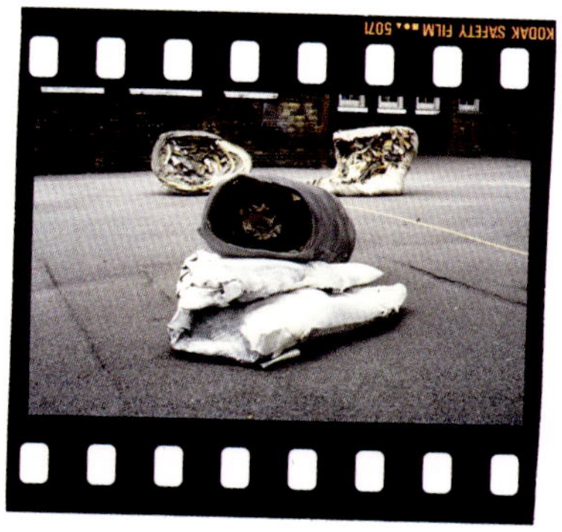

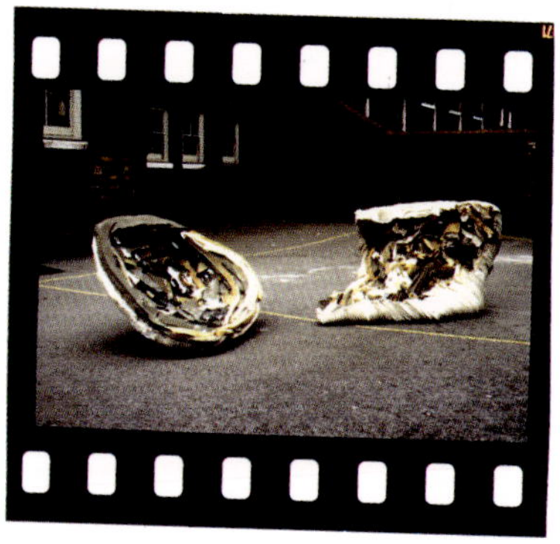

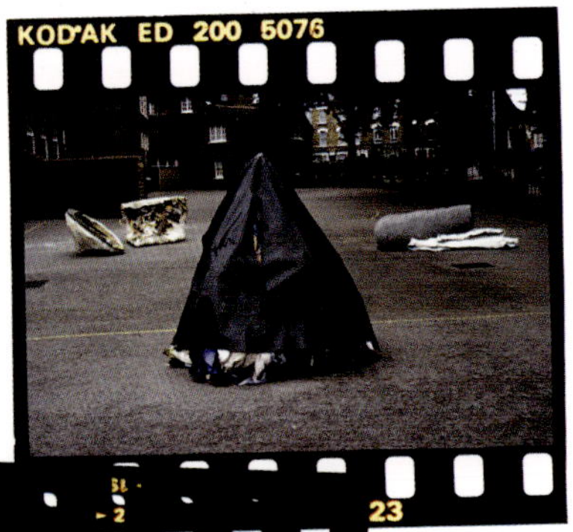

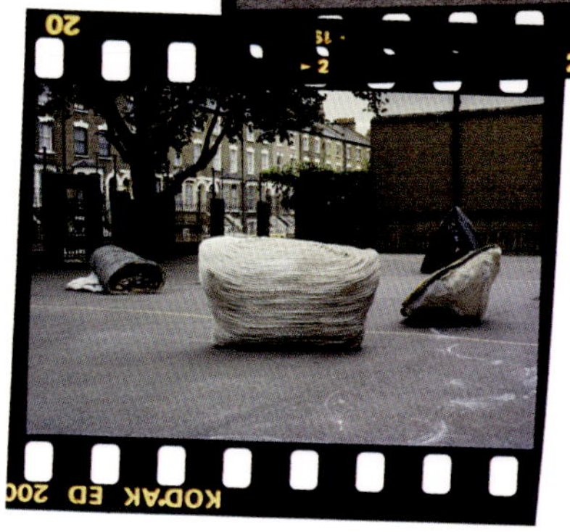

12 Barlow, "Big Bad Ugly", p. 39.

13 Barlow, Phyllida, "Hearsay, Rumours, Bed-sit Dreamers and Art Begins Today", transcript of paper (p. 3) given for "Next Generations – Current Sculptural Practice in the UK and Beyond", seminar to accompany *Early One Morning* exhibition at the Whitechapel Gallery, 20 July 2002.

> I decided to concentrate my energy on as intense a tactile experience as I could possibly get to, so I worked in the dark. I set up the materials so they were very close at hand, and the point of that was that for me sculpture is not about image – of course, image comes into it – but about the sensation of being there with an object, and your own time, the time needed to walk around an object, in relationship to the time of the object. That seems to be something to do with sensuality, the idea of touch, and for me this piece was important because I wanted the work to be absolutely about touch and not about image, where I excluded light from the studio in order to focus my attention on the touch of the materials – paper, fabrics, plaster and all sorts of things.[12]

The studio is a haptic space. It is this which brings Barlow's idea of the studio into close contact with other places where touch and handling is important. She touches upon this herself when talking about the reaction to the 1965 *New Generation* exhibition: "The studio could look beyond itself for inspiration. The kitchen, the dressmaker's, the garage, agriculture, road works, building sites and, of course, the bed sit, the home of most art students, could all provide processes to be plundered and appropriated as means to an end."[13] Such circumstances generate play. Seen alongside Phillip King's *Rosebud*, 1962, Barlow's *Strangers*, 1985, is stuffed with alternative possibilities: it is a wigwam of contingencies and a stand against the austere and empirical certainties of New Generation sculpture.

Phillip King
Rose Bud
1962

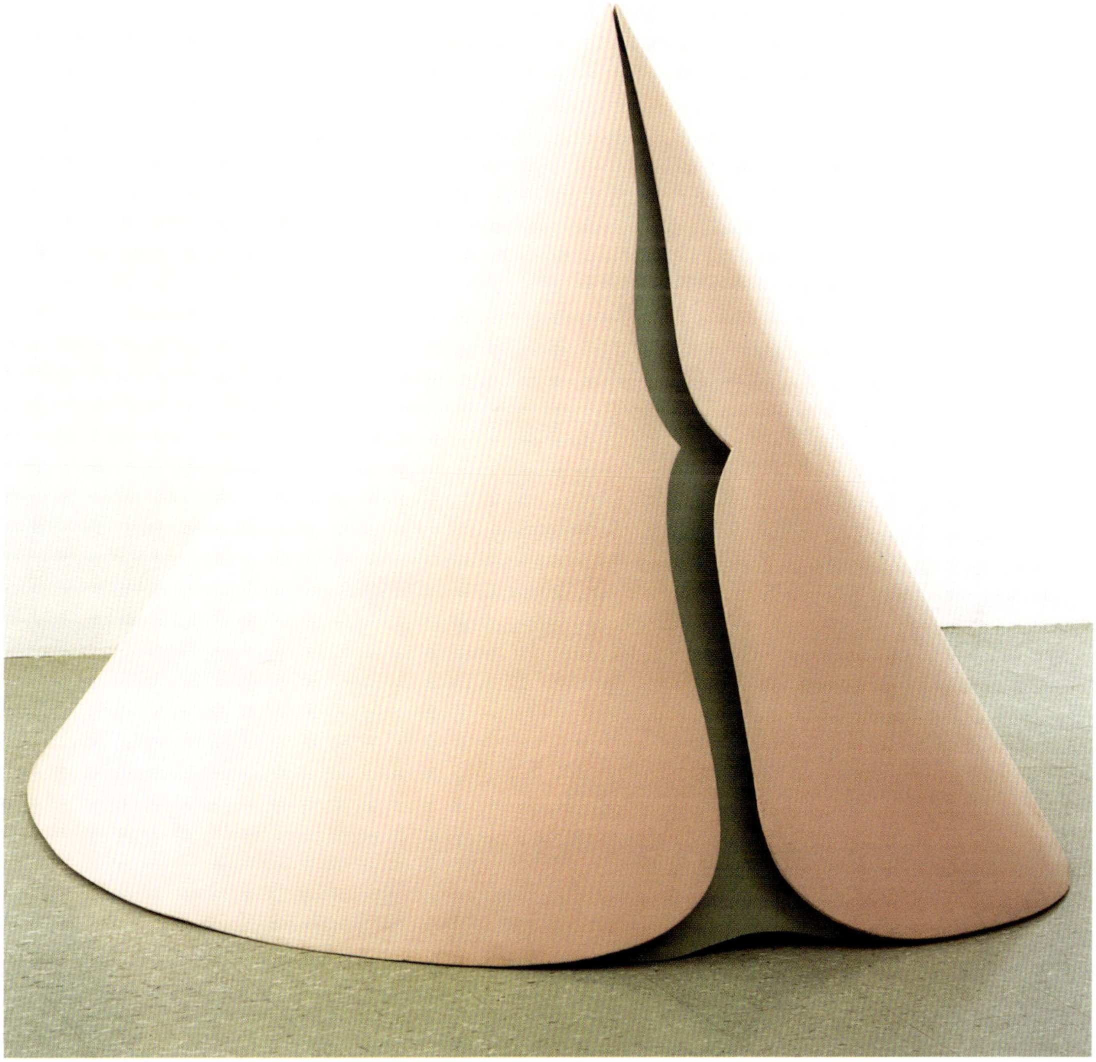

Below
Chair
Plywood, carbody filler, fibreglass, resin
120 x 150 x 150 cm
1968

Opposite
Object for an armchair
Blanket, curtain fabric, red tape, arm chair
100 x 150 x 100 cm
1994
Elbrook House, Ashwell, Hertfordshire

Barlow's studio is a place where new relationships and exchanges can occur. This is precisely the subject of her mid 1990s series, "Objects for...". There is *Object for a sitting room*, 1995, *Object for a television*, 1994, *Object for an ironing board*, 1993, *Object for a balcony*, 1994, *Object for a dressing table*, 1997 and *Object for a piano*, 1998. So where is the *Object for a studio*? There isn't one, because ultimately this is what all her work is, an 'oeuvre of objects for the studio'. But is it just a studio? Hasn't it been a studio-home all along? I think it has and that Barlow's studio is a studio-home in real and imaginary ways. It is next door to her house: her studio is her neighbour. The studio, like the home, is a private, intimate place. It is a place for a family of people and of things, who grow up and leave the nest, who get jobs and get exhibited.

It is also a place to kick off your shoes, put your feet up and start work. "Objects for..." is a series of works about the relationship between art and life, between art objects and other objects, between the studio and the home. Barlow has actually been match-making objects since the 1960s. Compare, for example, Barlow's early work *Chair*, 1968, with her *Object for an armchair*, 1994. *Chair* is made up of a wooden box chair and three Arp-like cushions, which have been modelled in clay and then cast in fibreglass resin. *Chair* is both severe and playful: it is an uncomfortable combination. It takes two not to tango. With *Objects for an armchair* things have got more relaxed, more mellow, more 'exuberant' perhaps. There is also now comedy, rather than just play: providing an upholstered foot stool for this object, stuck bolt upright in the armchair, is a wonderful touch.

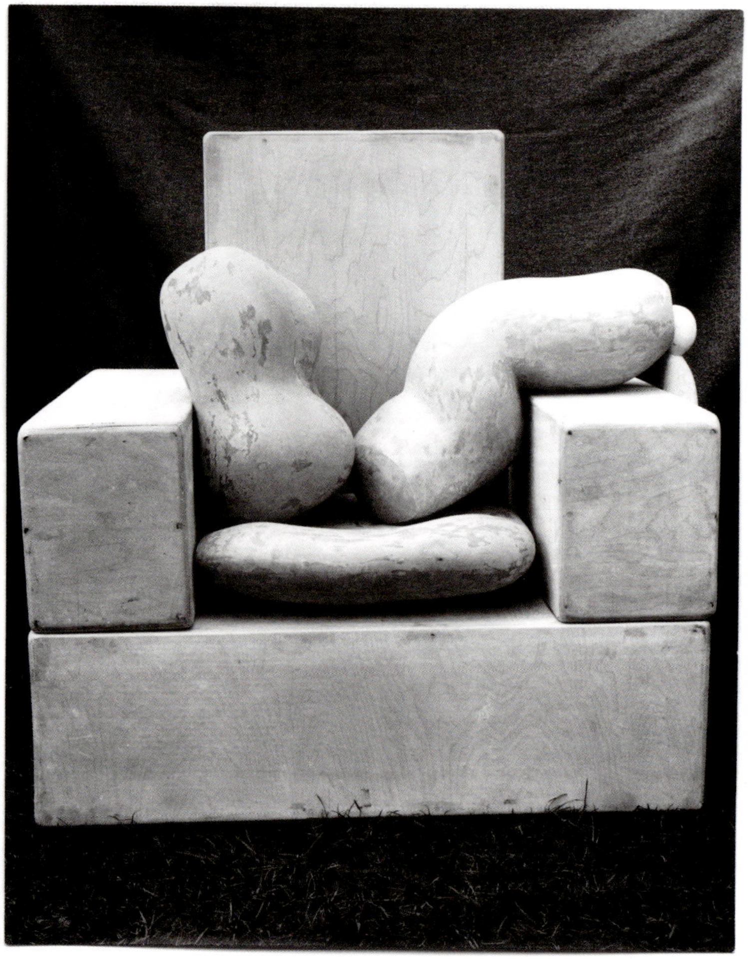

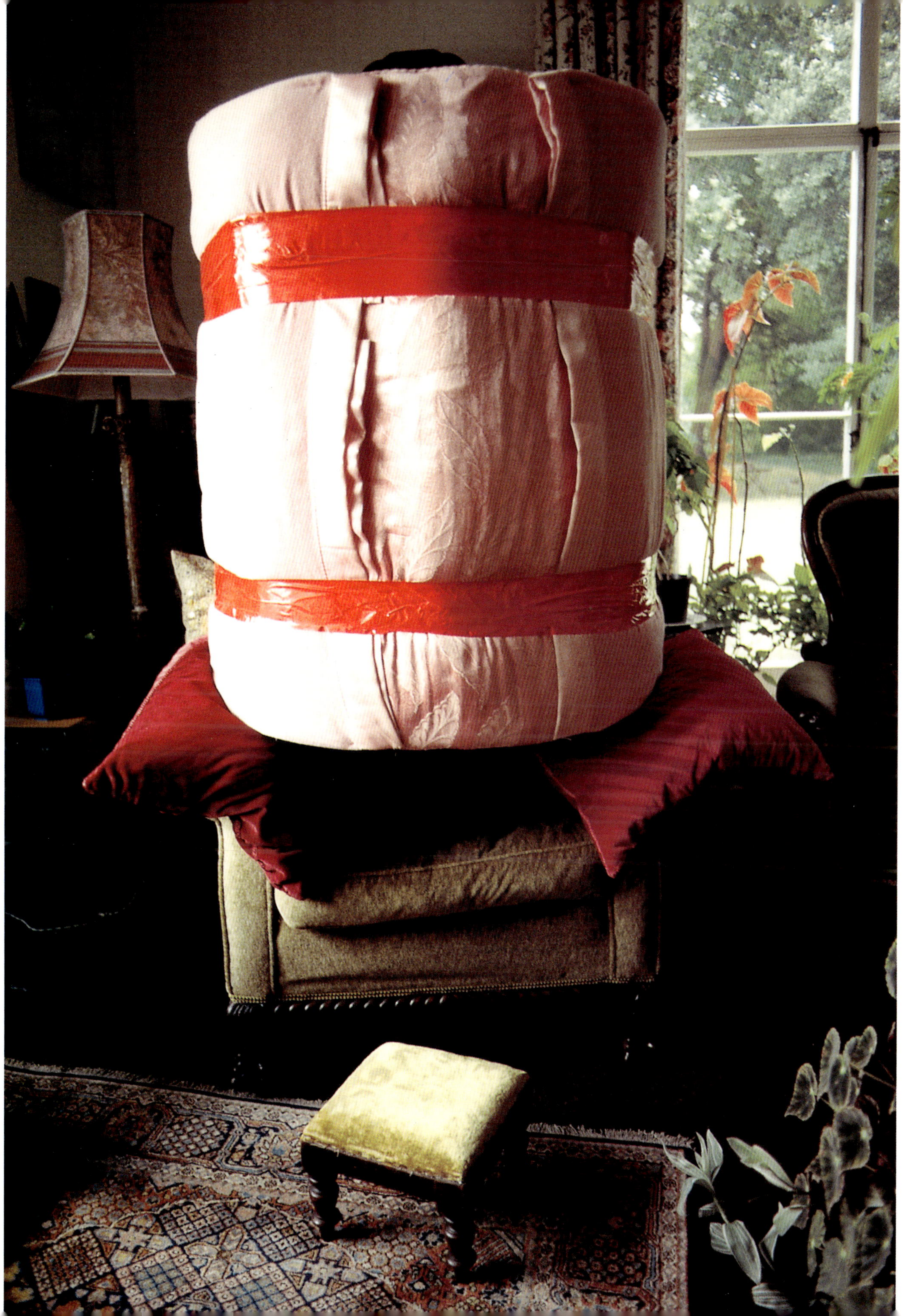

Object for a piano
Blanket, paint, wood, red tape, brown paper, rubber tubing, upright piano
100 x 200 x 210 cm
1999
Richard Salmon Gallery, *Furniture* curated by Paul Heber Percy, touring to Bluecoat Gallery, Liverpool; John Hansard Gallery, Southampton

Object for four-poster bed
Wood, paint, fabrics, threads, bedside table
50 x 180 x 60 cm and
20 x 180 x 90 cm
1994
Private address

Object for a street grit bin
Kitchen foil over bread
90 x 200 x 200 cm
1995
York Way, London, N7

The "Objects for..." series is, for me, some of the best work Barlow has made. They are so alive and say so much about her take on things and on the relationship between making sculpture and the studio-home environment. They are not about hatred or about enemies. The companions and friends she makes for things range from the absurd, to the comic, to the quietly and clumsily sinister. They are kinds of strange personal gifts to things. What do you give an object that has got everything? Do you give a wardrobe some clothes? No, you give it a suitcase.

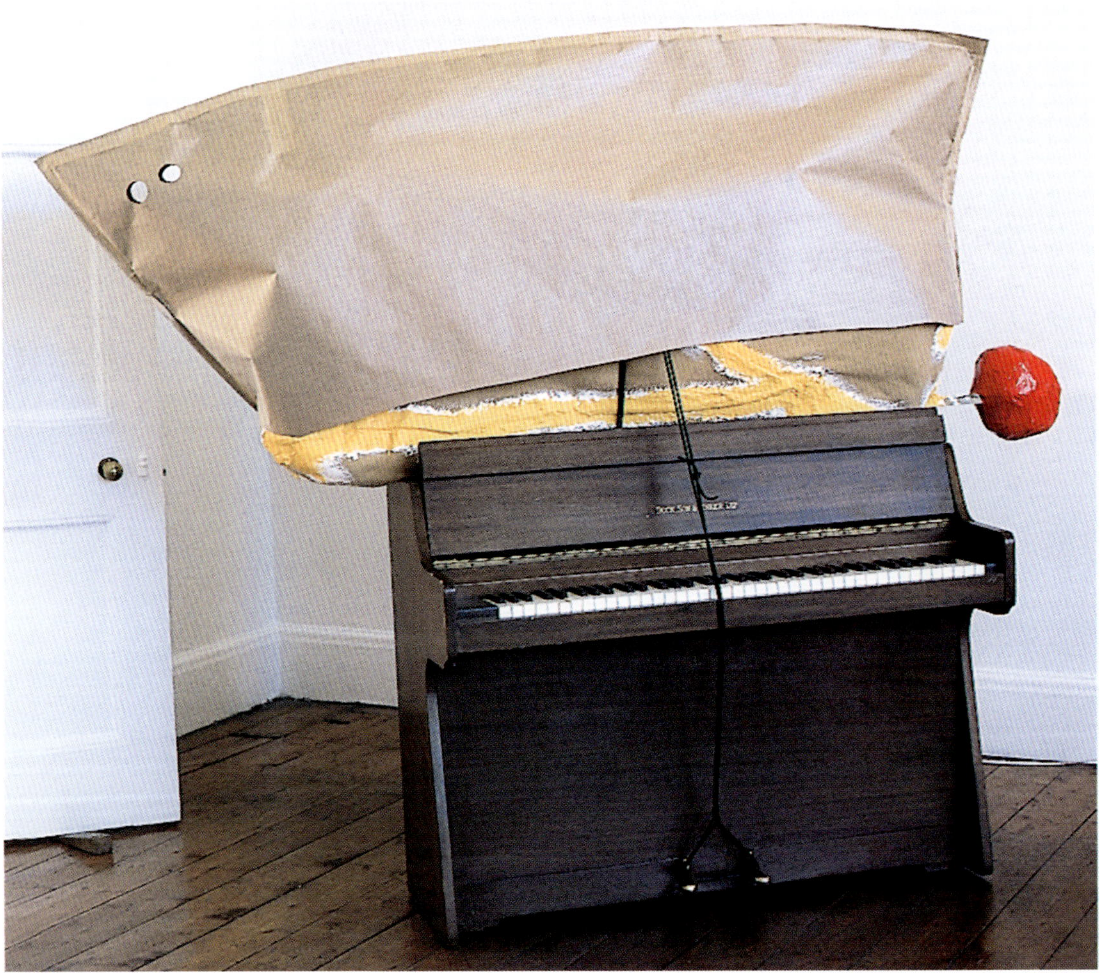

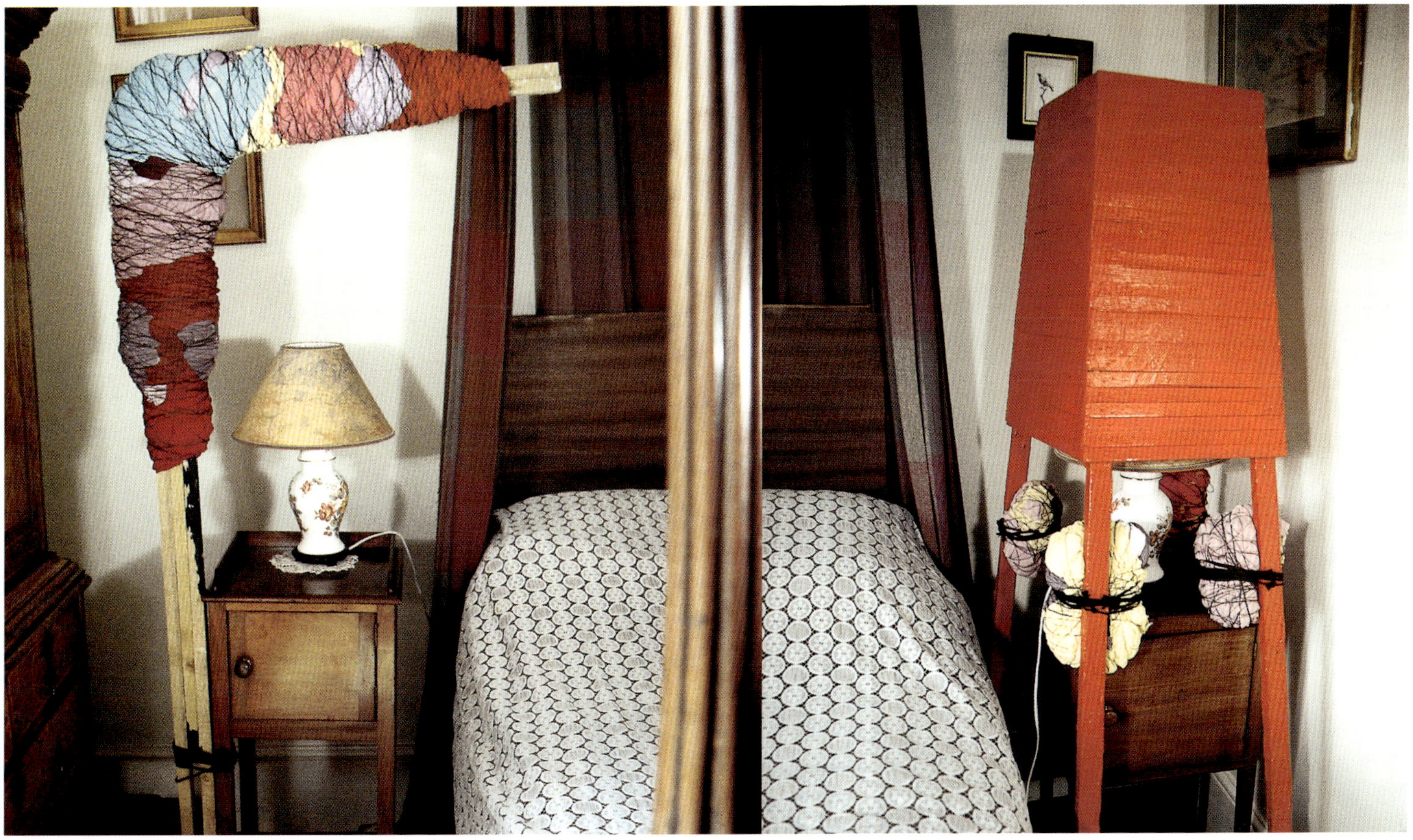

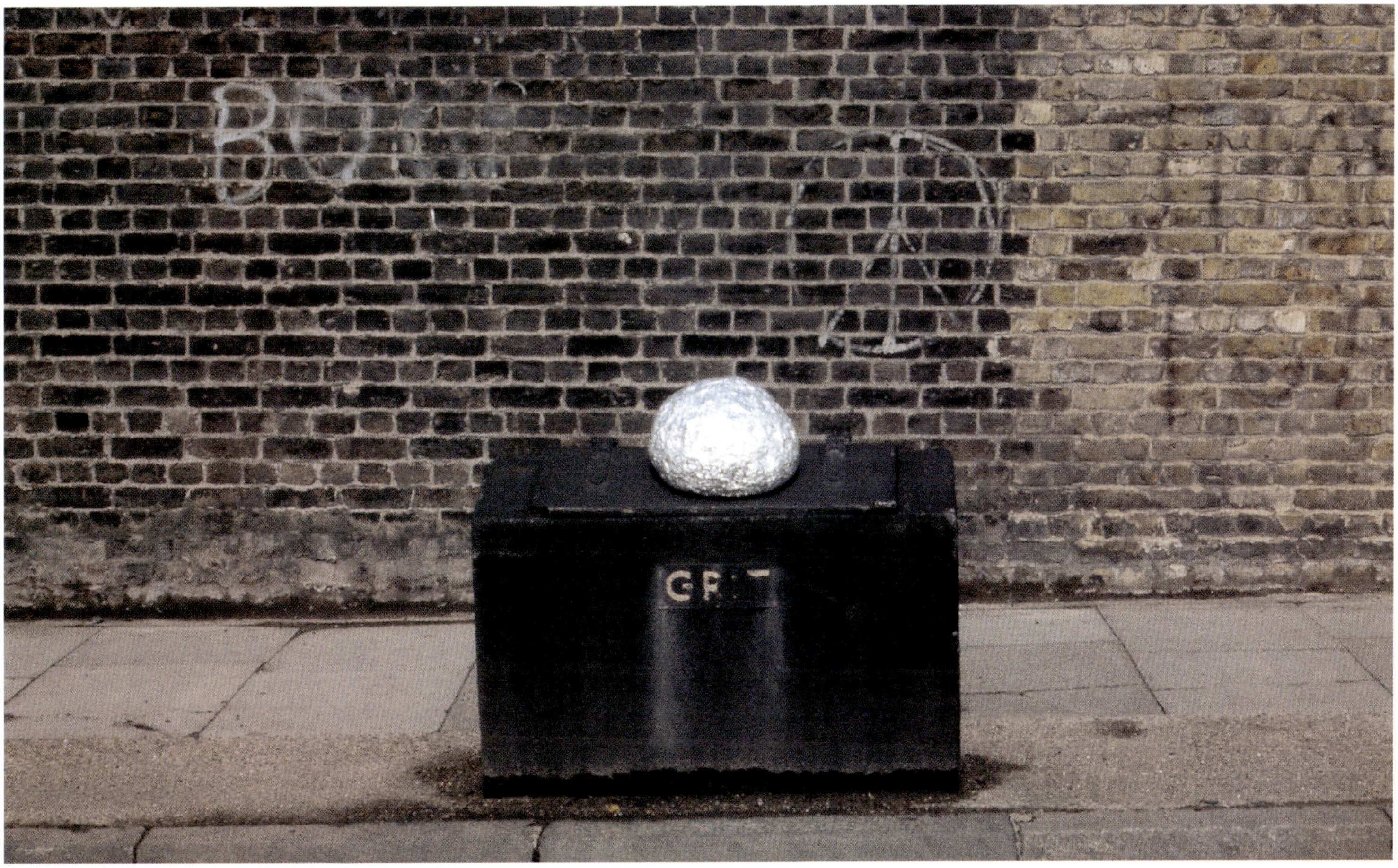

Object for an ironing board
Blanket, wood frame, wool,
mixed threads, ironing board
60 x 170 x 150 cm
1994
Private residence

Object for balcony
Clothing rail, curtain fabric,
plastic, flex
120 x 150 x 100 cm
1994
Private residence, Paris

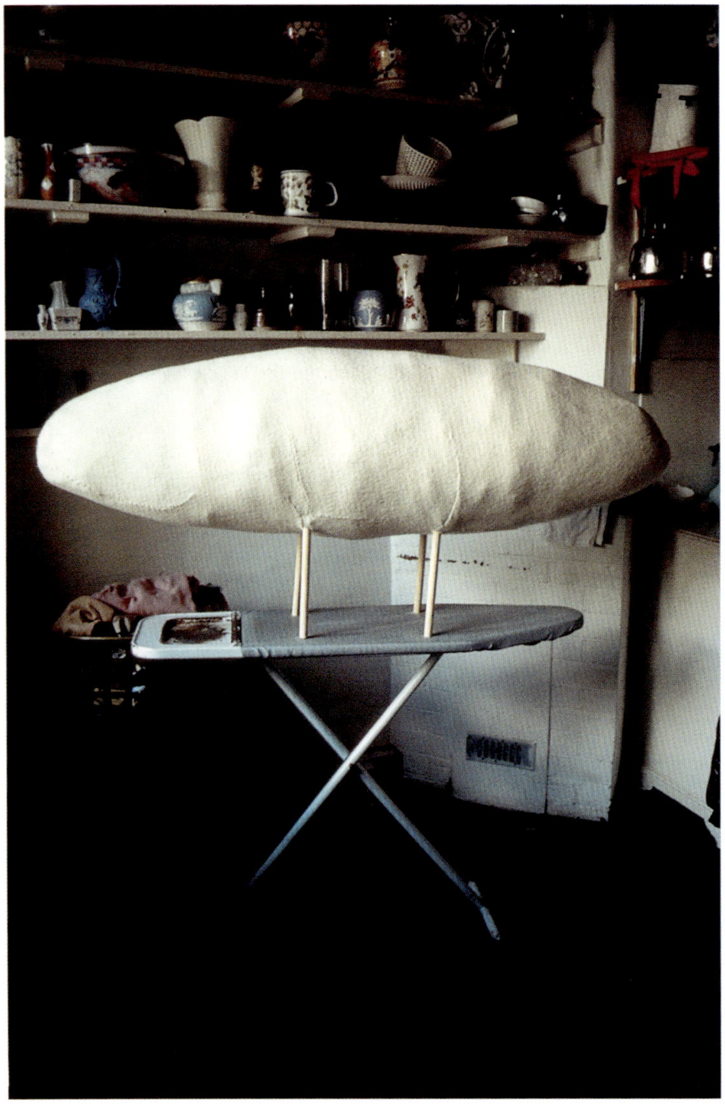

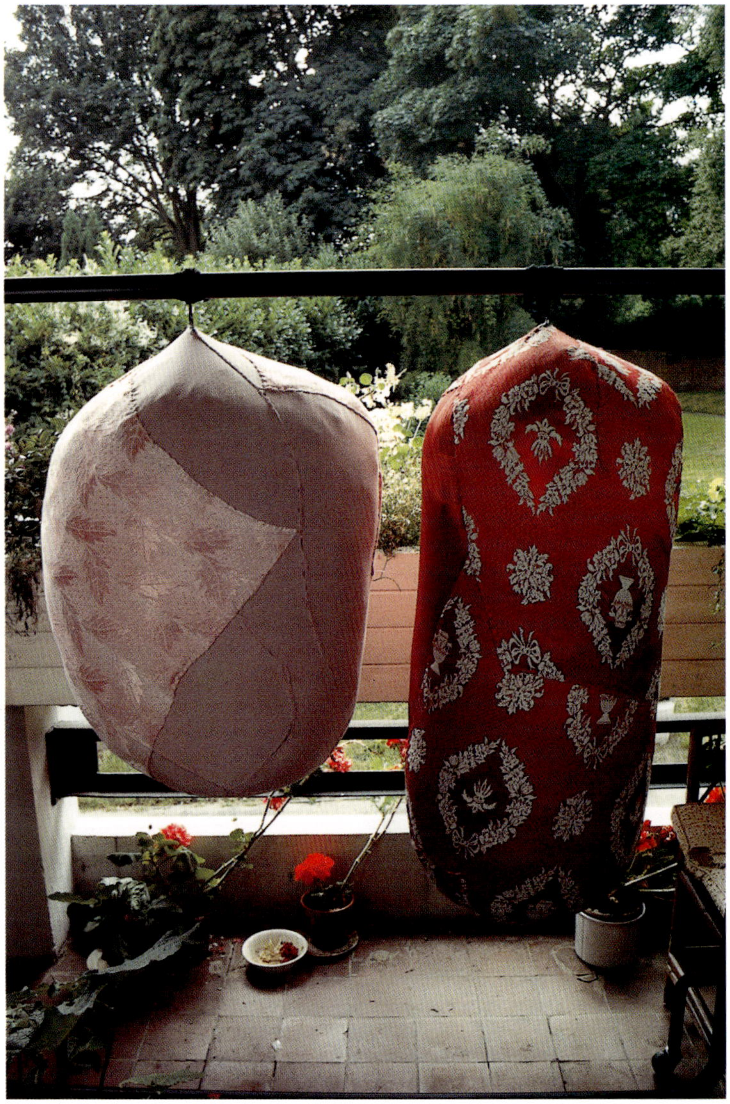

Object for street furniture
Blanket, paint
90 x 200 x 200 cm
1999
York Way, London, N7

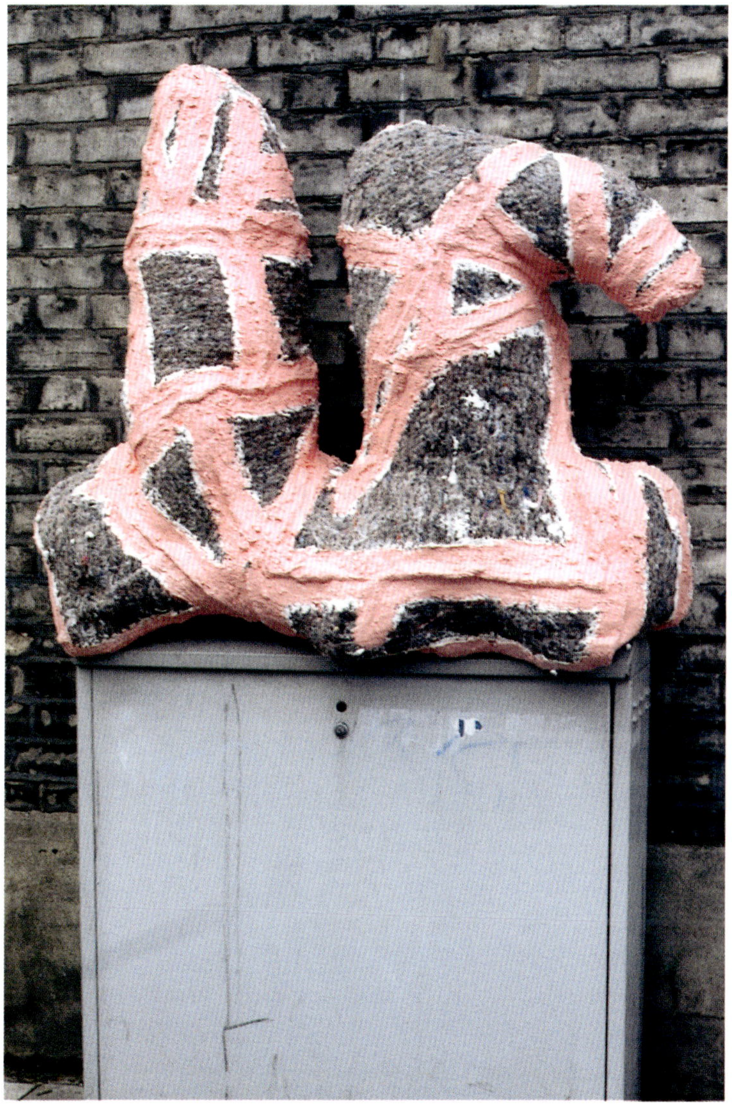

Object for a lamppost
Blanket, paint
90 x 200 x 200 cm
1999
York Way, London, N7

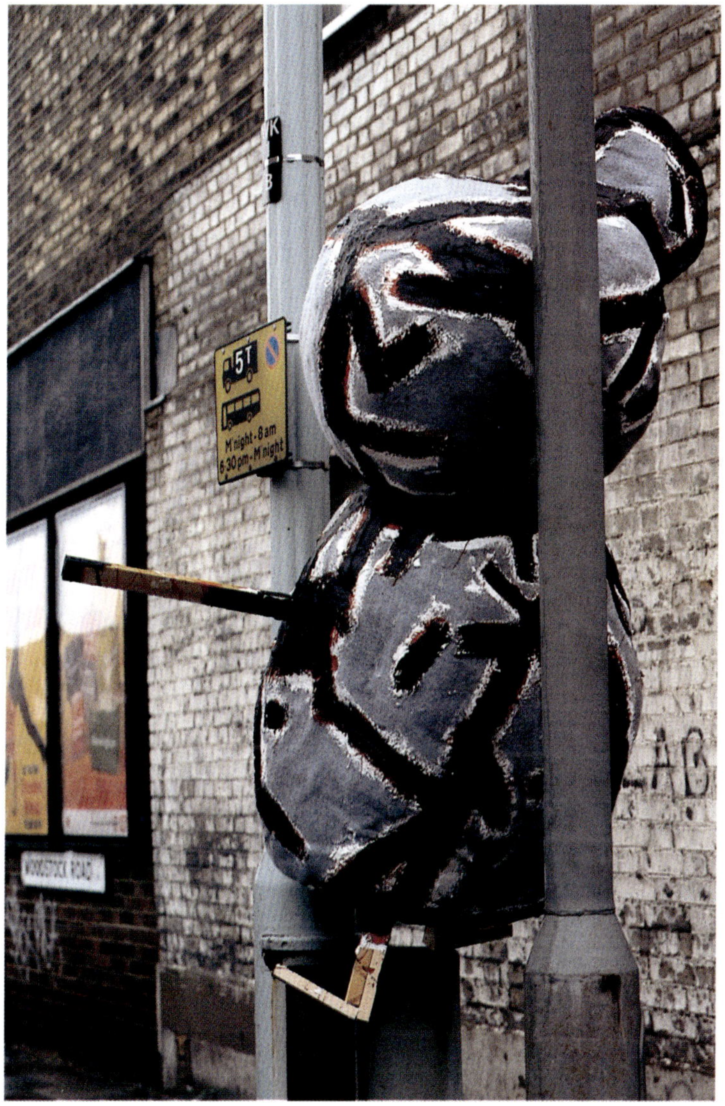

Object for air ducting
Plywood, paint, newspaper, rags, rubber, tubing
300 x 180 x 150 cm
1996
London Artforms, Roseberry Avenue, London

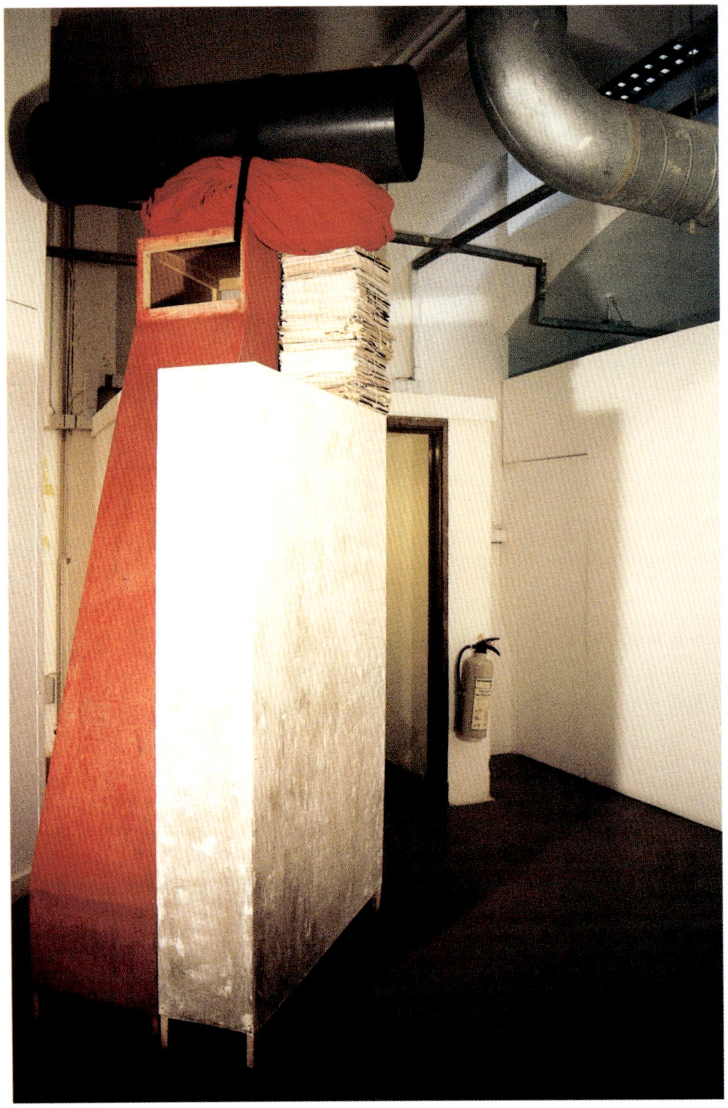

Object for the sitting room
Blue tarpaulin, rubber hose, sitting room
Diameter 100 x 150 cm high
1994
81 St Augustine's Road, London, NW1

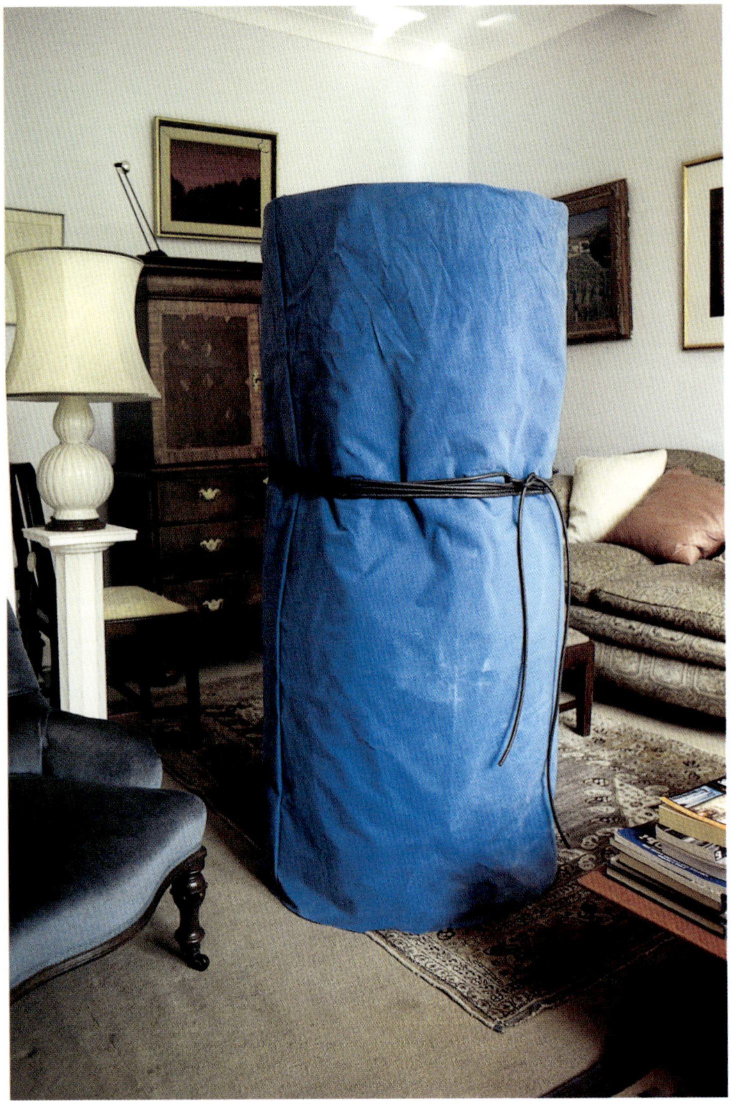

Object for the television
Dough over plaster,
television set
80 x 180 x 80 cm
1994
Private address

Object for a dressing table
Polystyrene, paint, garden netting,
foam off cuts, rags, industrial
binding, dressing table
120 x 200 x 200 cm
1997
Norwich Art Gallery, for *Barely Made*,
curated Jaqueline Poncelet

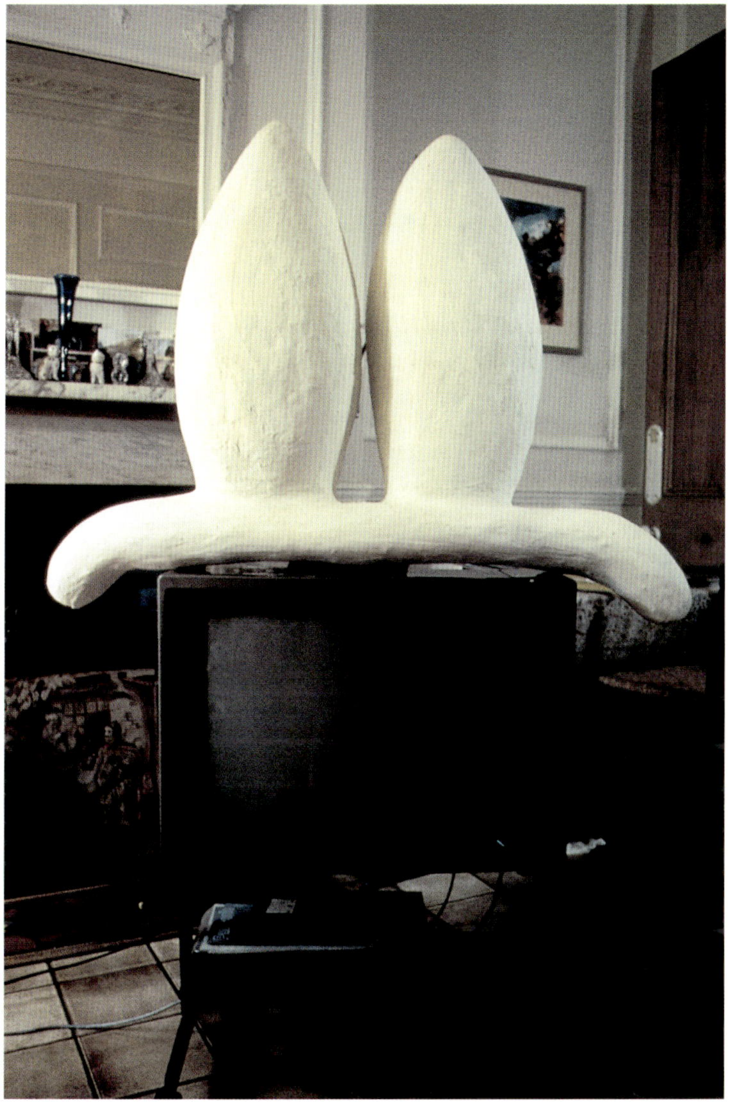

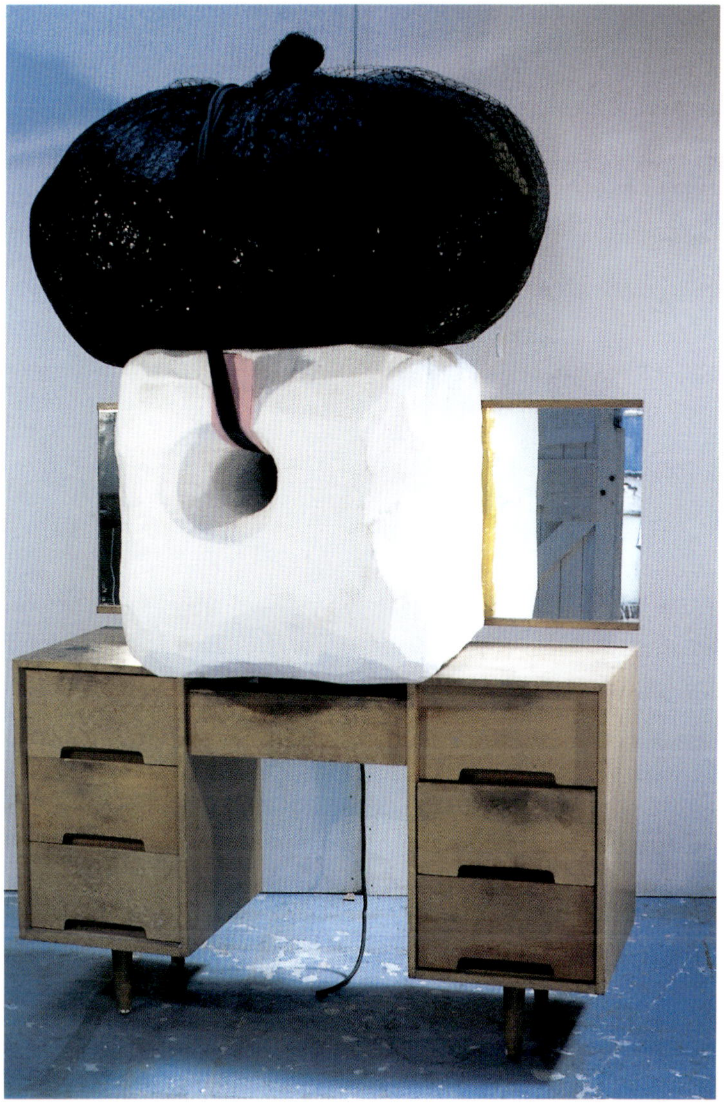

Installing Objects

14 Phyllida Barlow talk at the Henry Moore Institute, Leeds, in the 'Studio Lives – Contemporary Views' series, October 2001.

> I am still looking for the single object, the object that can exist on it's own. I am still looking for this. Perhaps there is no such thing.[14]

Sculpture, for Phyllida Barlow, is a relational art. It is about dialogues, correspondences, conversations, connections. Travelling by train from Leeds to Kings Cross, I have seen a lot of Phyllida Barlow sculptures recently. You get them at high speed, and you get them when you are pulling in and pulling out of stations. They nearly always come in groups, in ensembles. A grey signal box, a huge metal wheelie bin, some piping, a pile of wooden pallets, a stack of cables, some tyres, a large concrete cylinder and a section of scaffolding. They are randomly placed, but always have a kind of togetherness: the cables lean against the pallets, and the signal box looms over the scaffolding keeping an eye on the skip, which rubs shoulders with a stack of broken wooden crates. Such objects can take on imaginary relations through their placements, if you let them, which Barlow does. They assume compositions. Adrian Stokes once made a similar point about the formal relationship between the patterns of cows in a meadow and the positions of fielders on a cricket pitch. Indeed the role of place is far from incidental here. Those overlooked, unloved, scruffy, abandoned sites by the side of railway lines, are in turn the kinds of places that Barlow has shown her work, when she has shown outdoors. Dumping grounds. Barlow has a railway yard and railway track running at the back of her Finsbury Park house, behind her studio.

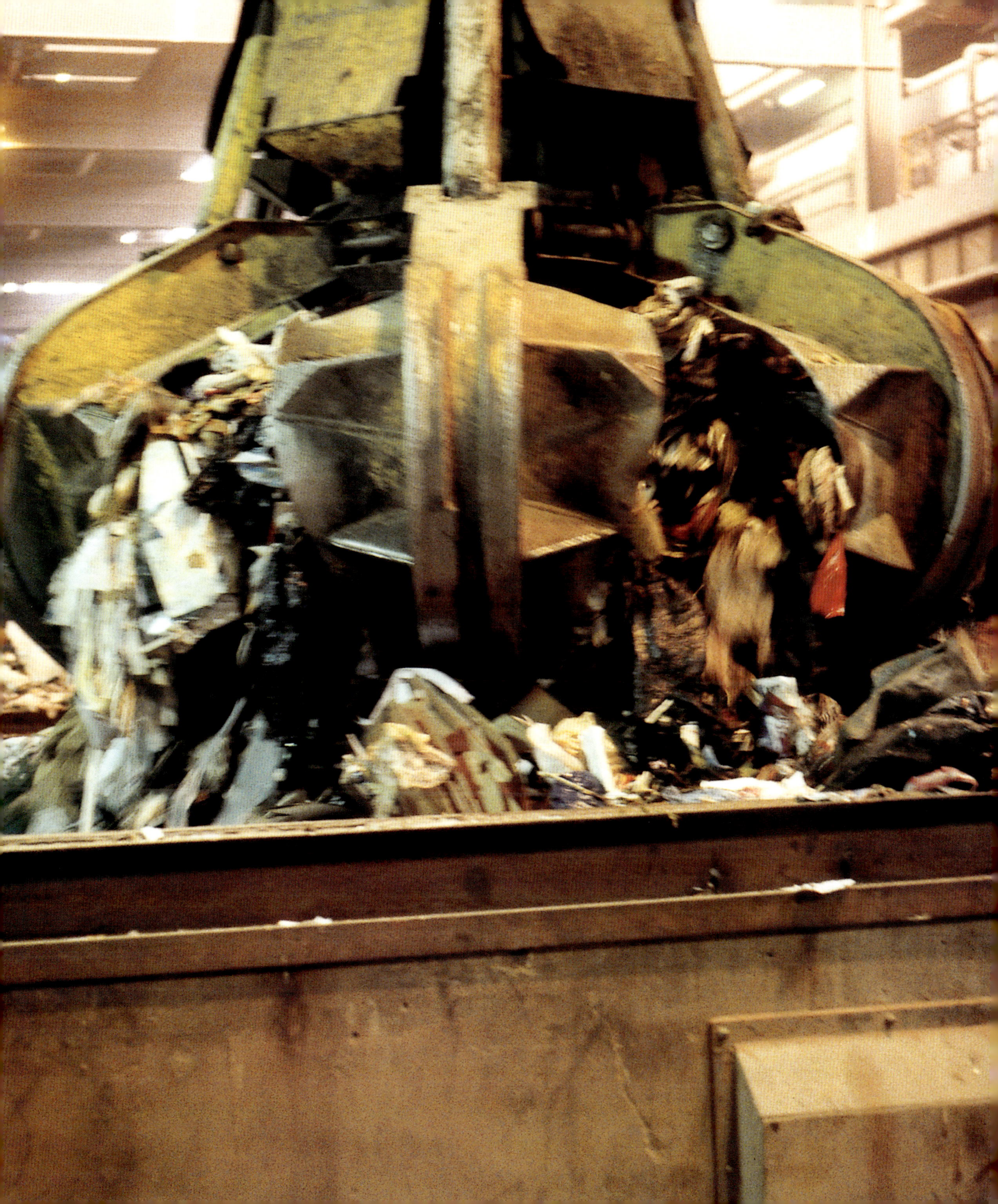

Untitled x 4
Hardboard, plywood,
filler, polystyrene,
paper, felt
900 x 900 x 300 cm
2001

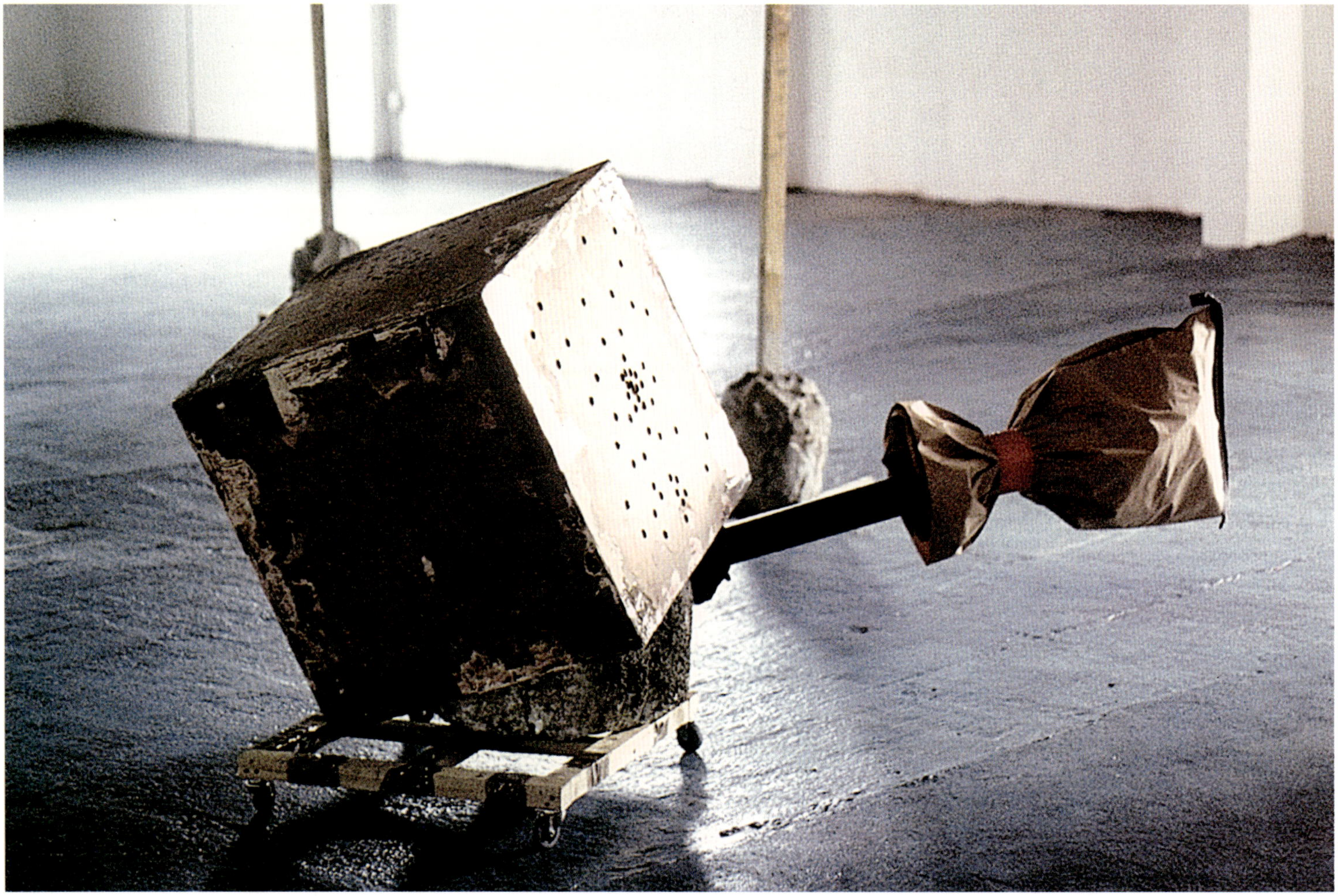

I am also, of course, talking about images here. Barlow clocks up many of these in her travels by train and by car. She has an extraordinary mental store room for these things and often works on them from memory back home at the studio. She doesn't use photography, or rather she did until she became frustrated with the way background incidentals (such a signage and hanging baskets) interfered with the combinations of objects she was interested in recording. Instead, she took to drawing (and drawing quickly in paint). One summer she created an archive of things she loved from outdoors. She did about two or three a day of these transformations, these replications, these 'bad copies', these approximate similes. These are colour shapes as much as anything else: an awkward cube of orange chats to an oval red. These drawings are settings for ensembles that try to evoke the three-dimensional life of things and to unflatten things.

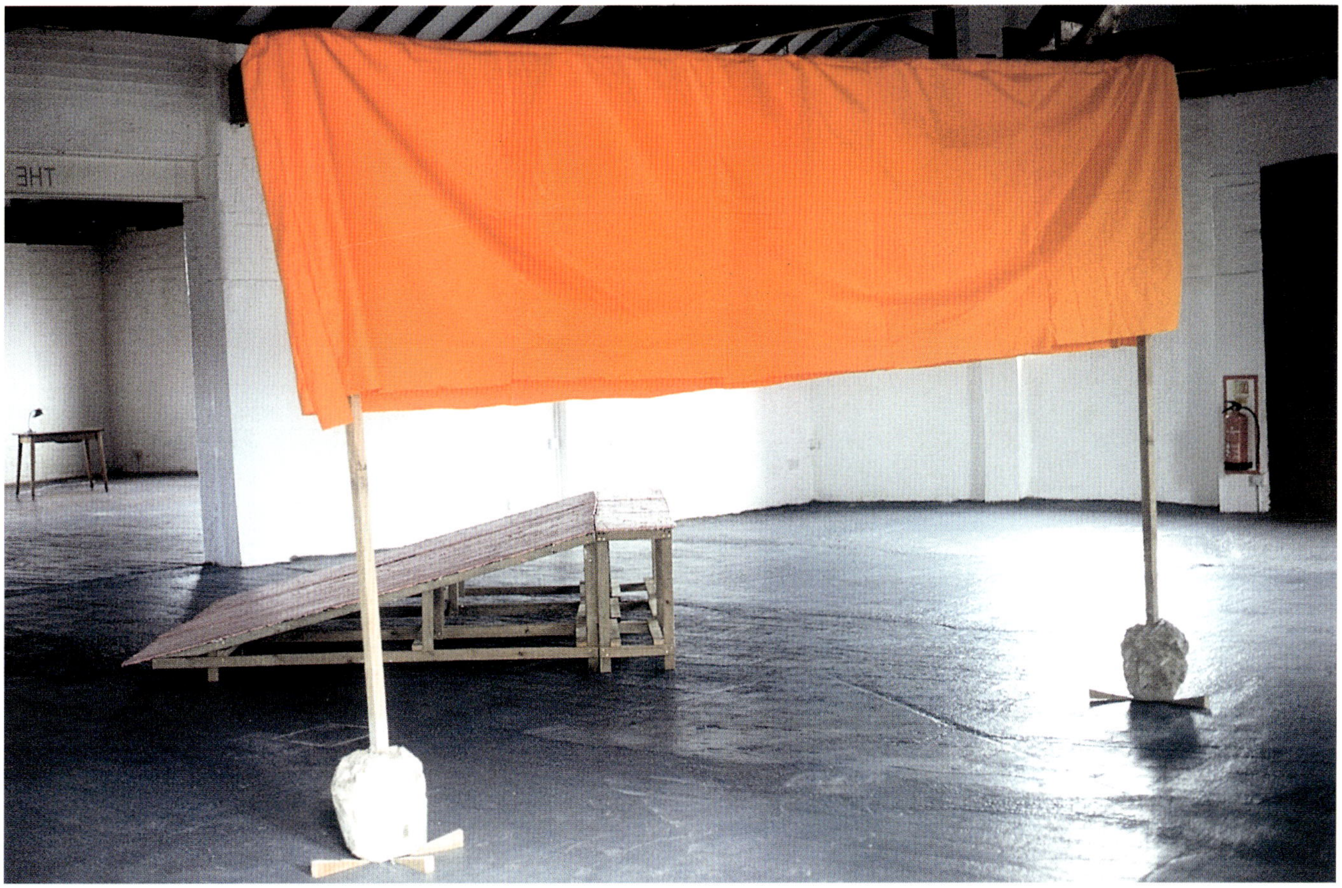

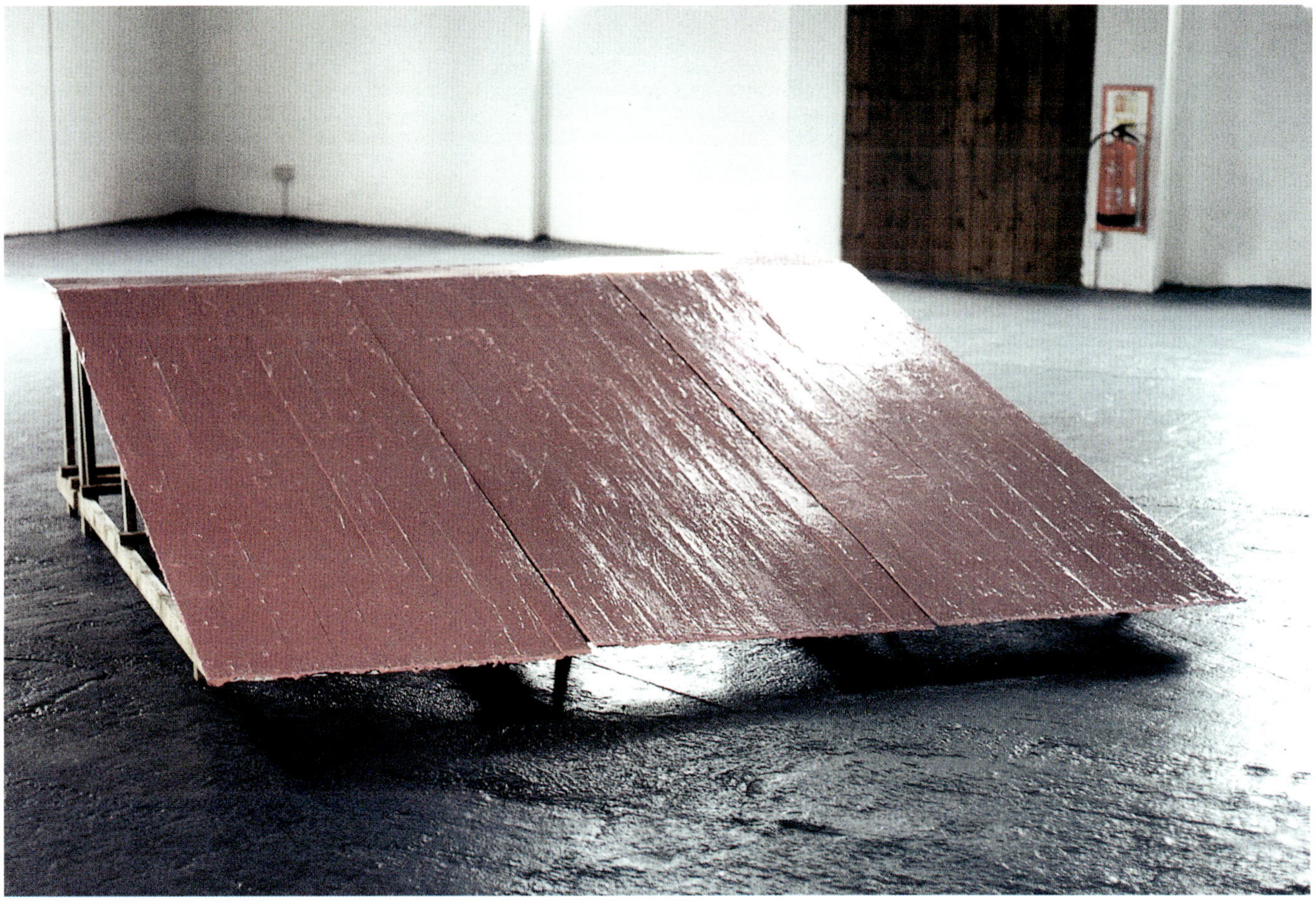

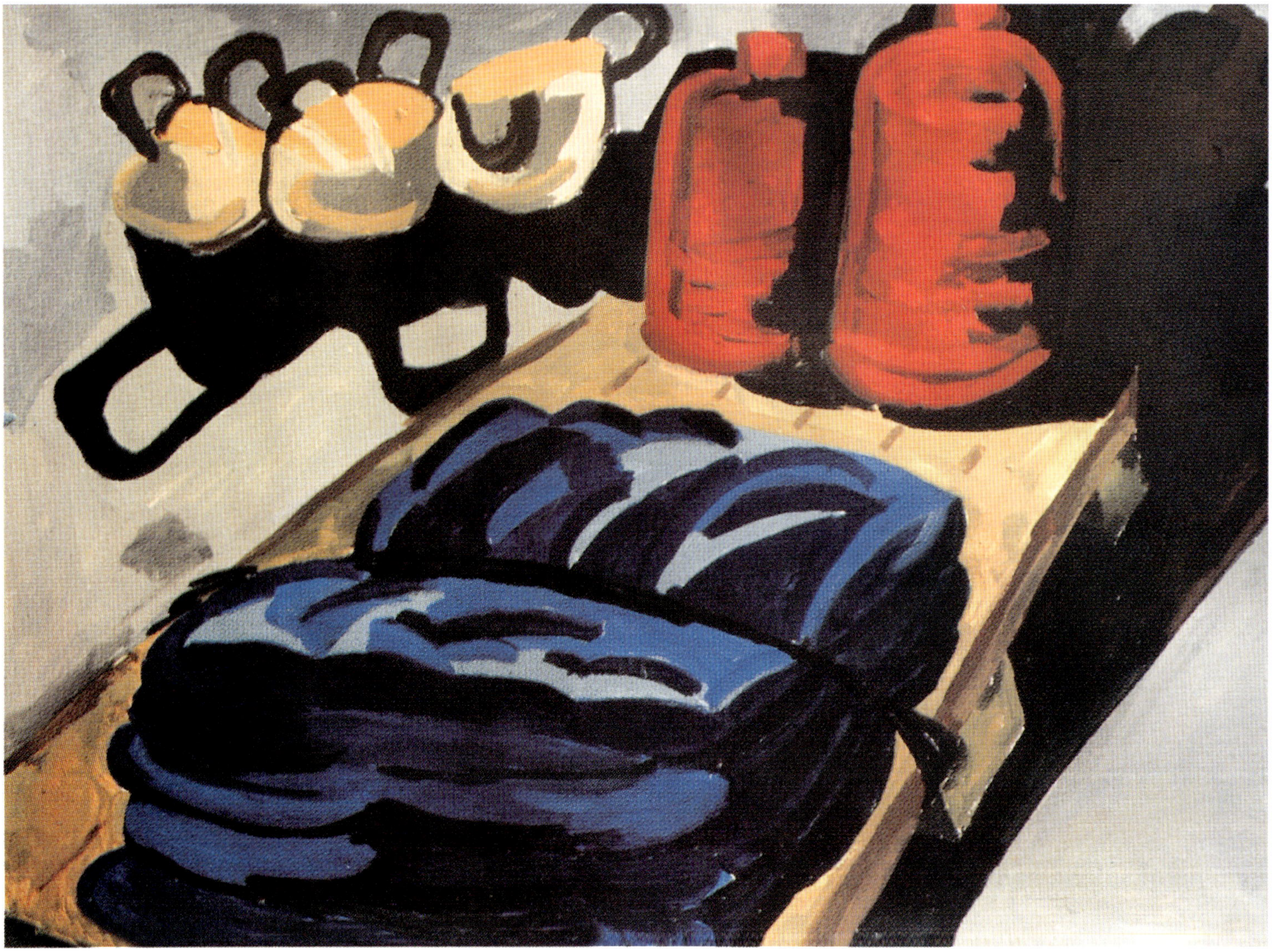

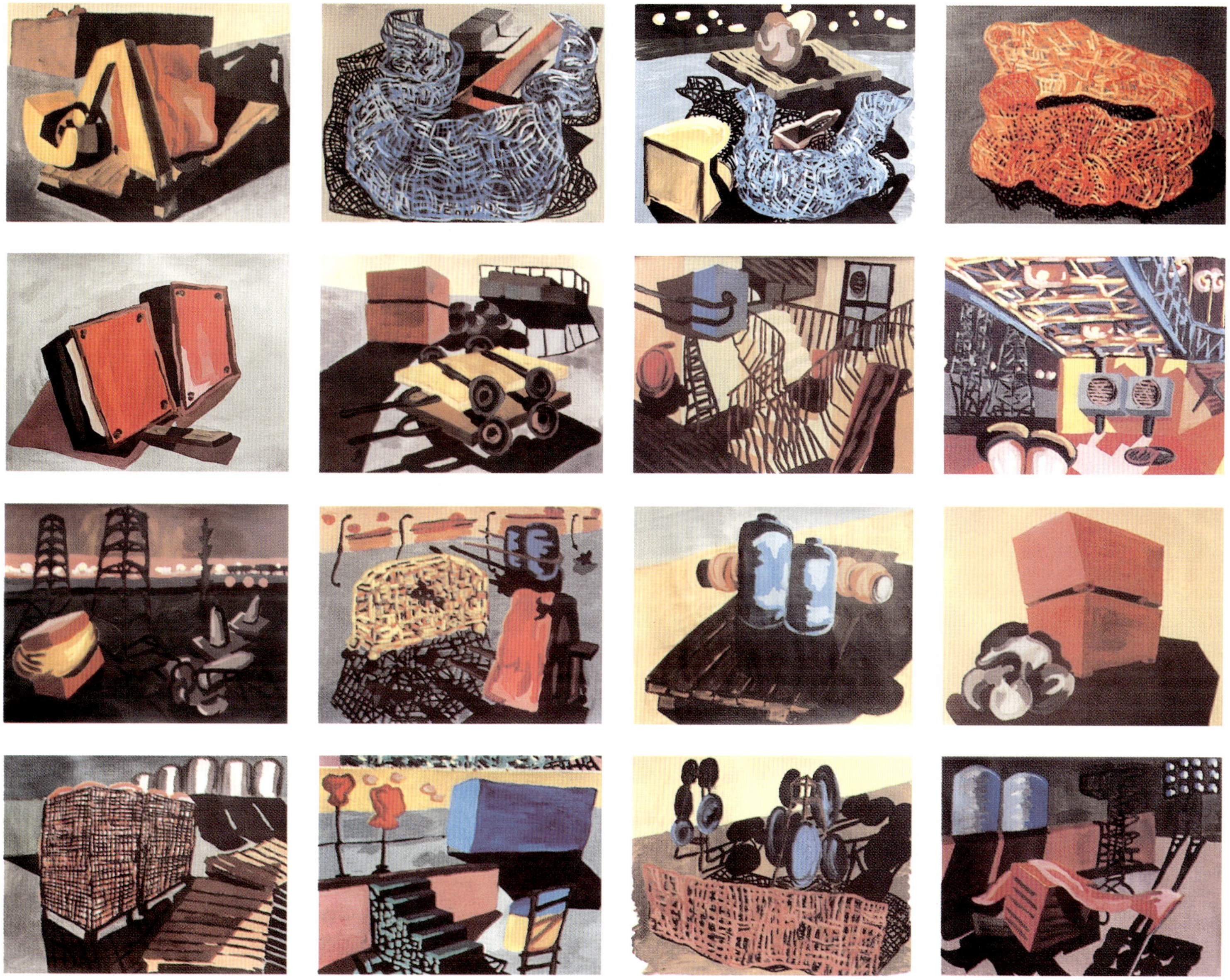

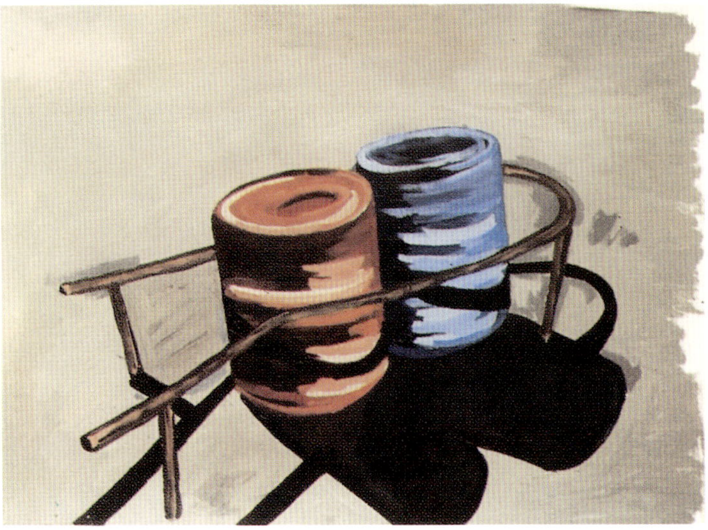
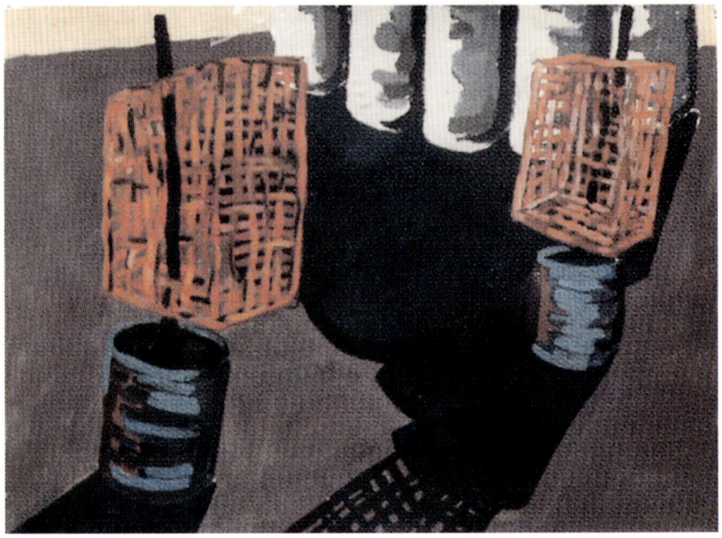
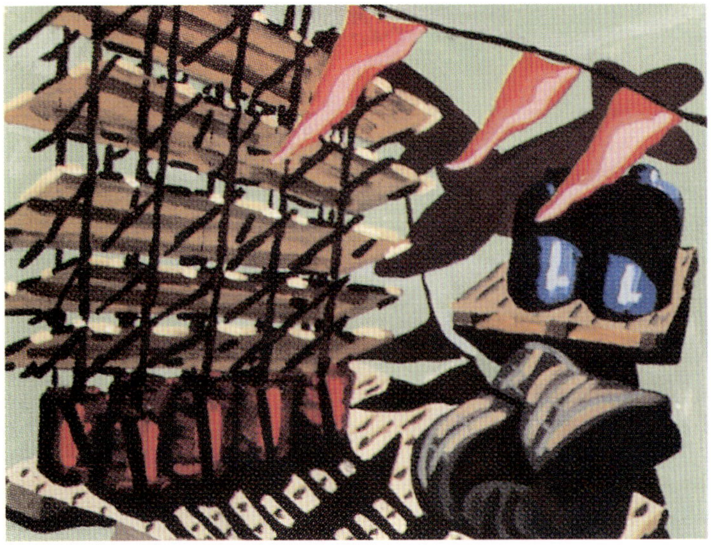
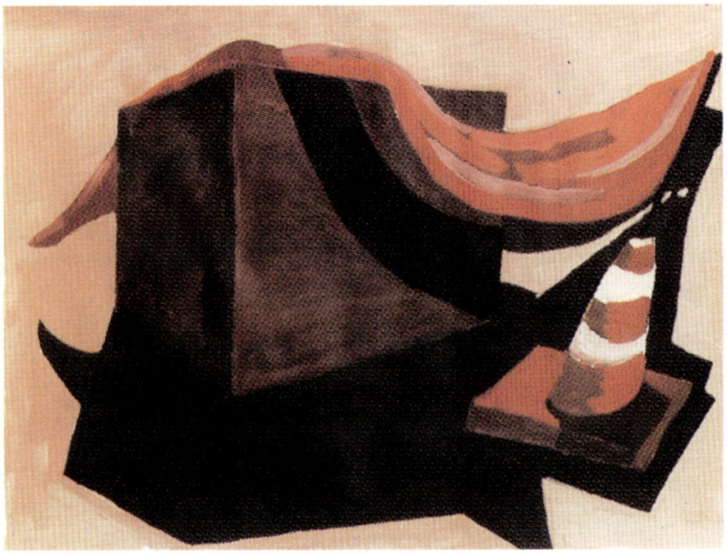
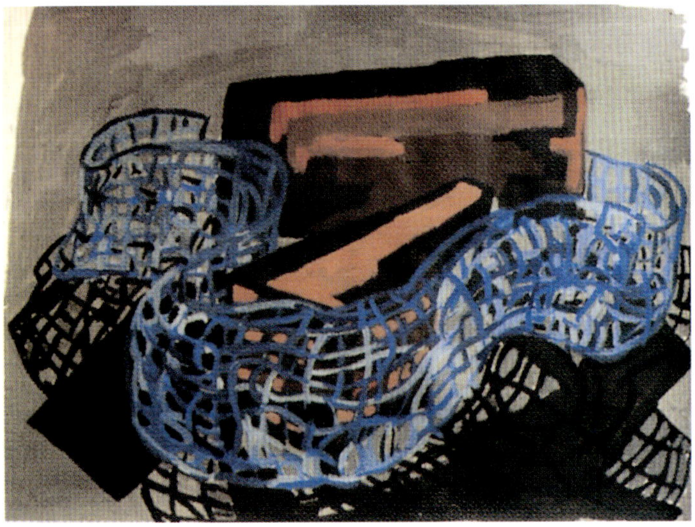
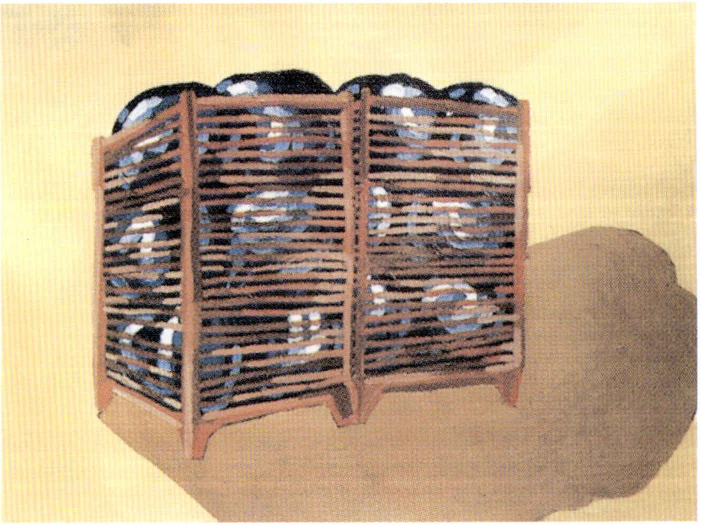

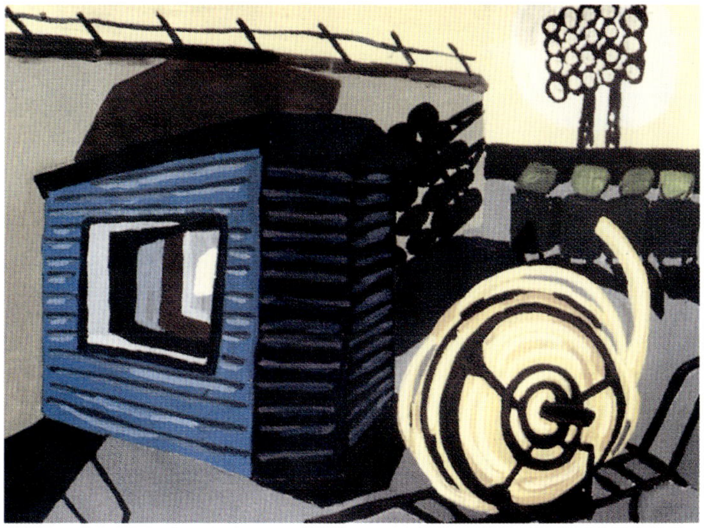
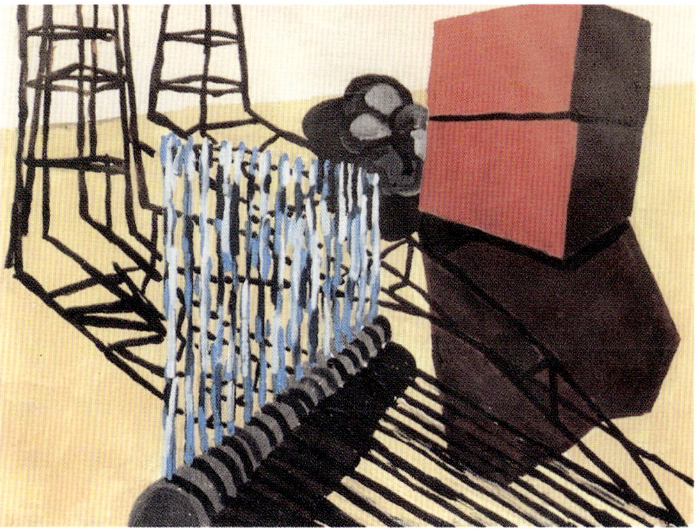
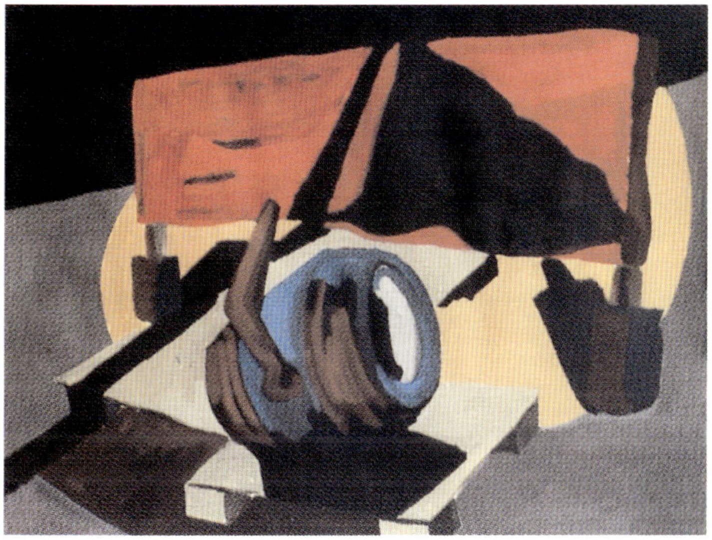
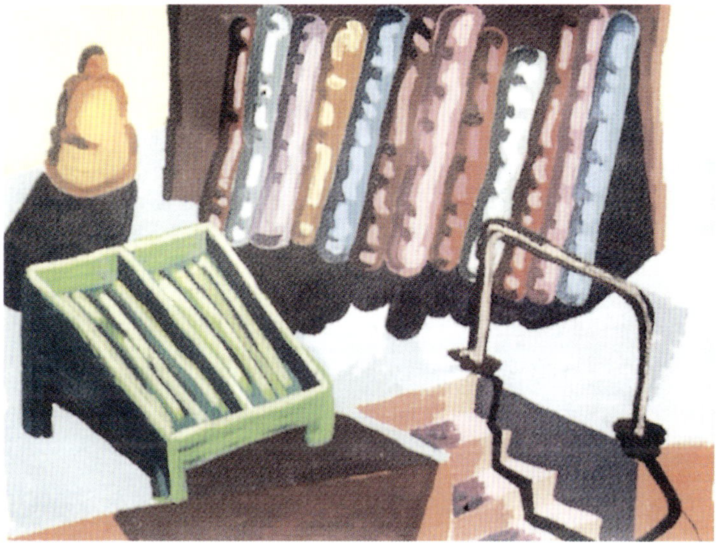
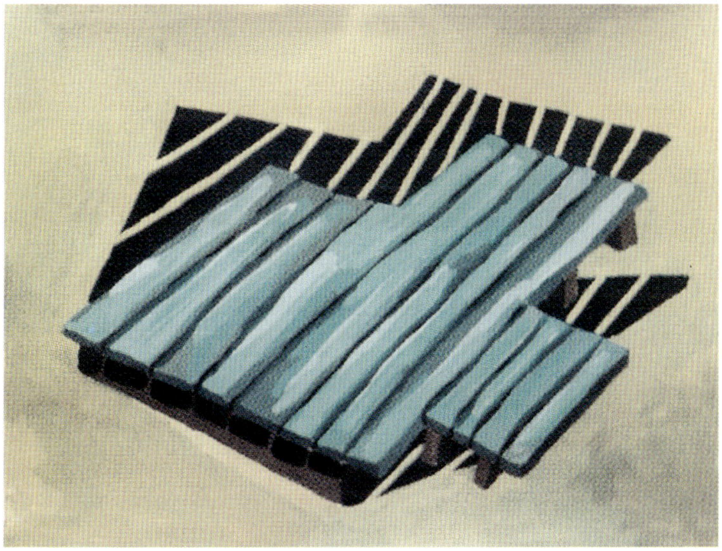
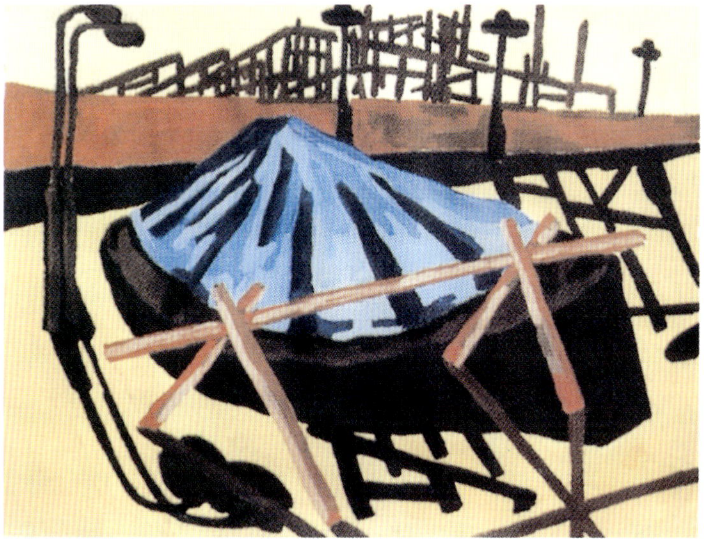

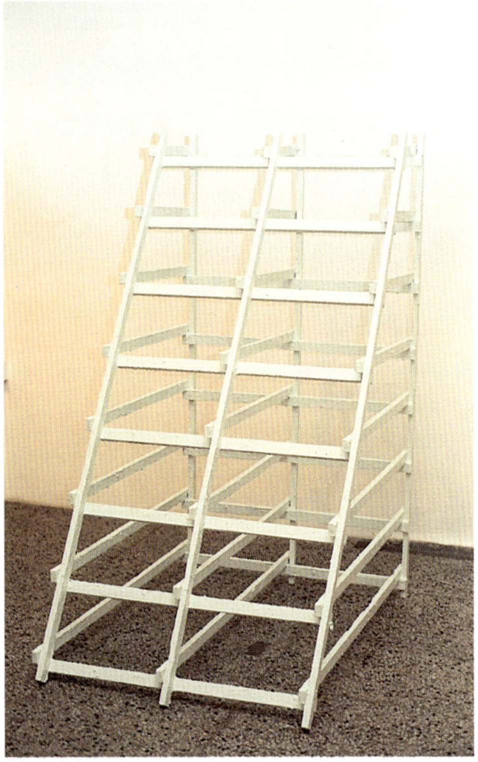
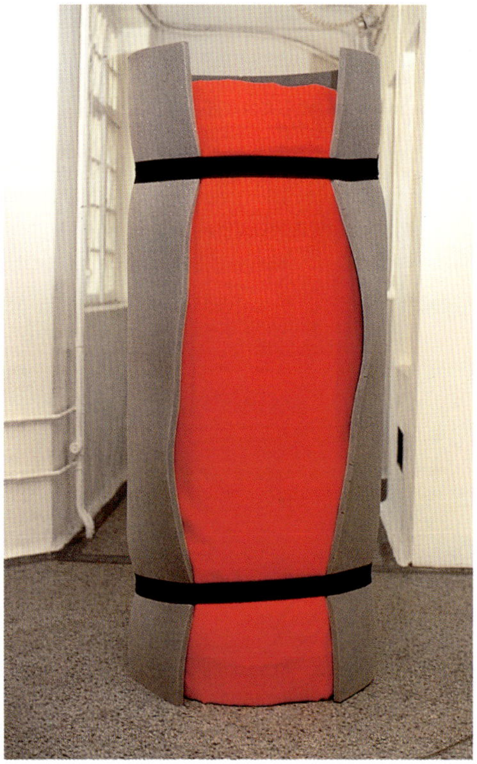
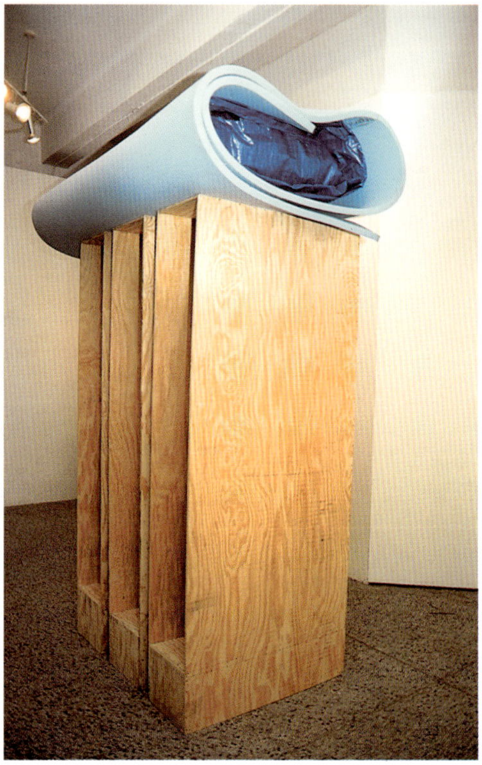

Across, Around, Up
Painted roofing timbers, upholstery foam, felt, elastic, packaging foam, tarpaulin, shuttering ply.
180 x 210 cm, 185 x 210 x 180 cm, 120 x 190 x 180 cm
1992
Diorama, Regent's Park, London

This is one way to read Barlow's approach to installation, a mode of sculptural activity that she has become well known for. Barlow has settled into an installation-based way of working over the last twelve or so years now, installing objects in groups and ensembles. Her 1992 exhibition (with Keith Wilson and Fernando Palma) at Regent's Park's Diorama in which she exhibited *Across*, *Around* and *Up* was a turning point. With these pieces, she found herself returning to sculpture and reclaiming her relationship with objects, after the experience of making *Deep*, 1991 – a failed work in which she tried to fill a whole space with boxes.

These three directional pieces (diagonal, vertical and horizontal) exhibited in 1992 would find themselves reconfigured and regrouped across a range of works and ensembles in the 1990s. *Depot*, a four-part work made for the Museum of Installation in 1995 is a key work. Like so many of Barlow's sculptures, *Depot* no longer exists. It was destroyed at the end of the exhibition, rather than stored. The storage was conducted during the exhibition itself – indeed the gallery was a kind of temporary storage space for this mobile group of objects. Storage depots are places not known for visitor-friendly arrangements. They are not image-conscious places of display; they are not places that put on shows. Barlow here has borrowed from their pragmatism and matter of fact attitude to stuff and generated a new kind of environment within her work that places interesting demands upon the viewer-visitor.

At the furthest end of the space, the two bound cylindrical components are joined at the base through a short jigsaw piece-like platform. This platform has the look of a plinth or stage. The viewer, however, is to walk around this stage and not to walk over it, joining in the ensemble's theatre. This platform-plinth is a way of linking and interlocking the two components, giving them a unity and mobility, and preventing the viewer from becoming a trespasser. Barlow does not like people touching her work, let alone joining in on the act. The grandstand-like component of *Depot*, a favourite structural motif in her sculpture of the 1990s, almost stands as a physical embodiment of this prohibition. This wooden structure is an instrument of spectacle turned into a non-functioning object of display. It could never take an audience (it would collapse under the weight) and stands its ground as a stubborn example to us all as we try to circumnavigate it and gauge its fixed, one-way view.

Depot
Painted wood, upholstery foam, canvas, industrial PVC tube, hardoard, red tape, rubber tubing, painted shuttering ply
Overall space/work:
600 x 240 x 1800 cm
1995
Museum of Installation,
Great Sutton Street, London

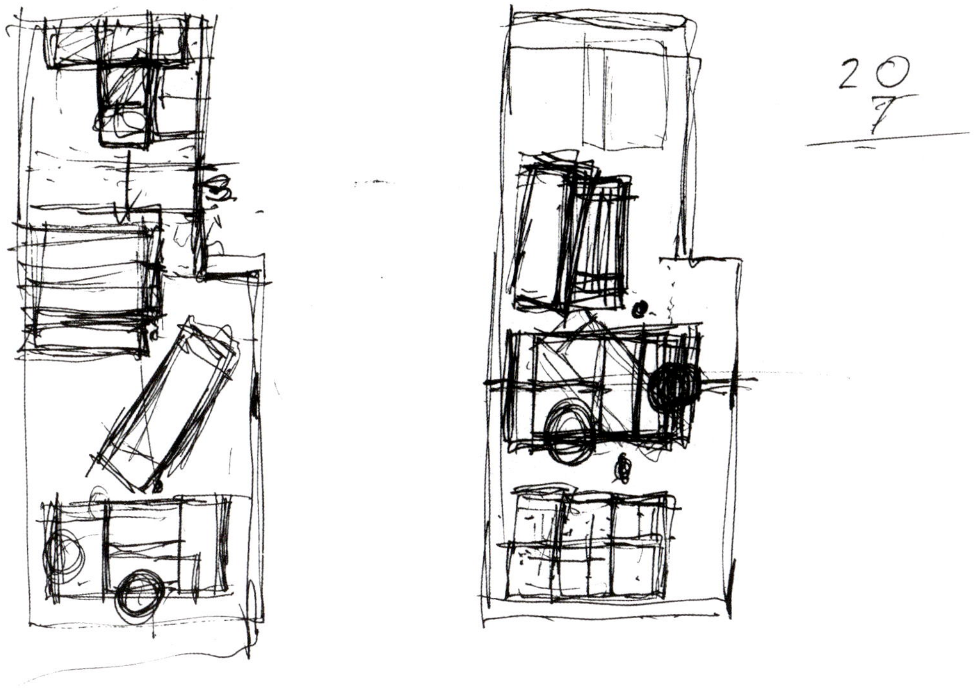

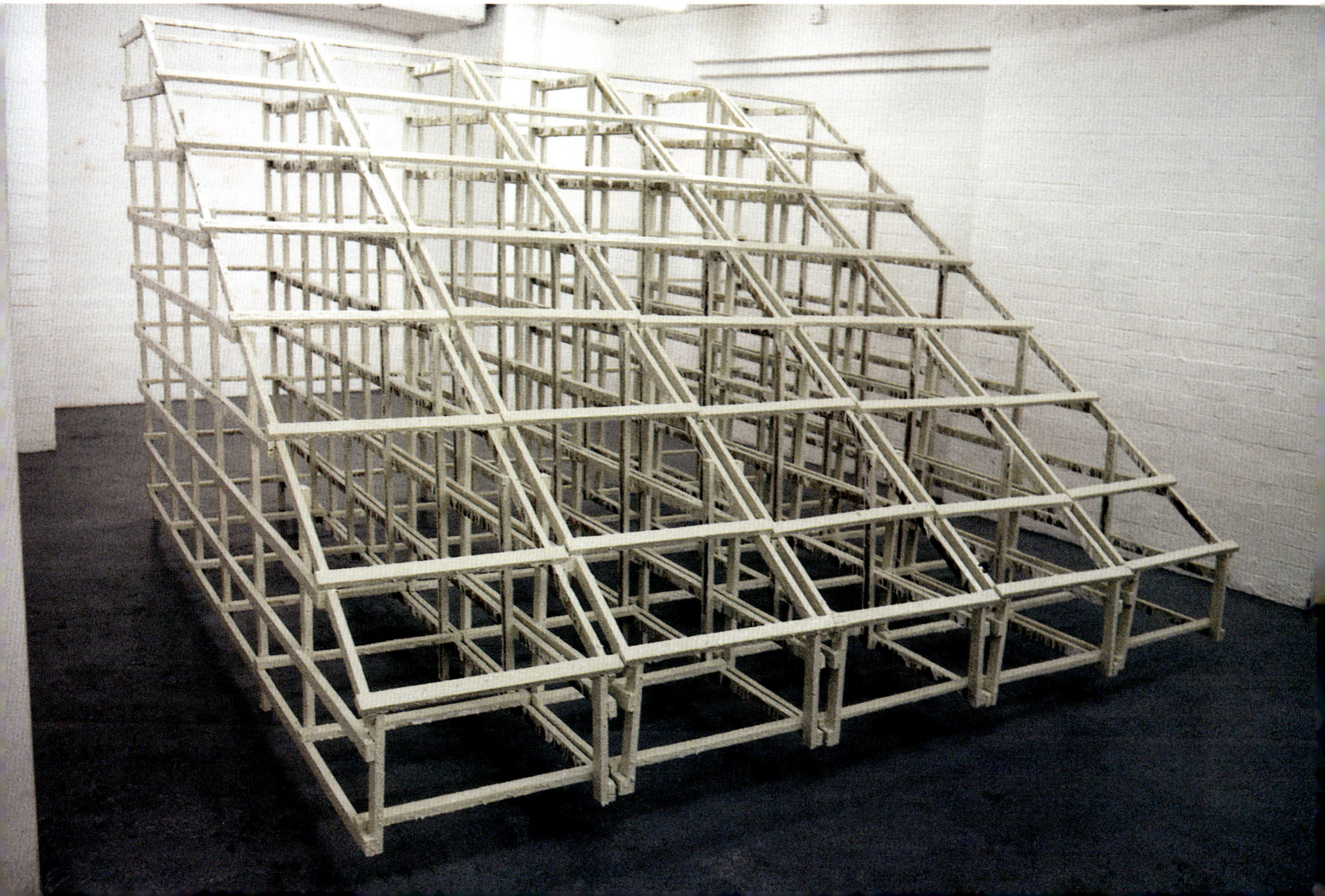

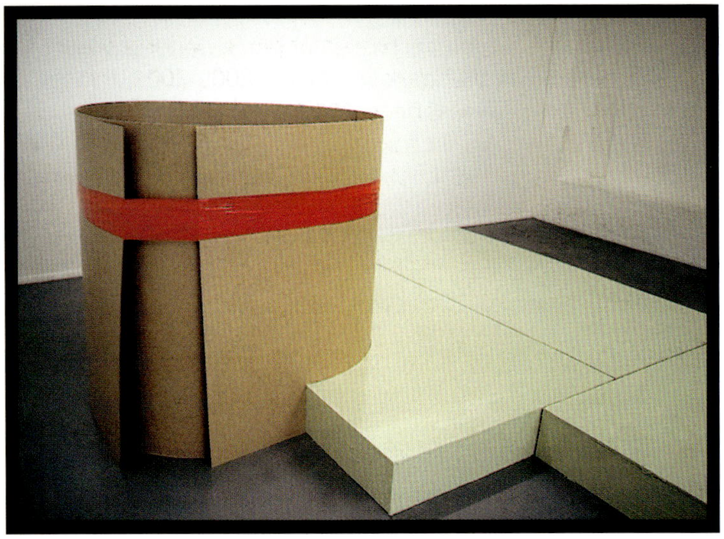

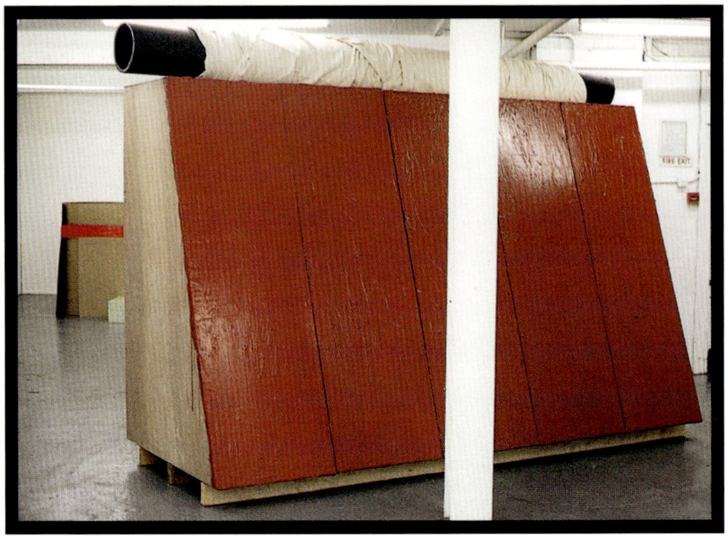

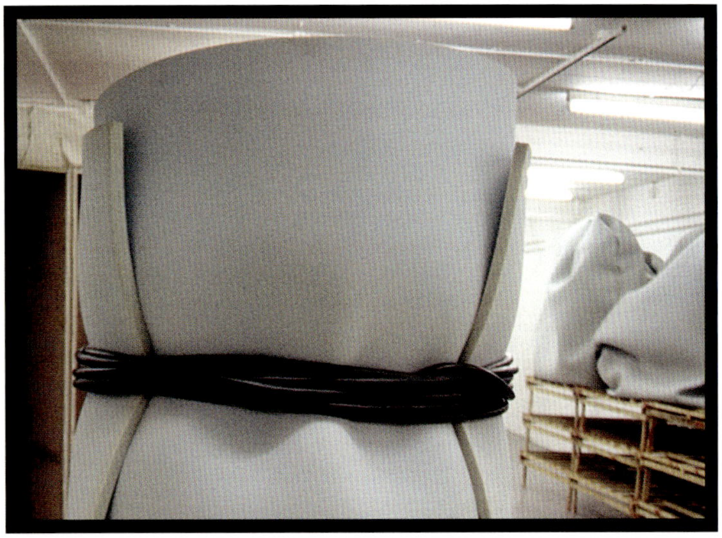

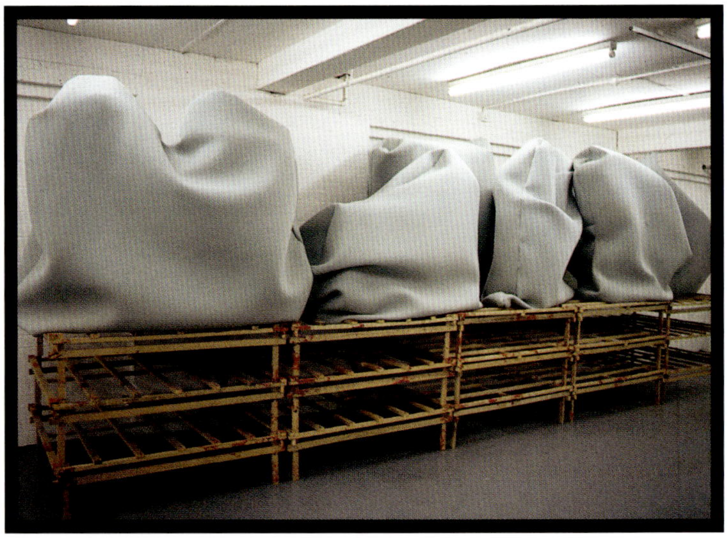

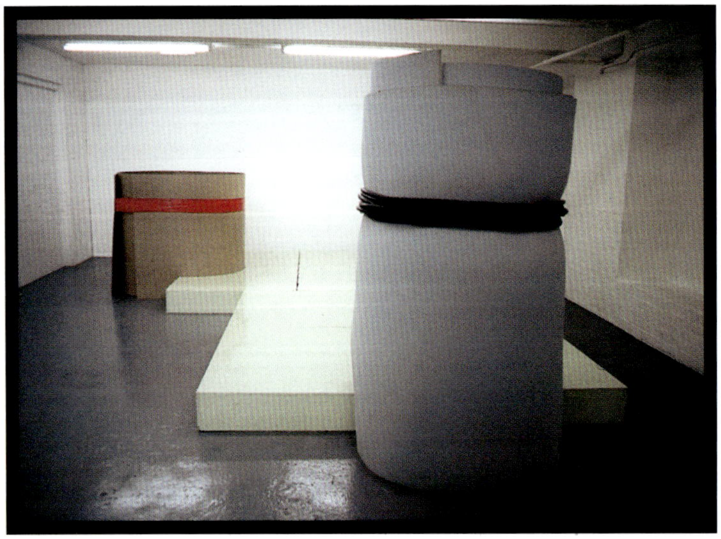

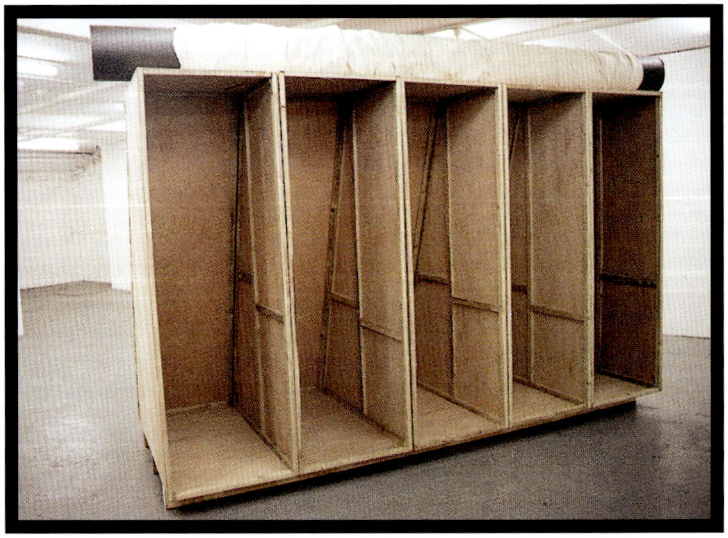

Barlow has often been seen as one concerned with narrative. In many ways however, Barlow is an anti-narrative sculptor. Her installed works do not have stories or plots, rather a poetry of formal correspondences and invisible threads. In *after dark into black*, 2000-2001, the ensemble is so dense and so tightly packed that it almost becomes a single work. Barlow showed this in the British Art Show at the time. It was, she said, a culmination of a decade of work. Characteristically, Barlow was not happy with it. Looking at it I ask her why and she talks about having tried to cram too much into it and it being too busy. *after dark into black*, however, is an extraordinary work. It has an operatic quality to it and is rich in colours, surfaces and forms. It has a self-referential life to it that forces the viewer to stand back and try and take it all in. It is both one work and an ensemble of works. Slightly to one side, there is an upright cylindrical structure bound in foam. “What’s inside it?”, I ask. She doesn’t tell me.

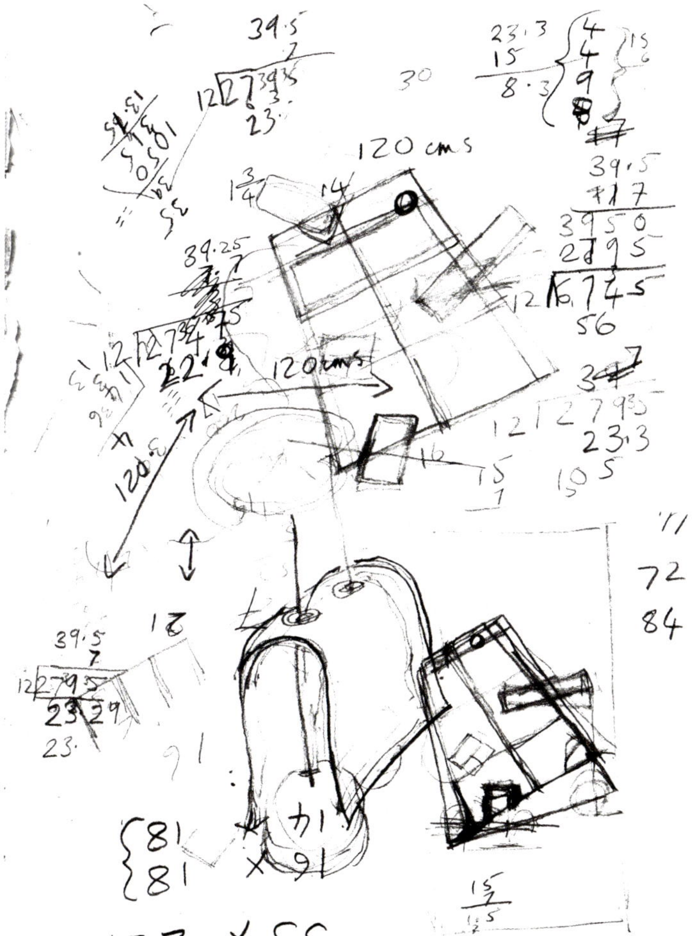

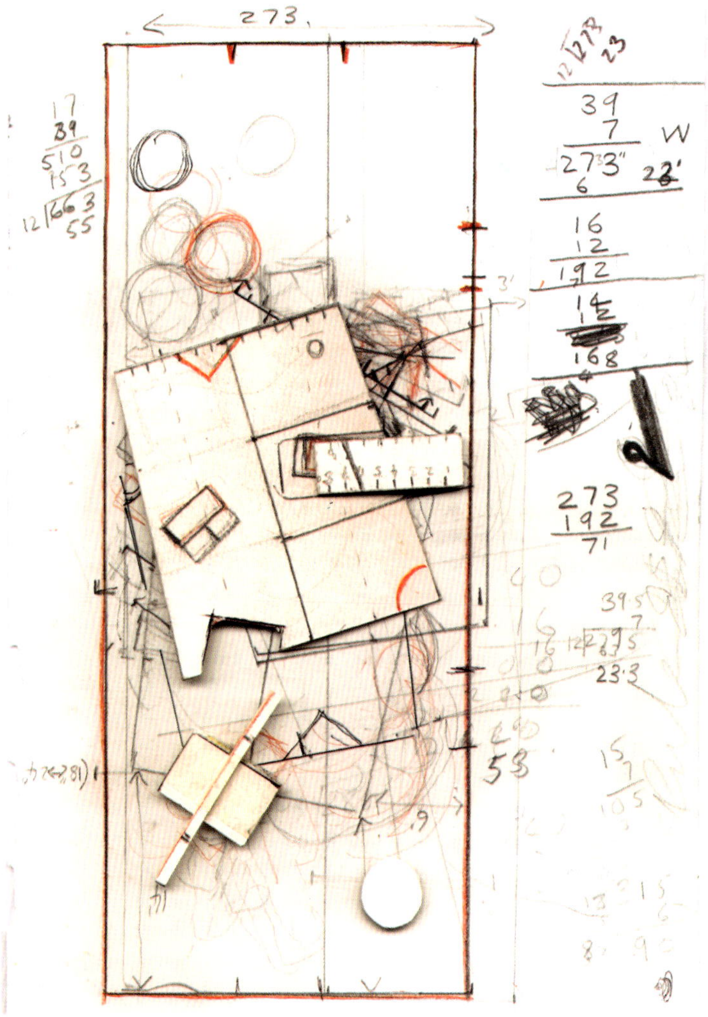

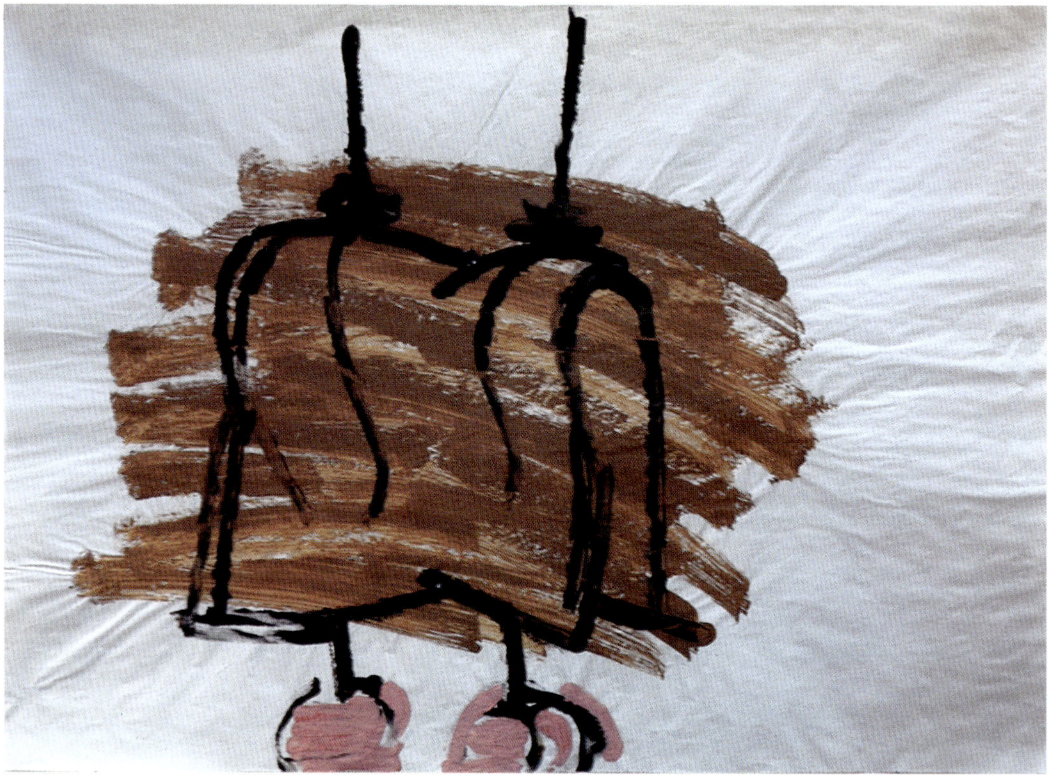

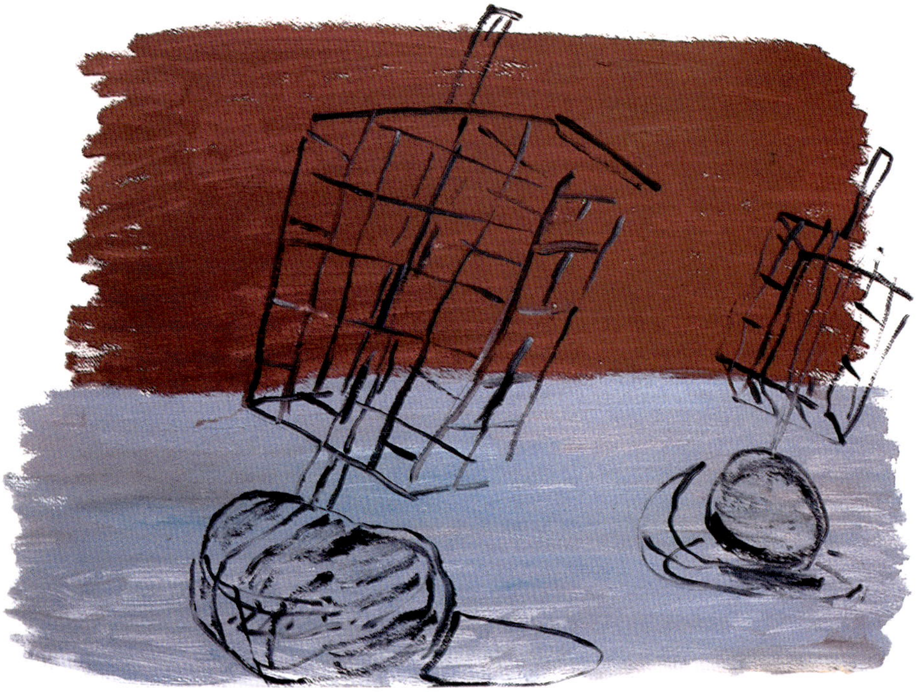

after dark into black
Hardboard, paint, felt, black mattress, plastic pipe, rubber tubing, painted fabric, paper, tape, roofing batons, stitched hessian, casters, plaster/concrete
Overall: 750 x 330 x 900 cm
2000-2001
Deen Gallery, Edinburgh, Scotland; Southampton City Art Gallery; CVA, Cardiff, Wales; The Gas Hall, Birmingham: UK

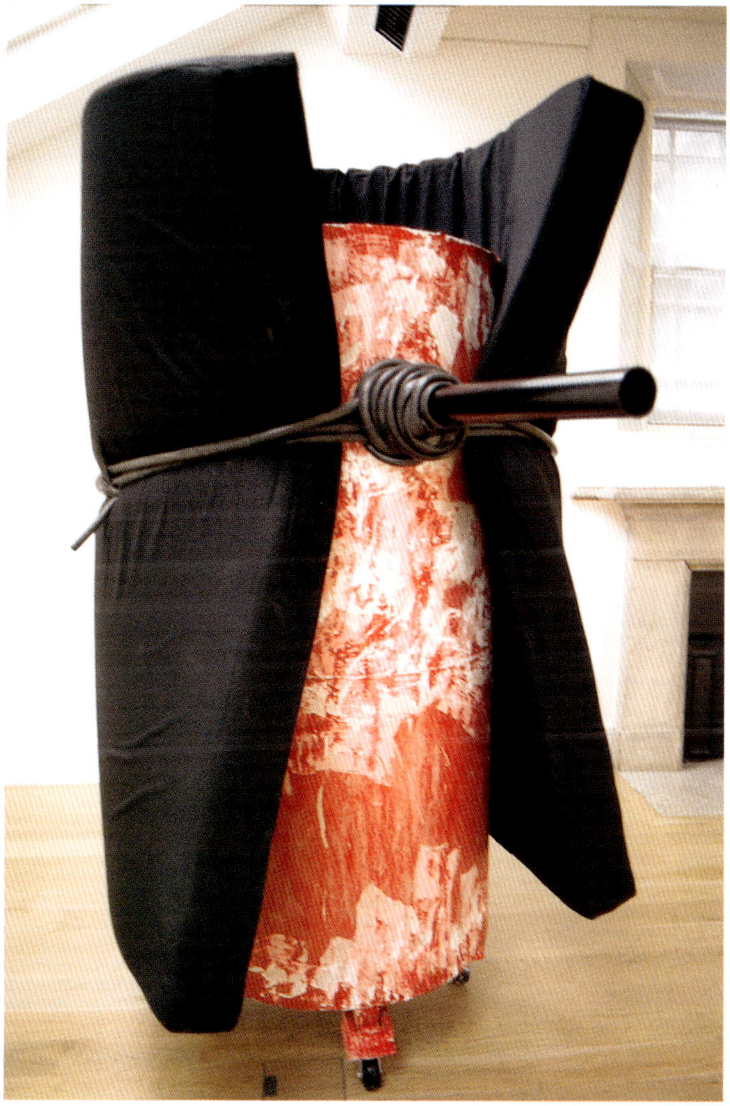

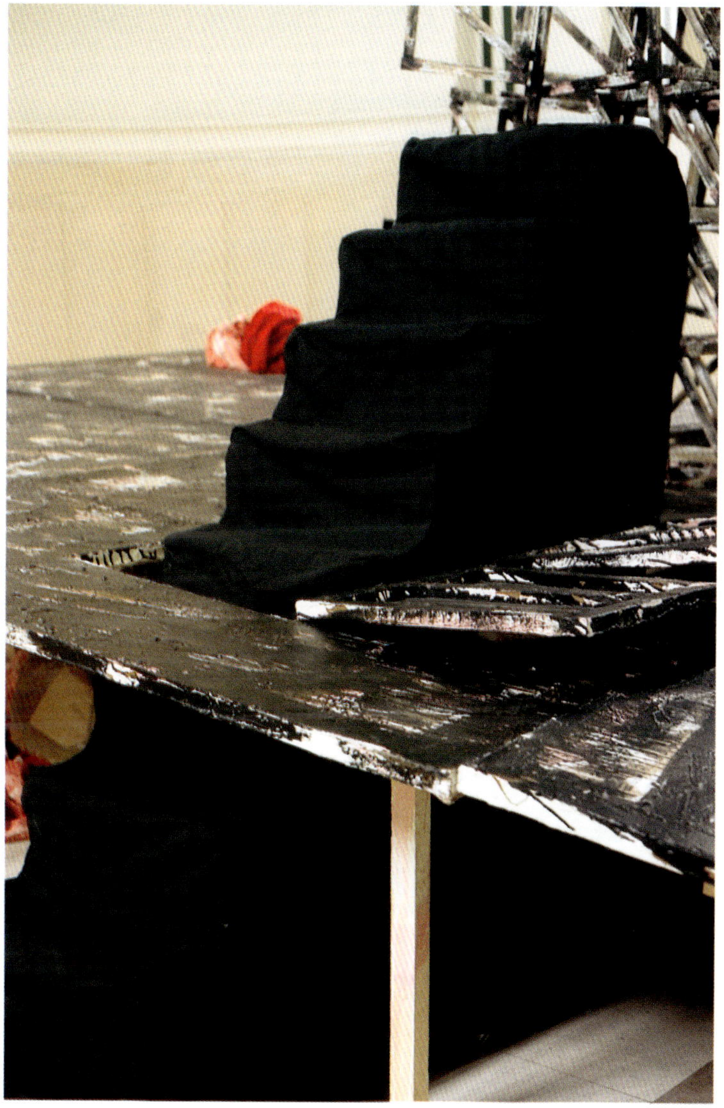

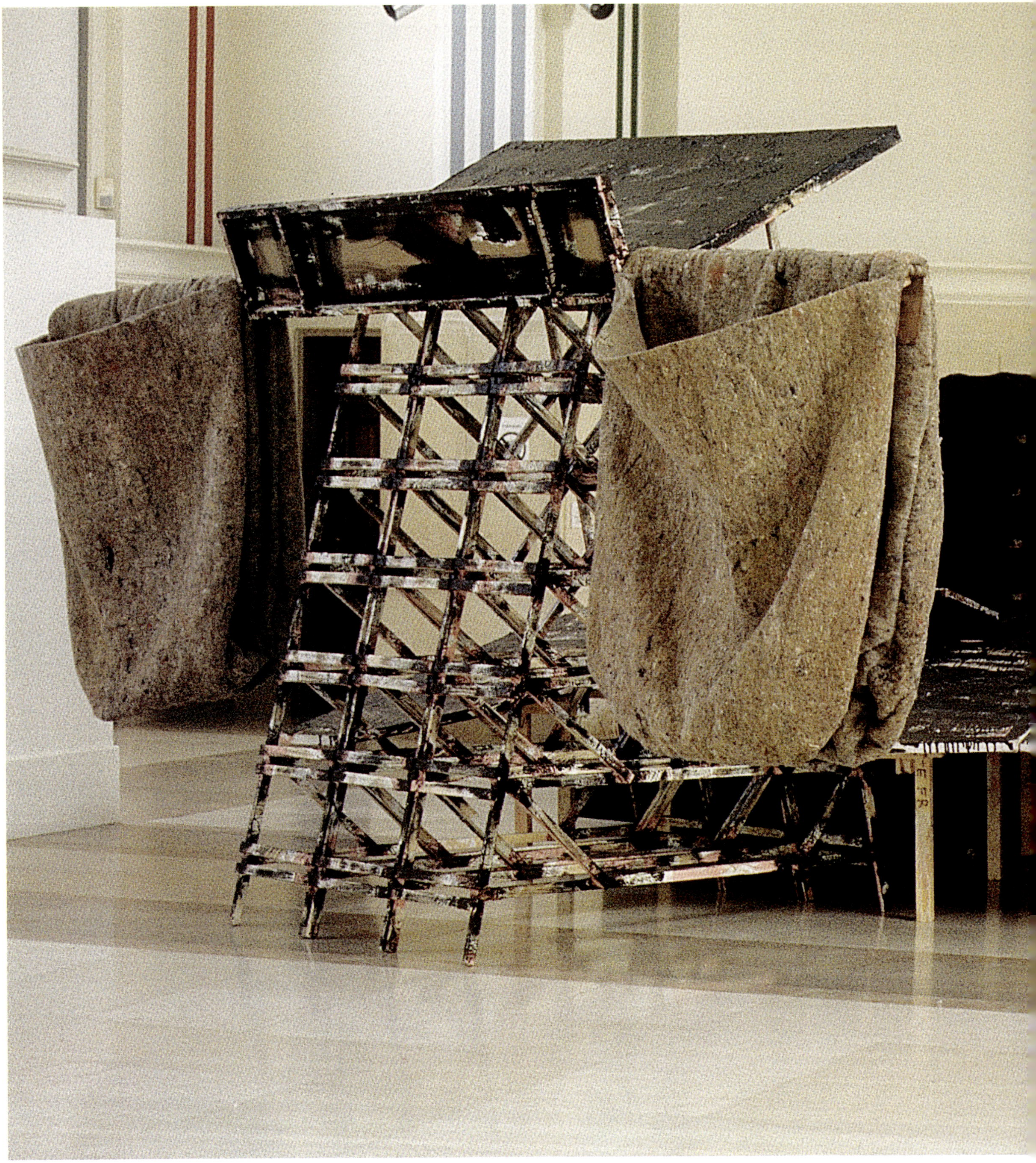

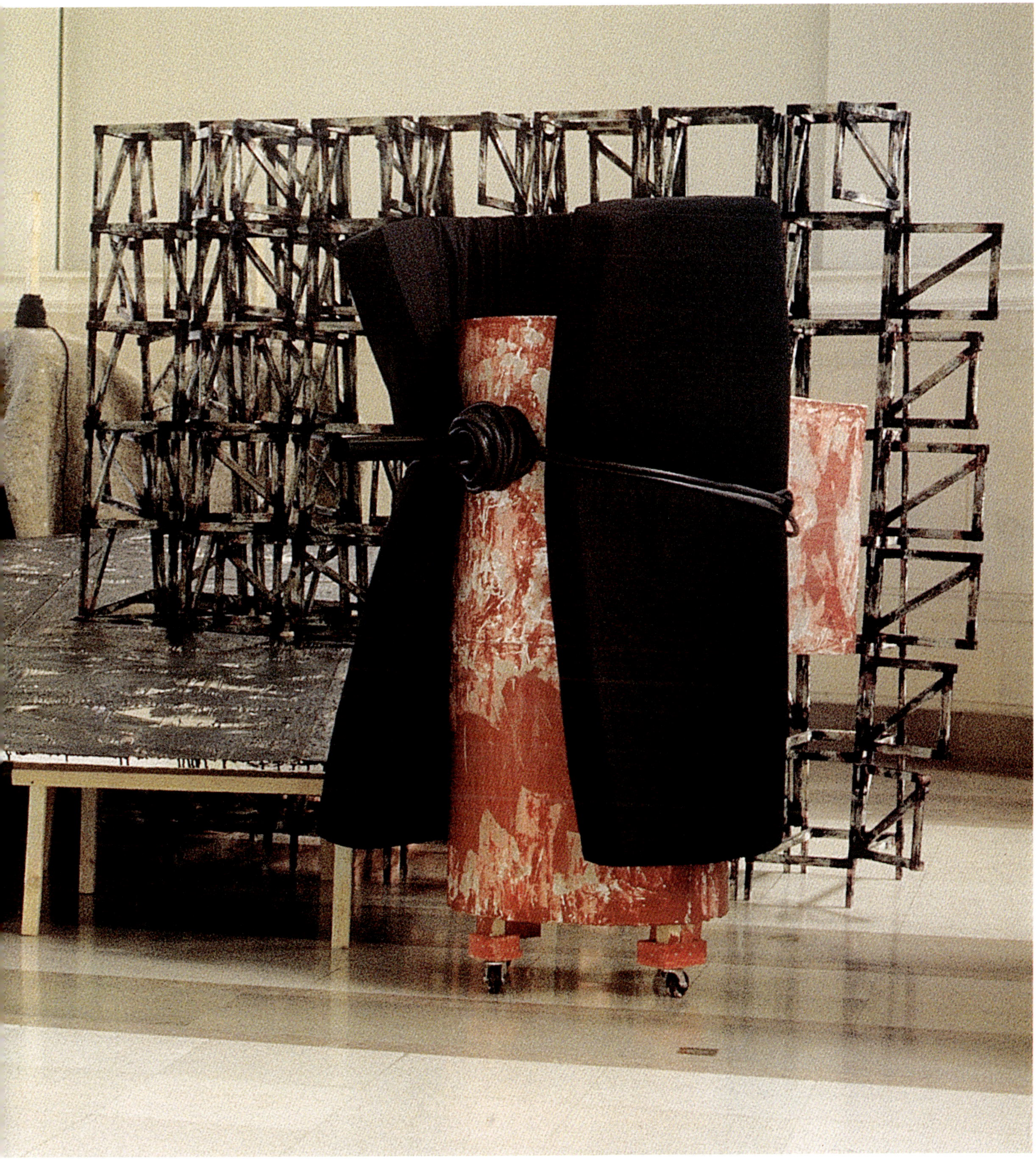

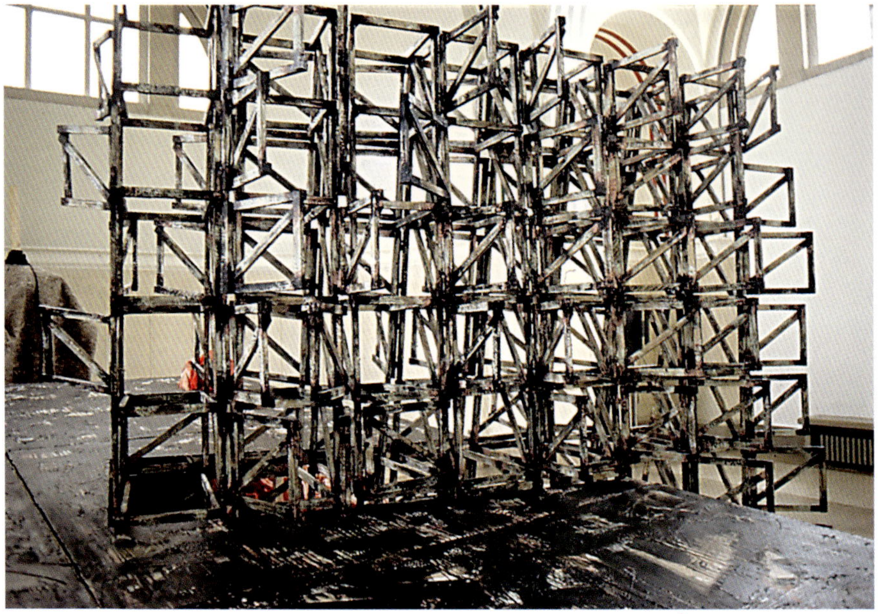

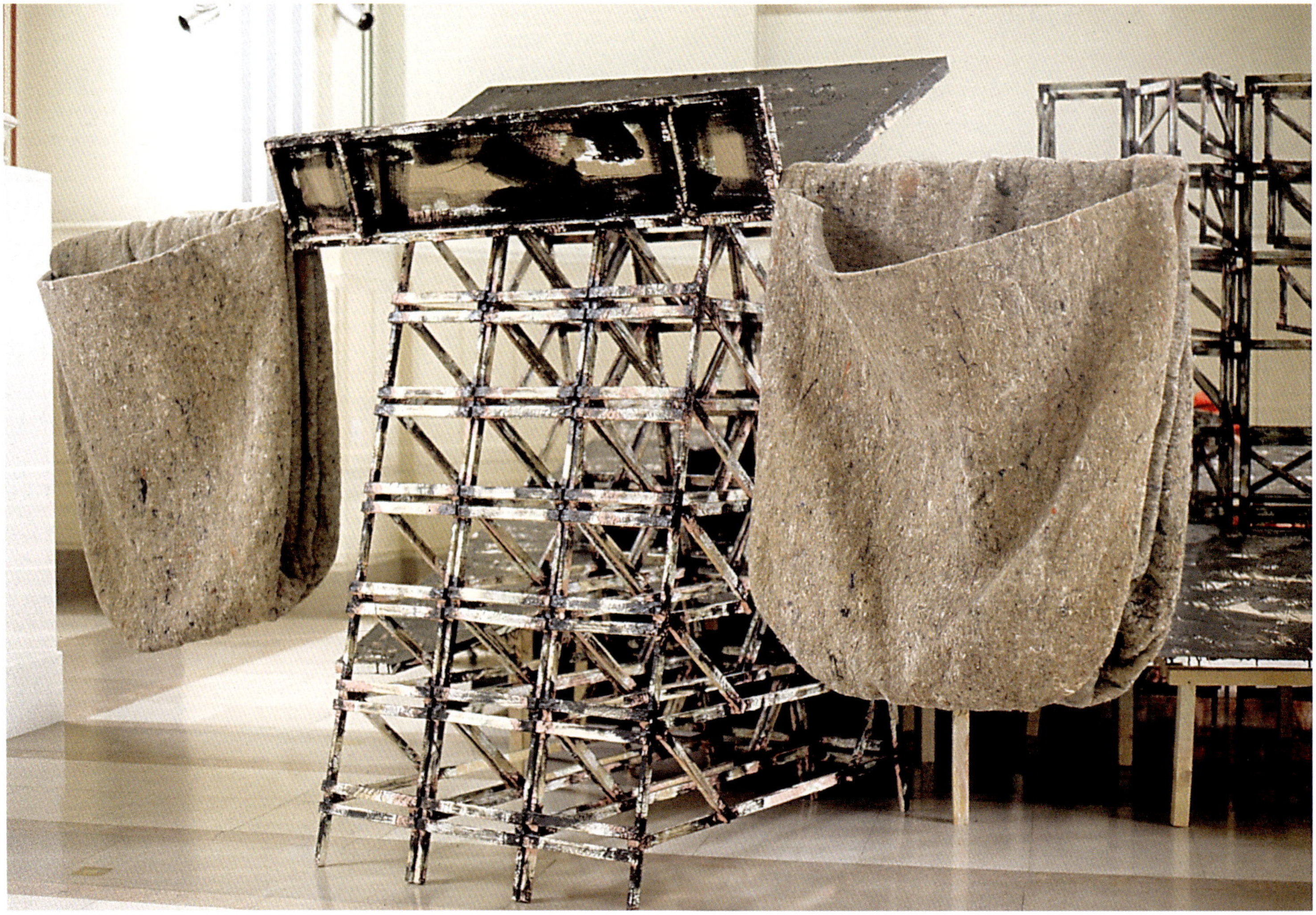

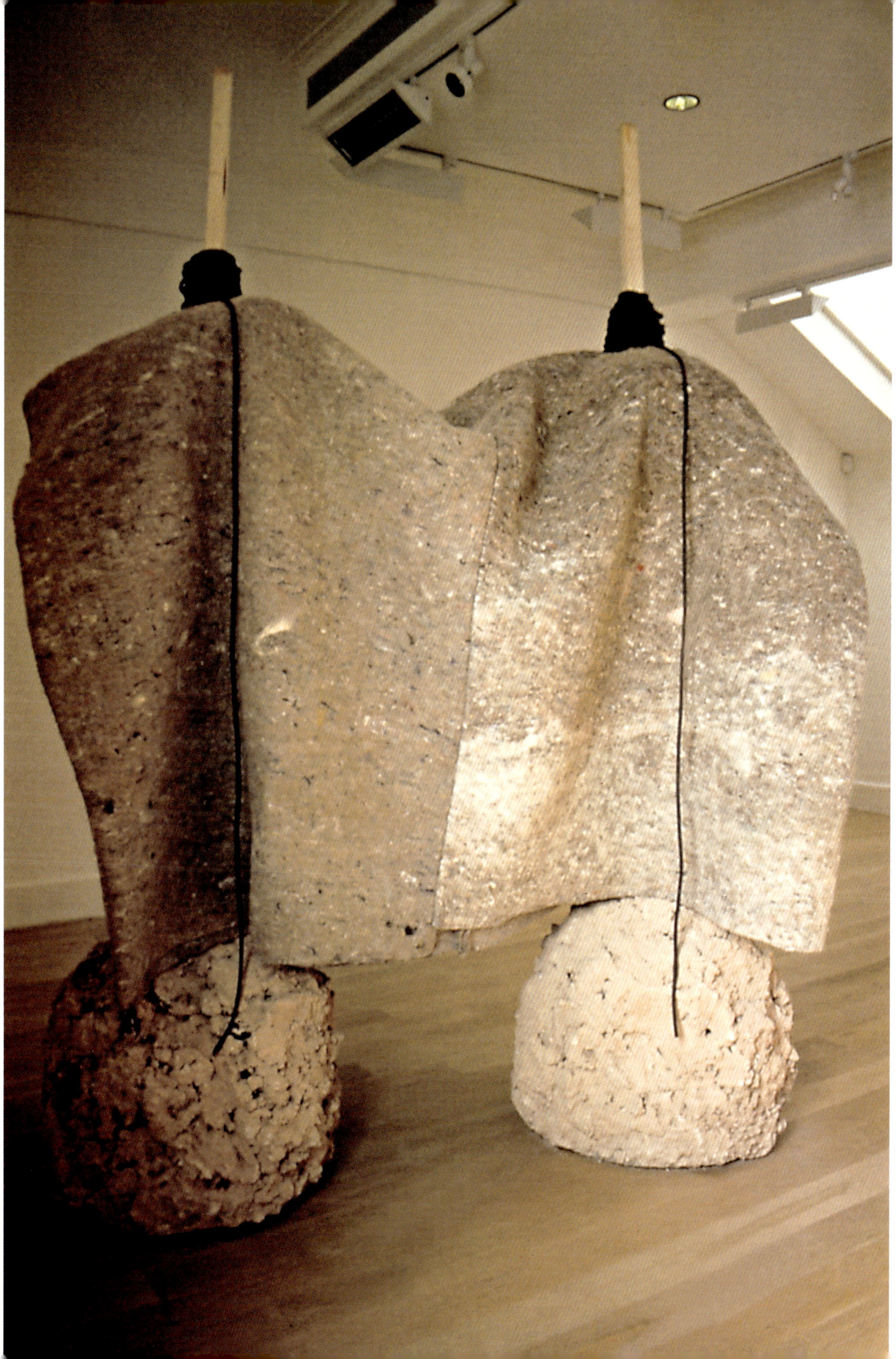

One & Two
Plywood, filled fabric cushions
210 x 210 x 180 cm
1992-1993

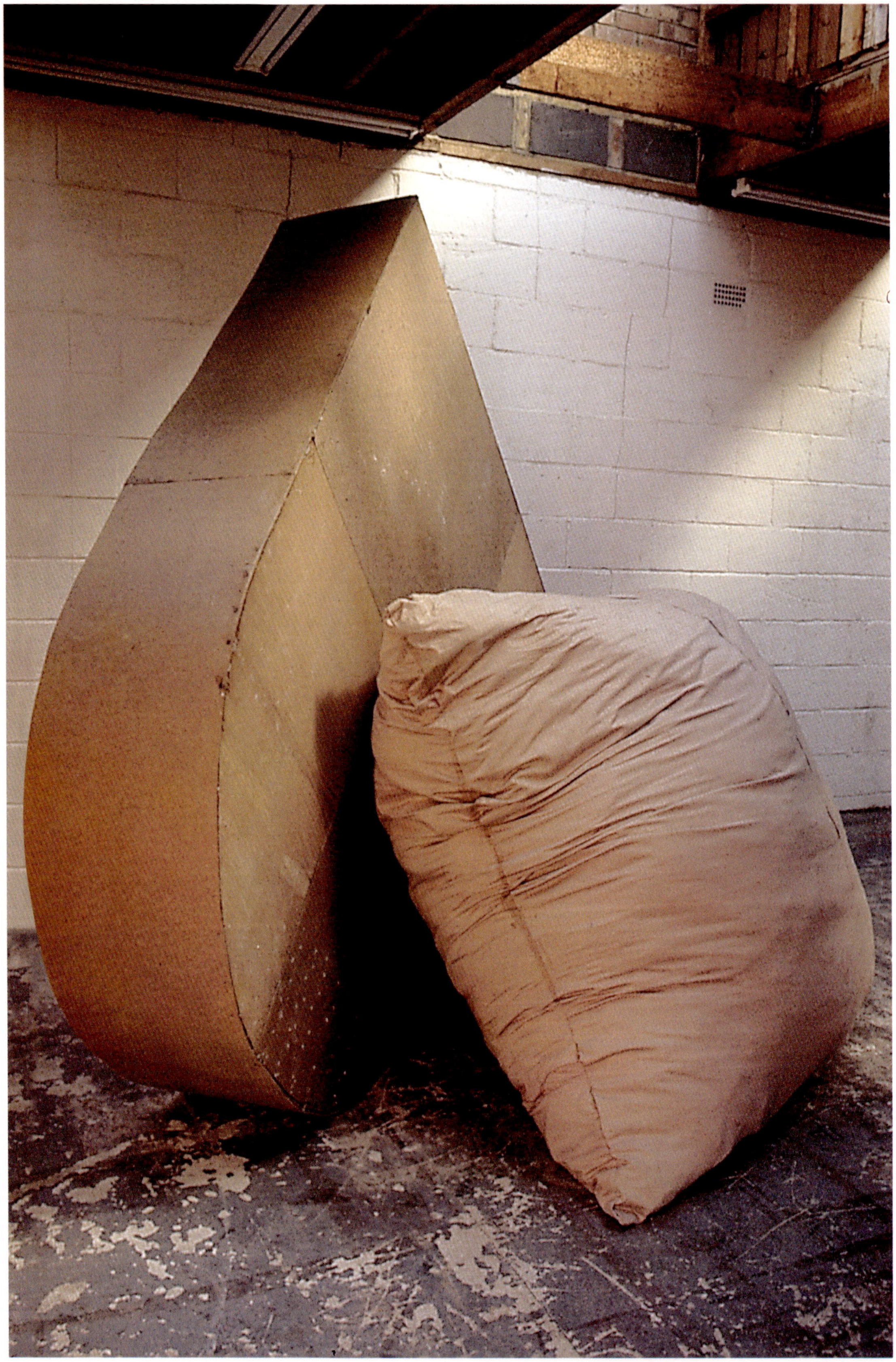

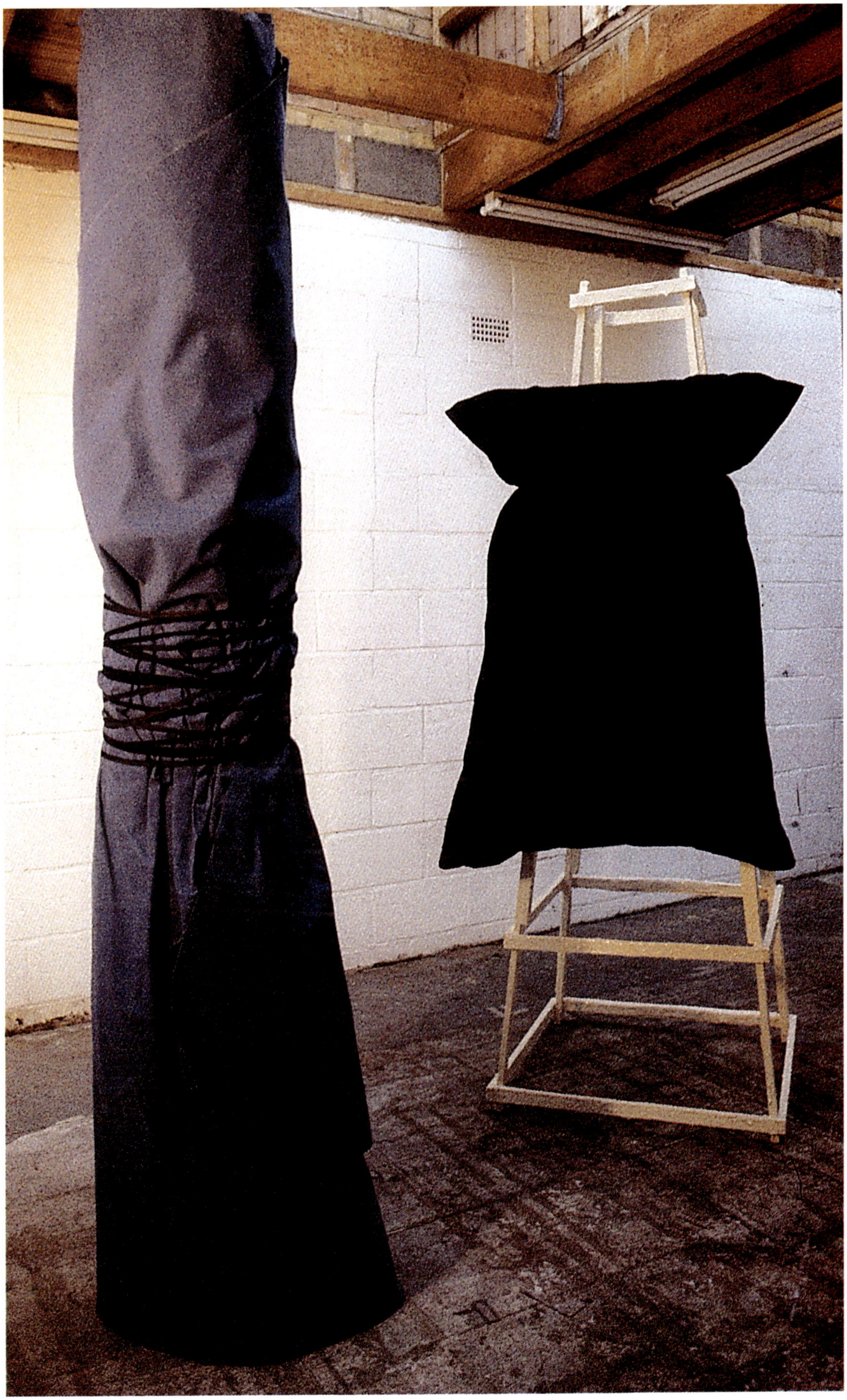

Left/foreground
Tied tarpaulin
Tied tarpaulin pipe, plastic, fabric, faom, rubber flex
300 x 120 x 120 cm
1992-3

Right/background
Bag on Frame
Paint, timber, filled fabric, cushion, rubber flex
240 x 120 x 120 cm
1992-3

The Sneeze of Louise

Phyllida Barlow

This essay is adapted from a slide-illustrated lecture on the sculpture of Louise Bourgeois and refers to work seen during 1995 in the exhibitions *Rites of Passage* at the Tate Gallery Millbank, London, *Louise Bourgeois* at the Musee d'Art Moderne de la Ville de Paris, and *Louise Bourgeois: Sculpture* and *The Prints of Louise Bourgeois* at the Museum of Modern Art, Oxford. The slide illustrated talk emphasised a narrative interpretation of the sculpture as well as identifying the rich formal concerns inherent to the work. The working title for the talk was "Telling Tales: interpreting Louise Bourgeois' sculptural narratives.

Whilst looking at Louise Bourgeois' *Cells* and *The Red Rooms* in the Musee de l'Art Moderne de la Ville de Paris and the Tate Gallery, London I thought about the devices artists have used during this century to frame and contain disparate things so as to bring unlikely, opposing or contrasting objects together as a unified experience – devices such as boxes, plinths, cages and, of course recently, the ubiquitous vitrine.

I recalled Marcel Duchamp's *Why Not Sneeze, Rrose Selavy* of 1921. As a small, neat object it is easy to remember. Its disparate collection of things are unified by a small, portable cage. The ring on top is just big enough for a finger to go through suggesting a container for the lightest of animals – small birds to be transported to and from market. It is therefore a portable object which, as such, clearly shows the signs of wear and tear.

It contains a collection of white cubes, apparently trapped. Though marble is a dense, heavy material the cubes masquerade perfectly as cubes of sugar. Protruding into the cubes are two objects: a thermometer and a cuttle bone. The thermometer is an instrument which measures and records the changes in body temperature, registering sickness or health, but here, as it nestles and probes into the cool deceitful cubes of marble sugar, what change is expected to be detected? Perhaps a rise in temperature would cause an explosion and the

Boxes
27 plywood boxes
Each 30 x 30 x 30 cm
1968

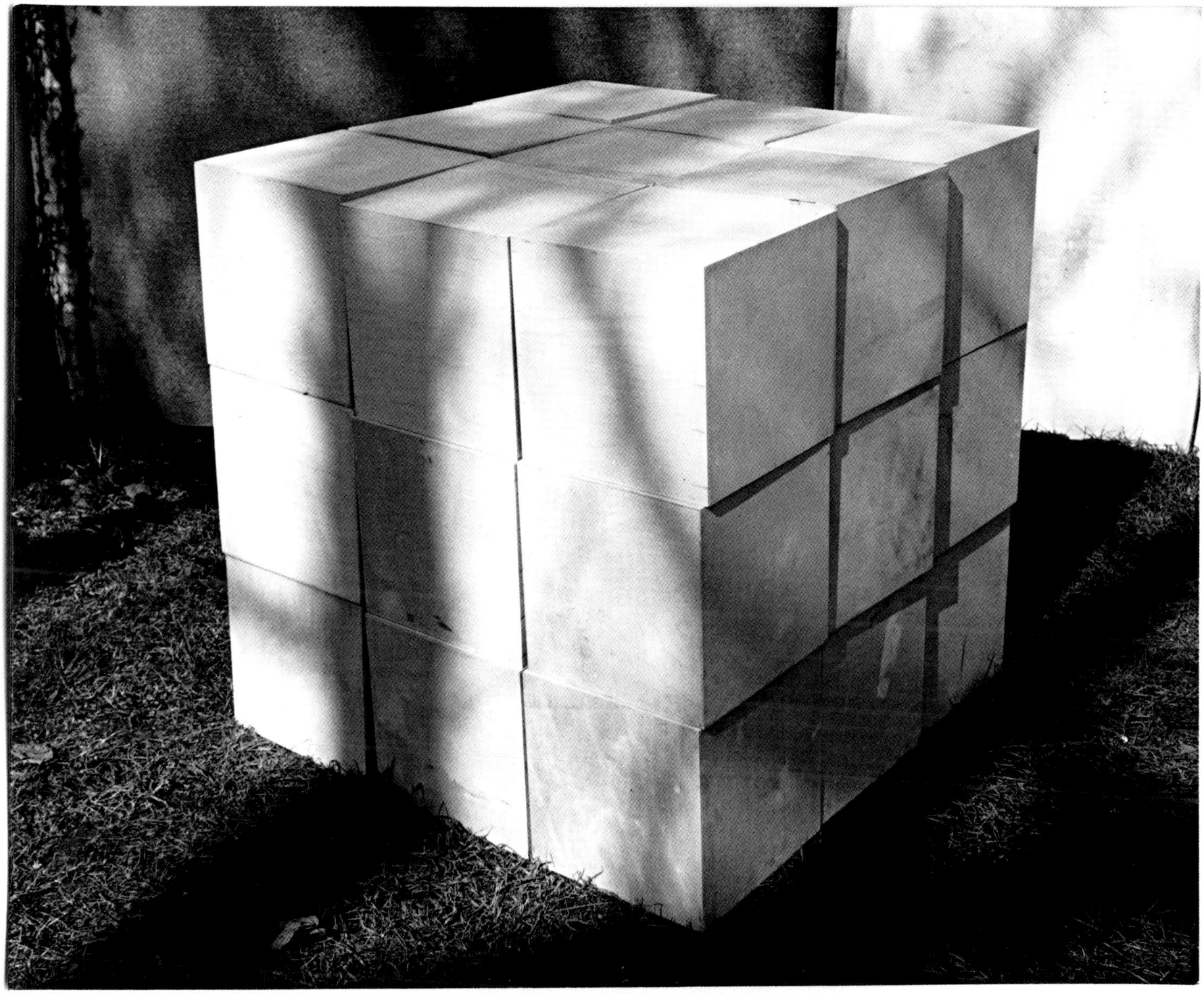

1 "Louise Bourgeois – In a Strange Way Things are Getting Better", an interview with Francesco Bonami, *Flash Art,* vol. xxvii, no. 174, January/February 1994, p. 39.

2 "Louise Bourgeois: Self-Expression is Sacred and Fatal – Statements", no. 45, p. 189 in Christiane Meyer-Thoss, ed. *Louise Bourgeois: Designing for Free Fall,* Amman Vertag A G, Zurich, 1992.

3 Meyer-Thoss, *Louise Bourgeois: Designing for Free Fall*, p. 200.

small cage and its contents would fragment into a powder of sugary marble-dust laced with beads of mercury, ground cuttle bone, tangled wire and shards of glass.

Is this an object held in time, poised to explode? The thermometer waits in anticipation for any change which indicates the impending explosion. What is the role of the cuttle bone? What is a cuttle bone – something found washed up on sea shores, or an object for pet birds to sharpen their beaks on? It is, in fact, the central bone of the cuttle fish, a squid-like animal which ejects ink when alarmed. Like the thermometer this residual object also indicates anticipation, but in its case it is the anticipation of fear, and the volatile consequences of that fear, an eruption of black ink. Gradually this small, portable cage-object becomes more and more like an ambiguous instrument with a sexuality which its title begins to reveal. More particularly, it reveals its absence of sex, its hoping for sex.

The sneeze, sometimes referred to as the next best thing to an orgasm, is the anticipated event and the disparate contents of the cage, in their different ways, mark time in anticipation of this longed for, desired event. At the moment when the thermometer registers a change as the cool marble sugar cubes become hot and the cuttle bone recalls its former status as the rigid inner bone of the warning, ink-squirting fleshy squid, the prolonged anticipation will be released in the craved for orgasmic explosion of a sneeze. Louise Bourgeois knew Marcel Duchamp and thought he was an unhappy man because "... all his life he could not make a woman sexually happy".[1] Perhaps this adds to the significance of this object's potent sexuality, for, as Bourgeois said in an interview with Christiane Meyer-Thoss, "...the sexual, and the absence of sex is everything".[2]

Duchamp's object is an object of measurement. It is in suspense, held in time, unfolding itself continuously at the same moment, a constant reminder of the longed for and the about to be. Its tension is borne out of its implications of an unfulfilled sexual longing told by its disguising and playful symbols. "All symbolic acts are pleasurable," said Louise Bourgeois. "People will not admit to that."[3] Though these symbols are playful what they symbolise is painful: the fearful experience of sexual longing when it is reciprocated by a dreaded and awesome sexual unfulfilment. I can recall *Why Not Sneeze* as an image. It is easy to remember. The work of Louise Bourgeois which reminded me of *Why Not Sneeze* I cannot recall as an image, and I find it difficult to remember. It demands that you are there with it.

The work I am referring to is *Cell (Eyes and Mirrors*), 1989-1993. This work reveals itself as you approach it and walk around it. And it is as an unfolding space and as an unfolding object that it arouses response. These unfolding qualities are time-based and seem to refute an image for a physically sensual experience which is to do with time, place and a all-pervading atmosphere of fear. It is the element of time which enables me to compare *Cell (Eyes and Mirrors)* with Duchamp's *Why Not Sneeze*. In both works I experience a suspension of time through objects which act as instruments of measurement.

With *Cell (Eyes and Mirrors)* the space unfolds as you walk around the sculpture. This is emphasised in the contrast between the predatory and watchful but unseeing gaze of the carved breast-like granite eyes and the ever watchful, all-seeing gaze of the mirrors which seem to record, hold and trap every movement beyond their immediate environment. As you walk around this sculpture you can experience an opposite view. As you look at, or more appropriately, watch the back of the granite eyes the front is revealed by the mirrors. This is a sculpture with eyes at the back of its head. As objects of continuous revelation the mirrors are instruments of surveillance which do not keep secrets, harsh devices of stark objectivity which capture, in real time, the presence of the viewer who becomes ensnared and trapped in the *Cell*'s interior space.

4 *Reperes: Louise Bourgeois Retrospective 1947-1984*, preface by Jean Fremon, Paris: Galerie Maeght LeLong, p. 27.

5 *Reperes: Louise Bourgeois Retrospective 1947-1984*, p. 27.

6 Meyer-Thoss, *Louise Bourgeois: Designing for Free Fall*, p. 128.

The mirrors are the gaze, the sight of the sightless granite. They are the instruments which register change. They monitor your changing movements and the unchanging movements of the objects they stand guard over within, just as the thermometer anticipates change in *Why Not Sneeze*. The boundary or container for this sculpture – the derelict structure of salvaged window frames from disbanded factory or office – act as a grid. Grids imply systems of order, means for measuring. As Louise Bourgeois has said: "With grids everything has a place, everything is welcome."[4] Like the well-used container cage of *Why Not Sneeze*, this worn and weathered container has recorded on it its passage through time. Both have time engrained within them and because of this they convey a sense of resignation. They can wait forever.

Cell (Eyes and Mirrors) is full of sight and no sight, a kind of blindness which is full of stillness, a state of waiting, but also of movement. The movements are caught in the reflective eyes of the mirrors which lie in wait to trap the stalking viewer and pull them into the gridded, interior space where "everything has a place, everything is welcome".[5] This blind and watchful anticipation is also full of fear, and, like 'Why Not Sneeze', full of the absence of sex. This absence is suspended in time which itself constitutes the fear in *Cell (Eyes and Mirrors)*. Louise Bougeois says: "My work is a very specific fight against fears, one at a time".[6] Here absence of sex arises out of fear of the awesome potency of the sexual, implied by the ripe, breasted forms of the granite eyes, and their accompanying voyeuristic mirrors, rather than out of the fear of the awesome impotency of the sex of *Why Not Sneeze*.

Man Ray's *Object to be Destroyed,* 1923, and Louise Bourgeois' *No Exit*, 1989, show how time can be manifested in objects and sculpture whose material and physical identities could seem to deny and to be incapable of referencing time. The forensic evidence of time in the sculptures of Louise Bourgeois is as emotively significant as the artist's explicit use of sexually charged forms and surfaces. As in *Why Not Sneeze* and *Cell (Eyes and Mirrors),* a similar anticipatory sense of time through measurement is present in *Object to be Destroyed* and *No Exit*. They are instruments of measurement. In the case of *Object to be Destroyed* a metronome reveals time as a beat, a rhythm. Time becomes malleable because its rhythm can be altered from faster to slower and back again. Time appears to pass quickly or slowly or, if the metronome stops, to stand still. All compete with our notion of time as a constant.

This is an ominous instrument object. Its alterable but unrelenting beat is emphasised by the ever-watchful photographic image of the eye, expediently attached to the metronome needle with a paper clip. Its cold, dreamy stare is both hypnotically alluring and fearsome in its concentration, an additional and accompanying menace to the rhythmic clockwork sound. It is an unavoidable reminder of a potential time bomb and a relentless advance towards a moment. This object's relevance to the sculpture of Louise Bourgeois is through the ever-watchful gaze of the image of the eye, and the association Louise Bourgeois makes in her sculpture with watchfulness, sleep and blindness. Implicit in these states is their relationship to sound, sound which alerts, awakens and reveals.

The potential to describe sound through objects which can evoke or associate themselves with sound rather than through objects which make sound as in *Object to be Destroyed* is evident in much of the sculpture Louise Bougeois of which *No Exit* is one example. The staircase of *No Exit* acts as a grid on which the tread of a foot could measure and beat out the rhythm of a quick or slow pace. This potential for sound is embedded within the wooden staircase's material physicality. Formally, *No Exit* is a sculpture with a clearly identifiable front and a back. It has an interior and an exterior. Also, it is phallic: the column of stairs is accompanied by two carved wooden spheres set on either side. This phallic arrangement, so essential to much of her sculpture, can take on and become female with characteristics of breasts and vagina.

As you approach this work, the carved spheres seem to be rolled back, like a newly opened up tomb, inviting entry. You can walk around the staircase and into the space it occupies – very different from *Cell (eyes and Mirrors)*. It is essential to do this in order to discover that at the back of the staircase is located a small hatch which reveals the space beneath the stairs. The ultimate secret space, it is the ideal hiding place, small, dark and highly charged with childhood inquisitiveness and fears. This under-the-stair space is inhabited by two casts of hearts supported on a steel rod. These are the sound of this work colluding with the already implied sound of the foot fall on the bare boards of the staircase. These casts act as a reminder of the beating, thumping heart. Like the foot fall on the stair it can change in rhythm and pace, signalling a combination of pleasure and fear, of calm and agitation. It reciprocates the bare boarded stairs' symbolic implications of the empty or deserted house, where anything and everything can lurk. The uncertainty where the staircase is going to or coming from evokes the dread of apprehension, the anticipation of the unexpected – a sound, a creaking board, or a movement, a fleeting shadow of something or someone unknown.

No Exit is full of suspicion. Arousing implications of time held and potential movement, its disparate elements are contained by a framed, screened space: the staircase is partly encircled by high wooden screens, offering another kind of unfolding space as experienced in *Cells (Eyes and Mirrors).* Screens, with their implications of privacy and intimacy, do not protect this particular space because it can be entered. The viewer is lured in to walk around at leisure, to experience the shifting evocations of time and movement contained in the bare boarded stairs and secret place beneath, and the could be and the about to be sound of the pulsating heart and beating foot fall.

The sculptural concerns of traditional formalism and material physicality paradoxically arouse their opposites, the powerful sensory and sensual responses of the non-physical and the non-material. The traditions inherent in the sculpture of Louise Bourgeois are deeply rooted in the Palaeolithic and twentieth century art of Europe. These traditions are exemplified by the sculpture of mid-twentieth century European artists. This is the dark heart of European sculpture which, after World War Two, sought a way to begin again by placing its trust in nature. Believing in nature as pure, simple and innocent provided the incentive to establish new beginnings for artists through which they could eradicate the horrors of war and its accompanying despotic totalitarianism and the genocide of the then recent past.

Etienne Martin's wood carving *Large Couple*, 1947, invents a primitive styled expression which equates with those qualities of nature believed to herald a better, purer future. Its heavy forms, dark shadows and cumbersome figuration are evidence of the grim aesthetics of mid-twentieth century European sculpture, in which well-learnt, crafted sculpture techniques and a formalism identifiable with ancient art were doggedly and uninspiringly deployed. Louise Bourgeois' *Untitled,* 1968-1969, is comparable to the Etienne Martin work, but is redeemed by its fluidity, its spillage and its sensual tactility, qualities which have the potential to give beauty to the monstrous. The arched form is curled over on itself, like a massive wave, to form deep, cavernous, concave, folded spaces at the centre of the work, the reciprocal womb-like form to the phallus/breast forms emerging as the top surface of the sculpture. These merged phallus/breast forms are endemic to her 50 years of making sculpture, from the totemic, breasted phallic sculptures of the 1940's and 50's, through to the hanging and suspended *Fillette,* 1968, the *Lairs* and the numerous pendulous cast rubber forms of recent years (1990s). Within this autonomous object there is the merging of the feminine and the masculine, between the phallus and the breast, between the swelling, growing forms and the excavated, cavernous space beneath. The enclosed spaces of the more recent *Lairs*, *Cells* and *Rooms* seem to have their origins in this monstrous object's interior space.

7 Meyer-Thoss, *Louise Bourgeois: Designing for Free Fall*, p. 123.

8 Meyer-Thoss, *Louise Bourgeois: Designing for Free Fall*, p. 69.

9 Meyer-Thoss, *Louise Bourgeois: Designing for Free Fall*, p. 69.

The glorious upheaval of the plaster forms of *Untitiled* so clearly portray Louise Bourgeois' relationship with fear that it becomes alarming to try to identify what this object is. It seems to exemplify the power of an autonomous object which defies a rememberable identity. As I have already noted, objects and sculpture can be either recalled as some kind of image, or be impossible to recall and so demand that you are there to experience them. The experience of objects and sculpture is inextricably linked to the real time required to look, walk around and consider. It is almost as if, in the absence of a human presence, the object would dissolve. This is very different from an object which presents itself as an image and can take on a pictorial equivalence.

The use of plaster is one of the liquid-to-solid materials with which Louise Bourgeois has had a continued relationship. Through it she reveals her marks of making, such as striations of finger marks drawn in the wet surface of the plaster during the process of modelling. Like all such marks they make evident her presence in the work, as if her emotions are drawn into the body of the sculpture. "My subject," she says, "is the rawness of the emotions, my medium is my materials. Plaster gives a lot to the doer. If you pour plaster it is going to set, go from liquid to solid, it has a life of its own, separate from the sculptor. The resistance of stone is total. Plaster and cement provides you with a kind of dialogue."[7]

Louise Bourgeois' language with materials and form have a symbiosis with how emotions find physical outlets through the body. This is powerfully communicated in *Untitled*. It is a kind of spewing up, a welling over of stuff with her mark so clearly smeared into the setting plaster. It is fearless about the non-beautiful but it does give beauty to the monstrous, endowing the fat, full and over-flowing forms with sensuality. *Untitled* shows how her subjectivity and her relationship with herself can be manifested through the most traditional of sculptural forms and techniques. "I have complete confidence in my inner self, the outer one is of no consequence to me."[8] This sculpture is raw and hot and her presence within it contrasts sharply with the distance she keeps from the more highly finished works where she employs a cool, mechanistic objectivity and her presence and closeness to the work is eradicated. *Untitled* is wild in its confrontation and fearless in its nameless identity.

Spiral Woman, 1951, is another example which clearly demonstrates the traditional roots of Louise Bourgeois' sculpture. The spiral, at one time used to inhabit every sculpture department as the exercise which demonstrated how a twisted, turning form, can reveal both its front and its back from any one point of view. The spiral with its turning of forms and space is more imaginatively achieved in *Cell (Eyes and Mirrors)* where the innovation of the mirrors reveal the back of the objects and their space from any one view point. *Cell (Eyes and Mirrors)* is a kind of spiralled space. *Spiral Woman* is mundane. However, Louise Bourgeois has continued to evolve the spiral form throughout her creative life as initiated in this earlier work. The fact that the spiral form of *Spiral Woman* is fixed to a metal support which holds it above the ground pre-empts the suspended form, such an important part of her repertoire which have distinguished the very differing identities for her sculpture. "Horizontality is a desire to give up, to sleep and be passive, to retreat. Verticality is affirmation, an attempt at a peaceful compromise and a desire for acceptance. Hanging and floating are states of ambivalence and doubt."[9]

Spiral Woman's simple construction of layered wood produces concave and convex forms. The excavated, cavernous forms of *Untitled* could have their origins in the concave spaces created by the spiral forms of the sculptures of this earlier time, and are evolved in works such as *Velvet Eyes*, 1984, and the recent *Nature Study 5, 1995*, with their deeply excavated spaces harbouring rounded, succulent forms. *Spiral Woman* does not touch the ground. The sculpture is placed in space surrounded on all sides by air, suggesting a kind of displacement. The object fixed on top of the sculpture implies a direction, like a compass needle, and gives this otherwise symmetrical object an asymmetry as well as disarming its abstract identity with a figurative implication. The extensive use of the spiral form, richly and inventively evolved, is an indication of the importance of the otherwise dull *Spiral Woman*.

The suspended form implied in *Spiral Woman* is fully realised in the hanging *Lair* (1986). This is the lair as a lure. Its pendulous form of solid, dense black rubber surveys the space in which it hangs through its eye, a square empty slot slicing through the bulbous body of the lair. The rounded form of *Lair*, now swollen, bellied out and assertive, is evolved from the earlier carved wood, phallic totems. The eye, the square slot of empty space – ambiguous because where something should be there is nothing – penetrates the dense rubber substance but does not unfold an interior space. Instead the viewer is taken cleanly through the body of the object to the other side. This empty eye slot is the lure, pulling the viewer into its sight in order to be taken through, with not even a glimpse of an unexpected interior space, for there is none. *Spiral Womans*' form turns anxiously in space. *Lair* confidently commands the space it inhabits, its empty eye turning on the space with radar precision. As with *Cell (Eyes and Mirrors)* the eye in *Lair* is also blind, but its absence is compensated for by its watchful menace which reciprocates its dark, predatory, suspended weight – a protectively sealed space which might harbour a deadly intent.

Maison Fragile, 1978, although an earlier work, could be the exoskeletal container of the bulbous form of *Lair*. *Maison Fragiles*' lean but perilous structure contrasts starkly with the ubiquitous rounded forms of carved marble and cast rubber and offers the meanest support and the slightest protection. Its insecurity is enhanced by its unstable lilt and its gangling height which argue with its table-like identity and structural economy.

Articulated Lair, 1968, merges the form and structure of *Lair* and *Maison Fragile* to become an interior landscape, a place full of dread – deathly, calm and still. Like *Lair* it recalls, in an entirely new and re-imagined way, the dark sculpture of the 1940s and 50s. In *Articulated Lair* those carved, totemic, breasted, phallic forms have evolved into pendulous, ripe, elongated forms of dense, black cast rubber. They are arranged simply as solo objects or in clusters, but instead of standing, as in those earlier works, they are now hung, housed and supported within the angles of the tall articulated, steel screens. If the hanging *Lair* is the lair as a lure then *Articulated Lair* is the lair as a place, an interior landscape and, as with *Cell (Eyes and Mirrors)* and *No Exit*, it is suspended in time.

With its institutional, functional painted steel walls and its yawning, cavernous cathedral-like space, *Articulated Lair* is a place of waiting, a cleaned and modernised development of the excavated space of *Untitled*. Most of all, however, it is a storage place for the equipment which hangs on the walls in dormant anticipation. And it is large, adult sized equipment, in alarming contrast to the size of the diminutive stool. These sexually charged objects relate ominously to the child's stool which sits in isolation at the centre of the space. The anticipation of how these pendulous objects might be used, or how they might have already been used, perhaps as weapons of defence or attack, or as ripe, succulent reminders of delight, (now morbidly inert) makes the identity of this child-visited place ambiguous. Is it a protective or an imprisoning place? Whichever it is, it is a place of waiting, whose sense of interior landscape is static and where all growth and potential for change is held still.

Like *No Exit*, *Articulated Lair* is also a sculptural object which can be walked around and walked through, enterable by one of two small doors incorporated into the structure. It has a similar rhythm of opening and closing forms as *No Exit*. The articulated screens are reminiscent of the articulated staircase. This lair is the ultimate secret place under the stairs but formidably enlarged to become that ominous space as experienced from a child's point of view. This is a place of total silence, a place of limbo and deathly suspense, without heartbeat or foot fall, where the empty stool waits for the child.

10 Meyer-Thoss, *Louise Bourgeois: Designing for Free Fall*, p. 194.

If *Articulated Lair* is dormant then *Cumul 1*, 1969, is awakening. And if the sexuality in *Articulated Lair* is in deathly fear of its ominous, perhaps abusive, potency, then the sexuality in *Cumul 1* is sensually awakening, an intoxication of drowsy rapture which creates a peaceful recognition of deep sex. The white marble is carved into a cocooning cloth: the enrobing cocoon of *Fillette* and of *Fragile Goddess* has become a membrane which now slips aside. Caressing the emerging phallic forms, it mutates into heavy lidded eyes laden with sleep. *Articulated Lair* is a death-like interior landscape. *Cumul 1* answers with the landscape of bliss, confident in its sensual and sexual drowsiness, a dormancy changing to wakefulness.

The carved marble cluster of phallus/breast forms are not only emergent but also merging their male and female identities. This is a harmonious landscape, where the moment of dawn is captured, a moment of waking which reciprocates the horizontality of this sculpture and the relationship to horizontality which Louise Bourgeois equates with sleep and the desire to give up, to succumb. For me, I interpret *Cumul 1*'s desire to give up as an easy abandon and the desire to sleep as a state of bliss. I referred to *Untitled* as a hot object in comparison to her precisely carved and smoothly surfaced marble and bronze sculptures. *Cumul 1* is a superbly carved and smoothly surfaced sculpture, the result of calculated and precise technique. The whiteness has a cool purity redolent of a classical elegance and taste which the rounded, swelling, overtly sexual forms rudely challenge with an indolent kitsch.

The Sneeze of Louise is the sexual charge in the sculpture, unpredictable in how, where and with what it will direct itself but rampant with an emotive and unashamed sculptural language: it exploits and explores the extremes of where she places herself in the work, intimately close or objectively and coldly at a distance.

Louise Bourgeois should have the last word: "It is not an image I am seeking. It's an idea. It is an emotion you want to create, and an emotion of wanting, giving, destroying."[10]

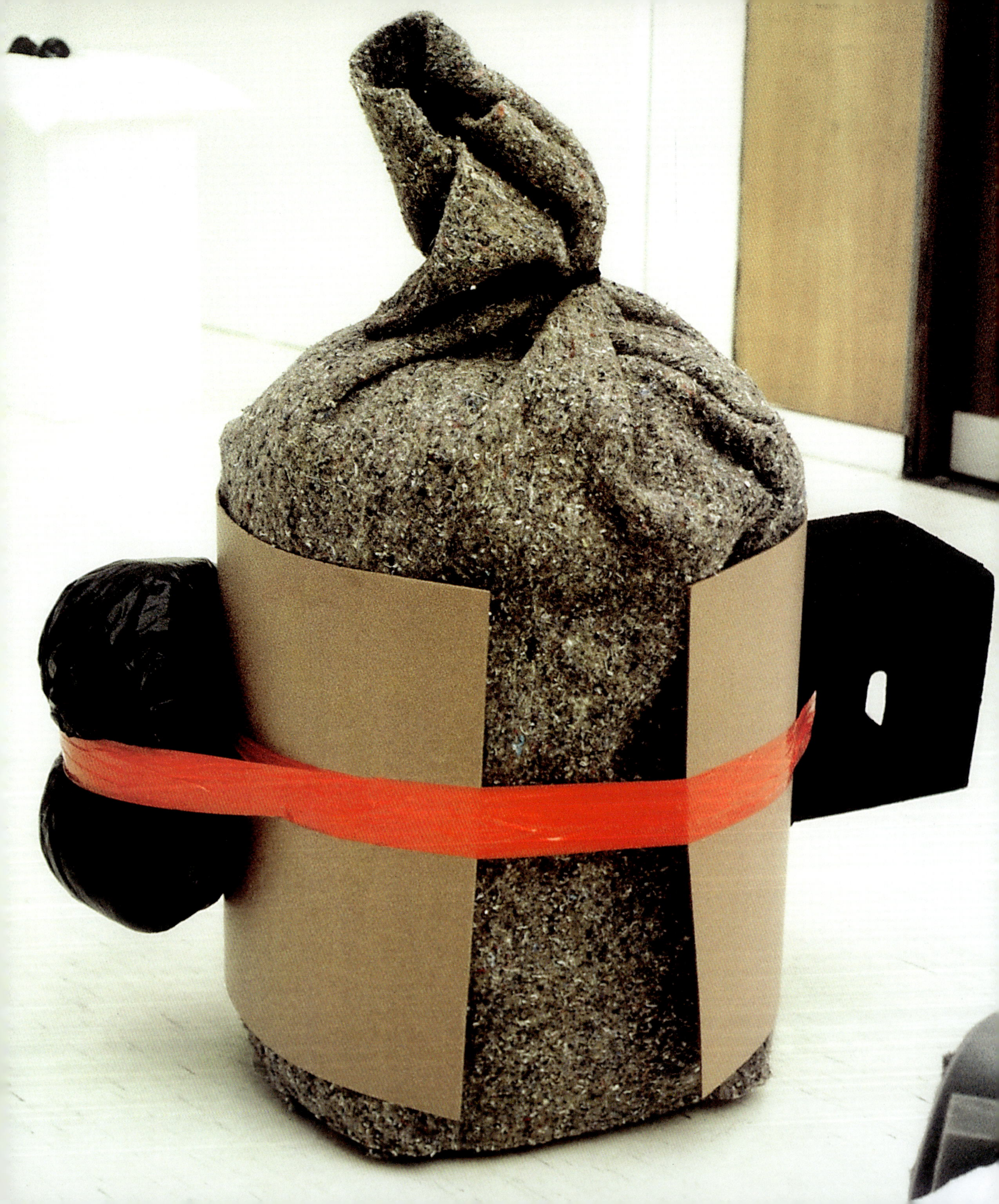

Little Drunks
Carpet felt, plastic container, tape, rubber tubing, polystyrene, plaster, brown paper
Each work: 60 x 100 x 120 cm (approx)
1998
Swiss Cottage Library, for *Touching Matters*

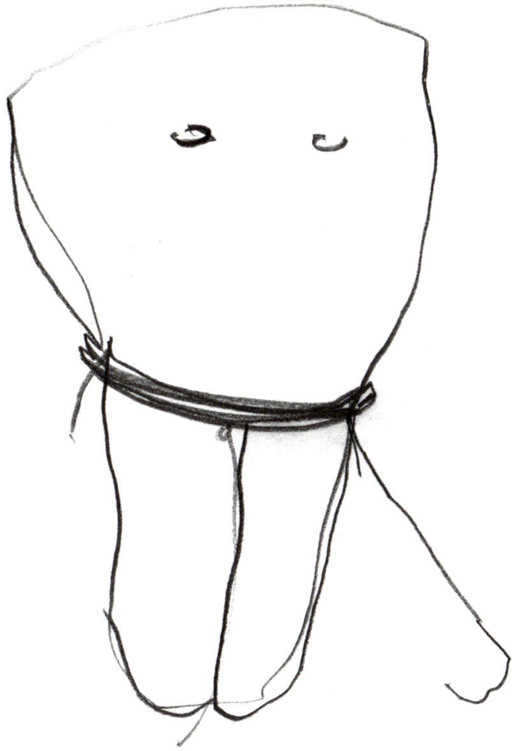

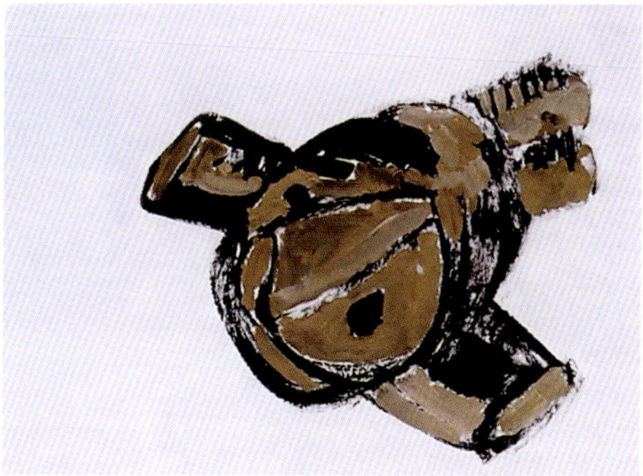

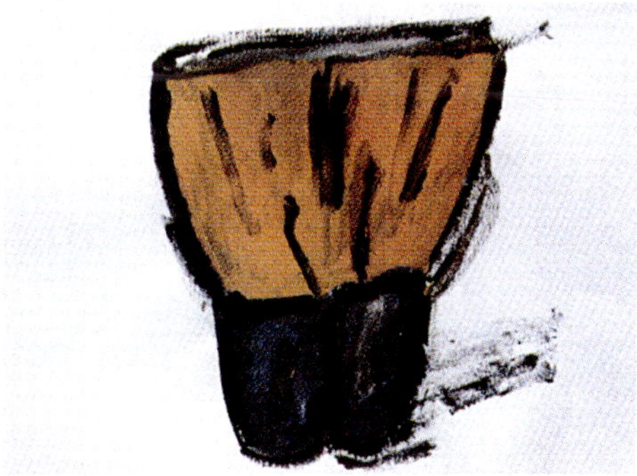

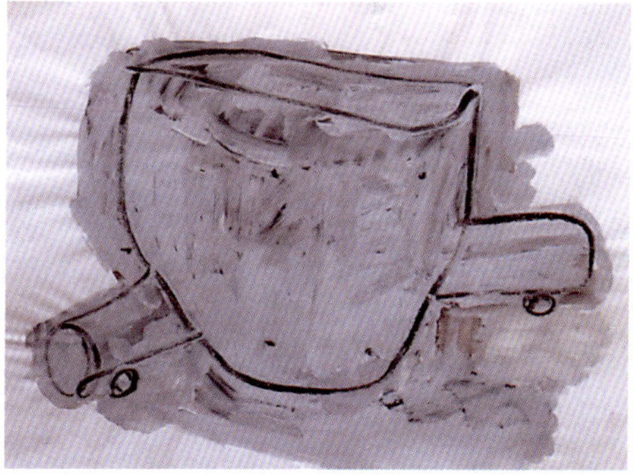

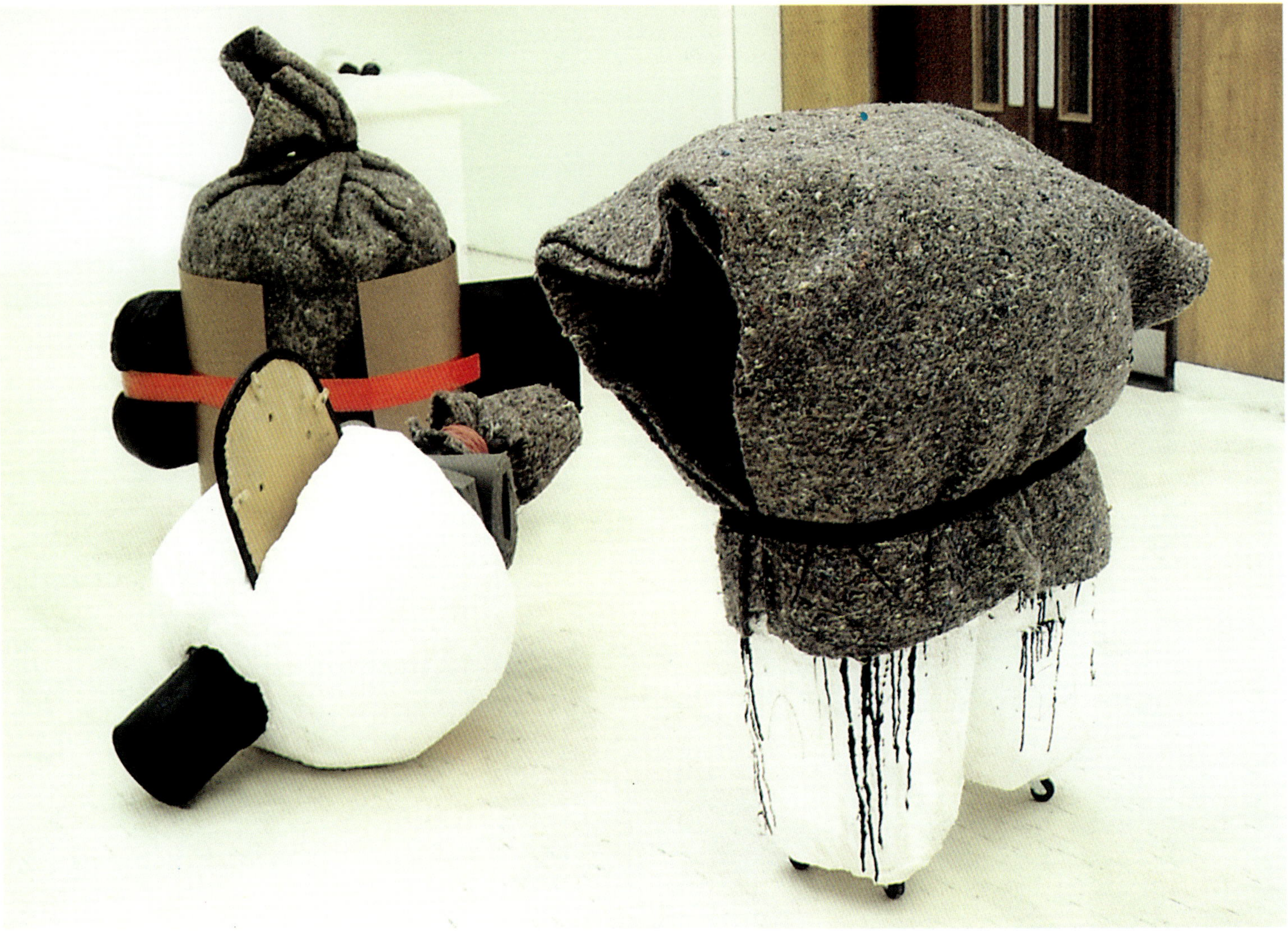

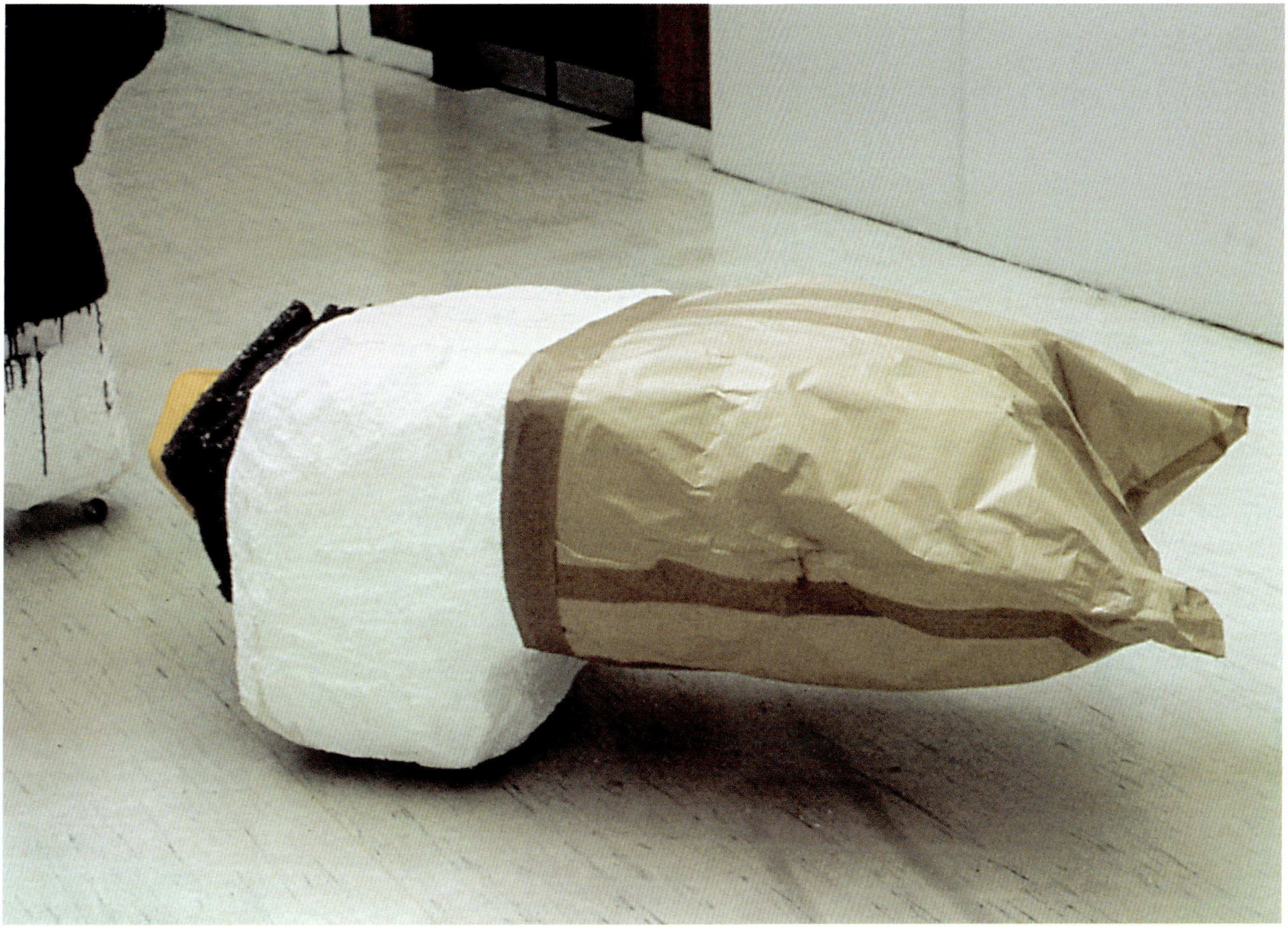

The Hatred of the Object

In this 30 minute talk I want to put forward and unravel a disparate collection of thoughts based on what I diagnose as “the hatred of the object”.

I believe that the studio, and in particular the sculptor’s studio, is somehow at the centre of this hatred, and to some extent the victim of it. My argument focuses on two kinds of traditional studios: the enlightened studio and the grim studio.

In the enlightened studio curiosity is fundamental to how ideas are explored, manifested through the physical manipulation of material, privately and intimately, where there is a slow evolution of processes, intellectual and practical, involving experimental approaches to concepts, techniques, forms and aesthetics. My experience of such a studio is that the artist is at the centre of this self-created world, independently selecting and discarding, and in control of the development and eventual showing to the outside world of their individual expression.

However, parallel to this ideal vision of the enlightened studio there is also a darker, predatory vision of the traditional studio, one which, I believe, stands in direct contention to the experimental needs and economic restrictions experienced by today’s artists, and this is the grim studio.

My understanding of this kind of studio is based directly on my art school experience at Chelsea School of Art, and then the Slade, in the early 1960s. I was given a traditional education in sculpture where I was taught a repertory of sculpture techniques. It was accepted that these techniques provided the young sculptor with all they needed to know in order physically to produce sculpture. And from my own experience, they constituted a somewhat grim ritual by which the student was initiated into the highly specialised and selective, even elitist, world of sculpture.

Therefore my education involved clay modelling, casting, plaster modelling, armature construction and assemblage with metal and wood. The emphasis was on self-sufficiency through hard work, preferably involving a great input of labour. Tutorials and seminars did not exist as such, but at the end of a long, and compulsorily hard day’s work everyone met up in the pub where there was avid talk but little discussion about the day’s events in the studio. Existentialism was the religion and hard drinking and hard working were the rules of the game.

However much I may have departed from this training, it is in fact deeply ingrained within me. The root of all my working methods seems to be somehow related to my early experiences with clay, which was very much my preferred

Untitled
Pigmented resin and fibreglass
75 x 75 x 75 cm each
1968

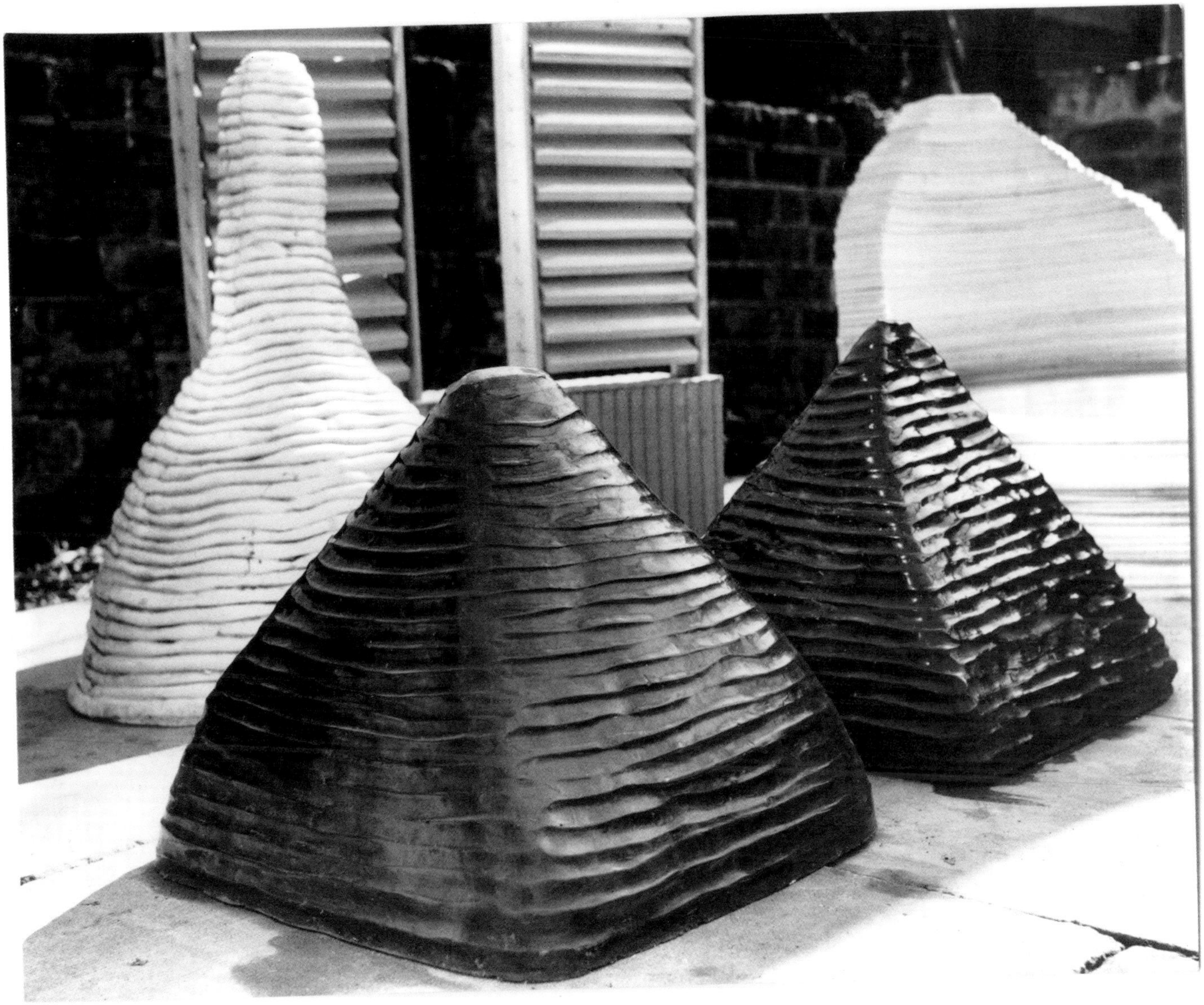

Bowl
Perspex, resin, fibreglass,
spray paint
Diameter 130 x 100 cm high
Each disc: diameter 40 x 20 cm high
1968

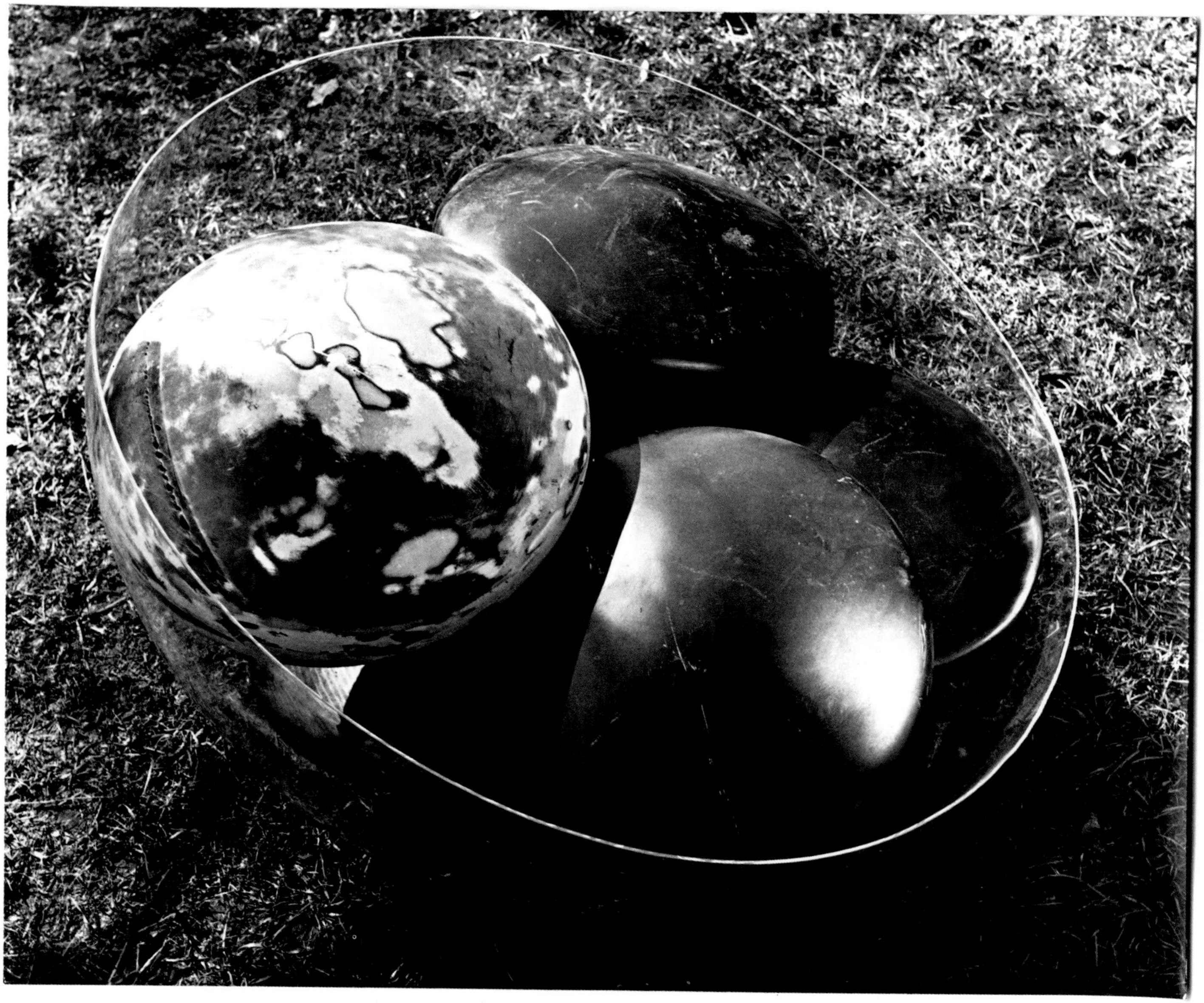

medium because it involved the least amount of technical equipment and kept processes close to the hand.

But more than anything else, this training provided me with the independence to make simply and expediently, enabling me to do so almost anywhere with the minimum of financial and physical resources. The emphasis which such an education placed on self-sufficiency had, despite its exclusivity and its all male domination, given me the confidence to set up my own studio in the simplest way and to begin to make work cheaply and conveniently. The privacy and the autonomy quickly lent itself to experimentation and to a drastic distancing from the more restrictive aspects of such an education.

I am grateful for my sculpture training because of the independence it instilled in me and, for better or worse, a certain kind of confidence in the most basic of making. Perhaps more important than anything else has been an appreciation of time: quite simply the time it takes to make something oneself. Sculpture can reflect this element of time, either in how one must move around it, that is, literally walk around it – a kind of stalking – or in what species of physical and material object it is, or in the processes involved in making it what it is and the time it has taken to achieve this. It is the fusion of these characteristics which makes sculpture, whether it be object or installation, project its own particular, inherent sense of time.

I am aware that what I experienced educationally was representative of the traditional studio in its grim and restrictive guise. As such, this kind of studio comes down to us loaded with cumbersome luggage – historical, aesthetic and moral. The grim studio like this is full of crap which necessarily and understandably has been purged by generation after generation. Especially now that increasing numbers of young artists are rejecting the financial burden of the studio and relying more and more on having their work produced via the desk and telephone, to be organised, managed and manufactured elsewhere. Reciprocally, ideas are submitted in proposal form or as scale models, thus short-circuiting the necessity for the experimental, time-consuming, trial-and-error processes that are so much part of studio culture. Instead, the emphasis is on a need for designed objects, the making of which can be delegated elsewhere – anywhere, that is, other than the studio.

In comparison to this way of producing a work, the studio in either its enlightened or its grim guise can seem to force a moral attitude to work – passing on an inheritance of a kind of Protestant work ethic in which is entrenched a strong sense of struggle out of which good must surely come. Attached to this disagreeable identity there can also be a resistance to and suspicion of experimentation which is understood as breaking rank with sculpture and which should therefore be expelled from the discipline of sculpture into a kind of purgatory. Such attitudes are backward looking, suggesting a grumbling, discontented relationship with the present and a denial of the fantastic, if difficult, choice of materials and techniques available to the sculptor, all potential for plundering in whatever way possible. To deny this potential further enforces the studio as the grim abode of the punitive, the repressive and the backward looking.

For me, the studio is deeply important: emotionally and practically. But it speaks trouble, and although I would not, could not, have it any other way, it can seem to be a shaming thing to be lumbered with, as if the party is going on elsewhere. The grim, traditional studio, rigidly rooted in the past, can now not only be expensive, but boring as well. Rent and amenities, along with the specialist traditional materials such as stone and bronze, cost a fortune, and the desire to limit mistakes in order to keep costs down demands a prescriptive attitude to working methods – paradoxically, not unlike those of artists who have rejected the studio.

Of course, there are many superb artists who use the studio, or not, in whatever way they like, enlightened or otherwise, and their work speaks for itself, being of imagination, originality and relevance.

But my proposition of the hatred of the object hinges on the perception of the traditional studio as an inheritance loaded with morality and stringent work ethics enforced for no good reason. Furthermore, where such a domain is thought to abide by rigid hierarchies of good and bad, right and wrong, these judgements seem to be passed according to the extent to which the artist can deposit evidence of struggle on their sculpture-object through the act of making.

Craft, and the hands-on hands-off debate emerges. Again, the spectre of the grim studio rises, claiming the high moral ground with its demand for the hand made, with the added insistence that maximum evidence of the mark of the artist be left on the work. Thus the essential need for the studio is justified – as the place where the object is processed through private and personal rituals of making. In this blinkered environment Duchamp has never existed, nor any attempt to acknowledge the wealth of iconoclastic gestures erupting out of twentieth century art which have kept the processes of sculpture awake and contentious.

Understandably a revulsion can set in. The object – the hot object – that is, the object loaded with the all-too-visible signs of the act of making, can repulse through its somewhat desperate need to attract. It becomes an object of emotional blackmail, persuading us to feel for it because it shows us so clearly the marks, wounds perhaps, caused through its struggle to come into existence. For those who are questioning the necessity for such agonised creativity, these objects arouse suspicion and eventually a kind of loathing because they rely on predictable mannerisms with which to generate a reaction.

Similarly, our culture abounds with objects demanding to be loved – but produced in a totally different way – that is, industrially designed and manufactured products. These are cool objects, hands-off maybe, but objects which impose a similar emotional blackmail to their opposite numbers, demanding to be bought, to be owned. These product-objects which saturate our daily lives infiltrate our emotions, often seductively and pleasurably. But on closer analysis they can also generate loathing as their true destructive or pollutant identities are revealed behind their fabulous disguise of, for example, rounded forms and glossy surface. The car is, of course, the supreme example.

Therefore my notion of the hatred of the object is born out of what I perceive to be a conflict between opposing species of sculptures: one hot, and the other cold. However, their supposed differences can, paradoxically, produce similar responses: both demand to be loved and needed, albeit in different ways, and yet both are infinitely capable of invoking the opposite response to the one intended – instead of love, hatred.

Not surprisingly, finding a way out of this conflict can not only be an attractive proposition but a necessary one. So abandon the studio with its dogged, backward looking, moral messages and abandon the product with its corrupt disguises and its economic dependency. Where else to move other than to take on production through delegation? Without a studio there can be liberation to explore and exploit diverse media through the specialist agencies, suppliers and manufacturers. The technology does not necessarily have to be learnt or directly experienced in order for the idea to be manifested: the work can be produced through delegation via desk and telephone or fax machine.

This position makes the technologies of computer and industrial design production available for artists to plunder without the burden of having to own or even learn how to use them.

There can be no need to engage physically or in tactile ways with the stuff with which the proposed work is to be made: it can all happen elsewhere. Again, anywhere but a studio. Such a distance from the manipulative production of the object seems to me to generate a genre of object-sculpture that is more pictorial than sculptural. Nothing exemplifies this more than the on-going use of the vitrine – a compelling, often mesmeric object in its own right – and when deployed as a device for framing and containing, one that becomes an art object with infinite possibilities, all dependent on the choice of thing to be placed within.

The vitrine is, at its most banal, not only a substitute for the plinth but the symbolic equivalent of the screen – that of television, film, computer, video, x-ray, radar and a host of others. It so conveniently and, funds permitting, so beautifully offers the real as the anti-real within a space that is pretence.

For me, the vitrine tidies up, cleans up. It makes safe the horrific so that objects of danger, disease, terror and violence can be shown as easily as objects of desire and seduction. Anything and everything can be tamed into submission once framed within and behind the glass defence.

It must be the vitrine's ability to accommodate anything and everything that makes it so compelling but, at the same time, it does more than this. It removes both viewer and artist from the work, it tames and sanitises and although it makes possible an astonishing choice of content, materially and technically, to be acted upon, in the end my response has been that, as a device, it deadens opinion, rendering the status of the object as a wild, messy, unpredictable, ugly, difficult thing to being cleansed, tamed, glamourised, polite. A shift from raw experience to managed spectacle.

Therefore the confrontation with raw experience and the unpredictable must be through the uncontained object, the wild object – one which can be approached close up, which can be walked around, experienced in real time. I believe this kind of object to be inherently difficult and more likely to be experienced as so, even as uncomfortable and confusing. And even more problematic, such an exposed object might fail to arouse any response whatever, because when so blatantly displayed it is not glamorous, and must stand up to close, uncompromising scrutiny through which all is revealed. This is very different from the vitrined object which can cunningly both mask and hide parts of itself, if so wished. The naked object, raw and exposed, does at least offer itself for opinion, showing that a risk has been taken even if it has perhaps failed.

Not so with the vitrined object. It can never fail. The object is repressed and once-removed. It becomes pictorial, framed and glazed – quite literally glossed by the shiny reflective glass. It seems almost more akin to photography than to the confrontationally presented object. It therefore becomes a made-easy experience.

Consequently, the vitrine, for me, induces disappointment: like the wild animal in captivity, the object is emasculated, the potential of its physicality reduced to a mere virtual identity. Vitrines are an invitation to remove the potency of an object,

Landscape
Plywood, car body filler
100 x 100 x 100 cm
1968

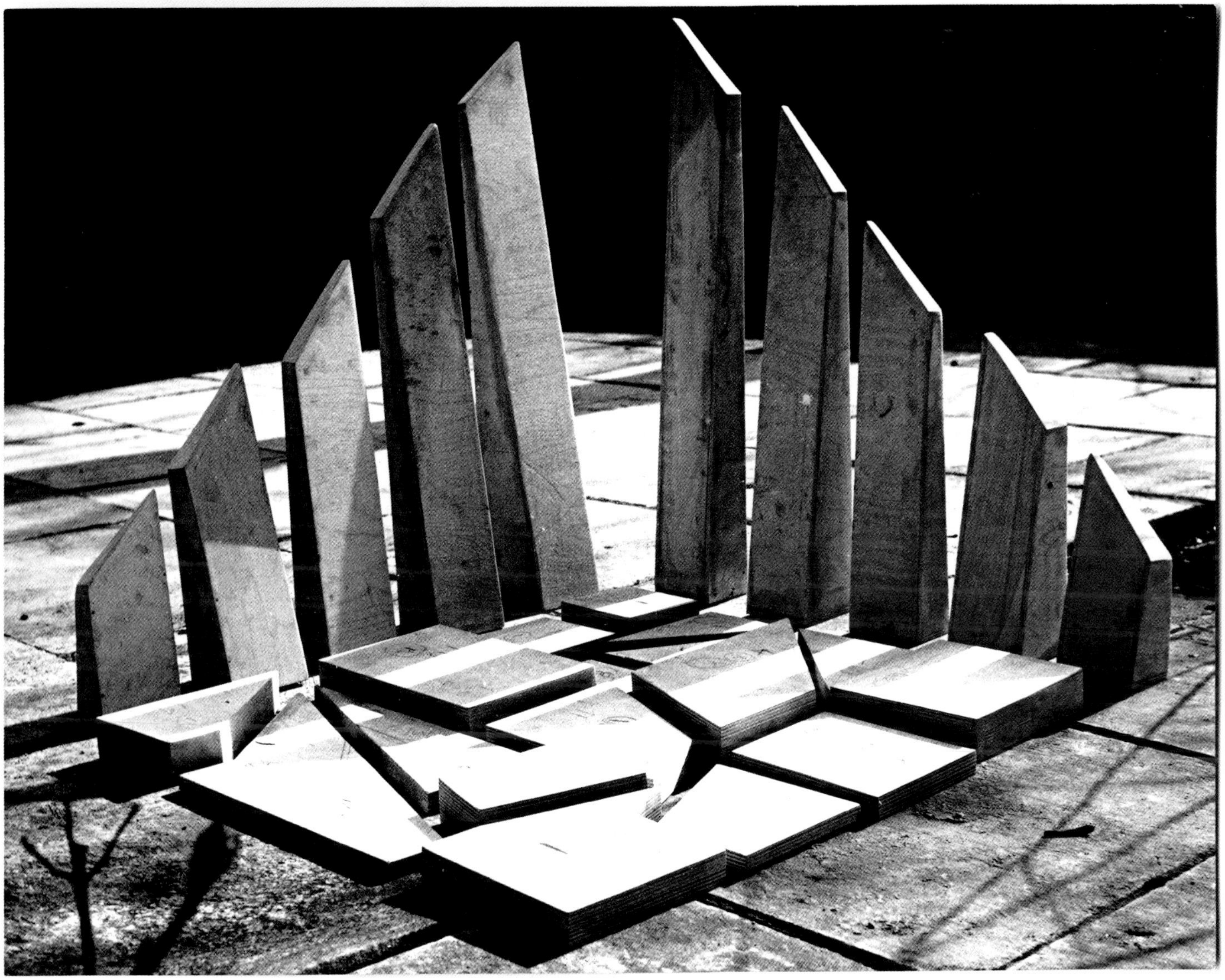

Head
Resin, fibreglass, plywood, filler
100 x 120 x 120 cm
1968

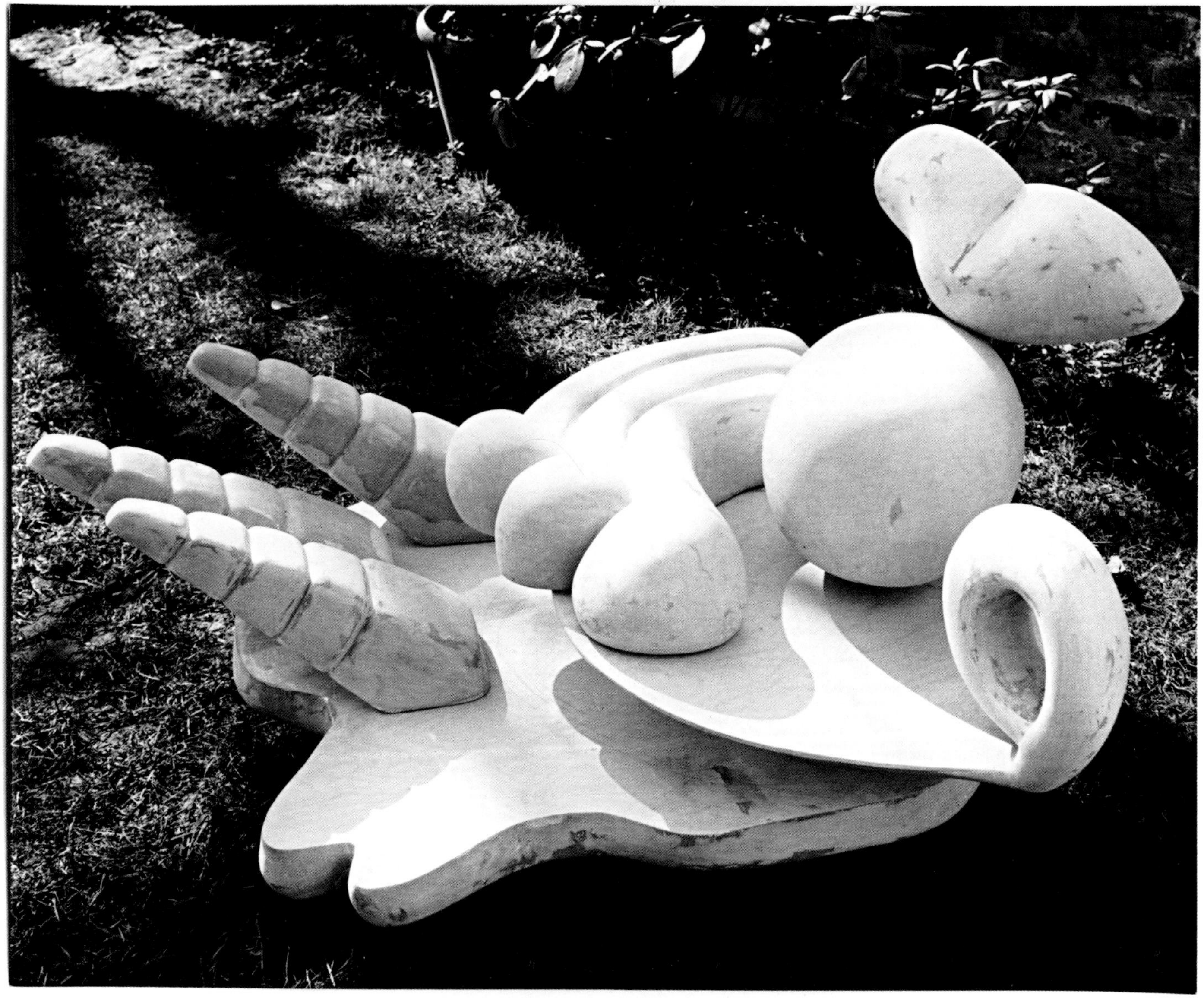

its repulsiveness, its seductiveness, its beauty or its ugliness – all hugely powerful characteristics in their emotional effect. These characteristics potentially invoke hatred because they perhaps remind us of the uncontrollable sides of ourselves and could be too strong to deal with. Therefore the vehicle of these emotions, that is the object, must, quite literally, be removed, put away, to be scrutinised from a safe distance and to function only as a reminder of possible threat.

The vitrine can reduce the material physicality of objects to a pictorial status. But the contention of the sculpture-object is to oppose the pictorial and to offer experience in real time – the time required by the object and its space to be walked around, through, across, using memory – to remember this part whilst you are experiencing that part – so that the work unfolds through the senses and is the antithesis of the pictorial.

The sensory aspect of sculpture is more than just the state of appearance. It is a whole relationship with the process of making and can engage with the non-visual as much as with the visual. The vitrine exemplifies how an object can be produced through delegation where there is no need for a studio: the work can be produced, through design and specification, by specialists. The contents, likewise, can be brought together through the appropriate research and if necessary, sponsorship. Without doubt there is considerable work involved, but little that demands the physical and tactile involvement with materials where processes of trial and error inevitably create sensory and sensual relationships with the emerging object. Because of this the vitrine triumphs. It is as free of historical luggage as a studio-produced object might be. In this way the vitrine, yet again, proves itself to be an enviable device.

Those artists who desire to make sculpture have chosen an increasingly difficult art form. When there are already so many objects in the world and so much manufactured stuff in production the sculptor is challenged from every side. Because of this, I consider sculpture to be a minority art form – preferably highly elitist – and in constant need of critical reassessment.

The burgeoning number of students taken on to sculpture courses indicates that only a few will pursue sculpture as rooted in the traditions I have described, both in how they will use a studio, an enlightened one I hope, and how they relate to making processes. For me, this is a healthy state of affairs.

Traditionally sculpture courses have offered only a few places, for practical reasons as well as those of demand. Since the idea of what sculpture can be has diversified, so have the numbers wishing to enter sculpture courses increased. The traditional object-maker, using hands-on processes and workshop techniques, is surrounded by performers, filmmakers and object-designers in an environment where proposals for sponsorship abound and the act of physical making is kept to a minimum. A rich symbiosis is generated in which the independence and close involvement of the maker is in contention with their opposite number – the delegator – and a tough co-existence is established between the two.

The delegated object, also the designed object, produced by specially chosen manufacturers or craft-persons, combined with the significant role of the vitrine, signal the importance of the written proposal in seeking out and achieving the artist's intended objective. This represents the reality of being an artist today, whereas crass economics can determine so much. The vitrine could be understood as being economically accommodating. Once made, admittedly probably at some considerable expense, anything can be placed within it, probably at less expense. If there are no studio overheads, (the vitrine would be factory produced), there would be little or no experimental making, no trial-and-error processes, therefore no outlay on materials, etc.. The written proposal would determine how and by whom and with what this object would be realised, and it could be no more expensive, probably less so, than the cost of maintaining a studio and all that goes on in it.

Without doubt, the vitrine is endlessly fascinating, but now familiarity is beginning to breed contempt – it has become an over-used and therefore, abused device. Aesthetically stunning, capable of beautifying anything from shit to sheep, and portraying the already desirable as unreachable and untouchable, the vitrine seems to have captured the imagination of artists and viewers alike, perfectly symbolising how we are now forced to experience aspects of contemporary life. Its glory is becoming muted, its message repetitive.

The vitrine clearly demonstrates the endless possibilities of making without making, signalling how the artist can be emotive whilst keeping their distance from their work, delegating its production and thus rendering the studio unnecessary.

Therefore the hatred of the object is manifested through the mistrust and abdication of the studio. The demise of the studio equates with a shunning of, and a hatred of the object.

In researching the sculpture of Louise Bourgeois I came face to face with my contention of the hatred of the object. Her sculpture has received unanimous appreciation in recent years, even more so since the *Rites of Passage* exhibition at the Tate, and the Paris retrospective, both showing the rich extremes typical of her work, which refutes type-casting and stylistic formulae. Her sculpture emerges without self-conscious strategies for making and unashamedly identifies itself with its roots in traditional sculpture processes of carving, construction, modelling and casting, so prevalent in the middle years, the 1930s and 40s, of the twentieth century in Europe when Bourgeois was just beginning as an artist. These processes are exemplified by the brooding, cumbersome sculpture of artists such as Etienne-Martin, Stahly, Zadkine and, to some extent Arp, who were her influential contemporaries. Because of its traditional roots, the sculpture of Louise Bourgeois is the antithesis of the hatred of the object, and from this point of view I am perplexed as to its popularity when it stands for everything which has been so drastically repudiated in the way I have described.

Perhaps it is because her work transcends the grim spectre of traditional practice, and is unpredictable and diverse enough to refute classification. Also, her art absorbs contemporary debate. There seem to be shrewd calculations made as to where she positions herself in the work: sometimes every trace of making is left evident and exposed on the surface of the object and at other times the surface is stretched and cleansed of all such marks, indicating an impeccable craft process. Similarly, appropriated objects, *objets trouves* and designed factory-produced objects co-exist in harmonious abandon with the overtly handmade.

This work stands unprotected, open and exposed, offering itself for the closest of scrutiny, strategically involving the viewer in very specific acts of looking, and all the while there is the sense of the work looking back, at times insolently answering back the viewer's gaze. This is sculpture which operates in total antithesis to the vitrine: the objects celebrate, reveal and confront the desirable and the repulsive, the beautiful and the ugly, the seductive and the repellent.
The sculpture, whether it is autonomous object or installation, contrives to meet the viewer with the demand to be investigated, to be walked around, pried into, stalked, looked under and over. These are object experiences that jolt us into seeking out comparisons, to find equivalents, emotional and physical which stir our imagination to question what we are looking at and what it is saying to us. There are no quick answers and no conclusions, just stark, undiluted confrontation with raw emotions.

Perhaps in the end the hatred of the object has had its day and maybe the tremendous acclaim awarded to Louise Bourgeois' sculpture is part of the hated object's demise. Perhaps the *tabula rasa* of traditional sculpture processes has been fulfilled and these processes can now be reclaimed and reinvested and their potential can be rediscovered. I would certainly welcome this as I do consider that these ancient processes are not necessarily an end in themselves but a means to an end. They provide independence and an appropriate, expedient and human antidote to the worlds of the virtual and the removed, the sanitised and the hands-off.

The hatred of the object is a fiction I have invented in order to understand and contextualise some of the issues emerging from contemporary art. Within my arguments are, possibly, some truths, but there is also a good deal of conjecture, some of it all too familiar. However, for me, the idea of the hatred of the object is important because it enables me to examine and make clear to myself the importance of the studio and its harbouring of those private acts of making which, however removed they may be, are in my case deeply rooted in the traditional sculpture processes of modelling, casting and construction. And I value them all the more because they are vulnerable to misinterpretation and abuse, and therefore easily dismissed and overlooked. Their co-existence with the productions of the delegators and the non-studio makers forces debate and a continuing critical exchange, ensuring that all acts of making are infinitely possible and necessary for a rich and challenging diversity of sculpture to be produced.

This text is taken from a paper presented at the *Sculpture, Method, Research* conference hosted by Central St Martins in September, 1995.
It was also published in *Matrix 3D*, Stuart Evans, Joanna Greenhill and Ingrid Svenson, eds., London: The Lethaby Press, 1997.

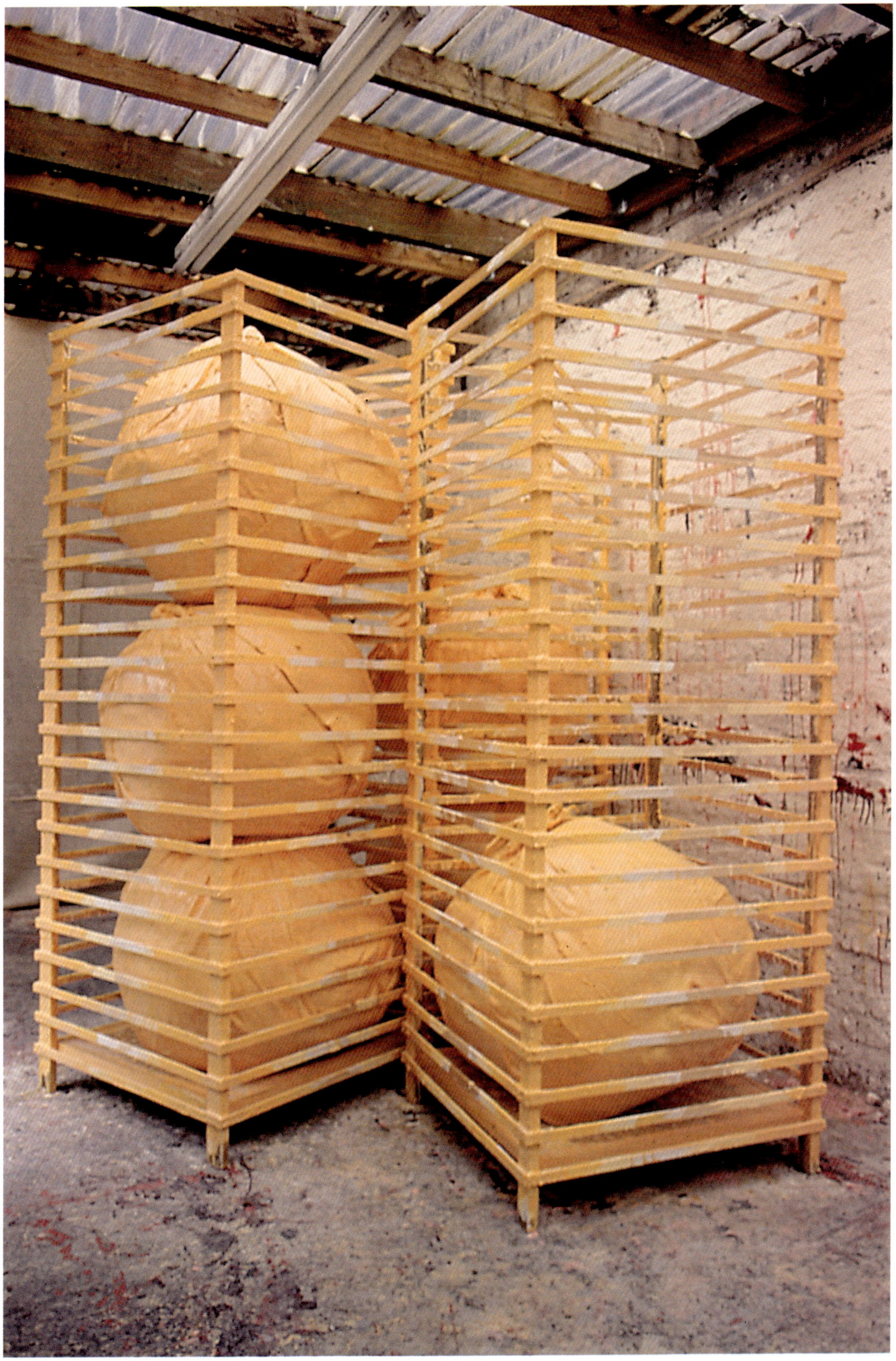

Untitled
Painted timber, canvas
210 x 210 x 240 cm
2001

Dawn till Dusk
Carpet felt, painted wood, painted hardboard, paint stripper, bitumen, canvas, cardboard, casters, brown paper, parcel tape, casters
Overall dimension of work/ space: 600 x 540 x 540 cm
1999
Royal Western Academy, Bristol, *Sculpture Triennial* curated by John Maine and Alison Wilding

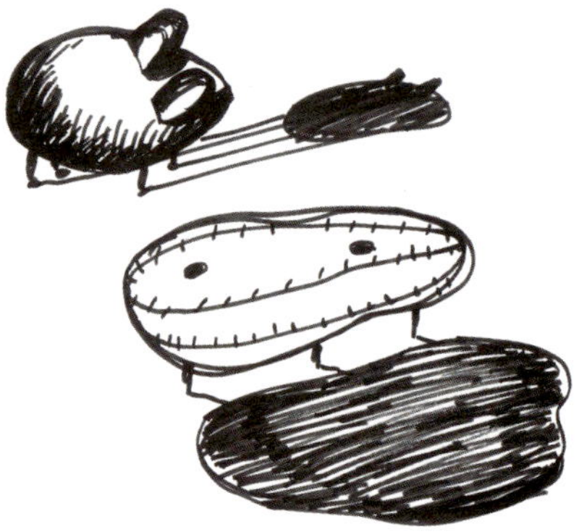

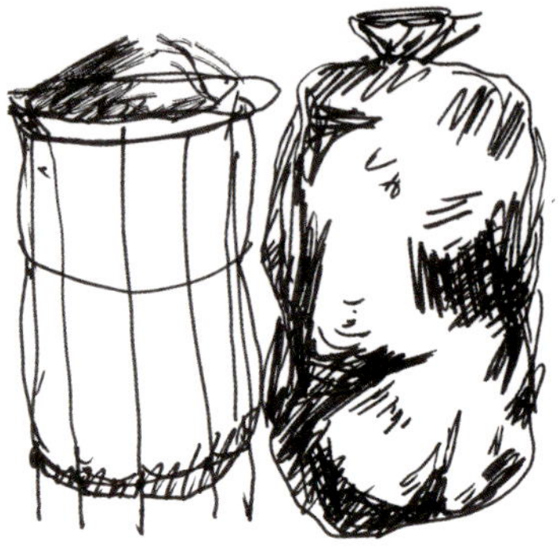

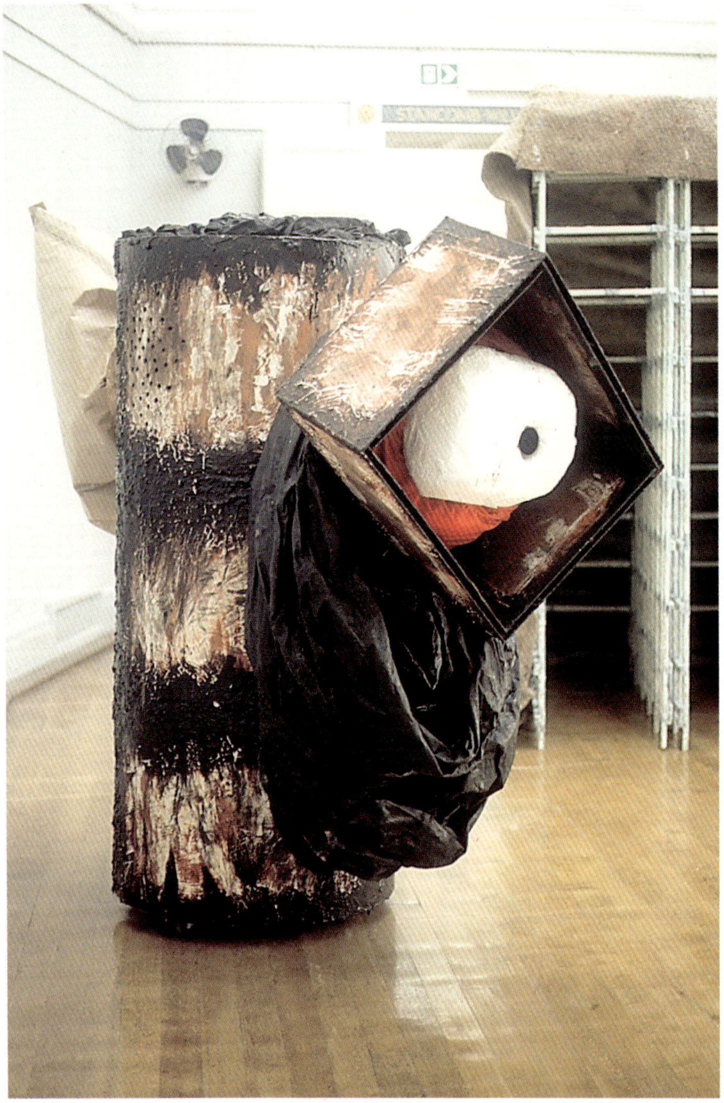

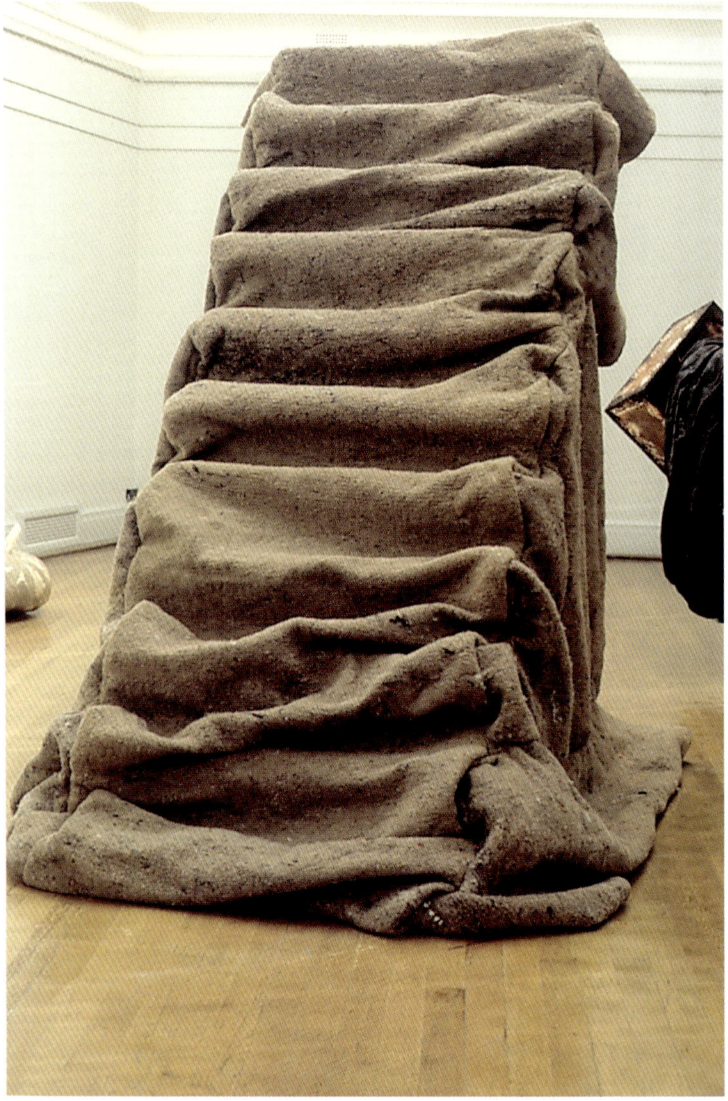

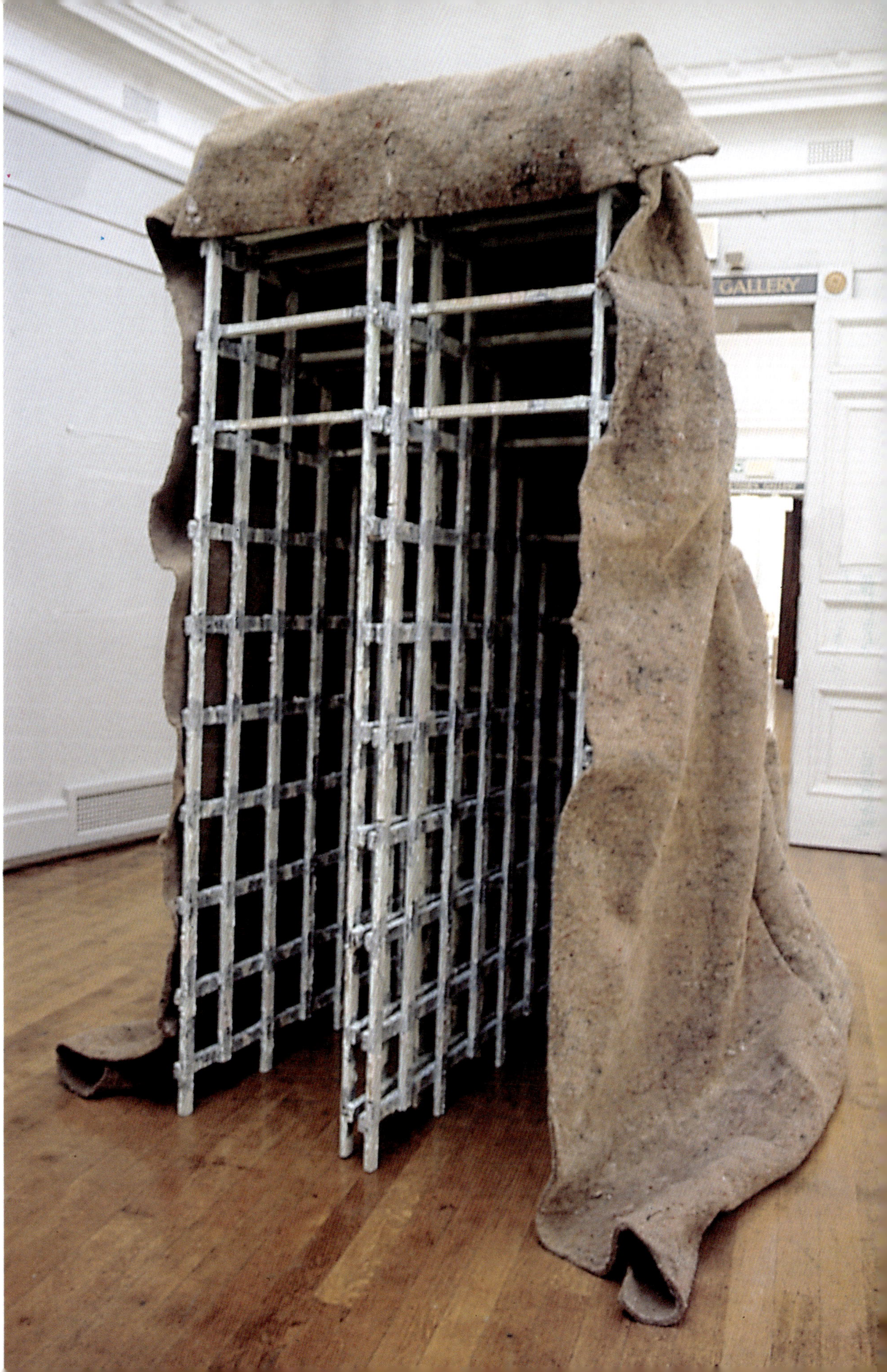
GALLERY

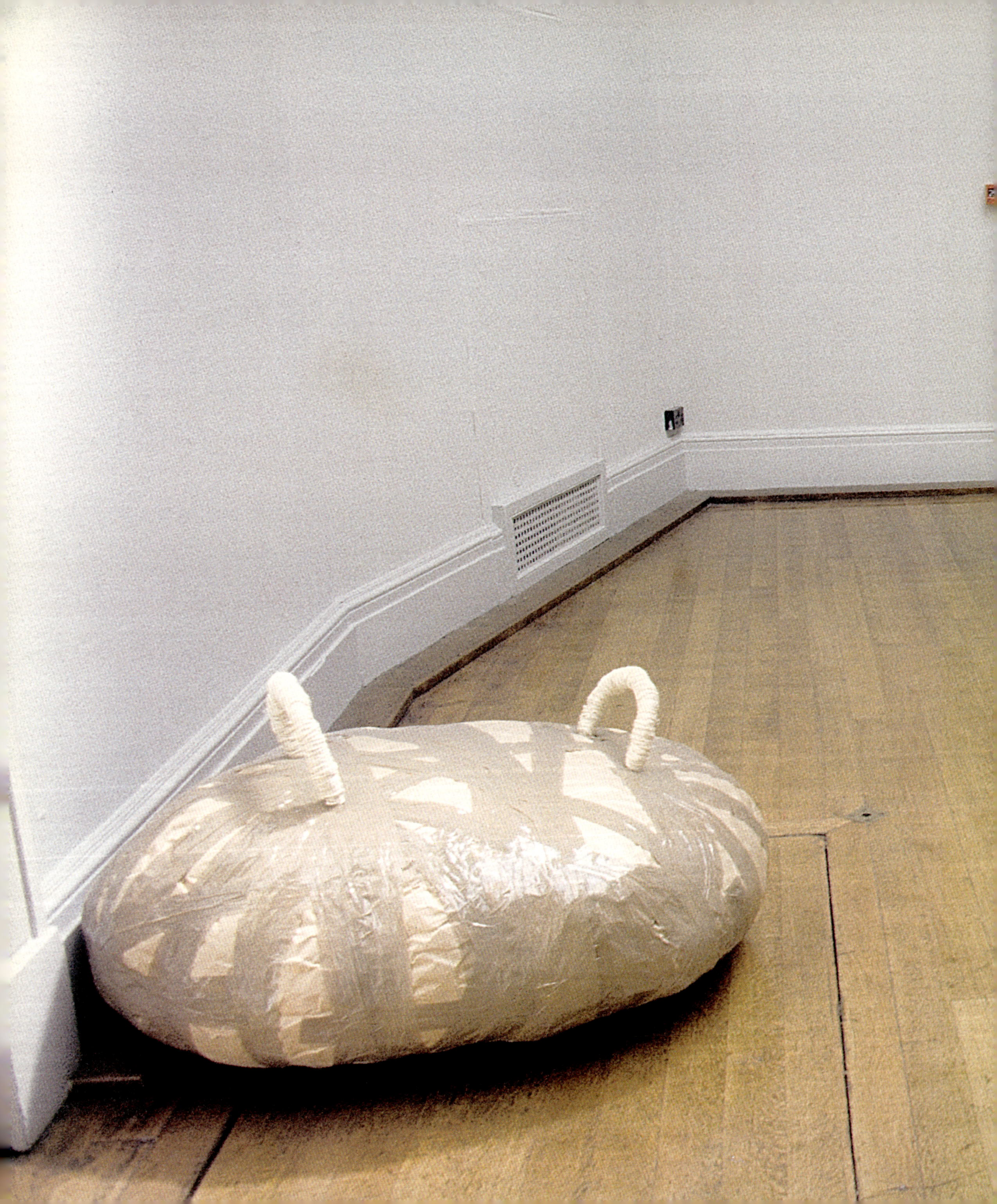

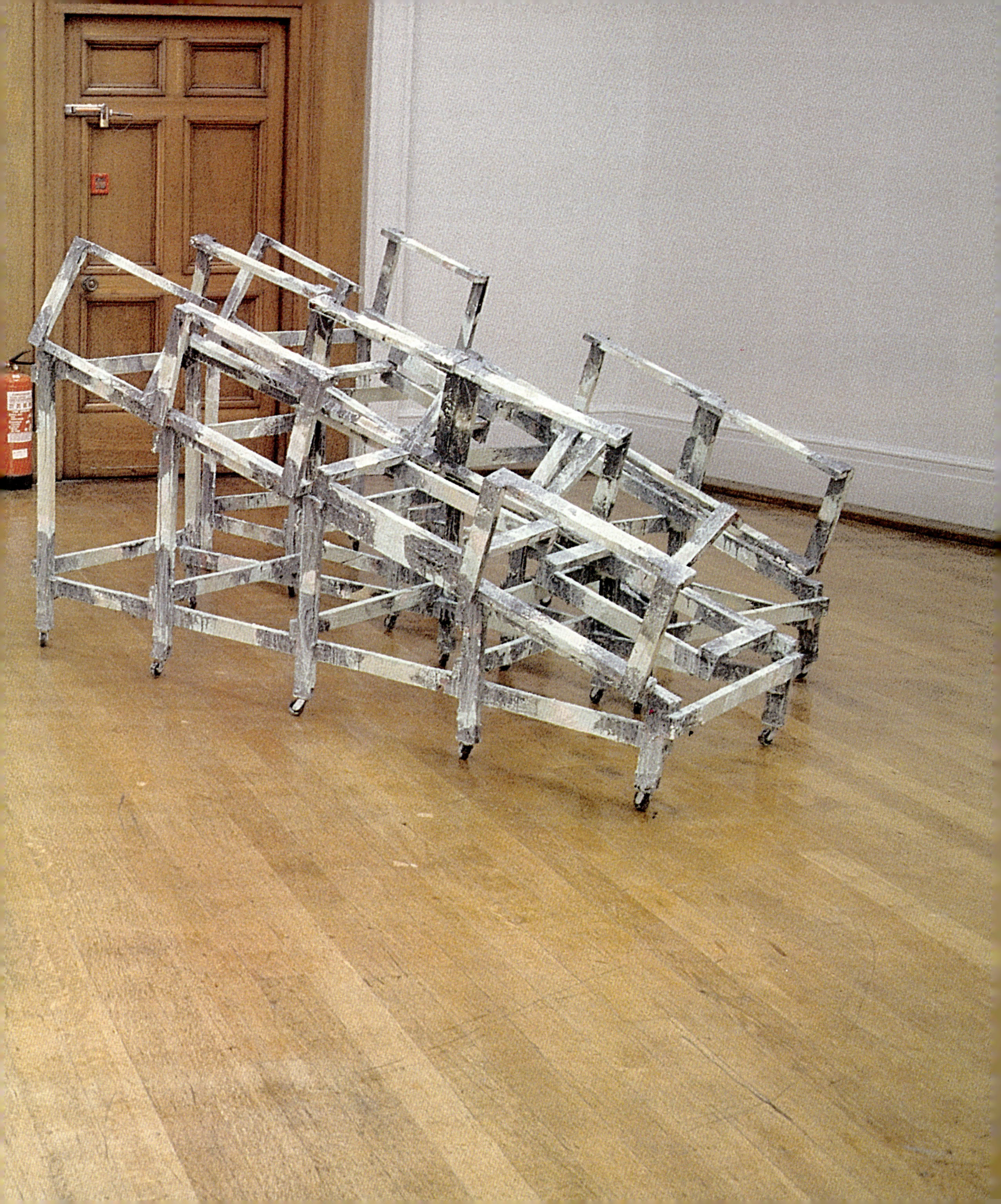

Travelling light: a brief analysis of the end of work and the triumph of the photographic colour transparency

While I was preparing for a talk recently, I decided to make a slide copy of Tony Smith's *Die,* 1962. The particular image I wanted to document was from the catalogue, *The Art of the Real,* accompanying the exhibition of the same title, which had toured from the Metropolitan in New York to the Tate in 1969. The image of Smith's *Die* shows the infamous black steel cube situated in an ambiguous space, which partly suggests a large urban garden and partly a rural environment. The cube itself is streaked and stained, anything but pristine, and placed awkwardly within the boundaries of the black and white photograph, printed on thin, now slightly yellowing, glossy paper. Wherever the location might be, the photograph clearly states that it is only a record, taken for expedient reasons. As a photographic document it proclaims that to know anything about what this work is really like, you will have to be there with it. The photograph is exactly that – a photograph – and as such makes absolutely no effort whatever to enhance either the appearance of the cube or its less than sophisticated environment.

In comparison, a more recent 1984 catalogue of other work produced in the 1960s and early 70s, now identified as Minimalism (interestingly nowhere in *The Art of the Real* is this particular word to be found), there is a reversal of priorities. Gone is the semi-domestic garden or rural setting. Instead, the photographs show clean, rectilinear spaces, representing the simplicity of the gallery, where any visual competition with the artwork has been removed, and the space, if it has to be shown, as with the Carl Andre floor pieces, does not interfere with one's reading of the work. In fact, the Sol Le Witts exist in a kind of cyberspace, so important has it been deemed, by this particular catalogue designer, to eradicate any kind of environmental intrusion.

The confidence shown by the 1984 catalogue in how the photographic images represent the work, as well as its overall design, inform us in no uncertain terms of what it believes the Minimalist ideal to be. That is, the cleansed photographs reflect Minimalist didacticism.

This 1984 catalogue heralds the rise of the fundamental importance attached to photographic representation for an understanding of the original work. The artwork serves the catalogue, which, in turn, re-presents, or re-offers the work on the conditions of the medium of catalogue production. As we all know, the catalogue has become an artwork in its own right. It is symbiotic with the work, forming a parasite/host relationship, where it can dictate the ideology that is most convenient, stylish, enhancing, sensational, of how it wants the artwork to be projected, and the most effective and successful way of achieving this within the available choices offered through the medium of catalogue production.

Therefore, there is no need to be there with the work; its representative, in the form of the idealised photographic image, presented through the object of the catalogue, can be believed to communicate far more than experiencing the reality of the work itself. But this displacement of the reality of the work by its alter ego, its photographic representation of itself, provides a model that I would question, and in which I feel an increasing lack of confidence, both as an artist and as a lecturer. This is despite the fact that I rely heavily on photography, not only.within my own work, but in discussing students' work, or when participating in the selection of applicants to the Slade, and elsewhere. Last week, for example, I looked at over 7,000 slides as part of the submission for the 1998 *New Contemporaries* exhibition.

This model I have referred to, I believe, demonstrates the relationship of the catalogue, and its partner, the photograph (particularly the colour slide), to what identifies and specifies professionalism. It is the absolute necessity of the colour slide that has enabled it to become the representative not only of the work photographed, but also of what creative position the artist is pursuing, so clearly manifested through the all-important choice of the how, the where, the when, and with what of the colour slide image. And it is through these choices imaged by the colour slide that the professional style of the artist can be identified. A young artist showing an image of their work in the manner of this photograph of Tony Smith's *Die* would be given short shrift because of their severe lack of professionalism. And such criticism could be justified because there would be genuine concern for how best such a student should represent their work as a photographic image.

The holiday brochure, the tourist industry's equivalent to the catalogue, also offers a visual representation of what is supposed to be the actual experience. The holiday can be represented through photographs shot in heavily staged and contrived studio settings, where blue skies and sandy beaches are nothing more than ingenious visual lies. The demand for more and more exotic and challenging forms of travel has to be responded to with the appropriate supply of journeys, tours, treks, outward-bound vacations, culture breaks, adventure holidays, luxury cruises, off-the-beaten-track adventures, scenic route tours, etc.. You name it and a tour operator will come up with the goods. Even climbing Mount Everest has to be booked years in advance to ensure that you have enough room, along with all the other climbers, to stand on its summit. It is still possible to travel as a free spirit without a specific destination, but there are plenty of dangers to be heeded and certainly the tour operators will be following close behind to see if they can exploit your example and turn it into another packaged opportunity.

Similarly, today, artists find themselves confronted by a plethora of choices – a choice of journeys, perhaps – to continue the metaphorical comparison with tourism. But underlying all these choices is the confrontation with the orthodoxy of professionalism. Therefore, if the choice an artist decides upon is to go it alone, shun the world and all that it involves, in order to make that decision, some kind of knowledge of what the art world is has to be recognised in order to shun it. But clearly, one way of avoiding any contact with the art world is to have absolutely no photographic documentation of your work. This would be the journey without destination.

So hugely important has the evolved form of art work documentation become, that without doubt, the catalogue, which exemplifies this evolution, has become a superb souvenir of the original artwork. It is the enticement for the reality, but it can also allow the dispensation of the reality. The tourist industry's plethora of brochures entice in the same way, and as long as the bookings roll in, little interest need be paid to the actual experience, undoubtedly longed for, and often wonderful, but possibly nothing like the advertised image. Therefore, whatever choice of journey the young artist decides upon, and whatever choice of journey mature artists have decided upon, the catalogue provides the zenith of professionalism in terms of how it records that journey, and it cannot represent that record without photographic documentation. These photographic images are not enough in themselves, for the catalogue does not only represent the work. The accompanying professions of curator, theorist, historian, plus the catalogue designer are also represented, to provide the information that authenticates the catalogue as the height of professionalism. The greater number of these satellite professions are represented, the greater the level of professionalism attained. It is a clear but highly flawed system. Its clarity, however, does in fact generate choice: the choice of whether you, as an artist, and in this case, young artists at art school, want to, or are able to measure up to the level of professionalism as manifested by these state-of-the-art catalogues.

The contemporary catalogue, with its outstanding photographic representations, is, in the context of a takeaway culture, the takeaway exhibition. Not only does it superbly represent the work, it re-presents the work in a compacted, portable book form, where the art objects within, whatever their original form – sculpture, painting, film, or whatever – become reduced to a single idealised portrait of that original work. This idealised portrait becomes the visual resource of information, so often used by art schools in particular, through which an artist's intentions become disseminated. The singular, highly reduced, cleansed, framed photographic image, without scale, without surface, without gravity, without time, without smell, without movement, without the contact between you and it, without so much, becomes the carrier of, and is responsible for, so much.

However, the reality of the package holiday, or the trek across Nepal, or the cultural tour down the Nile, can be a very different experience from the blue-skied, yellow-sanded image offered by the travel brochure. The violent stomach upset is definitely not featured! Nor the screaming child who has developed an uncontrollable aversion to sand. What neither the glowing brochure nor the seamless catalogue ever show is mistakes.

For me, mistakes are intriguing because they reveal something that was not meant to be revealed. On a holiday, or trekking adventure, this can be anything from a bloody nuisance to life-threatening disaster. But within art, it can be the meeting point of possibilities, generating a scheme of choices otherwise not only previously unconsidered, but also not thought possible. The ethos of the accident in art as a potential for a creative process can be a dubious ethos when the art accident becomes a kind of mannerism. Mistakes, I believe, are different, because the intention is one thing and the result another. Anyway, accidents are part of mistakes in so much as they reveal, change, divert, intervene, confront. Mistakes set up the kind of contention that demands a response, and the contention is that it is an unexpected response that is demanded. A new reality intervenes to question the previous pretence.

Mistakes provide subversion, and reciprocally, professional orthodoxy invites subversion. If the catalogue presents the height of professionalism, then there will be subversion in its orthodoxy. And this is what art schools can initiate. They can provide the critical framework in which young artists can test out their tolerance for the professional orthodoxy of the day. A young artist within art school who produces work that can seriously and effectively challenge and subvert the orthodoxy of professionalism is, I believe, achieving something significant, because he or she will be producing work that will not be dependent on what is already given. However, I am sure that the art machine, like the tour operator trailing the free-spirited traveller, will be quick off the mark to absorb this subversive act.

Essentially, the process within art schools is experimental, and because experiments embrace the mistake, they defy the memorial grandeur of the catalogue, simply because catalogues never show mistakes. The ever-present companion to mistakes is doubt. This is similarly absent from catalogue culture because essentially a catalogue is an advertisement and as such it must be promoting its product. It must offer the product's most successful identity, and because doubt would undermine that proffered conviction, doubt is therefore not a quality used by catalogues. But the process of discussion and critical analysis, as used within art schools, is one of both encouraging doubt and allaying it, and such prevarication between the two is, on the terms of the prevailing professional orthodoxy, unacceptable. However, the orthodoxy of professionalism has irrevocably established that the photograph, in particular a colour slide, is the single most important memento of the art school experience with which students leave.

But what makes art school documentation different, is its accommodation of mistakes, and the understanding and collusion between all concerned for the interest in mistakes, and doubt and enquiry and guesswork. These identities are constantly up for discussion, and critical analysis, but supported by the pleasure derived from the fact that there is the freedom to engage with them. Because the catalogue exemplifies a professional orthodoxy and as such cannot accommodate any hint of mistake or doubt, they become the representatives of failure. And this is the major flaw in the professional orthodoxy: its presumption of what is and what is not failure. For me, the emphasis on the immaculate, the unblemished and the eradication of process has displaced the sensuality of failure with the anaesthesia of success. Success, that is, exemplified by the professional orthodoxy of the catalogue. This is a success not based on discovery through experimentation, but success based on what is already known, and received through the photographic image.

The fact that professionalism, as exemplified through the catalogue, is identified through the perfection of the photographic image, is helpful in making young artists recognise and act on the importance of the production of good slide documentation of their work, but is absolutely no good for disseminating the wealth of innovative experimentation that evolves within art schools.

The catalogue clings to its orthodoxy, and as yet, there is no apparent reason why it should not, because it is so undeniably successful. But there are signs that its influence might be inhibiting the opportunities that art schools can provide for mistakes to be made and experienced. And where this influence is most noticeable is with the annual degree shows.

There does seem to be a dilemma where the degree show, which is the event at the interface between the art school and the professional world, is vulnerable to the rigidity of the professional orthodoxy as manifested by the catalogue, filled as it is with its cleansed images of works, inhabiting their equally cleansed hyper-spaces. The numerous imitations of this ideal make themselves evident every year in the inadequacies of these studio-turned-gallery spaces, not only endorsing the model for the degree show as the ubiquitous white cube, but also endorsing what the white cube represents as a professional ideal.

I hope that art schools can precipitate the challenge to the conventions of professionalism without lapsing into nostalgia for past solutions, or mimicking the ubiquitous white cube. It is a real challenge. So powerful are the instructions from outside art schools as to what constitutes professionalism that the innovation of a new form for what an exhibition could be confronts every young artist today. The fact is that the numerous exhibition spaces now available can make such a confrontation seem like a waste of time and creative energy, especially when the prevailing professional orthodoxy is interpreted as "exhibit or die". Therefore, to take the time, and to consider and demand particular conditions for how to exhibit in relation to the work, and how imaginatively to reinvent the exhibition orthodoxy, can seem like professional suicide. Therefore, I'm beginning to feel that the time when the convention of the degree show is changed, or developed, will be the time when the relationship between the experience and the reality of the art work and its representation as a photographic image will itself be changed, because of a recognition of the need to challenge what the relationship is between the art object and its image as representing a professional orthodoxy. I believe that it is within the relationship between the work and its photographic representation that the contention of professionalism – for what and for whom – will be, and already is being, argued, and out of which a reinvention of professionalism could appear.

In order to generate the confidence that can initiate change, there has to be the recognition of choice. I feel that despite the vast choice on offer in terms of materials, media, form, aesthetics, content and subject, the young artist can believe that they, in fact, have no choice, and therefore no confidence in the imaginative possibilities of how to put these choices back into the world through exhibition. And this is then reciprocated by a pessimism about how young artists perceive their future, as if there is only one route, and that is the idealised success route as represented, and demonstrated through the catalogue.

But as the hardened traveller, without the assistance of the ubiquitous tour operator, will tell you, there are numerous potentially successful routes along which the young artist can travel. The most important advice is probably that the young artist should get to know their temperament, and come to terms with that temperament so that they can travel appropriately, to find the journey that is most rewarding to them, and not feel obliged to travel to where they think everyone else is travelling. Because, like Everest's summit, it could be horribly overcrowded, or it could be an all-too-familiar sight-seeing tour, or an over-organised package holiday. On the other hand, if that is what is needed and wanted temperamentally, then that is where to go.

The fact is that there is a choice, and tourism is not the only way in which to experience the world – at the mercy of the tour operator and the travel brochure. And art schools have to throw caution to the wind and not be so controlled by the conventions of tourism, either through totally rejecting it, or by complete submission to it. The current professional orthodoxy is unashamedly ambitious in how it defines success, and in how it manifests that success through the catalogue and its cargo of photographic images. The art school should be able to present equivalent ambitions, through investigating what the choices actually are, so that it can manipulate to its advantage professional orthodoxy, and without academicising them, initiate how to change and subvert those orthodoxies for the creative benefit of all concerned. Professionalism in the visual arts is there to be evolved, and where better for this to happen than in art schools?

This text is taken from: *Issues in Art Education. The Dynamics of Now*, vol. 3, William Furlong, Polly Gould and Paul Hetherington, eds., London: Tate Publishing, 2000. Based on a paper submitted at the conference, *From Varying Positions*, held at the Tate Gallery in 1998, organised by the Wimbledon School of Art in collaboration with the Tate Gallery.

Untitled
Paint, wood
120 x 300 x 180 cm
2002

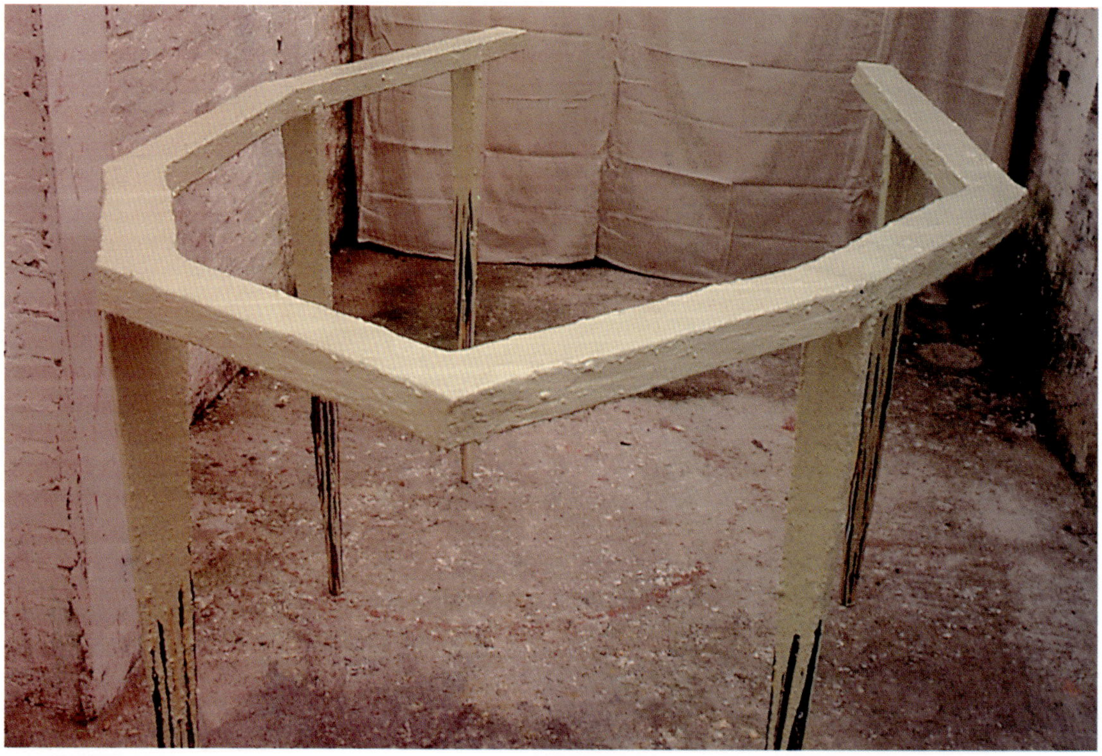

Discussion between Phyllida Barlow, Naomi Salaman and Alex Hartley from *Postcards on Photography*

Alex Hartley What struck me about what you were saying is that most of the artists I know no longer really experiment in a big way. The experiments are very little things, and most of the work which goes on in the studio is making work directly for exhibition. Experimentation happens on the periphery of the making process.

Phyllida Barlow I think that exhibitions are fantastically important, but I know a lot of these exhibitions aren't exhibitions, they're showing work and that's a big difference. There's such a hunger to be on that plane, where you must have all the accessories, like the catalogue. Whereas maybe the most important thing to do is to test the work out in some way? Then you can enjoy the luxury of not having to be involved in private view cards with an image on it and all that stuff.

AH When I left college I worked as an installation photographer for galleries. It was fascinating to see the priorities and the ambitions of the galleries … who would spend the most money on all that stuff … the idea of the currency of the transparency, and that the object doesn't really matter. Then you see that the invite stands in as the poor man's catalogue. Most people won't go to the show but they'll have had your little calling card.

PB I mean it's all very understandable in human terms. You want some sort of evidence, a souvenir that you've been there and done that. My feeling is that the camera has become the endorsing instrument.

Naomi Salaman Like the witness.

PB In a funny kind of way, and I know it's like pissing in the wind, but I suppose I am critical of that. It's almost as though, why not just admit that there's an audience of one, and it's you? I'm not suggesting that a slide shouldn't be taken but it seems that the trust is being put into something that is like a souvenir, rather than in the experience.

NS It's something we are thinking about with this catalogue because it will fail to represent the work. The difference between the experience and the representation in photorealism is inherent in the work. When the object returns to the photographic state it doesn't make any sense, there is too much missing.

PB The painted surface is the object, therefore by rendering it back to the very thing that it is being duplicitous about, makes it fail. That is such an interesting experiment in itself. You'd imagine that with the exercise of making the painting look like a photograph there would be no problem with it then being photographed. But that is absolutely where the problem lies.

AH As the photographer you'd have to be sure you lit the work to show the thickness of the canvas, and that it wasn't cropped in, show the surrounding area of the scene, etc.

NS But even if you took care to show the work in installation, the thickness of the canvas, the texture of the surface, you'd still be looking at a photograph.

PB I wonder whether there's this strange collusion between this idea of perfect finish and the camera. Is it a pointless thing to start to question? Another issue I think about is difficulty. The object which demands you walk all round it is a much more difficult act of looking than being able to sit and be given that act of looking already processed in some way. That's where I see a kind of slippage, where the camera takes on a high status because it's able to get rid of difficulties. That suggests to me that there *are* dangerous ways of looking at art.

AH Ugly work really suffers in terms of representation. Things which are about mass, things which are really ugly are really difficult to represent.

PB Absolutely, and this is the heart of the whole thing to me. I wonder whether there isn't a kind of forced bio-engineering going on, a kind of evolutionary process where difficult work, because of its lumpenness, its non-visual qualities, its sensual qualities of weight, coldness, hotness … the camera is unable to deal with those things. So could the reign of the camera make artists shy-off from difficult work, because the currency of the batch of slides has become so important. If somebody has got really involved in a whole set of processes or ways of making where they actually don't know where the hell to photograph it from, or what to photograph … let us say there's just a puddle on the floor where everything's happened. I mean, what the hell do you do with that? It's such a challenge that your work is about something that's disappeared. Does it no longer have a power if it doesn't show in this language of the camera?

NS When you were using the tourist metaphor, I kept thinking about the fear of wasting time which happens when you don't have a guide. Those blind alleys.

AH The catalogue validates the work and tells you it's worth looking at right from the beginning because someone has paid money for it to be included.

NS Do you ever pick up a calalogue to experience the work?

AH No, I guess not. But you can imagine you understand the work without having seen it.

NS I think there are valid ways of understanding and knowing work that do not have to take place with the work. To carry on with your terms, Phyllida, let's say you go to the gallery and have a completely 'anaesthetic' experience. In the most romantic extension of the idea that a direct experience of the work is the most rich one, the other side, is that it can be difficult to relate directly to the work.

PB Looking is very difficult: you're not going to be rewarded. If you talk about work through verbal language you're instantly rewarded by the quality of language that can give this charismatic description to something. But actually walking round a work is extremely slow, and can at times be boring. But catalogues are not boring objects.

AH Catalogues can be unbelievably exciting, but as a maker there's a desire to see the back of things which you're totally denied through catalogue shots. Not having the work means you can't look into it, see whether the finishes go all the way round, see whether you are being presented with just the perfect view or not.

PB The collusion of the camera with the artwork, and the resulting catalogue, has a convention about it that makes it almost seem as though the artworks are all functioning in roughly the same kind of spaces.

NS It democratises all sorts of artistic production.

AH Those installation shots are often complete artifice; to get 'the shot' that will show the exhibition… during the Summer galleries will set up the next five exhibitions two or three months in advance to take photographs for the catalogue. Twenty-five people working for a whole week, day and night, in order to get six photographs. The power of that shot is amazing. Somehow you're meant to imagine that the catalogue was produced really quickly. You're not really meant to question the catalogue. And most people won't see the show. In the way Phyllida talks about catalogues, I think of the gallery space. The architect and the catalogue designer are very similar. You imagine there's nothing, but that nothing shows the power of the space - such as Claudio Silverstrin and John Pawson, who designed a lot of the galleries which came up in the late 'eighties. It's meant to be invisible, but it says 'power'. The Castelli space, you see great art in that space over time, through lots of catalogues, but it's the architecture that you've seen more than the work. Even as the gallery space tries to become invisible, it becomes more visible.

There is a close connection between doing installation shots for galleries and the work I produce. It focused me on the power of these images. Some of the first work I did was using images taken from the review sections of art magazines where I touched out the work of the artist, leaving the gallery space. I was thinking about the power of the installation shot, and that people wouldn't see the show, but the world over would have some idea of it from the installation shot. *Viewer* was made specifically for Victoria Miro's space which is just like a shop, with glass frontage. *Viewer* mirrors how the gallery works, the lens and the object within it, which has another space, and how you interact with the piece brings attention back to the viewer and the space and how you interact with that space.

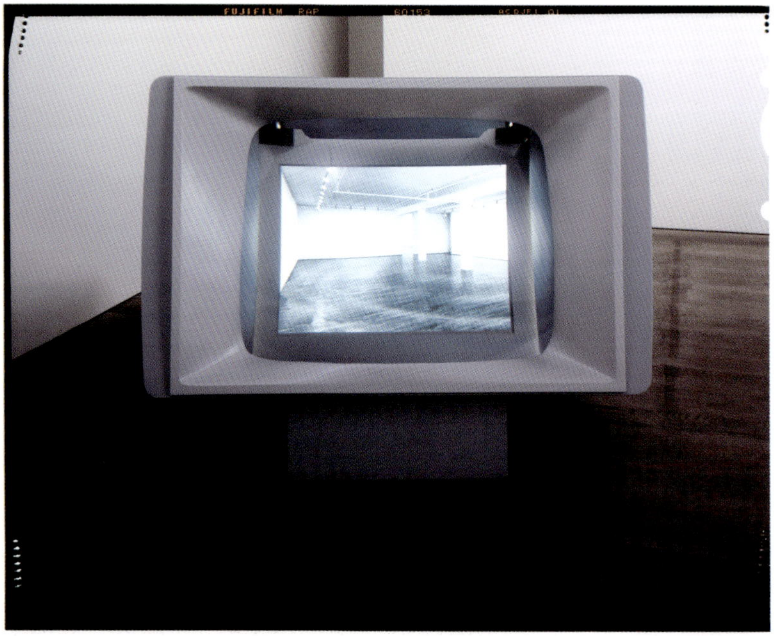

Alex Hartley
Viewer
MDF, perspex, paint, water, electrical components
225 x 205 x 160 cm
1997

NS But also, the space of the gallery is visible, and behind that is the office where they keep everything on slide. It's like making a huge version of the office. There is an inversion of scale and in what you end up seeing as art. As with *'Archival Disaster'* there is a sense of this inversion of invisibility to visibility.

AH *'Archival Disaster'* comes from the idea of the currency of the slide, and my running battle with my own disorganised archive of my work. I see it sculpturally: by blowing it up it will be a very physical object you have to deal with, and will totally divorce it from the original thing - it's a failed attempt to be organised and make representation.

NS It just has that feeling that a little disturbance in the archive, that's supposed to be just a document of the world, could then have this knock-on effect in the real world and that actual people or places might start falling over.

Phyllida, going back to 'the anaesthesia of success compared to the sensuality of failure', the modern cultural practice of sitting and watching TV. or the automatic image that the camera gives you could be described as a kind of anaesthetic, and takes away all those sensual aspects of the difficult slow process of looking. But the anaesthetic means that the operation can go ahead. On a certain level a deeper investigation of culture can take place, because that process of actually feeling the knife going in is taken away, so that then you can get to another level of culture which is discursive, or anyway, it's removed from this thing which you are obstinate about … being there. You don't want an anaesthetic in any way.

PB Success becomes anaesthetic because of the way that it publishes itself, whereas the sensuality of failure is quite private, you could say almost masturbatory; you know it's hidden from view. I just think it is necessarily overlooked by the professionals as an alive place of working. Whereas success often just means the publicity machine takes over, it looks like an artist's work you know … but it isn't.

NS That's what I wanted to say about this cold empty catalogue space you describe, that seems to present an idealised portrait. On the other hand, you can see it as an incredibly peopled space. Someone took the photographs, someone arranged the page, somebody designed the typeface … it's full of people. You can see it as being shovel fed something, but you can also see it as a lot of people being involved.

PB What fascinates me about all of this is the means by which things can be eradicated, the whole activity of what people do. What is that all about? I know it's about showing the artwork off to its best advantage, but I feel there's something else going on there, that's maybe about a chilling removal of everyone involved.

Discussion between Phyllida Barlow, Naomi Salaman and Alex Hartley, 14 September 1998, from the catalogue *Postcards on Photography*, Naomi Salaman and Ronnie Simpson, eds., Cambridge: Cambridge Darkroom Gallery, 1998, for the exhibition *postcards on photography – photorealism and the reproduction*.

Alex Hartley
Archival Disaters
ABS plastic,
MDF, aluminium
Dimensions various
1998

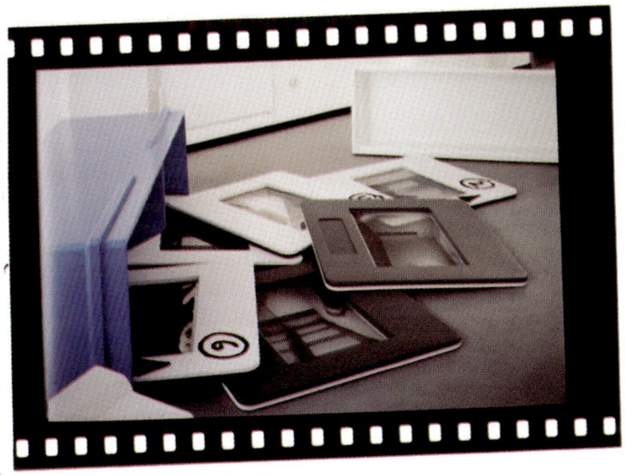

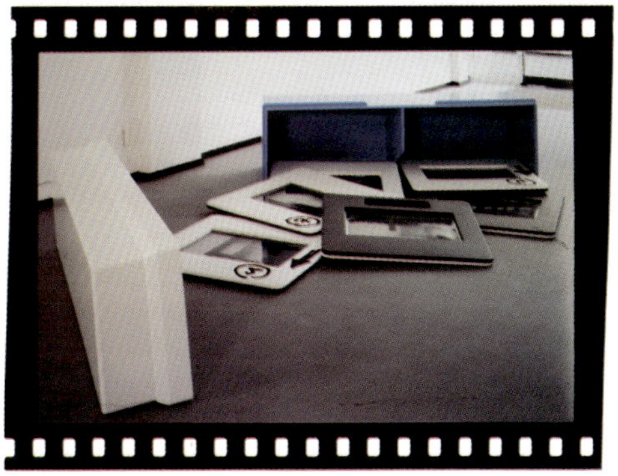

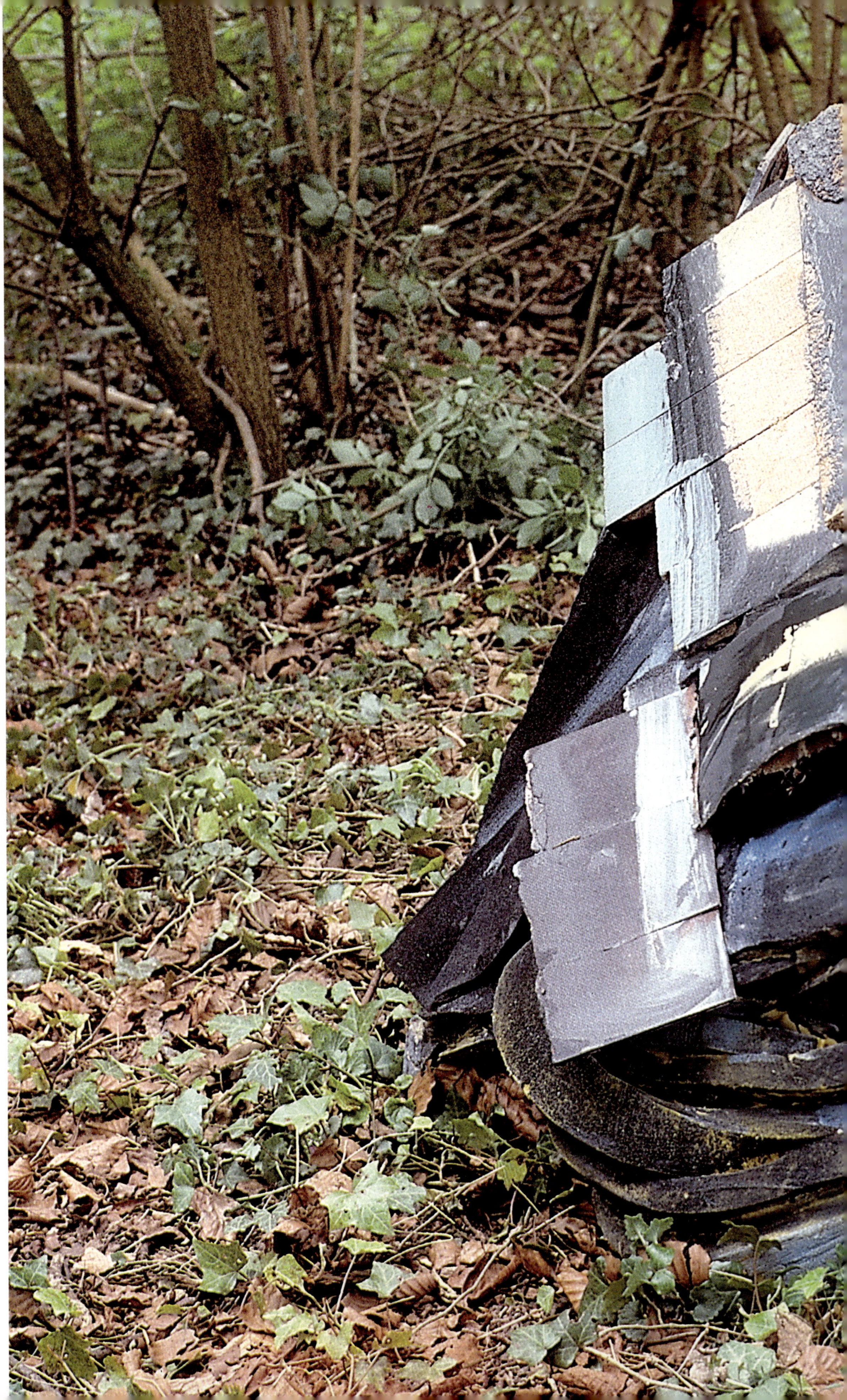

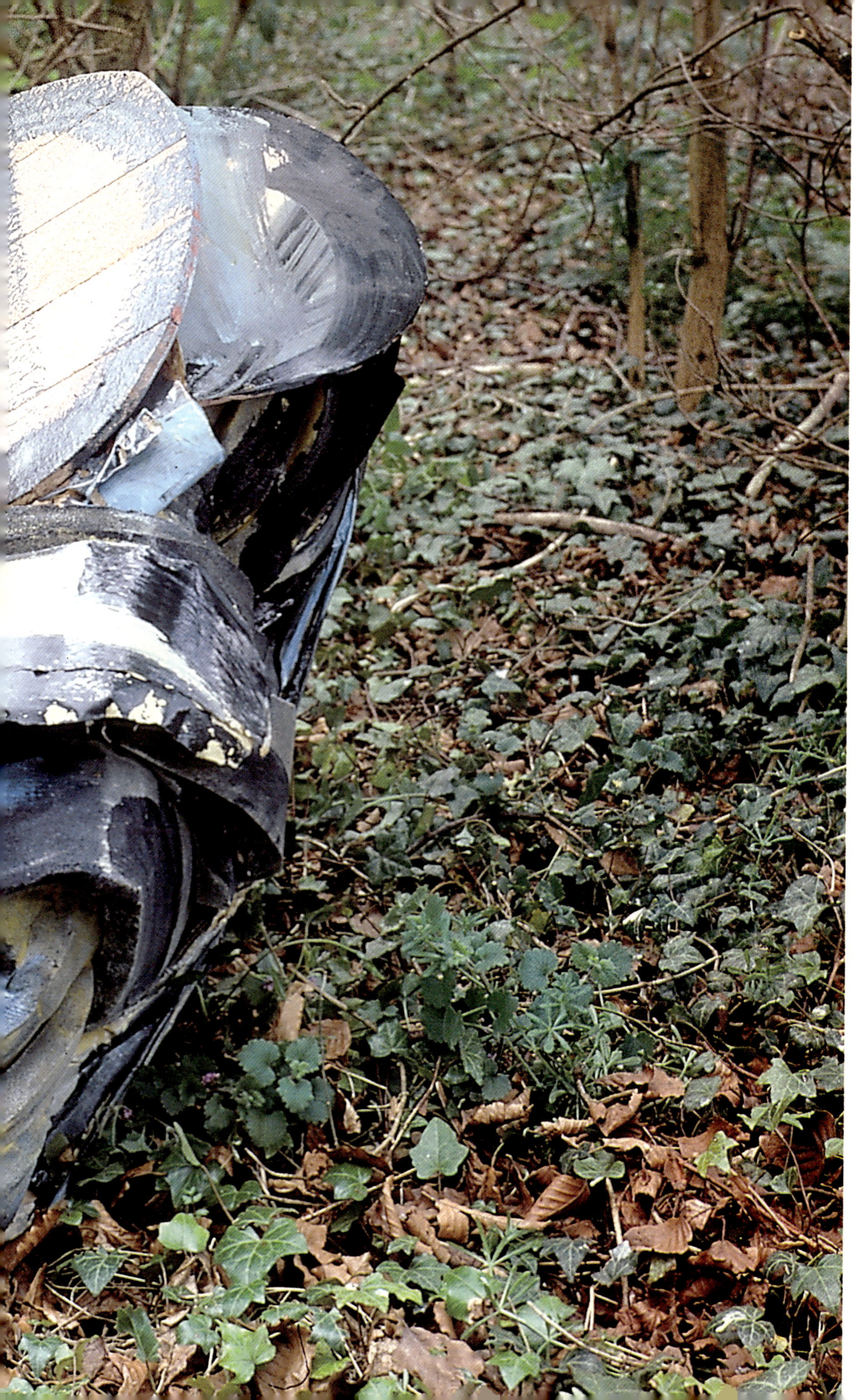

Previous and these pages
Touchpiece series
Hardboard, upholstery foam, string,
paper, latex, paint, formica
70 x 80 x 70 cm (approx)
1983-1989
Various locations

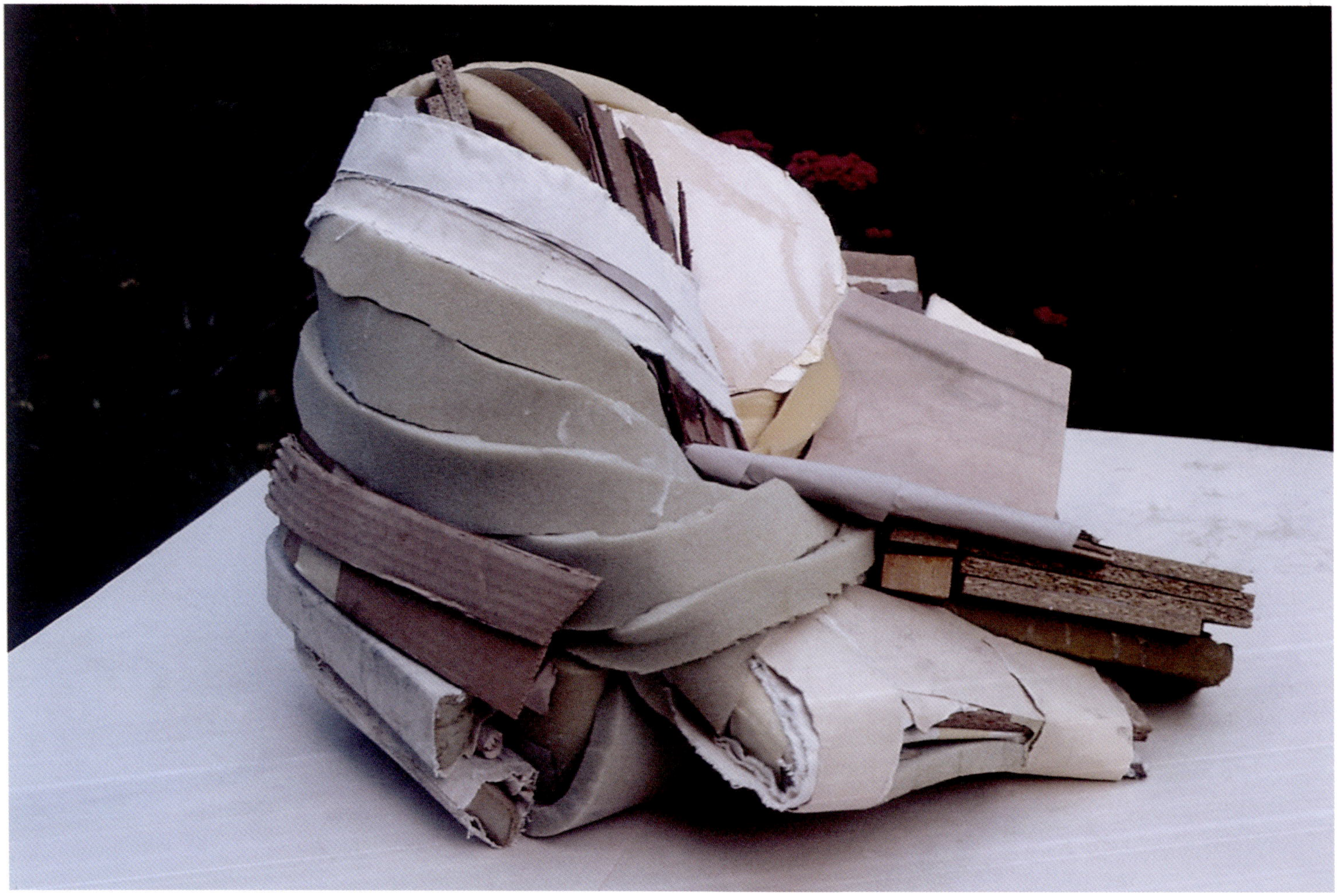

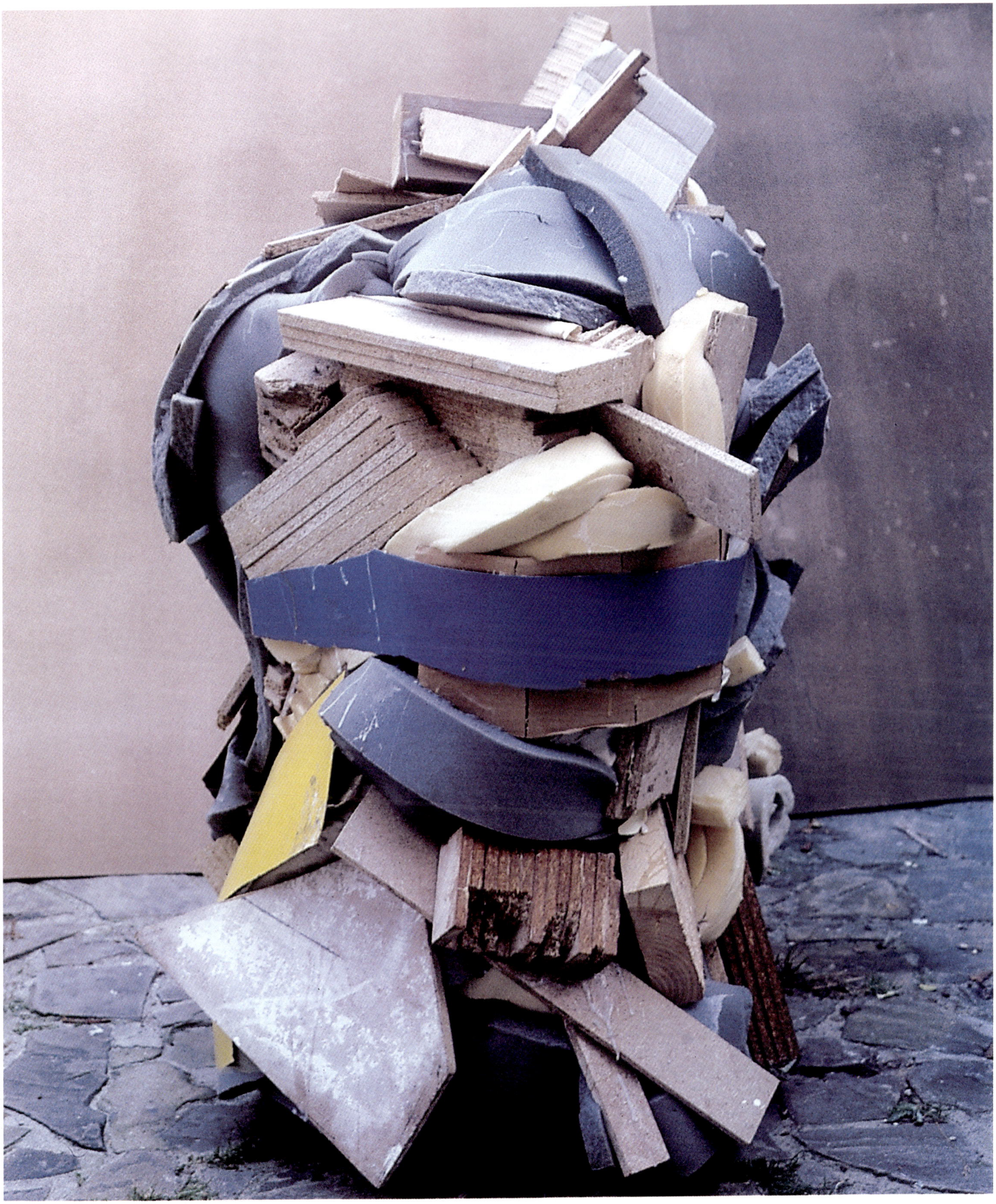

Touchpiece series
Paint, upholstery foam, paper,
canvas, wood, rope, rubber
140 x 150 x 140 cm (approx)
1984
Studio work

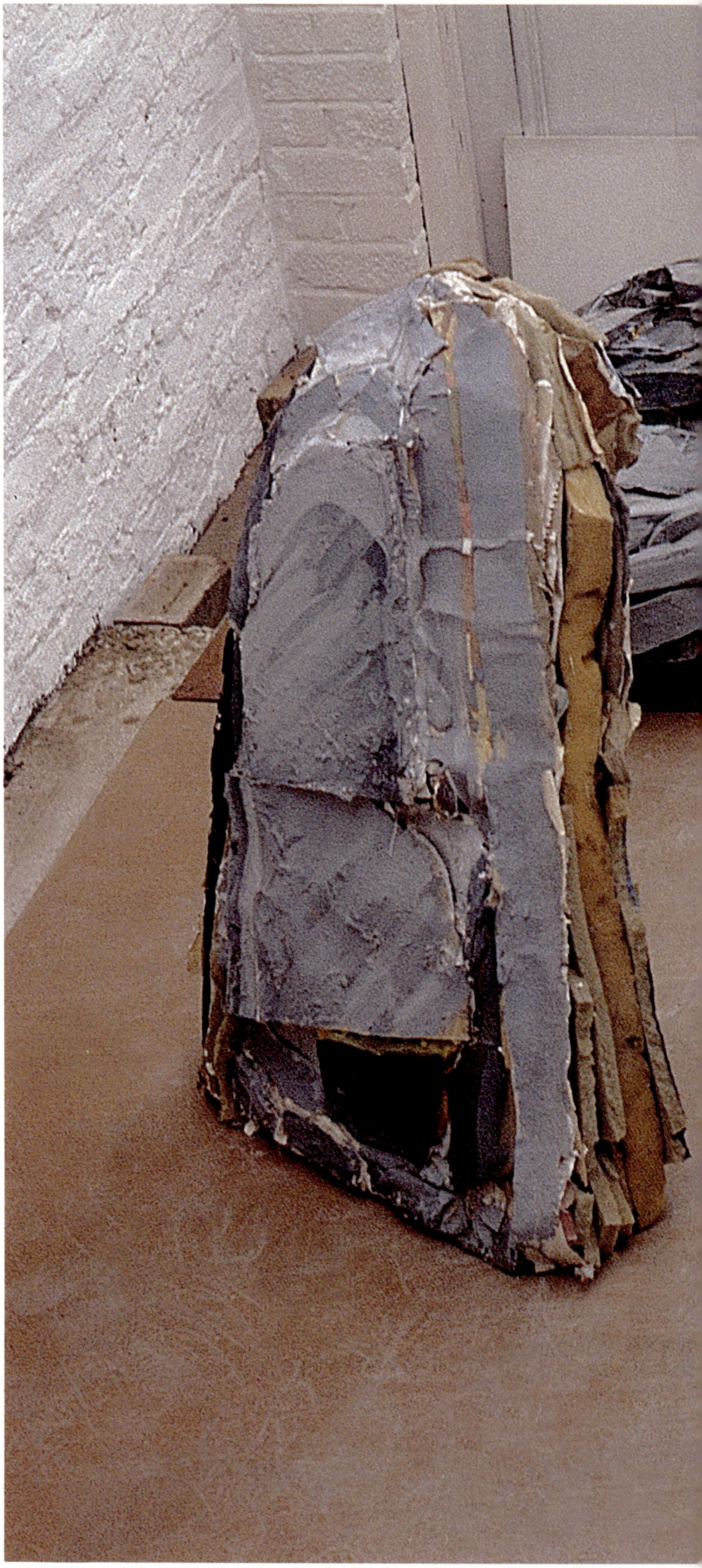

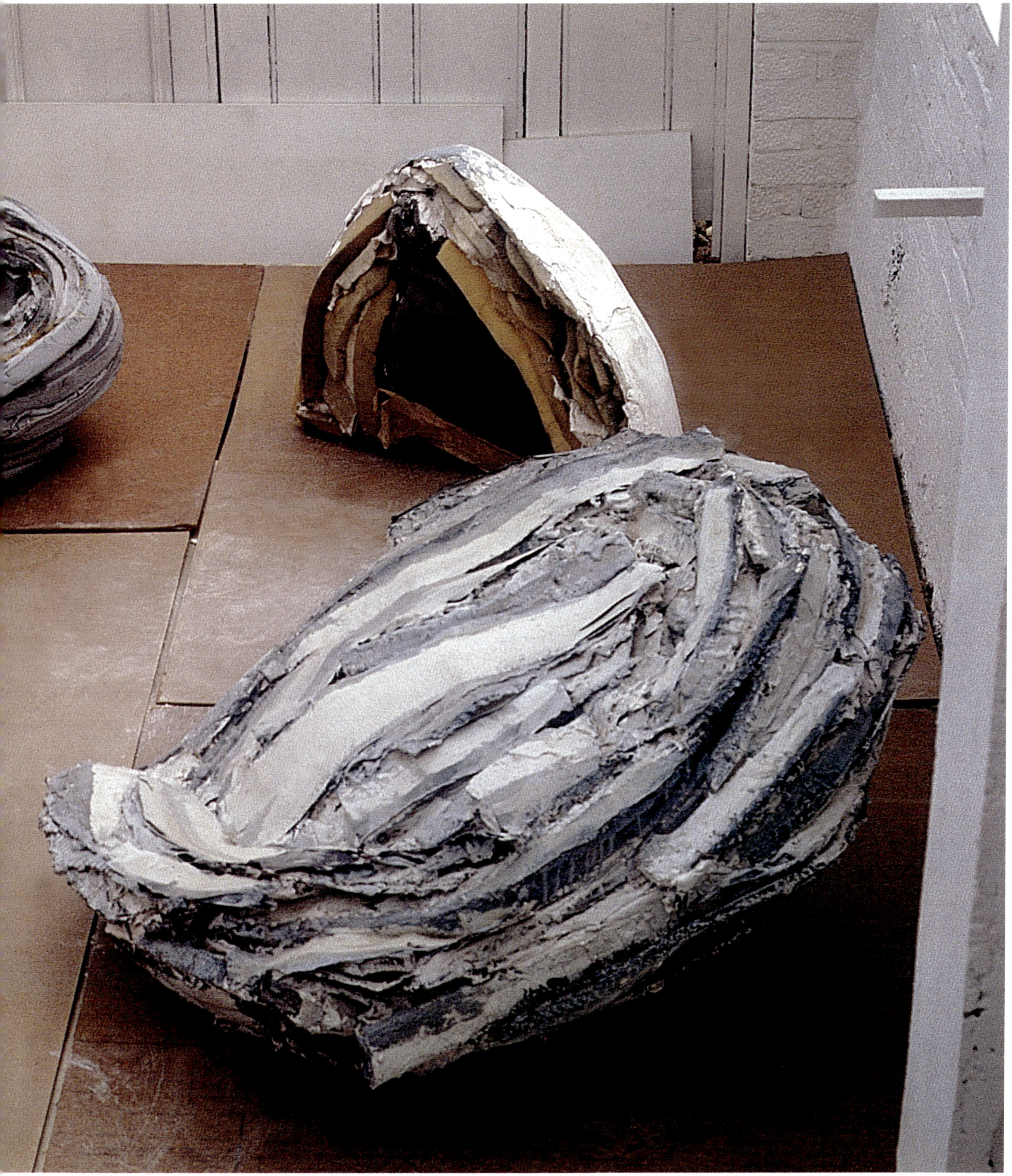

Hearsay, Rumours, Bed-sit Dreamers and Art Begins Today

I am having difficulty in pinning down what the significance of the 1965 *New Generation Sculpture* exhibition could be. I have resorted to compiling lists, lots of them, and each one with a different inflection. But the crucial thing has to be how to edit these lists into something relevant for this conference. And I keep on going back to the subject of the conference – is it, what is the future *for* sculpture, or the future *of* sculpture, or, maybe, does sculpture have a future? And who cares anyway.

The 1965 *New Generation* exhibition has stuck in my memory, but not because it was an exceptional artistic experience. The opposite is more the case. As Mary Horlock cites in her catalogue essay for this exhibition, *Early One Morning*, Bruce McClean referred to the 1965 exhibition as more of the same: New Generation sculpture was nothing more than Henry Moore with stripes. The exhibition was more relevant to its immediate past than to anything new. New Generation was a kind of mutton dressed as lamb.

Dominating my lists has been the word 'new'. New does signify clean, fresh, bright, unused, unopened, spotless, even pure. Certainly not second-hand, nearly new, borrowed. And when the new is spoilt, even in the slightest way, a tiny scratch on the new car body, or a spot of grease on new clothes, the entire effect is ruined, and the new becomes a ruin. To have removed the word 'new' from the title of the *New Generation* exhibitions would have lost everything: to have called them the "Next Generation" would have meant nothing, but would have been, in fact, nearer the truth.

And 'new' does also mean 'young'. Importantly, the *New Generation* exhibitions did herald the importance and excitement of showing new, young artists' work when previously there were few such exhibitions.

But despite the brightness and so-called newness of the *New Generation* exhibition, there was an inherent familiarity about it. A dullness took over: the stillness of the sculpture was bland, not atmospheric; its weight was leaden rather than illusionary; its colour, although its greatest asset, too reminiscent of what had been shown in the previous year's *New Generation* painting exhibition. The 1965 exhibition was destined to be short lived, and all too quickly it became consumed by institutionalism, its fate sealed into academicism.

The exhibition became a demonstration for how sculpture could be learnt. As an all male preserve, the *New Generation* exhibition offered a collection of workshop practices, born out of essentially male-based activities: welding, fibreglass and resin casting and construction, and semi-industrial assemblage. Sculpture as such provided an ideal for a 'school of sculpture' to be established, based on sheet metal assemblage and fibreglass and resin techniques, and exercises accompanying these would reveal all.

Also, there was this all-pervading suspicion, through rumour and hearsay of course, that all that was going on in New Generation sculpture, UK, had its origins in the USA, and those who had an inkling of this were disappointed in the claims bestowed upon the exhibition. Dominating the experience was not a sense of newness but more of an eclecticism culled from various of the moment, American styles. American art was what was craved: stripes, colour fields abounded within and without art schools making the exhibition several years overdue, and out of date quicker than it could have expected.

Therefore, going to see the current Tate Britain collection of 1960s New Generation sculpture re-stated exactly that sense of dull academicism, where crucial missing ingredients deny the possibility of a more enchanted experience. The emotional denial inherent to the work brought back how easily the New Generation sculpture had become fodder for designers who had plundered its bright, toy-like style for their own ends, making the work indistinguishable from the burgeoning Habitat domestic commodities, Galt's faddish, pseudo crafted toys, as well as packaging, textiles and new innovations with easy to assemble furniture and DIY, also a burgeoning, new industry.

The increasingly tedious debates about sculpture then: to plinth or not to plinth, the value of the laborious grind of making, truth to materials etc., etc., paled into more art school academicism as new rumours and hearsay of what was going on elsewhere began to filter through. And what was it that was being talked about and rumoured? Stories of works in deserts and excavations in derelict warehouses employing a different kind of labour: straight manual labour as seen on the street and building site: diggers and excavators, were being appropriated to make sculpture, whilst at the opposite end of the scale, resin and a new material, latex, were being used like paint, not as a substitute for bronze, but as stuff in its own right, to be dunked into, painted on cloth to make it rigid, moulded off rigid forms to make them soft, poured, spilt and thrown. Weight, mass, scale and size were all being usurped by gesture, touch and the here and now. And artists were taking to the streets, like so many others at that time, and foregoing the studio; anywhere and everywhere was a site, and anything and everything could be made into art. Excitement and imagination had arrived. By 1968, the New Generation exhibitions were dead history.

So, what is newness? Interestingly the current exhibition, *Early One Morning*, does not make such a claim, but, as the title suggests, offers energy, vitality and an anything goes exuberance. It clearly does delight, and, because it does not offer any definitions for sculpture – which the 1965 show became associated with – there is a free spirit about this exhibition. Whether this free spirit is new or not is another matter, but certainly the 1965 exhibition could make no such claim. All the old rules were firmly in place: craft, weight, formal autonomy, symmetry, asymmetry. The 'new' could be learnt, and art schools were where you went to learn it. A new academicism had been born, and an all male one at that! Freeness, imagination and surprise did seem to be missing from the 1965 exhibition. And as the hearsay and rumours increased from the USA and Europe, the more academic and institutionalised the British art scene seemed to become. The hearsay and rumours offered an entirely different experience, an experience rooted in the forbidden and despised notion of theatricality. No more the need for permanency, weightiness, handicraft, the learnt and to be taught restraints of what was and what was not sculpture. Instead, in with impermanency, temporariness, dematerialisation, the fugitive, the ephemeral, the here and now. Out with the welding shop and the learnable techniques and in with experimentation with anything and everything: materials and physicality were opened up for anything, everything, everywhere. And the artist him or herself could be anyone, and as such they could be subject and object of the work.

The beauty of the theatrical lay in its potential to take on anything, anywhere: the stage became container and protagonist for the work, and could be anything and everything. Absolutely anywhere could be appropriated as an art space.

Sculpture became the activity incarcerated within an art school, to be taught and learnt. The street and anywhere else became the time and the place. Creative freedom was reciprocal to the political activities raging around Europe and the USA. The incident, the act itself was the work, and how it would have permanency would be through its potential for rumour and hearsay, all of which could be endorsed by the most significant of reporters, the camera: the Super 8 movie camera and the 35 mm SR, and their rolls of black and white film. These were to become the most important travelling companions and accomplices to this ephemeral work.

So for me the legacy of the 1965 exhibition was not in the show itself but in what it spawned as an opposition to it. Sculpture continued to be made in studios but there was a burgeoning feminising of the processes, and a different take on labour intensivity was beginning to emerge. The studio could look beyond itself for inspiration. The kitchen, the dressmaker's, the garage, agriculture, road works, building sites and, of course, the bed sit, the home of most art students, could all provide processes to be plundered and appropriated as means to an end. Speculation was the game and time was of the essence. Why try to compete with the super-artists, and their corporate support: the former rebels, who had become the then established global exhibitors: the Smiths, Caros, Kings, Tuckers, yesterday's equivalents to today's Turrells, Violas, Christos, Pistolettos. Why devote hours to labour intensive activities when results could be produced immediately, as was beginning to be seen through the work of Hesse and Bourgeois. Why go to the macho means of production when twiddling your thumbs and putting things together from your immediate environment was all you could afford to do. What about staring at the bed-sit ceiling and dreaming up the wild, the wonderful and the way beyond from the patterns on the ceiling and making it become reality by any means possible? The smoothed out surfaces of the fibreglass and resin aficionados were becoming clichéd, let alone the fact that resin was carcinogenic, and therefore an unsuitable material to spend too much time with. All the more reason for speedy, direct application; all the more reason for hit and run techniques.

Theatricality and time became absorbed into all aspects of sculpture. Issues about the plinth blurred into comparative obscurity and irrelevance. Space became location and place, a material in its own right and the object could both occupy and disown that space: the object could be dematerialised. Its presence could, and can, for that matter, be manifested through its absence, and again the hearsay and rumours of such work were as important as the work itself. Again, it was and is the camera in all its guises which provided the evidence, and it is only evidence, of such work. Therefore, I believe, sculpture as a fundamentalist activity which could only tell the truth, the whole truth and nothing but the truth became tedious and irrelevant. Released from its history of permanency and absolute materiality, sculpture could fragment space, could be cinematic in its relationship to how to occupy space, and could fib and lie itself into its own reality. Objects could connect and interrelate over spaces that they would charge with atmospheric and moody resonances, and time had to be taken to experience the whole encounter: objects, space, time.

And so hearsay, rumours, bed-sit dreams and 'art begins today' attitudes came to stay and have stayed. Sculpture, for myself, still resides in the experience of unreality: the walking around of things that have no use in the world and which defy absolute categorisation and definition. I do not want to be told about things which I already know about, unless of course it is to be surprised, to be offered a glimpse of something which I could never conceive of being what it is. The fugitive and the ephemeral are still exciting; the place of where something might be and could be, whether that is brought into an official art space, or whether that is claiming somewhere else, is still exciting. And the here and now, which has to be the most exciting and enduring of sculptural experience, where once you have gone away from the object it somehow cannot quite be retrieved. It demands that you have to be there with it, to experience it, to know it.

Even though conceptual art raged like wildfire, and tried its hardest to establish its own domination, it could not override the enthusiasm for making-and-doing in its revitalised, theatrical form. It did have an influence, undoubtedly so, causing a wave of doubt and reconsideration of who art was for, where it should, and could be seen, with what, how, and why. Again, the dominant tool was the camera, and so a cross over between the mental and physical approaches to making became inextricably bound, and the rest is history.

Likewise with commodification: it may come and go, with its boxed, based and vitrined symptoms of conventionalism and conservatism; they may have abounded, and still do abound, incarcerating and taming aesthetics, and emasculating and caging form, as they do, where the wild, untamed and visceral is brought to heel under the whip of consumerist, product-led and commercially driven incentives. Importantly as well, hearsay and rumour have now found perfect accommodation within the catalogue, which has undoubtedly become the most important record, souvenir and take-away memorandum of what is shown: no catalogue, no exhibition? So what becomes of rumour and hearsay under these circumstances? Time will tell.

But the most significant influences on sculpture for the present and for its future do still remain beyond the institutions, firmly residing in the sphere of the artist him or herself. Where, with what, how, why, when, can still surprise, be momentary, difficult to access, or even be known about, but because of these difficulties and awkwardnesses, not despite them, hearsay, rumour, bed-sit dreamers, and art-begins-to-day attitudes, will prevail, and will be initiated and stimulated by the favoured art of the time, even by default, even for the sake of contrariness, even to stake out an opposition, all of which provides the resource and incentive for what will happen next.

The 1965 New Generation sculpture galvanised something: whether, through opposition, it was an anti-historicism and anti-institutionalism on one hand, which has not endured. Or whether it is the spirit of adventure centred on the individual and how he or she releases that, whatever their life experience, bed-sits or otherwise, which *has* endured. Whatever the influences from 1965 might be, if any, the future of sculpture always lies in the unexpected. Therefore, this most awkward, recalcitrant and unmanageable of art forms can be relied upon to make believable the imagination. Imagination has to be what is inherently new and surprising, and essential to sculpture, its past, its present and its future.

This text was presented as a talk at the *Early One Morning* exhibition seminar *Next Generations – Current Sculptural Practice in the UK and Beyond*, Whitechapel Gallery, London, July 20 2002. *Early one Morning* showcased 5 young British Sculptors: Gary Webb, Clare Barclay, Eva Rothschild, Jim Lambie and Shahin Ahrussinabi.

Reds, Bodything, Lie
Fabric, elastic, upholstery foam,
wooden frame, red felt, rubber
Each work: 100 x 120 x 120 cm
1995
Contemporary Arts Society,
Royal Festival Hall, London

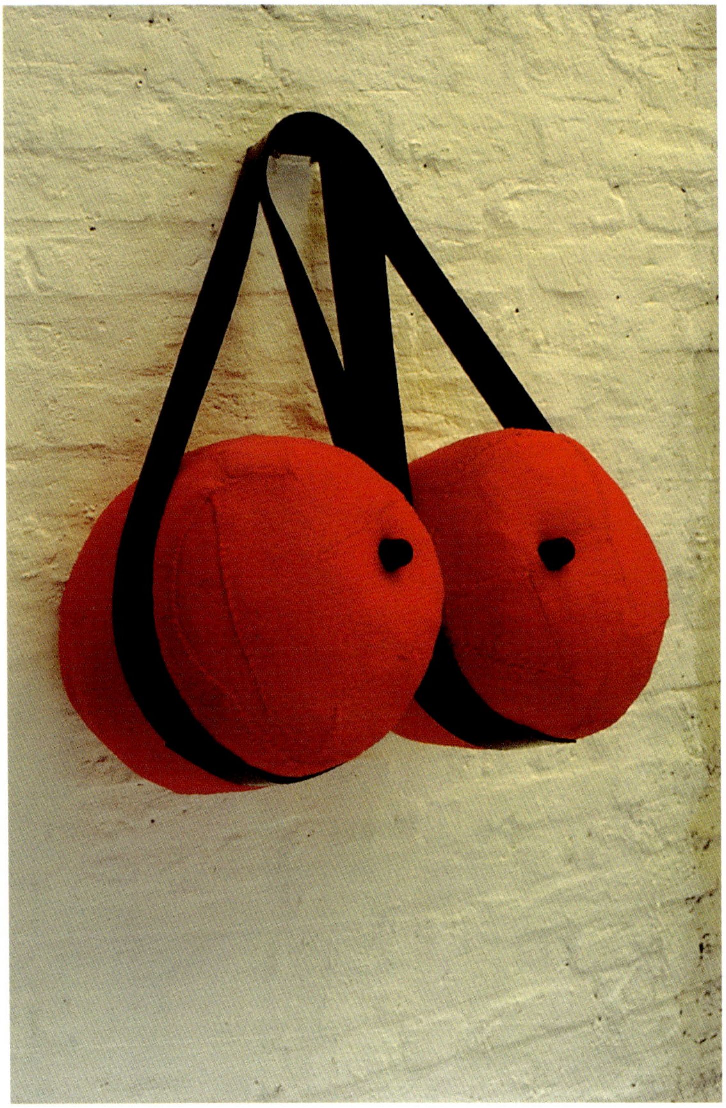

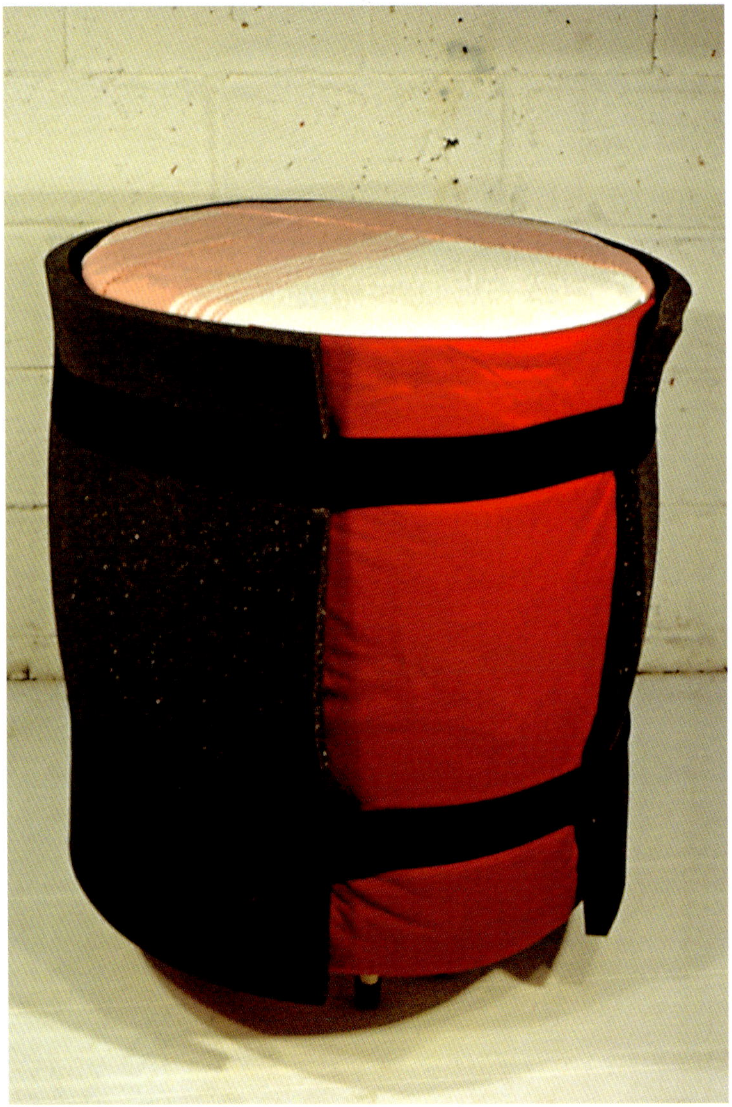

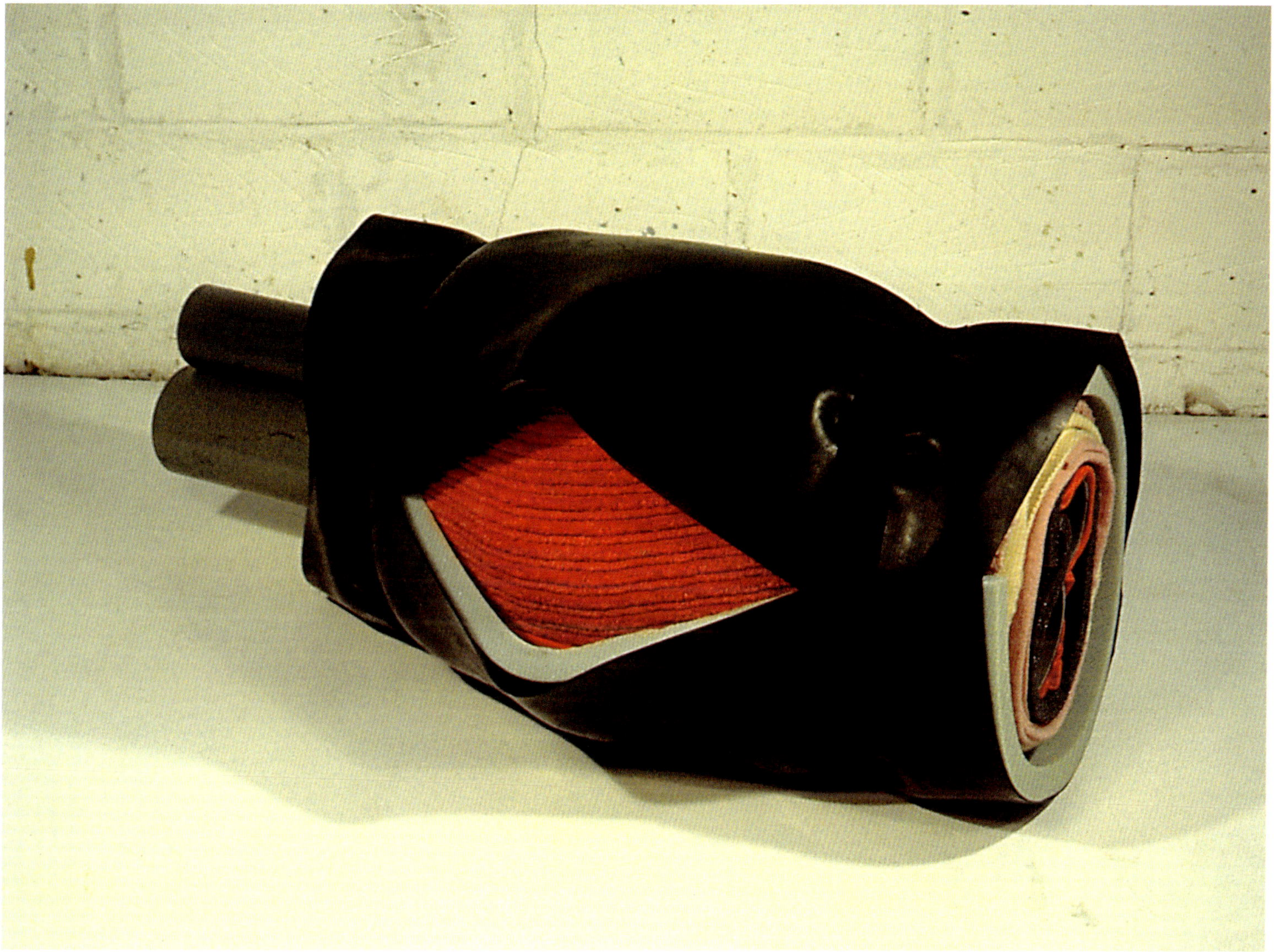

Lost for Words

Description and the thing described. A longstanding relationship which works well enough. Or does it? With sculpture rooted in process and touch and which evidence themselves as the essential experiences of the object itself, it can be difficult to translate such qualities into verbal language. The difficulty belongs to an expectation that what is said, what the words are, will have an absolute integrity when matched against the object itself. My contention is that the work of Eva Hesse repudiates verbal language, and particularly a language initiated by the process of naming.

The currency of sculpture which can use the language of naming becomes easily empowered by critical backup, and the more the work can be named, the more such naming renders the work's physicality and materiality redundant. The network of meanings which can be constructed from the associations with the sculpture's naming eventually displace its physical and material qualities with an image, and the more pictorial the object, the more easily achieved is its physical and material displacement.

Non-image based qualities, such as tactility, weight, texture, depth, height, width, darkness, light, smell, temperature, emptiness, fullness, and qualities inherent to materiality, physicality and process use descriptions such as stretchiness, fallingness, droopiness, rigidness, fatness, thinness.... Although apt enough, the problem is how to substantiate such descriptiveness, give it clout, equivalent to, but different from, the rich discourse which can be constructed around work which lends itself to being named. The semiotic chain generated from naming can also spawn numerous meanings to which equally numerous critical theories can be attached. Inevitably, I believe, such work acquires an intellectually superior identity than work which cannot invite such tactics.

Whilst in the USA, I sought out Eva Hesse's work. They were few and far between, but in the end I saw three. All were memorable. But how I came upon a section of *Sans II* (in the San Francisco Museum of Modern Art) has interested me: perhaps I was not concentrating, or at saturation point, but I did not notice it, when it was there in front of me. As it and I stood locked in a blank stare, I knew that to come across this work, as if by stealth, was the experience: there was, in fact, nothing surprising. Like many sculptors experiencing the work of Eva Hesse, everything is absolutely clear: the materials, their processes, how the grid-like form and structure could have been made, and the variegated discolouration of the ageing, resin-impregnated fibreglass.

The fragility of the work, its light saturated surfaces, its combined strict formalism with the undulating, slightly sagging edges, are Eva Hesse's signature; these are hers, and to such an extent that whenever such results reveal themselves within an artist's process, and alarmingly the work begins to look Eva Hesse-ish, he or she can have the knee-jerk reaction to back off, because the sense of pastiche can be overwhelming. Eva Hesse has invented a sculptural language which is so completely hers that it can be impossible to appropriate some of the processes, even though they are generic and available to anyone, for fear of stumbling upon an almost, but definitely not, Eva Hesse.

This near-copyright on materials and their processes creates a dilemma. Numerous experiments within art schools, usually at foundation course level, encourage using materials such as plaster, latex, cement, wax, resin, all liquid to solid materials. The point of these experiments is to get young artists to test out and experience the nature of materials, to find out what they do, to witness their time-based properties, and to experience the hands-on, the mess and all.

Once these processes have been discovered, what next? To make a series of near-miss Eva Hesses, because by this time, art students, new to such processes, will have been introduced to Eva Hesse, and, like an author condemned to an exam syllabus, these processes become identified with Hesse and with a coded message that this is 'emotional art' because it is wordless; it is primal: so, quite literally, it is as if nothing more can be said. But the narrative continues. Because such processes come packaged as emotional, the resulting work is delivered as 'personal', about 'feelings', as if no other art can claim such sanctity. And, as if things cannot get much worse, because of these claims, the resulting work, by default, refutes questioning or criticism. And a protected species is born.

This scenario explains something of the lack of a robust critical language which can compliment these processes, materials and resulting works. The claims that 'emotion' is evidenced through an appearance of tactility, materiality and process is dubious, but there is probably some truth in it as well. More importantly, there is this difficulty with making a critical and descriptive language work for the work itself, rather than avoid the work by jumping to critiques and theories culled from existing canons which substitute for the actuality of what is there.

So the work of Eva Hesse, as a generalisation, is not promoted in art schools beyond the most primary stages of an experience of sculpture, relegated, as I believe she is, to introduce and induct a sculptural language at a basic level, rather than to manifest a profound relationship to making, which reveals extraordinary depths of intellect, emotion and psychology. Her work, at worst, can be reduced to art school exercises to impress upon wary students the virtues of making: as a teaching aid to informality, the fun of playing with stuff, the emotiveness of spillages, splashes and mess, and the transformatory mysteries of processes. And having clocked these, it's then on to the real stuff, the stuff with meaning, as if meaning is somehow oppositional to emotion, and the processes of making.

remnant series: Dallas, 2003
Various tapes, card, plastic, newspaper, polyeurethane, wire, plaster, bread,
Dimensions approx: 30 x 30 x 30 cm
2003
for the Magnet School, Dallas

My initial blankness on meeting *Sans II* diffused slowly. Restlessness, anticipation, and an anxiety about missing a wonderful opportunity, were dissolved by the act of moving and looking. Dark and light, a rhythm, from one blurred, boxed form to the next, everything a repetition, but everything different, and the open-ended emptying out into the space beneath, which became full and supportive like an invisible plinth holding every side of the work, sealing interior, exterior and surrounding space into a symbiotic dependency.

By now I am as close to the work as I can be. A different mood prevails, a fear of disturbance: close up the work demands stillness and silence. There is a pulling inwards, as into long-frozen ice, an odd response, when the material itself has warmth. The chill is bewildering, at odds with the embedded hairs of the fibreglass, and the softly caramelised edges, and the aged, yellowing resin. It doesn't make sense, but then this is all in my mind, isn't it, and not really anything to do with the work.

But of course it is. Objects are emotive, because of their formalism, their structure, their place and time in relationship to ours. Upright and suspended things are different to collapsed and recumbent things, obvious enough, but being there with objects in these conditions influences our own condition, the way we look, move and behave. The memory of the work is not the same, however powerful, just as a text is not the work.

My description is identifying a paradox: the hotter the sense of touch, and the evidence of process, the cooler the resulting work. Tactility is duplicitous and misleading. Liquid to solid materials only have so much time in which they can be handled whilst they are setting: it is a one-hit relationship. And with a material like resin, if it has not set, due to a faulty mix, or too cold conditions, the process of restoring the surface to how you want it to be is excruciating. And there were such nightmares encountered with Hesse's working methods. To get dripping lengths of resin-sodden cloth to hang, drop, fall exactly so, working with its temperamental chemical reactions, as in *Untitled*, 1970 would have only permitted minimum contact of tactile, hands-on, activity. Resin's carcinogenic potential is now notorious.... Therefore, *Untitled*'s tactile heat is in stark contrast to the reality of its making where the resin impregnated fibreglass would have been as deftly, and as quickly manipulated as possible, in fact, as hands-off as possible.

Meanwhile, those supposedly coolest of cool objects of Donald Judd or John McCracken, of Koons or Hirst, have every inch of them handled, touched, manipulated, not necessarily by the artist but certainly by their fabricator.

The work of Eva Hesse is contradictory. If its materiality and process are the work, then these belie their pragmatism, offering paradoxes instead: where hot is cold, touched is untouched, anti-form is precision, and place is time. The work could not be more different and complex than its simplified interpretations within art schools, or its reputations which have mythologised its sensitivity, confusing it with sentimentality and nostalgia.

My conundrum is how to evidence through language what is there and the being there, a language which can have a critical status unencumbered by an over emotive rhetoric on one hand and an over laden theoretical position on the other. The work of Eva Hesse is gloriously nameless. But an Eva Hesse is unequivocally an Eva Hesse. For me, it cannot yield to a worded, semiotic process. Its paradoxes are its meanings. The work exists as if it has always been in the world. And, paradoxically, despite its unequivocal signature, it exists as if it could have been made by you.

This text was first presented as a paper at the *Eva Hesse Symposium*, Tate Modern, London, November 15 2002.

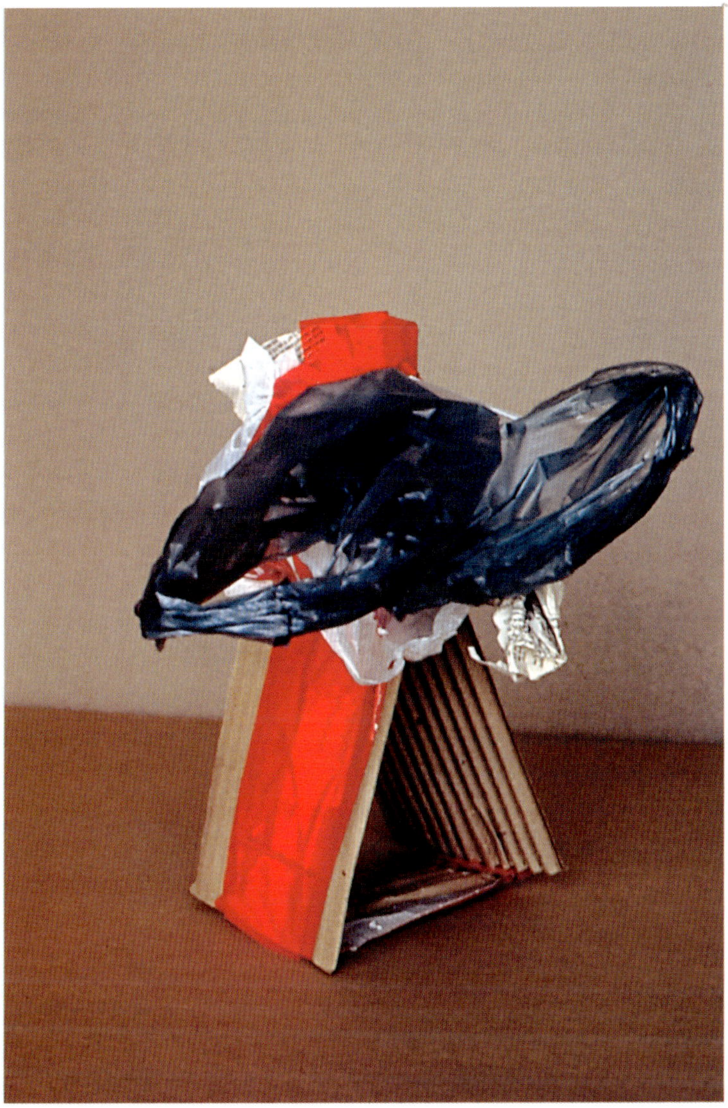
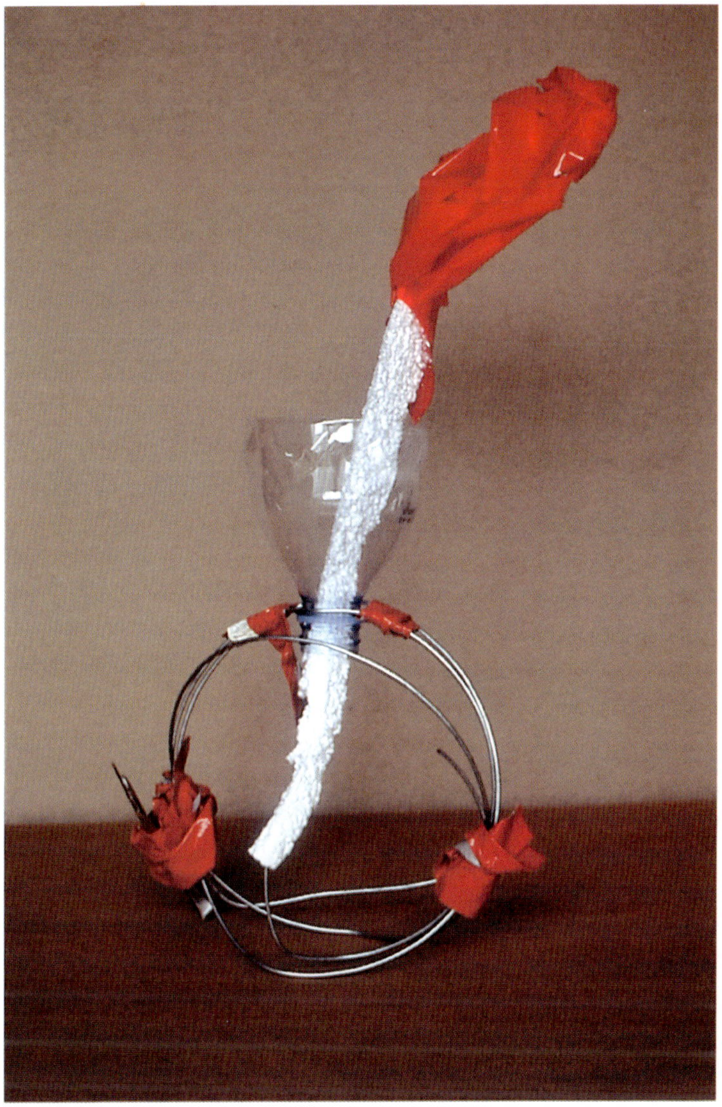
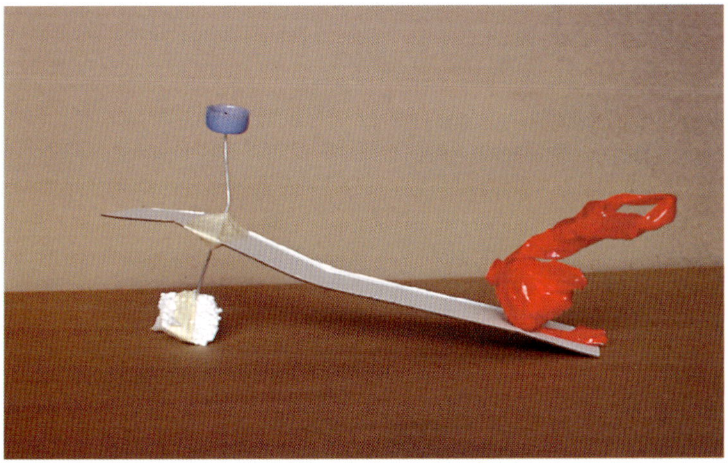
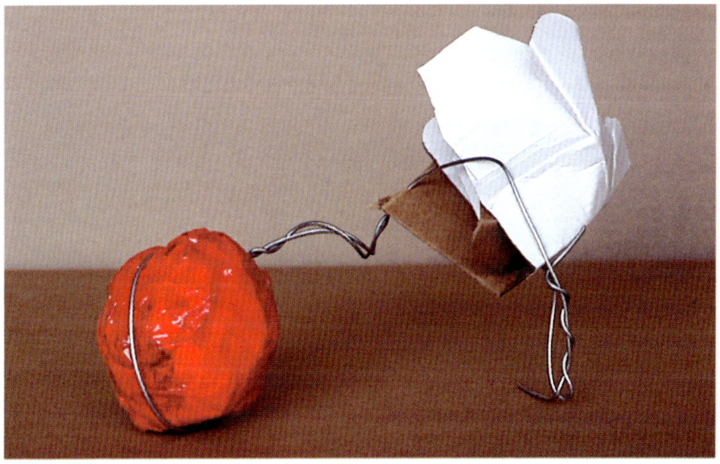

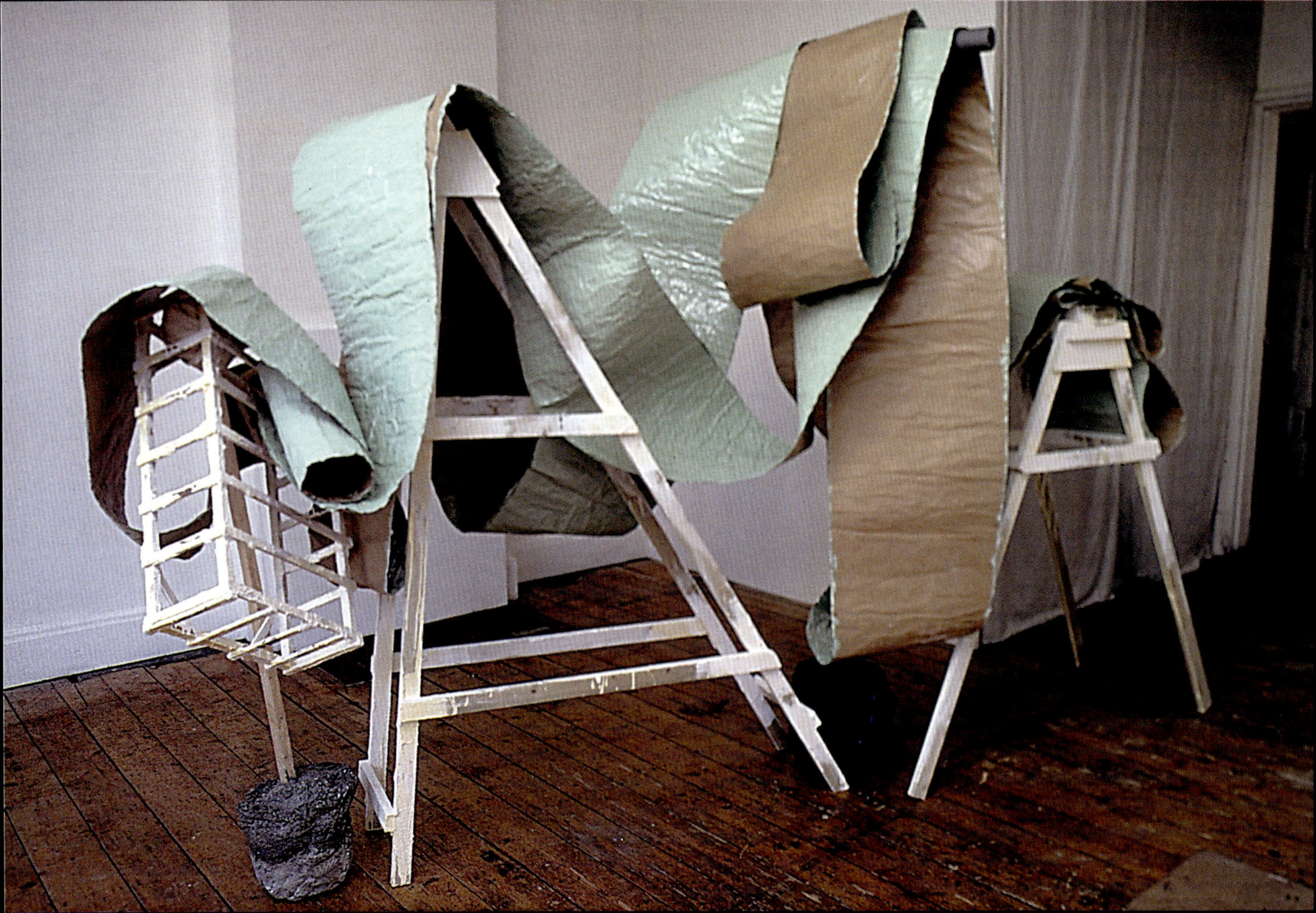

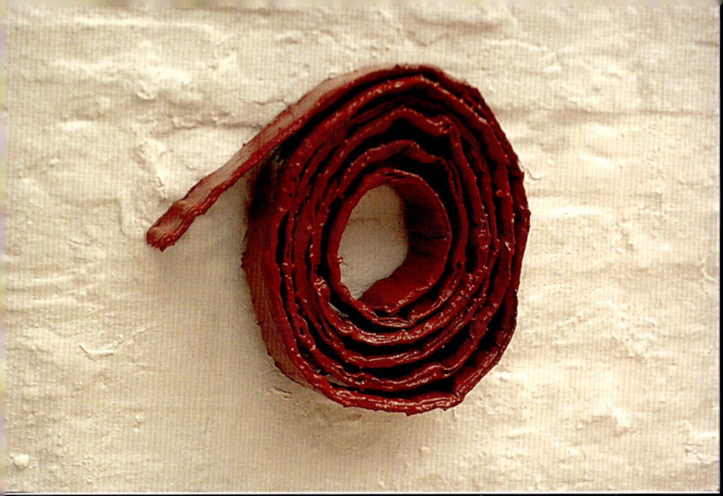

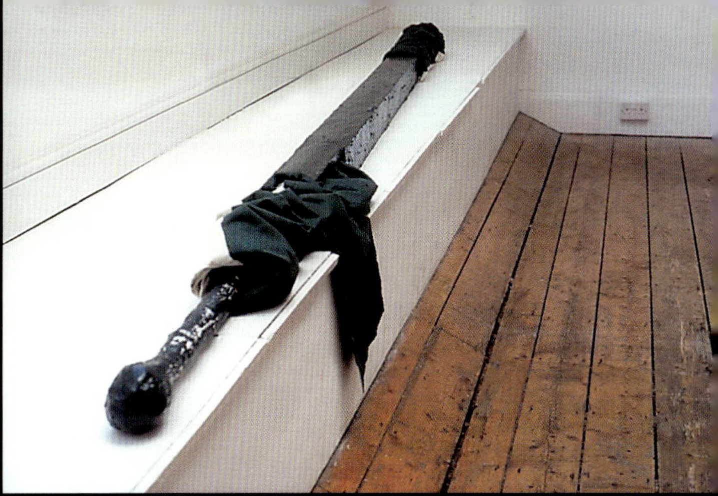

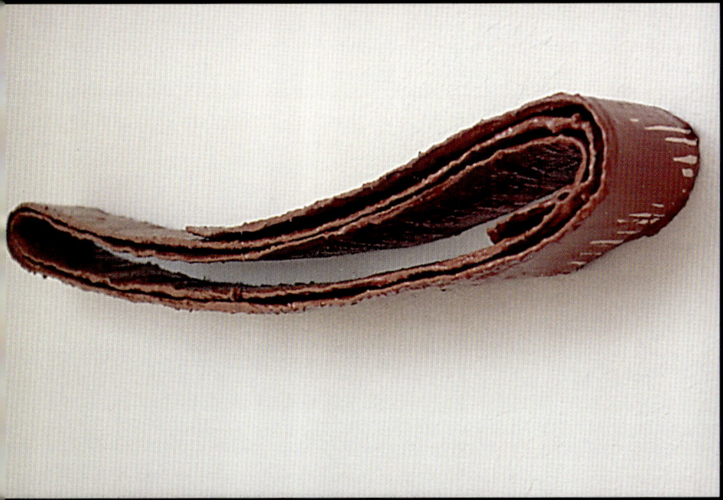

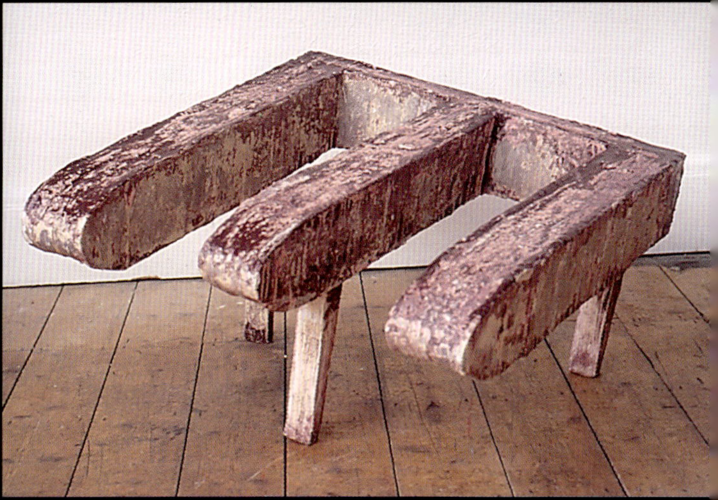

Clockwise
Untitled: canvas, latex, paint
20 x 20 x 150 cm

Untitled: wood, paint, felt, canvas, plaster, timber length
20 x 20 x 420 cm

Untitled: wood, paint, paint stripper, PVA
120 x 120 x 90 cm

Untitled: paint, wood
180 x 130 x 360 cm

Untitled
180 x 130 x 360 cm

Untitled: canvas, latex, paint
20 x 20 x 150 cm

All 2002
Richard Salmon Gallery, London

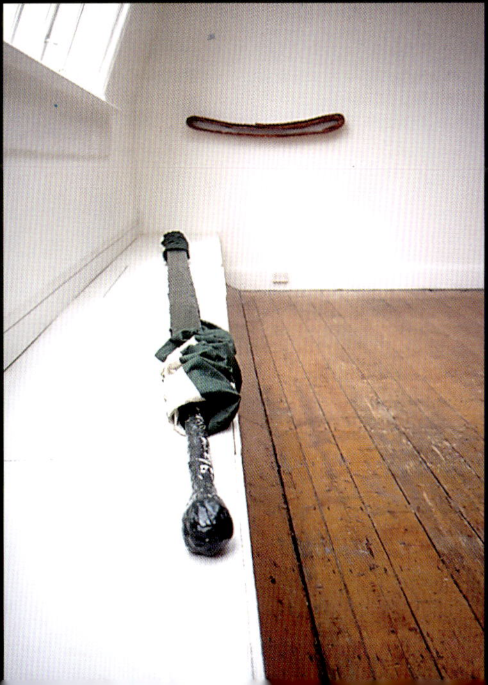

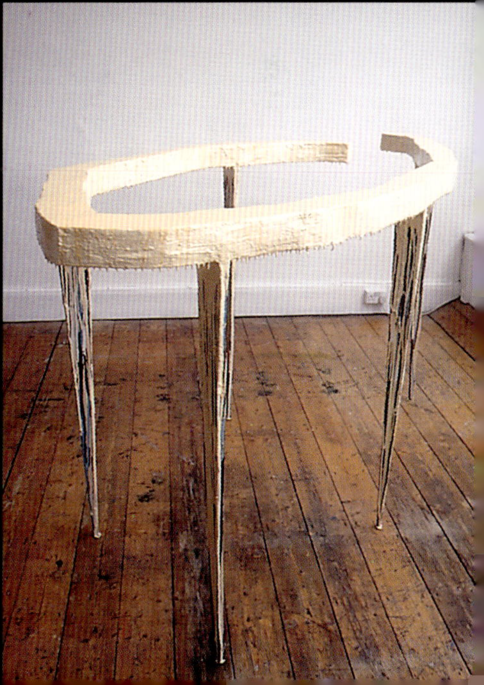

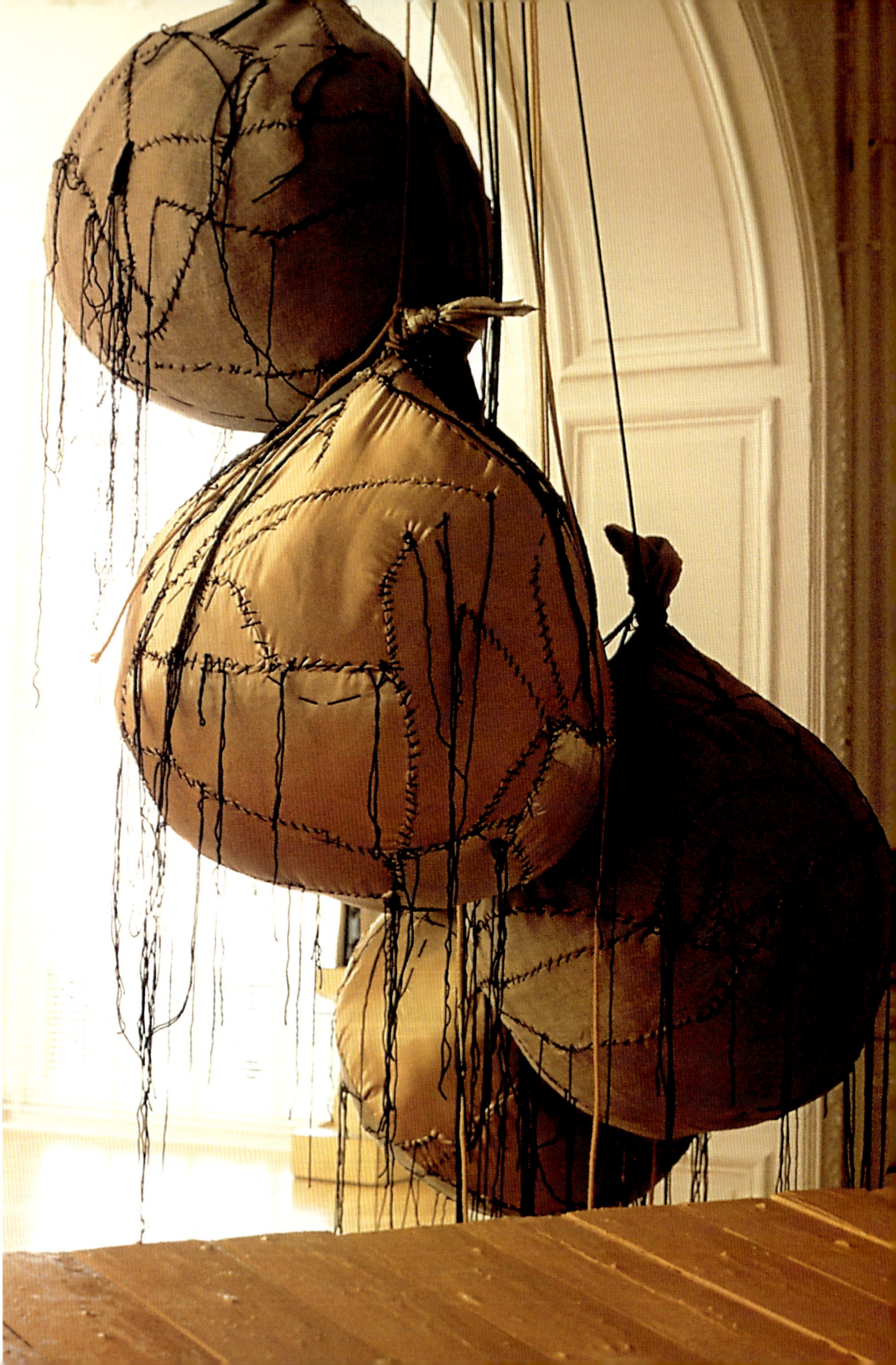

Untitled: metropole
Paint, timber boards, canvas, satin, wool, hessian, cord
180 x 150 x 300 cm
Five hanging padded spheres, each diameter 110 cm (approx)
Suspended from a height of 600 cm
2003
Metropole Gallery, Folkestone for *The Greatest Show on Earth*, curated by Peter Fillingham

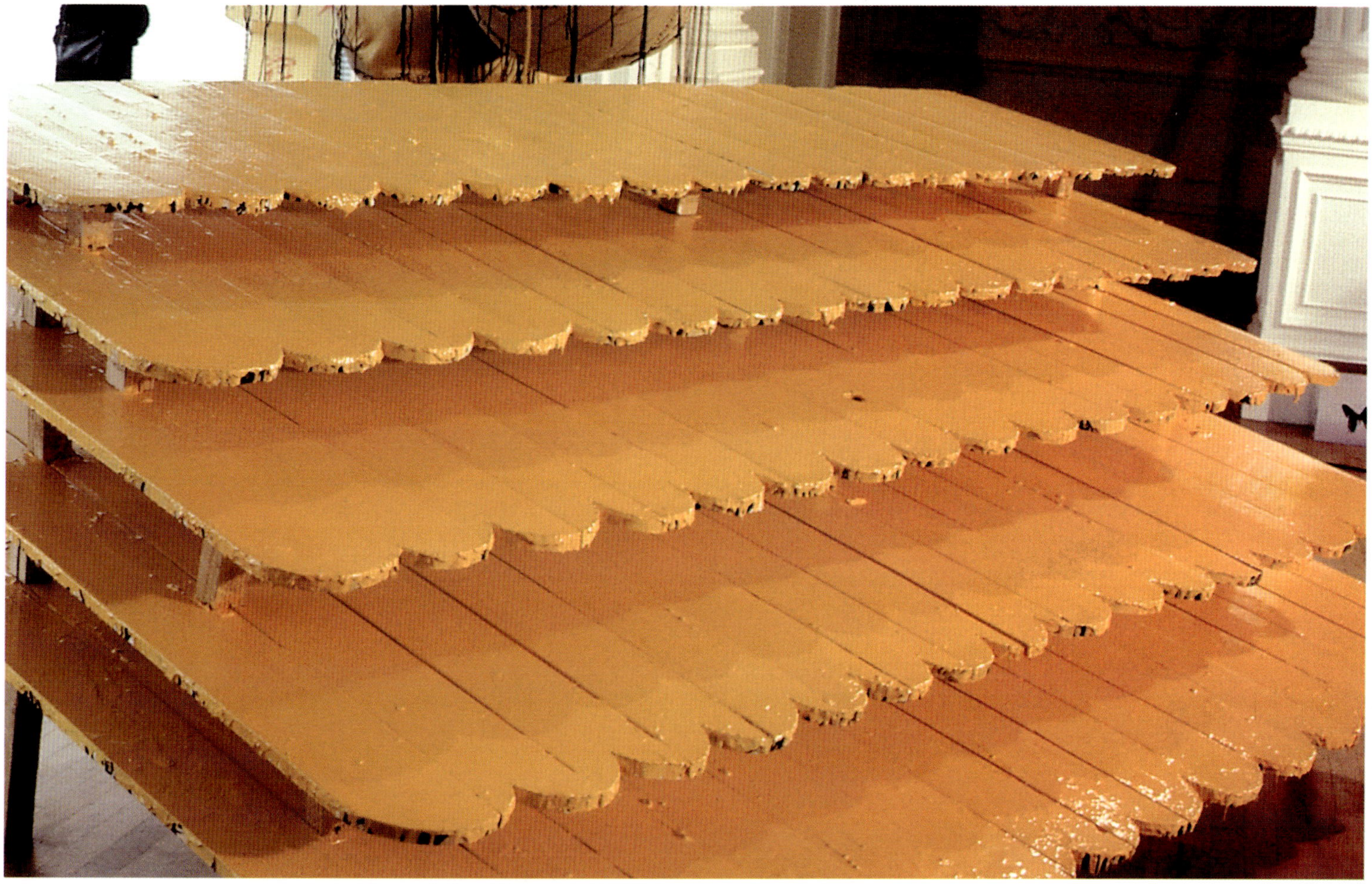

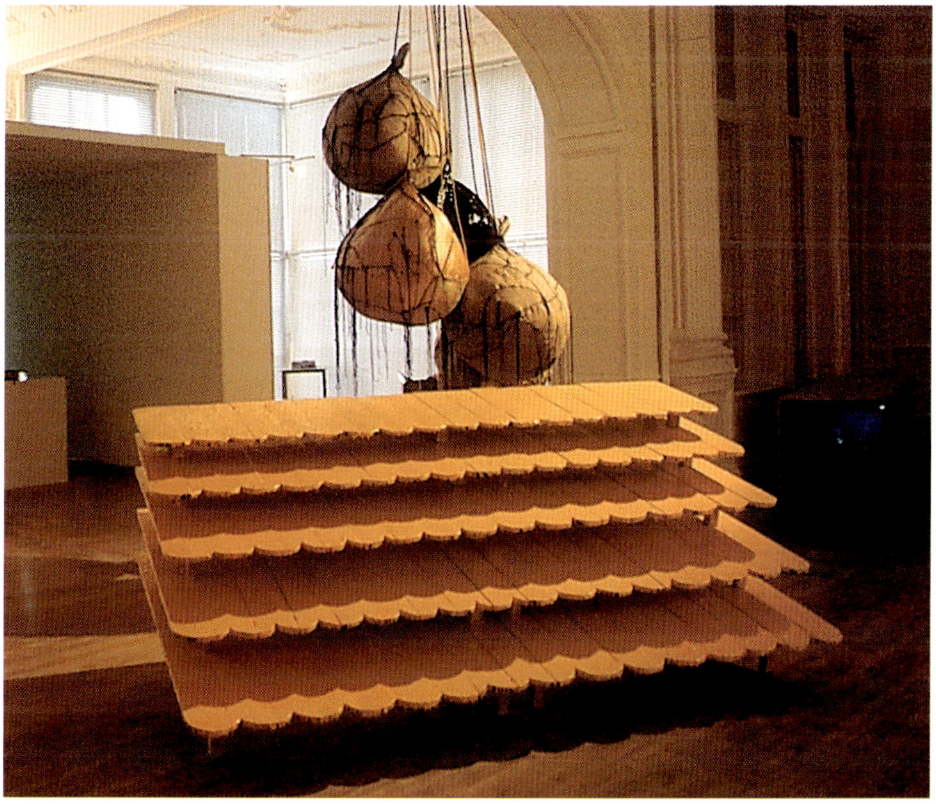

Sculpture Now

Wrecks
Studio debris, canvas, upholstery foam, wood, hardboard, chipboard, formica, paint
100 x 200 x 250 cm
180 x 200 x 190 cm
120 x 130 x 200 cm
1984
Bayfield, Norfolk

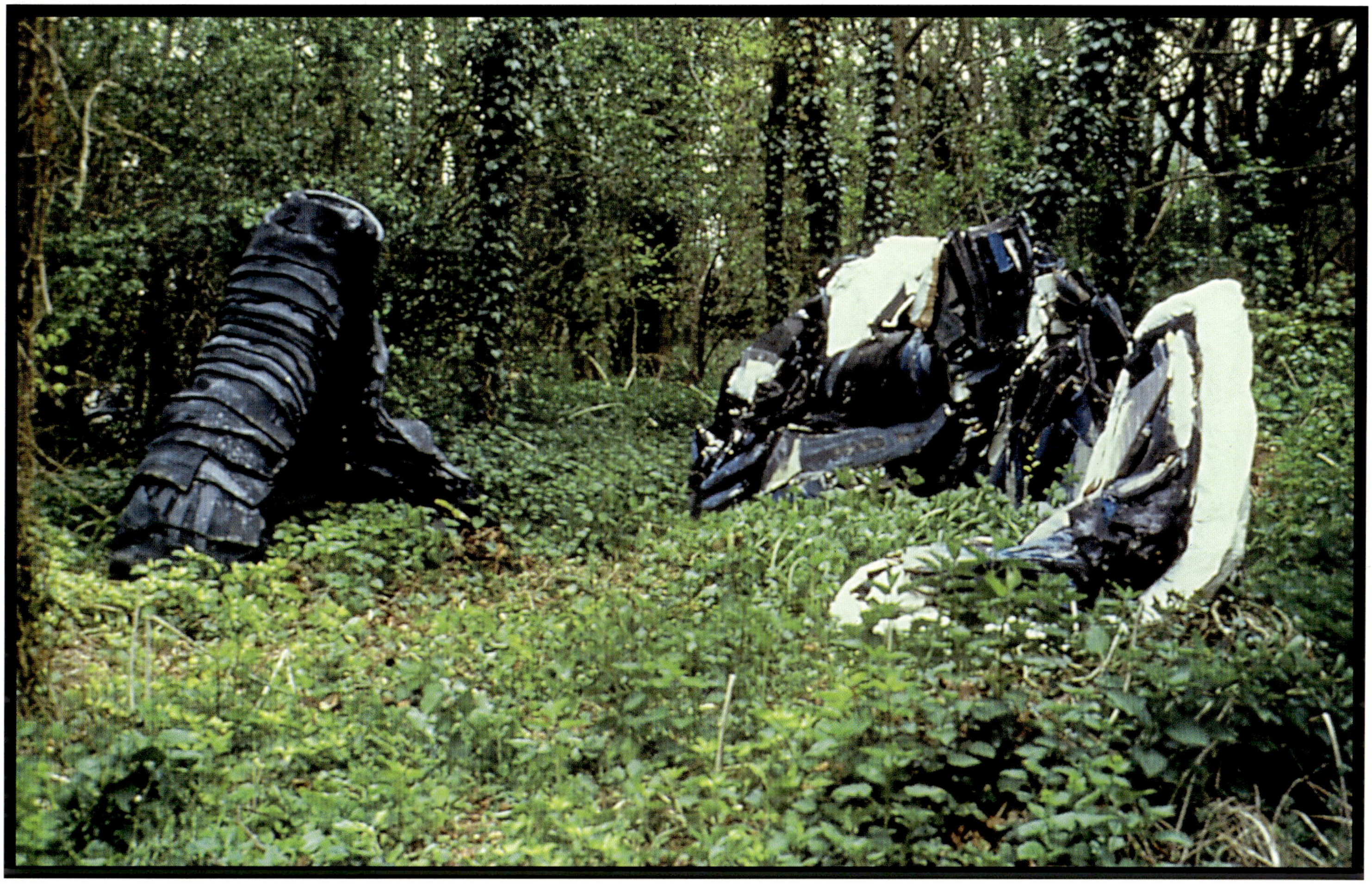

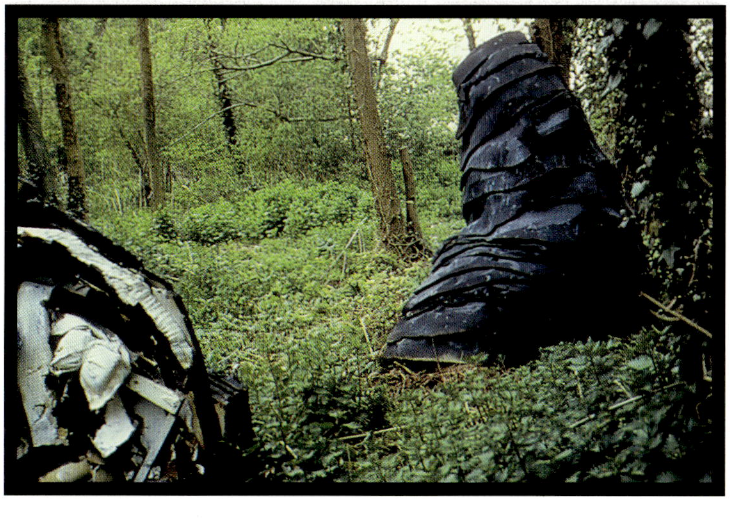

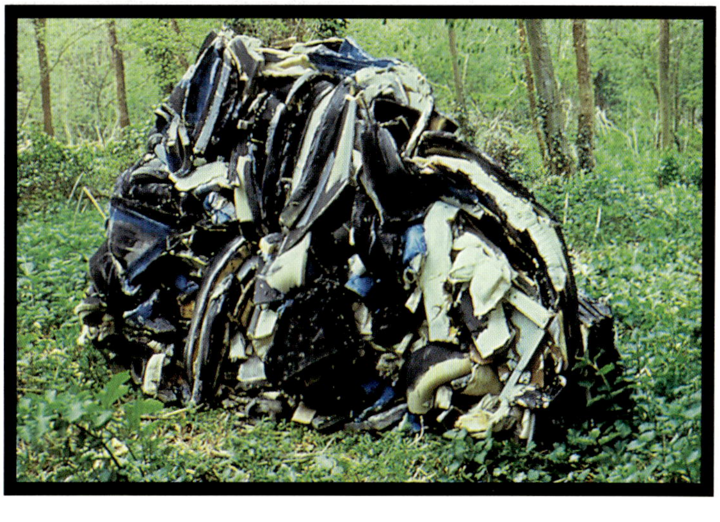

Mark Godfrey I've seen and been inside Serra's *Torqued Ellipses* at the old DIA when they were shown in Chelsea, and they were the most compelling sculptural experience I've had in terms of pure 'sensation' of space opening up and enclosing me.

Phyllida Barlow I don't know how a young artist will deal with the same kind of issues because those particular shoulders that Serra was standing on made it possible for him to work in a specific way with space, time and process. I don't know how we can do that in sculpture now.

Sotiris Kyriacou I would say you're doing that in your work a lot – the fact that you're creating works which encourage an awareness of context. Your work, or a lot of it, demands to be experienced from different viewpoints, and in the way that the viewer relates to it in time and space shares similar dynamics to Serra's.

PB But I think in trying to use those same concerns we are faced with a dilemma about how relevant those concerns are now when the use of space is much more politicised.

SK I think "restless" is a very good word to describe how your work and Serra's, demands a very active viewing engagement. I think that's political with a small "p".

Richard Deacon My experience of the Serras is also of having seen them in the original DIA space. What I did have a problem with is the idea of relevance and its relationship to experience – if I have an experience in front of something then how do I judge the relevance of that? I have bodily experiences in relationship to Serra's work and there seems to be an interchange between how I feel and the way the work reflects this.

The other question I had was when you say you wanted to make work like Serra, do you mean in the manner of or do you mean work that accesses the same experience?

PB I mean accessing the same experiences. It transcends verbal language describing the work and becomes an experience about your own bodily self with the thing that's actually there. It seems to have become very difficult to make work like that.

RD Well, it is difficult to make work like that anyway.

MG Is the reason it's difficult because it's already been done so well that a young sculptor may not be able to better what Serra has done? Or is it that that kind of work just no longer feels compelling in the same way? Recently I saw the work of a young sculptor whom I admire a lot, Simon Starling; the last show that I saw of his was at the South London Gallery and he constructed a huge waving curtain wall, which was not difficult to relate to some of Serra's works. But this curtain wall was printed with designs and the whole sculpture was actually about the genesis of this design and the narrative of how this object came about. So, in a way, he seemed to be someone who was offering a bodily experience of space but there was also a narrative or a semiotic content as to what the work was about.... On its own the curtain wall wouldn't be a compelling kind of work to make.

Laura Cull Isn't it arguable that Starling's piece is deconstructable in this way because it's to do with the process and the story behind the piece? It makes a very different object from the Serras, I think. There's a lot of current sculpture that seems to be mimicking the concerns of high modernism but, even though it visually relates to this, it is not actually engaging with the problems and experience the work proposes.

Raimi Gbadamosi I think maybe that is necessary in a world where most people consume sculpture through photographs and through reproductions they become interested in the notion of mimicking. If sculpture is flattened because of its constant reproduction then we enter into an engagement with a reproduction rather than the experience of the actual sculpture and if there is going to be an experience it is going to be incidental.

LC You have to be careful to avoid making a hierarchy between the representation of an experience and direct experience.

RG There ought to be a hierarchy between a representative experience and a natural experience; there's a difference between walking along the beach and reading about walking along the beach.

Charles Harrison I get a slight sense of a division of generations; on the one hand what we've got is a lot of talk of bodily experiences and being impressed by objects and so on, which I would associate with a kind of anxiety going back to the1960s – about how you make sculpture bigger and more important. Serra sorted that out, you make it heavier as well as bigger. Other people go round claiming things about the fantastic physical and bodily experiences they have in front of these things and that generates a kind of inflated, rather overexcited talk about the experience of sculpture. Along with that goes a kind of anxiety about how you might update that experience, which seems to me a very strange kind of question.

PB Why?

CH I'm not sure if what you're worried about is conditions of relevance in an experience. I'm not sure where you'll find your criteria, particularly for the relevance of the experience of standing in front of an object. Relevance seems to me a strange question). On the other hand we have some artists who are making work and using the umbrella of sculpture as a kind of protection for the work they make, and what they seem to be concerned to do – and I think with some justice – is to deflate that talk about experience and bodily sensation and so on, by just taking stuff away; a photograph will do or a representation of it will do or a text will do. What it will do for, is not to replace the experience but to deflate the chat about it and to slightly ironise that, which is one of the things you have to do if you want to go on making art. You've got to establish some kind of relationship with distance to the over-inflated talk of the previous generation so you do that with instruments that won't attach themselves in the same way.

MG Is it possible for the artist to progress even if they don't find the previous generation self-important?

CH I don't think it's possible for artists to progress at all.

MG As a critic, I find the Serras very compelling, but I am also interested in newer work out there. My reason for being interested in it isn't because it ironises or deflates the rhetoric that goes with the Serras.

SK The Serras are huge or big in scale but they are very modest in their demands in the sense that you can have this very strong empathy with them, but they also make you very self-aware of the context in which you and they are in and, therefore, there's this kind of modesty about them despite their scale.

CH I would have thought they depend – and this is not inconsistent with them being modest – on a certain aggression in relationship to the context that they are set up in. So they establish their autonomy partly by establishing their invasiveness.

William Potter I interpret them more as using the language of the whole space, embodying sculpture with the space; the architecture is still there but it's brought into the realm of the sculpture.

CH Can I ask what relevance means in this context? What do you mean by it, Phyllida?

PB I'm curious about what the sculptural experience is which I understand as non-visual.

CH You mean a specifically sculptural experience, as opposed to aesthetic experience or artistic experience?

PB Yes. If there is such a thing as a sculptural experience.

CH Let's just make this clear – this is an experience, a kind of experience if there is such a thing, that is provided by sculpture and nothing else.

PB When I was first a student at Chelsea, as a sculptor you learnt sculptural things, you learnt to carve etc., and there wasn't any concern that these things went anywhere else; they were in sculpture, but for me they had nothing to do with a sculptural experience. I had to wait until the early 1970s before things could be sculptural, not necessarily the physicality of the thing that was there, but the sensation of walking around something; something that might disappear, like Robert Morris' steam pieces.

WP Is it objects that actually give you that, or is that an attitude you take to a piece of work?

PB There *are* objects that give me that, but it is also becoming aware of what you could do with materials or how materials do not have to be permanent or last. And it is the space. There was a whole range of new ways of experiencing an artwork that weren't just about its visibility and standing in front of it and being able to name certain things about it. It was the actual physical sensation of being there.

CH This seems to be the problem with talking about a categoric experience which is specifically sculptural. That requires you to come up with some means of distinguishing between things which are sculpture and things which aren't. One of the things that happened in the late 1960s / early 70s was that a lot of people were wanting to try and explore certain kinds of experiences – or whatever you want to call it – they were interested in and they then extended definitions to cover them. So, you get Richard Long walking up and down and calling it sculpture, Gilbert and George doing interviews and calling them sculpture. And at the same time, Americans like Morris or whoever, were deliberately chipping away, rather didactically, at the fringes of the definitions and extending them to the point where they collapsed. What you want to talk about is a category of experience which is specific to sculpture. What you've got to do is find some way of drawing lines around an area, the fringes of which seem to infinitely expand. I'm not sure how you do that.

Naomi Salaman I have some sort of idea about this, it was to do with the initial difficulty I had addressing the questions you were posing or the way some of the arguments were set up. I came across a quote from Thierry de Duve, he says something about how 'Art' has taken over the place and the site of sculpture and painting, in lieu of craft-based disciplines. So, I thought maybe the relevance/irrelevance question can be framed instead as "sculpture isn't now", which means it's somehow underneath or buried slightly in the past, and maybe that's quite an interesting place for it to be because it's full of things that aren't now and maybe this relates to this quality of the experience that you're interested in. You might put sculpture up against photography

and say it's everything that photography isn't, it's everything that is a trace of tactility and sensuality....

PB Which I think photography can actually be....

NS Well, I'm not sure, maybe it can echo… I like the idea that the issues of sculpture that you're interested in can be located, somehow, in the remains of the discipline, the bits that haven't been taken up by contemporary art, these bits that lag behind, the bits that haven't come into words yet, the bits that still lag behind in the unusable remnants of a discipline like clay, things that haven't got words glued to them yet.

CH There are two possible conclusions, maybe three. One is that we are inescapably in the year of generic art, that in a sense, painting and sculpture degenerate to the point of being craft practices like pottery and stained glass and so on and they've had their day; Joseph Kosuth, heaven help us, is right and the problem for the artist is to simply question the definition of art and that's what art is; and what you do is produce ever more improbable objects and call them art and that's the game, one possibility. The second possibility is that the era in which we've had anxieties about the status of paintings and sculpture, since the mid 1960s I suppose, is a phase of transition into an impending period where we will have to come to terms with the various new media and forms of communication available to us, where artwork will sort itself out into appropriate kinds of media, or appropriate to the age in which we happen to be living. A third possibility is that things like carving and modeling will recover their status.

NS I think there are pedagogical issues, in terms of the discussion of how a work emerges, how it's discussed and validated, it's about what happens in studio seminars; it seems to me that the relationship of art education to the institution of art is another way into considering this problem of the sculptural experience.

PB Another way is to examine the kind of verbal language that is tolerated. Through a vocabulary that is immediately attached to something which can be academicised. We can go to the library, we can find numerous texts on the abject whereas to talk about somebody's passion for their work, without irony, seems really difficult or well nigh impossible....

NS But don't you also want a place that isn't already mapped out in terms of an academic or critical orthodoxy?

PB Yes.

NS That's a difficult place for us to describe....

PB Yes, I don't know what it is, that space or place, outside of making my work.

NS Well, like you said in one of your texts it's between failure and success, unmapped.

MG Phyllida, in one of your texts you differentiate between sculpture and the three-dimensional when you make a distinction between your practice and what you call the 'made easy', which I take to mean works by people like Damien Hirst or Marc Quinn or Jeff Koons....

PB Definitely not Jeff Koons.

MG … object-makers who place their work in vitrines, for whom the work is an image. And if that was prevalent in the 1980s and 90s, then I do see now a lot of artists who are making work where there is a return to a three dimensional encounter, but this is an encounter which has complexity, which isn't just about things in space, matter and material. Thomas Hirschorn would be an example, Rachel Harrison, the young American, is another example; but I was wondering how you situate those practices and whether they are compelling to you, because you started this discussion with an anxiety about what's happened to a practice like Serra's… but I see that there's a kind of continuum here.

PB I think those artists do take on that language and I think it's embellished, it's got great added narrative themes in it which gives it a kind of currency that's viable, critically viable. I'm curious to go back to what Naomi says about what happens when you strip away critical terms, narratives which seem to me to be like props to the work – and they're interesting props.

MG But saying you can strip them down is like saying you can have a Serra without the steel.

PB Actually that's an important point. I think one of the things that determines a work by Serra is the vast resources, financially, that enable a work to be made – and therefore what do people do when they don't have those financial resources. I think that this is a very relevant question to ask, because if that's where you're beginning to come to terms with that kind of language but what you're faced with is vastness and weight and money, it could completely alter the way in which you make or experience those kind of works.

SK But you're not expecting people to make clones of Serra and use the same materials and scale; you're expecting people who sympathise with Serra's concerns to actually make work in a different way.

MG Did you see the last Matthew Barney film which featured Serra remaking one of his thrown lead pieces? Barney's work is image-based – even his three dimensional work is image-based – I can't imagine wanting to spend that much time walking around it….

WP This is a different issue. I think to make an image three dimensional gives it a different currency, it makes it more expensive, it makes it heavier and can add a sense of importance to it.

RD I thought the Barney film was interesting and I thought that Richard Serra did quite a good job of deconstructing, but not destroying a piece of work I like a lot. Playing with a machismo image and allowing himself to be used as he did, rendered aspects of his mythology ironic, and he is obviously aware of this.

Anish Kapoor was on the radio on Sunday and he said something interesting – he said that artists don't make work they make mythology, and it is mythology that enables you to attach experience to the work. Phyllida seems to be starting from a slightly different position where she's wanting an experience to be imminent in the space independent from the object, from the thing itself, rather than something which is brought to it.

LC I must ask whether you felt that there was something to be mourned – about that generic art? I don't think there is.

CH I think that would depend on what you think the implications of it are and also on whether you think that is the condition we are currently in. I think Arthur Dante said that "art can be anything but not everything can be art" and that's the problem – whether we still potentially have distinct genres and the possibility to develop in distinct media, and so on,which may not necessarily look quite like those we are used to.

LC I suppose I am questioning whether it's a kind of linguistic engagement or whether it's an engagement about whatever sculptural values are, as a concept or as a label....

AH It's certainly an issue which goes directly to problems of definition and categorisation. How much do you want to protect, let's say, the concept of sculpture as it extends into areas that don't necessarily have the kind of craft and studio base which Britain has always been associated with? You can call them something else, for example, you could call the work of Richard Long for instance something other than sculpture. Does it matter if it gets called sculpture? And does it matter because one of the things we're trying to hold on to is a sense of history and tradition?

NS I think it's important to distinguish between mourning, that you, Laura, were talking about, because of the moving on, the modernisation....

LC ... and some kind of nostalgia.

NS Yes, exactly between mourning with nostalgia for some lost past, or what it seems to me that Phyllida keeps investigating or being a kind of voice for, which is about the bits that haven't been modernised, the bits that aren't included in the articulate form of what contemporary art is; they are bits which get left in an obsolete place. And that kind of obsolescence, is marginal, it is not interesting *per se* but it is a place where things can happen.

PB It seems to be where the language has got stuck, words like passion, they seem to be stuck in that obsolescence and that's what I find very difficult because it's as though there's a fear in giving those words a contemporary association or a contemporary place or relevance – it does come back to relevance.

NS It's not mourning, it's not nostalgia but there is this kind of campaign against something to do with the present

PB No I would really hate that, because I think the present is the only thing you've sort of got, in a way, so it therefore seems incredibly vital to be able to claim these things for now but not to claim them through nostalgia or mourning.

NS Maybe its a campaign against success, or some of the effects of success.

RG Going back to what you were saying earlier, Naomi, the idea about sculpture moving on to becoming something else. I feel that there is an emotional response to something which is sculptural. Language can only describe that experience when language and the art object become one and the same; then one can argue that the art object is wholly unnecessary because the word will do.

SK There seems to be a paranoia about defining different disciplines rather than what I keep calling the dynamics of the work, maybe we should be looking at different qualities or different things that we expect from an art work rather than trying to almost prescribe a discipline. The qualities that you find in Phyllida's work you can find in a lot of painting for example. I think that the viewer/work dynamic is paramount... how the work relates to the viewer and the viewer to the work, these things go beyond specific disciplines.

RD Phyllida has a sort of history of guerilla activity as a sculptor. Large work installed in unsanctioned spaces....

WP But you talk of that as a threatened activity, do you?

RD About three years ago, walking down Gower Street, builders were cleaning out a house and in order to do that with minimum disruption to the pavement, they constructed this extraordinary pyramid that filled the doorway completely, spilling down on to the street very neatly. This kind of blockage in the doorway – it could have been a work of Phyllida's – it was one of those occasions where you weren't quite sure, it was borderline, it had characteristic obsessiveness, and neatness that enabled one to invest it with all kinds of meaning. I'd been given freedom and also I'd been given references: x stacks up and y spreads out.

I was interested in Phyllida describing a despair about the difficulties of making things other than packages and the only reference she has is science fiction films for a kind of form-making, I found that interesting, it isn't about the contemporary, it's to do with ideas of the future.

PB Can I refer back to the Anish Kapoor interview – he said something which I thought was very surprising; he says that he makes his work entirely for himself and I thought this complicated his ideas on myth; I thought such an idea would always be retrospective and it's this retrospective luggage that I find complicated. Artists often argue for experimentation, and that suggests they are dealing with things that they don't know. That has set up a confused ideology which is rooted in a particular kind of art historical baggage. Becoming aware that you are emotionally and intellectually naked in a space that is actually very uncharted, is a very positive challenge. Rachel Harrison, for instance, I think her work is like a compendium of art historical references. Even with Simon Starling's work, which I like, I think there is a strong narrative or explication there that you can unpick with a fine toothcomb and every aspect of that narrative pulls rock solid, there are no cracks. I think this is to do with the kind of training artists get, that gives them these layers of vocabularies or layers of languages which they can then bind together in ever-increasingly intricate and intriguingly protective ways.

MG I can see why you could make a criticism of those people like Rachel Harrison for being sort of synthesisers of an approach to sculpture that might have existed in the 1970s and the 1980s, but with your own work you could also think about its roots in Arte Povera and also, maybe Hepworth. To what extent every work is always a compendium?

PB Totally....

Duncan McCorquodale In some ways, people looking at your work see it as being conservative, a throw back, whereas I see it more in the way that Richard Deacon is referring to it, as being something of a guerilla tactic, which is contemporary.

CH Why is something employing guerilla tactics in that sense assured of contemporaneity ?

DM I don't think it's necessarily assured of being contemporary, but if you're talking about a kind of purity of looking in relation to Richard Serra and that having to do with the 1970s, Phyllida's work doesn't sit very comfortably with that.

AH It's made of the wrong stuff, which is the significant difference.

DM The wrong stuff?

AH Yes, if Serra is your point of reference, for instance.

DM Yes, there is an aspect of the ephemeral about the work, it's made and then ends up being thrown away after being exhibited, but it's the way that Phyllida's work relates to a history of sculpture that makes it contemporary.

CH I'm still confused about where we're getting our context of contemporaneity and relevance from, I mean the terms are being bandied around a lot and I'm not at all sure about what anyone means by them.

MG I had a conversation with Phyllida the other day when I went to see her show in Surrey, and we were talking afterwards about art historians who have a very teleological conception that mediums progress or that art progresses and that developments happen and expand on what the previous generations have done etc.. According to such narratives, I see that certain people make sense now as contemporary and breaking new ground – I have named some people already like Starling, Hirschorn and Orozco. But then, I was confused, because I have some sympathy for those kinds of accounts, it is a sort of slap in the face when I go to Phyllida's show, it feels like contemporary work but it doesn't fit into any of those narratives of sculptural history that I am comfortable with.

LC It's maybe something to do with what you're up against…it's about being a bit slippery and being slippery in relation to the gallery system and about what's expected of you as an artist at the moment….

CH What often counts are the things that you're up against, and one of those things could be the gallery system, another thing could be the current state of the discipline if you know what the discipline is, and another thing could be the current consideration of criticism, or it could be the war in Iraq or it might be the new concepts of what the human body is or neuro-science.

LC Sure, but what I'm interested in with Phyllida's work is the particular enemies that she's battling against, the struggle that is going on there… that's how I understood the talk about guerilla tactics

PB Exactly, that's what I mean by relevance – it is what do you do as an artist, how you do things.

CH How you conduct yourself…?

PB How you make your work – does someone make it for you? Who does one make the work for?

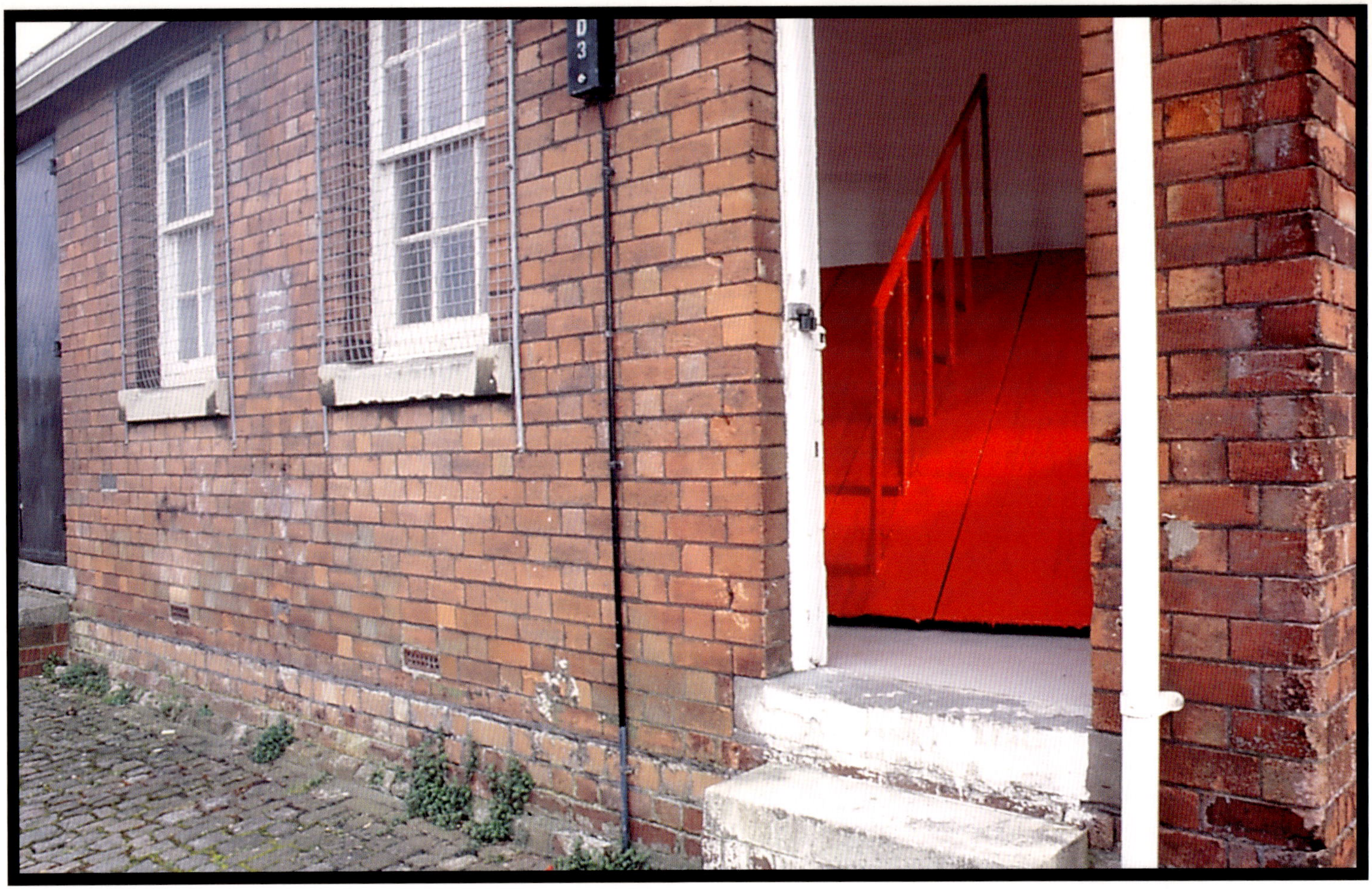

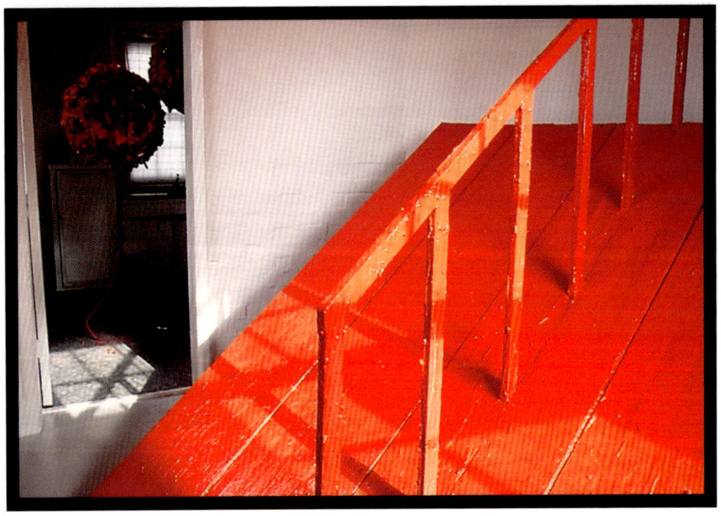

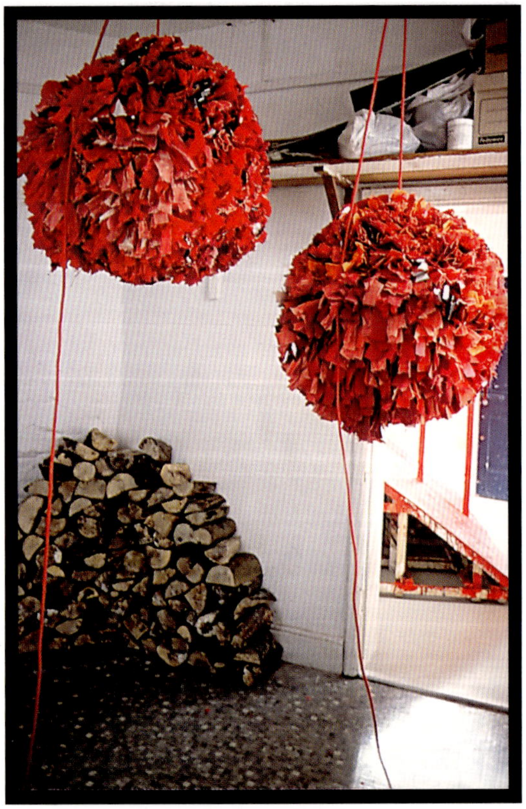

Fete
Timber boards, paint, paper, felt, fabric, foil, newspaper, cord
300 x 300 x 300 cm
120 cm diameter, suspended from a height of 400 cm
2002
Station, Phoenix Wharf, Bristol

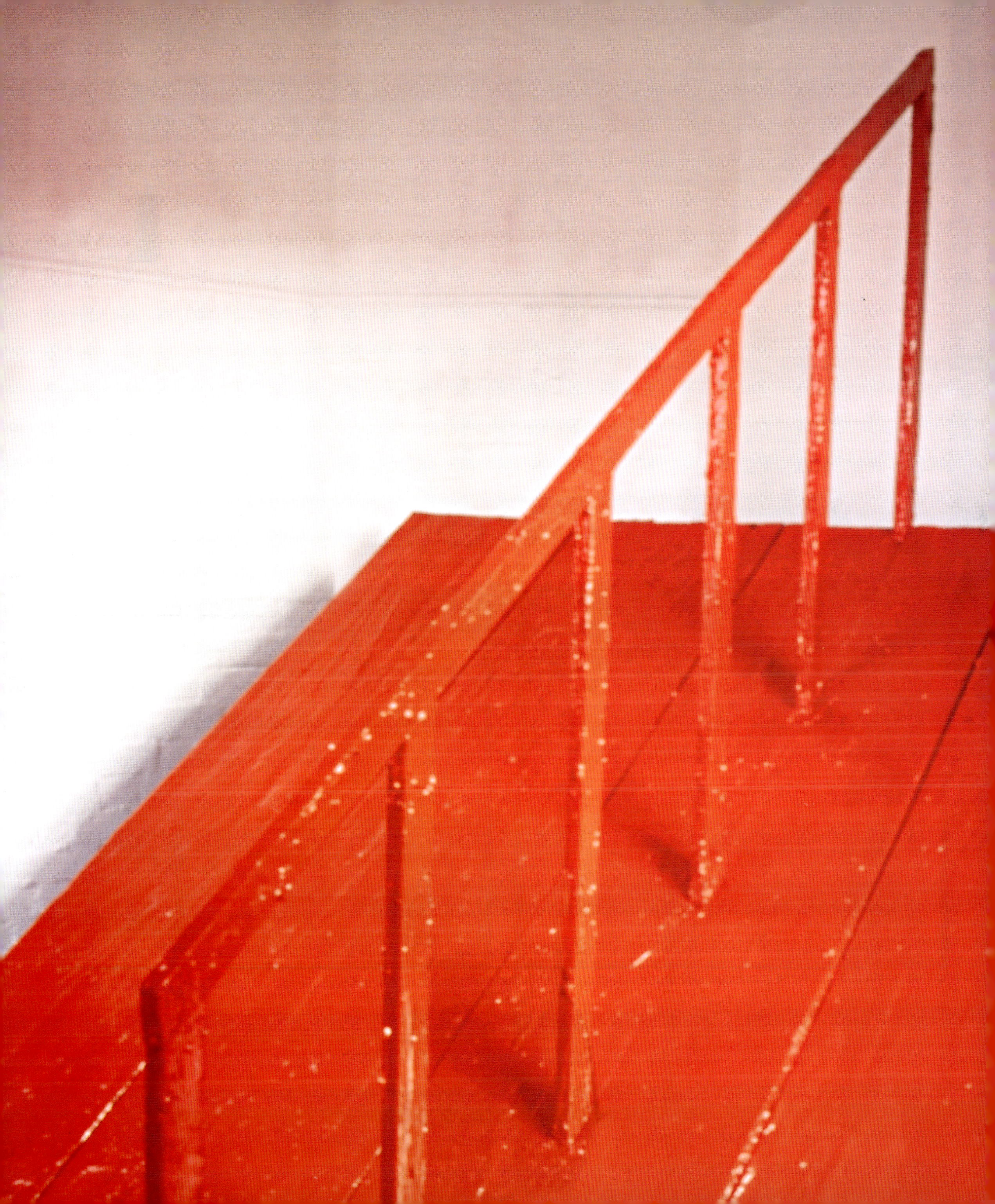

RD When I see something of yours that you've made it allows me to refer to these as being documents about possible experience rather than being photographs in themselves. But there is something slightly paradoxical in the fact that the works are transient and deliberately so, ephemeral products. Is there not a slight contradiction – or it may relate to your notion about negativity, to dematerialisation – between your quest for a kind of immanence in a sculptural experience. These photographs that will appear in the book, are not 'it', but all there is. So through photographs and occasional encounters, we build up a notion of what 'it' might be. There is a kind of withdrawal and – I was going to say lack of conviction, but I actually don't think that – an unwillingness to render permanent, or a feeling that perhaps it is impossible to render permanent.

PB A feeling that it is impossible is where I place it….

LC That's kind of saying that there is no 'it', there's not a final 'it'.

RD Well, no. I think that Phyllida seems to be saying that there is an 'it', but you can't see it.

LC Even when you encounter the object, that's not it?

RD Well, the object refers to 'it'; the photographs refer to 'it'.

NS Like you were saying, Richard, before, that artists create myth rather than produce work, I was just thinking, maybe, this book is an archive of documents that partially represents what has been done. Maybe the images stand for the myth that is produced; a series, evidence of events you missed, another something missing?

RD I think Phyllida, you are constructing an existentialist anxiety that actually isn't present in the experience of the work. It can be a false consciousness of what you suspect your work to be about.

PB No, I don't think it's a false consciousness, I think it can be a flawed dilemma because you are full of this longing to make and this longing to locate that is the driving force behind my work – the longing to actually engage physically with stuff and see what does happen, but it's also very important that there is a place for that, a location for it. And that's not always possible…. I might be the only one to see it. Students seem to be genuinely anxious about how they make work and the fact that most of the work that gets made now isn't seen – but I wonder, is that really such a worst case scenario or is that just a fact of creative life?

DM I'm not sure that it even matters as to whether there is more unseen art or not. I think the point holds that a lot of art isn't seen. You, Phyllida have a pedagogic interest, you are concerned about how your students are going to enter the system.

PB But I think that having absolute integrity and total honesty in relation to making work is a kind of impossibility, and maybe that's what I'm referring to, this flawed dilemma….

MG Because your work is ephemeral, it's destroyed after it's shown and doesn't exist other than in the image, etc. – well, a whole set of questions come in here, but I don't know if principles come with this and I don't know whether those principles pre-existed the moment before the work was made or whether they were just invented after the fact. If circumstances were different, if the work was sold, or preserved, would the ideas be different?

AH Or to put it another way would the work remain ephemeral if MOMA offered you a million dollars?

MG That's what I mean, the Tate might say they would like a work for their collection. At that point some of the ideas that go into the work alter, so what I'm saying is do the ideas come in at the end to sort of justify…

PB No, I think the driving force behind the work is actually to do it and being able to have a place to do it, whether that's of my own initiative or not. It's not been about existing in perpetuity. I haven't given a lot of thought about whether the Tate buys it or not, because this has not been on the table.

DM So how do you feel about your work in this context, Richard? Obviously, your's is a different sort of engagement when it comes to selling work.

RD I can be anecdotal about it. Much of the work I made at the end of 1960s, the beginning of 70s, was deliberately ephemeral and performance-based, but at the same time I also found myself fiddling around, which is a kind of habit, and making things that I thought were kind of interesting and that I wanted to present and be able to put in different places. And, in part, it may be that when you invest six months in making something, you end up with something that is fairly robust. Storage and sales are issues, being able to sell things on is, in my opinion, entirely helpful. It means there is more money to live on, and if you make things that are permanent, having someone come along who pays money for them is nice and reassuring. But whether the market place constructs a context, that gets on to a more difficult terrain and I think younger artists than myself are in a much more tricky situation because the market is hotter. When I was a student throughout most of the 70s, the market was pretty low key, so issues about selling didn't come into place until after I'd established how I wanted to make work, so it doesn't particularly disrupt the way I think about making work. But going back, Phyllida, do you think it would be possible to reconstruct some of your work on the basis of photographs?

PB I think my work has been as close to performance as it possibly can be and therefore I haven't known how I, or someone else, would deal with the reenacting of the performance, the re-making of a work. I think it is something that I would specify with the help of the images, but they wouldn't necessarily end up looking like those records, those documentations.

SK I don't think the perishability or ephemeral nature of your work is integral to it, or the only reason why it works.

PB No I think it's more about the action of doing, which brings about the issue of touch and even of deposit, the deposit of the artist on the work which is what I see my use of paint as being… I think the autonomy of the object has something to do with the fact that it's a kind of negative; it's to do with something I would describe as the non-pictorial. I can't date it exactly, but the intention of a lot of the work up until probably 1995 was as a performative event. And then, I think, I saw them as less performative and more sculptural, by which I mean they had an autonomy in their objecthood, they were there as mass, weight, actions and were to be experienced in the here and now.

LC I keep thinking about a phrase you said... "is there some sort of canceling out?"

PB Painting my work is like closing it down, sealing it and in a way rooting it to the spot.

DM In the same way as a patina does with other materials?

PB Yes, I suppose, it could be like a bronze or even the surface of a Richard Serra.

LC Yet it is a gesture still.

PB Yes, it's a gesture.... The surface of the sculpture has a very odd relationship with it – it almost removes the actual objectiveness of the object, it actually makes it, the surface, be something in its own right. It gives it a painterly identity. It's like that pillar there which is painted pale green, but that seems to be in competition with what one imagines its physicality might be. I don't believe that is just a shell, a pale green shell. I believe there is something beneath that painted greenness, there is a sort of duality working so I'm not sure which one wins, which one we'll see first or experience first, whether we experience the column as a weighty heavy supporting object first, or whether we experience it as a painted surface first – the two things seem to be switching. Those qualities about where sculpture starts to dissolve seem to me to be a really exciting place.

SK But your work has a kind of conceptual impermanence, in that the work can almost be experienced fresh every time you see it because it has this kind of constant refusal to be defined or described in any sort of way and what maintains your interest in it as a viewer is this constant toing and froing between the more sensual or narrative potentials or suggestive potentials of the work and its materiality and viewability from different points, its refusal to be reduced to any one particular aspect. So this notion of a physical impermanence is not integral to the success of the work, nor to understanding the work. So if you were to make a piece for the Tate, it would not be an unsuccessful piece by definition....

PB It wouldn't be unsuccessful because it has to last.... This impermanence thing seems to be an irritant, it is like using a very traditional trajectory, or being at the end of that trajectory and denying it at the last minute, which seems to make people feel there is something inherently dishonest in the whole activity. I'm curious about the morality at play here, having a book of photographs of work that doesn't exist.

CH Do you think there is a relationship between your interest in the notion of impermanence on one hand, and the fact that your work has run alongside a teaching practice on the other? If you are earning your money from teaching, you are not going to starve if you do not sell the work.

PB But there are still problems like storage. If you want to test out or experiment ideas or an action which is ongoing or repetitive which is to do with things like ramming and stuffing and crushing, and it is not just about the one-off thing you hold in your hand, it is going to get big, and there is the problem of how you are going to store that. Whether I'm teaching or not, storing massive amounts of materials has been totally unviable.

NS It is also a model of practice in a way. Maybe the finished work is not the result you are after....

PB There is an enormous doubt on my part about the validity or credibility of permanence.

NS That's a very gendered and provocative position to take up. I'm not saying that criticising permanence has not been done before, I'm saying that Phyllida's work sort of maintains a relationship to tradition but undermines some basic premises, whilst valuing bits of it. It's a practice in pieces, rather than a solid, monolithic thing.

PB Yes, I do see it as a practice in pieces, as if I am wanting to have a bit of everything.

NS We were talking earlier about a deflation, deflating the previous generation, and that is very much in terms of an Oedipal notion, you would replace the elders with your newer version of what is newness and contemporary it-ness; instead, what you promote is this constant falling back into pieces, constructing and then collapsing, something else is happening. It is something other than Oedipal, it is the...

PB … the Electra complex!

NS The Electra complex, you have to destroy the mother, break her into pieces in order to produce another kind of space, emotionally and physically....

Extracts of the round-table discussion on contemporary sculpture, Slade School of Art, London, 10 July 2003.

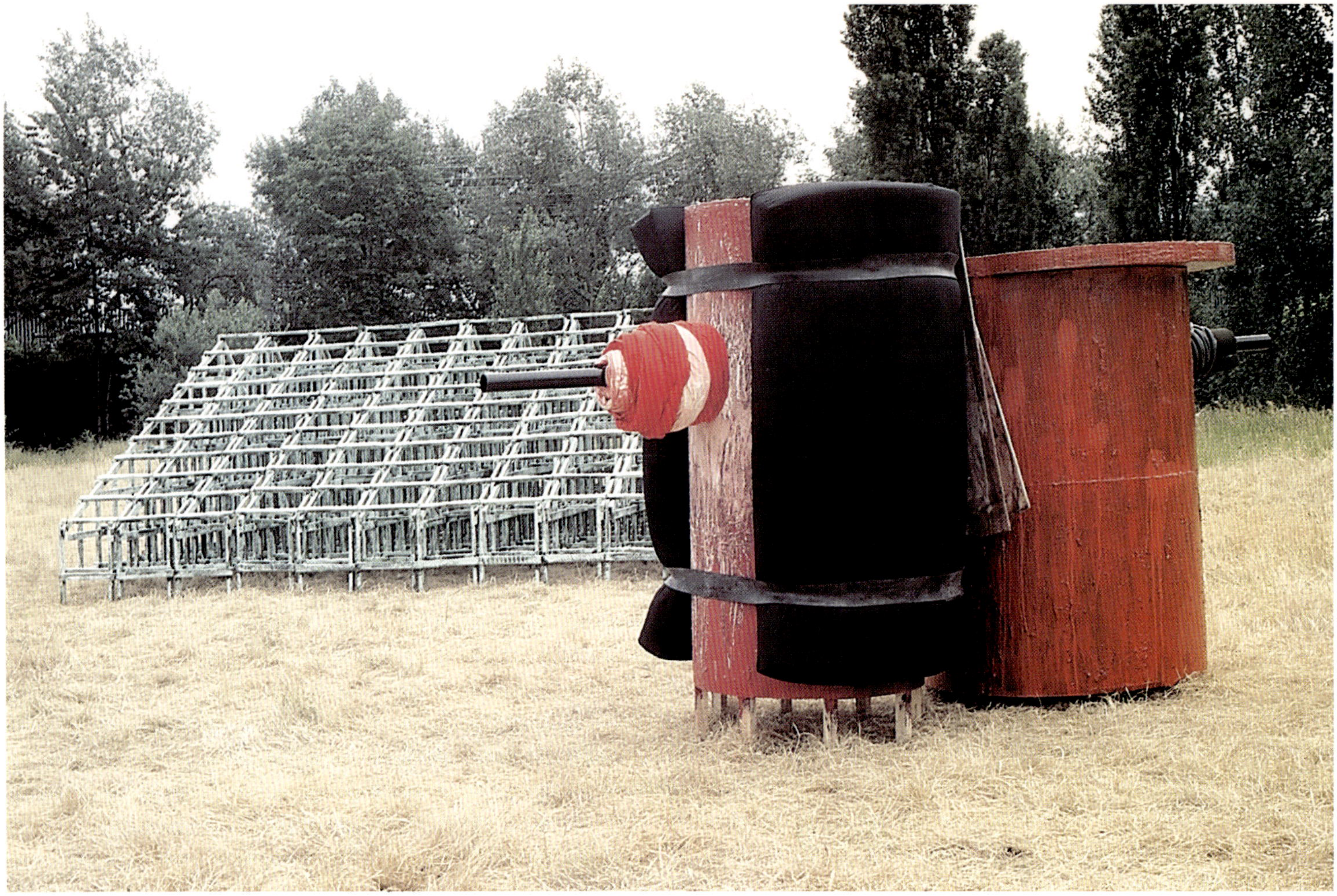

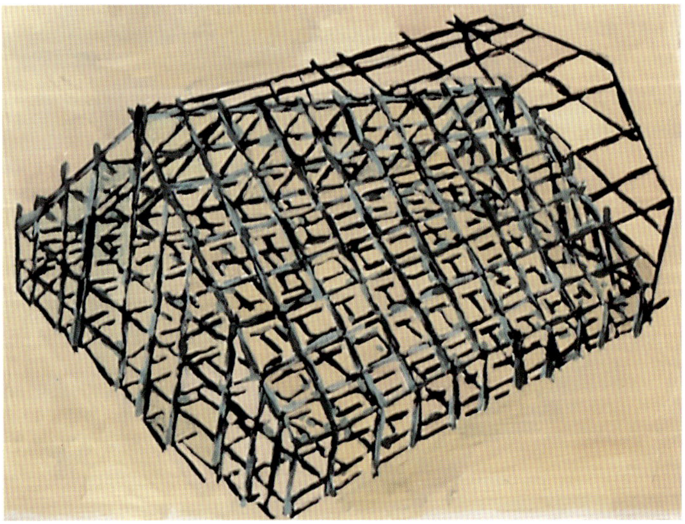

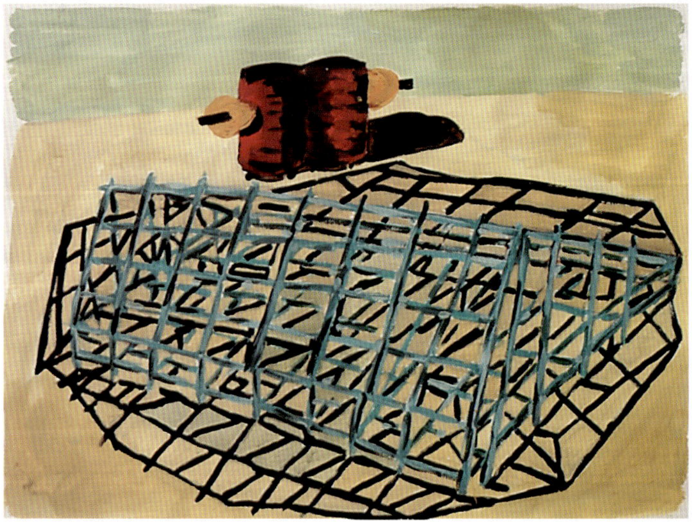

View
Paint, timber, hardboard, plastic tube, mattress, fabrics, elastic
Overall dimensions:
600 x 210 x 600 cm

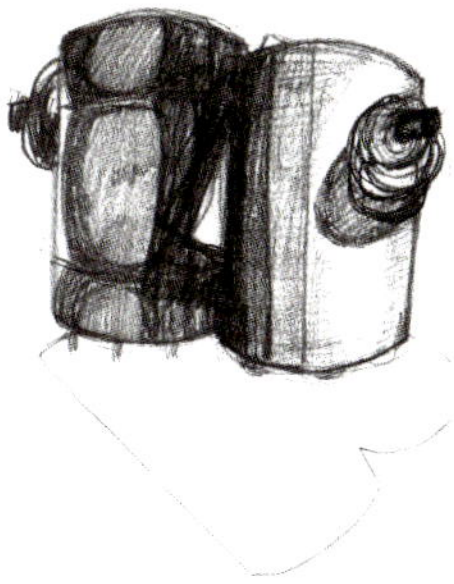

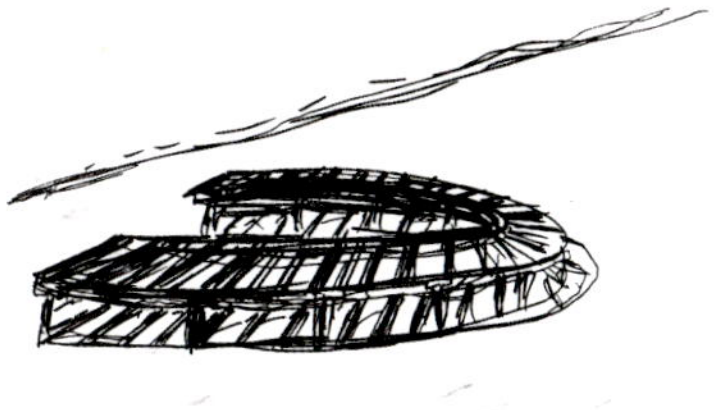

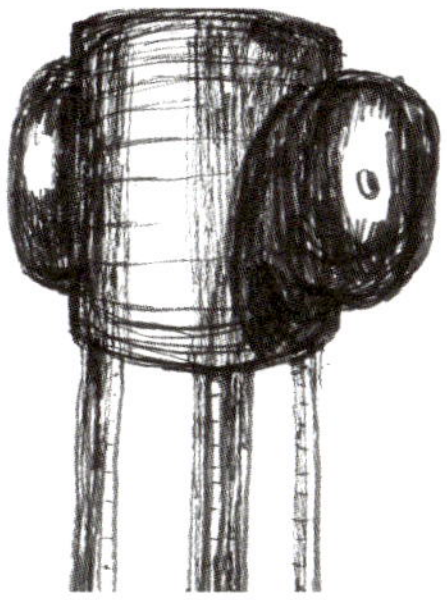

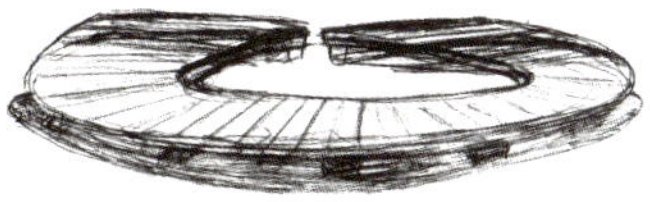

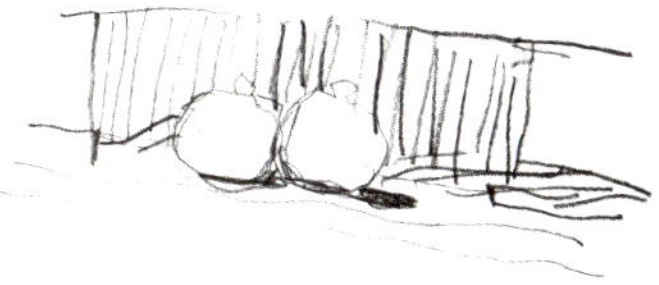

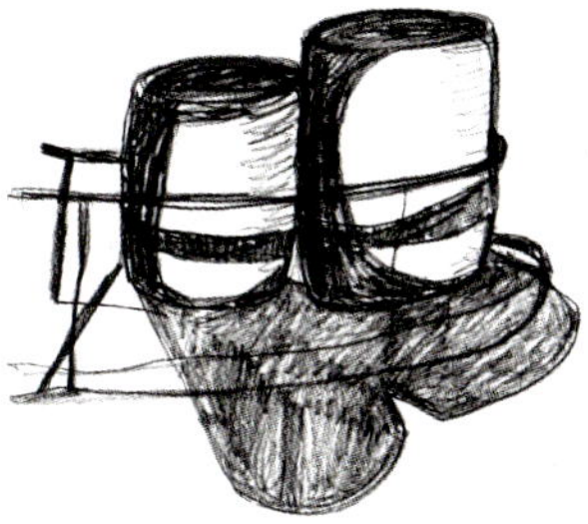

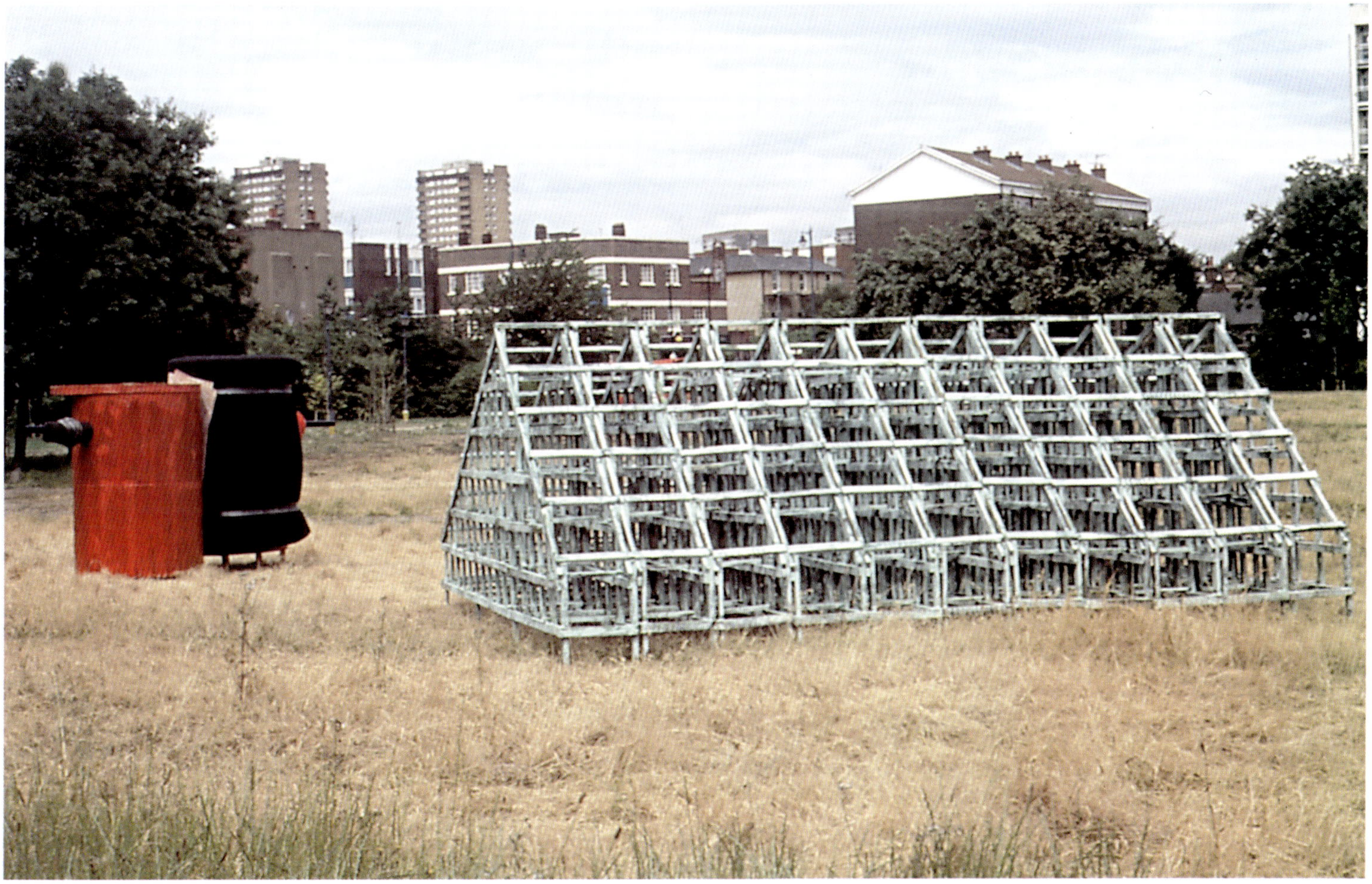

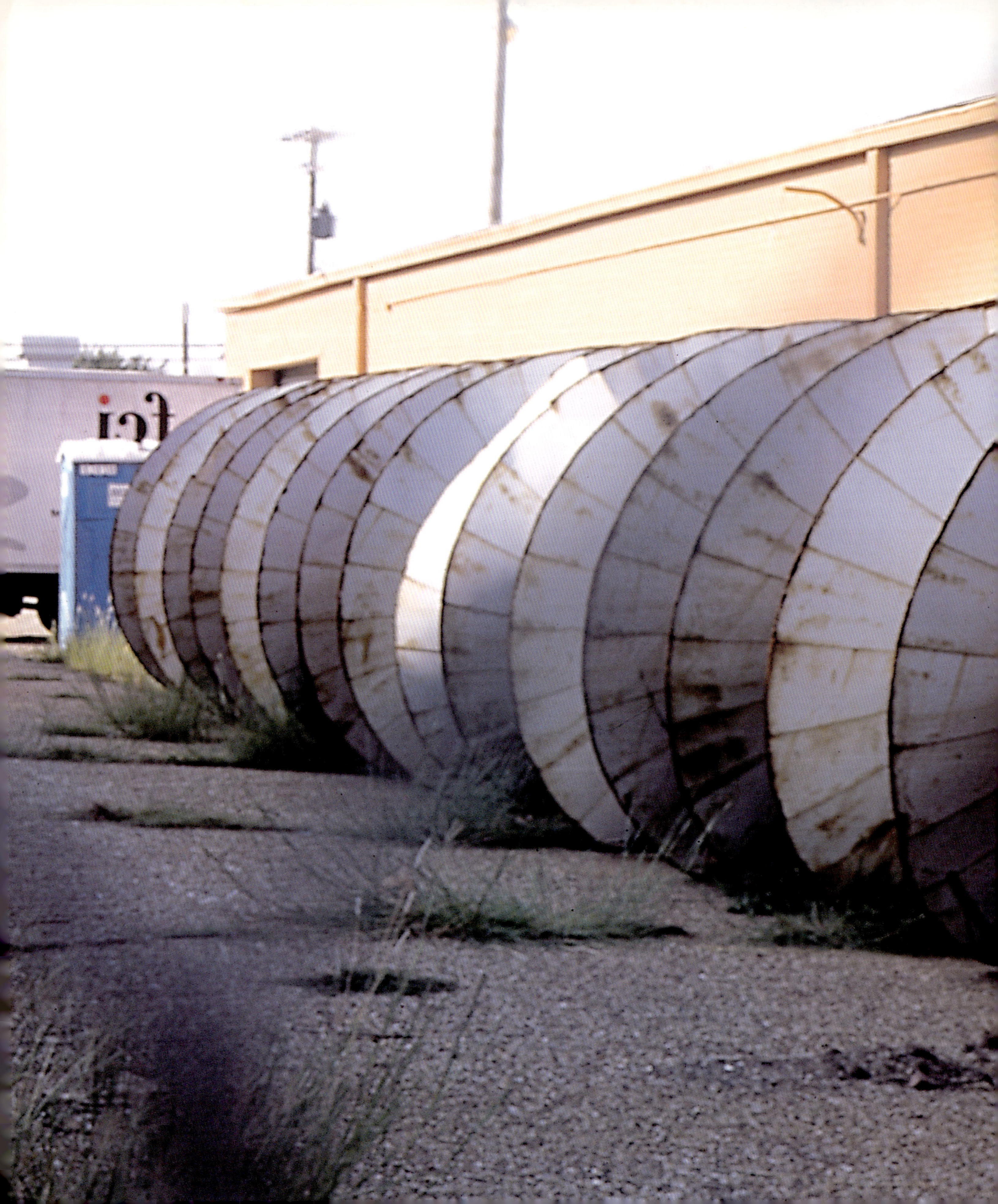

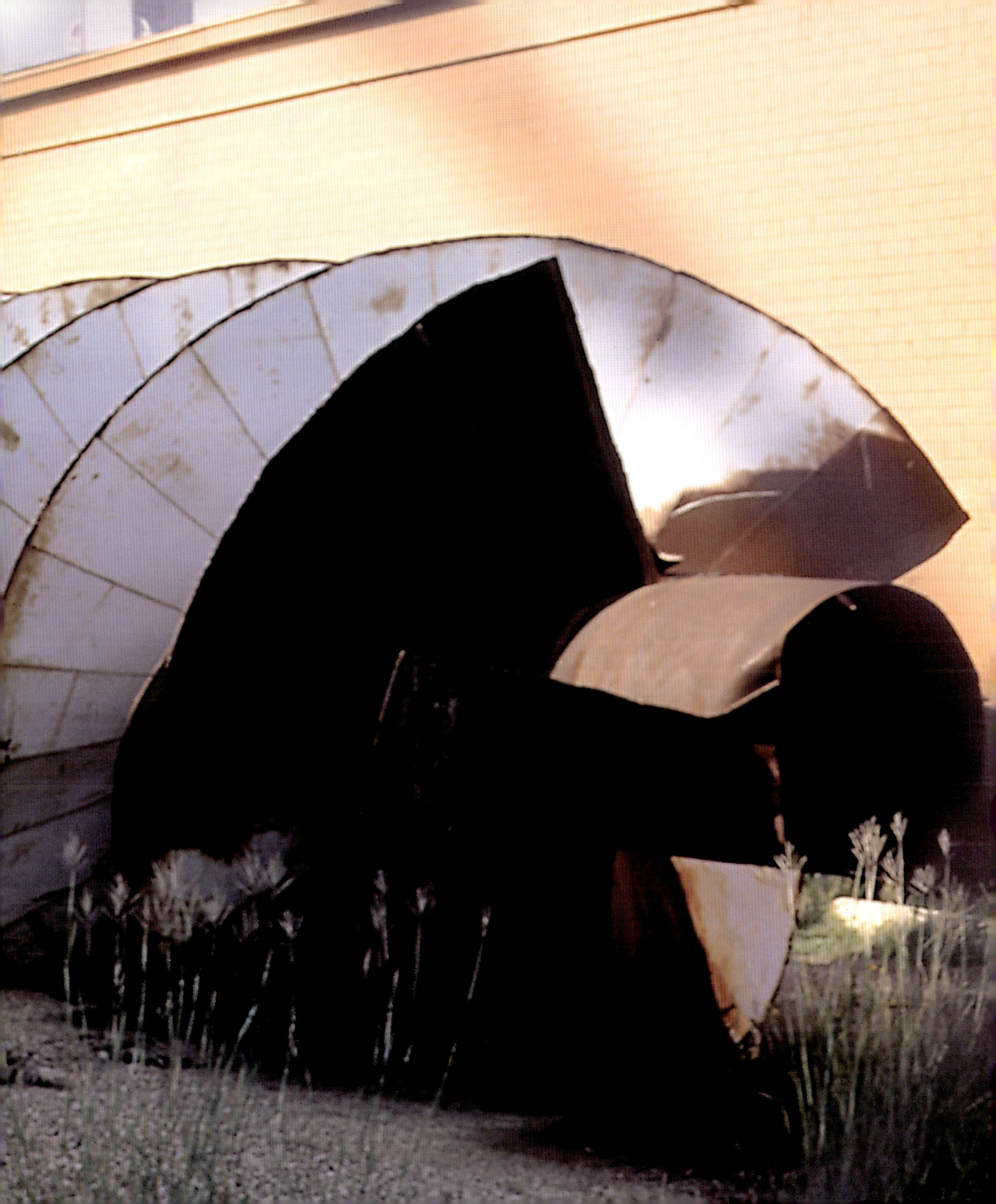

Objects for Objects series
'Sculptures for a Library'
Blanket, tape, thread, hardboard,
painted laths, canvas, paint,
Each work: 60 x 40 x 90 cm
(approx)
1995
Henry Moore Institute Library, Leeds

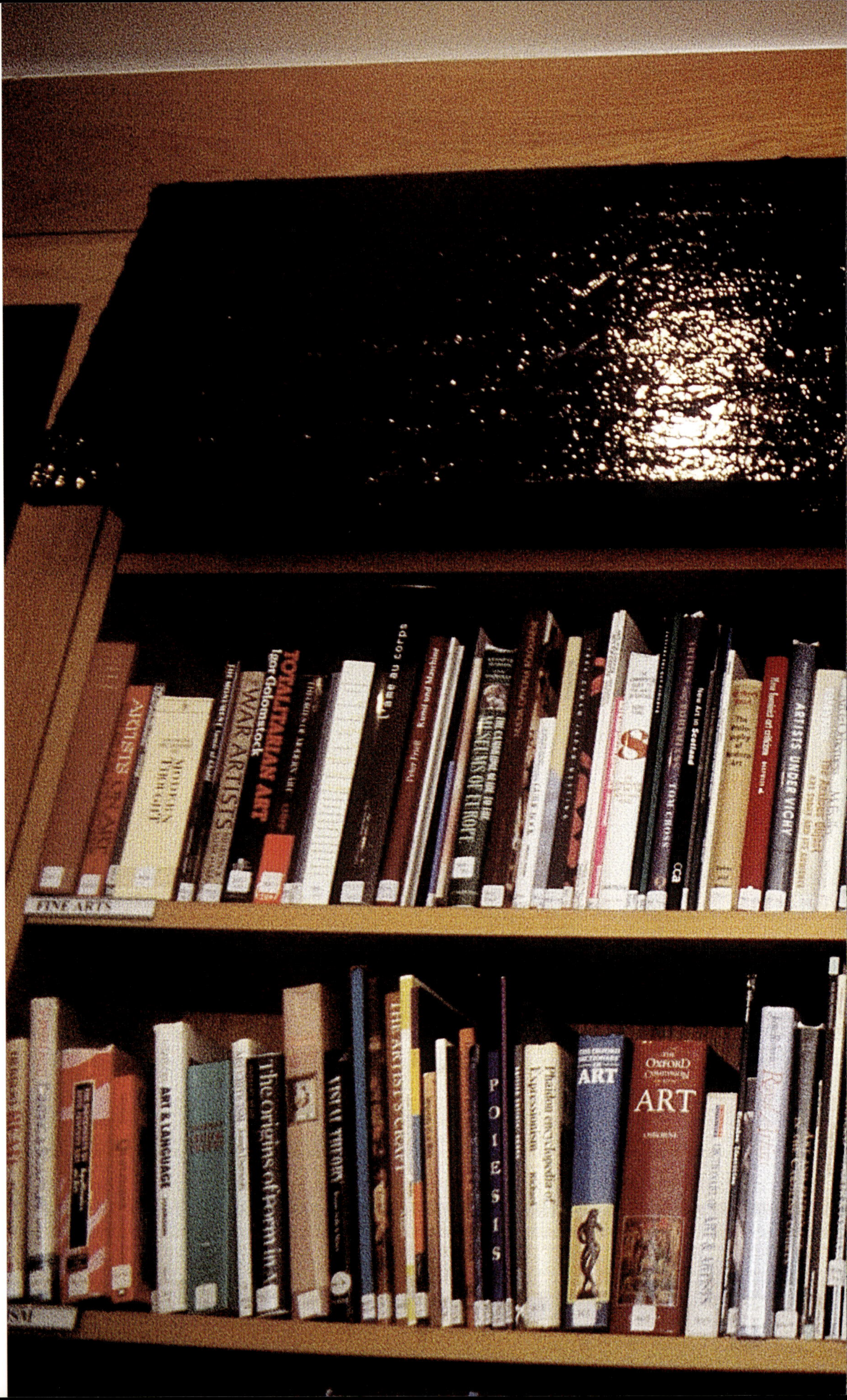

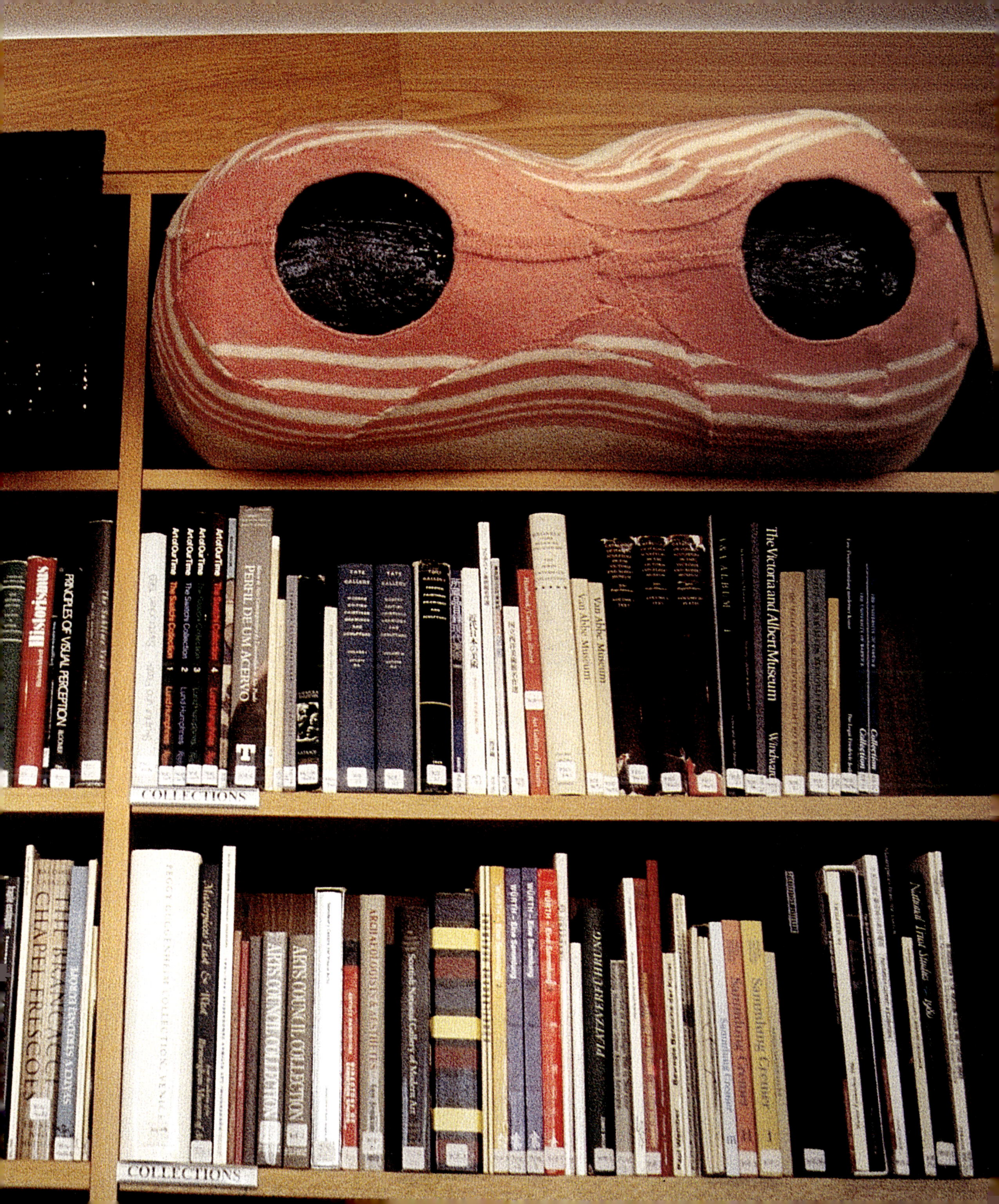
Historismus
PRINCIPLES OF VISUAL PERCEPTION
Art of Our Time
The Saatchi Collection
PERFIL DE UM ACERVO
TATE GALLERY
Van Abbe Museum
The Victoria and Albert Museum
COLLECTIONS
THE BRANCACCI CHAPEL FRESCOES
PEGGY GUGGENHEIM COLLECTION, VENICE
Masterpieces East & West
ARTS COUNCIL COLLECTION
Scottish National Gallery of Modern Art
PLATZVERFÜHRUNG
Sammlung Greiner
National Trust Studies 1980
COLLECTIONS

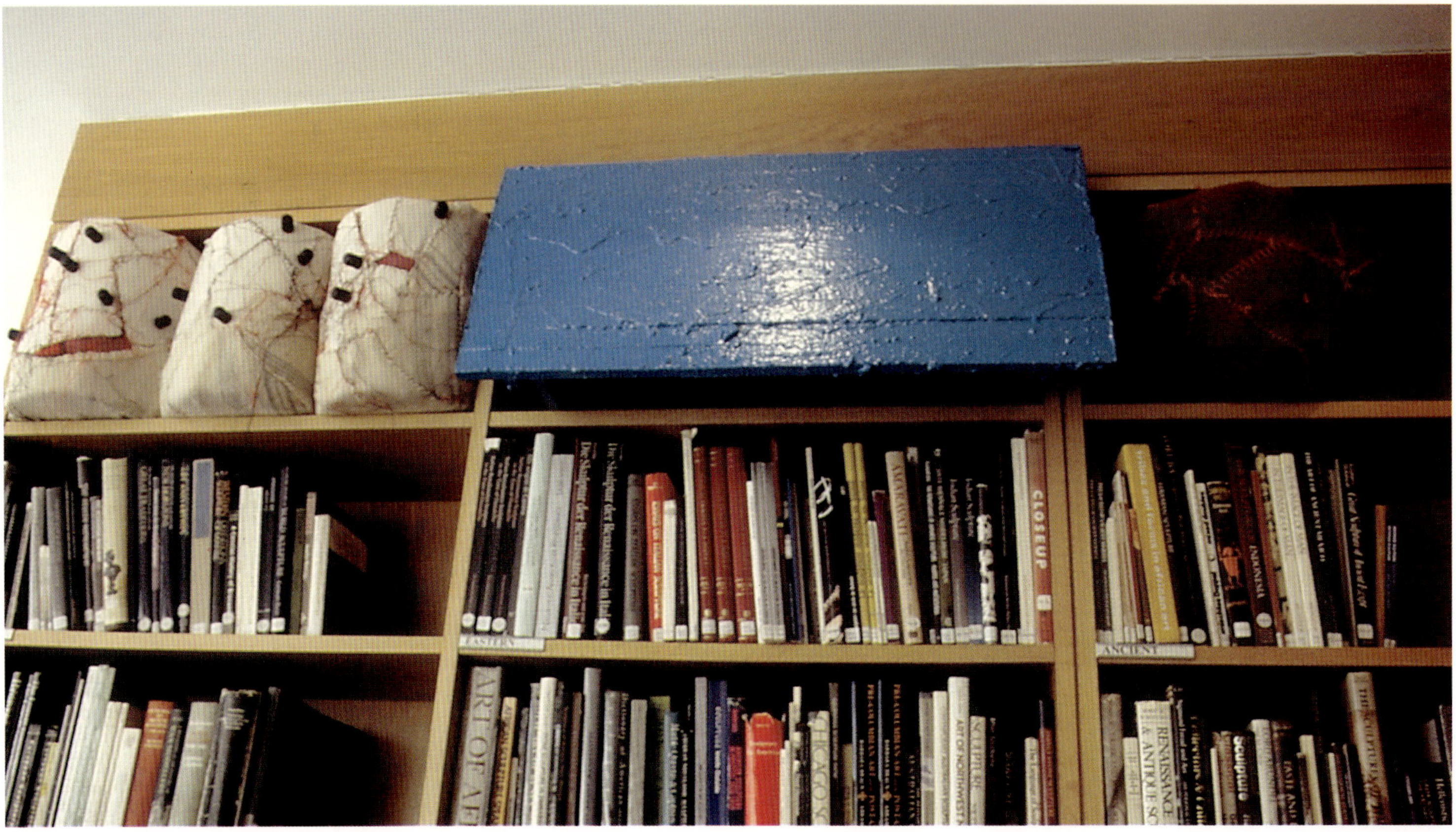
CLOSEUP

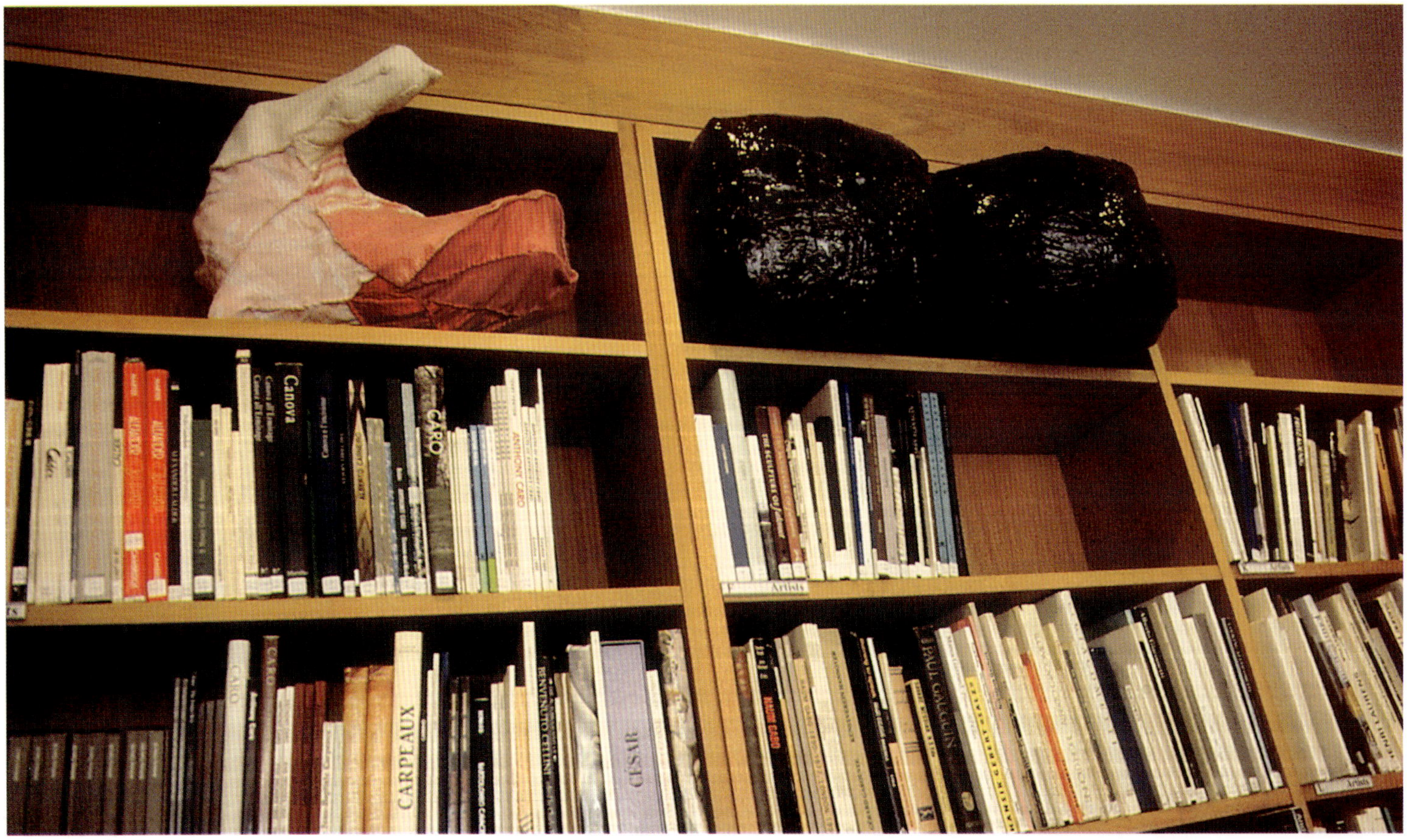
Canova
CARO
ANTHONY CARO
CARPEAUX
CESAR
PAUL GAUGUIN

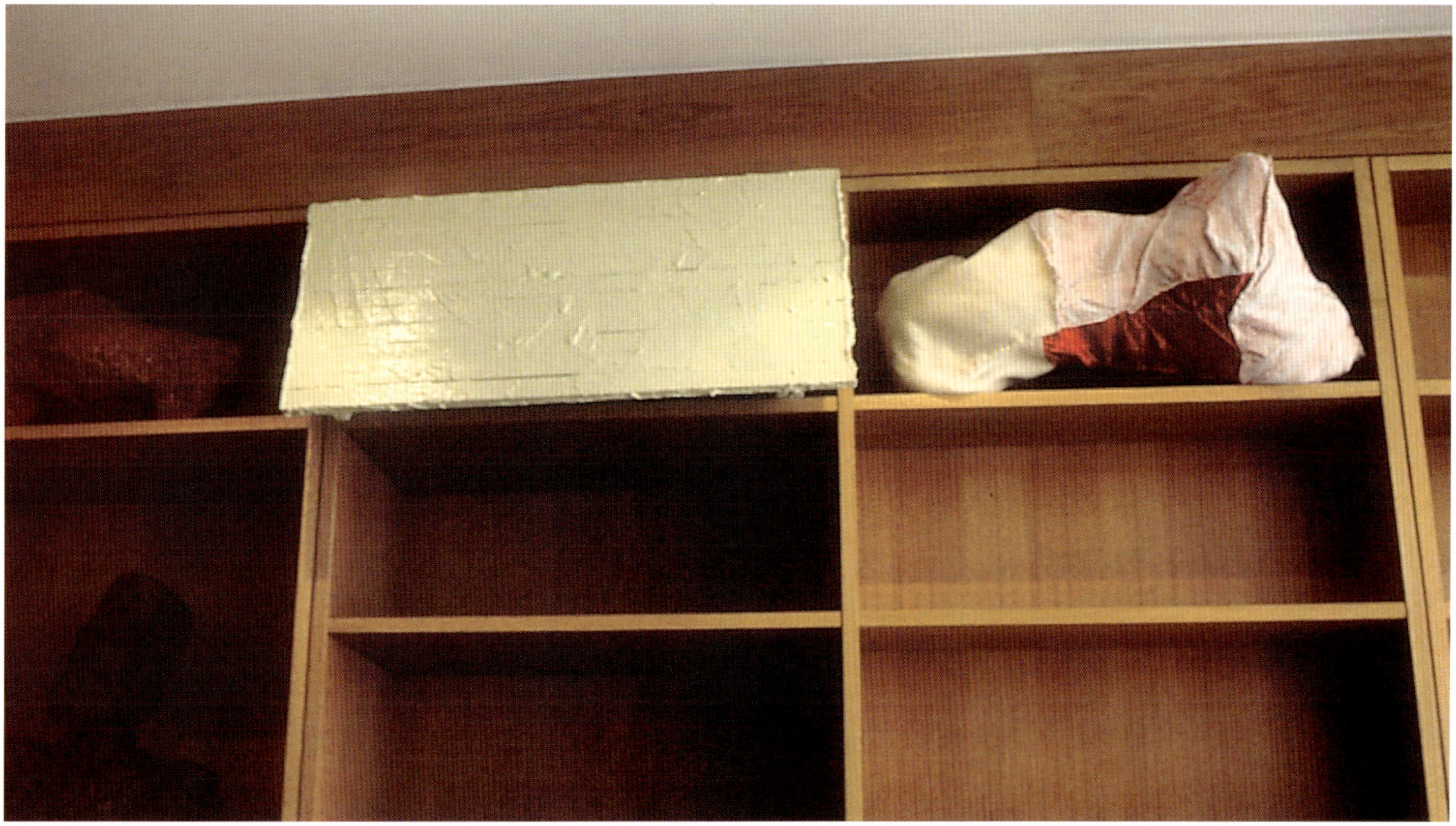

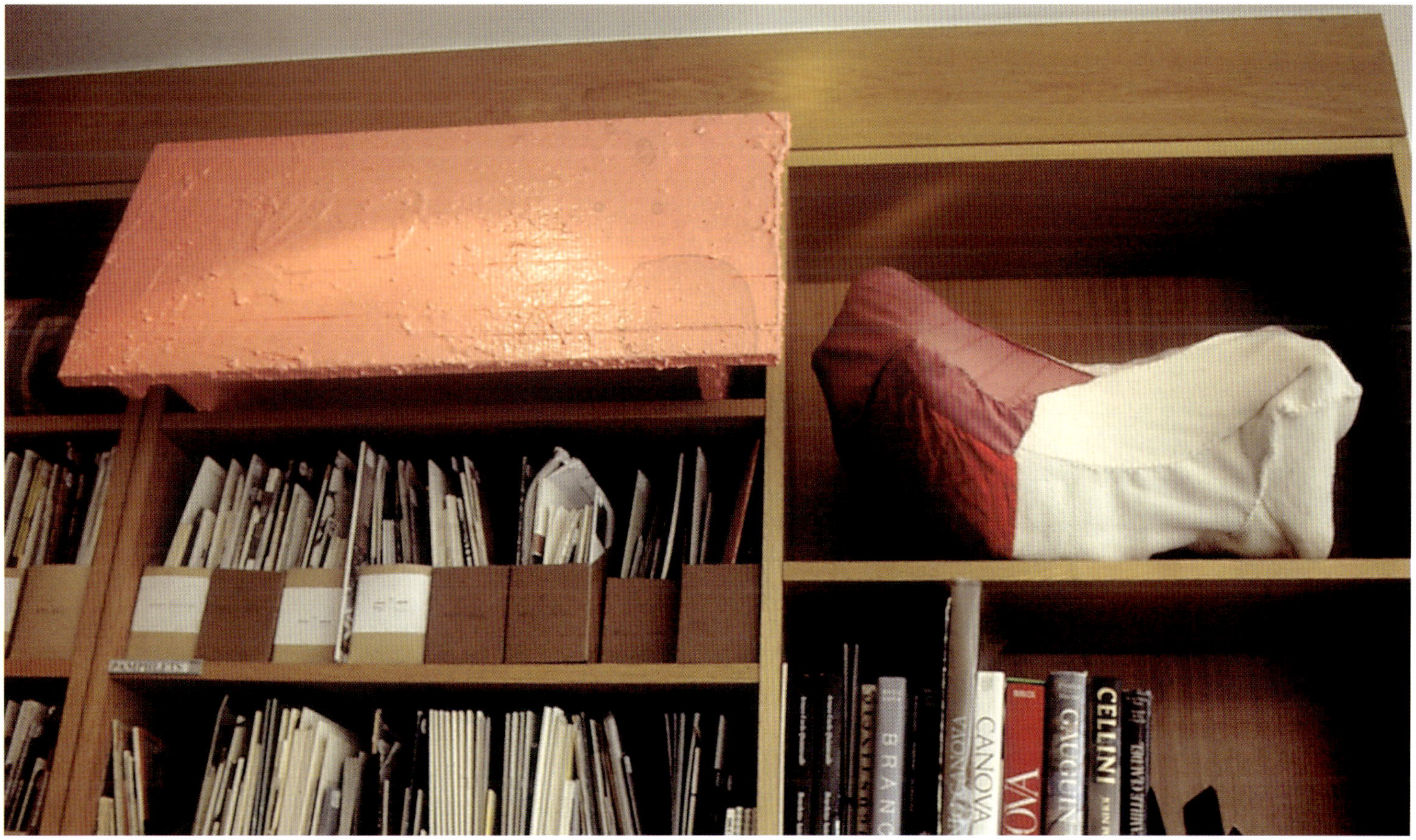
CANOVA
GAUGUIN
CELLINI

Biography

Phyllida Barlow

Born Newcastle-upon-Tyne, 1944
Lives and works in London
Studied at The Slade School of Fine Art, 1963-1966
Currently Head of Undergraduate Sculpture
Reader in Fine Art, Slade School of Fine Art
McDermott Visiting Artist to University of Texas at Dallas, 2003

Solo Exhibitions and Installations

2003 *Untitled (Dallas) 2003* University of Texas at Dallas Visual Art Gallery
2002 *New Sculpture*, Richard Salmon Gallery, London
Fête, Station, Phoenix Wharf, Bristol
2001 Knives in Hens, Set Design commissioned by the Attic Theatre Company, at Wimbledon Theatre, directed by Jenny Lee, written by David Harrower
1996 *Recall*, Marshall's Mill, Dean Clough, Halifax. Three Sculpture Installation
1995 *Depot*, Museum of Installation, London
(Objects for Objects series)
Sculptures for the Library, Henry Moore Institute, Leeds
1994 *In Place*, A series of privately commissioned site specific objects for *Objects for Objects*
Out of Place, Installation for a Country House Hallway, and *Installation for a Garage*
1991 *Plantation*, Commissioned by the Business Design Centre, Islington and the MOI, for Fresh Art
Deep, Museum of Installation, London
Closed (Vigil ii), RIBA Sculpture Court, Portland Place, London, curated by Lady Gibberd
1990 *Fall*, DEGW Offices, London, curated by Kapil Jarawala
1989 *Crowd*, Unit 1, Hermitage Road Industrial Estate, sponsored by Skyman Paper and Plastics
Wallworks, Wall Sculptures, Smith Jarawala Gallery
Vigil I, Three site-specific sculptures commissioned for Site3, The Churchyard, Windsor, SW Arts/Windsor Festival
1988 *Slope*, Site-Installation, The Gallery, Dean Cough, Halifax, Curator Paul Bradley for Sir Ernest Hall, Director
1987 *Expanse*, Installation Sculpture for Unit 7, curated by Nicola Oxley, Nico D'Olivera and Michael Petrie GLAA funding
Oracle, Installation for St. Peter's Churchyard, Cambridge. Kettle's Yard Residency. Supported Eastern Arts.
1985 *Wrecks*, Bayfield Norfolk
Ghosts, Mare Street, (Old Stocking Factory), London
Strangers, Finsbury Park, London, (school playground)
1984 *Scar*, Archway Road, (abandoned house, attic), London

Group Exhibitions

2003 *Shelf Life, 60 Minutes*, Studio 1.1, Redchurch Street, London
Location, Location, Location, Albury Arts, Potsford House, Guildford: *holed up: yellow, red, green, pink*
The Drawing Auction, The Drawing Room, Laburnam Street
The Greatest Show on Earth, Metropole Gallery, Folkestone
2002 *Harvey's Bodies*, Metropole Gallery, Folkestone, *Untitled Metropole*
Royal Academy Summer Exhibition, Invited Artist, curated by Alison Wilding
2001 *Station to Station, Spacex 2,* Exeter Maritime Museum, Exeter, Devon
Mile End Park Sculpture Exhibition, Mile End Park, Tower Hamlets, London, E8, *View*
2000-2001 *British Art Show 5, after dark-into black,* Commissioned by the Hayward Gallery, selected by Pippa Coles, Matthew Higgs, Jaqueline Poncelet, for a National Touring Exhibition, organised by the Hayward Gallery, London, supported by the Arts Council of England, 2000. Touring to Edinburgh, Southampton, Cardiff, Birmingham
1999 *Sculpture, Dawn till Dusk*, The Royal Western Academy, Bristol: six sculptors, selected by Alison Wilding and John Maine, for the Triennial Sculpture Exhibition
O Pas La-Surprising Places, Far Away, LAC:Lieu D'Art Contemporain, Narbonne, France, curated by Aude Herail Jaeger. Supported by the Henry Moore Foundation, FRAC, DRAC:Rousillon-Langudoc, British Academy, British Council, Richard Salmon Gallery, Vignobles James Herrick
Furnitue, curated by Paul Heber-Percy for Richard Salmon Gallery, London and touring to John Hansard Gallery, Southampton, Bluecoat Gallery, Liverpool
Dumbfounded, curated by Carmel Buckley, Battersea Arts Centre, London, touring to New York, Chicago, San Francisco: 2001-2002
1998 *Not Nothing Nowhere, after dark*:The Master Shipwrights House, Deptford, London, curated by Willy Robertson and Chris Mazieka, supported by Greenwich Millenium Regeneration, and private sponsors
Out of Place, 'Time and Time Again' Chapter Art Gallery, Cardiff, Wales curated by Nilofar Akmut, from the National College of Arts, Lahore, Pakistan, International Workshop, supported by the Arts Council of Wales, Pakistan Airline.
Touching Matters, The Gallery, Swiss Cottage Library, London, curated by Francois Dupre for the Women in Focus, commissioned by Camden Arts.
The Ugly Edge, (*Ugly Mugs*), The Henry Moore Institute Gallery, curated by Elizabeth Rosser, for the Ugly Edge Conference.
1997 *EAST International, 'Truce'*: Norwich School of Art, selected by Nicholas Logsdail and Tacita Dean, supported by the Arts Council of England.
1997-2000 *Musee Imaginaire*, The Box Project, Museum of Installation, curated by Nicola Oxley, Nicholas d'Olivera, Michael Petry, supported by the Arts Council, the Henry Moore Foundation, British Council, touring to Nottingham, Edinburgh, Birmingham (UK); Oslo, Stavanger (Norway); Berlin (Germany).
1997 *Barely Made, Objects for a Dressing Table*, Norwich Art Gallery, curated by Jaqueline Poncelet
1996 *9 Months2 Seconds*, Manhattan Lofts, Bankside, London, curated by Maria Marshall, supported by Bankside Business Development, Manhattan Associates Property
TRY, Gulbenkian Gallery, Royal College of Art, London, curated by the MA in VAA, Royal College of Art, supported by the Paul Hamlyn Foundation
1995 *Contemporary Arts Society Fair*, Royal Festival Hall, London.
The Gas Station, SPAT, a work commissioned by the Laboratory, Ruskin School of Drawing, Oxford University, curated by Paul Banaventura, for an Internet Exhibition: www.ruskin.sch.ox.ac.uk/lab supported by the Arts Council of England
1994 *Leich und Luft* Die Neuue Fabrik, Hamburg, Germany, curated by Andreas Ruthi and Ruprecht Racht
1993 *Shopping sensations*, Bradford City Art Gallery, toured from the Rothschild Centre, Croydon
1992 *Shopping Sensation, 'Home'* Rothschild Centre, Croydon. Curated by Jane Heath for the Disabled, supported by the Arts Council and Croydon Council
*Three Sculptors, 'Up Across Around'*Diorama, Regents Park, London

1990 *Seam*, commissioned by the National Garden Festival, Gateshead, curated by Isabel Vasseur, funded by the Arts Council and NE Arts.
MAAD Festival Cambridge, Collaboration with dancer Louise Tonkin, Kettle's Yard Gallery Cambridge
1988 *Houseworks, 'Fold'*, curated by Mark Dunhill, for 13 Clarynge Road, Bristol
1987 *The Shelf Show,'Muscle and Bone'*, Kettle's Yard, Cambridge
1986 *Casting an Eye, 'Engulf'*, curated by Richard Deacon and Alison Wilding for The Cornerhouse, Manchester
Third Generation, Canterbury festival Sculpture Exhibition
1983 *Tout Quarry Sculpture, 'Fill'*, selected by Philip King, Tout Quarry, Portland, Dorset
1979 *Sculpture in Action, 'Stacks*, South Hill Park, Bracknell, Berkshire
1978 *Twelve Sculptors at West Surrey, 'x2'*, West Surrey School of Art Gallery.
1977 *Three Sculptors in the Close, 'Four'*, The Close, Gloucester Cathedral
1976 *Contemporary Painting and Sculpture, 'Shedmesh'*, Camden Arts Centre
1975 *Drawings*, Gallery 21, London
1974 *British Sculptors, Attitudes to Drawing*, Sunderland Arts Centre
1972 *Sculpture at the University of Surrey, 'All and Everything'*, University of Surrey
1971 *Sculpture and Drawings, 'View', 'Chair', 'Wardrobe'*. Camden Arts Centre
Spectrum London, 'Sofa & floor & drawings', Alexandra Palace, London
1965 *Young Contemporaries, 'Table'*, ICA Galleries, London

Exhibitions Curated

1996 *Artists for a Day,*Dee Meaden: Flowers East, London
AD HOC, London Art Forms-16 artists
1992 *Three Sculptors,* Diorama, Regents Park, London. Phyllida Barlow, Fernando Palma, Keith Wilson.

Selected Exhibitions

2001 *New Ashgate Gallery-Contemporary Sculpture,* Selected by Phyllida Barlow, William Pye, Ed Tillotson
1999 *Kettle's Yard Open,* selected by Phyllida Barlow and Stephen Chambers
1998 *New Contemporaries*, Selected by Phyllida Barlow, Eddie Berg, Christine Hohenbüchler, Adrian Searle

Governorships

1997-2003 Byam Shaw School of Art, Director: Alister Warman

Selection and Awards Panels

2001 Nominator for the Arts Foundation Awards for 2001
Nominator for the Paul Hamlyn Awards, 2001
1999 Selector for the Kettle's Yard Open Exhibition, Cambridge
1998 Selector for the 1998 New Contemporaries: with Eddie Berg, Christine Hochenbuchler and Adrian Searle. Chair: Sacha Craddock
1996 Selector for the Prudential Awards for the Visual Arts: with Cedric Price, Richard Wentworth, chaired by Julian Forrester.
1994-1998 Selection Panel: British School at Rome, Fine Art Faculty Board
1993-1994 Selection Panel: British School at Rome, The Sargent Fellowship
1995 Nominator for the Sculpture Awards: The Arts Foundation [Panel of Award Winner: Melanie Counsell]
1990-1993 Selection Panel: The British School at Rome, Rome Scholarship
1992 Selector of Installation Art Section at 'Fresh Art', Islington Business Design Centre

Gallery Talks and Lectures

2003 *Aspects of Sculpture*, 3 lectures, University of Texas at Dallas
2000 *Spectacular Bodies, the History of Art and Science from Leonardo to the present day,* Hayward Gallery, Gallery Debate with Professor Michael Baum, Emeritus Professor in Surgery, and Visiting Professor in Medical Ethics, UCL, and Phyllida Barlow, Reader, Head of Undergraduate Sculpture, Slade School of Fine Art
Panamarenko, Hayward Gallery: Tuesday Gallery Talk
1999 *Pistoletto Retrospective,* Museum of Modern Art, Oxford: Gallery Talk
1998 *Playing with Paradox,* Opening Talk: Retrospective of the work of George Fullard, Kettle's Yard, Cambridge and Mappin Art Gallery, Sheffield
Louise Bourgeois: New Work, Serpentine Gallery, London
Out of Place, Gallery Talk for the visually impaired Chapter Art Gallery
1997 *Rose Finn Kelcey: New Work,* Camden Arts Centre, London
Tony Cragg: New Work, Whitechapel Art Gallery, London
1996 *TRY,* Sculpture-Dead or Alive Royal College of Art, London
The Sneeze of Louise, The Sculpture of Louise Bourgeois: Friday Review at Oriel Gallery (Arts Council of Wales), Cardiff
1995 *The Rites of Passage*, The Sculpture of Louise Bourgeois: The Tate Gallery, London
1993 *The Sculpture of Susana Salano,* Whitechapel Art Gallery, London
1991 *Pistoletto- a Retrospective,* Camden Arts Centre
1990 *Sightlines,* Gallery Talk on the installation *Seven Obsessions* at Whitechapel Art Gallery, London

Conferences and Panels

2002 *Eva Hesse Symposium: Tate Modern/Leeds University collaboration coordinated by Prof. Griselda Pollock:* 'Lost for Words', slide illustrated talk
Barnet Newman Study Day, Tate Modern/Open University, coordinated by Sophie Howarth and Gill Perry: edited version of 'Hearsay, Rumours, Bed-sit Dreamers and Art begins Today'
The Whitechapel Art Gallery: Next Generations: Current Sculptural Practice in the UK and Beyond: 'Hearsay, Rumours, Bed-sit Dreamers, and Art Begins Today', slide illustrated talk by Phyllida Barlow, in conjunction with the exhibition 'Early One Morning' and with Iwona Blaswick, JJ Charlesworth, and Niru Ratnam
Royal Academy of Arts: Architecture Forums; 'The City as Sculpture: From Skyline to Plinth' a slide illustrated talk for a panel discussion chaired by Richard Cork, with Anthony Gormley
2001 *NYU in London: Saturday Artists' Seminar*, organised by Naomi Salaman, Phyllida Barlow and Kathy Batista, Slide Talk: 'What is Public Art?'
Studio Lives: Contemporary Views by Artists: Henry Moore Institute, Leeds Slide Talk on the workand its relationship to the 'studio'
'Selector's Event': New Contemporaries, with Eddie Berg, Jennifer Higgie, at the Camden Arts Centre
2000 *Artistic Judgements: Quality in the Contemporary Visual Arts:* Organised by Southern Arts Board, Paper titled 'On Being Judged'

1999	*Public Art Debate: 'Art and Regeneration'*, Organised by Museum of Installationand Deptford X, Paper titled: 'Why Not a Tree'
	Sculpture Forum, Panel discussion on 'Sculpture': Triennial exhibition at the RWA, Bristol, chaired by John Maine
1998	*So, What is the Object?,* New Contemporaries Panel Discussion with Sacha Craddock, Michael Archer, Keith Tyson, Phyllida Barlow, Camden Arts Centre
	The Ugly Edge, organised by the Henry Moore Institute, Leeds, with Elizabeth Rosser, Mark Cousins, Phyllida Barlow, John Thompson Paper titled: 'Ugly Mugs, Hot Stuff and Cool Customers'
	From Varying Positions, What is to be Expected from Art Schools Now? Co-ordinated by Wimbledon School of Art at the Tate Gallery: Paper titled: Travelling Light, a brief analysis of the end of workand the triumph of the photographic colour transparency.'
	Touching Matters, Conversation between Phyllida Barlow and Angela Thwaite. The Gallery, Swiss Cottage Library 1998
1997	*Cloth,* 'Big, Bad, Ugly', a slide talk for the one day conference on Craft/Art?, Norwich Art Gallery
	Barely Made, Panel Discussion on the exhibition 'Barely Made', between Jaqueline Poncelet, Sussana Heron, Stephanie Bergman, Laura Godfrey Isaacs. Norwich Art Gallery
	Richard Tuttle Exhibition, Camden Arts Centre Artists Debate Art: Panel discussion with Richard Wentworth, Keith Wilson
1996	*Drawing:* 'Making Work Work': Slide talk on the sculpture of Phyllida Barlow for the Tate Gallery Summer School, co-ordinated by Silvia Le Haav
1995	*Louise Bourgeois Retrospective Sculpture and Prints,* Paper titled: 'The Sneeze of Louise' at MOMA, Oxford. Louise Bourgeois Symposium, St Anne's College, Oxford
	Matrix 3D Conference, Co-ordinated by Central St. Martins School of art: Sculpture Methods Forum with Tim Llewellyn, Richard Wentworth, Lewis Johnson. Paper titled: 'The Hatred of the Object'
1994	*The Future of Art Education,* Panel Discussion for Fresh Art at the Business Design Centre, Islington, with Phyllida Barlow, Ian Biggs, Margery Althorpe Guyton, chaired by Tim Marlowe
1993	*Ten Years at Tout Quarry,* 'Damage and Repair' Tout Quarry Sculpture Park, Portland, Dorset

Awards

2003	Henry Moore Foundation Award for Black Dog Publishing monograph
	Elephant Trust Award for Black Dog Publishing monograph
	Dean's Award: travel to the USA, for exhibition and lectures
1996	Dean's Fund Award, University College London, Research Award to travel to Lahore, Pakistan: International Art Education Workshop-National College of Arts.
	British Council Travel Bursary, to participate in the International Art Education Workshop at the invitation of the National College of Arts, Lahore
1995	Elephant Trust Award, for a four sculpture installation at the Museum of Installation, London

Bibliography

2003	*Sculpture,* Peter Suchin on Phyllida Barlow at Richard Salmon Gallery, April, Vol.22 No.3
2002	*Contemporary*, Tom Morton, Phyllida Barlow at the Richard Salmon Gallery, Nov. 2002, ISSN 14759853
	Royal Academy Illustrated 2002, Published by the Royal Academy of Arts: edited by Alison Wilding, ISBN 1903973104
2000	*British Art Show 5,* Published by Hayward Gallery Publishing. Introduction by Pippa Coles, Jaqueline Poncelet, Matthew Higgs, and texts by Tony Godfrey, Marcelo Spinelli and Helen Luckett. 2000, ISBN 1853322040
1999	*Furniture,* Copyright Richard Salmon, Joan Key, Paul Heber-Percy, Martin Herbert. 1999. ISBN 1873550111
	Contemporary Visual Arts, Issue 24, 'Dereliction Chic: Art & Domestic Places', Mark Gisbourne, pp.31-35. ISSN 10285040
	Dumbfounded Designed and Published by Alison Green. Texts by Alison Green, 'Ways of Communicating' and David Burrows, 'Dialogue between and Umbrella and a Sewing Machine'. ISBN 0953642003
	Triennial Sculpture Exhibition, Royal Western Academy. Edited and Forward by John Maine
	O Pas La, Surprising Spaces, Published by Aude Herail Jaeger London 1999. Essay Title, 'The Rise and Fall of His Majesty the Baby' by Christopher Kool-Want. ISBN 09535959000
1998	*Out of Place,* Catalogue and essay on the exhibition 'Out of Place' by Sunil Gupta, titled Inside/Outside-Surrounded by Four Women' Published by Chapter. ISBN 19000290228
1997	*EAST International,* Catalogue essay by Linda Morris. Published by Norwich Art Gallery. ISBN
1996	*try,* Catalogue and essay on the exhibition 'try', by Alexandra Bradley , Rosie Gunraj, Clare Manchester, Angela Murray, Hannah Redler. 1996
1995	*Looking Out for Picture Past,* Review by Elizabeth Rosser on the exhibition 'Depot' by Phyllida Barlow at the Museum of Installation. Women's Artists Magazine. No. 65. July/Aug
	Art and Design, 'British Art-Defining the Nineties', 'Womens Voices' by Nicola Oxley. pp. 68-70. No.41
1994	*Art and Design,* 'Art and the Natural Environment Acer Pseudoplantus' by Michael Petry. Pages 94/96. No.36
	Installation Art, Texts by Michael Archer. Edited by Nico D'Olivera, Nicloa Oxley, Michael Petry. Pages 66/67. Published by Thames and Hudson
1993	*Art and Design*, Installation Art. 'Earth Sites' by Nico D'Olivera, Nicola Oxley, Michael Petry. Pages 20/21. No.30
1991	*Art and Design,* 'New Museology'. The Third Annual Academy Forum. Michael Petry, Museum of Installation, Pages 14/15
1990	*Festival Landmarks '90,* Catalogue for the National Garden Festival, Gateshead, 1990 Edited by Isabel Vasseur and Geraldine Prince. Page 49
1988	*Performance Magazine,* 'Performance and Sculpture'. 'The Shadow of Apparatus' by Brian Catling. No.53. Apr/May.

Publications

2003 Text *'Testing for Lies'* for Edward Fellows' exhibition catalogue
Text *'a severe weather warning'* for Melanie Counsell's exhibition catalogue, Sête, France
Frieze: Picture: *'Mandy' 1952* with text

2002 *Slade Magazine,* Angela de la Cruz: notes from a studio visit, July 22, 2002 '…from the mouth to the tail'.
The Architectural Review: June 2002: The Royal Academy Forum; the city as sculpture: from the plinth to the sky, with speakers Anthony Gormley and Phyllida Barlow, text reproduced: 'In and Out of the City', June, 2002, p.90-91
The Sculptor Speaks: The Henry Moore Institute, a response written for the HMI Newsletter to the Institute's conference on its collaboration with the National Sound Archive production of an oral archive of sculptor's voices. Published by The Henry Moore Foundation. Co-ordinated by Liz Aston. Feb 2002

2001 *Artistic Judgements: a discussion about quality in the visual arts,* Southern Arts Board at St Catherine's College, Oxford. Paper titled 'On Being Judged'. Published April 2001, Southern Arts.

2000 *Issues in Art Education: 'The Dynamics of Now',* Paper titled 'Travelling Light: a brief analysis of the end of work and the triumph of the 35mm colour transparency'. Given by Phyllida Barlow for 'From Varying Positions', 1998, at the Tate Gallery, organised by Wimbledon School of Art. Edited by William Furlong, Polly Gould and Paul Hetherington. Published in 2000, by Tate Gallery Publishing Ltd.

1998 *Flattening the World*, Catalogue Text for an exhibition of the sculpture of Paul Mattocks, at The INAX Gallery, Tokyo104, Japan
at Sea, A Faxed conversation between Phyllida Barlow and Alison Wilding for the catalogue GROUNDED which accompanied the exhibition of the sculpture of Alison Wilding at the Northern Centre for Contemporary Art, Sunderland
Die Macht des Alters
Strategien der Meisterschaft. Telephone Texts between Christine and Irene Hohenbuchler and Phyllida Barlow, Marlene Dumas, Elfiede Jelinek, Margareta Schutte-Lihotzky, Lidwien van de Ven, for their work and catalogue for their exhibition at Kronprinzenpalais, Berlin; Kunstmuseum Bonn; Galerei der Stadt Stuttgart, Germany.
Postcards on Photography, 'Travelling Light: A brief analysis of the end of work and the triumph of the photographic' from an original talk for the catalogue 'Postcards on Photography' for the Photorealist exhibition at the Cambridge Darkroom Gallery, Cambridge curated by Naomi Salaman and Ronnie Simpson.
'Cloth', 'Big, Bad, Ugly' ed. Linda Morris, NSAD

1997 *MAKE: The Magazine of Women's Art:Soapbox,* 'How Does the F Word Inform your Teaching' No.77. Sept/Nov. Page 10
Matrix 3D Conference, Edited by Stuart Evans, Joanna Greenhill, Ingrid Swenson. The Lethaby Press, Central St Martins College of Art. 'The Hatred of the Object' by Phyllida Barlow
MAKE: The Magazine of Women's Art:Soapbox 'Is There Such a Thing as Maternal Imagination?' No. 75 April/May. Page 22

1996 *Hide and Seek,* Introduction to the sculpture of Auder Herail Jaeger and Alison Gajra for their exhibition 'SYZYGY' to Forderverein Aktuelle Kunst e. V, Munster, Germany, based on their collaborative exhibition 'Clandestine', London. Women's Art Magazine. No.69. Apr/May *SYZYGY,* as above, for 'Aktuelle Kunst' Zeitung herausgegeben vom Forderverein Aktuelle Kunst Munster e. V.
Braziers Summer Workshop, 'Out of Time' by Phyllida Barlow, for Braziers Workshop, Edited by Gill Ord, Andy Cohen, Sarah Davies, published by Braziers Park, Ipston, Oxon
Museum of Modern Art papers. Louise Bourgeois. Vol. 1
'The Sneeze of Louise' by Phyllida Barlow. An adaptation from a slide illustrated talk on the Sculpture of Louise Bourgeois. Edited by Ian Cole. Published by MOMA, Oxford

1995 *Feel Good Factor,* Review by Phyllida Barlow on the exhibition 'Feel Good Factor' of the work of Leila Galloway, Miwa Kojima and Rachel Chapman for Women's Art Magazine. No.64 May/June

1993-1994 *2B and 1,* Introduction to the work of Marco Bettoni, Hose Buitago, John Isaacs, for their touring exhibition to Milan, Italy, Barcelona, Spain, London, UK. Funded by the EEC Kaleidoscope fund

1993 *In Time*, A catalogue introduction to the sculpture of Hiroshi Watanabe for his exhibition at the A1 Gallery, Tokyo, Japan

1992 *Wall to Wall,* Television interview with Phyllida Barlow on the work of Alison Wilding, Turner Prize nominee, for Channel 4, 'Wall to Wall' Productions, for the Tate Gallery, London.

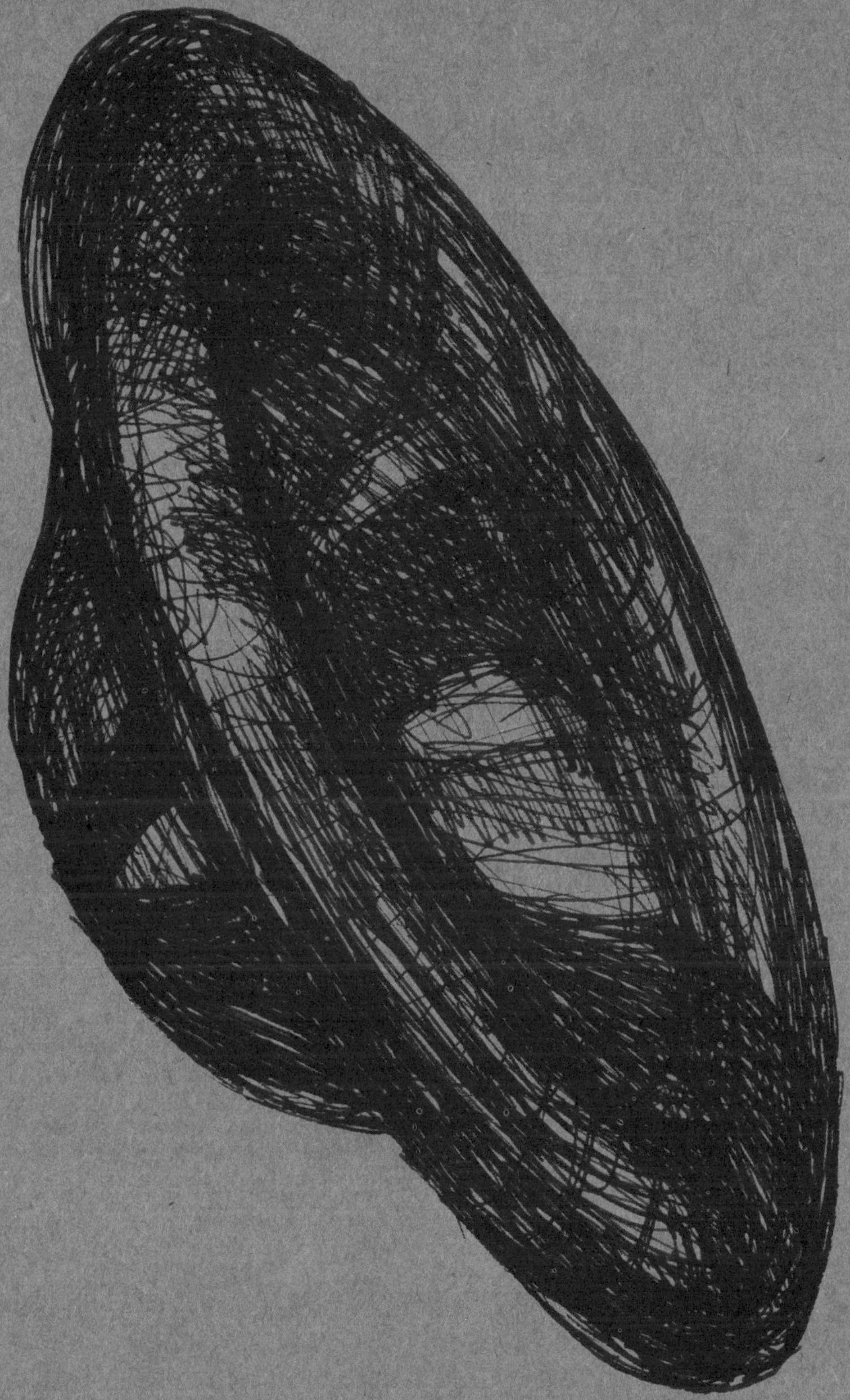

Picture credits

All works are by Phyllida Barlow unless stated otherwise.

All dimensions are width x height x length unless stated otherwise.

Tony Smith, **Die**, 1962. Steel Digital image © 2002 The Museum of Modern Art/Scala, Florence. © ARS, NY and DACS, London 2004.

Barry Flanagan, **Heap 4**, 1967. Hessian and sand. Courtesy the Arts Council Collection, Hayward Gallery, London and the artist.

Robert Morris, **Untitled (Threadwaste)**, 1968-1969. Threadwaste, asphalt, mirrors, copper tubing, and felt. © ARS, NY and DACS, London 2004. Courtesy Castelli Gallery, New York.

Louise Bourgeois, **Avenza Revisited II**, 1968-69. Plaster, plastic and wire on wooden base. Daros Collection, Switzerland, courtesy Cheim & Read, New York, photo: Jochen Littkemann.

Image of Phyllida Barlow from Camden Arts Centre Exhibition, photo: Tate Archive

Image of Phyllida Barlow from Twelve Sculptors of West Surrey, photo: Tate Archive

Bill Woodrow, **Twin Tub with Guitar**, 1981, © Tate, London 2003 courtesy the artist.

John McCracken, **Plank**,1966 (remade 1988). Polyester resin, fibreglass and wood, 96 x 29 x 4 cm. Courtesy Lisson Gallery, London, photo: Gareth Winters, London.

David Annesley, **Swing Low**, 1964, painted steel, © Tate, London 2003 courtesy the artist.

Anish Kapoor, **At the Edge of the World II**, 1998. Fibreglass and pigment, 800 x 800 cm. Courtesy Lisson Gallery, London, photo: John Riddy.

Richard Serra, **Snake**, 1998-99. Cor-ten steel. © FMGB Guggenheim Bilbao, photo: Erika Barahona Ede.

Marcel Duchamp, **Why not sneeze, Rrose Selavy?**, 1964 (replica of the 1921 original). New York, Museum of Modern Art (MoMA). © Digital image, The Museum of Modern Art, New York/SCALA, Florence, © Succession Marcel Duchamp / ADAGP, Paris and DACS, London 2003.

Alighiero E Boetti, **Lampada Annuale (Yearly Lamp)**,1966, Steel, 78 x 40 x 40 cm. Courtesy Sammlung Goetz, Munich.
Hans Haake, Standort Merry-Go-Round (German Merry-Go-Round), 1997. Courtesy the artist. © DACS, London, 2004.

Guiseppe Gabellone, **Untitled**, 1999, courtesy greengrassi, London.

Jacques Lipchitz, **Figure**, 1926-30. Courtesy Hirschhorn Museum and Sculpture Garden, Smithsonian Institution, Gift of Joseph H Hirschhorn, 1966, photo: Lee Stalsworth.

Louise Bourgeois, **Nature Study (Velvet Eyes)**, 1984. Marble and steel. Collection of Michael and Joan Salke, Boston, MA, courtesy Cheim & Read, New York, photo: Allan Finkelman.

Phillip King, **Rose bud**, Digital image © 2003 The Museum of Modern Art/Scala, Florence.

Drawing credits

Group 1
pages: 14, 17, 18, 75, 99, 101, 126, 129, 157, 159, 177 (top), 190, 241, 253, 255 Sketch Book Drawings
Variable media: ink, marker, acrylic, pencil
Dimensions variable
undated

Group 2
page 27
compressed charcoal on cartridge paper
50 x 75 cm
1976-1978

Group 3
page 42
pencil on cartridge paper
60 x 80 cm
1974-1977

Group 4
pages: 15, 77, 97, 118, 121, 131, 160, 177, 240
Acrylic on watercolour paper
Dimensions variable
undated

Group 5
page 54
Acrylic on brown kraft paper
80 x 80 cm (approx)
1998-1999

Group 6
Map Series
page 62
heavy watercolour paper, ink, pencil, felt tip pen, rubber
150 x 110 cm
1991

Group 7
Untitled Series
pages: 152, 153, 154, 155
Acrylic on watercolour paper
31 pictures, each 80 x 60 cm
2001

Cover image
Balloon

page 3
Oil Slick

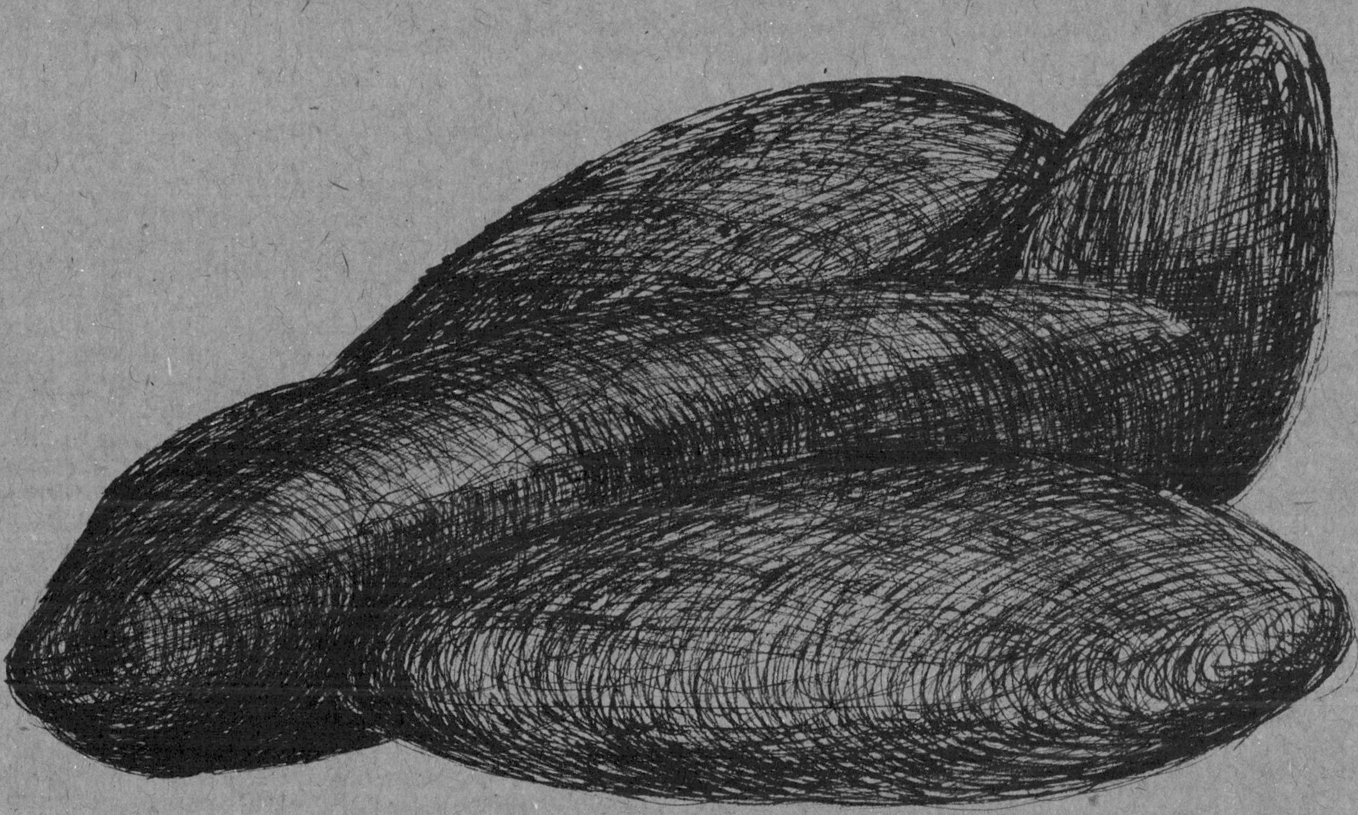

Acknowledgments

Phyllida Barlow would like to thank Richard Salmon of the Richard Salmon Gallery and Sotiris Kyriacou for their support and encouragement. Also, she would like to thank Alison Wilding for giving permission for the use of the faxed conversation, and Naomi Salamon for the use of the *Postcards* discussion, and Alex Hartley for the use of images of his work.

This publication has been made possible through the generous support of the Henry Moore Foundation, the Elephant Trust and anonymous donations.